ANTHROPOLOGICAL PAPERS OF
THE UNIVERSITY OF ARIZONA
NUMBER 71

Murray Springs

A Clovis Site with Multiple Activity Areas in the San Pedro Valley, Arizona

C. Vance Haynes, Jr., and
Bruce B. Huckell, Editors

CONTRIBUTORS

Larry D. Agenbroad
George C. Frison
C. Vance Haynes, Jr.
E. Thomas Hemmings
Bruce B. Huckell
Jim I. Mead
M. Steven Shackley
Lawrence C. Todd
Michael C. Wilson
Susan L. Woodward

THE UNIVERSITY OF ARIZONA PRESS
TUCSON
2007

About the Editors

C. VANCE HAYNES, JR., is Regents' Professor Emeritus at the University of Arizona and a member of the National Academy of Sciences. For the past 50 years he has specialized in the geochronology of the peopling of the Americas. After pursuing geological and engineering training at Johns Hopkins University and the Colorado School of Mines, Haynes obtained his doctoral degree from the University of Arizona in 1965 studying geochemistry and Quaternary geology. He has conducted field research at many of the important Paleoindian sites in North America and performed Paleolithic research in east Africa and the eastern Sahara. He has published extensively on these topics.

BRUCE B. HUCKELL is the Interim Director of the Maxwell Museum of Anthropology and Research Associate Professor in the Department of Anthropology, University of New Mexico. He received his BA and MA degrees in Anthropology at the University of Arizona, and in 1990 obtained his doctoral degree in Arid Lands Resource Sciences, a University of Arizona interdisciplinary program centered on human ecology in arid environments. Focusing primarily on late Pleistocene-Holocene hunter-gatherer paleoecology in western North America, and particularly the lithic technological organization of those groups, he has directed investigations at Clovis and Folsom sites in Arizona and New Mexico. He has published numerous articles on lithic technology and is the author of *Anthropological Paper* 59.

Cover: Photograph of the Murray Springs Site taken in 1967 by C. Vance Haynes, Jr. Image of *Mammuthus columbi* courtesy of Mary Stiner from the files of the Stanley J. Olsen Zooarchaeology Collections, original photograph by Marie Wormington. Illustration composed and rendered by Arthur J. Jelinek.

THE UNIVERSITY OF ARIZONA PRESS
Copyright © 2007
The Arizona Board of Regents
All Rights Reserved

This book was set in 11/12 CG Times
∞ This book is printed on acid-free, archival-quality paper.
Manufactured in the United States of America.

Library of Congress Cataloging-in-Publication Data

Murray Springs : a Clovis site with multiple activity areas in the San Pedro Valley, Arizona / C. Vance Haynes, Jr., and Bruce B. Huckell, editors.
   p. cm. – (Anthropological papers of the University of Arizona ; no. 71)
  Includes bibliographical references and index.
  ISBN-13: 978-0-8165-2579-9 (pbk. : alk. paper)
  ISBN-10: 0-8165-2579-X (pbk. : alk.paper)
  1. Murray Springs Clovis Site (Ariz.) 2. Clovis culture Arizona. 3. Clovis culture—San Pedro River Valley (Mexico and Ariz.) 4. Arizona—Antiquities. 5. San Pedro River Valley (Mexico and Ariz.)—Antiquities. 6. Excavations (Archaeology)—Arizona. 7. Excavations (Archaeology)—San Pedro River Valley (Mexico and Ariz.) 8. Fossils—Arizona. 9. Fossils—San Pedro River Valley (Mexico and Ariz). I. Haynes, C. Vance (Caleb Vance), 1928 II. Huckell, Bruce B.
E99.C832M87 2007
979.4'69–dc22   2007000205

Contributors

Larry D. Agenbroad
   Professor Emeritus, Northern Arizona
      University, Flagstaff, Arizona
   Director, The Mammoth Site
   Hot Springs, South Dakota

George C. Frison
   Professor Emeritus, University of Wyoming
   Laramie, Wyoming

E. Thomas Hemmings
   Northeast Geoarchaeology
   Acworth, New Hampshire

Jim I. Mead
   Department of Geology
   Northern Arizona University
   Flagstaff, Arizona

M. Steven Shackley
   Director, Archaeological XRF Laboratory
   Department of Anthropology
   University of California
   Berkeley, California

Lawrence C. Todd
   Department of Anthropology
   Colorado State University
   Fort Collins, Colorado

Michael C. Wilson
   Department of Geology
   Douglas College
   New Westminster, BC, Canada

Susan L. Woodward
   Department of Geography
   Radford University
   Radford, Virginia

Contents

PREFACE	xi	Weik Ranch Member (Stratum G_1)	49
Acknowledgments	xiii	Hargis Ranch Member (Stratum G_{2a})	51
		McCool Ranch Member (Stratum G_{2b})	52
1. CLOVIS INVESTIGATIONS IN THE SAN PEDRO VALLEY	1	Bakarich Ranch Member (Stratum G_3)	53
C. Vance Haynes, Jr.		Teviston Member (Stratum H) and Modern Arroyo Cutting	53
Clovis Site Discoveries in the San Pedro Valley	1	Curry Draw Member (Stratum J)	54
Discovery of the Murray Springs Site	6	Late Quaternary Paleoclimatic Interpretations	54
Murray Springs 1966-1971	8		
		3. MODERN VEGETATION OF THE MURRAY SPRINGS AREA AND THE UPPER SAN PEDRO VALLEY	57
2. QUATERNARY GEOLOGY OF THE MURRAY SPRINGS CLOVIS SITE	16	*Susan L. Woodward*	
C. Vance Haynes, Jr.		Modern Vegetation of Curry Draw	57
Geomorphology and Modern Conditions	18	Vegetation History	59
Stratigraphy of Curry Draw	28		
St. David Formation (Stratum X)	30	4. MOLLUSCAN FAUNAS OF THE SAN PEDRO VALLEY, ARIZONA	62
Nexpa Formation (Stratum Y)	31	*Jim I. Mead*	
Millville Formation (Stratum Z)	31	The Upper San Pedro River Valley	63
Murray Springs Formation and Emergent Water Table	31	Physiography and Biomes	63
Moson Ranch Member (Stratum D_1)	31	Modern Cienegas in Southeastern Arizona	64
Sobaipuri Member (Stratum D)	32	Methods of Study at the Fossil Sites	68
Coro Marl Member (Stratum E)	32	Fossil Molluscan Fauna	69
Fry Ranch Member (Stratum D_2)	34	Terrestrial Fauna	70
Kendall Ranch Member (Stratum E_1)	34	Aquatic Fauna	75
Graveyard Gulch Member (Stratum F_1) and Decline of the Water Table	35	Comparison of Fossil and Modern Assemblages	76
The Clovis Age Landscape	40	Habitat Reconstruction	78
Lehner Ranch Formation	44	Millville Alluvium (Z_2)	78
Clanton Ranch Member (Black Mat, Stratum F_2) and the Reemergence of the Water Table	45	Sobaipuri Mudstone (D)	78
		Coro Marl (E)	78
		Graveyard Sand (F_1)	78
Earp Member (White Marl, Stratum F_{2b}), the Ponding Facies	45	Clanton Clay (F_2)	79
		Donnet Silt (F_3)	79
Donnet Ranch Member (Stratum F_3) and Gentle Aggradation	47	Weik Alluvium (G_1)	80
		McCool Alluvium (G_{2b})	80
Escapule Ranch Formation, Times of Arroyo Cutting and Filling	49	Significance of the Faunal Record	80
		Evaluation of the Faunal Record	82

5. BURIED ANIMAL KILLS AND PROCESSING LOCALITIES, AREAS 1–5 — 83
E. Thomas Hemmings

Methods of Investigation — 83
Stratigraphy of the Clovis Occupation — 84
Vertebrate Remains — 85
  Bone Preservation — 86
Wolf Creek Deposits, Areas 1 and 2 — 86
  Vertebrate Remains — 87
    Area 1 Mammoths — 92
    Area 2 Mammoths — 93
    Bison — 93
    Camels — 93
    Horses — 94
    Canids — 94
  Artifacts — 94
  Charcoal — 94
  Area 1 and Area 3 Extensions — 94
    Charcoal — 95
    Flaked Lithic Debris — 95
  Overview of Areas 1 and 2 — 95
The Mammoth Kill, Area 3 — 96
  Occupation Surface — 96
  Vertebrate Remains — 97
    Mammoth — 97
    Bison — 103
    Canids — 103
    Rodents — 103
  Hearths — 104
  Artifacts — 104
    Bifaces — 104
    Unifaces — 106
    Utilized Flakes — 106
    Cobble Hammers and Manuports — 107
    Lithic Debris — 107
    Obsidian Nodules — 108
    Bone Tool and Worked Bone — 109
  Mammoth Processing — 111
    Bone Distribution — 111
    Butchering Sequence and Utilization — 111
  Bison Processing — 112
  Overview of Area 3 — 112
The Multiple Bison Kill, Area 4 — 114
  Occupation Surface — 114
  Bison Remains in Area 4 — 114
    Bone Preservation — 115
    Number of Individuals — 118
    Species and Size — 119
    Age Composition — 119
    Other Vertebrate Remains — 120
  Cultural Remains — 120
    Hearths and Depressions — 120
    Projectile Points and Lithic Tools — 121
    Bone Tool — 124
    Flaked Lithic Debris — 124
  Bison Processing and Utilization — 125
    Bone Distribution and Butchering Sequence — 125
    Cooking and Rendering — 127
    Meat and By-product Yield — 127
    Processing Task Unit — 128
    Procurement — 128
The Horse Kill, Area 5 — 129
  Clovis Occupation Surface of Area 5 — 131
  Vertebrate Remains — 131
    Horse — 131
  Artifacts — 132
    Projectile Points — 132
    Bifaces — 132
    Uniface — 132
    Utilized Flake — 134
    Pebble Hammer and Manuports — 134
    Flaked Lithic Debris — 134
  Overview of Area 5 — 135
Conclusions — 136

6. BISON AGES FROM DENTITIONS AT THE MURRAY SPRINGS CLOVIS SITE, ARIZONA — 138
Michael C. Wilson, Lawrence C. Todd, and George C. Frison

Dentitions — 138
  Group 1 (0.7 to 0.8 Year) — 139
  Group 2 (1.8 Years) — 139
  Group 3 (2.7 to 2.8 Years) — 139
  Group 4 (3.7 to 3.8 Years) — 142
  Group 5 (4.7 to 4.8 Years) — 142
  Group 6 (5.7 to 5.8 Years) — 143
  Group 6+ — 143
Radius — 143
Conclusions — 143

7. THE HUNTING CAMP AT MURRAY SPRINGS — 146
Larry D. Agenbroad and Bruce B. Huckell

Preliminary Investigations, 1969 — 146
Area 7, 1970 — 148

Areas 6 and 7, 1971	149
Discussion	155
Clovis Artifacts from Areas 6 and 7	155
Bifacially Flaked Implements	155
Projectile Points	155
Bifaces	156
Unifacially Retouched Implements	157
End Scrapers	158
Gravers	159
Laterally Retouched Flake Tools	159
Blades and Blade Tools	160
Retouched Blades	160
Utilized Blades	161
Blade Fragments	161
Clovis Cores	162
Obsidian Nodule	162
Clovis Debitage	162
Archaic Period and Younger Artifacts	164
Archaic Period Bifacially	
Flaked Artifacts	164
Projectile Points	164
Bifaces	165
Archaic Period Unifacially	
Retouched Pieces	166
Archaic Period Cores	166
Archaic Period Debitage	166
Artifacts of Uncertain Age	166
Debitage of Uncertain Age	167
Ground Stone Artifacts	167
Pottery	168
Overview of Areas 6 and 7	168
8. **CLOVIS LITHIC TECHNOLOGY: A VIEW FROM THE UPPER SAN PEDRO VALLEY**	170
Bruce B. Huckell	
Debitage from Murray Springs	171
Methods of Study	171
Cluster Descriptions	172
Area 1 and Area 1 Extension	173
Area 2	174
Area 3	174
Area 3 Extension	176
Area 4	177
Area 5	178
Flakes Not Assigned to Clusters	179
Discussion	179
Area 6 and Area 7	180

Flakes Not Assigned to Clusters	184
Discussion	184
Clovis Flint Knapping at Murray Springs	184
The Clovis Industry	185
Raw Material Sources	186
The Biface Mode	189
Bifaces	189
Projectile Points	194
Clovis Point Production	197
Clovis Point Repair	199
The Flake and Flake Tool Mode	201
Laterally Retouched Flakes	203
Composite Flake Tool	204
Gravers	204
End Scrapers	204
Unretouched Implements	205
The Blade and Blade Tool Mode	205
Blade Technology	208
The Expediency Mode	209
Discussion	210
9. **CLOVIS PALEOECOLOGY AS VIEWED FROM MURRAY SPRINGS, ARIZONA**	214
Bruce B. Huckell and C. Vance Haynes, Jr.	
Clovis Diet: Specialists, Generalists, Or Other?	215
Theoretical Perspectives on Large Mammal Hunting	215
Clovis Subsistence in the San Pedro Valley	217
African Elephant Behavior and Implications for Mammoth Hunting	218
Weaponry Design and Technological Organization	219
Subsistence Strategies	221
Clovis Land Use and Mobility	221
Clovis Site Structure in the San Pedro Valley	222
Lithic Raw Material Evidence	222
Extinction and Murray Springs	224
Evidence from the San Pedro Valley	224
Extinction and the Black Mat	225
AFTERWORD	
Does the Past have a Future at Murray Springs?	226
C. Vance Haynes, Jr.	

APPENDIX A. Radiocarbon Dating at
   Murray Springs and Curry Draw   229
     C. Vance Haynes, Jr.
   Standard A-B-A Pretreatment   229
   Dating the Clovis Occupation   230
   Multiple Fraction Radiocarbon Dating
     of the Black Mat (F_2)   231
   Dating the Coro Marl   237
   Dating the Sobaipuri Member   237
   Conclusions   239

APPENDIX B. Nature and Origin of the
   Black Mat, Stratum F_2 240
     C. Vance Haynes, Jr., with Contributors
   Chemical Evaluation of the Black Mat
     Deposit at Murray Springs   242
       (*Raymond N. Rogers*)
   Pyrolytic Gas Chromatographic Mass
     Spectrometry Analysis   245
       (*Artur Staniekwicz and Erik Tegelaar*)
   ^{13}C-NMR Spectral Analyses of the
     Black Mat Samples (*Jerry A. Leenheer*)   247
   Overview   247

APPENDIX C. Sources of Obsidian at the
   Murray Springs Clovis Site: A Semi-
   quantitative X-Ray Fluorescence Analysis   250
     M. Steven Shackley
   Instrument Methodology and
     Source Description   250
     The Cow Canyon Source   251
   Discussion   252

APPENDIX D. Vertebrate Specimens
   from Murray Springs Areas 1–5   255
     E. Thomas Hemmings
   Areas 1, 3, 4, 5,   255
   Area 2   263

APPENDIX E. Geological and Archaeological
   Investigations at Murray Springs, Area 9
   and Trench 13N   266
     Bruce B. Huckell and
     C. Vance Haynes, Jr.
   Background to the Research   266
   Testing in Area 9   267
   Black Mat Testing at Trench 13N
     and Area 9   269
   Summary and Conclusions   270

APPENDIX F. Identification Numbers of
   Illustrated Artifacts from the Murray
   Springs Site   273
     C. Vance Haynes, Jr.

APPENDIX G. Murray Springs Project
   Field Personnel, Volunteers, and
   Site Visitors   276
     C. Vance Haynes, Jr.

REFERENCES   279

INDEX   299

ABSTRACT, RESUMEN   307

COLOR ILLUSTRATIONS

Following page 48

Plate 1. Topographic map of the Murray Springs Clovis Site as of 1998

Plate 2. Stratigraphic column and ^{14}C chronology of Curry Draw correlated with earlier stratigraphic designations

Plate 3. Photogeologic map of the Murray Springs Clovis Site area

Plate 4. Stratigraphic profiles of Trenches 1, 9, and 24

Plate 5. Stratigraphic profile of the north wall of the South Branch of Curry Draw

Plate 6. Stratigraphic profiles H, I, and J in Area 2

Plate 7. Stratigraphic profiles D, C, G, and N in Area 1

Plate 8. Paleogeologic map of the Clovis-age surface

Foldout 1. Stratigraphic profiles of Trenches 4, 15–19, 21, 22, and 25

Foldout 2. Stratigraphic profiles of Trenches 10–14, 20, 26–28, 32, and Line X of Area 3

Following page 176

Plate 9. Distribution of flake clusters within the Area 3-2 knapping locus

Plate 10. Distribution of flake clusters within the Area 3-3 knapping locus

FIGURES

1.1. Map of southeastern Arizona showing the San Pedro River Valley from Mexico to the confluence with the Gila River — 2
1.2. Map of the upper San Pedro Valley from Mexico to Benson, Arizona, showing locations of sites and grass circles — 3
1.3. Topographic map of the Murray Springs site showing excavation areas, stratigraphic trenches, and profile locations — 4
1.4. Views of Murray Springs Areas 1 and 2 — 7
1.5. The mammoth skeleton in Area 3 — 8
1.6. Views of Murray Springs Areas 1 and 3 — 9
1.7. Views of Murray Springs Areas 1 and 3 — 10
1.8. Views of Murray Springs Areas 4, 5, and 6 — 11
1.9. Views of Murray Springs Areas, 3, 4, 5, and 7 — 12
1.10. Views of Murray Springs Area 8 — 13
1.11. Views of Murray Springs Area 8 — 14
1.12. Fossil teeth from Area 8 discovery trench on National Geographic Society flag — 14
2.1. Time-stratigraphic column for the St. David Formation of the San Pedro Valley — 17
2.2. Map of the Curry Draw area showing the Murray Springs Site, trenches, and grass-floored circular depressions — 18
2.3. Shaded relief map of the Murray Springs Site — 19
2.4. Aerial views of the Curry Draw area — 20
2.5. Generalized geologic cross section of Curry Draw at the Murray Springs Site — 21
2.6. Views of special features of the Curry Draw area — 22
2.7. Part of the San Rafael de Valle grant mapped in 1902 by Philip Contzen — 23
2.8. Views of some modern environments — 25
2.9. Aerial photographs of Curry Draw during a 67-year interval — 26
2.10. Arroyo stratigraphy of the Escapule Ranch Formation in Curry Draw — 29
2.11. Coro marl (Stratum E) type section at Profile A in the north wall of the South Branch — 33
2.12. Detailed stratigraphic profiles of the Graveyard sand channel (Stratum F_1) in the north wall of the South Branch (Profile B) of Curry Draw — 35
2.13. Photographic panorama of the F_1 channel at Profile B, close-up of the F_1 channel sand, and proboscidean long bone in Stratum D_2 — 36
2.14. Large pieces of charcoal in the top of the F_1 channel sand in Area 2 — 36
2.15. African elephants digging water holes at Wankie Reserve, Zambia — 37
2.16. Views of the Clanton Ranch Member (black mat) F_{2a} and the Earp Marl Member F_{2b} facies — 38
2.17. Map of Area 8 showing anomalous features associated with Conduit 2 — 43
2.18. Profile of bioturbation in Area 7 — 44
2.19. Close-up view of the black mat and Donnet silt (F_2 and F_3) — 45
2.20. Geologic cross section of the Graveyard sand channel (F_1) and the Donnet Ranch channel (F_{3a}) in Trench 22 — 47
3.1. Shrub species characteristic of the Chihuahuan Desert surrounding Curry Draw — 58
3.2. Curry Draw, with mesquites and rabbitbrush — 58
3.3. Willows and cottonwoods in Curry Draw — 58
3.4. Woodcutter Draw, a drainage on the Whetstone surface — 58
3.5. Generalized cross section of the natural vegetation and its edaphic controls in the lower San Pedro Valley near Curry Draw — 59
4.1. Map of southeastern Arizona and adjacent areas of New Mexico and Sonora, Mexico — 62
4.2. Babocomari (Brophy) Cienega showing ponding and nearby marsh area — 64
4.3. Sheehy Springs, San Rafael Valley, showing the plains grassland to desert grassland surrounding the narrow cienega — 64
4.4. Sphaeriid clam habitat at the gravel-bottomed pond at Sheehy Springs — 67

4.5. Pond and shore habitats surrounded by an encinal (oak) woodland at Sylvania Springs, Huachuca Mountains ... 67
4.6. Map of Curry Draw at the Murray Springs Site showing molluscan and Pollen Profile sample locations ... 69
4.7. Generalized cross section of Curry Draw at Murray Springs showing the stratigraphic positions of the 19 molluscan matrix samples ... 69
4.8. Scanning electron microscope photographs of fossil molluscs ... 74
4.9. Simpson's faunal similarity index used to compare modern molluscan assemblages with fossil assemblages ... 77
4.10. Graph illustrating the changes in number of aquatic and terrestrial molluscs for the stratigraphic layers at the Murray Springs Site ... 80
5.1. View across the South Branch of Curry Draw at the Murray Springs Site ... 87
5.2. Mammoth remains in Area 2 ... 87
5.3. Distribution of remains in Area 1 ... 88–89
5.4. Distribution of remains in Area 2 ... 90–91
5.5. Mammoth remains from Areas 1 and 2 ... 92
5.6. Bison upper left forelimb from Area 2 ... 93
5.7. Distribution of remains in Area 3 ... 98–99
5.8. Distribution of remains in Area 3 Extension and Area 1 Extension ... 100–101
5.9. Excavation of the occupation surface in Area 3 ... 102
5.10. Mammoth tracks on a low-lying part of the occupation surface in Area 3 ... 102
5.11. Partial carcass of a mammoth on a high part of the occupation surface in Area 3 ... 102
5.12. Mammoth upper molars from Area 3 ... 103
5.13. Lithic artifacts from Area 3 ... 105
5.14. Lithic artifacts from Area 3, reverse sides ... 105
5.15. Debitage from Area 3 ... 108
5.16. Marekanite nodules from Area 3 ... 109
5.17. Mammoth bone shaft straightener from Area 3 ... 110
5.18. Worked bison long bone fragment ... 111
5.19. Distribution of remains in Area 4 ... 116–117
5.20. Bison skeletal elements from Area 4 ... 118
5.21. Bison skeletal material from Area 4 ... 118
5.22. Lithic artifacts from Area 4 ... 122
5.23. Lithic artifacts from Area 4, reverse sides ... 122
5.24. Cobble hammer from Area 4 ... 124
5.25. Worked bone gaming(?) piece and burned bone from Area 4 ... 124
5.26. Utilized flakes and debitage from Area 4 ... 125
5.27. Distribution of remains in Area 5 ... 130
5.28. Lingual view of upper and lower right cheek teeth of the horse from Area 5 ... 131
5.29. Lithic artifacts from Area 5 ... 133
5.30. Lithic artifacts from Area 5, reverse sides ... 133
6.1. Bison lower dentitions from Murray Springs compared with dentitions from the Hawken Site ... 141
6.2. Age Group 3 bison lower dentitions from Murray Springs, Area 4 ... 142
6.3. Age Group 5 bison lower dentitions from Murray Springs, Area 4 ... 142
6.4. Age Group 6 and Group 6+ bison lower dentitions from Murray Springs, Area 4 ... 143
7.1. Murray Springs Site area showing locations of Areas 6 and 7 ... 147
7.2. Portions of Area 7 cleared, swept, and excavated showing the grid system and subgrid designations ... 148
7.3. Excavated pits that may have been Archaic period wells in Area 7 ... 150
7.4. Distribution of remains in Area 6 ... 151
7.5. Distribution of remains in Area 7 ... 152–153
7.6. Paleotopographic map of Areas 6 and 7 ... 154
7.7. Clovis bifacial artifacts from Areas 6 and 7 ... 157
7.8. Clovis unifacial artifacts from Areas 6 and 7 ... 158
7.9. Clovis blade tools from Areas 6 and 7 ... 160
7.10. Archaic period artifacts from Areas 6 and 7 ... 165
8.1. Locations of Clovis knapping loci in Areas 3, 4, 5, and the extensions of Area 1 and Area 3 ... 172
8.2. Locations of Clovis and Archaic knapping loci in Areas 6 and 7 ... 181
8.3. Schematic diagram showing Clovis lithic technological organization ... 186
8.4. Refitted flake groups that allow measurement of biface widths ... 190

8.5.	Histogram of biface widths from refitted flake groups and biface fragments	191		molluscan samples, carbonate radiocarbon ages and Profile Y	238
8.6.	Complete and fragmentary bifaces from Murray Springs	192	B.1.	Pond clays just under the black mat, showing shrinkage cracks on the Clovis surface	242
8.7.	Clovis points and fragments from Murray Springs	196	B.2.	Sample 18AZ94 pyrolysed at 800°C for 10 seconds	246
8.8.	Clovis points and fragments from Murray Springs	196	B.3.	^{13}C-NMR Spectrum of the black mat	248
8.9.	Clovis point breakage and repair options based on specimens from the San Pedro Valley	200	C.1.	Archaeological obsidian sources in the Southwest	251
			C.2.	Ternary plot for Southwestern net intensity obsidian data	252
8.10.	Unifacially retouched flake tools from Murray Springs	202	C.3.	Net intensity peak count bivariate plot of Cow Canyon source material and Murray Springs obsidian artifacts	254
8.11.	Composite flake tool from Murray Springs	204			
8.12.	Clovis retouched and utilized blade tools from Murray Springs	206	E.1.	Locations of Area 9 and Trench 13N black mat sampling area	267
8.13.	Clovis large blade tools and possible blades from Murray Springs	207	E.2.	Distribution of horse teeth and bone fragments in Area 9	268
8.14.	Clovis expedient tools from Murray Springs	210	E.3.	Murray Springs Trench 13N stratigraphic profile with ^{14}C sample locations numbered	270
A.1.	Detailed stratigraphy of interbedded Clanton clay stringers and Earp marl at Trench 13N and Trench 18 in Area 8	236	E.4.	Murray Springs Area 9 headcut stratigraphic profile and microstratigraphic columns A and B for sediment sampling	271
A.2.	Type section of the Coro member at Profile A showing locations of				

TABLES

4.1.	Murray Springs Site fossil assemblage and the present indigenous molluscs of the upper San Pedro Valley	65	5.4.	Age estimates for ten bison lower dentitions from Area 4	119
4.2.	Molluscan assemblages from three springs in southeastern Arizona	70	5.5	Illustrated Clovis lithic tools and debitage from Murray Springs, Area 4 and Area 5	121
4.3.	Murray Springs Site molluscs that are either absent or now inhabiting oak woodland to oak-pine woodland	70	5.6.	Estimated weights of body parts, organs, and contents in eleven bison from Murray Springs, Area 4	128
5.1.	Variation between knapping areas and general surface collection from Area 3	109	6.1.	Bison lower dentitions from Area 4	139
5.2.	Estimated weights and percents of carcass weight of body parts, organs, and contents of a 5,450 kg mammoth cow	112	6.2.	Measurements of lower bison teeth from the Murray Springs Site	140
			6.3.	Measurement of radius from the Murray Springs Site	144
			7.1.	Fire-cracked rock concentrations in Areas 6 and 7	150
5.3.	Comparison of observed numbers of skeletal elements with original numbers in eleven bison from Area 4	115	7.2.	Clovis artifacts from the Murray Springs camp, Areas 6 and 7	156

7.3.	Cultural and material attributes of debitage from the Murray Springs camp, Areas 6 and 7	163	8.9.	Attributes of thirteen blades and blade tools from Murray Springs	205
7.4.	Archaic period and younger artifacts from the Murray Springs camp, Areas 6 and 7	164	A.1.	Curry Draw radiocarbon ages arranged stratigraphically by locality	232–235
8.1.	Attributes of the Murray Springs flake clusters	173	A.2.	Multifraction radiocarbon ages of Clanton clay and Earp marl microstrata in Trench 13 North and Trench 18, Area 8	235
8.2.	Flakes not assigned to clusters in Areas 1, 3, 4, and 5	179	B.1.	Analysis of black mat samples from Trench 18, Area 8	241
8.3.	Flakes not assigned to clusters in Area 7	184	B.2.	Atomic absorption analysis of black mat	241
8.4.	Major raw materials identified from knapping loci at Murray Springs	187	B.3.	Chemical composition of the acid-soluble component of the black mat	241
8.5.	Biface widths from distally overlapping flake groups	189	C.1.	X-ray fluorescence data for obsidian specimens from the Murray Springs Clovis Site	253
8.6.	Measurements of bifaces and biface fragments from Murray Springs	191			
8.7.	Attributes of nineteen Murray Springs Clovis points	195			
8.8.	Attributes of twenty-three unifacially retouched flake tools from Murray Springs	201	C.2.	Rb, Sr, Zr and Rb, Nb, Zr X-ray fluorescence data for the Cow Canyon obsidian source, Arizona	253

Preface

Murray Springs is an ancient Clovis site with multiple activity areas in the San Pedro Valley of southeastern Arizona. This volume reports on the interdisciplinary research conducted during six consecutive summer field seasons (1966-1971) of excavations at Murray Springs. A subsequent monograph will describe similar research at the Lehner Site and other Clovis sites in the immediate area during 1963-1968, 1974-1975, and 1980 to provide an integrated view of the prehistoric occupation of the San Pedro Valley 13,000 years ago. As far as we can tell, Clovis people were the first human beings to come to the geographical area known as southeastern Arizona.

Clovis is the name given to the earliest well-defined cultural complex found in the archaeological record of North America. It is recognized by the presence of the Clovis projectile point, a fluted biface on which channel flakes have been removed from the base and flutes extend longitudinally up from the concave base on both sides for a distance equivalent to the width of the base or more (Haynes 1980b, 1982b), producing a biconcave transverse basal cross section. This knapping innovation is thought to facilitate hafting the point snugly in a split or notched foreshaft. Such an interpretation is supported by the fact that most Clovis points have their basal edges ground up both sides as far as the longer of the two flute scars or channels, matching the extent that sinew lashing would likely extend. Dulling these edges prevents cutting the sinew when it is tightly wrapped around the point.

Surface finds of Clovis points are known from all of the conterminous United States and the Interior Plains of Canada, but in situ stratified sites are rare. Clovis points were first found in situ with mammoth remains in 1932-1933 in a terrace of the South Platte River near the railroad siding of Dent north of Denver, Colorado (Figgins 1933). At that time the three Clovis points found there among the bones of 12 mammoths were considered to be simply larger versions of the Folsom points found with an extinct form of bison (*Bison antiquus*) near Folsom, New Mexico in 1926-1928. However, the second discovery of Clovis points in situ in 1936 in Blackwater Draw, New Mexico, showed them to occur with mammoth bones stratigraphically below Folsom points with bones of *Bison antiquus* (Cotter 1937). The larger, more robust fluted points with skeletal remains of mammoths came to be known as Clovis points (Howard 1943: 223-233), after the nearby town in eastern New Mexico, and the more delicate fluted points with bison were named after the type site near Folsom, New Mexico. Sellards (1952) later defined the Llano complex as mammoth hunters and the Folsom complex as bison hunters. However, subsequent finds of Clovis points with bison skeletons at the Clovis type site (Hester 1972: 46-47), more recently at the Jake Bluff Site in Oklahoma (Bement and Carter 2004), and at Murray Springs as reported here, have made Sellard's definition of the Llano complex obsolete. Instead, the term Clovis "technocomplex" has been used in recent times. Here it is simply referred to as the Clovis complex.

After the Dent discovery in 1932 and Clovis in 1936, the next stratified Clovis site discovery was in 1937 near Miami in the Texas panhandle where three Clovis points and a scraper were found with bones of at least five mammoths (Sellards 1952). In 1952 near Naco, Arizona, the skeleton of a single mammoth was unearthed with eight Clovis points in direct association (Haury and others 1953). Naco was the first Clovis site found west of the continental divide. The Lehner Site was discovered three years later and only 17.7 km (11 miles) to the northwest of Naco (Haury and others 1959). Excavations there in 1955-1956 yielded 13 Clovis points and 8 other stone tools among the bones of 9 mammoths. Charcoal from two hearths produced the first radiocarbon dates for Clovis and indicated an age of about 11,200 radiocarbon years before present (B.P.). Following Stuiver and others (1998), 11,200 B.P. calibrates to about 13,150 calendar years. Except where indicated otherwise, all radiocarbon ages hereafter are stated as uncalibrated ages B.P. (before present being 1950).

In 1960 a mammoth skeleton was found with non-diagnostic stone tools southwest of Rawlins, Wyoming. A fragment of ivory from here, the U. P. Mammoth Site, provided an age of about 11,200 B.P. (Irwin and others 1962). Two years later, three Clovis points were found associated with the skeleton of a mammoth in Domebo Branch, Oklahoma (Leonhardy 1966). Buried logs in the deposit yielded ages of about 11,000 B.P. In the early 1960s, a radiocarbon age at the type site of about 11,170 B.P. was obtained on an organic layer contemporary with the Clovis occupation (Damon and others 1964).

Up to the 1960s, age estimates for Clovis ranged from 10,000 B.P. to more than 15,000 B.P. The tight clustering of radiocarbon ages between 11,000 and 11,200 B.P. was unexpected yet it was consistent with the similar stratigraphic position of these buried Clovis sites (Haynes 1970). In the early 1960s, Broecker and Farrand (1963) radiocarbon dated the Two Creeks interstade, a period of glacial recession in the Great Lakes area, to about 11,800 B.P. The appearance of Clovis sites in the interior of North America only a few hundred years after the Two Creeks recession led to the suggestion that an ice-free corridor, proposed earlier by Johnston (1933), had opened up between the Laurentide and Cordilleran ice sheets during the Two Creeks interstade and allowed Clovis progenitors to move into the interior from Alaska (Haynes 1964). This interpretation became the "Clovis First" model of the peopling of the New World (Haynes 1966) that is being challenged today by several potential pre-Clovis finds of the past 30 years (Madsen 2004). However, the evidence for pre-Clovis is just as equivocal today as it was then for similar claims of the previous 35 years (Haynes 1969, 1971), but the search must continue.

If some of these potential pre-Clovis sites are indeed validated by more compelling evidence, we have an interesting situation in the Americas where there are several cultural complexes represented by widely different artifacts or assemblages that suddenly, at about 11,500 B.P., give way to or become a single complex, that is the Clovis complex. Until potential pre-Clovis sites are unequivocally demonstrated, we assume that the Clovis complex represents the first peoples to succeed in subsisting in Arizona, if not the conterminous United States.

The geologic situation in the upper San Pedro Valley provides an unmatched opportunity to study the Clovis culture and its relationship to the environment of a specific region at closely spaced points in time 13,000 calendar years ago. A combination of fortunate circumstances has made this opportunity possible, not the least of which has been the role of local amateur archaeologists. Fred and Marc Navarrete, Edward F. Lehner, Slim Leikem, and Louis Escapule not only recognized the importance of the sites they found but had enough concern for the advancement of knowledge to report their discoveries to professional scientists. Throughout the half century during which these Paleoindian studies have taken place in southeastern Arizona, the University of Arizona and the Arizona State Museum have always had a few faculty and staff who specialize in Pleistocene studies involving geology, paleontology, palynology, geochemistry, and other disciplines in support of archaeology.

Another benefit of this work has been the graduate students who contributed to the fund of knowledge through theses and dissertations based on the San Pedro Clovis sites. Susan Woodward (1969) wrote a master's thesis on the modern vegetation of Curry Draw (modified for Chapter 3 herein); Jeffrey Saunders' (1970) master's thesis considered the proboscideans of Arizona; Tom Hemmings' (1970) doctoral dissertation reported on the archaeology of the Murray Springs Site (modified for Chapter 5); and Jim Mead's (1979) master's thesis recorded the late Quaternary molluscan fauna of the San Pedro Valley (modified for Chapter 4). Combining pollen analyses with multivariate statistical techniques, David P. Adam completed a doctoral dissertation in 1970 that modeled the San Pedro Valley vegetation changes associated with the alluvial deposits during and after the Clovis presence (Mehringer and others 1971). Furthermore, there have always been enthusiastic students and amateur archaeologists who would volunteer their time and effort to help with the investigation of a new fossil locality or archaeological site. It is to these dedicated people that we hope this work will do justice (see Appendix G). Preliminary reports on each field season are published in the *National Geographic Society Research Reports* (Haynes 1973, 1974, 1976, 1978, 1979, 1980a, 1981). This volume, of course, is not the last word. There is no end to the number of things that could and should be done to answer specific questions about many aspects of the Quaternary history of the San Pedro Valley. Investigations are continuing and many more will be done as time goes on, so there is never really a *final* report.

To keep this monograph to a manageable size, two major contributions have been set aside for publication in the sequent volume on the Lehner Site in which we plan to summarize the entire San Pedro Valley Paleoindian research. The opus on the palynological investigations ("Pollen Analysis of the Lehner Site, Southeastern Arizona," by Peter J. Mehringer, Jr., David P. Adam, and Paul S. Martin 1966) is based principally on investigations conducted at the Lehner Site in 1963 (Mehringer and Haynes 1965) and includes the Martin-Schoenwetter-Mehringer pollen profile in Curry Draw (Mehringer, Martin, and Haynes 1967) integrated with the multivariate community model of Adam's (1970) dissertation. This work was compiled in draft form in 1972 and approved for publication by the U.S. Geological Survey in 1993.

The other major work is the "Late Pleistocene Vertebrates of the San Pedro Valley, Arizona" by Jeffrey J. Saunders. His draft was completed in 1983 and includes the vertebrate fauna from the Murray Springs, Lehner, Escapule, Naco, Leikem, and Navarrete Clovis sites as well as other finds of Rancholabrean fauna without cultural association. He also reports on the Schaldack, Donnet, and Hurley mammoth skeletons that lacked associated artifacts.

Another significant contribution is by Richard Hereford and Julio Betancourt entitled "Historic Geomorphology of the San Pedro River: Archival and Physical Evidence." The report is to appear in a volume titled *Riparian Area Conservation in a Semi-Arid Region*, edited by Juliet Stromberg and Barbara Tellman.

In addition to chapters by the editors, this monograph includes the work of eight contributors, a few of whom had completed their parts more than 30 years ago. Since the end of archaeological excavations 35 years ago, we have all been involved in various activities ranging from career moves to other important projects that prevented the manuscripts from being completed until recently. The result is a publication containing contributions that would have broken new ground and set new standards had they been published at the time. Meanwhile the archaeological profession has progressed, especially with regard to analytical methods and anthropological theory that augment the study of hunter-gatherers. We have chosen to publish these contributions in their current form, however, rather than ask the authors to revise them to current disciplinary interests. To do so now with many authors far removed from the Murray Springs project in both space and time would only further delay publication to the unforeseeable future. What is presented here may be considered historic in terms of the discipline as it stood in the 1970s. However, the knowledge gained from the Murray Springs project remains especially vital today for understanding the Clovis people and the world they knew.

We dedicate this work to the mentors who showed us the way: Paul E. Damon, Emil W. Haury, John F. Lance, Paul S. Martin, E. B. Sayles, Terah L. Smiley, and Raymond H. Thompson.

Acknowledgments

In late March 1966, soon after Vance Haynes and Pete Mehringer had found the mammoth occurrences and coordinated with Emil Haury, Ted Smiley, and Ray Thompson, Haynes called Dr. Leonard Carmichael, Vice-President for Research and Exploration at the National Geographic Society (NGS). After describing our finds and explaining their potential loss to erosion during the upcoming summer rains, he said, "a research proposal would be given serious consideration." On 19 May Ed Snider, NGS, called to inform Haynes that the Executive Committee had approved his proposal for an emergency grant. Less than a month later, the excavation of the Murray Springs Site began. The NGS Committee for Research and Exploration approved annual grants thereafter until 1971 when the archaeological excavations ended. Haynes was funded for an additional year to complete geochronological investigations.

Support for geological investigations was provided by the National Science Foundation through grants GP-5548, GA-1288, GA-12772, and GA-35625. Administrative support was provided by the Geochronology Laboratories and the Departments of Geosciences and Anthropology at the University of Arizona as well as by the Arizona State Museum, Tucson. Initially all vertebrate paleontological specimen collecting was coordinated by John F. Lance at the University of Arizona. On his transfer to the National Science Foundation in Washington, this task was taken over by Everett H. Lindsay and doctoral candidate Jeffrey J. Saunders. Peter J. Mehringer took charge of paleoecological investigations.

The Murray Springs Site was on the property of the Little Boquillas Ranch owned by the Kern County

Land Company (KCL) of Bakersfield, California until 1970 when it became a part of the Tenneco West Corporation, Houston, Texas. Both corporations granted us free access and Boquillas foremen Ed LeViness and Bozman Haver said we could do whatever we needed to do as long as it did not interfere with their cattle operations. In 1986 through land trade-offs, the Bureau of Land Management (BLM) acquired the Murray Springs Site as a part of what became in 1988 the San Pedro Riparian National Conservation Area (SPRNCA). Since then, BLM archaeologist John Herron followed by Jane Pike Childress have been wonderful overseers of both the Murray Springs and Lehner Clovis sites. Both did a great deal to facilitate scientific research since the formation of the Conservation Area. BLM administrators and field personnel, including Ray Brady, Jesse Juen, William Childress, Jack Whetstone, Gary Stumpf, and archaeologist Gay Kinkade to name a few, have all been very cooperative and supportive.

The Friends of the San Pedro are a group of volunteers dedicated to the preservation of the natural ecology of the SPRNCA. In 1990, with limited funds provided by the BLM, they constructed graveled pathways to and through the activity areas of the Murray Springs Site and built two wooden foot bridges over Curry Draw arroyo. In subsequent years, Jane Childress led a BLM project that provided weatherproof signs for self-guided tours that in excellent fashion explained the archaeology, geology, and ecology of the site area. In 1997 National Park Service archaeologist Catherine H. Spude prepared an assessment of the Clovis sites in the San Pedro Valley and recommended inclusion of all of them in a National Historic Landmark proposal.

Because Moson Road had not yet been constructed, access to the site for the six years of our archaeological excavations was by a dirt road across state land leased by the Bella Vista Ranch owned by Andrea Cracchiolo of Sierra Vista and Tucson. He was enthusiastic about our work and was happy to give us access across his state lease. Since his death at age 102, his son Joseph has continued this cooperation.

In 1968 Craig Fisher of NBC News produced a television documentary on "The First Americans" in which the Murray Springs project played a major role. NBC's Hugh Downs visited the site and narrated the production as Tom Hemmings and Vance Haynes escorted him through the site's activity areas and demonstrated the spearthrower or atlatl. We are pleased that the University of Arizona played a part in this educational production.

In addition to honoring our mentors and the avocational archaeologists mentioned here and in Chapter 1, we owe a debt of gratitude to many others for support in one form or another. These people include Peter J. Mehringer and David P. Adam, longstanding friends and colleagues whose palynological studies in the San Pedro Valley were state of the art at the time. Archaeologist Jonathan Gell did excellent plane table mapping of the site area, shown in Figure 1.3. Vertebrate paleontologist Everett H. Lindsay provided much help and advice in the collection and curation of the vertebrate specimens.

The U.S. Army at Fort Huachuca aided in providing aerial photographs of the site area and the length of Curry Draw. These photostrips, provided by Col. Bud Morris, were taken from Mohawk photo reconnaissance aircraft and provided the base maps for geologic mapping. During a visit by an Army helicopter we traded a tour of the site for a ride from which we could take aerial photographs of the excavations. Also, the Commanding Officer of the Fort arranged for access to the artillery range so we could excavate the Hurley mammoth in 1967 and survey for other sites.

In 1966 Alfred Weik, who lived across the river from Edward F. Lehner and the Lehner Site, provided his services in cutting Trench 1, the bulldozer trench. The backhoe trenching and overburden removal at the archaeological excavations were expertly performed by Jim Smith of Sierra Vista. Jim was able to execute remarkable feats with his backhoe and not go below the "black mat." The one time the mat was penetrated occurred with a substitute operator. Fortunately, he missed the rear end of the Area 3 mammoth and we were able to stop him before any serious damage occurred. Epoxy preservative was furnished free of charge by the Jones-Dabney Company.

Help with radiocarbon dating was provided by Austin Long (University of Arizona), Sam Velastro (University of Texas), and Herbert Haas (Southern Methodist University). Additional analyses of black mat samples in Appendix B were provided by Michael J. Holdaway (atomic absorption), James L. Bischoff (chemical analyses), and Jesse Ballenger (mechanical analyses and chemical pretreatment).

In 1967 Fred Wendorf (archaeologist) and Claude C. Albritton (geologist) from Southern Methodist

University brought 16 students to Murray Springs to make microstratigraphic studies and assist with geologic mapping in the San Pedro Valley. Students included Jon Gibson, Charles Nelson, Parker Nunley, David Hurst Thomas, Robert Thorne, and Dorothy Washburn. All of the Clovis tools and projectile points from the site were expertly cast by the late Allen Eichenberger of Hannibal, Missouri. The fine line drawings of the lithic artifacts presented in Chapter 8 were done by the late Lucille R. Addington of Dallas, Texas. J. David Kilby, Department of Anthropology at the University of New Mexico, drafted Figure 8.11.

Obsidian hydration measurements were provided by L. J. Foote and Clement W. Meighan, University of California at Los Angeles. Initial obsidian sourcing was by neutron activation analysis by A. A. Gordus through arrangements made with James B. Griffin and Edwin N. Wilmsen, University of Michigan.

Wood identifications were provided by R. C. Koeppen, Forest Products Laboratory of the U.S. Department of Agriculture; Vorsila L. Bohrer, University of Arizona Herbarium; James E. King, Department of Geosciences, University of Arizona, and Lisa Huckell, a Research Affiliate with the Maxwell Museum of Anthropology, University of New Mexico. A major work on the fossil pollen of southeastern Arizona by Peter J. Mehringer, Jr., David P. Adam, and Paul S. Martin will be a significant part of a subsequent volume on the Clovis occupation of the upper San Pedro Valley.

We are deeply indebted to James P. Holmlund, owner, and W. Randy Haas, Western Mapping Company, Tucson, for rendering the grayscale maps and for processing many of the line drawings. Their interest in computerizing the San Pedro Valley landscape for the benefit of geologists and archaeologists has provided an accuracy to this presentation that we did not possess 35 years ago. Randy Haas processed Figures 1.1, 1.3, 2.2, 2.3, 2.9, 5.3, 5.4, 5.7, 5.8, 5.19, 5.27, 7.1, 7.4, 7.5, 8.1, 8.2, E.1, E.2, and Color Plates 1, 9, and 10. The skillful computer colorization of Plates 2–8 and Foldouts 1 and 2 is the work of Jim Abbott of SciGraphics, Tucson; he also processed Figs. 2.1, 2.5, 2.12, 2.17, 2.18, 2.20, 8.4, A.1, A.2, E.3, and E.4. Most of the line drawings were originally drafted by Ron Beckwith of the National Park Service Western Archeological Center, Tucson. E. Thomas Hemmings drew the original illustrations for Figures 5.17 and 5.18.

Figures were supplied by the authors of each chapter and photographs were taken by C. Vance Haynes, Jr., unless otherwise indicated. Jannelle Weakly, photographer at the Arizona State Museum, Tucson, took the photographs for Figures 5.22, 5.23, 5.25, 5.29, and 5.30. G. Michael Jacobs, Senior Archaeological Collections Curator, Arizona State Museum, gave us invaluable assistance in locating artifacts and checking field numbers with ASM artifact numbers. With the kind advice and help of Alan Ferg, Archivist in the Arizona State Museum, we have placed referenced manuscripts pertaining to various aspects of Clovis studies in the San Pedro Valley prepared by several researchers working with Haynes in the "C. Vance Haynes, Jr., Papers" in the Archives of the Arizona State Museum, University of Arizona, Tucson.

The color plates were made possible by a generous gift from Joseph L. and Ruth Cramer. Funds for the color cover were kindly supplied by William J. Robinson.

We are most appreciative of the many crew members and volunteers who prevailed through six hot summers to uncover the Clovis living floor and expose bones and artifacts that had not seen the light of day for 13,000 years. The crew members, volunteers, and site visitors for each field season are presented in Appendix G.

Our sincere thanks are expressed to Michael B. Collins and Stuart Fiedel for their thoughtful examinations and suggestions for improvement of the draft chapters of this volume. The original manuscript benefited from the expert word processing of Doris Sample, Ellen Stamp, and Barbara Fregoso of the Department of Anthropology at the University of Arizona. Carol Gifford, editor of the *Anthropological Papers*, did a superb job of technical editing and formatting this volume. Without her expert advice and tireless effort, this publication, like the Clovis artifacts, might not yet have seen the light of day.

C. Vance Haynes, Jr., and Bruce B. Huckell
December 2006

CHAPTER ONE

Clovis Investigations in the San Pedro Valley

C. Vance Haynes, Jr.

In 1966 on a fine, sunny spring day, typical of Arizona's San Pedro Valley (Fig. 1.1) in late March, Peter J. Mehringer, Jr., and I were studying alluvial deposits in an arroyo at a place known as Murray Springs (Fig. 1.2, Site 5) when we discovered two concentrations of very large animal bones in the upper reaches of the vertical-sided gully. To use an expression of the late John Lance, our good friend and then professor of vertebrate paleontology at the University of Arizona, the deposits were "chucky jam full" of bones. We deduced that the bones exposed at the first locality found that day (Fig. 1.3, Area 1) were all of mammoth. At the second locality (Area 2), camel, horse, and bison as well as mammoth appeared to be represented in a buried bone pile. But what excited us most was the stratigraphic context of the mammoth bones at Area 1. It was essentially the same as at the famous Lehner Clovis Site also in the San Pedro Valley and only 17 km (10.5 miles) to the south (Fig. 1.2, Site 2). The Clovis occupation surface at Lehner was covered by 10 cm of a black organic clay, the "black mat" (Stratum F_2). The bones at Murray Springs, as at Lehner, were under and in contact with the black mat.

CLOVIS SITE DISCOVERIES IN THE SAN PEDRO VALLEY

In 1951 Fred and Marc Navarrete discovered the Naco Clovis Site (Fig. 1.2, Site 1) in Greenbush Draw, a major tributary of the San Pedro. An interdisciplinary team of scientists, archaeologists Emil W. Haury, E. B. Sayles, and William W. Wasley of the Arizona State Museum, geologist Ernst Antevs, and paleontologist John F. Lance of the Geochronology Laboratories, excavated the Naco Site and reported a total of eight Clovis points directly associated with the incomplete skeleton of a single mammoth (Haury and others 1953).

Four years later in 1955–1956 Edward F. Lehner and the same scientists from the University of Arizona found 13 Clovis projectile points among the bones of nine mammoths under about 2 m of alluvial sediments near Lehner's ranch house (Fig. 1.2, Site 2), 17 km (10.5 miles) northwest of the Naco Site. The first radiocarbon ages for the Clovis culture, about 11,160 B.P., were obtained from two hearths at the Lehner Site (Haury and others 1959). Radiocarbon ages in this volume are presented in uncalibrated years before present (B.P.) with reference to the year 1950 except where calibrated ages are specifically mentioned (see Appendix A).

During the summers of 1974 and 1975 the Murray Springs team returned to the Lehner Site to excavate mammoth bones exposed by trenching in 1963 (Mehringer and Haynes 1965) and to search for an associated Clovis hunters' camp (Haynes 1982c). We did not find a camp site, but the excavations exposed the bones of three more mammoths in addition to bones of bison, camel, bear, and rabbit, all associated with an ancient stream channel (Agenbroad and Huckell 1981) that Haury and others (1959) called Mammoth Kill Creek.

An important find was a large but shallow roasting pit where a rabbit and parts of a bear and young mammoth had been cooked. The Clovis occupation surface provided 12 samples of charcoal that were radiocarbon dated and averaged 10,940 ± 40 B.P. (Taylor and others 1996). However, only a few stone tools came to light. Numerous small flakes were found where tools had apparently been resharpened by retouching the edges. Several flakes are of the same

Figure 1.1. Map of southeastern Arizona showing the San Pedro River Valley from Mexico to the confluence with the Gila River. Shaded relief image derived from USGS National Elevation Dataset (accessed 20 October 2005 at http://seamless.usgs.gov): image courtesy of Western Mapping Company, Tucson.

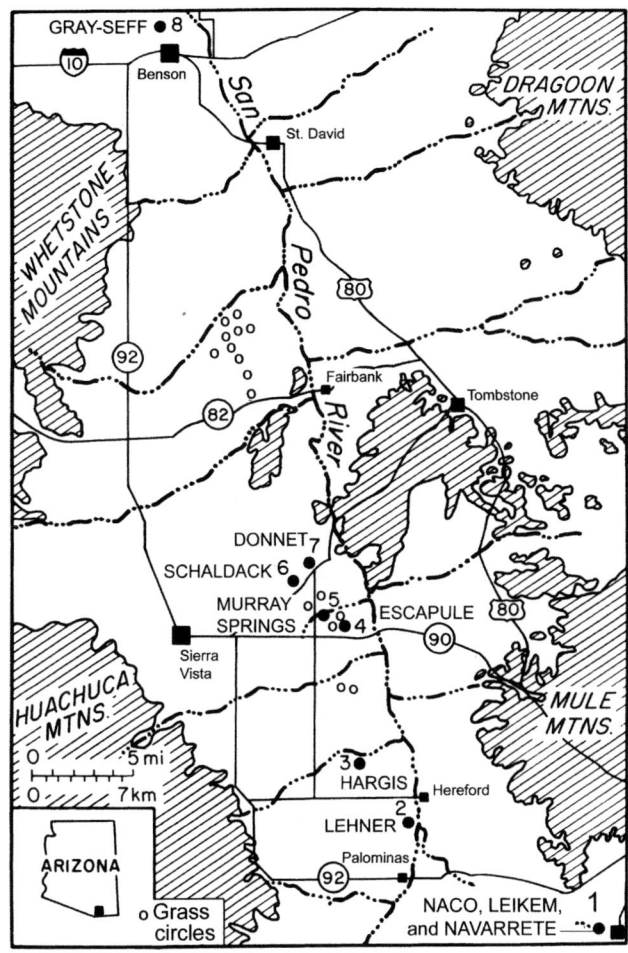

Figure 1.2. Map of the upper San Pedro Valley from Mexico to Benson, Arizona, showing locations of sites (●) and grass circles (○) described in Chapter 2.

material as two unifacial tools found 7 m away during the 1955–1956 excavations.

As at Murray Springs, the Clovis occupation surface was overlain by the black mat. At many places the black mat and younger units were riddled with rodent burrows. At least three generations of burrows could be distinguished on the basis of the color of the redeposited strata in their fills and their cross-cutting relationships.

The Escapule Clovis Site (Fig. 1.2, Site 4; Fig. 2.2), located only about 2 km (1.2 miles) southeast of the Murray Springs Site, consisted of the partial skeleton of a mammoth with two Clovis points in the rib cage (Hemmings and Haynes 1969). It was discovered by Louis W. Escapule in the early 1960s and professionally excavated in 1967. The bones were covered by the black mat (Stratum F_2) as at Murray Springs and Lehner.

Two other sites that should be mentioned in considering Clovis utilization of the San Pedro Valley are the Leikem and Navarrete sites. The Leikem Site, stratigraphically of Clovis age, was discovered in 1964 by Slim Leikem and reported to the University of Arizona by Howard Hamm. Mammoth bones were exposed in Greenbush Draw 1 km (0.6 mile) upstream (east) of the Naco Site (Fig. 1.2, Site 1) and on the opposite side of the draw. A Clovis point was found by Maureen Hogan, a six-year-old girl, who after school was playing in the backdirt from a stratigraphic backhoe trench that I placed far enough away to avoid the exposed bones. The trench did indeed avoid the exposed bones, but the skeleton of a second mammoth in a much better state of preservation was encountered by the backhoe. The complete Clovis point showed no evidence of wear from stream transport and was coated with carbonate blebs as occurred on the bones. No additional artifacts were found in our scientific excavations (Johnson and Haynes 1967).

We will never know for certain, but the point was probably associated with the bones of this second mammoth, which extended from the ancient stream bank to the ancient streambed where the skull lay. All were buried by a dark brown mudstone, an upstream facies of the black mat. In working out the stratigraphy I mapped both sides of Greenbush Draw between the Leikem and Naco sites, which showed both to be associated with the same ancient stream channel. The stratigraphy is clearly correlated with the other Clovis sites in the valley.

The second site stratigraphically of Clovis age was found in 1973 by Marc Navarrete, who with his father had discovered the original Naco Site. The Navarrete Site (Fig. 1.2, Site 1), as it is called, lies only 50 m upstream from the Naco Site and in the same bank. It was excavated by Emil Haury and Bruce Huckell and consisted of a few bones of two mammoths in the same buried channel as the Naco Site (Huckell 1981). A reworked projectile point fragment, found in the same channel deposit and half a meter from a pelvis, is apparently a contemporarily reworked portion of a Clovis point, but the diagnostic basal portion is missing. A slotted bone tool was next to a mammoth scapula exposed in the modern streambed, but from the manifest degree of leaching and calcification it is prob-

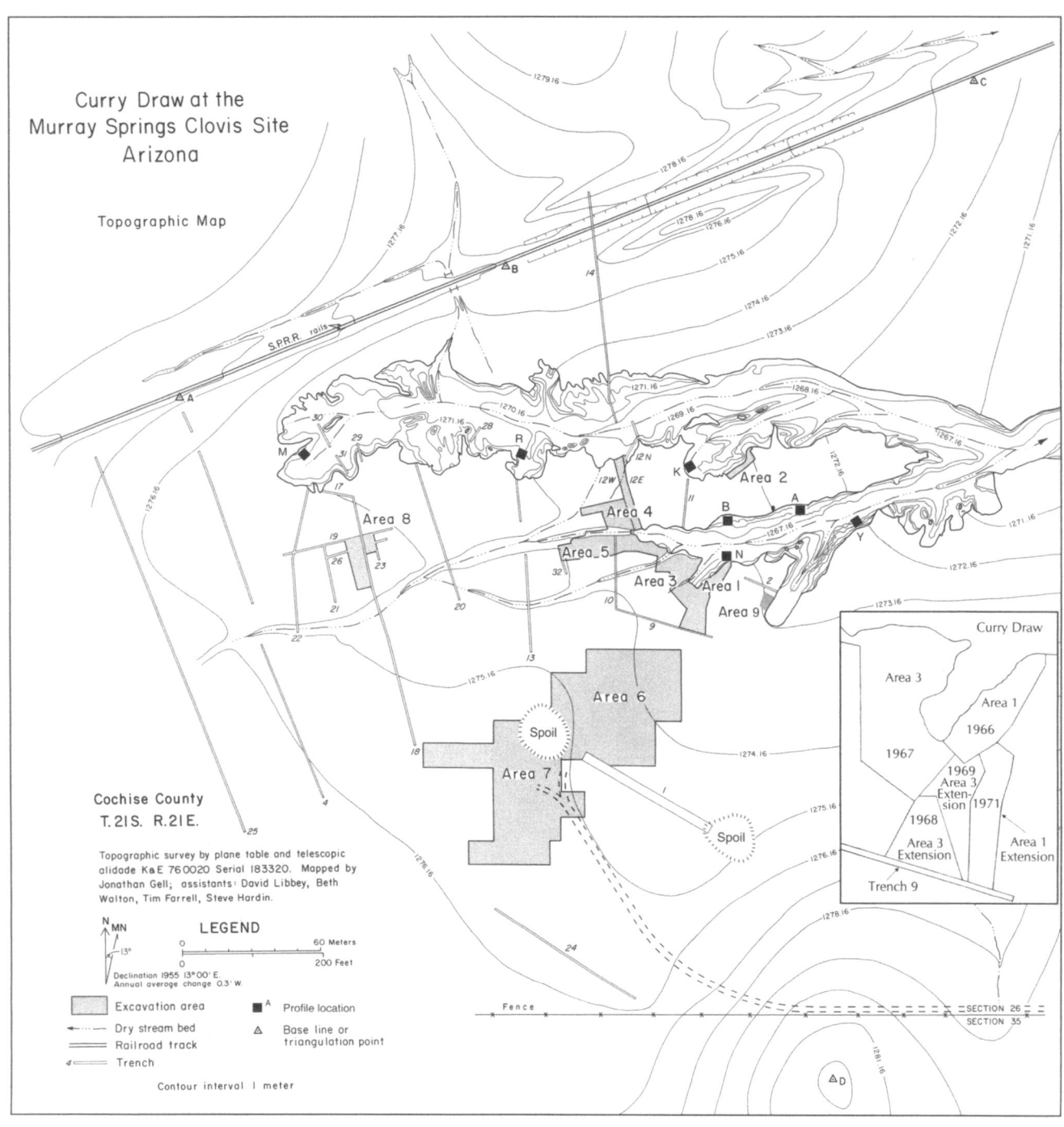

Figure 1.3. Topographic map of the Murray Springs Site showing excavation areas, stratigraphic trenches, and profile locations. Inset shows years of excavation in Areas 1 and 3.

ably contemporaneous with the mammoth bones and therefore part of a Clovis compound tool.

If we consider the Leikem and Navarrete sites to be Clovis, more than a fourth of the known stratified Clovis sites occur in the San Pedro Valley within an area only 32 km (20 miles) long. The others are scattered across the conterminous United States (Haynes 1980b; Stanford 1999), but, as explained in Chapter 2, the concentration of sites in the San Pedro Valley may be attributed in part to geologic factors of burial and erosion.

Until the Naco and Lehner discoveries the earliest archaeological evidence for the human occupation of southern Arizona had come from the Sulphur Spring Valley, the next major valley to the east of the San Pedro Valley (Fig. 1.1). In the 1930s E. B. Sayles and Ernst Antevs defined the Cochise culture on the basis of a sequence of preceramic sites in alluvium of Whitewater Draw and the San Pedro Valley (Sayles and Antevs 1941). Milling stones and rock-lined fire hearths occurred in the earliest stage, called Sulphur Spring, and bones of extinct Pleistocene animals were believed to be associated with it. Charcoal from a hearth was eventually dated by radiocarbon as 9350 ± 160 B.P. (A-67 bis., Damon and Long 1962). Questions regarding the relationship of the food gatherers of the Sulphur Spring stage to the hunter-foragers of the Clovis culture were raised but not answered by the Naco and Lehner excavations. Haury favored the hypothesis that Clovis was older than Sulphur Spring rather than a seasonal or functional facies of it (Haury and others 1953; Haury and others 1959). During subsequent excavations at the Lehner Site in 1974–1975 (Haynes 1982c), we found scattered artifacts of a post-Clovis occupation in situ at the top of the black mat that dated approximately 9700 B.P. The artifacts, clearly not Clovis, are attributable to the Early Archaic Sulphur Spring stage of the Cochise culture (Agenbroad and Huckell 1981), as is a well dug through the black mat. Sulphur Spring artifacts appear at least eight hundred years later than Clovis, and their temporal placement is further supported by Waters' (1985, 1986) reinvestigation of the Sulphur Spring type site.

At the time of the Naco Site discovery in 1951 there were only three other buried Clovis sites known, all east of the Continental Divide. The Naco and Lehner discoveries, the first ones west of the Divide, not only increased the number of stratified Clovis sites known at that time to five (Haynes 1964), but greatly expanded our knowledge of the Clovis culture (Haury and others 1959). Obviously they were skilled hunters of mammoth, bison, and probably other Pleistocene big game as well, but they also hunted smaller game as we learned later during renewed excavations at the Lehner Site (Haynes 1982c). Their distinctive "trademark," the Clovis fluted point, is a specialized projectile unique to the New World; surface finds have been made throughout the North American continent south of the late Pleistocene ice border (Anderson and Faught 2000; Haynes 1964). With the exception of a few bone and ivory tools, no perishable artifacts are positively associated with any Clovis site. The only human skeletal remains are a few skull and postcranial fragments of a child from the Anzick Clovis Site in Montana (Lahren 2001; Lahren and Bonnichsen 1974).

The remarkably similar chronostratigraphic position of the buried Clovis sites and their relatively brief existence, confined to between 11,000 and 11,500 B.P. by radiocarbon dating, led to the consideration that Clovis progenitors may have entered the New World from Asia after the deglaciation of the prairie plains of Canada at the end of the Pleistocene epoch (Haynes 1964, 1966). They may have been the first Americans and a factor in the extinction of the late Pleistocene (Rancholabrean) megafauna (Martin 1967).

As of the early 1960s the climate and environment of Paleoindians in the New World was not well understood and the interpretation of what was known was controversial (Antevs 1962; Martin 1963a). Peter Mehringer and I, then graduate students at the University of Arizona, attempted to shed new light on these problems by conducting new palynological (Mehringer) and geochronological (Haynes) studies in the San Pedro Valley. With encouragement from Emil Haury, Paul Martin, "Ted" Smiley and Ed Lehner we started in 1963 by reexposing the stratigraphy at the Lehner Site for collection of stratigraphically controlled radiocarbon and pollen samples. This work indicated a climate during Clovis time only slightly more mesic than today and produced enough encouraging results (Mehringer and Haynes 1965) that we extended these investigations to other Holocene alluvial deposits, including several where Paul Martin and his students had recovered useful assemblages of fossil pollen (Martin 1963a).

One such deposit was at Murray Springs where E. B. Sayles in 1953 had located mammoth bones and nearby a "heavily carbonaceous" organic deposit dated 8250 ± 200 B.P. (Wise and Shutler 1958, A-69). Although unsuccessful in relocating the mammoth bones, Paul Martin and James Schoenwetter (Martin 1963c) obtained a pollen record reflecting a warm, moist climate between radiocarbon samples that dated 8300 B.P. and 4000 B.P. This is essentially the Altithermal, a time Antevs (1948, 1962) proposed as having been hot and dry. In hopes of settling this problem Mehringer and I excavated a fresh profile of the arroyo wall and collected more pollen samples and radiocarbon samples (Appendix A). Our results essentially substantiated the warm, moist period of Martin's results but, as explained later, the record has turned out to be more complex than previously thought. We found that the 8300 B.P. date was on a redeposited mud ball and that the warm, moist period was between 5500 B.P. and 4000 B.P., post Altithermal (Mehringer and others 1967). No Altithermal period alluvial pollen record has been found because of a 2000-year hiatus in the stratigraphic record between 8000 B.P. and 6000 B.P.

DISCOVERY OF THE MURRAY SPRINGS SITE

Up to the spring of 1966 our several visits to Curry Draw (what we then called Murray Springs Arroyo) had been to the Martin-Schoenwetter pollen profile and the ruined Murray homeplace, at a spring about 100 m upstream, but not beyond. In extending the mapping of late Quaternary deposits in tributaries downstream in the San Pedro Valley from the Lehner Site, we were anxious to see what the rest of the arroyo looked like, so on that fine spring day we explored farther upstream in Curry Draw. Toward the headcut (Fig. 1.3) we found a layer of black organic clay, the "black mat" (Appendix B), identical to the black mat exposed at the Lehner Site atop the bones and artifacts (Fig. 1.4a).

The contrast of 5 cm to 15 cm of black clay over pale shades of greenish gray and reddish brown alluvium was spectacular, and its similarity to the Lehner Site stratigraphy prompted me to remark that all we had to do was find mammoth bones under the black mat and we could convince the National Geographic Society that we likely had another Clovis site. Within minutes of my remark we spotted mammoth bones under the black mat in a tributary gully (Fig. 1.4b). A few minutes later we explored the northern branch of the arroyo and found the second concentration of bones in a stratigraphic situation that was not as clear as the first (Fig. 1.4c). It was a very good day!

In a proposal to the National Geographic's Committee for Research and Exploration, I emphasized that if one were prospecting for a Clovis site, and essentially we were, the signs could not have been better. Buried Clovis sites are so rare and so important for understanding the origin and lifestyle of potentially the earliest inhabitants of the New World that a prospect like Murray Springs had to be tested. The Research Committee agreed, so less than three months after the site's discovery, the excavations began.

Initially we had intended to turn archaeological excavation of the site over to a colleague so I could concentrate on the geology and radiocarbon dating while Mehringer concentrated on pollen investigations. None of our archaeological colleagues were available, but a promising graduate student in the Anthropology Department at the University of Arizona, E. Thomas Hemmings, was looking for a suitable project for his doctoral dissertation. Tom had training in geology as well as field experience in archaeology and was interested in Paleoindian studies. So, using techniques I had learned from Henry Irwin and Cynthia Irwin-Williams at the Hell Gap Site in Wyoming, we began the excavation of Murray Springs, Areas 1 and 2, on 6 June 1966 with a crew of energetic and interested graduate students (Appendix G). Our objective was to uncover the Clovis living floor as carefully as possible in order

Figure 1.4. Views of Murray Springs Areas 1 and 2. (Unless noted otherwise, photographs are by C. Vance Haynes, Jr.)

a. David Libbey is examining sediments in the headcut of the South Branch of Curry Draw, 1966. The base of the black mat marks the Clovis occupation on the latest Pleistocene erosional surface. The contact between the St. David Formation below and the Millville alluvium above is at the top of Libbey's hat.

b. Vance Haynes is examining the mammoth bones in the discovery tributary, 1966, at what became Area 1. (Photograph by Peter J. Mehringer, Jr.)

c. Peter Mehringer is exiting the tributary in 1966 at the second bone discovery that became Area 2 later that year. The white bed is a marl facies of the black mat.

d. Beth Walton, Darell Clark, and Steve Hardin (top to bottom) excavating the Area 1 mammoth, 1966. The shovel is standing in backdirt filling the tributary arroyo.

e. Bones of the Area 1 mammoth stacked in a pile, consisting of a scapula resting on a lower jaw with a vertebra on top of the scapula.

f. David Libbey is inspecting Area 1 during an early stage of excavation in 1966. What appear to be mammoth footprints occur in foreground.

g. Peggy Davis and Bill Daniel (*background*) excavating the bone pile in Area 2, 1966.

h. Helicopter view of Area 1, Trench 9 (*foreground*) and Area 2 (*background*) near the end of the 1967 field season.

to observe the spatial relationships among artifacts, bones, and features such as fire hearths. The black mat aided precise excavation because it blanketed the Clovis occupation surface and broke cleanly away from it upon excavation by trowel, dental pick, or fingernail.

MURRAY SPRINGS 1966–1971

The accomplishments of the first field season during the summer of 1966 (Haynes 1973) included the excavation of a partial mammoth skeleton (Mammoth 1) in Area 1 (then designated Locality 1; Fig. 1.4*d*) and a few associated biface thinning flakes and worked pieces of stone. The lithics confirmed the presence of humans there at 11,000 B.P. according to a radiocarbon date obtained on ash (*Fraxinus*) charcoal. Further evidence of humans was suggested by the apparent stacking (Fig. 1.4*e*) of a mammoth scapula on a lower jaw and a vertebra on top of the scapula (Chapter 5). We considered numerous elephant foot-size depressions over much of the Clovis occupation surface to be mammoth tracks (Fig. 1.4*f*). Part of a mammoth skull in a lower deposit appeared to be much older, and therefore unrelated to the artifact horizon; it was left in place for later excavation. Our excavations in Area 2 revealed a pile of bones of mammoth, horse, bison, and camel but no artifacts (Fig. 1.4*g*).

I began detailed geologic mapping of the arroyo, which we learned was called Curry Draw on the 1902 land survey map by Philip Contzen of the U.S. Survey Department (Chapter 2, Fig. 2.7). We found the bones and artifacts to be associated with an ancient spring-fed stream system that had eroded its way through a late Pleistocene lake deposit. The only disappointing aspect was the almost total lack of significant amounts of fossil pollen in more than 100 samples collected and analyzed by Mehringer. Much of the vegetational history had to be derived from elsewhere (Mehringer and others 1971), but the extant vegetation along Curry Draw was studied by Susan L. Woodward (Chapter 3; Woodward 1969) to provide a basis for comparisons.

Between the 1966 and 1967 field seasons Louis Escapule, who was born and raised in the Tombstone area, showed us three additional localities nearby where he had found mammoth bones over several years of searching for archaeological sites in the San Pedro Valley. Another occurrence of mammoth bones was found by CWO William S. "Stanley" Hurley on the Fort Huachuca artillery range. During the 1967 field

Figure 1.5. The mammoth skeleton in Area 3 exposed in 1967. North-south line crosses the lower teeth and ends at nail in tusk at north end.

season, in addition to continuing the excavations at Murray Springs, we excavated partial mammoth skeletons at what we called the Hurley, Schaldack, Donnet, and Escapule sites (Haynes 1974). The last site, which contained two Clovis points found by Louis Escapule and his family, has been reported elsewhere (Hemmings and Haynes 1969).

As the excavations expanded we changed designations from "localities" to "areas," so the initial discovery Localities 1 and 2 became Areas 1 and 2 (Fig. 1.4*h*) and new areas of excavation were numbered in sequence. During the 1967 excavations at Murray Springs (Haynes 1974) we uncovered a nearly complete mammoth skeleton in Area 3 adjacent to Area 1 (Fig. 1.5). The crew at first named it Big Earl until paleontologist Jeff Saunders told us that Eloise would be more

Figure 1.6. Views of Murray Springs Areas 1 and 3. *a*, Morris Eckhardt exposing a pile of lithic flakes in Area 3, cluster 2, 1967. *b*, Mammoth bone shaft wrench exposed in 1967 shows dark staining where in contact with the black mat and no staining on that portion of the handle exposed a centimeter or two below the contact (photograph by Barney Burns). *c*, Numerous elephant foot-size depressions in Area 3 between the carcass of the mammoth in left background and the water hole, just off the bottom edge of the photograph, are believed to be mammoth tracks; view is to the northwest; backdirt pile is in the tributary headcut. *d*, Mammoth tracks and the water hole (*arrow*) were exposed by removing the black mat of the Clanton clay (Stratum F_{2a}) and the Earp marl (Stratum F_{2b}) from the southern part of Area 1; Afifa Hassan with wheelbarrow is in Area 3 Extension; John Bower is troweling the floor; directly behind him is Rob Pardee and Fekri Hassan is troweling at back wall.

appropriate. Between her and some bison remains were one Clovis point, the tips of two others, several stone tools, and hundreds of flakes produced by shaping and sharpening stone tools (Chapter 5). Many of these waste flakes occurred as discrete concentrations of specific lithic materials, each representing the debitage produced by a single flint knapper (Chapter 8). Some concentrations were so tight that many flakes of a particular pile were in contact with each other (Fig. 1.6*a*), attesting to the undisturbed condition of the 11,000 B.P. Clovis occupation surface. This degree of site integrity is unprecedented in Paleoindian archaeology.

The most remarkable artifact find of 1967 was a shaft wrench of mammoth bone (Fig. 1.6*b*) similar to some found with Paleolithic mammoth hunting cultures of Eastern Europe (Haynes and Hemmings 1968). It occurred in an area with a dense concentration of what we believe to be mammoth footprints (Fig. 1.6*c*). Perhaps it had been trod upon by a mammoth because part of the handle had broken off and was slightly below the erosional contact (the Clovis occupation surface) on what at one time was a muddy surface (Chapter 5).

A significant find in the western edge of Area 1 was what was most likely a shallow well or water hole (Fig. 1.6*d*) dug to the side of the stream bed, possibly by a mammoth, much as elephants do today in Africa and Asia during periods of drought (G. Haynes 1991:

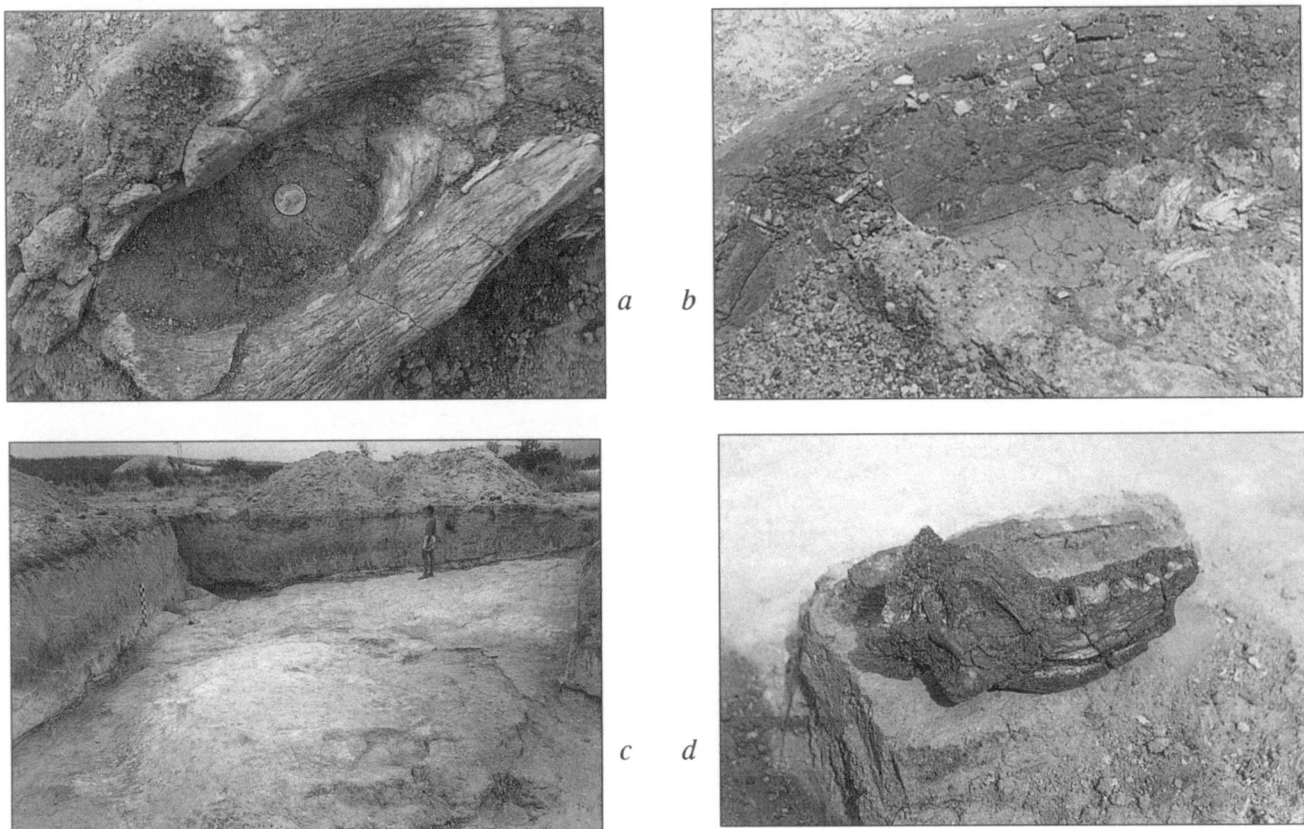

Figure 1.7. Views of Murray Springs Areas 1 and 3. *a*, Mud-cracked puddle clay in the obturator foramen of the pelvis of the Area 1 mammoth probably represents the last rain event before deposition of the black mat (Stratum F_{2a}). *b*, Mud-cracked puddle clay by tusk of the Area 3 mammoth, from same rain event as in *a* (photograph by Helga Teiwes, Arizona State Museum). *c*, Tom Naylor examining the Area 3 Extension in 1969; back wall is the south wall of Trench 9 and exposes lenticular cross section of the F_1 channel sand; thalweg of the F_1 channel (Wolf Creek) runs along the east (*left*) side. *d*, Jaw of dire wolf (*Canis dirus*) occurred on the Clovis surface in Area 3 between the water hole and the shaft wrench, 1967.

124–126). This feature, as well as mud cracks (Figs. 1.7*a*, *b*, B.1) and the indicated drop in the water table, led to the interpretation that a significant drought occurred about 11,000 B.P. (Haynes 1991). The Clovis age stream traversing Areas 1 and 3 (Fig. 1.7*c*) we named Wolf Creek because a dire wolf jaw (*Canis dirus*; Fig. 1.7*d*) was found in the left bank near the water hole. In 1969 Area 3 was extended southward (Area 3 Extension) to Trench 9 (Fig. 1.3) and in 1971 Area 1 was extended southward (Area 1 Extension), both with diminishing returns of artifacts (Haynes 1978).

Our exposure of the exact topographic surface that was walked upon by Clovis people was made possible by the fact that soon after occupation the water table rose to the surface in the low areas on and around the ancient stream channels. These areas were covered by the black organic clay deposit, the algal "black mat" (Chapter 2 and Appendix B) that contrasts sharply in both color and texture with the underlying sediments. Therefore, the Clovis level could be traced anywhere in the site by simply following the lower contact of the black mat (Stratum F_2). I call it the Clanton Ranch Member of the Lehner Ranch Formation (Chapter 2) after the Clanton Ranch house, the ruins of which are near the mouth of Curry Draw (Fig. 2.2). Because the Clantons were among the "black hats" or bad guys at the notorious O.K. Corral shootout in Tombstone, the name seemed appropriate for the black mat. White marl facies of Stratum F_2, described later, are called the Earp Member after the home of the "white hats" in

Figure 1.8. Views of Murray Springs Areas 4, 5, and 6. *a*, Cathy Ungar excavating bison rib cage in Area 4, 1968. *b*, Area 4 with crew in the expanded Trench 12, 1968 (photograph by Noye M. Johnson); white high ground (*lower right*) is Coro marl; Clovis hearth dated 10,760 B.P. is dark patch in depression in front of wheelbarrow; flake cluster A4–1 extends from the wheelbarrow onto the Coro marl. *c*, Westerly overview of Areas 4 and 5 with prehistoric well exposed in the west wall of Area 5, 1970; dark area (*center foreground*) is the headcut of the South Branch filled with back dirt (black mat). *d*, Clearing of the surface at the Clovis camp in Area 6 began in 1969; cottonwoods (*far middle ground*) are in Curry Draw; quarries of black silicified limestone occur in the saddle of the Lewis Hills (*background*).

Tombstone, realizing, of course, that the Earps were apparently not totally free of misdeeds.

It is the black mat that is responsible for the unusually high degree of site integrity. Wherever overlain by it the Clovis surface has remained virtually undisturbed since 11,000 B.P. This fortunate situation has allowed an estimated 98 percent of the artifacts to be exposed in the precise places where they were lost or abandoned about 13,000 years ago. Every significant artifact was recovered and photographed in situ before being plotted, removed, and catalogued in the field. Where the black mat is absent, as on high ground, the ancient surface is disturbed to varying degrees by insect and rodent burrowing (bioturbation, see Chapter 2).

By the end of the 1967 season Clovis artifacts had been found on the surface up to 80 m south and west of Area 1, and rain-induced caving of the south headcut exposed a bison bone bed under the black mat and on the Clovis occupation surface of what became Area 4 (Fig. 1.3). Therefore, during the 1968 field season (Haynes 1976) we exposed a multiple bison kill in Area 4 (Fig. 1.8*a, b*) northwest of Area 3, possibly a horse kill in Area 5 southwest of Area 4 (Fig. 1.8*c*), and expanded excavations into Areas 6 and 7 (Fig. 1.3) where the presence of surface artifacts led us to suspect a hunting camp might exist (Fig. 1.8*d*, Fig. 1.9*a*). A direct tie between the camp and the bison kill was demonstrated by the occurrence of an impact-produced

Figure 1.9. Views of Murray Springs Areas 3, 4, 5, and 7. *a*, Southerly view of excavations of the Clovis camp in Area 7 shows 2-m squares of the random sampling pattern laid out in 1971; the back dirt pile of Trench 24 crosses the East Swale, which extends to the cluster of soapberry trees on the intermediate horizon. *b*, Helicopter view of excavations in Areas 3, 4, and 5 in 1971; vehicles at west (*left*) edge are parked at Trench 32. *c*, Where the black mat (Stratum F_2) thickened in the northwesterly part of Area 5, it covered numerous small depressions probably made by bison in a muddy swale (photograph by E. Thomas Hemmings in 1970). *d*, In the Clovis camp in Area 7, some artifacts such as this Clovis point base occurred on remnants of the contact between the Coro marl and the Donnet silt in spite of significant bioturbation.

flake in Area 4 that fit the impact flake scar on a broken Clovis point found 73 m away, and presumably discarded, in the Area 6 camp. The reverse situation was discovered later by Bruce Huckell (Chapter 8, Fig. 8.2) in the laboratory, suggesting that an impact flake had been inadvertently carried 140 m from the bison kill to the camp in Area 7 (Fig. 1.9*a*), probably in a piece of meat.

Two clearly defined fireplaces or hearths were found in the Area 4 bison kill, one of which (Fig. 1.8*b*) yielded the only charcoal radiocarbon age (10,760 B.P.) positively related to a Clovis feature. As explained later, the age is probably about 100 years too young because of contamination. Another 20 charcoal dates are most likely directly related because the samples occurred on the Clovis surface or in the top sediments of the buried Clovis age stream channels, the Graveyard sand (Stratum F_1; Appendix A).

In 1968 excavation of the bison kill area was extended to the north by widening Trench 12 (Fig. 1.8*b*) and to the south (Fig. 1.9*b*; Haynes 1978). This produced two Clovis points, a blade, two bifaces, and numerous flakes. The lowest part of Area 5 was covered with small depressions that probably are bison

Figure 1.10. Views of Murray Springs Area 8. *a*, Conduit 1 exposed by Trench 18 became a buried mound as compaction lowered the surrounding ground (see text). *b*, Large mammal bones were common in Stratum D_2 around the sides of Conduit 2 where Rosa Portell-Ferrer is cleaning bone. *c*, Gerald Kelso (with hat) and Jeff Saunders observing Conduit 2 near the center of which a 75-cm diameter area of soft sand outlined by tape (Feature 1) may be where Clovis people recovered water. *d*, About 10 m south of the conduits a 75-cm diameter excavation exposed by removing the black mat may have been an attempt at well digging that was abandoned when the much better source was found in Conduit 2 described in *c* above (see Fig. 2.17).

tracks or a mixture with other tracks (Fig. 1.9*c*). Two prehistoric wells, one exposed in the west wall of Area 5 (Figs. 1.8*c*, 5.27), are estimated to be about 3,000 years old based on the stratigraphic position of the surface from which they were dug (see Foldout 2, following page 48).

During the final two field seasons (1970–1971) at Murray Springs, Larry D. Agenbroad took over as site foreman while Hemmings completed his dissertation. Our attention focused on the Clovis camp (Area 6 and the adjacent Area 7) and a fossil spring (Area 8) encountered by stratigraphic Trench 18 (Fig. 1.3) west of the main excavations at the end of the 1969 field season. In addition to concentrations of flakes, the camp site produced scrapers, knives, and basal portions of Clovis points (Fig. 1.9*d*), the kinds of artifacts that

Figure 1.11. Views of Murray Springs Area 8. *a*, Removal of the weakly cemented sand (Stratum D_2) from Conduit 2 revealed concentric layers of relatively more cemented sand with bones and teeth; the dip in the black mat at the top of the mound may be where Clovis people collected water. *b*, Ten anomalous rocks, cobble to boulder size, occurred on Sobaipuri mud north of Conduit 2; eleven others were found 10 cm to 70 cm below the contact with the black mat (see Fig. 2.17); these rocks may have been stepping stones. A single biface thinning flake occurred with remnants of a bison jaw by the white tags at the right edge of the photograph.

Figure 1.12. Fossil teeth brought up by the backhoe (from Area 8 discovery trench) on the National Geographic Society flag include horse (*lower left*), bison (*upper left*), camel (*top center*), mammoth (*lower right*), and miscellaneous specimens (*upper right*) with the canine of a large cat.

would be expected in a hunting camp (described in Chapter 7).

Excavations in Area 8 were directed by vertebrate paleontologist Jeffrey J. Saunders, who had been in charge of the vertebrate studies since 1967, and archaeologist-palynologist Gerald Kelso, who had been with us in 1966 and 1969 (Saunders and Kelso 1971). Excavations in the feeder sand (Stratum D_2) of one of two spring conduits (Figs. 1.10, 1.11), both of pre-Clovis age, revealed hundreds of bones and teeth of several Pleistocene animals (Fig. 1.12). The springs were probably most active between 30,000 and 15,000 years ago when they fed the lake or pond (Strata D and E) that covered the Murray Springs Site area during the late Pleistocene glacial period. There appears to have been an attempt here by Clovis people to find a source of water when it was low soggy ground (Chapter 2).

From the interdisciplinary investigations at Murray Springs we learned that Clovis people successfully hunted bison and mammoth along the banks of a spring-fed creek (we named it Bison Kill Creek) about 11,000 B.P. (Plate 8) during a brief drought (Haynes 1991), even though the riparian environment was somewhat more mesic (higher water table) than it has been in the recent past. They carried lithic raw material with them in the form of bifaces (Hemmings 1970) that could serve as chopping and cutting implements and that were further worked, on the spot, into tools suitable for the task at hand (Chapter 8). Fifty to 150 meters away from the kill areas they maintained a temporary hunting camp where they apparently processed some of the meat, hide, and bones taken during the hunt and repaired their tools and weapons.

Fortunately most of the Murray Springs Clovis Site lies within a complex stratigraphic framework. These strata are like pages in the book of time for Curry Draw. Reading and interpreting these pages, the task of the geologist, allows one to place the Clovis events in their proper place in the stratigraphic framework and, in collaboration with others, to reconstruct the paleoclimatic and paleoecological changes that occurred during the deposition, pedogenesis, and erosion of the strata. The geologic investigations presented next in Chapter 2 clarify the stratigraphic framework and provide evidence with which to estimate the geologic-climatic processes that formed it.

CHAPTER TWO

Quaternary Geology of the Murray Springs Clovis Site

C. Vance Haynes, Jr.

The Murray Springs Clovis Site is located in Curry Draw, a small tributary of the San Pedro River. The San Pedro is the middle of three rivers that flow northward through southeastern Arizona to the Gila, a major tributary of the Colorado River. From its headwaters near Cananea in Sonora, Mexico, the intermittent to ephemeral San Pedro River extends northward 241 km (150 miles) to join the Gila River at Winkelman (Fig. 1.1). As defined here, the upper San Pedro Valley extends northward from south of the border with Mexico to the town of Benson and lies between the Dragoon and Mule mountains on the east and the Whetstone and Huachuca mountains on the west (Fig. 1.2). Precipitation across the total drainage area of 11,610 square kilometers (4,483 square miles; with 1,803 square kilometers or 696 square miles in Mexico) averages 38 cm (15 inches) but is only about 28 cm (12 inches) at the lower elevations (Roeske and Werrell 1973). Most of the rain falls during the summer monsoon season with a second peak of more general rains occurring in the winter.

The structural control for the San Pedro Valley is not well defined. It is a part of the basin and range geomorphic province in which mountain blocks of older rocks are separated by down-dropped blocks forming basins filled with younger sediments (Morrison 1985, 1991). A few large earthquakes occurred within the historic period (DuBois and Smith 1980). The Huachuca Mountains, the highest of the bordering ranges, support pine, fir, and aspen at their summits (2,920 m), which are 1,990 m higher than the riverbed at Charleston. The gently sloping surfaces extending from the base of the mountains to the inner valley are referred to as bajadas or pediments. These slopes vary in length from 10 km to 30 km (6–19 miles) and are broken by bedrock hills such as the Charleston and Lewis hills on and near the axis of the valley.

The bajadas overlie either the Granite Wash alluvium of Robert Gray (1965, 1967) or less defined pediment-cap alluvium all overlying a deep valley fill composed of alluvium, playa sediments, and ancient soils (paleosols) known as the St. David Formation (defined by R. Gray 1965, 1967), which is of Pliocene-Pleistocene age (Fig. 2.1; N. Johnson and others 1975). The oldest part of the basin fill is of Miocene age and rests in places against tilted Miocene beds, thus dating the last major episode of tectonism.

Curry Draw is an easterly flowing tributary of the upper San Pedro River in Cochise County, Arizona (Fig. 2.2). The arroyo, which appears as a second order unnamed drainage on the Lewis Springs 7.5 minute Quadrangle, exposes the Murray Springs Clovis Site in the SW¼ of the SE¼ of Section 26, R21E, T21S (31°34'13"N, 110°10'40"W). The site, at the confluence with the East Swale tributary (Figs. 2.2, 2.4a–d), is 3.3 km (2 miles) from the San Pedro River but is best reached from Moson Road by taking the Murray Springs Site road east-northeastward along an abandoned Southern Pacific railroad grade that parallels the draw for 1 km (0.62 mile). Since 1988 the site has been a part of the San Pedro Riparian National Conservation Area of the Bureau of Land Management and is signed for self-guiding tours.

The Murray Springs Clovis Site (Fig. 2.3; Plate 1, following p. 48) is unique in that it contains three distinct activity areas where a band of Clovis hunters killed mammoth (Areas 1 and 3) and several bison (Areas 4 and 5) and occupied a small camp site (Areas 6 and 7) during two or three brief visits 13,000 years ago. The buried occupation surface is clearly displayed

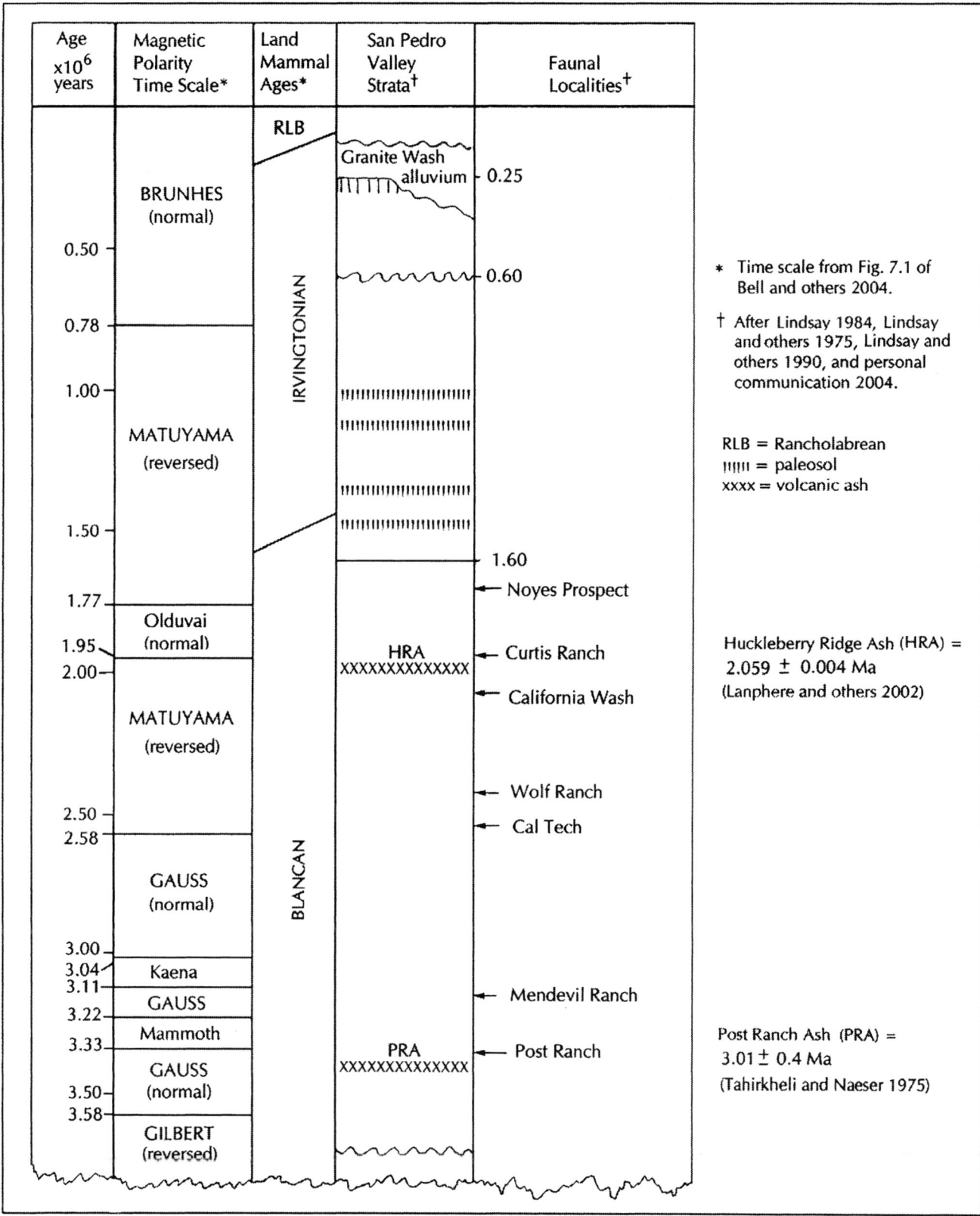

Figure 2.1. Time-stratigraphic column for the St. David Formation of the San Pedro Valley, modified after Lindsay and others 1990.

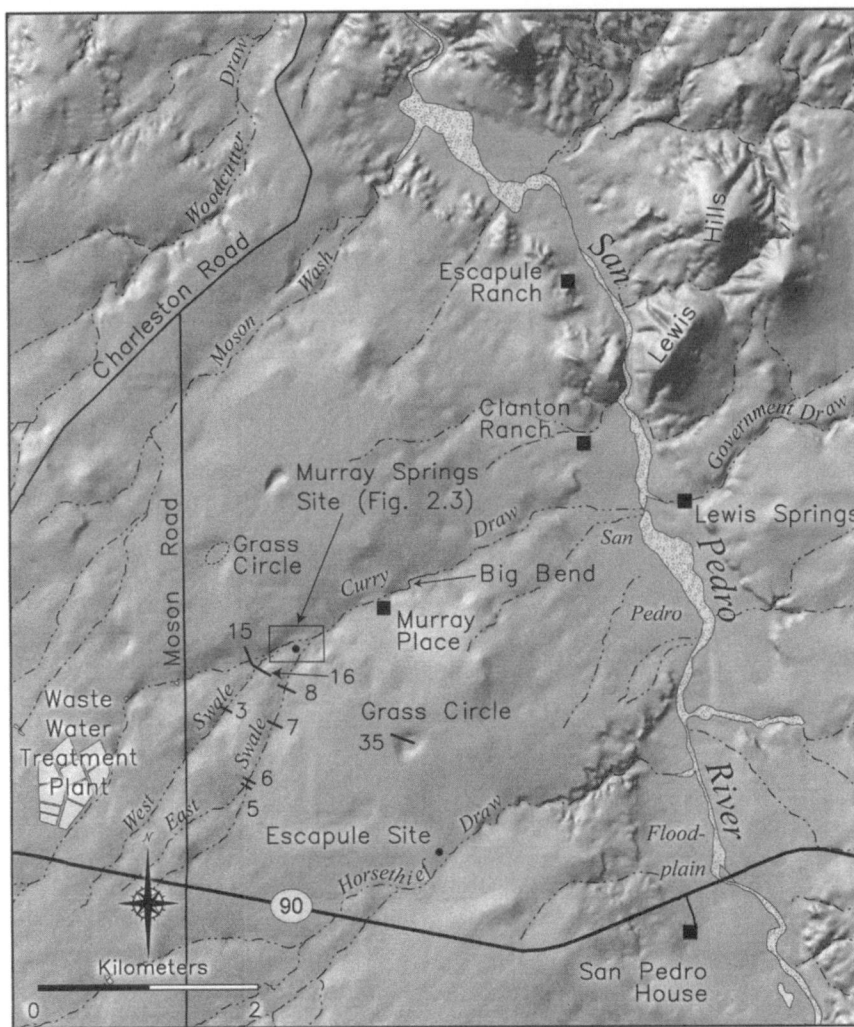

Figure 2.2. Shaded relief digital elevation map of the Curry Draw area showing the Murray Springs Site, trenches outside of Figure 2.3 box, and grass-floored circular depressions between Horsethief Draw and Moson Wash. Ancient quarries for black silicified limestone occur in the saddle of the Lewis Hills, "Limy Hill" on Figure 2.7.

in the arroyo walls as an erosional contact at the base of a distinctive black organic mat, Stratum F_2 (Clanton Ranch Member of the Lehner Ranch Formation) that preserved artifacts and extinct animal bones in their original positions and mammoth tracks (Figs. 1.4f, 1.6c) as they were left 13,000 years ago (Haynes and Hemmings 1968). The late Quaternary stratigraphic framework (Fig. 2.5; Plate 2), more complete than at any of the dozen known Clovis sites in stratigraphic context, is impressive because of the marked color contrasts of the sedimentary strata and the excellent exposures along 2.6 km (1.6 miles) of arroyo walls between the site and the San Pedro floodplain to which the stratigraphy is directly traceable. Correlations throughout the upper San Pedro Valley are augmented by about 120 radiocarbon dates (Appendix A, Table A.1). Prior to this book, the Murray Springs Site has been reported on only briefly in the publications cited in Chapter 1 and in Haynes and Hemmings (1970).

GEOMORPHOLOGY AND MODERN CONDITIONS

Curry Draw, with two headcuts separated by 1 km (0.6 mile), is a typical discontinuous gully in which the lower headcut, at the Murray Springs Site as of 1967, had moved at an average rate of 30 cm per year and in spurts of as much as 10 m during a particular storm period. However, in 1998 a summer storm caused the headcut to migrate more than 30 m upstream. Two northward-flowing tributaries, the East and West swales (Figs. 2.2, 2.4), remain essentially undissected, except that a headcut had started up the East Swale about 15 m and exposed mammoth bones (Fig. 1.4b)

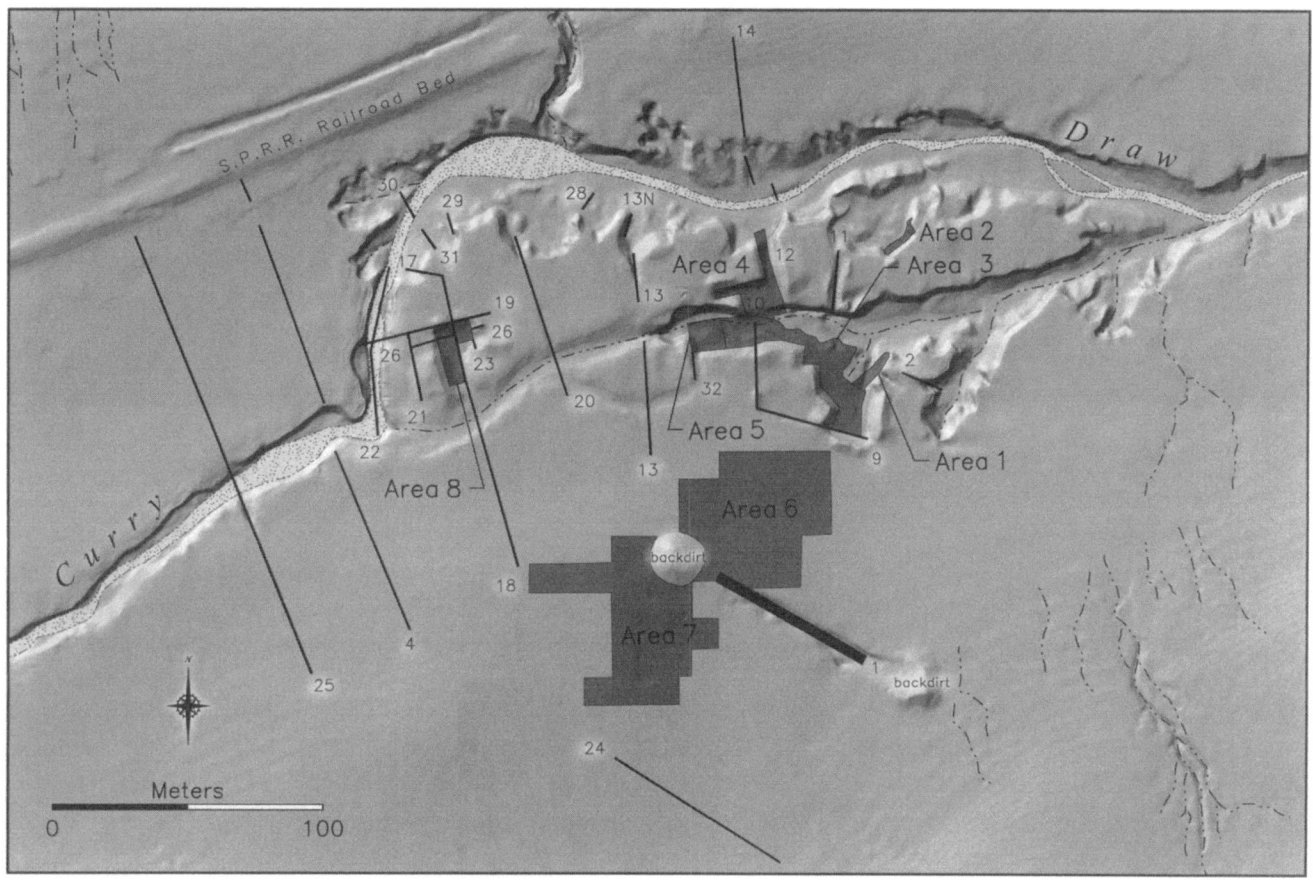

Figure 2.3. Shaded relief digital elevation map of the Murray Springs Site showing the North and South branches of Curry Draw, the archaeological excavation areas, and the stratigraphic trenches (based on 2002 aerial photogrametry).

sometime between Paul Martin's visit to the Murray Place in 1959 and the time that Mehringer and I discovered them in 1966 (Chapter 1).

The local upland (the Tombstone surface of Bryan 1926 and Plate 10 in Gilluly 1956) is an ancient bajada extending from the Huachuca Mountains to the inner valley. Along Curry Draw the Tombstone surface is being eroded by slope retreat extending westward from the San Pedro inner valley as well as from the tributary valley sides (Fig. 2.4e, f). In the site area an alluvial gravel veneer, the Nexpa gravels (Stratum Y), unconformably overlies the St. David Formation as strathterrace remnants (Figs. 2.5, 2.6d). As described later, slightly higher areas of Tombstone surface in the Curry Draw area contain shallow circular depressions called "grass circles" because of the desert grassland communities preserved in them (Figs. 2.2, 2.4e, f, 2.6a–c; Chapter 3). The only significant tributaries of upper Curry Draw, the East and West swales just mentioned, are undissected and filled with middle to late Holocene alluvium of the Escapule Ranch Formation (Plates 3 and 4; Foldout 1). The two swales are not traceable beyond about 3 km (1.85 miles), where they merge with the Tombstone surface and lose their identity. The gentle slopes between remnants of the Nexpa gravels and the Holocene alluvial fills are in some places difficult to identify and map as either St. David Formation or Millville alluvium because of pedogenic modification and a thin veneer of lag gravel and slopewash alluvium.

The stratigraphy and geomorphology of Curry Draw reveal an unusually complete record of late Quaternary depositional, pedological, and erosional events (Fig. 2.5) controlled by changing climate. If water table levels with respect to channel configuration and sediments can be taken as approximate indicators of fluvial

20   *Chapter 2, C. Vance Haynes, Jr.*

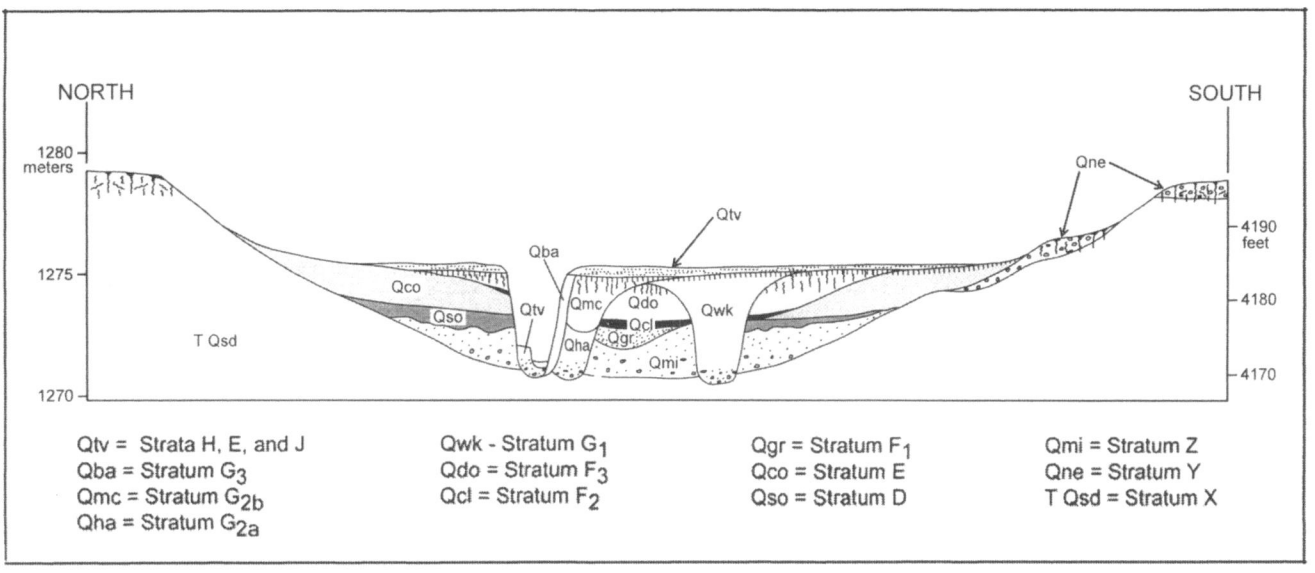

Figure 2.5. Generalized geologic cross section of Curry Draw at the Murray Springs Site. Elevations are approximate and vertical scale is exaggerated.

discharge conditions, some gross indications of late Quaternary climate change can be read from the alluvial stratigraphy.

Historic accounts of what the San Pedro River looked like before arroyo cutting have already been mentioned and are more thoroughly covered by Cooke and Reeves (1976), Hereford (1991, 1993), and Hereford and Betancourt (In preparation). However, there are few if any published accounts of how the tributary valleys appeared.

The Murray Springs Clovis Site is named for the homeplace of William "Pink" Murray and family located at a point of spring discharge along the floor of Curry Draw (Fig. 2.2). The late Grace McCool, who compiled Cochise County history for many years (McCool 1967), told me in 1981 that the Murray Place was occupied earlier by Joe Curry and his family, who in 1882 refurbished an abandoned adobe building at a spring, and that the location (Fig. 2.7) had been a watering station for the pre-Civil War Tucson freight

◄─────

Figure 2.4. Aerial views of the Curry Draw area.

a, Easterly view down Curry Draw to the San Pedro River in the background where the Lewis Hills can be seen on the east side. The Murray Springs Site is at the confluence of the East Swale (*lower right*) and Curry Draw. Trench 4 is in the foreground. The abandoned railroad grade that parallels the north side of the draw later became the modern access road.

b, Near vertical view shows the undissected East and West swales, tributaries of entrenched Curry Draw. The furrows paralleling the swales are a root-knifing operation to remove desertscrub done in 1966 in preparation for aerial seeding with an exotic grass (*Eragrostis lehmanniana*) to improve the range for cattle.

c, 1980 Peter Kresan aerial photograph, westerly view, up Curry Draw showing Moson Road crossing the draw and the north end of the Huachuca Mountains (*background*).

d, 1971 aerial view showing stratigraphic backhoe trenches and the Murray Springs archaeological excavations at the Curry Draw-East Swale confluence. Area 8 excavation is left of center. The Clovis camp (Areas 6 and 7) is the light area below and right of center.

e, Westerly view showing an entrenched grass circle within Chihuahuan desertscrub on the Tombstone surface. Slope retreat (*foreground*) is eroding the Tombstone surface. Murray Springs excavations (*right middle*) are at the East Swale-Curry Draw confluence. Desertscrub has been artificially replaced by Lehman's lovegrass (*Eragrostis lehmanniana*) in the light area.

f, View south-southeast showing the San Pedro floodplain (*background*), entrenched grass circle (*right middle ground*), and the Murray Springs excavations (*left foreground*).

Figure 2.6. Views of special features of the Curry Draw area. *a*, Aerial view of trench in grass circle of yucca grassland surrounded by Chihuahuan desertscrub. *b*, Westerly view across grass circle showing early stage of trenching through yucca grassland. *c*, Dennis Stanford examines the compound paleosol in the grass circle trench in 1967; the mollic epipedon is probably a local manifestation of the Donnet silt (Stratum F_3); see Appendix A, Table A.1, for bulk sediment radiocarbon dates in the black A horizon. *d*, A Stage IV petrocalcic horizon in Nexpa gravels (Stratum Y) is exposed by the railroad cut north of Trench 14. *e*, In 1967 the road into the site, along the Tombstone aqueduct pipeline (buried), passed through a pasture seeded with Lehman's lovegrass in 1966 after the area had been root-knifed. *f*, A repeat photograph in 2006 shows how well the Chihuahuan desertscrub has reclaimed its territory.

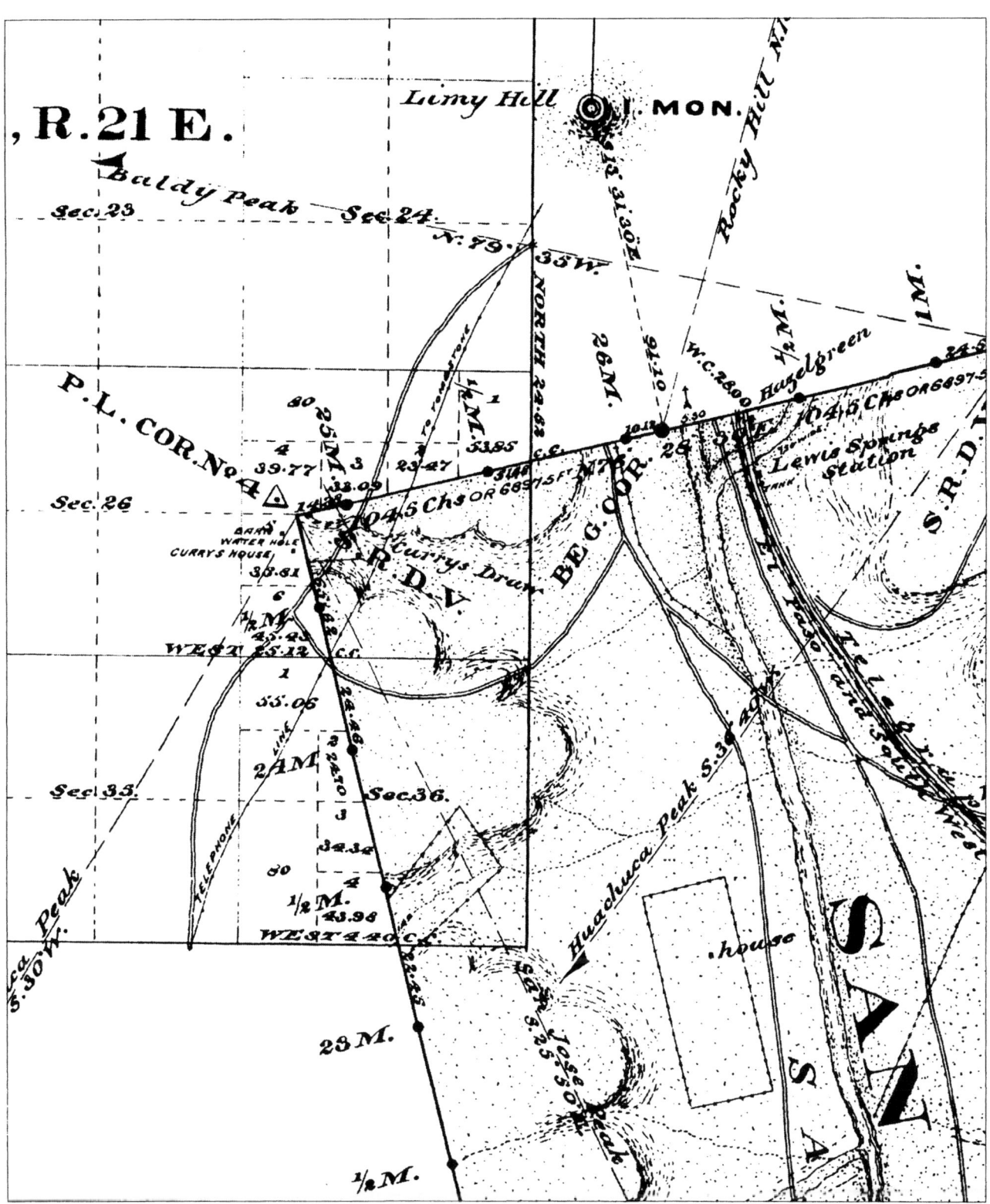

Figure 2.7. Part of the San Rafael de Valle grant mapped in 1902 by Philip Contzen of the U.S. Survey Department shows "Currys Draw" and home site that later became the Murray Place.

company of Tully-Ochoa. The Curry house, barn, and water hole are shown on "Currys Draw" on the 1902 Plot of the San Rafael del Valle land grant by Philip Contzen, U.S. Survey Department (Fig. 2.7). It is not known when the Murray family took over the Curry Place, but Pink reportedly worked as a foreman for Col. W. C. Greene, who owned the adjacent San Rafael del Valle grant (Sonnichsen 1974; 17,353.86 acres granted to Rafael Elias Gonzales in 1827) as well as the Murray Springs property. After Greene's death in 1911, some of his holdings in Cochise County were acquired by the Boquillas Land and Cattle Company.

According to local residents, the old Murray Place was a grassy swale where dairy cows were pastured before 1913 when the Murray family moved to Tombstone. Correspondence with Pink's oldest son Henry reveals that up to the time they moved, there were two cottonwood trees, a "boxed in" spring, and a hand-dug well 25 to 30 feet deep that never went dry, and no arroyo (Henry P. Murray, personal communication with P. J. Mehringer 1967 and C. V. Haynes 1981).

In 1968 the late Ernest B. Escapule, who knew Pink Murray, recalled that the arroyo cut to the Murray Place in 1916 when excessive runoff deepened the ruts of a wagon road that led down the middle of the grassy swale. On the other hand, in 1969 the late Albert Thomas, a longtime rancher on the east side of the valley, stated that the San Pedro cut to Wolf Ranch (San Pedro House on Highway 90; Fig. 2.2) in 1926 and that the headcut in Curry Draw was just below the Murray house in 1929. The Fort Huachuca spur of the Southern Pacific Railroad was placed along the north side of Curry Draw in 1913 by the El Paso & Southwestern Railroad Company (E. J. Horley, personal communication 1980).

Now the mostly dry arroyo (Fig. 2.8a) is 3 m deep at the homeplace, where large cottonwood trees flourish and water frequently emerges along 30 m or more of the sandy bed (Fig. 2.8c). Today this is the Murray Spring, but remnants of a wood-lined hand-dug well on the right bank are probably from the well that provided water for the Murray household before arroyo cutting. The detailed nature of the Murray Spring before arroyo cutting is not known. Presumably the name was applied to seeps along the grassy floor of the draw. Today organic sediments of the Bakarich Ranch Member (Stratum G_3) exposed in the arroyo walls indicate it was essentially a small cienega before the latest episode of entrenchment. Throughout much of the period from 1966 through 1969 the arroyo bed at the Murray Place remained wet (up to 20 cm of standing water at times, Fig. 2.8c), but was dry most of 1970 and 1971. Even when dry, water is encountered within 20 cm to 30 cm of the surface as revealed by miniature water holes dug by small animals (Fig. 2.8b). The shallow aquifer is very likely perched.

The two branches of Curry Draw converge about 120 m downstream of the Murray Springs Site (Figs. 1.3, 2.3; Plate 3). The earliest aerial photograph of the area shows the South Branch headcut to be about 850 m upstream from the Murray Place in 1935 and the North Branch headcut about 300 m beyond that (Fig. 2.9a). By 1955 the South Branch headcut had advanced 55 m, reaching the East Swale, and the North Branch headcut had advanced 60 m farther upstream (Fig. 2.9b). U.S. Army photographs taken in 1966 (Fig. 2.9c) show the South Branch headcut had moved about 60 m, and the North Branch headcut had moved

⎯⎯⎯⎯⎯⎯⎯⎯⟶

Figure 2.8. Views of some modern environments.

a, Dry bed of Curry Draw ~ 0.3 km above the Murray Place, 1976.

b, Animal-dug water holes in the dry bed of Curry Draw, July 2002, are typical of small animals seeking water at depths up to 30 cm below the bed surface.

c, Bruce Huckell observes spring discharge in the floor of Curry Draw at the Murray Place in 1981 that forms ponds up to 20 cm deep dammed by cottonwood roots. In 1970 and 1971 this reach was dry and wide enough for a jeep to pass. By the late 1970s an inset terrace formed, covered by the deer grass (*Muhlenbergia rigens*) shown here.

d, Perennial spring-fed discharge of Government Draw at Lewis Springs in 1967 may be a modern analog of Bison Kill Creek just before it dried up during Clovis time.

e, Pond fed by natural effluent at Babocomari Cienega in 1972 may be a modern analog for the Murray Springs Site's black mat (Stratum F_2) deposition during the Younger Dryas cold period.

f, The undissected swale of Turkey Creek in 1971 above O'Donnell Cienega is a modern analog of what Curry Draw might have looked like at the end of Donnet silt (Stratum F_3) deposition about 8000 B.P.

g, Aerial view of the San Pedro River in Mexico a few kilometers south of the border in 1967. Northwesterly view shows perennial flow meandering across a floodplain with back swamps and abandoned meanders. The terrace above the floodplain is of much older valley fill sediments.

a b c

d e

f g

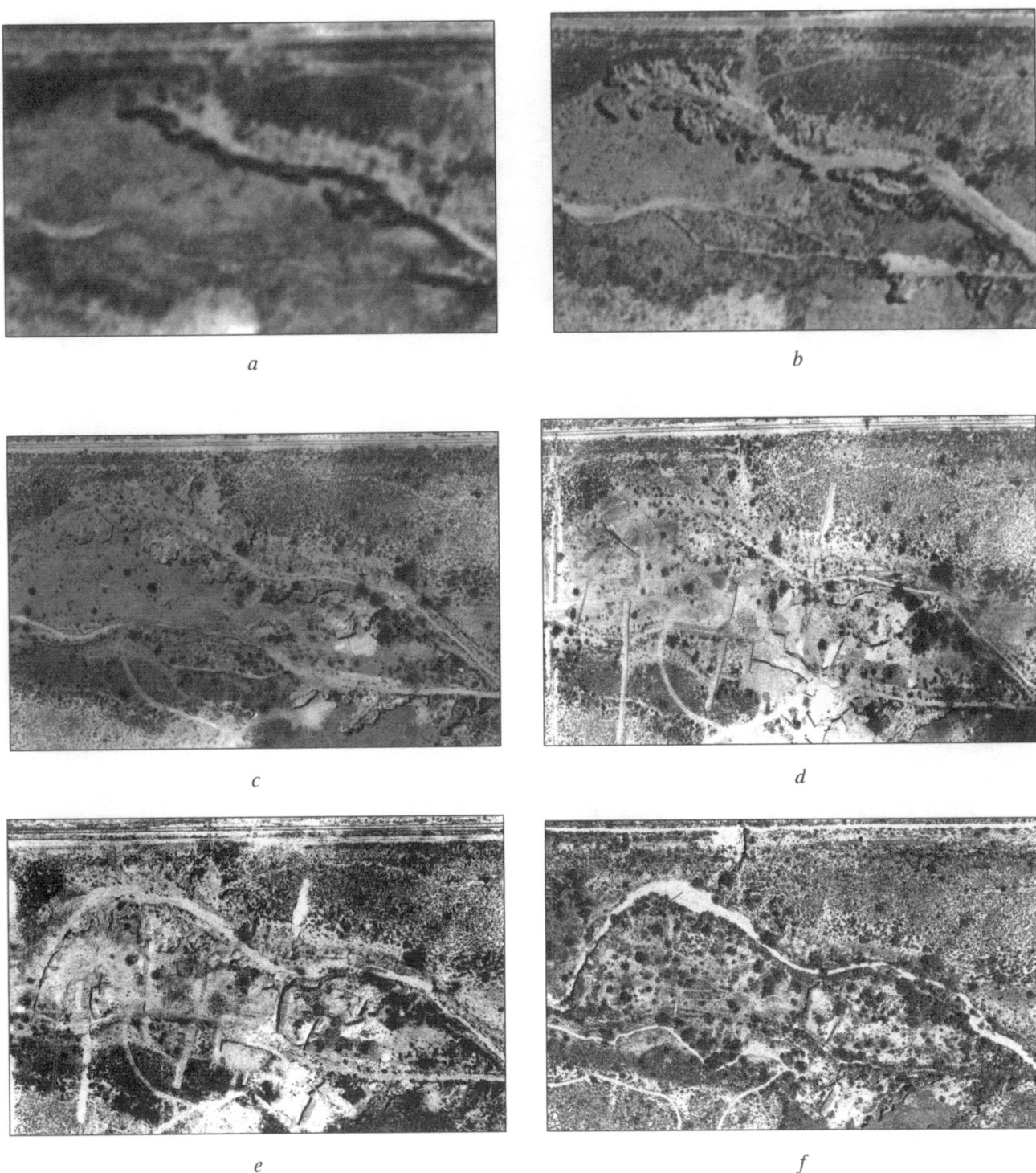

Figure 2.9. Aerial photographs of Curry Draw during a 67-year interval. *a*, 1935 U.S. Soil Conservation Service photograph SCS-701. *b*, 1955 U.S. Geological Survey photograph DXH-5N-90. *c*, 1966 U.S. Army Combat Surveillance School photograph. *d*, 1969 U.S. Army Combat Surveillance School photograph. *e*, 1973 Cooper Aerial Surveys photograph. *f*, 2002 photograph by Engineering and Environmental Consultants for the Bureau of Land Management.

less than 10 m. As mentioned in Chapter 1, rains of 1967 caused a retreat of 3 m that exposed the bison kill area in the south headcut, which moved an additional 27 m by 1973 (Fig. 2.9*e*). To protect the site from erosion, Trench 22 (Figs. 1.3, 2.3) was deliberately not completely filled in when the project ended; the intent was for Trench 22 to divert discharge to the North Branch and away from the South Branch headcut, an event that began during high discharge in 1983. Discharge events of the 1990s have caused the North Branch headcut to migrate more than 100 m farther upstream by following and widening Trench 22 to the main channel of Curry Draw. The most damaging event occurred in 1998 when a significant amount of discharge at the head of Trench 22 topped the bank at the right angle bend and flowed to the south headcut, causing it to move about 2 m headward (Figs. 2.3, 2.9*e, f*; Plate 1).

The upstream headcut was about 80 m west of Moson Road in 1966, but was buried during construction of the road in 1972 (Fig. 2.2). It had moved no more than 10 m or 20 m between 1955 and 1972. Between 1935 and 1955 it moved about 270 m.

In 1966 most of the land south of Curry Draw was deep plowed ("root-knifed" by a large bulldozer pulling a one-inch-thick steel knife blade between two rippers a few inches below the surface) to destroy the Chihuahuan desertscrub (Chapter 3) with the hope that aerial seedings of an African grass (*Eragrostis lehmanniana*; Bock and others 1986) would displace the whitethorn acacia, creosote, and tarbush and reestablish desert grassland (Fig. 2.4*b, e*). The experiment produced three or four years of good grass (Fig. 2.6*e*) before desertscrub began to reestablish itself, and today it is clearly the winner (Fig. 2.6*f*).

The root-knifing operation, by ripping up the caliche (petrocalcic horizon) with furrows paralleling the contours, must have greatly increased the infiltration capacity of the ground to the south of the draw, thus practically eliminating overland flow for a few years. Overland flow in the swales, most of which were not root-knifed, occurred in the summer of 1969 when a local thunderstorm created overland flow that spilled over the north wall at the North Branch headcut. Little or no flow occurred over the South Branch except where it was joined by the East Swale, despite the fact that there is about ten times more catchment area to the south than to the north. Typically, summer thunderstorms are very localized. Recent runoff has caused significant headcut migration up the East Swale, which exposed bone, but no artifacts, below the black mat in Area 9 (Appendix E).

Discharge down Curry Draw was further curtailed by the construction in 1966 of a tank dam 2.7 km (1.67 miles) upstream of the Murray Springs Site. Despite isolating 44 percent of the catchment, the tank seldom had water in it. In 1980 the area between Moson Road and the tank dam was converted into sludge ponds for waste water from the Sierra Vista sewage treatment plant (Fig. 2.2). This has recently been converted to an infiltration site for treated waste water.

From the time we discovered the Murray Springs Clovis Site in 1966 until 1971, it was possible with 4-wheel-drive vehicles to motor up the arroyo bed from the mouth of Curry Draw all the way to the site and the North Branch headcut. Since then, inset terrace alluviation along the wet stretch has made the bed too narrow, and bunches of a tall native deer grass (*Muhlenbergia rigens*) have grown on the inset terrace (Stratum J), which is as much as a meter high in places (Fig. 2.8*c*). Why is aggradation taking place today along the spring-fed reach?

The alluviation may have resulted from the approximately 300 cubic meters of screened backdirt that we had dumped into the south headcut by 1969, but this sediment charge could not have been much different from what had been produced naturally by the erosion and migration of the headcuts. Aggradation is obviously promoted by the growth of grass along the moist reach. Once the grass started reducing flow velocity and trapping sediment, the process became self-enhancing and may continue unless the power of a flash flood exceeds the resistance threshold caused by the grassy inset. The growth appears to be due to a sustained increase in the level of the local water table. There could be three reasons for this: (1) an increase in rainfall, (2) increased infiltration due to the root-knifing, or (3) infiltration of the treated water upstream. The first and second seem less likely to be main factors, because the discharge records for the San Pedro at the Charleston bridge show no unusual increase and therefore no unusual increase in rainfall. In fact, from 1965 to 1970 it is below the mean (Hereford 1993, Fig. 33). According to the Sierra Vista city service department, excess effluent at the water treatment plant was used to irrigate about 300 acres of alfalfa in the Curry Draw catchment, but this would probably not provide adequate infiltration to account for the rise of what is most likely a perched aquifer at the spring at the Murray Place. Direct recharge via the holding ponds to a shallow aquaclude appears to be the main cause.

The late Quaternary stratigraphy of Curry Draw is well exposed along the nearly vertical walls of the arroyo (Fig. 2.10). The geology along Curry Draw was mapped at a scale of about 1:1000 on aerial photographs taken by the U.S. Army Combat Surveillance School at Ft. Huachuca. This reconnaissance mapping, along with stratigraphic sketches, will be the subject of a separate report by Robert L. Laury and me.

Though the late Pleistocene strata are readily recognized and differentiated in the field, the middle and late Holocene alluvial sediments are so similar that differentiation requires careful mapping of their contacts in order to observe their cut-and-fill relationships. Where the contact relationships are obscured, radiocarbon age or diagnostic artifacts may have to be relied on for placement in the stratigraphic sequence. Pedogenic development may also be definitive. Because the cut-and-fill sequence of these subparallel channels is best observed in exposures at right angles to the stream axes, seven backhoe trenches, up to 4 m deep, were cut across the abandoned floodplain of Curry Draw in the site area at intervals of 20 m to 40 m and ranging in length from 76 m to 198 m (Figs. 1.3, 2.3). Twenty-seven shorter backhoe trenches and a bulldozer trench were placed at strategic locations to determine the detailed stratigraphic relationships of the sedimentary units (Plate 4; Foldouts 1 and 2). The walls of the excavations provided additional stratigraphic profiles (Plates 6, 7). The arroyo wall of the north wall of the South Branch is shown in Plate 5. Most of the profiles have a vertical exaggeration of twice the horizontal scale and were mapped by measurements with respect to level lines whose elevations were tied into the site datum at Station D (Fig. 1.3). Measurements along the trench level lines are shown at 4-m spacing along the bottom of most profiles and elevations above mean sea level (AMSL) are shown along the sides. Plate 3 is a photogeologic map of the Murray Springs Site. (Plates, Foldouts follow p. 48.)

STRATIGRAPHY OF CURRY DRAW

In the latest code of stratigraphic nomenclature (North American Commission on Stratigraphic Nomenclature 1983), it was proposed that Quaternary strati-

Figure 2.10. Arroyo stratigraphy of the Escapule Ranch Formation in Curry Draw.

a, The channel of Weik Ranch Member (Stratum G_1) is exposed in the right bank of the South Branch of Curry Draw at the Murray Springs Site. Here the ancient channel of the East Swale, on the left, has removed the eastern edge of the Area 1 Clovis site. The basal channel sand and gravel contains redeposited Coro marl (white masses) and Millville alluvium. Mehringer's 10-cm-interval pollen sampling of G_1 is visible on the left. Black oxidized wood fragments from the channel provided a radiocarbon age of 5750 ± 250 B.P. (Appendix A, Table A.1). See Plate 7, Profile N.

b, At the Big Bend of Curry Draw (Fig. 2.2) a right bank tributary alluvial fill of Weik alluvium (Stratum G_1) is inset against fine grained facies of Millville alluvium (Stratum Z).

c, Trench 17 exposed the channel of the Hargis Ranch Member (Stratum G_{2a}) where it truncates Donnet silt (F_3), F_{3a} channel, and black mat (F_2). See Foldout 1, Trench 17.

d, View downstream in Curry Draw about 200 m below the confluence of the North and South branches. Peter J. Mehringer is pointing out McCool alluvium (G_{2b}) in the right bank exposure. The dark (reddish brown) paleosol at the top is in part due to slopewash redeposited from Millville alluvium of the valley sides. Teviston alluvium (H) caps the sequence.

e, At a slight bend in Curry Draw ~ 350 m downstream of the confluence, a left bank exposure shows a channel fill of Hargis alluvium (Stratum G_{2a}) overlain by lower McCool alluvium (Stratum G_{2b1}). Caliche of the St. David Formation forms the buried bank shown at the lower right. Mehringer's pollen sampling column is in the center of the channel. Carbonized plant remains from near the base of the channel dated 4000 ± 130 B.P. (Appendix A, Table A.1).

f, The first left bank tributary at a railroad trestle ~ 50 m downstream of the Big Bend exposes a cut-and-fill inset sequence of three strata. Hargis alluvium is overlain by McCool alluvium, which is overlain by a lower terrace of Curry Draw alluvium (J).

g, About 100 m below the junction of the North and South branches the right bank of Curry Draw exposes McCool alluvium showing laminated pond mud in the lower part and loamy alluvium in the upper. Part of the sag in the middle of the exposure is due to compaction (see h).

h, Compaction of the laminated muds of lower McCool alluvium is apparent where the muds have settled over a caliche boulder or bench. Bands are offset by several microfaults. Mehringer's pollen sampling profile is visible at left.

graphic formations be defined on the basis of their bounding discontinuities (erosional contacts) and called alloformations. This basis for definition is what many Quaternary stratigraphers have traditionally used for defining both formations and some members within formations. Herein I have defined the Nexpa, Millville, Murray Springs, Lehner Ranch, and Escapule Ranch formations on the basis of significant erosional disconformities that truncate paleosols at the top of each formation. Therefore, geologic time is accounted for by the sequence: deposition, followed by stability and soil formation, followed by erosion with members being made up of different strata within formations.

The terms alloformation and allomember are cumbersome to use and, for readers less familiar with geology, here I revert back to the use of formation and member in Quaternary mapping but using the same criteria for defining alloformations and allomembers. In the descriptions that follow, field designations of strata are designated as capital letters with lower case letters and subnumerals designating substrata. This chapter is an update of the geology I discussed earlier (Haynes 1987). A chart of the stratigraphic column is presented in Plate 2, which serves as a color index for Plates 2–8 and Foldouts 1 and 2 following page 48.

St. David Formation (Stratum X)

In Curry Draw the late Quaternary stratigraphy (Figs. 2.1, 2.5) is best displayed and most complete between the Murray Springs Clovis Site and the mouth at the San Pedro floodplain (Fig. 2.2). In some places the arroyo walls rise as much as 6 m (Fig. 1.4a) above the sandy bed. At a few places along the base of the wall are exposures of reddish brown mudstones; hard, cemented, coarse sands; and white marls and caliches of the St. David Formation, designated in the field and on the detailed cross sections as Stratum X (Plate 2). Within Curry Draw and other tributaries, the buried surface of the St. David Formation represents an erosional topography buried by Nexpa gravels (Stratum Y) along the upper slopes and by the Millville Formation (Stratum Z) along the ancient valley floor.

In most exposures the St. David sediments are more indurated than the younger deposits, although there are parts of the Millville that resemble beds in the St. David. However, on the basis of facies changes and contact relationships, these are readily differentiated. The St. David carbonates exposed by Curry Draw are distinctly more dense and harder than the Coro marl in the Murray Springs Formation. On fresh exposures a trench-shovel blow usually rings on the former and makes a dull thud on the latter. The St. David carbonates in this area appear to be lacustrine in origin, occur in dish-shaped lenses, and contain a higher percentage of calcium carbonate as opposed to sandy caliches associated with zones of pedogenic calcification or ground water deposition (R. Gray 1967; Smith 1994).

An erosion-resistant carbonate bed in the St. David Formation in the headcut of the first right-bank tributary 100 m downstream from the confluence of the North and South branches of Curry Draw helps to maintain a vertical headcut. At a bend 200 m farther downstream, the modern channel has cut through a buried meander bend of an earlier channel. The short cutoff has exposed alternating beds of olive green mudstone and white carbonate of the St. David Formation. A similar exposure has, in recent years, appeared in the downstream end of what we call the "Big Bend" (Fig. 2.2). The left bank used to be late Holocene alluvium from top to bottom, but erosion of the wall has removed the Holocene alluvium and exposed an older wall of Millville alluvium with St. David Formation at the base.

A sand facies of the St. David Formation consists of poorly sorted, medium to coarse, arkosic sandstone cemented by coarse crystalline calcium carbonate. It appears to be a product of groundwater cementation and occurs as resistant low knobs in a few places along the channel of Curry Draw. At Area 1 of the Murray Springs Site it is exposed by recent erosion of the right bank. According to well drillers, this facies is widespread in the subsurface of the San Pedro Valley.

Exposures of the St. David Formation along U.S. Highway 90 near where it crosses the San Pedro at BLM's San Pedro House (Fig. 2.2, the Wolf Ranch locality of Johnson and others 1975) reveal a sequence of mudstones, marls, sands, and gravels containing a late Blancan fauna (Harrison 1978). Its paleomagnetic age straddles the Gauss-Matuyama boundary (Johnson and others 1975). Good exposures occur in Horsethief Draw (Fig. 2.2), north of U.S. 90, because of deeper incision there than in Curry Draw. Gravel lenses that crop out on the slopes above the San Pedro floodplain between Curry and Horsethief draws can be mistaken for Nexpa gravel straths; most are, but some are interbedded within the St. David Formation, as can be observed in the Horsethief Draw exposures.

Nexpa Formation (Stratum Y)

As ancestral Curry Draw eroded into the St. David Formation, it left gravel straths at several levels above the channel. I call these the Nexpa Formation after the ancient Sobaipuri name for the San Pedro Valley (Di Peso 1953b: 23). Remnants of the Nexpa gravels (Stratum Y) occur along the valley slopes as patches of coarse gravels (Fig. 2.5; Plate 3) with varying degrees of carbonate cementation, ranging from essentially none to a stage IV petrocalcic horizon (Gile and others 1966). This last stage is exposed by a railroad cut north of the North Branch at the Murray Springs Site (Fig. 2.6d). The pebble to cobble gravel is engulfed in calcium carbonate and is capped by a laminar horizon 2 cm to 4 cm thick. Strath remnants of Nexpa gravels south of Area 7 and capping the low hill with Datum D (Fig. 1.3), although not as calcareous as in the railroad cut, show stage II to III calcification. In some places carbonate coatings have been partially leached away from tops of clasts.

The gravel clasts are subangular to rounded and composed of metavolcanics, quartzites, and chert. The metavolcanics show varying degrees of weathering from thin (~ 2 mm) rinds to nearly complete alteration, although the latter clasts are rare. The valley slope topography along Curry Draw is in part controlled by the armoring effect of the Nexpa gravels. Some gravel caps have nearly completely eroded away, but their former presence is indicated by concentrations of dispersed-cobble lags on local high spots.

The Nexpa gravels were a poor source of lithic raw material for prehistoric cultures, but a few widely scattered clasts of quartzite and chert show flake scars, probably of human origin. Such objects have been mistaken for Paleolithic artifacts of great age but none occur in situ within the Nexpa Formation. Most of these appear to be the result of nothing more than prehistoric testing of this surface material and dropping it upon learning of its poor quality.

Millville Formation (Stratum Z)

Following a long period of net degradation, represented by the Nexpa straths at descending elevations, the regimen changed to one of net aggradation. This is represented in the upper San Pedro Valley by the Millville Formation, named after the ruins of the 19th century mill site on the right bank of the San Pedro River near the Charleston road bridge where it is represented by a 12-m terrace. Along Curry Draw the Millville Formation (Stratum Z) is composed of brownish red, muddy sand and sandy gravel in the upper reach near the Murray Springs Site (Fig. 2.5; Plate 5). Muddy sand and sandy mudstones over basal gravel appear downstream in the Big Bend area where the maximum observed thickness is about 8 m (Fig. 2.10b). A buried sandy mudstone terrace remnant (Stratum Z_1) at the base of Stratum Z_2 produced a Rancholabrean microfauna (Lindsay 1978, 1984) but is probably beyond the limit of radiocarbon dating. A tusk, presumably of mammoth, was found in Millville gravel at meter 36 in the left bank of the South Branch of Curry Draw in the Murray Springs Site area about 30 m above the junction with the North Branch (Plate 5b).

The Millville alluvium in the site area has been examined in detail by Laury (Laury and Haynes 1977). The poor sorting, paucity of fluvial bed forms, and rapid facies changes suggest flashy discharge and bank collapse in the upper reach. Finer facies and fluvial bedding become more prevalent down stream. At the Big Bend, clay lenses with pelecypod shells indicate low stream velocity and perhaps ponding. Whereas the thickness of the Millville alluvium in the site area does not exceed that of the Holocene alluvium, its channel is five times wider. The Millville was probably deposited by an ephemeral stream that reworked portions of the St. David Formation and gravels from the Nexpa straths. As a result, rapid facies changes occur laterally as well as longitudinally. The irregular top of the Millville in Curry Draw is without evidence of weathering, and the sharp contact with overlying units appears to be erosional at all exposures but with relief of only 1 m to 2 m.

Murray Springs Formation and Emergent Water Table

The Moson Ranch sand, Sobaipuri mudstone, Fry Ranch sand, Coro marl, Kendall Ranch sand, and Graveyard sand members make up the Murray Springs Formation of late Pleistocene age. These were times of spring discharge feeding ponds and marshes.

Moson Ranch Member (Stratum D_1)

The Moson Ranch Member (Plate 2) is named after one of the prominent 19th century ranches in the San Pedro Valley (McCool 1967: 11; Sonnichsen 1974).

Light brown to white calcareous sand of the Moson Ranch Member (Stratum D_1) occurs as an irregular discontinuous layer up to 50 cm thick on top of the Millville alluvium and in sharp contact with the overlying Sobaipuri mud (Stratum D). In Area 1, the Clovis age Graveyard sand (Stratum F_1) appears to be derived in part by the reworking of Stratum D_1 (Plate 7). The contact with the top of the Millville is commonly gradational, suggesting derivation by reworking. In several places along the natural exposures provided by the arroyo walls there are irregular, elongated, subhorizontal zones within Millville alluvium (Stratum Z) of a white to light gray friable, silty, gritty sand similar to muddy sand in the Millville alluvium but without the clay fraction. These appear to be extensions of Stratum D_1 into Stratum Z and are localized to areas near spring conduits described later. As we indicate (Laury and Haynes 1977), they appear to be the result of the winnowing of clays via the horizontal movement of groundwater through Millville alluvium when it was saturated.

The excavation of Trench 18 exposed a buried spring conduit of medium to coarse sand that came up through Millville alluvium and interfingered with Stratum D (Foldout 1). This conduit-sand facies of the Moson Ranch Member (Stratum D_1) contained bone remnants and numerous teeth of horse, bison, mammoth, camel, bear, large cat, and wolf (Figs. 1.10–1.12). These finds led to the full scale excavation of Area 8 in 1970 and 1971, which revealed two conduits, one with three coalescing feeders, containing abundant Rancholabrean faunal remains (Saunders 1983). Here the Sobaipuri mudstone wedges out over the mounded conduit sands (Stratum D_2), but some lower portions intertongue with them. These stratigraphic relationships suggest that fluidization and reworking of Millville alluvium (Stratum Z) by the horizontal flow of ground water led to the formation of Stratum D_1 and artesian discharge to Stratum D_2 (Fry Ranch Member) and to a pond or lake in which the Sobaipuri mud and Coro marl were deposited.

Sobaipuri Member (Stratum D)

When Fray Marcos de Niza in 1538 entered Nexpa, the San Pedro Valley, he found it occupied by the Sobaipuri Indians living near modern day Fairbank (Bandelier 1929; Di Peso 1953b). The Sobaipuri Member of the Murray Springs Formation consists of olive green mudstone that varies from nearly pure clay to sandy clay with dispersed fine pebbles. It is clearly a shallow pond or lake sediment with a mixed lacustrine and terrestrial molluscan fauna (Chapter 4). Its thickness is commonly about 20 cm but varies widely from 2 cm to nearly 2 m across relatively short distances of 10 m or less due to the paleotopography of the top of the Millville Formation (Plate 2; Foldouts 1 and 2). The thicker portions display diffuse lamina of various shades of olive green and include a dark gray to brown organic clay band (Substratum D_0) that yielded a radiocarbon age of 29,000 ± 2000 B.P. in Trench 12N (see Fig. 2.16a; Foldout 2, Trench 12N). A humate date of 19,000 ± 1600 B.P. is apparently contaminated with younger humates of nuclear age carbon (Appendix A, Table A.1).

The teeth of Rancholabrean megafauna are fairly common along the basal contact of the Sobaipuri mudstone and occasionally in the Moson sand (Saunders 1983). Small squeeze-ups of the mudstone into overlying strata occur in several places, as described below.

Coro Marl Member (Stratum E)

The Sobaipuri Member is conformably overlain by the white Coro marl (Stratum E), named after a chief of the Sobaipuri (Di Peso 1953b: 23). It is composed of up to 2 m of white chalk beds. Profile A (Fig. 1.3), Stratum E type section, is a short backhoe cut into the north wall of the South Branch (Fig. 2.11; Plate 5b) for the purpose of describing the Coro marl and sampling it for pollen and molluscan studies (Chapter 4) and for radiocarbon dating (Appendix A, Fig. A.2). In the lower meter individual marl beds, 20 cm to 40 cm thick, contain dispersed mollusc shells and are separated by olive green clay bands up to 1 cm thick, some containing numerous mollusc shells. In some exposures along the natural arroyo wall two bands merge, pinching out the intervening marl. In other places the lower clay band merges with Stratum D, indicating that the deposition of Stratum D and the lower half of Stratum E are interrelated and probably penecontemporaneous. Squeeze-ups of D into E (Plate 5a, Station 16 W; Appendix A, Fig. A.2) probably occurred at a time when the strata were still semifluid or plastic and appear to be miniature diapirs due to the geostatic load of the Coro marl on the Sobaipuri mud. At 52 W on the north wall profile of the South Branch (Plate 5a), a squeeze-up has pushed out laterally to form a lacolithlike lens between marl beds. Other squeeze-ups are apparent in the headcut moving up the East Swale in Area 9 (Appendix E, Fig. E.4).

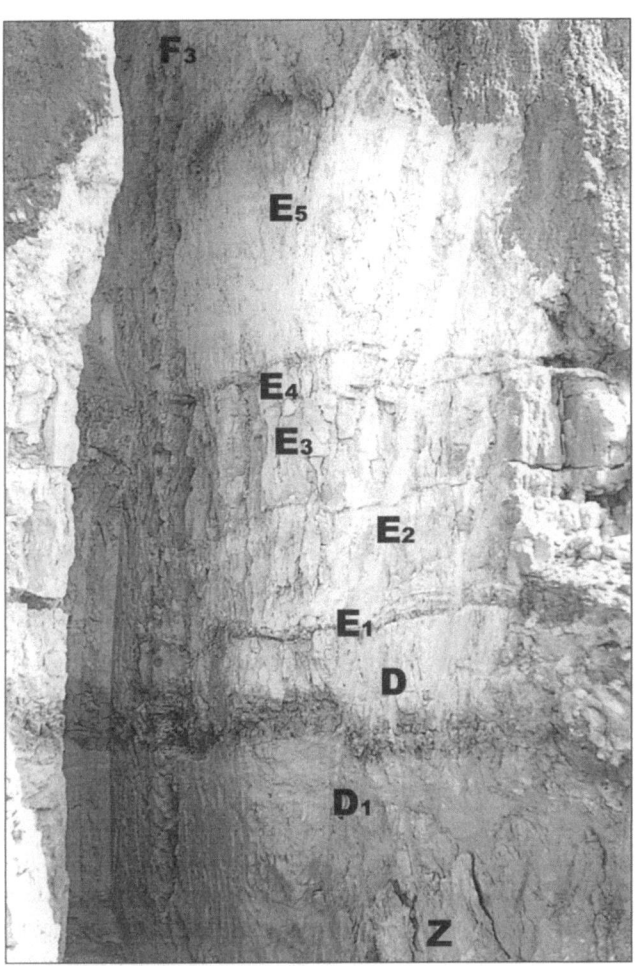

Figure 2.11. Coro marl (Stratum E) type section at Profile A in the north wall of the South Branch, showing Sobaipuri mud (Stratum D) as parting muds and overlying Moson sand (D_1) and Millville alluvium (Z). Nails at 10-cm spacing in back of cut are Mehringer's 1966 pollen sampling profile. Mead's mollusc samples for Stratum E were also collected here. Figure A.2 in Appendix A shows sample locations and radiocarbon dates.

At Profile A the upper 80 cm of Stratum E is a massive white marl that grades upward into light gray, very calcareous, silty fine sand of the Donnet silt (Stratum F_3), described later. This 20-cm thick gradational contact zone is caused by strong pedogenic development during the middle to late Holocene. This pedogenesis has contaminated the radiocarbon samples from at least the upper half of Stratum E with pedogenic carbonate and humic acids.

The radiocarbon ages of the carbonate fractions of the Coro marl range from 9780 ± 140 B.P. and 10,430 ± 160 B.P. at the top to 21,000 ± 500 B.P. near the base. Organic fractions sampled at Profile Y on the south wall (Fig. 1.3) opposite Profile A yielded respective radiocarbon ages ranging from 11,880 ± 250 to 27,560 ± 2300 B.P. All of these ages are shown on Figure A.2 (Appendix A) with the organic fraction values (all SMU dates) in proper stratigraphic position. Identical sampling was done here by Joseph Liddicoat to test for paleomagnetic excursions; unfortunately, the signals were too weak. Additional carbonate ages of 10,480 ± 200 B.P. and 13,310 ± 190 B.P. were obtained from laminated marls separated by mud partings in Trench 1 (Plate 4) between Areas 6 and 7. The younger value is too young probably due to illuviation of younger pedogenic carbonates or exchange with atmospheric CO_2.

Subsequent radiocarbon dating of mollusc shells from the Coro marl by Pigati yielded an age range from ~ 25,000 B.P. to ~ 13,000 B.P. As explained by Pigati and others (2004), these shells are believed to be more reliable than the carbonate and organic ages presented in Appendix A. Clearly the Coro marl represents a late glacial (Wisconsinan) high water table supporting a lake or pond surrounded by marshland.

As mentioned previously, the underlying dark gray to brown organic clay in the Sobaipuri Member (Substratum D_0) has a residue age of about 29,000 B.P. and a humate age of about 19,000 B.P. due to contaminant humic acids. The earliest radiocarbon date from the stratum stratigraphically younger than the Coro marl is 12,940 ± 390 B.P. from charcoal in the Graveyard channel sand (Stratum F_1). This is a single value from Area 1, but all 11 other charcoal values are between 10,710 ± 160 B.P. and 11,190 ± 180 B.P. (Appendix A, Table A.1). It is possible that the older charcoal is a relict of an earlier bed load in the F_1 channel. Support for this interpretation comes from the Lehner Site, where an alluvial sand (Stratum F_{1a}) cut through Coro marl has radiocarbon ages on two charcoal concentrations averaging 13,850 ± 90 B.P. (Haas and Haynes 1975). Therefore, the age of the Coro marl is bracketed between about 14,000 B.P. and 28,000 B.P.

The lithology of the Coro marl and Sobaipuri mudstone as well as their abundant molluscan fauna indicate a lacustrine origin (Chapter 4). This observation and the facies relationship with the spring conduit sands in Area 8 suggest the lake or pond was spring fed. It is probably significant that the Coro marl pinches out within 10 m of the spring vents (Plate 8). The absence appears to be by nondeposition rather than by erosion. Clays settled out to form the Sobaipuri mud until conditions (increase in pH, temperature, water hardness, or a combination thereof, probably in conjunction with algae) changed to favor calcium carbonate coprecipitation, though with brief returns to conditions for the parting muds to form during the first half of Coro marl deposition. The mixed terrestrial and lacustrine molluscan fauna suggests the pond was shallow, but how deep we cannot assess. There is no obvious impoundment for water in the geological situation downstream. In fact, the lateral distribution of the Coro marl expands downstream right to the edge of the inner valley of the San Pedro River, suggesting that Curry Draw was apparently an arm of a larger lake or marsh along the axis of the San Pedro River Valley.

Earlier I presented the possibility that the Coro marl represented a large Pleistocene lake in the San Pedro Valley (Haynes 1968b) extending from the Lehner Site northward at least to the Cerros Negros outcrop near Mammoth (Fig. 1.1). Due to a lack of confirmed shore features as well as other reasons, this hypothesis has been abandoned. Recent investigations of molluscs and ostracodes from the Coro marl (Pigati and others 2004) have led to the suggestion that it may be a cienega (wet meadow deposit) rather than a pond or lake. However, I find a wet meadow difficult to reconcile with the massive, white, high calcium carbonate content and with the laminar structure of the lower part of the Coro marl containing Sobaipuri mud partings. To me the data indicate a pond or lake surrounded by marsh land as occurs in some cienegas, for example, Babocomari Cienega (Fig. 2.8e). On the other hand, the upper part is less massive with differential hardnesses giving a "cottage cheese" like aspect to the marl. These conditions, plus the contamination indicated by the radiocarbon values, indicate desiccation and pedogenesis, suggesting that in the terminal phase of deposition the pond may have converted to a wet meadow before desiccation and erosion leading to the F_1 channel of the Graveyard sand.

Fry Ranch Member (Stratum D_2)

Between Stations 32W and 40W of the north wall of the South Branch of Curry Draw (Plate 5a) there is poorly sorted, muddy, calcareous sand (Stratum D_{2b}) overlying a very calcareous sandy mud (Stratum D_{2a}) that occurs as a lens between the Coro marl and the Sobaipuri mudstone adjacent to the Graveyard channel sand (Figs. 2.12, 2.13). This relationship, not obvious in earlier studies, is based on profile cleanup and tedious remapping in 1994. The age of Stratum D_2, here called the Fry Ranch Member (after a local old time ranch) of the Murray Springs Formation, is bracketed between the Sobaipuri mudstone and the Coro marl. Therefore, it was deposited after 29,000 B.P. and before the end of deposition of the Coro marl. Disarticulated mammoth bones exposed in this stratum (D_{2b}) throughout the 1970s (Figs. 2.12a, 2.13b) are now missing due to erosion and pilfering. The member appears to be a spring-laid deposit at the edge of a conduit that was either removed by the arroyo or that may yet remain behind the arroyo wall as an extension of Area 2. The overlying Coro marl here may be the younger of two phases identified by Pigati and his colleagues (2004). The conduit sands of the Area 8 spring vents are also designated Stratum D_2 as described below (pp. 42–44).

Kendall Ranch Member (Stratum E_1)

This member of the Murray Springs Formation is named after a historic ranch near Tombstone as well as Kendall Station, an earlier name for Fairbank (Carmony 1995). In Area 2, mapping of Stratum E_1, the Kendall Ranch Member, around the base of the excavations is shown in Plate 6, Profile J. Stratum E_1 is an irregular lens of calcareous sand between Stratum F_1 above and Stratum E below, between map Stations 17 and 28. From Station 21, the Fry Ranch Member (D_2) extends southeastward to Station 13 as a tongue within the Sobaipuri mudstone and is believed to derive from the same spring conduit at depth, as just proposed. Westward between Stations 33 and 38, Stratum E_1 extends below our excavation and appears to derive from another spring source. The stratigraphic relationship indicates that E_1 is younger than D_2 but may have resulted from a reactivation of a spring vent from artesian discharge following erosion of the Coro marl. Therefore, the age of Stratum E_1 must be between that of the youngest Coro marl and the oldest Graveyard channel sand (F_1), discussed in the next section, and therefore between about 13,000 B.P. and 14,000 B.P.

Sometime during the late Wisconsinan artesian pressure declined and the pond in Curry Draw shrank, became a wet meadow, and eventually dried up, exposing the Coro marl to subaerial erosion. The Coro marl is truncated by the initial formation of a drainage

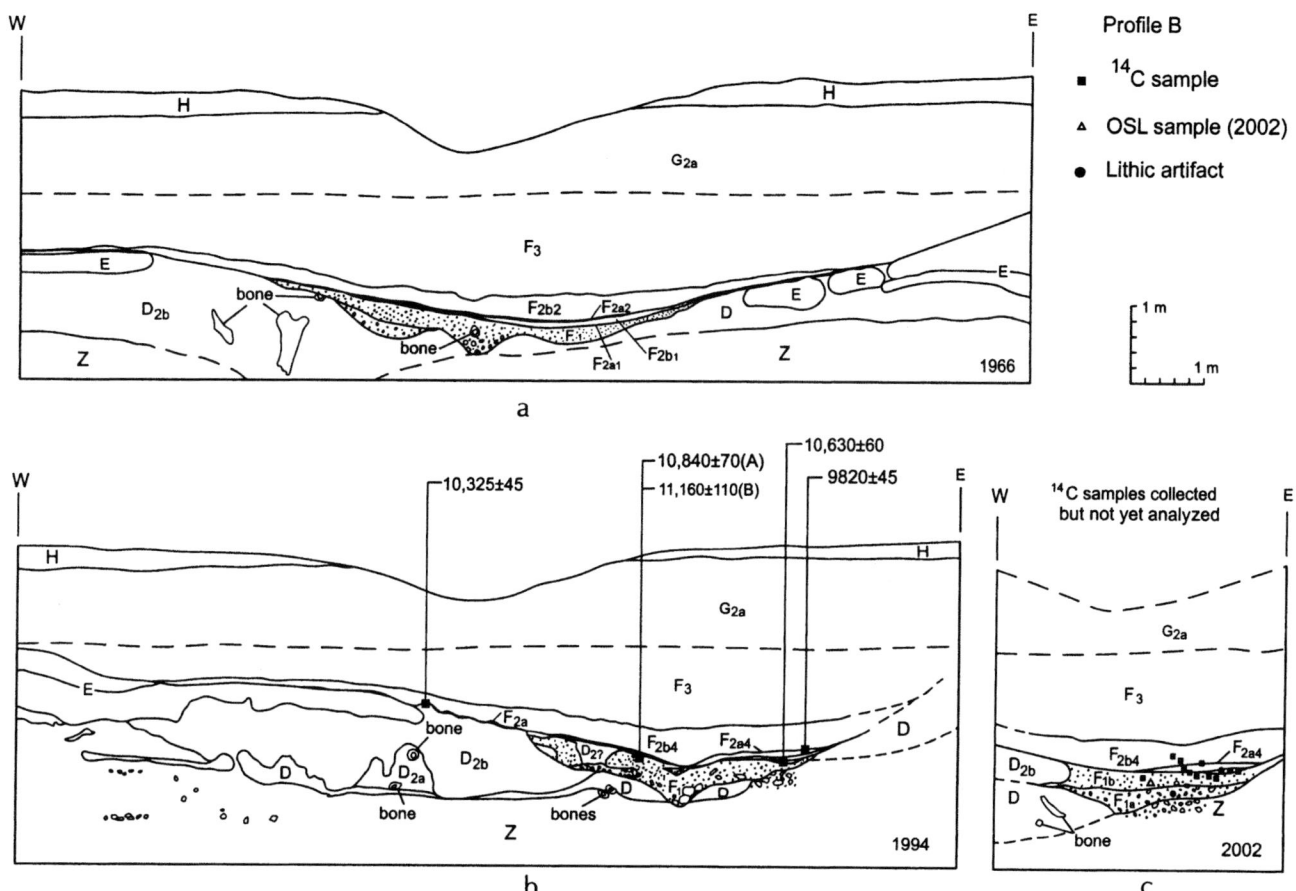

Figure 2.12. Detailed stratigraphic profiles of the Graveyard sand channel (Stratum F_1) in the north wall of the South Branch (Profile B) of Curry Draw in three different years showing variations due to erosion.

system, perhaps by seepage and sapping as the bottom muds dried out, but the Graveyard Gulch channel eventually cut through the Coro marl and Sobaipuri mud (Figs. 2.12, 2.13). The shallow channels of Stratum F_1 were the result of this net decline of the water table during late Wisconsinan time.

Graveyard Gulch Member (Stratum F_1) and Decline of the Water Table

The shallow channel of the Graveyard Gulch Member (Stratum F_1), with low gently sloping banks, is cut into the older strata. The basal contact is part of a widespread erosional surface that formed the Clovis-age landscape (contact Z_1 and Z_{1-2} of Haynes 1984, 1998b). The Graveyard channel sand is gray to greenish gray, poorly to moderately well sorted, medium to coarse subangular to subrounded arkosic sand occupying a shallow channel 3 m to 6 m wide and up to 0.5 m thick.

A modern analog might be the spring-fed lower reach of Government Draw (Fig. 2.8d) that enters the east side of the San Pedro River near Lewis Springs (Fig. 2.2; Haynes 1981). This, plus the fact that Stratum F_1 contains many bones of extinct animals (Saunders 1983), led me to name it the Graveyard Member after Graveyard Gulch, a drainage near the cemetery and ruins of Charleston (Fig. 1.1). In Area 2 the buried F_1 channel widens to an anomalous width of 12 m with a maximum thickness of 0.7 m where it overlaps the stratum E_1 spring-laid sand (Plates 6 and 8). An unusual thickness of nearly 1 m coincided with the massive bone concentration of Area 2 (Fig. 1.4g). As stated previously, this may have been an artesian spring.

No artifacts were found in situ in Area 2, and Hemmings (Chapter 5) suggests that some of the bones may be discards from Clovis activities upstream. There is also the possibility that some of the bones occur in or were reworked from underlying Stratum E_1. During the

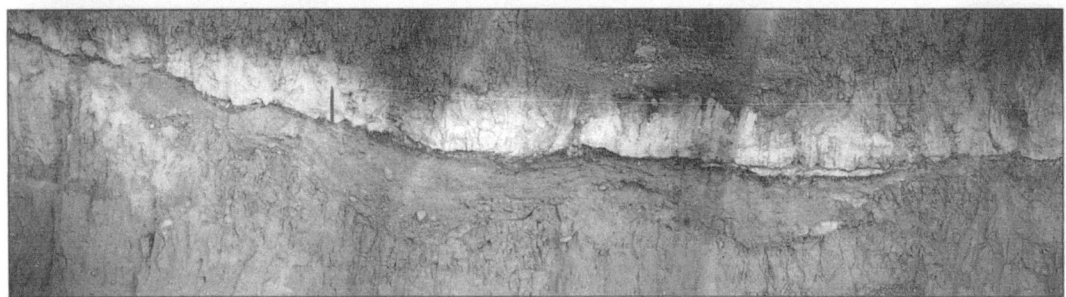
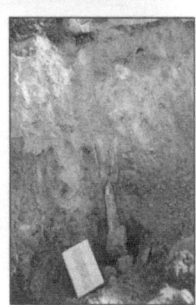

Figure 2.13. *Top*, Photographic panorama of the F_1 channel at Profile B in the north wall of the South Branch. *Left*, Close-up of the F_1 channel sand, showing a thin lens of Earp marl (F_{2b1}) between two stringers of black mat (F_{2a1} and F_{2a2}; see Fig. 2.12). Black specks in upper F_1 are charcoal fragments. *Right*, Proboscidean long bone in Stratum D_2 below and left of the F_1 channel. Photographs taken in 1966 (*top* and *left*) and 1968 (*right*). See Figure 2.12 for stratigraphic designations.

time the Graveyard channel was active, E_1 was undoubtedly saturated and very soft. In fact, there may have been artesian seepage in Area 2 during F_1 time, making it an area of deep quicksand and a place to be avoided by Clovis people.

Charcoal, mostly of ash wood (*Fraxinus* sp.), was abundant in Stratum F_1 in Area 2, occurring in large fragments and concentrated masses in a few places (Fig. 2.14) but only as natural concentrations in the ancient streambed, not in man-made fire hearths as in Area 4. Five radiocarbon ages from F_1 in Area 2 range from $10,840 \pm 70$ B.P. to $11,190 \pm 180$ B.P. (Appendix A, Table A.1).

The best exposure of the Graveyard channel occurs in the north bank of the South Branch of Curry Draw (Figs. 2.12, 2.13; Plate 5a), where it is an extension of the F_1 channel of Wolf Creek from Area 1 directly across the arroyo (Plate 3). In the north wall profile it is

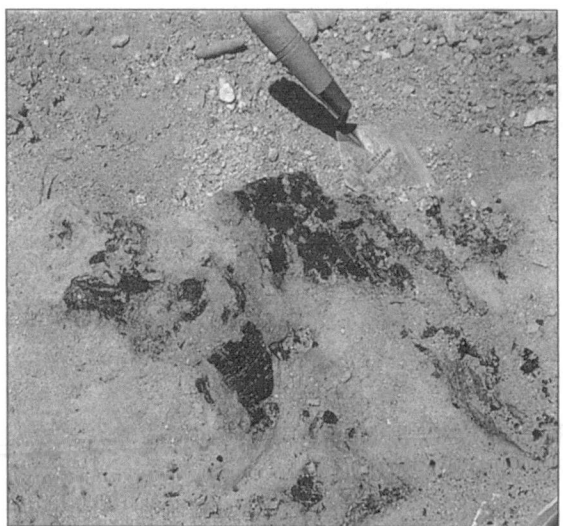

Figure 2.14. Large pieces of charcoal in the top of the F_1 channel sand in Area 2 are ash (*Fraxinus* sp.) wood.

seen as an irregular lens, 6 m wide and 40 cm thick at the thickest point between Stations 28 and 34. The channel fill consists of soft coarse sand with rust-colored iron stains and dispersed charcoal over lenses of gravel, probably lagged from the Millville alluvium.

The F_1 channel has been removed between the north and south banks of the South Branch of Curry Draw by headward erosion (Plate 3). It occurs in the tributary gully that had cut about 15 m into the East Swale and exposed the Area 1 mammoth at the time of our discovery in 1966. An aerial photograph taken in 1955 (Fig. 2.9b) indicates that 11 years earlier the headcut of Curry Draw was 40 m downstream. Therefore, in fewer than 10 years a significant part of the Murray Springs Clovis Site may have been lost to erosion before anyone knew it was there. Furthermore, the eastern part of the Clovis occupation surface in Area 1 was truncated by the erosion of the Weik alluvial channel (G_1) sometime between 8000 B.P. and 7000 B.P. (Plate 7, Profiles D and N). Subsequent excavation in Area 9 east of the G_1 channel yielded no Clovis artifacts, indicating that the Clovis site ended within the area now occupied by the G_1 channel fill (Appendix E).

In the discovery locus of Area 1 the Graveyard channel contained the partial skeleton of an adult mammoth (Saunders 1983) and four nondiagnostic artifacts (Chapter 5). In the order of discovery, this is the first mammoth found (Fig. 1.4b, e). Bone fragments were dispersed throughout the full 40-cm thickness of the channel sand and reworked Millville alluvium (Z_1; Plate 7, Profile C) and were scattered along the very low banks composed of Sobaipuri mudstone, Moson sand, and Millville alluvium (Plate 8). Many bone fragments occurred within these older units, indicating they had a soft, plastic consistency at the time of penetration, which may have been in part caused by trampling as this area was covered with mammoth tracks (Fig. 1.4f), described later.

The skull of what may be a pre-Clovis mammoth was discovered under a meter of Sobaipuri mudstone at the base of the east wall of Area 1 (Plate 7, Profile D). It was in a tusk-down orientation and therefore probably reached at least a meter or more into Stratum Z_1. There is the possibility that this skull belongs to the first mammoth and that it had sunk into the older sediments at a time when they were saturated and soft mud. However, penetration below a meter is difficult to imagine unless a mammoth foot inadvertently forced it down in walking through. There is no stratigraphic evidence for this event and mammoth bones are relatively common in Stratum D elsewhere in the site. It remains a possibility because whereas we did find the mandible, we did not find the skull of the Area 1 mammoth; we assumed it had been eroded away by the tributary headcut.

On the arbitrary boundary between Area 1 and Area 3 Extensions there occurred a 50-cm-deep irregular depression about 6 m west of the axis (thalweg) of the Wolf Creek (F_1) channel (Figs. 1.6d, 2.16e). Graveyard channel sand occurred anomalously upslope around the depression (Plate 7, Profile G) from which it was apparently scooped up and out. The area was covered with smaller circular depressions believed to be mammoth tracks (Fig. 1.4f). Therefore, the larger depression appears to be a water hole or well (Plate 8) dug by mammoths during a time of drought (Haynes 1991). The water hole was probably significantly deeper originally, considering that an unknown amount of compaction has occurred. Similar features are known from Africa where elephants excavate water holes (Fig. 2.15).

Four charcoal radiocarbon ages from Stratum F_1 in Area 1 range from 12,930 ± 390 B.P. to 10,710 ± 160 B.P., if an anomalously young age of 8770 ± 70 B.P. is omitted (Appendix A, Table A.1). The older value may also be anomalous, considering the Stratum F_1 ages from Area 2 and from other places at Murray Springs yet to be discussed or, as mentioned earlier and more likely, it could be a relict from an earlier F_1 bedload.

Figure 2.15. African elephants digging water holes at Wankie Reserve, Zambia. (Photograph by Gary Haynes and used with permission.)

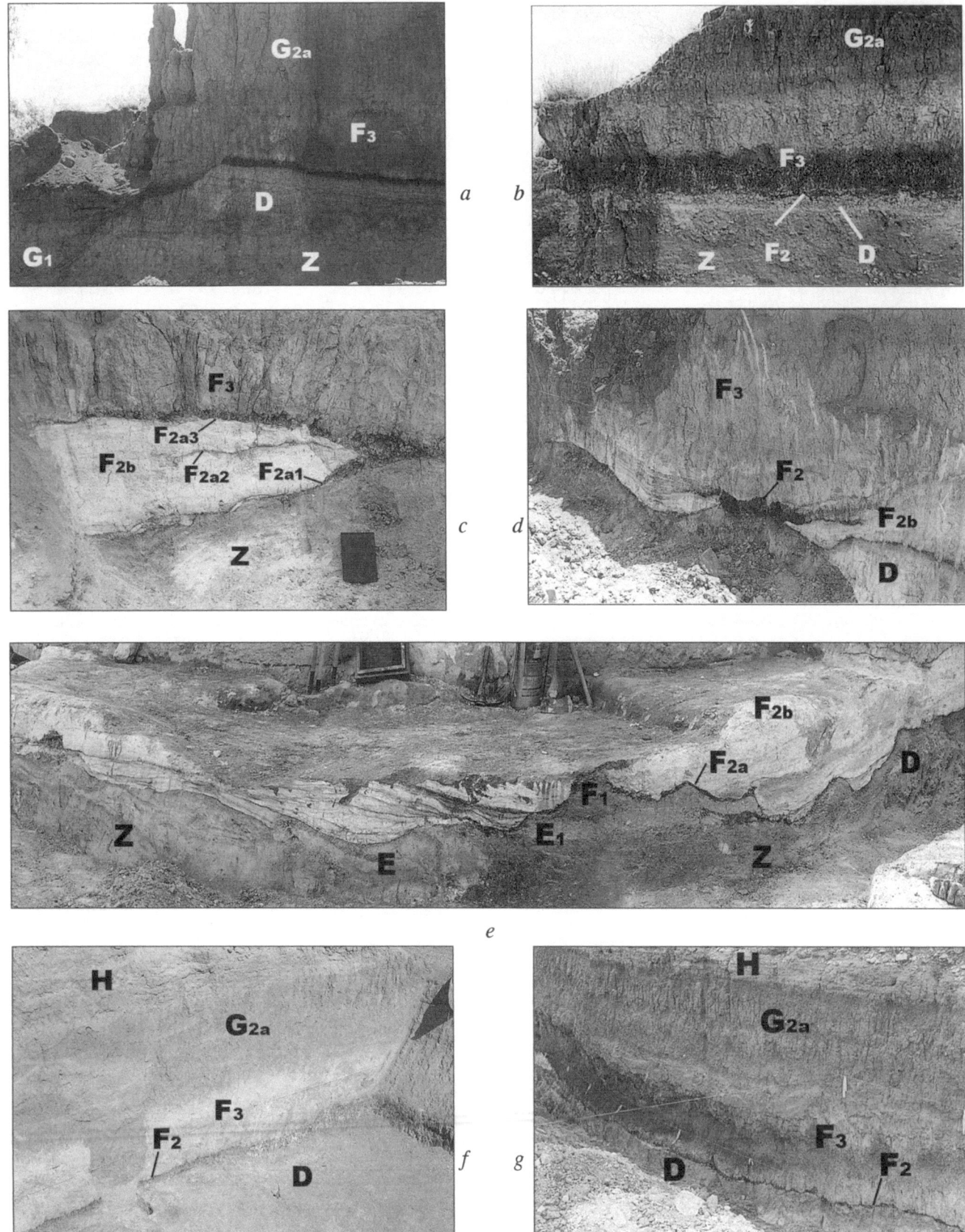

Several occurrences of the Graveyard channel sand crop out on small erosion remnants along the south bank of the North Branch of Curry Draw, indicating the position of the main branch of the Clovis-age creek, Bison Kill Creek (Plate 8). Short trenches (28, 29, 31, 33, and 34 in Figs. 2.3, 7.1) were cut to trace this ancient channel and collect charcoal (Plate 3). Dispersed gravel lenses were probably eroded from Stratum Z and are essentially channel lag deposits. The F_1 channel in Trench 28 contained interbedded sands and sandy clay lenses and charcoal dispersed throughout its 1.3-m thickness (Foldout 2, Trench 28). Three radiocarbon ages on the charcoal are $10,930 \pm 170$ B.P., $10,790 \pm 150$ B.P., and $10,740 \pm 190$ B.P. Stratum F_1, encountered by the north end of Trench 20, produced a charcoal radiocarbon age of $10,890 \pm 180$ B.P. (Foldout 2).

The ancient creek represented by the F_1 channel is called Bison Kill Creek because of its proximity to the bison kills of Areas 4 and 5 (Plate 8) and to maintain a tradition initiated by Haury who called the same age (F_1) channel at the Lehner Clovis site Mammoth Kill Creek (Haury and others 1959). At Murray Springs, the tributary F_1 channel with the mammoth kills of Areas 1 and 3 is called Wolf Creek (Plate 8) because of the wolf (*Canis dirus*; Fig. 1.7d) remains found there (Saunders 1983).

In Area 1 a lens of cream-colored marl (F_{1c} in Plate 7, Profile C), full of snail shells, was originally thought to be a fragment of displaced Coro marl that had been eroded and "melted" down by the stream action of Wolf Creek. However, the molluscs are an assemblage considerably different from that of typical Stratum E marl (Chapter 4). A radiocarbon age on the carbonate fraction of the shells is $12,820 \pm 450$ B.P. As mentioned in Appendix A, shell carbon is commonly contaminated, but certain species from Coro marl appear not to be significantly contaminated (Pigati and others 2004). I now believe this marl may be the result of carbonate precipitation in a small, spring-fed pond within the Graveyard channel that preceded final aggradation of the channel sand and, in conjunction with the 12,930 B.P. age of charcoal in the channel, indicates that cutting of the channel had occurred before 13,000 B.P.

The deposit that buried the F_1 channel and the Clovis occupation surface (Fig. 2.16) is the combined Clanton Ranch Member, the black mat (Stratum F_{2a}), and its marl facies, the Earp Member (Stratum F_{2b}). Overlying this deposit is the Donnet Ranch Member (Stratum F_3) that nearly filled the valley of Curry Draw (Fig. 2.5). These deposits make up the Lehner Ranch Formation.

The contact between the Murray Springs Formation and the overlying Lehner Ranch Formation is the erosional contact upon which the black mat (Stratum F_2) lies. It is the bounding discontinuity that marks the bottom of the Lehner Ranch Formation. At the top of the Graveyard sand, the Clovis-age stream channel, the contact is considered conformable whereas away from the Graveyard channel the contact is an erosional hiatus of as much as 3,000 years.

Under the strict definition of alloformation, the contact between the Murray Springs Formation and the

Figure 2.16. Views of the Clanton Ranch Member (black mat, F_{2a}) and the Earp Marl Member (F_{2b}) facies.

a, North end of Trench 12N exposes black mat (F_2) on Stratum D, which is truncated by the Stratum G_1 and Stratum G_{2a} channels. Note lenses of redeposited F_2 in G_1. Mehringer's pollen sampling is at 10–cm intervals.

b, Thickened black mat in the South Branch headcut is due to 25–cm thick dark gray cienega soil at the base of the Donnet silt (F_3) overlying 2–5 cm of black Clanton clay (F_2) overlying crenulations (animal tracks?) in the Sobaipuri mud (D) on Millville alluvium (Z). The upper 65 cm of F_3 (light gray) is overlain by Hargis alluvium (G_{2a}).

c, South wall of Area 1 in 1966 shows how the F_2 black mat split into stringers of black Clanton clay separated by white Earp marl (F_{2b}). Notebook for scale measures 19 cm by 14 cm.

d, In the east wall of Area 2 a lens of black mat extends northward and southward as stringers of black Clanton clay separated by white Earp marl. See Plate 6, Profile J.

e, Photo panorama of the east side of Area 1, 1967, shows a 2–mm to 10–mm thick black Clanton clay draped over the mammoth-track topography of the water hole (*right side*) and overlain by white Earp marl containing stringers of Clanton clay piching out downstream within Earp marl. See Plate 7, Profile G, for detailed stratigraphy.

f, West wall of Area 5, an extension of the west wall of Trench 32 (Foldout 2), exposes an Archaic period well. It bottoms in Millville alluvium under the black mat that thickens in the lower area (swale) to the north and covered microrelief due to animal (bison and horse?) tracks. See Fig. 1.8c for a more northerly view.

g, Backhoe Trench 12 (Foldout 2) was expanded to extend Area 4 excavations to the North Branch of Curry Draw. This exposure displays the swale between Bison Kill Creek to the north and main Area 4 to the south. Note Clovis surface covered by black mat truncates the white marl of Stratum E. The Donnet silt (F_3) is overlain by Hargis alluvium (G_{2a}) overlain, in turn, by Teviston alluvium (H). Level line tags are at 1–m spacing.

Lehner Ranch Formation would be placed at the base of the Graveyard Member. However, I place it at the top making the Graveyard channel deposit (Stratum F_1) the uppermost member of the Murray Springs Formation because it contains the last remnants of Rancholabrean fauna and marks the end of Clovis presence in the region. Mammoth, horse, camel, American lion, dire wolf, and Clovis are all abruptly absent from the stratigraphic record before deposition of Stratum F_2, the black mat. It is, therefore, an ideal Pleistocene-Holocene boundary that is recognizable throughout the region wherever the black mat occurs (Haynes 1982a). Before discussing the Lehner Ranch Formation in detail, the Clovis landscape it buried and the Clovis occupation on the contact between the Murray Springs Formation and the Lehner Ranch Formation need to be discussed.

The Clovis-Age Landscape

Just before the Clovis people first arrived in the Murray Springs area it probably was a spring field where water oozed from grass- and sedge-covered slopes to feed the shallow brook of Bison Kill Creek (Plate 8). Wolf Creek may have been fed by a spring seep about 60 m upstream from Area 7 where spongy tufa crops out; water emerging in Area 2 may have created quicksand, and Area 8 was a soggy spring field.

The analysis of fossil pollen (Mehringer and others 1971) at the Lehner Site indicates that the top 10 cm to 15 cm of the Graveyard channel sand was deposited in an ephemeral stream flowing through a cienega with grasses, composites, cheno-ams, and a few sedges bordered by a gallery forest of alder, ash, walnut, and hackberry trees much like Government Draw today (Fig. 2.8d). On uplands away from the site, pinyon pine, juniper, and oak trees were near enough to contribute to the pollen rain as at Sheehy Springs in the San Rafael Valley today (Chapter 4). Most of the charcoal fragments from the Graveyard sand (Fig. 2.14) at the Murray Springs Site have been identified as ash (*Fraxinus* sp.; Vorsila Bohrer, personal communication 1968, 1969; R. C. Koeppen, personal communication, 1968, 1969). R. C. Koeppen states that ash is excellent firewood.

From Mead's analysis of the molluscs (Chapter 4), both aquatic and terrestrial forms were abundant in some portions of the Graveyard sand, which, at Murray Springs, contained the last occurrence of woodland species molluscs. At the Lehner Site, woodland pollen persisted for another two millennia (Mehringer and others 1966), perhaps because of its proximity to the uplands at the base of the Huachuca Mountains.

Plate 8 is a paleogeologic map of the site area during Clovis time. The substrate is the Millville alluvium along the creek bottom, Sopaipuri mud around spring seep areas, and Coro marl farther away from the spring areas. Bison Kill Creek and Wolf Creek joined a few meters north of Area 2. In most places the creek beds had eroded into the Millville alluvium, which provided much of the sand and gravel bed load. In the channels there were very few Clovis artifacts, but most of them and the charcoal were in the upper 10 cm of the Graveyard sand or on top of it. Only in Area 1 did some artifacts occur deeper than 10 cm in F_1 and D_1 (Plate 7, Profile C), probably due to animal trampling. The mammoth tracks in Areas 1 and 3 were pressed into the channel sand and into the mud on both sides of the channel of Wolf Creek (Figs. 1.4f, 1.6c) and between the Area 1 mammoth and the Area 3 mammoth where they end. They appear to represent different sizes of mammoths, suggesting that the Area 3 mammoth was not alone as she walked over the bones of the Area 1 mammoth, passed by the water hole, and finally moved to the low rise where we found her partially articulated skeleton (Fig. 1.5). The channels were never active again after the Clovis occupation because tracks in the sand were not washed out. The water table had fallen and stream flow had ended, presumably due to drought (Haynes 1991). Shortly after the Clovis occupation the site went under water when Stratum F_2 was laid down, seemingly like a blanket over the Clovis landscape.

The first mammoth hunt may have resulted in the killing or scavenging of the Area 1 mammoth, because some of the bones underlay the surface covered with mammoth tracks made by later visits of mammoths, perhaps including the Area 3 mammoth. Clovis presence in Area 1 is revealed by four flakes, some of which may have been used as cutting tools (knives; Chapter 5), and a chunk of obsidian from the Cow Canyon area 300 km (186 miles) to the northeast (Appendix C). There was also an anomalous stack of bones (Fig. 1.4e) in which a scapula resting upon a lower jaw with a spinal vertebra on the scapula suggest the hand of man. There were no projectile points associated with the Area 1 mammoth, so there is no strong evidence that it was killed by man. Whereas elephants today are known to fondle the bones of their dead (Moss 1988), they are not known to stack them other than fortuitously at die offs (G. Haynes

1991). In fact, they usually just drop them and move on. The carcass may have been scavenged by humans. On the other hand, if it was a kill, artifacts may have been removed by erosion, because some of the western part of the skeleton, presumably including the skull, was removed by the modern tributary headcut (the discovery headcut), and the middle Holocene G_1 channel cut to within 3 m of it from the eastern side (Fig. 2.10a). Could the artifacts be nothing more than a part of the scatter pattern associated with the Area 3 carcass, 12 m to the west, and the stacking a result of children's play? Probably not, because the artifacts were all below the surface covered by tracks of the last mammoths and within D_1 reworked by the F_1 channel (Plate 7, Profile C). Therefore, the artifacts slightly predate the drop in the water table and the death of the Area 3 mammoth.

The Area 3 mammoth skeleton was nearly complete and more or less articulated except for the hind legs, one of which was missing (Figs. 1.5, 5.7). The skeleton was resting on its left side and was surrounded by artifacts, including a projectile point and two point tips (Chapter 5). A 4-m-wide swath of mammoth tracks covered the low ground around a shallow water hole or sump (Fig. 1.6c, d) and extended 11 m upslope in a northwesterly direction to the low hill with the mammoth skeleton (Figs. 1.6c, 5.10). Although the scavenging of a natural death cannot be precluded, we believe, on the basis of the projectile points, that this mammoth was most likely attacked and killed at this watering place (Chapter 5) during a time of drought (Haynes 1991).

The fact that some of the mammoth tracks were preserved in the Graveyard channel sand indicated that the streambed was inactive, because any discharge would have wiped out tracks in the channel sand of Stratum F_1. Even the water hole or well must have been dry, because there was no mud layer in it. Instead, clayey coarse F_1 sand occurred on the slopes around the well (Fig. 2.16e; Plate 7, Profile G) where it had apparently been scraped up by mammoths digging for water, much as elephants do today in dry streambeds during droughts (G. Haynes 1991). Hemmings (Chapter 5) describes this Stratum F_1 sand as a slope facies extending several meters west of the thalweg and pinching out against the rise where the Area 3 mammoth was found (Plate 8). Apparently mammoths had done a lot of scraping in and around the streambed. Further evidence of drought is the fact that the thalweg of the F_1 channel of Wolf Creek is 6 m east and *upslope* of the water hole. Had any discharge occurred later it would have diverted more channel sand to the water hole. Instead we found the F_1 increment of sand in the water hole had been scraped up and out (Plate 7, Profile G).

In excavating the Area 1 mammoth a small depression formed by an obturator foramen of the pelvis was found to contain a thin (~ 3 mm) layer of brown mud (Fig. 1.7a) that had cracked into typical polygonal segments upon drying. A similar depression occurred in the curvature of a tusk of the Area 3 mammoth (Fig. 1.7b). Mehringer's analysis of the mud from the pelvis revealed a pollen spectrum that is essentially modern (Mehringer, personal communication 1966). Our interpretation at the time was that the mud was modern and perhaps derived from the floor of a recent ant gallery, as commonly occurs in the alluvial deposits. However, in excavating Areas 3, 4, and 5 in subsequent years we found other small depressions containing thin layers of cracked mud covered by the black mat. In a few places where the black mat overlay clay substrates, careful removal and blowing with compressed nitrogen revealed more polygonal mud cracks (Appendix B, Fig. B.1). At the time no significance was attributed to these features so no further pollen analyses were made, but now in light of the evidence for drought the cracks may be evidence of the last wetting of the surface before final desiccation and subsequent deposition of the Clanton clay. The sequence of events may have been as follows.

1. Death of the Area 1 mammoth and penetration of bones and artifacts into the streambed during the final saturation of the F_1 channel and reworked D_1 sand.

2. Drop of the water table during drought.

3. Killing and butchering of at least 11 bison by Clovis people.

4. Excavation of the water hole, presumably by mammoths.

5. Death and defleshing of the Area 3 mammoth, presumably by Clovis people.

6. Formation of small puddles during a brief rain.

7. Desiccation and formation of mud cracks.

8. Extinction of the megafauna.

9. Rise of the water table and inundation of Wolf Creek and Bison Creek valley bottoms.

10. Deposition of the black mat, Stratum F_{2a}, the Clanton clay followed by Stratum F_{2b}, the Earp marl with stringers of black mat.

The bison kill in Areas 4 and 5 (Figs. 1.3, 1.8b–c) occurred 10 m to 40 m northwest of the Area 3 mammoth and near a muddy swale between Wolf Creek and Bison Kill Creek (Fig. 2.16g). Bone preservation was poor and most bones were compressed due to overburden pressure (Fig. 1.8a). Trench 12 and Profile K (Foldout 2) reveal a broad shallow swale whose axis extends from Area 4 to Area 2. Upslope the swale extends to the north side of Area 5 (Plate 8), which was covered with bison hoof-size depressions in Sobaipuri mudstone (Fig. 1.9c). These were absent from higher ground. A shallow basin-shaped Clovis hearth occurred in Area 4 adjacent to the swale and off the edge of a low outcrop of Coro marl (Fig. 1.8b). It contained burned bone fragments and charcoal that yielded a radiocarbon age of 10,760 ± 100 B.P., which is believed to be a minimum age because of incomplete removal of black mat from the charcoal (Appendix A, Table A.1). Another hearth in the southern part of Area 4 (Fig. 5.19) has not been dated.

Several shallow basin-shaped depressions that occurred in Area 3 and Area 4 are thought by Hemmings to be where bison rolled and dusted themselves (Chapter 5). Historically these have been called buffalo wallows (Roe 1951). The dated hearth in Area 4 may be where Clovis people used one of these buffalo wallows for a roasting pit (Chapter 5; Hemmings 1970).

Another feature of the Clovis landscape was apparently a shallow depression over the spring conduits of Area 8. Today this buried surface is a hill (Fig. 1.10a) rather than a depression because of topographic inversion due to differential compaction. The evidence of compaction is inferred from the present expression of the stratigraphy associated with the spring conduits (Foldout 1, Trench 18; Foldout 2, Trench 26). The D_2 conduit sand (Fry Ranch Member) forms a mound over which the Clanton clay (Stratum F_2) black mat is thicker than in the low ground around the mound (Fig. 1.10a). Everywhere away from this area the black mat is always thickest in low areas, either as black mat (Fig. 2.16a, b) or its marl facies (Fig. 2.16c, d, e), and thins over the higher areas. A probable explanation for the anomalous thickening over the mound of spring feeder sand is differential compaction. Medium to coarse sand, free of clay, will not compact nearly as much as saturated clay or mud upon dewatering. As the water table started its net decline about 15,000 B.P., the compaction of Millville alluvium, Sobaipuri mudstone, and Coro marl very likely significantly exceeded that of the conduit sands, eventually producing a topography that is inverted over the conduits. This situation appears to have occurred after deposition of the black mat and after deposition of the lower part of the overlying Donnet silt (Stratum F_3). It may have occurred between 8000 B.P. and 7000 B.P. when the water table had significantly declined. During Clovis time the conduit area would have been a shallow, perhaps seepy, depression in which, after Clovis departure from the area, the black mat subsequently formed and covered the bottom of the depression to a greater thickness than on the sides.

The only artifact found in Area 8 was a biface thinning flake near a cluster of horse and bison teeth near the west wall (Figs. 1.11b, 2.17). Thirty-one anomalous cobble to boulder-size rocks, 10 cm to 20 cm across, were impressed into the Sobaipuri mud and the conduit sand (D_2), perhaps as stepping stones (Fig. 1.11b). Another stone exposed by Trench 19 was about 20 cm below the F_2/D contact. These stones appear to be related to Feature 1 (Figs. 1.10c, 2.17), a 75-cm diameter circular area of well-sorted sand of finer grain size than the Stratum D_1 conduit sand. This feature appears to be a subconduit, but may have been part of a Clovis well.

Feature 2, an anomalous excavation approximately 13 m south of the spring conduits, consisted of a circular depression also ~ 75 cm in diameter and 10 cm deep (Figs. 1.10d, 2.17). Feature 2 had been excavated from the surface of Sobaipuri mudstone down to the brown layer therein. The black mat (Stratum F_2) extended down the near-vertical sides and across the nearly flat floor. Remains of three horse teeth were exposed in the floor. This anomalous feature is apparently an abandoned well excavation, undoubtedly by Clovis people. Its diameter, like Feature 1, is similar to the Clovis well discovered at the Clovis type site, Blackwater Draw, New Mexico, in 1964 (Haynes and others 1999) and a Clovis feature found at the Aubrey Site, Texas (Ferring 2001).

The stones impressed into the Sobaipuri mud and the conduit sand suggest that the area of the conduits was soggy, whereas the aborted well suggests drier conditions nearby. Apparently Clovis activity in Area 8 was directed toward finding water. What we interpreted as a subconduit near the center of Conduit 2 probably served as a Clovis well. It consisted of a shallow depression the same diameter as the aborted well but filled with soft, well-sorted sand (Foldout 1, Trench 18). The black mat actually protruded into this feature (Fig. 1.11a) from which Clovis people perhaps dipped out water.

A cross section through Feature 1 and the concentration of rocks (Fig. 2.17, X-X') show the stone alignment to extend from the Clovis age surface on the north

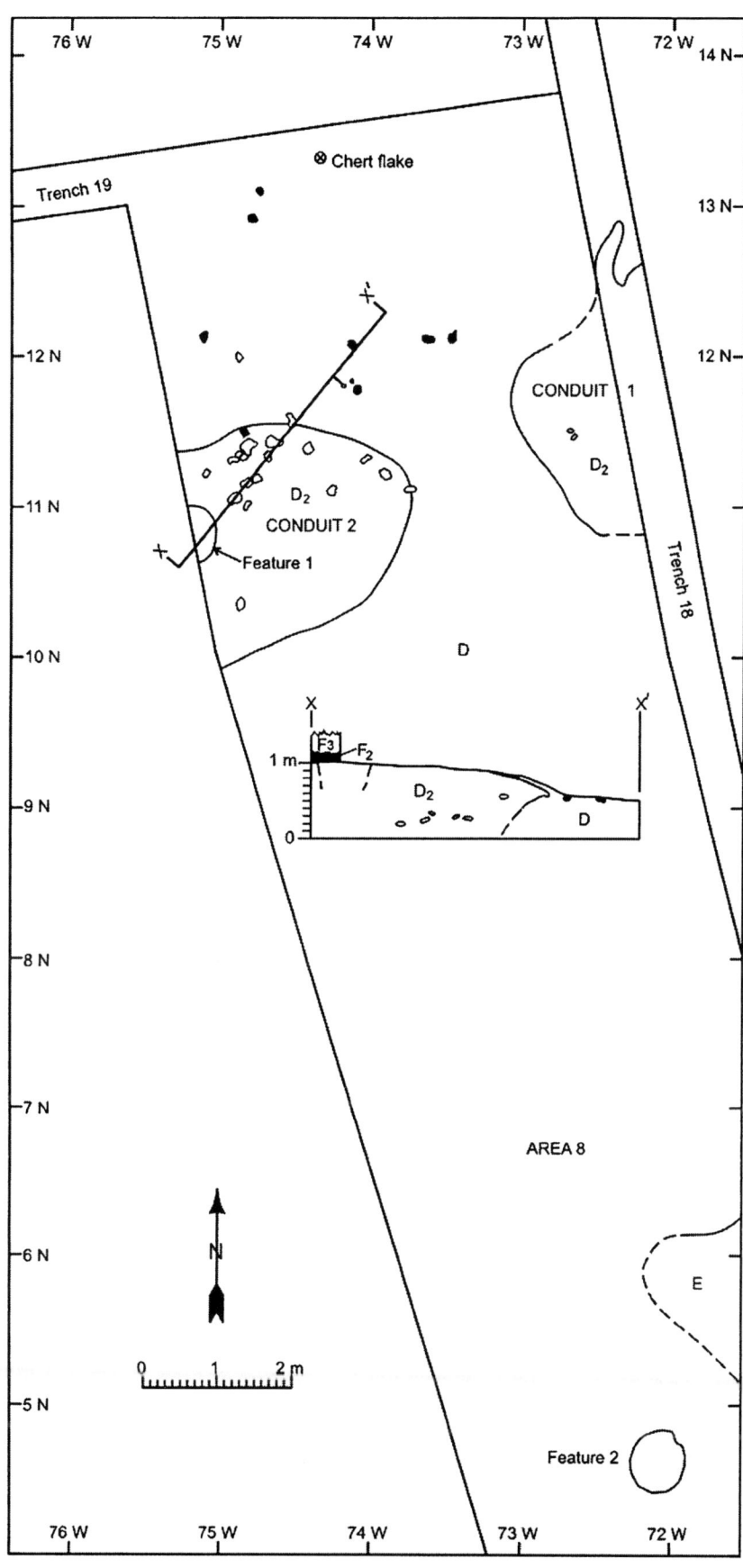

Figure 2.17. Map of Area 8 showing anomalous features associated with Conduit 2. Anomalous stones are indicated as blackened for those in contact with the black mat (Stratum F_2) and open outlines for stones below F_2 as shown in the cross section X–X'. Feature 1 may be a water source for the Clovis visitors and Feature 2 may be an aborted excavation for a well (see text and Figs. 1.10, 1.11). Two stones occurred in Conduit 1, and the chert flake was the only knapped artifact found in Area 8. Bone and tooth distribution not shown.

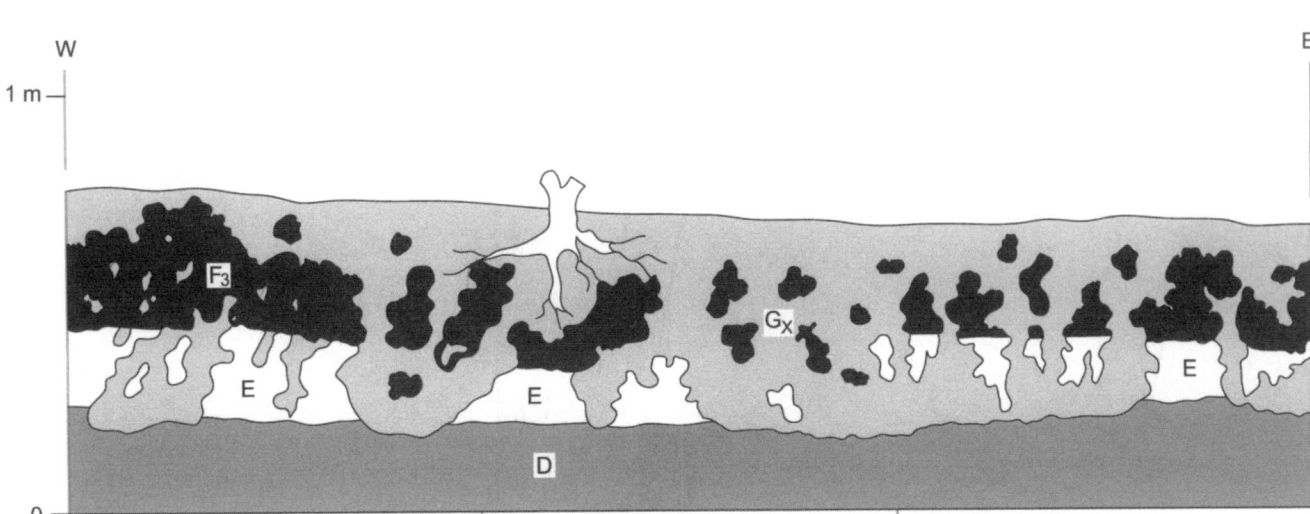

Figure 2.18. Profile of bioturbation in Area 7 (north wall of Grid EE-5 on the 5 east-west line of Square 24 and half of Square 23) shows remnants of the Clovis occupation surface as the contact between Donnet silt (F_3) over Coro marl (E) over Sobaipuri mudstone (D). Stratum G_x is a bioturbated mixture of strata G_1, G_2, and F_3.

side of Conduit 2 into the D_2 sand and toward Feature 1. However, the depth of the stones of as much as 70 cm below the Clovis surface suggests that they sank into the conduit either as they were being stepped on or afterward. If afterward, the sinking may be associated with the rise in the water table that led to black mat deposition. Rising water may have fluidized the conduit sand, allowing the stones to sink.

The Clovis hunting camp (Areas 6 and 7) is located on an eroded surface of Coro marl between Wolf Creek (the East Swale) and Bison Kill Creek (Curry Draw) near their confluence (Plates 3, 8). Many of the stone tools found in Areas 6 and 7 reflect camp type activity: end scrapers, blades shaped for multiple uses, and basal portions of broken Clovis projectile points (Chapter 7). These artifacts, along with thousands of flakes, occurred in a very bioturbated mixture of Donnet silt with Coro marl and slopewash alluvium. This example of bioturbation (Fig. 2.18) is caused by about 12 millennia of insect, root, and small animal activity within 20 cm to 30 cm of the surface. Excavation revealed a few artifacts to be on the tops of remnants of Coro marl and under remnants of Donnet silt (Fig. 1.9d). The Clovis-age surface on the higher ground was buried by the Donnet silt. This is consistent with the fact that the black mat is absent from the camp area because it does not extend beyond the low areas of the inner valleys.

Whereas the intense bioturbation moved artifacts vertically, up to 50 cm in a few examples, it apparently did not move them horizontally enough to destroy the horizontal concentration (Chapter 8). The depth of bioturbation was limited by the Sobaipuri mudstone, which was not significantly penetrated by either rodents or insects. The rounded bottoms of two buried circular pits in Area 7 extended about 15 cm into the Millville alluvium (Chapter 7, Fig. 7.3). The cause or purpose of these pits could not be positively determined. They most likely were dug during the later Cochise preceramic occupation in evidence in Area 7. In the western part of Area 7, the middle portion of a mammoth long bone was exposed on the surface (Fig. 7.5a). The preservation was too poor for identification of the particular element. At first sight the bone was difficult to distinguish from caliche. However, it is possible that the bone is one of the elements missing from the Area 3 mammoth and it could have been carried 125 m to the campsite by Clovis people. A fragment of a mammoth tooth was found in the northern part of Area 7 (Fig. 7.5a).

Lehner Ranch Formation

The drought that stopped the flow in the Clovis-age creek beds was the culmination of a net decline of the water table that began at least 14,000 years ago when the upper Coro marl was the bottom ooze of a marsh or cienega. The drop of at least 3 m was reversed with the deposition of the black mat, the Clanton Ranch Member of the Lehner Ranch Formation (Figs. 2.5, 2.16). The

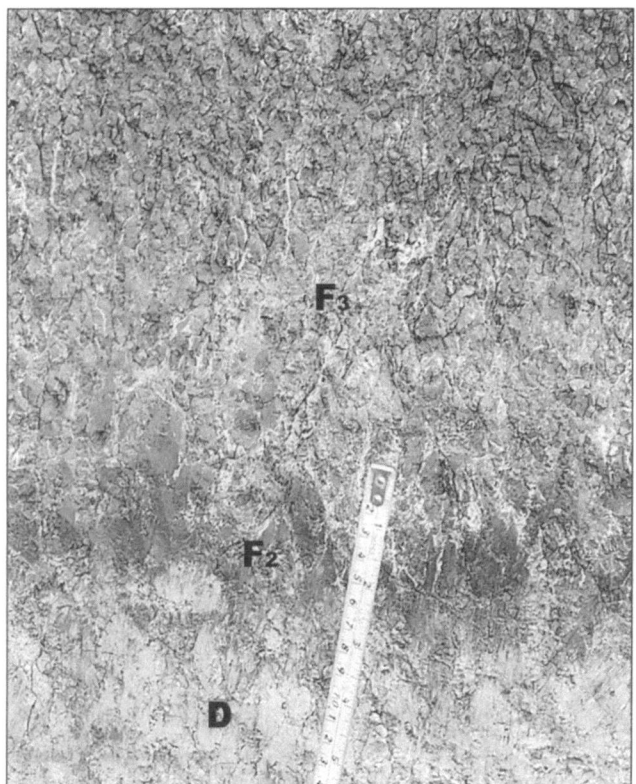

Figure 2.19. Close-up view of the black mat and Donnet silt (F_2 and F_3). Stratum F_2 is the black basal 5 cm resting on Stratum D and below basal Stratum F_3, both showing fine to medium irregular blocky pedogenic structure with filament and ped coatings of calcium carbonate and white fungus.

rise of the water table occurred in such a way that there was not any significant flow along Wolf Creek in Areas 1 and 3. If there had been flow, the mammoth tracks in the sandy creek bed of these areas would have been washed away. Instead, they were simply inundated.

Clanton Ranch Member (Black Mat, Stratum F_2) and the Reemergence of the Water Table

The Clanton clay or black mat (F_{2a}) is composed of very organic silty clay, mostly montmorillonite (Appendix B). As made evident by pyrolytic analysis by chemist Raymond Rodgers in Appendix B, the organic matter is probably derived from algal blooms occurring in ponds and wet ground around ponds. Subsequent pyrolytic analysis by Stankiewicz and Tegelaar (Appendix B) of a thin stringer of F_{2a} from a different location indicates organic carbon derived mainly from plant detritus with algae making a relatively minor contribution. The plant detritus occurs on slopes away from low areas with standing water, indicated by the carbonate facies, Stratum F_{2b} (Fig. 2.16c–e). Carbon 13 nuclear magnetic resonance (^{13}C NMR) analysis by Leenheer (Appendix B) supports Rodgers' interpretation of an algal origin for the black mat. Oxidized plant detritus appears to be a lesser component.

Typically, the black mat is 2 cm to 10 cm thick (Fig. 2.16a, e, g), with very strong, fine to medium angular blocky ped structure (Fig. 2.19). The peds are coated with filaments of calcium carbonate and, in some areas, with additional filaments of a white leathery fungus that upon drying can be mistaken for a carbonate coating. The internal pH of peds is 6.5 to 7.0. Values on the acid side of neutral (<7.0) are otherwise rare in the calcareous environment of the other sediments.

The black mat thins to nothing as it is followed stratigraphically upslope and ends at elevations of 1 m to 1.5 m above the Graveyard sand (Stratum F_1) of the creek beds. Downslope it appears to thicken to as much as 20 cm or more as in the north side of Areas 4 and 5 (Fig. 2.16b). However, in these areas only the basal black (2–5 cm) is true Stratum F_2 (Fig. 2.19). The upper, very dark gray (15–20 cm) is basal Donnet silt (Stratum F_3) in places with a component redeposited from F_2 (Foldout 2, Trench 13N).

Earp Member (White Marl, Stratum F_{2b}), The Ponding Facies

In lower areas the black mat bifurcates into thin (2 cm or less) stringers (Stratum F_{2a}) separated by grayish white soft, pulverent marl, the Earp marl (Stratum F_{2b}), of nearly pure calcium carbonate (Fig. 2.16c–e). In Area 2 the Earp marl is nearly 1 m thick (Plate 6) and distinguishable from Coro marl by being softer, slightly less white (very light gray), and, of course, stratigraphically younger. In the northeast end of Area 2 the black stringers converge to form a "knot" of 5-cm to 10-cm thickness (Fig. 2.16d). In Trench 13N this pinching and swelling of F_{2b} marl between several stringers of F_{2a} black mat reaches an extreme degree (Appendix A, Fig. A.1a, b). This situation offered an exceptional opportunity for microstratigraphic profiling and sampling for radiocarbon analysis as described in Appendix A.

A cross section of the F_1 channel is best exposed in the north wall of the South Branch (Plate 5) where the relatively gentle slope of the sides of the ancient valley of Wolf Creek are clearly outlined by the thin black mat overlying the eroded surface of the Coro marl. Upslope the sides of the buried valley are obscured by pedogenic processes, but downslope the black mat (F_{2a}) goes under a 35-cm thick deposit of white marl (F_{2b2}) and bifurcates over and under a thin (5 cm) lens of white marl F_{2b1} (Figs. 2.12, 2.13).

In Area 1 the water hole was coated with a thin (~ 1 cm) black mat (F_{2a1}) and covered by nearly 1 m of F_{2b} marl with several very thin stringers of black mat that thinned out down gradient (Fig. 2.16e; Plate 7, Profile G). The uppermost black mat (F_{2a1}) is obscured in the highest areas by pedogenic processes associated with the aggradation of the Donnet silt. Radiocarbon ages for upper F_2 range from a carbonate date of 10,250 B.P. near the middle, a black mat stringer age of 9020 B.P., to a carbonate age of 8057 B.P. at the top of F_3 (Plate 7, Profile G); the last two are minimum values.

The black mat occurs upstream in Curry Draw as buried erosional remnants exposed by most of the cross valley trenches (Foldouts 1, 2) and in a natural exposure in the right bank about 80 m farther upstream than the junction with the West Swale. Downstream it is exposed in a few places high in the arroyo walls and in tributary catchment areas as far downstream as the cottonwood gallery that begins 1 km below Area 1. Farther down, the arroyo walls are either younger alluvium of the Escapule Ranch Formation or the older Millville alluvium. The black mat also occurs in every major tributary of the west side of the San Pedro River from Lehner Ranch Arroyo to Graveyard Gulch and in the catchment of some minor tributaries (Haynes 1968b). Remnants occurring farther down the San Pedro Valley get progressively higher above the modern channel, reaching nearly 200 m at Cerros Negros where a remnant occurs above a thick outcrop of Coro marl (Agenbroad 1967).

My original interpretation of the black mat had been that it formed on wet soggy ground with standing water only in the lowest areas where the marl precipitated (Haynes 1991). However, it may be that it all formed in very shallow standing water, because some water depth would be likely for algal blooms of sufficient size to account for the observed thicknesses as well as the laminated structure of the Earp marl. When originally deposited and before dewatering and compaction, the mats were probably considerably thicker than they are now.

How Curry Draw came to be inundated is another question that requires further research. I originally believed that the water table rose gradually to allow a carpet of vegetation, perhaps low sedges, to grow and stabilize the surface such that the mammoth tracks were preserved without being eroded by running water. However, it is difficult to imagine this happening without at least a trickle of water along the thalweg filling up and breaking through the mammoth tracks. We found no evidence that this occurred. Instead, it is more likely that at the time the tracks had dried out there was enough calcium carbonate present to at least weakly cement the sediments and preserve the microrelief as the water table rose.

The possibility that a pond rose in Curry Draw starting downstream is unlikely because the highest occurrences transverse to the axial drainages are not at a constant elevation. Instead, they get lower in the downstream direction and higher upstream. Furthermore, there appears to be no time-transgressive age gradient. Perhaps precipitation preceding the reemergence of the water table resulted in the washing of silt and clay from adjacent slopes, through vegetation acting as a filter, to lowlands, covering the microtopography of the mammoth tracks. These would have soon been inundated by the emergent water table and mixed with algae. In the lowest areas, water depth may have exceeded 1 m.

A fairly rapid rise is postulated by the fact that the skeleton of the Area 3 mammoth is essentially intact. The disarticulated hind legs are probably the result of Clovis activity. From observations of elephant remains in Africa, Gary Haynes (1991: 188) found that carcasses deflesh in a matter of days, after which the carcasses begin to collapse and bones eventually get dispersed. Large animal predators speed up the bone dispersal process and even other elephants can contribute to the process by fondling bones of their relatives. The degree of articulation of this skeleton suggests that it was inundated soon after its death, perhaps in as little time as two weeks (Gary Haynes, personal communication).

Because the black mat invariably occurs both under and over the Earp marl facies, it most likely represents shallow water at the beginning of formation about 10,800 B.P. and at the end around 9700 B.P. If this interpretation is correct, then the stringers within the Earp marl may represent intermediate periods of shallower water. On the other hand, the stringers could represent redeposited black mat or organic debris washed from adjacent slopes during periods of stronger precipitation.

The radiocarbon ages for the black mat and Earp marl (Appendix A, Table A.1) are essentially identical to the radiocarbon ages for the Younger Dryas climatic reversal, a return to a glacial climate that interrupted deglaciation at the end of the Pleistocene (Berger 1990). The effect at Murray Springs appears to have been a water table rise due to colder temperatures that reduced evapotranspiration and perhaps to increased precipitation. In the latter case, the type of precipitation was probably gentle enough to prevent slopewash sedimentation other than by clay and silt. Gentle precipitation would support plant growth that would act as a sediment filter for runoff as well as prevent slope erosion via rills and runnels. These conditions appear to have existed during black mat time throughout the upper San Pedro Valley.

The analysis of fossil pollen at the Lehner Site (Mehringer and others 1971) indicates a cienega environment for black mat time, with the closest modern analog being parts of the Empire Cienega in the Sonoita Valley (Hendrickson and Minckley 1984; Martin 1963c). However, the inner valley was covered by open water and may have appeared as Babocomari Cienega does today (Fig. 2.8e).

Donnet Ranch Member (Stratum F_3) and Gentle Aggradation

The Donnet silt, named for an old ranch, is believed to be an eolian deposit. The end of Stratum F_2 black mat time is represented by desiccation and weak to moderate erosion of the black mat and, in a few places along Bison Kill Creek, entrenchment into the Graveyard sand. This brief period of discontinuous reactivation of the F_1 channel is seen at the north end of Trench 13N, where redeposition of the black mat is clearly indicated by a reversal of radiocarbon ages in the reactivated channel (Foldout 2, Trench 13N; Appendix A). This reactivation is also apparent in Trench 17 (Foldout 1) and Trench 28 (Foldout 2), but is best displayed by the recent widening of Trench 22 (Fig. 2.20). This localization of the areas of reactivation and the lack of a continuous gully indicate a brief episode of erosion (thalweg incision) as or before deposition of the Donnet silt began. The localized channel deposits are designated Stratum F_{3a} and are referred to as the Donnet channel phase.

Sedimentary analysis by Davis (1975) indicates that the Donnet Ranch Member (Stratum F_3) of the Lehner Ranch Formation is a clayey silt with secondary calcifi-

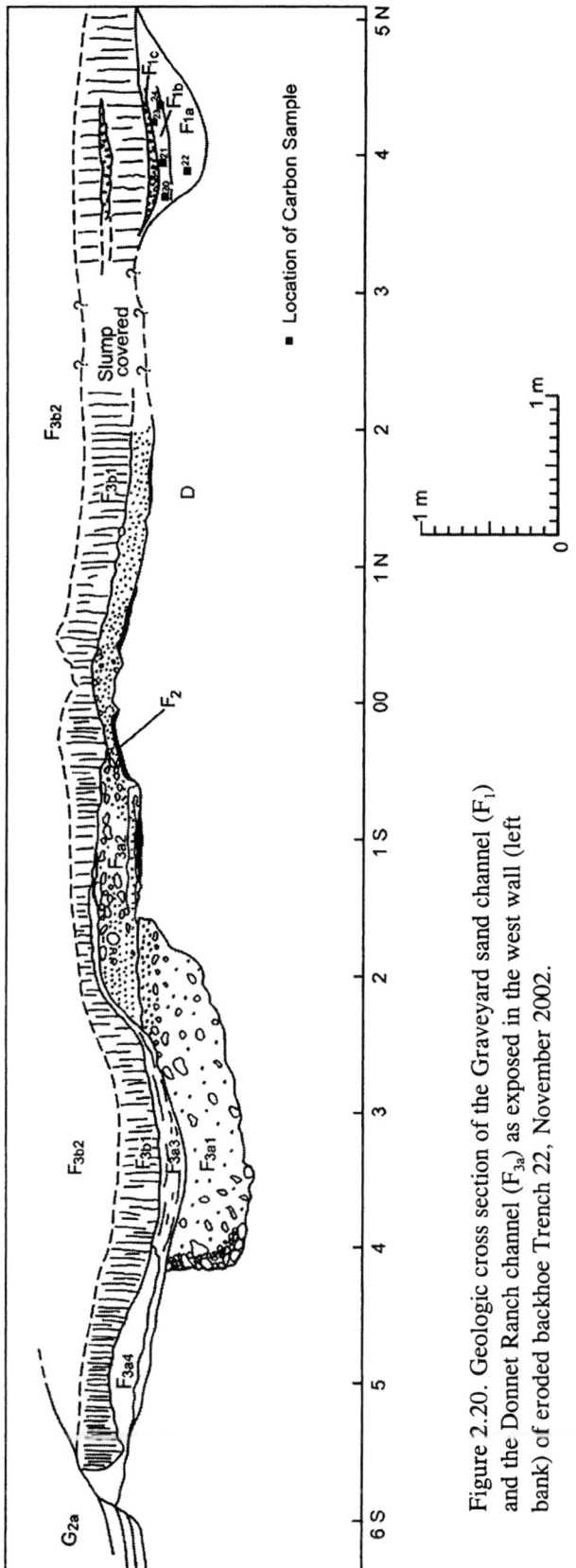

Figure 2.20. Geologic cross section of the Graveyard sand channel (F_1) and the Donnet Ranch channel (F_{3a}) as exposed in the west wall (left bank) of eroded backhoe Trench 22, November 2002.

cation. It is a cement-gray, firm, massive sediment that was deposited over the black mat to depths of more than 1 m in low areas. The color grades from very dark gray in the basal 2–20 cm, in contact with the black mat (Figs. 2.16b, 2.19), to light gray in the middle, to brownish gray in the soil zone (weak mollic epipedon) at the top. Donnet silt extends laterally beyond the black mat and filled the shallow valleys of Bison Kill and Wolf creeks (Fig. 2.5) until they became swales with nearly level floors, much as the valley of Turkey Creek appears today (Fig. 2.8f). Where Stratum F_3 thins out on uplands away from the valley floors, as in the Clovis camp area, it is thoroughly bioturbated by a combination of insect, small mammal, and root activity (Fig. 2.18).

An eolian source of the fine sand, silt, and clay of Stratum F_3 was evaluated by Davis (1975), who concluded that erosion of the Coro marl of adjacent slopes was more likely the source, although an eolian source could not be precluded. The light gray color and high calcium carbonate content (up to 36%) suggested derivation from Coro marl, the clastic content of which has yet to be quantified and analyzed. However, much of the Donnet carbonate is secondary and a significant eolian component is suggested by the regional distribution of the Donnet silt.

Along Curry Draw Stratum F_3 occurs over and extends laterally beyond Coro marl, thinning out on the upper slopes of the valley and on benches such as in Areas 6 and 7, the Clovis encampment site. This burial of the Coro marl indicates that it was inadequate as a sole source of sediment for deposition of Donnet silt. Furthermore, a perched valley in the Charleston Hills 7.4 km (4.6 miles) to the northeast contains Donnet silt, but there are no outcrops of Coro marl upslope as potential sources of sediment for Donnet silt.

Additional evidence of an eolian source is the sedimentary fill in the "grass circles." These are circular depressions on the Tombstone surface near the inner valley of the San Pedro River (Fig. 2.4e, f). They are most numerous on the west side of the valley west of Fairbank and the old Boquillas railroad station (Fig. 1.2). Four occur near Murray Springs: two to the north between Curry Draw and Moson Wash and two to the southeast between Curry Draw and Horsethief Draw (Fig. 2.2). The shallow depressions are "islands" of desert grassland communities within a "sea" of desert-scrub (Chapter 3).

In 1966, trenching across the larger of the two grass circles (Fig. 2.6a-c) southeast of the Murray Springs Site revealed a sinkholelike solution depression in a dense caliche (stage IV petrocalcic horizon). The top stratum is 10 cm of gray powdery silt, a soil that occurs at other localities in the San Pedro Valley, including the Murray Springs Site. It has been informally referred to as a desert A horizon but without the vesicles of a vesicular horizon. Below this the depression is filled with 30 cm to 70 cm of gray to dark gray sandy clay loam that resembles the Donnet silt modified by pedogenesis (Fig. 2.6c). This mollic epipedon is welded to a much older Bt horizon of variable thickness consisting of up to a meter of red, strongly prismatic, sandy clay that pinches out laterally between the caliche and the loam. Radiocarbon ages of the organic fractions of bulk samples from the middle of the top half of the loam are 1890 ± 130 B.P. for the residue (humins) and 3020 ± 90 B.P. for the humic acids (humates). The middle of the lower 30 cm produced radiocarbon ages of 4340 ± 140 B.P. for the residue and 6540 ± 190 B.P. for the humic acids (Appendix A, Table A.1). These are mean residence ages for pedogenesis, and the older values are minimums because contaminant humic acids cannot be removed from indigenous humic acids by standard chemical pretreatment (Appendix A). Therefore, the loam hosting the pedogenic development is very likely the Donnet silt. As it extends beyond the grass circle and onto the Tombstone surface, the loam becomes less organic and lighter in color, characteristics that are more typical of Donnet silt. Farther away, it rapidly thins out and loses its identity, and any vestiges of it have been obliterated by bioturbation. Coro marl cannot be a source because it was never deposited on the Tombstone surface.

These observations indicate that the Donnet silt is an eolian deposit that blanketed the landscape and that was redeposited as thicker sections in valley floors and low areas by slopewash from the uplands to gentle aggradation in the lowlands. Eolian deposition and slopewash aggradation of the valley floors may have been penecontemporaneous. The paucity of clasts larger than fine sand in the thick, massive sections of Donnet silt and the absence of significant channel facies indicate gentle erosion from adjacent slopes and slow aggradation over 1,600 radiocarbon years, from about 9600 B.P. to 8000 B.P.

If the Donnet silt once blanketed the landscape to depths of at least 10 cm, the substrate for plant growth was quite different during the early Holocene from what it is today on the Tombstone surface. The Chihuahuan desertscrub growing today is in part due to the edaphic effect of near-surface occurrences of highly calcareous petrocalcic soil horizons (caliche) of the lower slopes of the Tombstone surface and the Nexpa gravels. As one proceeds up the slope of the Tombstone surface toward the Huachuca Mountains, a strong red paleosol occurs in arkosic, much less calcareous, alluvium-colluvium that forms the substrate for desert grassland vegetation. This vegetation may have extended all the way to the edge of the inner valley of the San Pedro River during the time the Donnet silt was accumulating and perhaps earlier. Even in historic times, grasses were much more abundant in the Lewis Springs area than they are today (Hastings and Turner 1965).

The pollen evidence from the Donnet silt at the Lehner Site (Mehringer and others 1971) indicates an early mesic or cienega type of local environment near the base. That environment was followed by a net trend toward ever-increasing xeric conditions up section up to the time of entrenchment between 8000 B.P. and about 6700 B.P. (Mehringer and Haynes 1965).

Escapule Ranch Formation, Times of Arroyo Cutting and Filling

Sometime after 8000 B.P., arroyo entrenchment occurred throughout the upper San Pedro Valley beginning a period of epicyclic cutting and filling that persists to the present. The Weik Ranch, Hargis Ranch, and McCool Ranch members (Plate 2) represent arroyo fills of similar alluvium but of different ages that are difficult to distinguish without either clear contact relationships or archaeological content and radiocarbon ages.

Weik Ranch Member (Stratum G_1)

At Murray Springs Area 1, the channel of the Weik alluvium (Stratum G_1), named for the Weik Ranch across the river from the Lehner Site, is exposed in the south wall of the South Branch where it has cut away a part of the F_1 channel and the Clovis occupation surface (Fig. 2.10a). Gravel and coarse sand, occupying the basal 30 cm of the channel, are overlain by 60 cm of intermixed, redeposited Millville sand and gravel and fragments of Coro marl derived from collapse of the banks of the G_1 channel (Plate 7, Profile N). This basal fill is overlain by 1.4 m of banded, very calcareous, sandy muds, muddy sands, and sandy marls all overlain by 1.5 m of gray to brownish gray, massive, clayey fine sand and silt with strong, fine to medium, prismatic soil structure typical of cienega soils. A natural concentration of carbonized plant fragments about 40 cm below the top of the pond sediments provided a radiocarbon age of 5750 ± 250 B.P. on organics in silt and 5520 ± 200 B.P. on humic acids, both probably minimum values. Higher in the section a concentration of carbonized plant remains in the lower part of the cienega soil provided a humate date of 5630 ± 130 B.P. (Plate 7, Profile D). These ages are essentially the same as those from the Martin, Schoenwetter, and Mehringer Pollen Profile from below the Murray Place (Appendix A). They confirm the correlation as Stratum G_1.

This fill sequence reflects an initial channel bed load of gravel lagged from Millville alluvium and buried by bank collapse sediments. This load is followed by slopewash sedimentation into a pond or marsh within the draw, in which each sedimentary band reflects a different source area of erosion of an adjacent slope or a different depth of erosion. The colors and relatively high clay and carbonate content indicate Coro marl, Sobaipuri mud, and Donnet silt as the dominant source sediments. The light brown and gray colors are consistent with this interpretation.

The overlying gray, clayey fine sand and silt appear to be additional slopewash sediments deposited over the pond sediments when the water table was near the surface. At this time upper Curry Draw was a cienega, perhaps something like Leslie Creek Cienega (Hendrickson and Minckley 1984) today. The pollen profile from the Weik alluvium at the Lehner Site is consistent with this estimation (Mehringer and others 1971), as is that from Curry Draw (Mehringer and others 1967).

Although the Weik alluvium is not exposed in the North Branch of Curry Draw, its former presence there is revealed by the stratigraphic trenches placed across the valley. Only remnants occur in Trenches 15, 25, 12N, 14, and 27 (Foldouts 1, 2) and indicate a buried alluvial fill of gray, muddy sands and sandy muds. Subsequent erosion by the G_{2a} (Hargis alluvium) channel has removed most of the basal channel facies and all of the uppermost beds.

Downstream from the south headcut of Curry Draw the pond facies of Weik alluvium is exposed in the two tributary headcuts cutting into the right bank at the mouth of the East Swale (Fig. 2.3; Plate 1). In the first reentrant, cross sections of the left bank of the G_1 channel are exposed in both sides and clearly indicate the direction of the channel to be essentially west to east, parallel to modern Curry Draw. This being the case, the channel cross section just described at Area 1 must be either a reentrant caused by hydraulic inertia at a right angle bend or a branch channel. If the latter, it did not reach the present north wall of Curry Draw, so must have also turned eastward to link up with the other channel somewhere before the present junction of the North and South branches of Curry Draw. Samples of dispersed flecks of carbonized plant fragments from about 1.7 m above the base of the pond or marsh sequence in the second reentrant downstream provided a radiocarbon age of 6400 ± 100 B.P. (Appendix A, Table A.1).

A remnant of the G_1 channel occurs in the left bank of the South Branch of Curry Draw 45 m upstream of the junction of the two branches (Fig. 1.3; Plate 5b). Here the Weik alluvium contains the same pond or marsh facies as the other exposures upstream. The Weik alluvium is not exposed downstream for some 500 m, where it then appears in the right bank opposite a wooden wingdam placed by the Southern Pacific Railroad to deflect stream flow from undercutting the road bed. Here the pond facies, while thinner than upstream, is black and more organic. By tracing the black layer upslope and upstream for about 25 m, it can be seen to derive from remnants of the black mat (Stratum F_2) overlying Coro marl. The black color is obviously derived from redeposited black mat, and fragments of Stratum F_2 occur in the sand and gravel at the base of the channel, much as at Martin's Pollen Profile I that I discuss below and in Chapter 1 and Appendix A. About 10 cm of coarse fluvial sand separate the lower pond deposits from a thinner upper set that is dark gray. The two dark layers merge upslope and are overlain by a grayish brown cienega soil.

Between here and the Murray Place, the Weik alluvium is not readily distinguished from Hargis and McCool alluvium because of intense bioturbation that created loose rubbley silt extending to about 30 m east of the Murray Place. This right bank exposure is the location of the original Martin and Schoenwetter Murray Springs Pollen Profile I (Martin 1963c) that was resampled by Mehringer and me before we explored upstream in 1966 (Mehringer and others 1967). It will be referred to as the MSM (Martin, Schoenwetter, and Mehringer) Pollen Profile. A 10-cm thick layer of tan sand separating two layers of dark gray pond beds is undoubtedly the same sand as that just described for the upstream section. This readily allows correlations between the two locations. Radiocarbon ages for the lower layer of pond beds support the correlations and are 5890 ± 270 B.P. on bulk sediment and 5500 ± 400 B.P. on naturally carbonized willow wood. The bulk sediment samples of the upper layer provided ages of 4230 ± 290 B.P. and 4120 ± 490 B.P. (Appendix A, Table A.1).

An erosional unconformity separates Weik alluvium from overlying silty sand alluvium containing a hearth with a slab metate laid over it. Charcoal from the hearth provided an age of 1550 ± 90 B.P. On this basis, the overlying sediment is the upper part of Stratum G_{2b}, the McCool alluvium. This is disconformably overlain by about 30 cm of reddish brown, laminated silt and sand of the Teviston Member (Stratum H).

Farther downstream at the beginning of the Big Bend (Fig. 2.2), a fine-grained facies of the Millville alluvium is overlain by approximately 1 m of light brown Weik alluvium that deepens to about 4 m where it grades into a tributary channel fill of calcareous muddy sand alluvium with numerous clasts of rolled caliche fragments (Fig. 2.10b). This markedly different facies is due to the tributary's drainage area where caliches (petrocalcic horizons and marls) had been exposed in the past just as they are today. Erosion of exposures of caliche produces caliche rubble that eventually gets washed into the drainages.

The east (right) wall of the tributary extends out into Curry Draw where it bends sharply to the north, hence our field name of the Big Bend. This 75-m expanse of vertical wall provides the best stratigraphic exposure in Curry Draw for units older than the Lehner Ranch Formation. A succession of insets reveals that the St. David Formation is truncated by the contact with Millville alluvium, which is overlain by the Moson sand and Coro marl, which are truncated by the G_1 channel filled with gray Weik sand and gravel alluvium showing much redeposition from older units. In fact, redeposited fragments of mammoth bone and black mat have been observed in this channel fill at the Big Bend. Near the left bank of Curry Draw, before it turns back eastward again, there is an erosion remnant of Weik alluvium that becomes an island during high flow stages. This coarser-grained facies of Weik alluvium is exposed intermittently in the right bank downstream, but most of the left bank exposures are of Hargis and McCool alluvial units.

The marked facies changes in Weik alluvium from pond and cienega sediments in upper Curry Draw to fluvial sand and gravel downstream is fairly typical of middle to late Holocene alluvial fills in the tributaries of the upper San Pedro. The cause of damming to produce the ponds is unknown. Antevs (1941) invoked beaver dams because beaver are known to have been prevalent in the San Pedro Valley during the 19th century (Pattie 1905; Rodgers 1965). Though no evidence has been found to substantiate Antevs' beaver pond hypothesis, nothing has been found to refute it. I know of no beaver bones being found in Holocene alluvium in the area, but we did find, in the south wall of Area 4, a large sand-filled cavity in Hargis alluvium that could have been a beaver's stream bank den.

Other possible explanations for ponding in arroyos are tectonic tilting and bank collapse. There is no evidence to indicate any late Quaternary tectonic tilting (Morrison 1985), and it is unlikely because pond sediments occur in arroyo fills on both sides of the river. Damming by bank collapse in narrow channels is a real possibility for small localized ponds or charcos (Bryan 1928b), but probably not for such extensive ponds as those indicated for Weik alluvium in Curry Draw. This leaves beaver dams as a likely cause.

In all exposures the pond or marsh sediments are overlain by cienega soils, and pollen profiles through Weik alluvium show more xeric vegetation up section (Mehringer and Haynes 1965). These signs indicate a net lowering of the water table with time. Any reach of a drainage with the water well below the surface of a grassy swale becomes unstable and ripe for arroyo cutting because the threshold for entrenchment (Bull 1991: 10) has been lowered to a critical state. Any irregularity such as a soil crack, grass clump, or the like can become the initial point for headcut formation (Leopold and others 1964).

Hargis Ranch Member (Stratum G_{2a})

After about 4200 B.P. entrenchment occurred along the main channel of Curry Draw but not up the East Swale and only part way up the West Swale. The backhoe trenches across Curry Draw in the Murray Springs Site area reveal that entrenchment of G_{2a} followed the G_1 channel and removed most of the Weik alluvium from the North (main) Branch (Foldouts 1, 2). Aggradation of the Hargis Ranch Member of the Escapule Formation (Stratum G_{2a}) began shortly before 4000 ± 130 B.P., based on radiocarbon analysis of oxidized plant humates from a left bank exposure 60 m above the railroad wingdam in Curry Draw (Fig. 2.10e). Farther downstream, 470 m from the San Pedro River, charcoal from an aboriginal fire hearth in the lower half of the left bank provided a radiocarbon age of 3190 ± 80 B.P. These are the only radiocarbon ages considered reliable from Hargis alluvium in Curry Draw. Elsewhere in the upper San Pedro Valley there are six radiocarbon dates from Hargis alluvium that, along with those from Curry Draw, indicate aggradation between 4000 and 3000 B.P. (Haynes 1968b).

Trenches 25 and 4 reveal Hargis alluvium to consist of at least 5 m of interbedded medium to coarse arkosic sands, sandy muds, and sandy fine to medium pebble gravels (Foldout 1). The basal portions of the G_{2a} channel (G_{2a1}) were not exposed in Trenches 25 and 4. However, sandy pebble to cobble gravel probably occurs within 1 m below the trench floors because in Trench 14 about a meter of sand and gravel of the G_{2a1} channel, containing fragments of Strata D, E, and F_2, rests unconformably on St. David Formation (Foldout 2).

Hargis alluvium is exposed in the left bank of the North Branch from the headcut to about 50 m beyond the junction with the South Branch. It forms the right bank only from Trench 12N to a few meters below Area 2 (Plate 3). In the central part of the channel (Foldout 1, Trenches 4 and 25) the upper 60 cm is a reddish brown clayey, silty fine sand with moderately strong, medium prismatic pedogenic structure, suggesting a textural B horizon. However, laterally this stratum (G_{2a3}) thins out toward the sides of the channel, indicating a lens of sediment filling a swale. Therefore, the B horizon is partly pedogenic and partly cumulic in that much, if not most, of the clay is derived from slopewash. It is overlain by a 10–cm thick desert A horizon, consisting of a gray silt similar to what occurs in the grass circle at the top of the fill. This gray silt A horizon also occurs on the Weik alluvium fill of the East Swale and on Coro marl forming the left bank of the G_1 channel adjacent to the South Branch of Curry Draw (Appendix A, Fig. A.2, Profile Y). Humins from this soil provided a radiocarbon age of 1340 ± 120 B.P. and the humates dated 1570 ± 80 B.P. These data indicate that the gray silt is a sedimentary deposit covering a wide area on surfaces of different lithologies older than 1500 B.P. Therefore, it is not a pedogenic horizon per se, such as a leached horizon. It is most likely a cumulic A horizon, much like a vesicular horizon but without vesicles, developed in an eolian silt that blanketed the area sometime before 1500 B.P. but after the final aggradation of Hargis alluvium was completed about 3000 B.P.

Trench 32 (Figs. 1.3, 2.3), forming the west wall of Area 5, exposed a prehistoric well that had been excavated through middle Hargis alluvium (G_{2a2}) before aggradation of the upper Hargis alluvium (G_{2a3}; Fig. 2.16f; Foldout 2). A second well was found about 1 m east (Fig. 5.27). Both wells were dug perhaps between 3000 and 2000 B.P. and ended in Millville alluvium 12 cm below the bottom of the black mat. A light brown clay layer in the bottom of both wells suggests that they held water.

Below Area 2 the left bank exposures of Hargis alluvium reveal a succession of 5-cm to 20-cm thick bands of reddish brown and light brown, calcareous sandy gravels, sandy muds, and muddy sands totaling 4.2 m over sandy channel gravel. Farther downstream these beds grade into interbedded fluvial sand and sandy gravels with a 15-cm band of yellow to orange iron staining about 1.2 m below the surface. This horizontal band of discoloration crosses lithologies and is probably the result of precipitation of hydrated iron oxides at the capillary fringe of the water table. The iron-stained band also is exposed in Trench 27 (Plate 1; Foldout 2). Also in this trench, a distinct disconformable contact separates a lower set of fluvial gravel, sand, and mud from an upper set of similar lithologies. A 1-cm thick charcoal lens in the top of the lower set, 1.5 m above the base of the channel, provided a radiocarbon age of 4890 ± 60 B.P., an age more typical of upper Weik alluvium and about a millennium later than the same stratigraphic position in the G_1 channel in Area 1. Either G_1 channel aggradation was delayed in the North Branch or the charcoal is redeposited from Weik alluvium into the G_{2a1} channel. Whereas the reddish brown colors are consistent with the latter interpretation because lower Weik alluvium in this part of Curry Draw is more frequently gray in color, redeposited charcoal is usually dispersed rather than concentrated in a lens. Until this question can be resolved by more radiocarbon dating, the lower set will be considered middle Weik alluvium (Stratum G_1) overlain by Hargis alluvium (G_{2a}).

Farther downstream the Hargis alluvium exposed in the left bank about 60 m above the wingdam consists of 70 cm of banded sands and muds of a pond overlying more than 40 cm of channel sands and gravels. The pond sediments are conformably overlain by 80 cm of claycy sand alluvium bearing a cienega soil (Fig. 2.10e). Humates from carbonized plants near the bottom of the pond sediments have a radiocarbon age of 4000 ± 130 B.P. The Hargis alluvium is unconformably overlain by 1 m of poorly sorted, silty sand, slopewash alluvium of the McCool Member (Stratum G_{2b}). Down the remainder of Curry Draw it is difficult to tell Hargis from McCool alluvium without either having them in contact in a cut-and-fill (inset) relationship or having enough radiocarbon dates to clearly separate them by age.

In the right bank of the first north-bank tributary east of the Big Bend, two alluvial units are separated by an erosional contact that removed part of the lower stratum (Fig. 2.10f). Although there are no radiocarbon ages from this locality, the units are considered to be McCool alluvium (G_{2b}) over Hargis alluvium (G_{2a}) on the basis of lithological similarity to these units upstream. However, the possibility of the lower unit being Weik alluvium (G_1) cannot be precluded.

McCool Ranch Member (Stratum G_{2b})

The right bank of Curry Draw immediately below the junction with the North and South branches provided an excellent exposure of the McCool Member (Stratum G_{2b}) of the Escapule Formation (Fig. 2.10g). Approximately 1.5 m of layered reddish brown to pale reddish brown sandy muds and muddy sands of an ancient pond overlie roughly 30 cm of a basal channel gravel and are conformably overlain by 90 cm of calcareous clayey loam of a cienega soil. This in turn is conformably overlain by about 1.8 m of a grayish brown, poorly sorted, loamy sand slopewash alluvium with dispersed cobbles and pebbles. Differential compaction of the pond sediments is in evidence where the bands of sediment can be seen to rise in segments over a caliche boulder (Fig. 2.10h). Each segment is offset by microfaults.

At the downstream end of these deposits, they grade into poorly sorted, muddy sand alluvium with dispersed pebbles. A tributary arroyo entering Curry Draw from the south separates this section from one on the downstream side that contains more gravels derived from caliche rubble as both dispersed clasts and as lenses. Apparently the coarse load was carried to Curry Draw by the tributary. This raises the possibility that the tributary discharge could have dammed the main draw and caused the pond sedimentation just described, an event that might be tested by backhoe trenching in the left bank above and below the mouth of the tributary.

Poorly sorted light gray slopewash alluvium, probably of the McCool Member, occurs as the upper 40 cm to 90 cm of both banks in the reach with the cottonwood gallery from 40 m below the wingdam to the Murray

Place. In this reach the upper 1 m is thoroughly mixed by intense bioturbation. Its identification as McCool alluvium is based on an estimated correlation to the MSM pollen profile section some 30 m east of the Murray Place. As mentioned earlier, the Weik alluvium at the MSM profile is unconformably overlain by McCool slopewash alluvium with a radiocarbon age of 1550 ± 90 B.P. for the base of what probably is the upper third of the maximum McCool thickness.

Exposed in the right bank of the first north bank tributary (at a railroad culvert) east of the Big Bend are four alluvial units inset one against the other (Fig. 2.10f). The depositional sequence is probably Hargis alluvium overlain by McCool alluvium, as stated previously, with Bakarich alluvium (Stratum G_3) forming an inset 3-m terrace. Inset against this is a 2-m terrace of Stratum J, representing a post-Teviston brief episode of aggradation after cutting of modern Curry Draw. The opposite bank (right) of Curry Draw is composed of poorly sorted, gravelly sand of the Weik alluvium over St. David Formation. Farther downstream the alluvial strata of the Escapule Formation have not been differentiated except at the location of Profile 26 where the radiocarbon age of 3190 ± 80 B.P. on hearth charcoal indicates the stratum is Hargis alluvium.

In Curry Draw the only radiocarbon date for McCool alluvium is the 1550 ± 90 B.P. age for the hearth charcoal at the MSM pollen profile mentioned previously and estimated to represent about 67 percent of the total aggradation of Stratum G_{2b}. Hearth charcoal exposed by Trench 9 dating 1758 ± 85 B.P. was thought to be in upper G_1. However, the age indicates the hearth was probably in a pit dug from the surface of G_1 (Plate 3). Radiocarbon ages for McCool alluvium elsewhere in the upper San Pedro Valley indicate an age range of about 2000 to 1000 B.P. on the basis of 12 dates (Haynes 1968b).

Bakarich Ranch Member (Stratum G_3)

At the Murray Place (Fig. 2.2), inset against older Escapule alluvium, there are about 3 m of layered gray, organic sandy muds bearing a cienega soil in the upper beds. Carbonized plant remains from about 2 m below the surface provided a radiocarbon age of 500 ± 80 B.P. Farther downstream at Profile 23, as already mentioned, there are about 3 m of muddy sand alluvium forming a terrace inset against McCool alluvium. These are the only occurrences of the Bakarich Ranch Member (Stratum G_3) of the Escapule Ranch Formation in Curry Draw. They indicate a brief episode of cutting soon after 1000 B.P. and filling to sometime after 500 B.P. Four other radiocarbon dates in this period occur in the upper San Pedro Valley (Haynes 1968b).

The Bakarich alluvium appears to represent a brief episode of arroyo cutting and filling that did not progress very far up the few draws in which it has been recognized. It has not been analyzed for pollen or snails as far as I am aware, but its exposure at the Murray Place would be a good location to sample for paleoecological data because of a relatively high organic content.

Teviston Member (Stratum H) and Modern Arroyo Cutting

At the Murray Springs Site up to 60 cm of reddish brown, soft, laminated silty sand covers most of the swale formed by the top of Escapule alluvium (Plates 5–7), and medium to coarse pebble gravel facies cover parts of the center of the swale (Foldout 1, Trench 4; Foldout 2, Trench 12). This, the Teviston alluvium (Stratum H), could be traced up Curry Draw to its upper headcut before the construction of Moson Road required its filling. Teviston alluvium caps the tops of most of the arroyo bank exposures all the way down Curry Draw, and the stratum joins similar alluvium on the floodplain of the San Pedro River (Hereford 1993).

The North Branch headcut at the Murray Springs Site may have been initiated at the downstream end of the Teviston gravel where water velocity would increase coming down the nickpoint at the toe of the gravel lobe (Packard 1974). Whether or not this actually happened, Curry Draw became a typical discontinuous arroyo (Leopold and others 1964) because another headcut started up the draw from the mouth as explained earlier. Furthermore, another headcut about 1 m high occurs in Curry Draw southwest of its intersection with Highway 90. The headcut of the South Branch started to form about 150 m downstream from the toe of the gravel lobe sometime before the 1935 aerial photograph was taken (Fig. 2.9a). The fact that Teviston alluvium occurs farther up Curry Draw beyond the headcuts, over swales throughout the upper San Pedro Valley, and as alluvial fans on the historic floodplain of the San Pedro River (Hereford 1993) indicates that it is a result of widespread but localized gullying in swales.

In Greenbush Draw Teviston alluvium at Camp Newell at Naco (also known as Camp Naco) buries the military post's trash dump. The post was active from 1911 to 1925, but most of the diagnostic artifacts are of the period 1912 to 1921 when the camp was most active (Hart 1980). In 1964 I interviewed Mrs. Newell, who lived at Camp Naco when her father, J. J. Newell, owned the land on which the garrison was built. She claimed that the entrenchment of Greenbush Draw in 1922 was the result of the Army growing beans and hay in the swale; it is likely deposition of Teviston alluvium and modern arroyo cutting were penecontemporaneous.

The cause of Teviston alluviation may be related to several factors that occurred after the turn of the century. The land was heavily overgrazed by this time, the population had increased significantly, and desertscrub had displaced grassland (Rodgers 1965). Reduced vegetation, perhaps in conjunction with more intense rains, allowed slopewash alluvium to accumulate in swales and form alluvial fans where tributaries debouched into swales and onto the floodplain of the San Pedro River. Arroyo cutting may have occurred in response to more intense rain storms compared to more gentle rains (Leopold 1951), perhaps reflecting summer versus winter precipitation.

Curry Draw Member (Stratum J)

Curry Draw alluvium (Stratum J) occurs as a 2-m to 3-m alluvial terrace within the floor of entrenched Curry Draw (Fig. 2.8c) and as slopewash sediment deposited against the upslope (north) side of the railroad embankment along Curry Draw (Plate 3). In the draw the Stratum J terrace with the deer grass (*Muhlenbergia rigens*) on it at the Murray Place was not as well developed before 1971 as it is now (Fig. 2.8c). It is a younger facies that formed after the Stratum J terrace at the confluence of the North and South branches at the Murray Springs Site (Plate 5c) and after that at Profile 23 (Fig. 2.10f). Either or both of these could be complex response terraces as defined by Schumm (1973).

LATE QUATERNARY PALEOCLIMATIC INTERPRETATIONS

There are very few data on which to make paleoclimatic estimates for the time before deposition of the Murray Springs Formation. All that can be said regarding deposition of the Millville alluvium is that flashy discharges occurred in the upper reaches of Curry Draw and low energy discharges occurred in lower reaches. Lithologically Millville is similar to the arroyo deposits of the middle and late Holocene but with a much larger volume of sediment than any Holocene arroyo fill, suggesting deposition in an interglacial, perhaps Sangamon. The type section for Millville is the 12-m alluvial terrace at the Charleston Bridge and below the mill site ruins of Millville. It is capped by a red oxisol with a stage 3 carbonate horizon. Another possibility is that it represents an early Wisconsinan interstadial. However, the paleosol on the Millville terrace seems to be too strong for this late age.

In any case, the overlying Sobaipuri mud and Coro marl clearly represent high water tables, artesian discharge, and ponding during the Wisconsinan late glacial. The late glacial maximum would fall within the upper middle of the Coro marl. By about 15,000 B.P. the marsh became a wet meadow, and by 14,000 B.P. it had dried up and formation of the Graveyard channel had begun, coinciding with the net retreat of the continental glaciers. At the same time as deglaciation progressed, the Graveyard channel deepened and reached its largest configuration by 13,000 B.P. (Figs. 2.12, 2.13). It may have been in a state of dynamic equilibrium during Oldest Dryas, Bølling, and Older Dryas time. By Allerød time channel alluviation appears to have weakened as the water table began a fluctuating trend of net decline during the Clovis drought, perhaps with a rebound during the Intra-Allerød Cold Period (IACP).

When Clovis people first arrived at the Murray Springs Site 13,000 years ago, they found a shallow valley floored by the eroded surface of Sobaipuri mudstone and the Coro marl (Plate 8). The sandy drainages of Bison Kill Creek and Wolf Creek supported a riparian habitat apparently dominated by desert ash trees but probably included other riparian trees such as walnut, hackberry, and cottonwood. Low swales in Sobaipuri mud were soggy areas near spring vents and probably supported cienega vegetation such as composites, chenoams, sedges, and grasses, as Mehringer and others (1971) found in the Lehner Site pollen record. For slightly higher ground on the eroded surface of the Coro marl, we have no good evidence of what would be growing there during the Clovis visits. The edaphic effect of the high calcium carbonate substrate is especially compatible with today's Chihuahuan desertscrub, but desertscrub is unlikely to have been there 13,000 years ago.

Evidence indicates the Clovis people visited the site area at least two, and possibly four, times during a brief period of a decade or less. At first they found the Graveyard sand channel saturated but with little or no stream flow. Bones and artifacts were not transported by water action. By their last visit the streambed was dry and disrupted by animals, mostly mammoth, digging for water. By the time of their departure, the Rancholabrean megafauna, except for bison, was a thing of the past.

Mammoths, mastodons, three varieties of horses, at least two varieties of camels, dire wolves, American lions, tapirs, and others all disappeared from North America by 10,900 B.P. The cause of Pleistocene extinction remains a controversial issue (Martin and Klein 1984). Predation by humans was undoubtedly a significant factor, but it cannot account for the death of half a dozen or so young mammoths within the upper San Pedro Valley that are without any association with artifacts (Haynes 1998a). Drought appears to be another factor (Haynes 1991). In the San Pedro Valley this extinction event occurred in a geologic instant, perhaps too sudden to have been caused by human predation, drought, or disease. Something happened around 10,900 B.P. that we have yet to understand. Clovis people disappeared from the stratigraphic record as well, perhaps to become the Folsom technocomplex (Huckell 2003) elsewhere during the Younger Dryas period.

In any case, Curry Draw, as well as other low areas in the San Pedro Valley, was inundated as the water tables rose to the surface during the Younger Dryas climatic reversal between 10,800 B.P. and 9700 B.P. This rise in the water table appears to have been caused by more effective recharge as glacially cold temperatures reduced evapotranspiration from more widespread and gentle rains during the Younger Dryas. People of the Cochise culture may have arrived in the area as the black mat accumulated. Black mat deposition ended about 9700 B.P. as a weak erosional event (F_{3a} channel) redeposited black mat in some areas.

Deposition of Donnet eolian silt (F_{3b}) began as slopewash accumulation in cienegas and at the same time as the Preboreal of Europe. Donnet deposition continued but with increasing aridity until it stabilized as grassy swales that underwent pedogenesis before arroyo entrenchment ensued sometime between 8000 B.P. and 7000 B.P.

The widespread arroyo cutting in the American Southwest that occurred between 8000 B.P. and 6000 B.P. coincides with what Antevs (1955) called the Altithermal and defined as a warm dry period within the middle of the postglacial paleoclimatic record. The Altithermal in the San Pedro Valley may be characterized as a period of widespread arroyo cutting due to more intense rainfall, rapid runoff, high evapotranspiration, and lowered water tables. As a result most of the early Holocene alluvium of the master drainages such as the San Pedro and Santa Cruz rivers was removed by bank erosion during the Altithermal. Remnants of early Holocene alluvium occur mainly in the upper reaches of the tributary drainages, hence the preservation of the San Pedro Valley Clovis sites. Whereas there is no pollen record for the period between 8000 B.P. and 6500 B.P., the record from the Donnet silt at the Lehner Site shows progressive change from an initial relatively wet cienega phase at about 9500 B.P. to more xeric vegetation toward the top at about 8000 B.P. and leading to the aridity that prompted Altithermal arroyo cutting.

As the climate became more mesic, about 6000 B.P. as indicated by the MSM pollen profile in Curry Draw, aggradation occurred throughout the San Pedro Valley as the water tables rose in response to increased recharge from rainfall characterized by more frequent rains of the summer monsoons. As a result, arroyos aggraded with the poorly sorted flashy discharge type of sediments and, in places, with pond type sediments, possibly behind beaver dams. Weik alluvium (G_1), the stratigraphic manifestation of this process, is the first of several arroyo sedimentary fills, such as Hargis and McCool deposits, that characterize the late Holocene epicycles of arroyo cutting and filling recognized by Antevs (1955) and Bryan (1941) and his students. The process appears to be controlled by water table fluctuations (Haynes 1968a; Karlstrom 1988) resulting from the epicycles of high and low frequencies of cyclonic or monsoonal storms perhaps related to the frequency of El Niño events (Waters and Haynes 2001). Radiocarbon dating indicates that the frequency of arroyo cutting and filling has increased with time (Waters and Haynes 2001).

The last episode of significant arroyo cutting began in the middle of the 19th century but dominated the 1880s and 1890s as overgrazing occurred throughout the American west. The penecontemporaneity of these events led to the arguments of whether climate change (Bryan 1941) or overgrazing (Antevs 1955) was the dominant cause of arroyo cutting. I see water table fluctuations in response to climate change as the ultimate control (Haynes 1986). As long as drainages are effluent there is no arroyo-type incision going on and transverse cross sections show shallow valleys with gentle slopes such as the Graveyard channel (F_1) at Murray Springs. With climate change to more xeric conditions many streams become influent, that is, water tables bulging upwards to intersect dry streambeds and sustaining flow only when adequately recharged during the rainy season. At the beginning of the xeric part of the cycle many valleys are at the aggraded stage with valley floors being grassy swales. As water tables fall the swales become increasingly unstable such that intense runoff from a torrential rainfall can cross the threshold for erosion and make headcuts. Through time during this xeric regime headcuts form throughout the drainage system and eventually discontinuous headcuts merge to form the steep-sided arroyos so apparent today throughout the American west.

The process is exacerbated by overgrazing that reduces vegetative cover thereby increasing runoff, which, in turn, increases discharge. Arroyo deepening is commonly limited by more resistant older strata but widening continues as long as stream banks consist of the softer sediments of late Pleistocene and Holocene alluvium.

The existence of undissected grassy swales indicates that the process of arroyo cutting and headcut migration has not yet been completed, examples being the East and West swales of Curry Draw. As stated earlier, the draw itself was a grassy swale perhaps with a small cienega at the Murray Place in 1913. When wagon wheel ruts concentrated storm flow, a headcut developed and arroyo cutting began in this reach. It also began in the upper reaches, as headcutting there led to deposition of the Teviston alluvium (H). As emphasized by Cooke and Reeves (1976), anything that concentrates flow, such as wheel ruts or cow paths, can cause the threshold for erosion to be crossed. It is these conditions that ultimately exposed the Clovis sites of the San Pedro Valley to discovery.

In summary, the Murray Springs Formation is the result of the emergent water tables coincident with the last glaciation and with the net decline of the water tables during deglaciation. Clovis people arrived on the scene as water tables fell to their lowest level in more than 30,000 years. They and the Pleistocene megafauna disappeared in an instant of geologic time for reasons that are not understood. Water tables again emerged at the surface as glacial climate returned during the Younger Dryas, represented by the black mat (F_2) of the Lehner Ranch Formation. The Donnet silt (F_3) accumulated from eolian deposition and slopewash during the early Holocene transition to the later Holocene period of arroyo cutting and filling manifested by the Escapule Ranch Formation.

The San Pedro Valley may have been devoid of people for several centuries following the Clovis exploration of the valley. The Early Archaic Cochise people appear to have arrived in southeastern Arizona by 10,000 B.P. (Waters 1986) with the appearance of the Sulphur Spring people during Clanton clay and Donnet silt deposition. Thus began the cultural development that led to the Chiricahua Middle Archaic occupations of the Weik and Hargis depositions and eventually to the Late Archaic San Pedro people during deposition of the upper Hargis alluvium and lower McCool alluvium. Ceramics make their appearance in the archaeological record during the McCool alluviation. When the Spanish appeared on the scene, aggradation of Bakarich alluvium had been in progress for at least two centuries. As the cattle industry developed during the late 19th century (Bailey 1998), drought conditions exacerbated by overgrazing led to the erosion and arroyo cutting still in progress. With no hope of regional water tables rising significantly, it is unlikely that current arroyos will aggrade and fill their channels to the grassy swale stage in the foreseeable future. What aggradation does occur, as with the Curry Draw Member, is probably due to special local conditions as well as a complex response to discharge events. Today the environment of Curry Draw described in Chapter 3 has persisted with minor changes since the early 20th century. Before that the area had more desert grassland and less desertscrub (Hastings and Turner 1965).

Note: Chapters 1 and 2 by C. Vance Haynes, Jr., have undergone continuous modifications and additions since the original drafts in 1982.

CHAPTER THREE

Modern Vegetation of the Murray Springs Area and the Upper San Pedro Valley

Susan L. Woodward

Murray Springs, an archaeological site of considerable significance in New World prehistory, provides evidence for the coexistence of Pleistocene mammalian fauna and *Homo sapiens* in the upper San Pedro River Valley of Arizona. Paleontologists and anthropologists, geologists and ecologists have all worked to reconstruct the topography, climate, and vegetation of the land across which ancient peoples roamed in search of large game.

Interpretation of past conditions and relationships, however, depends in large measure on an understanding of present ecological patterns and processes. This knowledge is especially helpful for reconstructing Pleistocene vegetation, which in turn is often used as an indicator of Pleistocene climates and faunas. This chapter provides a record and an analysis of the vegetation along Curry Draw and adjacent areas in the vicinity of the Murray Springs Site as it existed in the late 1960s. Consideration is given to short-term and long-term environmental changes throughout the upper San Pedro Valley. Against this record, modern pollen rains are analyzed and the Pleistocene pollen record for the region is interpreted (Woodward 1969).

MODERN VEGETATION OF CURRY DRAW

Curry Draw emanates today from a broad zone of waist-high woody desert shrubs (Fig. 3.1). Three plant species predominate: creosotebush (*Larrea tridentata*), whitethorn (*Acacia vernicosa*), and tarbush (*Flourensia cernua*). Mesquite (*Prosopis juliflora*) joins the assemblage in favored locations on the finer soils of the interfluves. Whereas the geographic limits of creosotebush delineate the distribution of all the warm deserts of North America, tarbush and whitethorn are characteristic only of the Chihuahuan Desert, the core of which lies to the east and south from the Rio Grande Valley in southwestern New Mexico to Chihuahua and Coahuila, Mexico (Schmidt 1979). Other less common shrubs on the interfluves also have Chihuahuan affinities: *Koeberlinia spinosa*, *Condalia spathulata*, *Rhus microphylla*, and *Parthenium incanum*. Succulents are virtually absent, the only species of any consequence being *Opuntia leptocaulis*.

The monotony of the vegetation is broken along the drainages. Curry Draw flowed, in however intermittent and unchanneled a manner, at the surface in a grassy swale until the 1900s, depositing a narrow band of sand and gravel (Stratum H) along its once marshy trace. Swales of sacaton (*Sporobolus wrightii*) and tobosa grass (*Hilaria mutica*) persist headward of arroyo-cutting and along the terraces left by downcutting.

These same two grass species also occur in small "grass circles" 100 m to 200 m in diameter along incipient drainages on the interfluves (Fig. 1.2). Pockets of fine alluvium have collected in apparent solution depressions in the petrocalcic horizon of the older surfaces of the San Pedro basin (Chapter 2). Tobosa grass and an occasional yucca or palmilla (*Yucca elata*) occupy the deeper soils at the center of these depressions, and a concentric ring of sacaton indicates the shallower alluvium at the fringe. Littleleaf sumac (*Rhus microphylla*) and mesquite form a final, outermost circle (Woodward 1972).

Figure. 3.1. Shrub species characteristic of the Chihuahuan Desert surrounding Curry Draw (creosotebush, whitethorn acacia, and tarbush).

Figure 3.3. Willows and cottonwoods now grow in Curry Draw where the water table is near the surface.

Figure. 3.2. Curry Draw. Tall shrubs on banks are mesquites; rabbitbrush dominates the arroyo bottom.

Figure 3.4. Woodcutter Draw, a drainage on the Whetstone surface, supports walnut trees as well as desert willow, ash, hackberry, and soapberry.

The vertical-walled, flat-floored arroyo that Curry Draw has become provides habitat for a number of riparian species (Fig. 3.2), including rabbitbrush (*Chrysothamnus nauseosus*), Brickell bush (*Brickellia floribunda*), bush muhly (*Muhlenbergia rigens*), and seep willow (*Baccaris glutinosa*). Willow (*Salix gooddingii*) and cottonwood (*Populus fremontii*), which require large quantities of water at or near the surface throughout the growing season, mark the shallowest water tables and sites of springs (Fig. 3.3).

Above the lower headcut, phreatophytic mesquite and littleleaf sumac hug the banks, drawing pendulate water from the silts remaining from former marsh deposits and sending long taproots into channel stores. Individuals may attain heights of close to 6 m (nearly 20 feet).

About 3.2 km (2 miles) north of Curry Draw is Woodcutter Draw, which has undergone less downcutting than Curry Draw during the 20th-century episode of channel entrenchment. Vegetation along this wash is strikingly different from that of Curry Draw or the other incised drainages in the vicinity (Fig. 3.4). Woodcutter Draw supports tall walnuts (*Juglans major*), soapberries (*Sapindus saponaria*), hackberries (*Celtis reticulata*), ash (*Fraxinus veluntina*), and desert willow (*Chilopsis linearis*), as well as a tangle of smaller trees and shrubs including mesquite, littleleaf sumac, catclaw (*Acacia greggii*), and rabbitbrush. In the absence of springs, moisture availability is too low for cottonwoods and willows in the wash. The hydro-

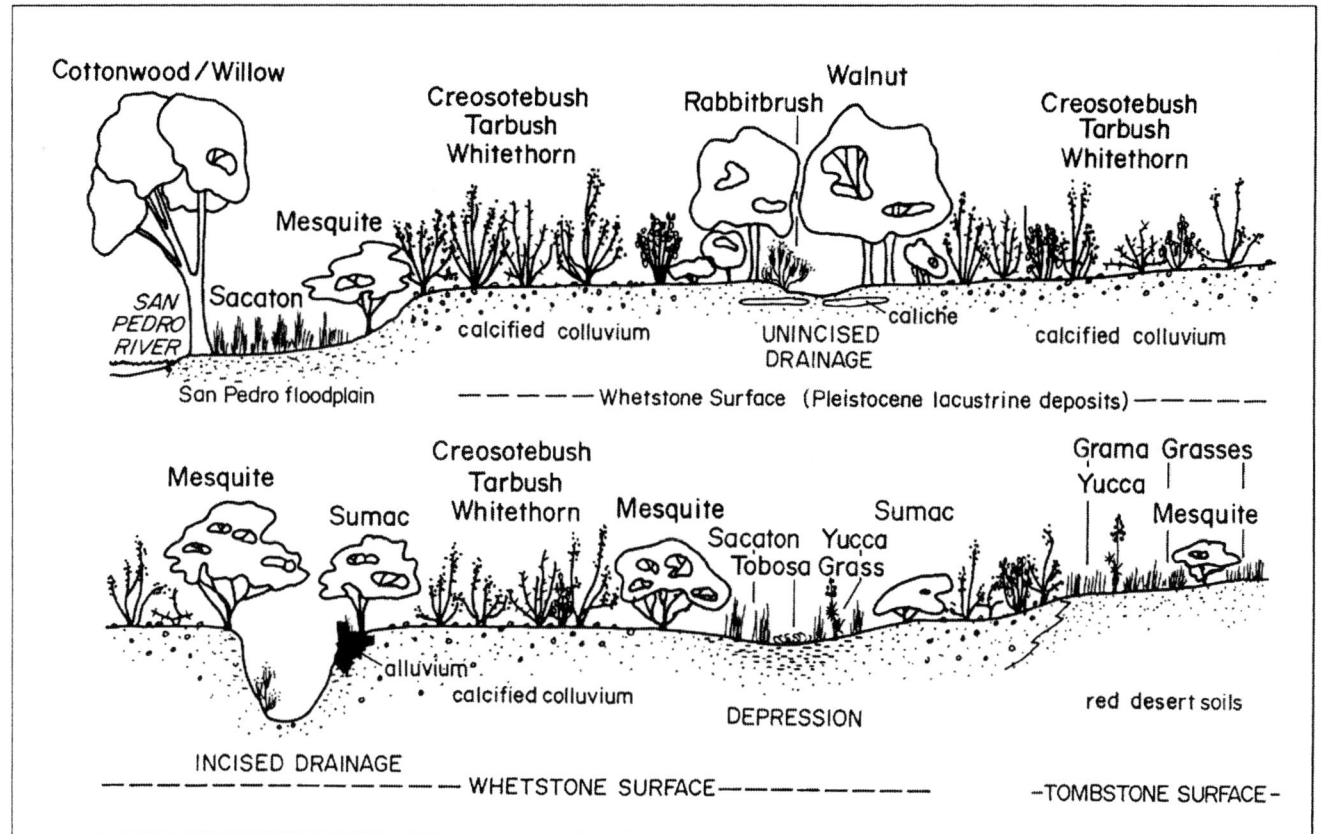

Figure. 3.5. Generalized cross section of the natural vegetation and its edaphic controls in the lower San Pedro Valley near Curry Draw.

phytic species that do occur draw their moisture from perched water tables and from beneath layers of caliche, which, while reducing percolation, also retard evaporation.

The distribution of species in the Curry Draw area is reproduced at a macroscale along the San Pedro River (Fig. 3.5). Cottonwood and willow line the stream, permanent in this part of its course. On the San Pedro floodplain grow sacaton and other grasses; mesquite outlines the distant edge. A break-in-slope marks the beginning of calcareous valley fill (the terraces and other geographic surfaces; Chapter 2), and with it begins the dominance of creosotebush, whitethorn, and tarbush. This zone continues along Curry Draw on the exposures of Coro marl (Stratum E).

VEGETATION HISTORY

During the second half of the 19th century the desert basins of the American Southwest underwent marked environmental changes. Whether a consequence of severe overgrazing or climatic oscillations or both (for example, Gardner 1951; Hastings and Turner 1965; Hereford 1993; Martin 1963c; Whitfield and Anderson 1938), a period of channel entrenchment began. During the next 100 years, southeastern Arizona experienced significant vegetation changes (see D. R. Harris 1966 for literature review). Desert grasslands suffered invasion by woody shrubs in the San Pedro Valley and elsewhere, as documented in Hastings and Turner's (1965) now classic volume, *The Changing Mile*. Is the Chihuahuan Desert vegetation of the Curry Draw area, then, an artifact of the last century? I think not.

If the physical geography of the Chihuahuan Desert proper is compared with that of this outlier of Chihuahuan vegetation in southeastern Arizona, many similarities are apparent. Perhaps most significant is the precipitation regime. The three North American warm deserts can be differentiated on the basis of the seasons of precipitation maxima. The Mohave Desert, under the influence of the Pacific High, experiences a winter maximum and dry summers. Most of the Sonoran Desert (the Vizcaino subdivision excepted) benefits from double maxima, gleaning moisture from Pacific frontal storms in the winter and again from convectional storms associated with the summer monsoon off the Gulf of Mexico. The Chihuahuan Desert lies too far to the east to extract much moisture from Pacific-generated winter storms and instead receives at least 55 to 60 percent of its annual moisture during the six warm months of the year (Schmidt 1979).

The San Pedro Valley actually lies in a transitional zone between Sonoran and Chihuahuan regimes. Lewis Springs, opposite the confluence of Curry Draw and the San Pedro River, receives 50 percent of its annual precipitation (295 mm) during the two months of July and August (Green and Sellers 1964). Other stations in the upper San Pedro Valley receive from 67 to 75 percent of their moisture between May and October (McDonald 1956).

The high elevation (approximately 1,280 m at Curry Draw) of the San Pedro Valley also makes the environment more like Chihuahuan high plains (over 1,200 m) than the lower Sonoran basins (below 900 m; Schmidt 1979). This elevational difference significantly affects winter temperatures and thereby limits the distribution of Sonoran species, which cannot tolerate lengthy periods of below freezing temperatures (Hastings and Turner 1965). Interestingly, the ecotype of creosotebush occurring in the San Pedro is that characteristic of the Chihuahuan Desert (with a chromosome number of $N=13$) and not the geographically closer Sonoran type (with a chromosome number of $N=26$; Yang 1970). Whether the prevailing genotype is the product of migration or adaptation is not clear.

The occurrence of Chihuahuan species on the calcified soils of the lower bajadas and other geomorphic surfaces repeats a phytogeographic pattern reported on limestone substrates in the mountains flanking the San Pedro Valley (Wentworth 1981), in the Swisshelm Mountains in the Sulphur Spring Valley to the east (Bradbury 1969), and in the Santa Catalina Mountains some 100 km to the west (Whittaker and Niering 1968). This correlation between carbonate bedrock and species with Chihuahuan affinity occurs in both Madrean and Sonoran floristic provinces and is strong enough and reliable enough for the latter to serve as an indicator of the former (Bradbury 1969).

In the neighboring Mule Mountains the Chihuahuan community differs in richness from the Madrean communities on granitic soils, showing a much lower diversity of herbaceous species and a slightly greater diversity of shrub species. Overall a physiognomic xeromorphism typifies the limestone flora, indicating that calcareous soils provide a more xeric habitat, which selects for desert species (Wentworth 1981). Outliers of Chihuahuan desertscrub are peculiarly suited to these habitats, because they evolved on limestone-derived soils (Muller 1947; Wentworth 1981) in a region of cool winters and a summer precipitation maximum.

Written records of pre-arroyo-cutting vegetation in the Curry Draw area exist in the form of survey notes of the Public Land Office surveys of 1879, 1901, 1902, and 1911 (Woodward 1972). Curry Draw was reconnoitered in 1901, when it was a wash two chains wide (40 m). Repeatedly the field notes mention dense undergrowth and the presence of "tesota" (whitethorn), "sage" (tarbush?) and "greasewood" (creosotebush). Only the floodplain of the San Pedro, surveyed the following year, had an "abundant growth of rich and nutritive grasses."

Although Public Land Office records indicate no major changes in vegetation on the Whetstone surface and the calcareous soils of other surfaces of the San Pedro Valley since the turn of the century, shrub invasion onto the desert grasslands of the noncalcareous red soils of the Tombstone surface is unequivocal. Public Land Office surveys record the presence of "scattering mesquites" and yuccas and presumably grasses. The "grass circles" evident today are not relics of these former upland grasslands in which perennial grama grasses (*Bouteloua* spp.) would have been dominant, but are expressions of local edaphic conditions where a deep alluvium has been colonized by floodplain species like sacaton and tobosa grass (Woodward 1972). Today, except where the natural vegetation has been destroyed and the area seeded with exotic grasses, the Tombstone surface is dominated by the Chihuahuan triumvirate: creosotebush, whitethorn, tarbush.

Although the existence of Chihuahuan desertscrub in the San Pedro Valley prior to arroyo-cutting can be documented, the time of initial establishment in the area is uncertain. Van Devender and Spaulding (1979: 707) believe that the immigration of Chihuahuan desertscrub to the northernmost extent of its distribution area occurred only in the late Holocene and represents the "last major vegetation change in the Southwest induced by climate." Their hypothesis is based on the requisite summer rainfall maximum, which they feel could not have been realized until the Laurentide ice sheet had dissipated. As the ice retreated in the early Holocene, summer precipitation increased in the Southwest and by the middle Holocene was probably greater than at present, indeed sufficient to support grasslands. Xeric habitats and desert communities developed in the drier climate of the late Holocene. The pollen record from Murray Springs Pollen Profile 1 (Profile 30) suggests that the transition to desertscrub began around 1500 B.P. in the upper San Pedro Valley (Mehringer and others 1967).

The comparative photographs of Hastings and Turner (1965) document an increase in density of desert shrubs on lower portions of the valley and their spread onto higher elevations since 1890, but the nature of the vegetation from 1500–200 B.P. is not known. Photographs taken in the 1890s depict a vegetation affected by centuries of human activity in the valley. Two features of these photographs are noteworthy: the low percentage of cover by either grasses or shrubs and the absence of large trees even along the San Pedro River. From at least 800 to 400 B.P. the Native American population of the desert is believed to have been more numerous than all the people inhabiting the area in the 1880s (Hastings and Turner 1965). The Sobaipuris, who lived along the upper San Pedro, were agriculturalists who also hunted, gathered, and fished (Di Peso 1953b). Wood was the only source of fuel and must have been quickly and widely depleted by these people. Mesquites, which represented a valuable food source, perhaps were protected. The Sobaipuris numbered more than 2000 in 1697, but were decimated by the diseases and Apache depredation that accompanied Spanish settlement in the first half of the 18th century (Di Peso 1953b), and the valley was essentially abandoned by 1762 (Hastings and Turner 1965).

A brief period of prosperity began on the Boquillas and San Rafael del Valle grants in the late 1820s, when large herds of cattle and other livestock were built up. However, Apaches again disrupted life in the valley, and these large ranches were abandoned by 1846. Some of the livestock remained, and numerous herds of feral cattle were reported along the river in the 1850s (Hastings and Turner 1965).

With the Gadsden Purchase of 1853, the area became part of the United States. Silver was discovered at Tombstone in 1878, and the appetite of the mines and smelters for wood soon impacted the surrounding mountains (Bahre and Bradbury 1978; Rodgers 1965).

The 1880s marked the major period of cattle raising in the valley. In 1883, there were some 68,000 head of cattle in all southeastern Arizona; by 1890 some 235,000 grazed in the San Pedro Valley alone (Hastings 1959). Summer rains failed in 1891 and 1892, and an estimated 50 to 75 percent of the cattle died (Hastings and Turner 1965). At about the same time, channel-cutting began on the San Pedro and its tributaries. In both cases, channels have been discontinuous, but local water tables were lowered by as much as 12 m (Bryan 1928a).

Did this episode of overgrazing, denudation of woodlands, drought, and lowered water tables culminate in a shrub invasion, or did consequent economic collapse permit a degree of recovery in the natural vegetation? Ecological relationships suggest that Chihuahuan desertscrub, at least on the Whetstone and other surfaces with calcareous soils, is an edaphic climax. It probably developed long before Europeans exploited the resources of the valley, but long after Clovis hunters pursued a now extinct megafauna near the San Pedro.

Note: This chapter is based on "Vegetation of the Murray Springs Area, Cochise County, Arizona," an unpublished Master's thesis by Susan L. Woodward, 1969, University of Arizona, Tucson.

CHAPTER FOUR

Molluscan Faunas of the San Pedro Valley, Arizona

Jim I. Mead

In 1955–1956 when the Arizona State Museum, led by Emil W. Haury, excavated the Lehner Site in southeastern Arizona (Haury and others 1959), the study of past environments of the arid Southwest was still in its infancy. Much was learned with the pioneering excavation of this Clovis site, located in the upper San Pedro River Valley (Fig. 4.1). A decade later, excavations at the nearby Clovis site at Murray Springs concentrated on the analysis of the alluvial stratigraphy and radiocarbon samples (Chapters 1 and 2; Haynes 1968b, 1973), on the Clovis activity areas and artifacts (Chapters 5, 7, 8), and on the fossil flora and vertebrate fauna (Mehringer and others 1967, 1971; Saunders 1974, 1977). One aspect of the multidisciplinary study that received less attention until later field seasons was the collecting and identification of the fossil molluscs.

These terrestrial and aquatic invertebrates were not widely incorporated into paleoenvironmental reconstructions in the Southwest until the mid-1960s (Metcalf 1962; Metcalf and Smartt 1997; Taylor 1967). It was not fully understood what information molluscs could add to paleoenvironmental reconstructions, nor who knew the Southwestern molluscs thoroughly enough to study them. Fossil pollen in stratified sites representing the past 20,000 years, while of great interest and an important paleoecological tool, was rarely recovered in this arid region (Hevly and Martin 1961; Martin 1963a, 1963b; Martin and Mehringer 1965; Mehringer and others 1966, 1971). In contrast, fossil molluscs occurred essentially throughout most alluvial records. The stratified alluvial deposits at the Lehner and Murray Springs sites were notably rich in mollusc shells, and therefore provided an excellent opportunity for an independent reconstruction of the paleoenvironments (Mead 1991).

Figure 4.1. Map of southeastern Arizona and adjacent areas of New Mexico and Sonora, Mexico. Features shown are the upper watersheds of the San Pedro and Santa Cruz rivers and Willcox Playa (Pluvial Lake Cochise) in the internally drained Sulphur Spring Valley.

[62]

The original study of most of the fossil molluscs recovered from the Lehner and Murray Springs sites was limited to the shell identification; a priminary list was included in portions of two abstracts by Russell (1970, 1971) and in the Arizona check list of living molluscs by Bequaert and Miller (1973). Brief mention of the molluscs from the Lehner Site was incorporated into a report about a pollen study (Mehringer and Haynes 1965). There is no detailed environmental reconstruction based on the numerous late Pleistocene molluscs from either the Lehner Site or the Murray Springs Site. This report combines J. C. Bequaert and R. H. Russell's identifications and my verification of the molluscs from the Lehner and Murray Springs sites, along with my interpretation of their paleoenvironmental significance (also see Mead 1991).

THE UPPER SAN PEDRO RIVER VALLEY

Physiography and Biomes

The ecological implications of the fossil molluscan assemblages from the Lehner and Murray Springs sites are important in helping to understand the past environments of the upper San Pedro Valley as well as the rest of southeastern Arizona. The headwaters of the San Pedro River lie 37 km (23 miles) south of Arizona in Sonora, Mexico (Fig. 4.1). The intermittent river flows northward within 2-m to 8-m high banks, 225 km (140 miles) to its confluence with the Gila River, itself an east-west tributary of the Colorado River, at Winkleman, Arizona. Unless otherwise stated, mention of the San Pedro watershed refers to the upper 112 km (70 miles) of the San Pedro Valley from Cananea, Sonora, to Benson, Arizona.

This region is physiographically part of the Mexican Highland Province of North America. Most of the mountain ranges have one or more prominent peaks with only two more than 2,735 m (9,000 feet) in elevation. The watershed in Sonora is formed by three principal mountain ranges: Sierras de San Jose, Magallanes, and Cocospera (Fig. 4.1). In Arizona the Dragoon and Mule mountains form the eastern watershed, and the Huachuca, Mustang, and Whetstone mountains form the larger catchment of the western watershed (Fig. 1.1).

The highest and most extensive mountain range in the upper San Pedro Valley is the Huachuca Mountains, west and north of which are the low, rounded Canelo Hills and the intermittent Babocomari River, a major tributary of the San Pedro River. The inner valley of the San Pedro receives runoff from numerous arroyos draining all the surrounding mountains. The Huachuca Mountains have more major tributaries entering the watershed than any other range. Sources of water for the valley, other than the seasonal rainstorms, are a few springs along the edge of the floodplain in the inner valley, especially near the town of St. David, and in the watershed of the Babocomari River.

The environmental gradients of the San Pedro Valley are complex due to the topographic extremes. In general, for the mountains bordering the San Pedro River, there exists an upward transition from Chihuahuan Desert vegetation to coniferous forest (Chapter 3; Lowe 1964; Wallmo 1955; Wentworth 1981, 1983). These local environmental extremes mean that there is also a wide variety of habitats providing for a diverse malacofauna. Names used for biotic communities generally follow those in Brown and Lowe (1974; also see Lowe 1964).

On the basis of distinctive molluscan faunas, the Nearctic Region may be clearly separated into eastern and western divisions, each subdivided into faunistic provinces (Binney 1885). Although the provinces have been modified a number of times (Henderson 1928, 1931; Pilsbry 1939–1948), each new decade of field collecting and compiling of check lists provides more refined boundaries.

The San Pedro River Valley is in the south-central portion of the Southwestern Molluscan Province (Bequaert and Miller 1973). Distinguishing features of this province are the molluscs *Sonorella*, *Ashmunella*, *Holospira*, and *Chaenaxis*. The most striking feature of the fauna from this province is its complexity (Bequaert and Miller 1973). The fauna are a heterogeneous assemblage of disparate genera and species (although limited in number), combining a wide variety of distributions with diversified origins. The province also has an unusually high proportion of endemic taxa (Bequaert and Miller 1973). These endemics, also known as precinctive taxa, are those genera and species not living beyond the limits of the province and are the overwhelming majority of species (192 of 234 native species, or 82%). Arizona has 155 indigenous molluscs (128 land snails and slugs, and 27 freshwater taxa), and 68 percent are endemic to the province (Bequaert and Miller 1973).

Modern Cienegas in Southeastern Arizona

There are numerous springs and cienegas in southeastern Arizona (Fig. 4.1) with molluscan faunas comparable to those of the Lehner and Murray Springs sites. Probably the largest active spring in the upper San Pedro is the cienega near the town of St. David. Unfortunately, at this time the molluscs from this complex cienega have not been thoroughly studied.

The well-known Babocomari (Brophy) Cienega (Fig. 4.2) borders the Babocomari River at 1,390 m (4,560 feet) elevation. This extensive marsh occupies an area in the floodplain approximately 1,200 m by 400 m and contains one main spring with numerous seeps throughout the area. Riparian trees and shrubs generally cluster near the water courses and a large pond, and open marshes make up most of the area. In recent years erosion threatened to trench the cienega, so a dam with an adjacent pond was built. Mollusc collections were made by J. C. Bequaert, R. H. Russell, A. R. Mead, and J. I. Mead in 1969 (Table 4.1).

Sheehy Springs at 1,440 m (4,750 feet) elevation (Figs. 4.3, 4.4) is located below the first terrace east of the upper Santa Cruz River, San Rafael Valley, Santa Cruz County. The active spring area, approximately 500 m by 100 m, may at one time have included 25 percent again as much area (as marked by the extent of the dried black soil extending upslope from the active zone) as it does now. I do not know whether this indicates the spring's discharge area has reduced in size through time or if it has shifted its location. Approximately one-fourth of the present active spring area is a cienega sedge (*Carex* sp.) and grass mat. The remaining portion, especially along the stream, is cienegalike with numerous narrow-leaf cottonwood (*Populus angustifolia*) and sycamore (*Platanus wrightii*) trees. A pear orchard with about 20 trees and a raspberry patch were probably introduced to the area in the 1800s by the owners of a ranch, now abandoned, on the terrace south of the spring. Numerous small ponds occur in the spring area, the largest near the pear orchard. The low, wet area is immediately surrounded by plains (short grass prairie) to desert grassland with occasional small mesquite shrubs (*Prosopis juliflora*) and rabbitbrush (*Chrysothamnus nauseosus*) occupying the slopes and top of the terrace. Plains grassland to oak woodland occurs within 1 km (0.6 mile) of the springs. Mollusc collections of the

Figure 4.2. Babocomari (Brophy) Cienega showing ponding and nearby marsh area. Many microhabitats are included within the area shown.

Figure 4.3. Sheehy Springs, San Rafael Valley, the headwaters for the Santa Cruz River, showing the plains grassland to desert grassland surrounding the narrow cienega.

cienega area were made by J. I. Mead and C. V. Haynes in 1975, J. I. Mead in 1976, J. I. Mead and R. S. Thompson in 1976, 1977, and 1978 (Table 4.1). Collecting living and late Holocene-age molluscs has continued with fieldwork during 2001–2004 in much of the San Rafael Valley by H. D. Dyer and J. I. Mead.

Table 4.1. Murray Springs Site Fossil Assemblage and the Present Indigenous Molluscs of the Upper San Pedro Valley
(List does not include the larger land snails)

	Escapule Formation				Lehner Formation						Murray Springs Formation				Millville Formation		NOTE		
	McCool Alluv. G_{2b}		Weik Alluv. G_1		Donnet Silt F_3		Clanton Clay F_2		Graveyard Sand F_1 ?		Coro Marl E		Sobaipuri Mudstone D		Alluv. Z_2				
Total No.	1732		314		3297		1597		1638		5496		435		114				
	%	N	%	N	%	N	%	N	%	N	%	N	%	N	%	N	1	2	3
Thysanophora hornii																			x
Microphysula ingersollii																		x	x
Euconulus fulvus	0.20	5	1.90	6	0.10	5	6.50	104	1.90	32	0.70	40	0.20	1				x	x
Glyphyalinia indentata																		x	x
Nesovitrea electrina					0.50	19	11.10	177	2.10	35								x	
Hawaiia minuscula	6.50	114	5.00	16	7.70	257	0.06	1	2.10	36	0.01	1			1.70	2		x	x
Zonitoides arboreus									0.20	4								x	x
Striatura meridionalis																		x	x
Vitrina pellucida alaskana																		x	
Deroceras laeve	0.60	12	0.30	1	1.10	39	1.70	27	2.60	44	0.07	4			46.40	53		x	x
Discus whitneyi									3.50	58								x	x
Discus shimekii																		x	
Helicodiscus eigenmanni																		x	x
Helicodiscus singleyanus	0.20	5	7.90	25	0.50	17	0.50	8	3.30	55	0.01	1						x	x
Punctum californicum									5.40	90								x	x
Radiodiscus millecostatus																			x
Succinea sp.	3.10	54	3.80	12	0.70	26	0.20	4	5.90	97	22.80	1258	31.40	137	6.10	7		x	x
Oxyloma sp.	0.20	4					3.90	63	0.50	9	0.50	29	1.10	5			x		
Gastrocopta pentodon	6.20	109	22.90	72	62.00	2046	51.40	821	14.30	235	3.80	214	1.80	8				x	x
G. pilsbryana																		x	x

Table 4.1. Murray Springs Site Fossil Assemblage and the Present Indigenous Molluscs of the Upper San Pedro Valley (*Continued*)
(List does not include the larger land snails)

| | Escapule Formation | | | | Lehner Formation | | | | | | Murray Springs Formation | | | | | | Millville Formation | | Note | | |
	McCool Alluv. G_{2b}		Weik Alluv. G_1		Donnet Silt F_3		Clanton Clay F_2		Graveyard Sand F_1 ?		Coro Marl E		Sobaipuri Mudstone D		Alluv. Z_2					
	%	N	%	N	%	N	%	N	%	N	%	N	%	N	%	N	1	2	3
C. quadridens																		x	x
C. ashmuni																		x	x
C. cochisensis																		x	x
C. prototypus																		x	x
C. dalliana							1.10	19										x	
C. cristata	1.70	30	9.50	30	4.10	138	0.30	5	2.20	37	0.07	4			1.70	2		x	x
C. pellucida	0.05	1																	
C. armifera									0.90	15	0.01	1					x	x	x
Chaenaxis tuba																			
Pupoides albilabris	0.60	12	2.80	9	1.20	40	0.10	3	0.40	7					2.60	3		x	x
P. hordaceus									0.06	1					0.80	1		x	x
Pupilla blandi			6.00	19					2.50	42	2.10	119	2.90	13				x	x
P. muscorum									1.40	23	3.20	181	0.90	4				x	x
P. hebes			1.50	5							0.09	5							x
P. syngenes	0.30	6	14.60	46	17.80	590	0.10	2	2.50	41	1.00	56	0.40	2				x	x
Vertigo milium	0.40	8	13.30	42	0.09	3	0.40	7	7.90	131	8.70	480	7.80	34	5.20	6		x	x
V. ovata																			
V. modesta	0.20	5	2.80	9	0.03	1	0.2	4	2.80	47	8.40	466	3.90	17			x	x	
V. berryi							1.50	25	0.90	16	0.10	6					x		
V. elatior			0.30	1	0.20	8	8.80	140	5.10	85	1.40	79					x		
V. ventricosa																			
?Columella columella																		x	
Vallonia perspectiva			0.30	1					3.50	58					8.70	10		x	x
V. cyclophorella									2.80	47	0.20	14	0.40	2				x	x
V. gracilicosta									4.60	76							x		x
Cionella lubrica									1.00	18									
Fossaria techella									0.06	1									
F. obrussa	7.10	123	2.20	7	2.60	89	0.80	14	0.70	12	0.80	47	0.20	1				x	
F. parva	0.20	4			0.30	10	0.80	14	4.40	73	34.10	1879	28.90	126	0.80	1		x	x
F. modicella									0.60	10								x	
Stagnicola caperata									0.10	2					0.80	1			
Physella virgata	0.80	15			0.10	6	1.70	27	0.60	10	0.03	2						x	x
P. humerosa	0.05	1							0.06	1								x	x

66 Chapter 4, Jim I. Mead

Table 4.1. Murray Springs Site Fossil Assemblage and the Present Indigenous Molluscs of the Upper San Pedro Valley (Continued)

	Escapule Formation				Lehner Formation						Murray Springs Formation				Millville Formation		NOTE		
	McCool Alluv. G$_{2b}$		Weik Alluv. G$_1$		Donnet Silt F$_3$		Clanton Clay F$_2$		Graveyard Sand F$_1$?		Coro Marl E		Sobaipuri Mudstone D		Alluv. Z$_2$		1	2	3
	%	N	%	N	%	N	%	N	%	N	%	N	%	N	%	N			
Gyraulus parvus	50.00	867	3.10	10	0.06	2			2.80	46	8.30	460	11.70	51				x	x
Helisoma tenue																		x	x
Drepanotrema aeruginosum																		x	x
Promenetus umbilicatellus	0.40	8																x	
Ferrissia fragilis									0.10	3								x	
Pyrgulopsis cf. longinqua							0.60	11	1.10	19								x	x
Pisidium casertanum	4.70	82	0.30	1	0.03	1	4.50	73	3.70	61	1.30	72	4.10	18	2.60	3		x	x
P. compressum	11.30	197							0.80	14					20.10	23		x	x
P. walkeri	4.00	70	0.60	2			4.10	66	1.70	28	1.40	78	3.60	16	1.70	2		x	x

NOTE: 1, Absent in Arizona; 2, Recent in Arizona; 3, Known recent in upper San Pedro drainage. List does not include the larger land snails.

Figure 4.4. Numerous sphaeriid clams inhabit the gravel-bottomed pond at Sheehy Springs. Note the abundant leaf litter and the near-shore habitats.

Figure 4.5. Pond and shore habitats surrounded by an encinal (oak) woodland at Sylvania Springs, Huachuca Mountains.

Sylvania Springs, 25 km (15.5 miles) northeast of Sheehy Springs, also feeds the headwaters of the Santa

Cruz River and emerges from Scotia Canyon, Huachuca Mountains, at 1,870 m (6,150 feet) elevation. Discharge from the four small springs feed what used to be open water ponds, but due to encroaching vegetation only the largest pond still contains deep, open water. The ponds were built by the homesteader of the nearby Peterson Ranch from natural ponds or seeps of unknown original size. A dense tall grass and sedge community borders the largest pond (Fig. 4.5), which contains chara (*Chara* sp.) with tufa forming along the pond edge. An oak-pine woodland closely borders the narrow community surrounding the pond. Mollusc collections were made by J. Marshall in 1951, W. B. Miller, J. C. Bequaert, and R. H. Russell in 1968, and J. C. Bequaert, C. V. Haynes, Jr., and R. H. Russell in 1968 (Table 4.1).

METHODS OF STUDY AT THE FOSSIL SITES

Stratigraphic layers at the Lehner and Murray Springs sites have been sampled for molluscs over a period of many years, but not in a consistent manner. A. J. Lindsay (1958) recovered molluscs from the alluvial layers at the Lehner Site in the mid-1950s; these samples were presumably part of a study of the fossil pollen. The alluvium at the Lehner Site was again sampled for molluscs by J. C. Bequaert in 1963 and by R. H. Russell in 1971. It is not certain how many matrix samples were taken by these collectors, but at least seven alluvial lots were recovered that produced molluscs: three samples from the Coro marl (Stratum E), one sample from the Clanton clay (Stratum F_2), and three samples from the Donnet silt (Stratum F_3). Chapter 2 describes the geology of the Murray Springs Site in Curry Draw.

At the Lehner Site, Bequaert and Russell recovered matrix samples from the arroyo embankments and from the walls left from stratigraphic trenches excavated in 1963 (Mehringer and Haynes 1965). The Lehner Site was again extensively excavated in 1974 and 1975, at which time I sampled 21 localities within the newly exposed alluvium. Two samples of matrix were removed from the Millville alluvium (Stratum Z), one sample from the Sobaipuri mudstone (Stratum D), four samples from the Coro marl (Stratum E), one sample from the Graveyard sand (Stratum F_1), two samples from the Clanton clay (Stratum F_2), three samples from the Donnet silt (Stratum F_3), one sample from the Weik alluvium (Stratum G_1), and three samples from the McCool alluvium (Stratum G_{2b}). No molluscs were recovered from the Hargis alluvium (Stratum G_{2a}) at this site.

Sampling for molluscs at the Murray Springs Site was initiated in 1968 by Bequaert and V. Haynes, with further laboratory work being done by Bequaert and Russell. Nineteen samples of matrix were collected between the base of the Sobaipuri mudstone and the top of the McCool alluvium from four stratigraphic sections (Nos. 5, 6, 8, and 9, Figs. 4.6-4.7) made originally for pollen sampling. The Sobaipuri mudstone was sampled twice from the brown clay at the base of the section adjacent to Pollen Profile 6 (Profile A, Fig. 1.3). Samples of the overlying white marl and mudstone from the Coro marl were collected from the middle of the section and at seven other positions up section (Fig. A.2). The Graveyard sand (Sample 10), the lower and upper portions of the Clanton clay (Samples 11-12), and the Donnet silt (Samples 13-15) at the lower contact with the Clanton clay were all collected near Pollen Profile 8 (Figs. 4.6-4.7). A channel fill sample (16) was taken from the middle of the Weik alluvium adjacent to Pollen Profile 5 (Fig. 2.10*a*). Three McCool alluvium samples (17-19) were removed adjacent to Pollen Profile 9, the first from pond muds and the second and third from 90 cm and 70 cm respectively higher in muddy alluvium (Fig. 2.10*g*). Additional mollusc samples from the Millville alluvium were recovered by E. H. Lindsay at the "Big Bend" in Curry Draw.

All of the alluvial samples were screen washed (1.5 mm mesh) with water to remove alluvial matrix and then sorted for molluscs, a procedure similar to that described by LaRocque (1966) and Jaehnig (1971). Molluscs were identified by Bequaert, except those of the Lymnaeidae, which were identified by Russell. Bequaert's identification of the Sphaeriidae essentially follows the criteria set forth by Herrington (1962) and used by LaRocque (1970).

Both Russell and Bequaert believe that for the present, *Lymnaea* should be separated into *Lymnaea s. s.*, *Stagnicola*, *Fossaria*, and others. After my own identifications and verifications, I accept Bequaert and Russell's identifications of the molluscs from the Lehner and Murray Springs sites. The taxonomy of the living gastropods has changed since the original draft of this chapter. The names and taxonomy used here follow the current usage in Turgeon and others (1998)

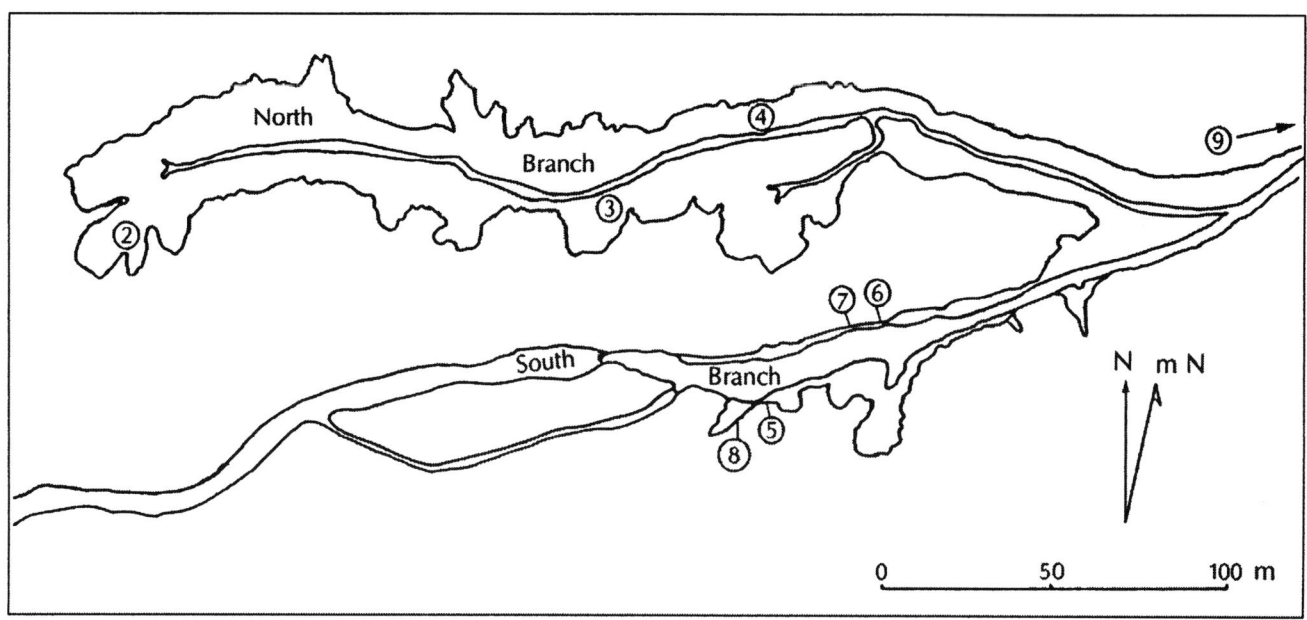

Figure 4.6. Map of Curry Draw at the Murray Springs Site showing molluscan sample locations and Pollen Profile locations 2–9 of Mehringer and others (1966).

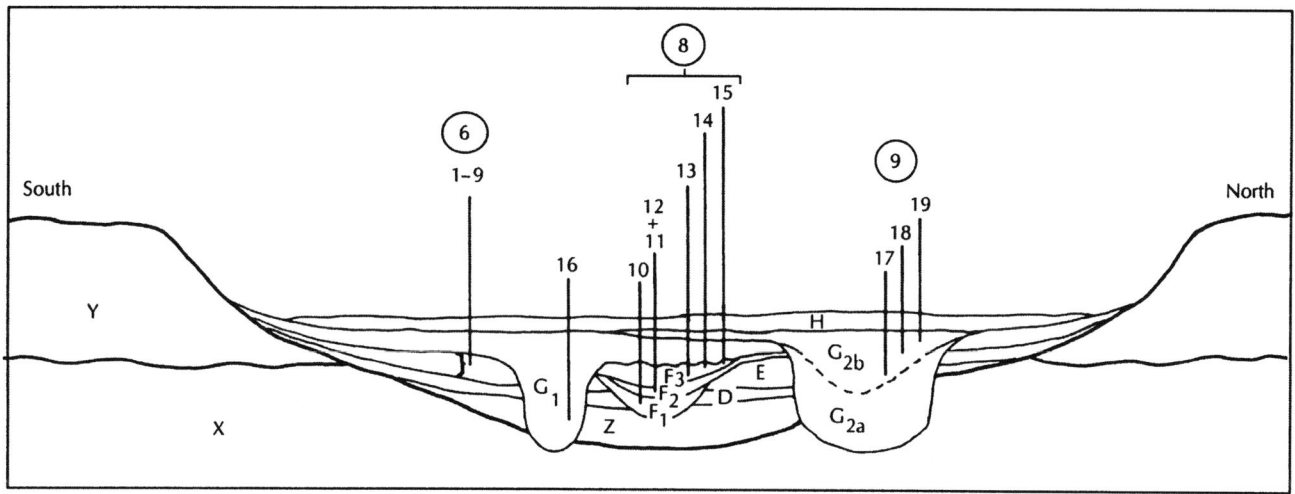

Figure 4.7. Generalized cross section of Curry Draw at Murray Springs showing the stratigraphic positions of the 19 molluscan matrix samples.

and at the website of ITIS (Integrated Taxonomic Information System:
http://www.itis.usda.gov/index.html).

FOSSIL MOLLUSCAN FAUNA

In the systematic list of the fossils, following Table 4.3, recovered from the Lehner and Murray Springs Clovis sites, the modern or recent localities of the fossil species are given first. The left-hand margin numbers refer to the ordering in Bequaert and Miller (1973). Recent localities were obtained primarily from Bequaert and Miller (1973) with some verifications and additions from my own field work; additional references are sometimes cited. A species' preferred habitat is based on its local habitat only, or, in the case of locally extirpated species, its closest extant habitat. Stratigraphic localities for the fossils refer to the vari-

Table 4.2. Molluscan Assemblages from Three Springs in Southeastern Arizona (x = present)

Taxon	Babocomari (Brophy) Cienega N = 14	Sheehy Springs N = 14	Sylvania Springs N = 23
Thysanophora hornii	–	–	x
Euconulus fulvus	–	–	x
Glyphalinia indentata	–	–	x
Hawaiia minuscula	x	x	x
Zonitoides arboreus	x	–	–
Striatura meridionalis	–	–	x
Deroceras laeve	x	x	x
Helicodiscus singleyanus	–	–	x
Punctum californicum	–	–	x
Catinella cf. vermeta	x	–	x
Succinea sp.	–	x	–
Gastrocopta pentodon	x	x	x
Gastrocopta pilsbryana	–	–	x
Gastrocopta pellucida	x	x	–
Gastrocopta ashmuni	–	–	x
Gastrocopta cochisensis	–	–	x
Gastrocopta cristata	x	x	–
Gastrocopta prototypus	–	–	x
Gastrocopta dalliana	–	–	x
Pupoides albilabris	–	x	–
Vertigo milium	–	–	x
Vertigo ovata	x	–	x
Vertigo ventricosa	–	–	x
Vertigo gouldi	–	x	x
Vallonia perspectiva	–	–	x
Cionella lubrica	–	–	x
Pyrgulopsis cf. longinqua	–	–	x
Fossaria obrussa	x	–	–
Fossaria parva	x	–	–
Physella virgata	x	x	–
Gyraulus parvus	–	x	–
Helisoma tenue	x	–	–
Drepanotrema aeruginosum	x	–	–
Musculium transversum	x	x	x
Pisidium casertanum	–	x	–
Pisidium compressum	–	x	–
Pisidium walkeri	–	x	–

Table 4.3. Murray Springs Site Molluscs that are Either Absent (—) or Now Inhabiting (x) Oak Woodland to Oak-pine Woodland

Taxon	In drainage at higher elevation	McCool Alluvium	Hargis Alluvium	Weik Alluvium	Donnet Silt	Clanton Clay	Graveyard Sand, 11,000 B.P.	Coro Marl	Sobaipuri Mudstone	Millville Alluvium
Zonitoides arboreus	x	–	–	–	–	–	x	–	–	–
Discus whitneyi	x	–	–	–	–	–	x	–	–	–
Punctum californicum	x	–	–	–	–	x	x	–	–	–
Oxyloma sp.	–	–	–	–	x	x	x	x	x	–
Gastrocopta prototypus	x	–	–	–	–	–	x	–	–	–
Gastrocopta armifera	–	–	–	–	–	–	x	–	–	–
Pupilla muscorum	–	–	–	–	–	–	x	x	x	–
Pupilla hebes	x	–	–	–	–	–	x	x	x	–
Pupilla syngenes	x	–	–	–	–	–	?	x	–	–
Vallonia perspectiva	x	–	–	–	–	–	x	?	?	x
Vallonia cyclopherella	x	–	–	–	–	–	x	x	x	–
Vallonia gracilicosta	–	–	–	–	–	–	x	–	–	–
Cionella lubrica	x	–	–	–	–	–	x	–	–	–
Ferrissia fragilis	–	–	–	–	–	–	x	–	–	–
Pyrgulopsis cf. longinqua	x	–	–	–	–	x	x	–	–	–
Pisidium walkeri	x	x	–	–	–	x	x	x	x	x
Pisidium compressum	–	x	–	–	–	–	x	?	?	x

NOTE: Hargis Alluvium was not sampled.

ous members of the formations at the Lehner and Murray Springs sites (Tables 4.2, 4.3; Chapter 2; Plate 2). The following abbreviations are used: Millville alluvium (Z); Sobaipuri mudstone (D); Coro marl (E); Graveyard sand (F_1); Clanton clay (F_2); Donnet silt (F_3); Weik alluvium (G_1); McCool alluvium (G_{2b}). An "*" indicates that the species was not associated directly with mammoth (*Mammuthus*) as previously stated in Bequaert and Miller (1973).

Terrestrial Fauna

HELICARIONIDAE
83. *Euconulus fulvus* (Muller) 1774
    Lehner: E.
    Murray Springs: D, E, F_1, F_2, F_3, G_1, G_{2b}.
This species occurs throughout Arizona except in the low, hot region around the lower Colorado River, Yuma and La Paz counties. In southeastern Arizona it is found generally in the woodland and higher communities above 1,830 m (6,000 feet) elevation. *Euconulus* is found in the San Pedro Valley mainly in the oak-pine woodland. It is not reported from Sonora, Mexico, although it is expected to be found there. It has been recovered from New Mexico, Trans-Pecos Texas, and northwestern Chihuahua, Mexico.

ZONITIDAE

85. *Nesovitrea electrina* (Gould) 1841
    Lehner: D, E, F_3.
    Murray Springs: F_1, F_2, F_3.

This species is widespread throughout Arizona, perhaps the most common land snail species in the state. It occurs from 1,250 m to 2,430 m (4,100 to 8,000 feet) elevation in southeastern Arizona and in the San Pedro Valley. Biotic requirements are varied; it occupies the xeric desertscrub of the valley and extends up into the chaparral.

87. *Zonitoides arboreus* (Say) 1816
    Lehner: E, F_2.
    Murray Springs: F_2.

At present the species lives throughout most of Arizona, occurring mainly in the wooded mountains above the desert communities, staying below the timberline. It is common in the San Pedro Valley between from 1,520 m to 2,735 m (5,000 to 9,000 feet) elevation. In the Huachuca Mountains, *Z. arboreus* is found from the oak grassland communities up into the pine forests. The species has not yet been discovered in Sonora, Mexico.

LIMACIDAE

90. *Deroceras laeve* (Muller) 1774
    Lehner: E, F_3.
    Murray Springs: Z_2, E, F_1, F_2, F_3, G_1, G_{2b}.

A native of Arizona, this slug is widespread in the state above 1,370 m (4,500 feet) elevation. In the Huachuca Mountains it is known from desert grassland communities up into the oak woodland above 1,830 m (6,000 feet) elevation in Miller, Brown, Tanner (Garden), and Huachuca canyons. It can also be found in the lower reaches of the San Pedro, such as the marshy areas of Babocomari Cienega at 1,370 m (4,500 feet) elevation. Interestingly, the species has yet to be discovered in Sonora and Chihuahua, Mexico, although it is known from farther south.

DISCIDAE

91. **Discus whitneyi* (Newcomb) 1864
    Murray Springs: F_1.

This snail is found throughout Arizona from 835 m to 3,650 m (2,750 to 12,000 feet) elevation. In the southeastern part of the state it is usually observed above 1,830 m (6,000 feet) elevation, but in the Huachuca Mountains it can be found from 1,520 m to 2,430 m (5,000 to 8,000 feet) elevation. Although it lives in a wide variety of habitats, in the Huachuca Mountains it is common in the oak woodland and chaparral community up through the oak-pine woodland. The species is known from Chihuahua, Mexico, but is not yet recorded from Sonora.

HELICODISCIDAE

94. *Helicodiscus singleyanus* (Pilsbry) 1889
    Lehner: E, F_2, F_3.
    Murray Springs: E, F_1, F_2, F_3, G_1, G_{2b}.

The distribution of this species is incompletely understood because it is often confused with *Hawaiia minuscula*. It is widespread in Arizona from 730 m to 2,650 m (2,400 to 8,700 feet) elevation. In the San Pedro Valley this small snail is usually found in the desertscrub up through the oak woodland communities and is also known from Sonora.

PUNCTIDAE

95. *Punctum californicum* Pilsbry 1898
    Lehner: F_3.
    Murray Springs: F_1, F_2.

This very small snail is widespread in Arizona from 1,220 m to 2,890 m (4,000 to 9,500 feet) elevation. In the San Pedro Valley it is found in the Dragoon and Huachuca Mountains, usually in the desert grassland through oak woodland and chaparral communities from 1,680 m to 1,830 m (5,500 to 6,000 feet) elevation. The snail is also common in leaf litter in the oak woodland of the Canelo Hills at 1,680 m (5,500 feet) elevation and at Sylvania Springs on the south side of the Huachuca Mountains. The species is not known from Sonora.

SUCCINEIDAE

-- *Succinea* spp. Draparnaud 1801
    Lehner: E, F_2, F_3.
    Murray Springs: Z_2, D, E, F_1, F_2, F_3, G_1, G_{2b}.

Most malacologists believe that genitalia are required for specific identifications within this genus; however, some paleontologists have observed some identifying characteristics of fossil shells. A number of species are present and widespread in Arizona, including in the San Pedro Valley.

-- *Oxyloma* sp. Westerlaund 1885
    Lehner: D, E, F_2.
    Murray Springs: D, E, F_1, F_2, G_{2b}.

As with most genera and species of Succineidae, the genitalia are required for specific identification. The genus *Oxyloma*, with its distinctive shell morphology and anatomy, is widespread in the recent fauna of most of the Nearctic, but at present does not live in Arizona.

PUPILLIDAE
103. *Gastrocopta pentodon* (Say) 1822
    Lehner: D, E, F_2, F_3.
    Murray Springs: D, E, F_1, F_2, F_3, G_1, G_2.

If *G. tappaniana* is considered a synonym, the species is widespread in Arizona, usually from 1,370 m to 1,980 m (4,500 to 6,500 feet) elevation. Within the San Pedro Valley, it is found in the Huachuca Mountains from 1,600 m to 1,830 m (5,250 to 6,000 feet) elevation in the desert grassland, oak woodland, and chaparral communities and at Babocomari Cienega, but it is not known from Sonora.

108. **Gastrocopta prototypus* (Pilsbry) 1899
    Lehner: E, F_3.
    Murray Springs: F_1.

Knowledge of the present distribution of this snail is fragmentary. Within the San Pedro Valley it is known from the Huachuca Mountains in Ash Canyon at 1,520 m to 1,830 m (5,000 to 6,000 feet) elevation, and from the Dragoon Mountains in Stronghold Canyon at 1,420 m to 1,610 m (4,700 to 5,300 feet) elevation. The species lives in riparian, oak woodland, and chaparral communities. Although found in central Mexico, this species is not known from Chihuahua or Sonora.

110. *Gastrocopta cristata* (Pilsbry and Vanatta) 1900
    Lehner: D, E, F_2, F_3.
    Murray Springs: Z_2, E, F_1, F_2, F_3, G_1, G_{2b}.

This species is common in southern Arizona, living predominantly from 760 m to 1,370 m (2,500 to 4,500 feet) elevation. In the San Pedro Valley, it occurs mainly in moderately arid areas, around 1,370 m (4,500 feet) elevation, within the oak woodland and plains grassland. The species is a pronounced thermophile. The only record in Sonora, Mexico, for this species is from river drift in the Rio Yaqui, Rio Sonoyta, and Rio Bavispe.

112. *Gastrocopta pellucida* (Pfeiffer) 1841
    Lehner: E, F_3.
    Murray Springs: G_{2b}.

This species is widespread in Arizona, but lives mainly from 335 m to 1,980 m (1,100 to 6,500 feet) elevation. Within the San Pedro Valley, it lives in desertscrub, oak woodland, and chaparral communities up to 1,980 m (6,500 feet) elevation. The species is very common throughout Mexico, including Sonora, Chihuahua, and Baja California.

-- **Gastrocopta armifera* (Say) 1821
    Lehner: E, F_2, F_3.
    Murray Springs: F_1.

This species does not live in Arizona at present (Bequaert and Miller 1973). The nearest recent locality is in the Sacramento Mountains of New Mexico, at 2,190 m (7,200 feet) elevation. According to A. L. Metcalf (1962, 1970), the snail is restricted to montane forest or grasslands. LaRocque (1970) indicates that the species lives in grass, shrubs, or wooded areas along river banks. Both authors imply that the species requires moderate moisture, although not necessarily flowing water.

114. *Pupoides albilabris* (Adams) 1841
    Lehner: E, F_2, F_3.
    Murray Springs: Z_2, E, F_1, F_2, F_3, G_1, G_{2b}.

This fairly large, distinctive snail is widespread in Arizona today, mainly from 455 m to 1,770 m (1,500 to 5,800 feet) elevation. In the San Pedro Valley, the snail is found along the river, and within the Whetstone Mountains at 1,280 m (4,300 feet) elevation, the Dragoon Mountains at 1,520 m (5,000 feet) elevation, and the Huachuca Mountains. It inhabits a wide variety of communities, but is common in the desertscrub, the chaparral, and through the oak-pine woodland communities.

115. *Pupoides hordaceus* (Gabb) 1866
    Murray Springs: Z_2.

This snail is widespread in Arizona today, between 1,220 m and 1,830 m (4,000 to 6,000 feet) elevation. In the San Pedro Valley it lives in desertscrub, chaparral, and oak woodland communities. It is not known to occur in Sonora, Mexico.

116. **Pupilla blandi* Morse 1865
    Murray Springs: F_1.

The species is fairly common in the northern, eastern, and southeastern portions of Arizona, from 1,520 m to 2,735 m (5,000 to 9,000 feet) elevation. In the San Pedro Valley, it is recorded from the Dragoon Mountains, living in grassland to oak woodland communities.

117. *Pupilla muscorum* (Linne) 1758
    Lehner: E, F_1.
    Murray Springs: D, E, F_1, G_1.

Pupilla hebes is related to and readily confused with *Pupilla muscorum*. The latter species probably lives in suitable areas at the higher elevations north of the Mogollon Rim in central Arizona. The only well-documented living population for the species is from the San Francisco Mountains at an elevation of 3,660 m (12,000 feet). In New Mexico the species is recorded as living above 2,040 m (6,700 feet) elevation. Within the Palearctic the species can be found in the warmer climates, but in the Nearctic the species stays in the boreal habitats. It is not known to live in Mexico.

118. *Pupilla hebes* (Ancey) 1881
    Lehner: D, E.
    Murray Springs: D, E, F_1.

P. hebes is widespread in Arizona highlands from 1,520 m to 3,350 m (5,000 to 11,000 feet) elevation. Within the Huachuca Mountains it is recorded from Ramsey Canyon at 1,710 m (5,600 feet) elevation and near Miller Peak at 2,735 m (9,000 feet) elevation. Locally it is found in oak woodland, chaparral, and pine forest communities.

119. *Pupilla syngenes* (Pilsbry) 1890
    Lehner: E.
    Murray Springs: E, G_1.

This species is found in Arizona only in the highlands and mountains from an elevation of 1,370 m to 2,735 m (4,500 to 9,000 feet). Within the San Pedro Valley, it is reported from the Mustang and Dragoon mountains above an elevation of 1,680 m (5,500 feet) elevation and in the Huachuca Mountains above 2,135 m (7,000 feet) elevation. The species is common in chaparral and oak woodland communities. It is not known from Mexico.

121. *Vertigo milium* (Gould) 1840
    Lehner: D, E, F_2, F_3.
    Murray Springs: D, E, F_1, F_2, F_3, G_1, G_{2b}.

This species is known in Arizona from only two localities, one being in the Huachuca Mountains in Tanner (Garden) Canyon at 1,830 m (6,000 feet) elevation. It lives at least in the oak woodland community and possibly in others. The species is not known from Sonora, Mexico.

122. *Vertigo ovata* (Say) 1822
    Lehner: E, F_2, F_3.
    Murray Springs: Z_2, D, E, F_1, F_2, F_3, G_1, G_{2b}.

This species is rare in Arizona, occurring only in a few locations. In the Huachuca Mountains it is found in Ash Canyon and Tanner (Garden) Canyon, both above 1,830 m (6,000 feet) elevation. At least it lives in oak woodland community, but can also be found in the marsh-riparian habitat of the Babocomari Cienega at 1,370 m (4,500 feet) elevation. It is recorded from drift of the Rio de Sonoita, Sonora, Mexico.

-- *Vertigo berryi* (Pilsbry) 1919
    Lehner: E, F_2, F_3.
    Murray Springs: D, E, F_1, F_2, F_3, G_1, G_{2b}.

This species is not known to live in Arizona at present, although it is found in Baja California.

-- *Vertigo elatior* Sterki 1894
    Lehner: E.
    Murray Springs: E, F_1, F_2.

This species (Fig. 4.8*b*) is not known to live in Arizona at present. The closest living population is in the Sacramento Mountains, New Mexico. It has been suggested that *V. elatior* and *V. ventricosa* may be synonyms and that *V. binneyana* may be closely related to *V. elatior* (Bequaert and Miller 1973). Fossil specimens of *V. ventricosa* and *V. elatior* from the Lehner Site appear to be very similar, whereas *V. binneyana* appears to be distinct.

-- *Vertigo ventricosa* (Morse) 1865
    Lehner: D, E, F_2, F_3.
    Murray Springs: E, F_1, F_2, F_3, G_1.

This species (Fig. 4.8*a*) is very rare in Arizona today, with the only possibly living community being at Sylvania Springs at 1,870 m (6,150 feet) elevation in the Huachuca Mountains.

-- *Vertigo binneyana* Sterki 1890
    Lehner: F_2.

A living population of this snail (Fig. 4.8*c*) is not known in Arizona, although the species is recorded in New Mexico. Very little is known of the species, which is similar to *V. elatior* and *V. ventricosa* (see Bequaert and Miller 1973 for discussion of conspecific species).

Figure 4.8. Scanning electron microscope photographs of fossil molluscs: *a, Vertigo ventricosa; b, Vertigo elatior; c, Vertigo binneyana; d,* cf. *Omalodiscus pattersoni*. All snails are from the Lehner Site. Molluscs are 1.5 mm in length.

VALLONIIDAE

126. *Vallonia perspectiva* Sterki 1893
   Lehner: E, F_3.
   Murray Springs: Z_2, F_1, G_1.

This species is widespread in the Arizona highlands, and in the San Pedro Valley it occurs mainly at elevations from 1,580 m to 1,975 m (5,200 to 6,500 feet). In the Huachuca, Mustang, and Whetstone mountains it lives predominantly in the chaparral and the oak and oak-pine woodlands. The snail is found in Sonora and Chihuahua, Mexico.

127. *Vallonia cyclophorella* Sterki 1892
   Lehner: Z_2, E, F_3.
   Murray Springs: D, E, F_1.

This species is more boreal and more restricted in habitat tolerance than *V. perspectiva*. It occurs in Arizona mainly in the northern plateau regions, but also lives in certain mountains in the southern part of the state. In the Huachuca Mountains it is found near Miller Peak at 2,850 m (9,200 feet) elevation. Bequaert told me that this snail was not recovered at Sylvania Springs as was reported in Bequaert and Miller (1973). Although living today in all the states of the Southwest, the boreal snail is not known from Mexico.

-- *Vallonia gracilicosta* Reinhardt 1883
   Lehner: E, F_2, F_3.
   Murray Springs: F_1.

There is no verifiable evidence that this snail is alive at present in Arizona; all records appear to be of fossils, either in situ or in drift. This species is present in New Mexico in the Sacramento Mountains above 2,280 m (7,500 feet) elevation (Metcalf 1967). It is not known alive from northern Mexico.

CIONELLIDAE

128. *Cionella lubrica* (Muller) 1774
   Lehner: E, F_2, F_3.
   Murray Springs: F_1.

First described as the genus *Helix* and often cited as *Cochlicopa*, this Holarctic species is widespread in Arizona from an elevation of 1,370 m to 3,040 m (4,500 to 10,000 feet). In the San Pedro Valley, the snail is known to live in the Huachuca Mountains from an elevation of 1,580 m to 2,800 m (5,200 to 9,200 feet) and in the Dragoon Mountains from an elevation of 1,430 to 1,710 m (4,700 to 5,600 feet), predominantly in the chaparral, oak woodland, and pine forest.

Aquatic Fauna

LYMNAEIDAE

130. *Fossaria techella* Haldeman 1867
    Murray Springs: F_1.

This aquatic snail is often placed in the genus *Stagnicola* (see previous comments and Bequaert and Miller 1973). Today this species is not found alive in the San Pedro Valley, although it is present in much of Arizona from 1,475 m to 1,750 m (4,850 to 5,750 feet) elevation. It is known from Sonora, Mexico.

132. *Stagnicola caperata* (Say) 1829
    Murray Springs: F_1.

Like the previous species, this one is not found alive in the San Pedro Valley, but is somewhat common over the state as a whole in elevations from 1,930 m to 2,765 m (6,350 to 9,100 feet).

133. *Fossaria obrussa* (Say) 1825
    Lehner: D, E, F_2, F_3.
    Murray Springs: D, E, F_1, F_2, F_3, G_1, G_{2b}.

Although not known from Sonora, Mexico, this species is found over much of Arizona in permanent seeps, ponds, cienegas, certain riparian areas, and irrigation canals. In the San Pedro Valley it is known from Babocomari Cienega at 1,370 m (4,500 feet) elevation, where it is common in permanent ponds and edges of ponds in the desert grassland.

134. *Fossaria parva* (Lea) 1841
    Lehner: E, F_2, F_3.
    Murray Springs: Z_2, D, E, F_1, F_2, F_3, G_1, G_{2b}.

This snail is known from northeastern to southeastern Arizona, but it is not reported from Sonora, Mexico. In the Huachuca Mountains this species is found in Ash Canyon at 1,520 m (5,000 feet) elevation, and is known from Sylvania Springs and Babocomari Cienega. The snail is also known as *F. dalli*, a fossil reported from the San Pedro Valley (Taylor 1966) as well as many other states.

135. *Fossaria modicella* (Say) 1825
    Murray Springs: F_1.

This species is not known from the San Pedro region, but it is found living in the northeastern part of the state from 1,070 m to 2,130 m (4,500 to 7,000 feet) elevation. It is known from Imuris, Sonora, Mexico, and may well be located in other permanent ponds in that state.

PHYSIDAE

136. *Physella virgata* (Gould) 1855
    Lehner: E, F_3.
    Murray Springs: E, F_1, F_2, F_3, G_{2b}.

This snail is located in all counties in Arizona and lives in suitable habitats from 305 m to 2,650 m (1,000 to 8,700 feet) elevation. Within the San Pedro Valley, it can be found in wet areas from 1,220 m to 2,650 m (4,000 to 8,700 feet) elevation. This species is known from northern Mexico.

137 *Physella humerosa* (Gould) 1855
    Lehner: F_2.
    Murray Springs: F_1, G_1.

This species has not been verified as living in Arizona at present, but it is known alive in New Mexico and northern Mexico.

PLANORBIDAE

138. *Gyraulus parvus* (Say) 1817
    Lehner: E, F_2.
    Murray Springs: D, E, F_1, F_3, G_1, G_{2b}.

This species is widespread in Arizona lakes and ponds. Within the San Pedro River region it is known from the Canelo Hills at 1,680 m (5,500 feet) elevation.

-- *Helisoma anceps* (Menke) 1830
    Lehner: F_2.

This species is absent from Arizona at present. West of the Rocky Mountains it is found in permanent aquatic habitats from Oregon to northwestern Mexico.

-- cf. *Omalodiscus pattersoni* (Baker) 1938

This species (Fig. 4.8*d*) is absent from Arizona at present. Only one shell was recovered from the Lehner Site that is assignable to *Omalodiscus pattersoni* (previously placed in *Anisus* and *Gyraulus*). The identification of this species from the San Pedro is of importance because the species is extinct and has not been recorded previously from Arizona, other than as a fossil recovered in modern drift of the San Pedro River at Fairbank, Cochise County (Bequaert and Miller 1973).

The fossil from the Lehner Site is incomplete, containing only three whorls. Taylor (1958) describes *Omalodiscus pattersoni* as containing up to 5½ whorls (the maximum number for *Gyralus* is 4 whorls) that very slowly and regularly enlarge. Both sides of

Omalodiscus pattersoni are almost planar, whereas *Gyraulus* has convex whorls and usually a concave left and convex right side. *Omalodiscus pattersoni* has a quadrangular aperature and *Gyraulus* an ovate aperature. The specimen from the Lehner Site (Fig. 4.8d) has no aperature preserved; however, both sides of the shell are planar, neither appearing as those of *Gyraulus*. More complete specimens are needed before there can be an unequivocal identification of this extinct species from the Lehner Site.

ANCYLIDAE
142. **Ferrissia fragilis* (= *Laevapex californica*) (Tryon) 1863
    Murray Springs: F_1.

This genus is not found in the San Pedro Valley at present but is the only limpet known from the Recent in Arizona. The closest known living populations are from Knipe (now known as O'Donnell) Cienega, Canelo Hills, and from Sabino Canyon, Santa Catalina Mountains, near Tucson.

HYDROBIIDAE
146. *Pyrgulopsis* cf. *longinqua* (Gould) 1855
    Lehner: F_3.
    Murray Springs: F_1, F_2.

This snail is restricted to springs and flowing streams. In the San Pedro Valley it is found in the Huachuca Mountains in Ash and Tanner (Garden) canyons and at Sylvania Springs. The family is not well understood in Arizona or northern Mexico (Nations and Landye 1984).

SPHAERIIDAE (includes Pisidiidae in ITIS)
147. *Musculium* (= *Sphaerium*) *transversum* (Say) 1829
    Lehner: E.

This "finger-nail" clam is not found in the San Pedro Valley at present, except for the Babocomari Cienega. It is rarely observed in any of the southeastern Arizona springs and cienegas like Sheehy Springs and Knipe Cienega in the nearby Canelo Hills. The species is known from Chihuahua and Sonora, Mexico.

149. **Pisidium casertanum* (Poli) 1791
    Lehner: E, F_2, F_3.
    Murray Springs: Z_2, D, E, F_1, F_2, F_3, G_1, G_{2b}.

This little clam is found widespread in Arizona from 1,070 m to 2,750 m (3,500 to 9,050 feet) elevation.

Living in permanent and usually stagnant water, it can tolerate moderate seasonal desiccation. In the nearby San Rafael Valley and Canelo Hills, this species is found in Sheehy Springs and Knipe Cienega at 1,510 m (4,950 feet) elevation. In the San Pedro Valley, it is known from Babocomari Cienega and from ponds in the Huachuca Mountains from 1,370 m to 2,130 m (4,500 to 7,000 feet) elevation. The species is not recorded from the ponds and cienegas of Sonora, Mexico.

150. *Pisidium compressum* Prime 1852
    Murray Springs: Z_2, F_1, G_{2b}.

Although living predominantly in northern Arizona, this species can be found living in southeastern Arizona springs and cienegas, such as the Sheehy Springs and Knipe Cienega in the nearby Canelo Hills. This species is not known from the San Pedro Valley, but is known from Sonora, Mexico.

152. **Pisidium walkeri* Sterki 1895
    Murray Springs: Z_2, D, E, F_1, F_2, G_1, G_{2b}.

This species is found over much of Arizona, but is not known alive in the San Pedro Valley. It is found in Sheehy Springs and Knipe Cienega in the nearby Canelo Hills.

COMPARISON OF FOSSIL AND MODERN ASSEMBLAGES

A comparison of the present molluscan assemblages from the three springs and cienegas (Table 4.1) with those fossils of the various sedimentary units examined from the Clovis sites should indicate possible environmental similarities and dissimilarities. There are a number of coefficients widely used in biogeographical studies to estimate faunal similarities. One is Simpson's coefficient, 100 x C/N1, where C is the number of taxa in common between the two sites and N1 is the number of taxa in the site of lowest diversity (Simpson 1965). This coefficient is biased toward the less diverse fauna. Taylor (1960) found this coefficient useful in analyzing the late Cenozoic molluscan faunas of the High Plains. Pierce (1975) found a second index, that of Dice (Sneath and Sokal 1973), to be the most useful. The problem with this index is that the coefficient ignores the species absent from both faunas. Another index is Jaccards's coefficient (100 x C[N1 + N2 - C]), which is similar to

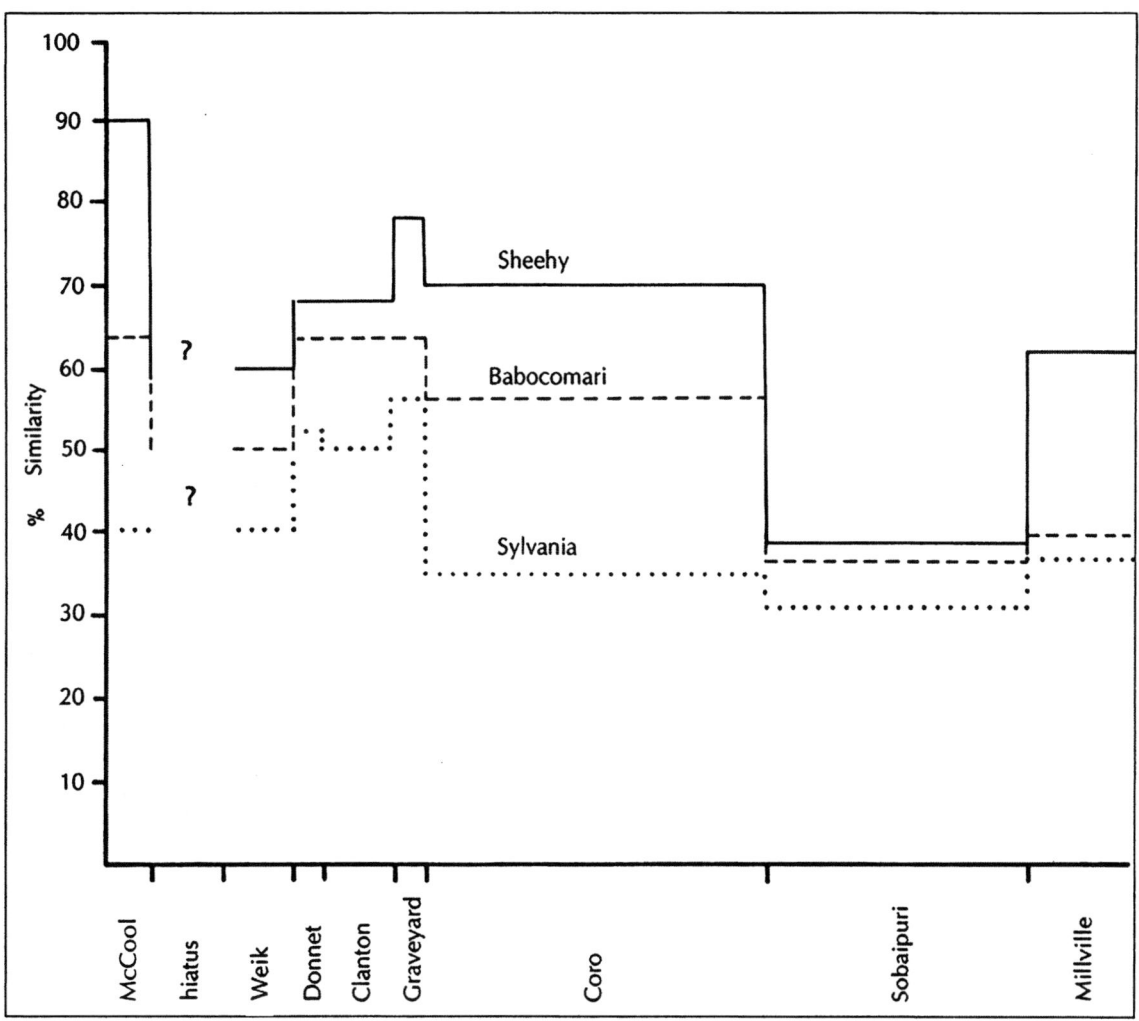

Figure 4.9. Simpson's faunal similarity index used to compare the modern molluscan assemblages from Babocomari Cienega, Sheehy Springs, and Sylvania Springs with the fossil assemblages from the Lehner Site and the Murray Springs Site.

Simpson's in that the number of species from both faunas is considered. However, Simpson's and Jaccard's coefficients can give contradictory results for the same set of data (Fallaw 1977, 1978; Flessa and others 1978). Simpson's coefficient was chosen for this report to test faunal similarities between the strata from the fossil sites and the modern springs because of the differing number of taxa between the localities. Simpson designed this index to work with localities having differing numbers of taxa. In contrast, Jaccard's index works best with localities having nearly equivalent numbers of species.

Of the three modern springs chosen for comparison, Sheehy Springs (Fig. 4.9) shows the highest correlations to most of the strata at the Murray Springs Site. The similarity coefficient indicates that the Murray Springs Site was similar to the modern sites during the time of deposition of Stratum F_1, the Graveyard sand (13,000–11,000 B.P.). The Stratum E Coro marl (27,500–14,000 B.P.) at both Murray Springs and Lehner was similar to the modern Babocomari Cienega and Sheehy Springs. A definite decrease in similarity to the modern sites occurs from the Stratum D Sobaipuri mudstone (32,000–27,500 B.P.) to the Coro marl at both sites. Another apparent decrease in faunal similarity occurs during deposition of the Weik alluvium (Stratum G_1; 6,000–4,000 B.P.), but an increase in similarity occurs during deposition of the McCool alluvium (Stratum G_{2b}; 3000–1000 B.P.). Because these modern faunas are related to the local water regime, the faunal similarities in the Clovis sites may also be interpreted as related to local water regime. If this is true, then intervals between 27,500 B.P. to 11,000 B.P. at both Clovis sites, and from 3000 B.P. to 1000 B.P. at the Murray Springs Site, were similar in faunal terms to an active spring with associated cienega and ponds. Therefore, a decrease in similarity between the modern sites and the fossil sites would indicate a decrease in available spring-related habitats, probably accompanying a decrease in discharge either from artesian springs or from seeps. Buried spring feeders at the Lehner and Murray Springs sites are related to the Sobaipuri mudstone and Coro marl (Chapter 2).

HABITAT RECONSTRUCTION

Millville Alluvium (Z_2)

The hard clayey sand and gravel stratum probably represents flashy streamflow and bank collapse as well as ponding. Less is known of this stratum as compared to the remaining younger strata. Only one species of mollusc (terrestrial) was recovered at the Lehner Site. Thirteen species of fossil molluscs (5 aquatic and 8 terrestrial) were collected from the strata at the Murray Springs Site. All are living in the San Pedro drainage today except for *Stagnicola caperata* and the two clams *Pisidium compressum* and *P. walkeri*, all of which are aquatic species. *Pupoides hordaceus* is common in and above the desert grassland in the San Pedro Valley at present; however, as a fossil it is found only in the Millville alluvium. Approximately half (46.4%) of the assemblage is comprised of the slug *Deroceras laeve*. The next most abundant fossil taxon (20.1%) is *Pisidium compressum*, which is locally absent but can be collected live in the San Rafael Valley. Generally the terrestrial assemblage representatives can be found in desert grassland to oak woodland. The presence of *Vallonia perspectiva*, *Pupoides hordaceus*, and *Stagnicola caperta* indicate a modern equivalent of a desert grassland to oak woodland near springs. The aquatic assemblage appears to be in situ, based on the relative shell ages and good preservation. In summary, the Millville alluvium probably represents a stream with intermittent ponds surrounded by a moist desert grassland to oak woodland.

Sobaipuri Mudstone (D)

The Sobaipuri Member of the Murray Springs Formation at the Lehner Site contains eight species of molluscs (1 aquatic and 7 terrestrial). At the Murray Springs Site, the Sobaipuri Member contains 15 species of molluscs (5 aquatic and 10 terrestrial). Most of these species may be found within the San Pedro today except for *Oxyloma* sp., *Nesovitrea electrina*, *Vertigo ventricosa*, and *Vertigo berryi*, which are now absent in Arizona, and *Pupilla muscorum*, *Pisidium walkeri*, and *Fossaria obrussa*, which are found in other regions of Arizona. All the terrestrials currently are found only in oak woodlands, oak chaparrals, or higher elevation habitats in Arizona. The terrestrial snail *Succinea* spp. makes up 68 percent of the assemblage at the Murray Springs Site. No habitat reconstruction is made from these shells because they are not identified to species. The good preservation and the long age range of the assemblage indicate they are in situ. The Sobaipuri Member at the two sites apparently represents ponding areas, based on *Gyraulus parvus*, *Fossaria obrussa*, and the bivalves *Pisidium* spp., with an oak woodland-plains grassland to oak woodland habitat at least on the fringes of the ponds.

Coro Marl (E)

The Coro marl, the middle member of the Murray Springs Formation, contains 32 fossil molluscan species at the Lehner Site (6 aquatic and 26 terrestrial). At the Murray Springs Site this stratum contains 24 species of molluscs (6 aquatic and 18 terrestrial). Forty-six percent of the total number of molluscs at the Murray Springs Site are aquatic species, whereas only nine percent are aquatic at the Lehner Site. Seven terrestrial species recovered from the Coro marl are currently absent from Arizona. Progressing from the time represented by the Sobaipuri mudstone to the Coro marl at both sites, there was a slight increase in the number of aquatic species and a large increase in the number of terrestrial species. The Coro marl represents a definite ponding phase with an oak woodland-plains grassland to an oak-pine woodland nearby, possibly only on the fringes of the site.

Graveyard Sand (F_1)

No molluscs were recovered from the Graveyard sand, the upper member of the Murray Springs Formation, at the Lehner Site. There is some question whether the mollusc-matrix sample from Area 1 at the Murray Springs Site is correctly assigned to the Graveyard Member. The matrix was sampled from a marl lens located within the Graveyard sand and, as Haynes (Chapter 2; Plate 7, Profile C, Stratum F_{1c}) points out, it is possible that the marl lens, and therefore the molluscs, is actually a portion of the Coro marl that somehow was incorporated into the Graveyard sand by erosion and undercutting of the marl. Haynes (Chapter 2) estimates the end of Coro marl deposition at no later than 13,000 B.P. and the beginning of Graveyard sand deposition at no earlier than 13,000 B.P. As a test the shell carbonate from Sample 10 was radiocarbon dated as 12,820 ± 140 B.P. (SMU-190), indicating it could be from either source. However, as pointed out in Appendix A, this value could be too old due to the hard water effect or too young due to chemical exchange with rain water high in nuclear age radiocarbon. As explained in Chapter 2, Haynes now believes the F_{1c} marl is a valid part of the F_1 channel deposit. This conclusion is based, in part, on the faunal assemblage being atypical for the Coro marl, as explained next.

The Murray Springs Sample 10 contains 40 species of molluscs, almost twice the number from any other unit on the site. Of the 40 species recovered from the locality, 20 species are different from those from the seven matrix samples of the Coro marl. Of the 44 species recovered from all the strata at the Murray Springs Site, only 10 were recovered from Sample 10. Samples of molluscs from Sample 10 were sent to Gifford H. Miller (personal communication 1979) with the hope that his work with amino acid racemization would help clarify the stratigraphic assignment of the problematic sample. The allogenic:isogenous ratio of molluscs from Sample 10 and of those from the Coro marl are discordant, implying that the Sample 10 molluscs are either from the Graveyard sand or from an entirely different Pleistocene marl. For now, the Area 1 molluscs are assigned to the Graveyard sand, but future work at the Murray Springs Site or at other sites in the San Pedro Valley may prove otherwise.

Forty species of molluscs (13 aquatic and 27 terrestrial) were collected from the marl lens in the Graveyard sand at the Murray Springs Site. Six of the taxa are absent today in Arizona. Of the six, *Vallonia gracilicosta* and *Gastrocopta armifera* are not found in younger units at the site, although they do occur in younger and older units at the Lehner Site. The assemblage is rich in aquatic species. The relative age range and the shell preservation indicate that the assemblage is in situ. Eight of the 13 aquatic species are not found within the drainage today. The freshwater limpet, *Ferrissia fragilis*, is uncommon in the Holocene of Arizona. The Graveyard sand from both Clovis sites contains the only record of the limpet. Habitats for modern representatives of the fossil assemblage range from desert grassland (*Helicodiscus singleyanus*) to pine forest (*Vallonia cyclophorella*); however, most species have an oak woodland preferred habitat. The Graveyard sand definitely indicates a time of local ponding with areas of open water. The sediments and the wide diversity of the taxa indicate little transportation prior to deposition. The immediate area around the water appears to have been a mixed oak woodland-plains grassland to an oak woodland habitat.

Clanton Clay (F_2)

Twenty-two species of molluscs were collected from the Clanton clay at the Lehner Site (6 aquatic and 16 terrestrial). Twenty-two species of molluscs were collected from the Murray Springs Site (6 aquatic and 16 terrestrial). Six of the terrestrial and three of the aquatic taxa from the Lehner Site are absent in Arizona. The modern habitats of the species recovered as fossils range from the desert grassland to mixed oak woodland-plains grassland to oak woodland. The *Pisidium* spp. bivalves and the aquatic snails, such as *Pyrgulosis* cf. *longinqua*, indicate ponding and flowing water. The vegetation around the wet areas may have been a desert grassland to a mixed oak woodland-plains grassland.

Donnet Silt (F_3)

The Donnet silt of the Lehner Formation contains 27 species of molluscs (6 aquatic and 21 terrestrial) at the Lehner Site and 18 species of molluscs (5 aquatic and 13 terrestrial) at the Murray Springs Site. Approximately 95 percent of the recovered shells from the Lehner Site and 89 percent from the Murray Springs Site are terrestrial snails. The few aquatic species indicate occasional ponding. The ponding did not occur throughout the sedimentary history of the stratum, based on the absence of the pond-loving clams *Pisidium compressum* and *P. walkeri*. The one occurrence of *P. caseranum* helps support the thesis of occasional ponding. This is the only clam found at the site that can tolerate dry mudflats during occasional dry spells. The water at the site during this period may have occurred predominantly as seepage and was only rarely free-flowing and ponding. Interestingly, the Donnet silt at the Lehner Site has the only in situ occurrences of the extinct species *Omalodiscus pattersoni* in the San Pedro Valley. Because of its tentative identification and single occurrence, I have decided not to place any paleoenvironmental significance on its recovery. The overall assemblage seems to indicate a trend to a more xeric period. Whether this trend occurred rapidly and throughout the valley or just at the two sites cannot be determined at this time.

Weik Alluvium (G₁)

The Weik alluvium at the Lehner Site produced no molluscs; however, at the Murray Springs Site the stratum produced 19 taxa (4 aquatic and 15 terrestrial), all from channel fill sediments. Fossils eroded from the older deposits, such as *Pupilla syngenes*, *Pupilla muscorum*, *Vertigo ventricosa*, and *Vallonia perspectiva*, appear to be contaminants. It is difficult to determine the local site habitats. Less than three percent of the assemblage is made up of aquatic forms, which tends to indicate the presence of some ponded water, especially given the few but persistent occurrences of *Pisidium walkeri*. Although these could be from flood debris or older deposits, interbedded pond muds and marls do occur in the Weik channel (Chapter 2). The terrestrial shells indicate a desert grassland to a mixed oak woodland-plains grassland habitat around the site.

McCool Alluvium (G₂ᵦ)

No molluscs were recovered from the Hargis alluvium at the Lehner Site. Some of the sediment of the McCool Member at Murray Springs may have come from the nearby Tombstone surface. *Oxyloma* sp. and *Gastrocopta pellucida* are regarded as contaminants. There are 22 molluscan species (9 aquatic and 13 terrestrial) from the stratum at the Murray Springs Site, with approximately 78 percent of the assemblage aquatics. This indicates a period of ponding, but how long it occurred cannot be determined. The terrestrial snails indicate a mixed habitat between a desertscrub, desert grassland, to a mixed oak woodland-plains grassland.

SIGNIFICANCE OF THE FAUNAL RECORD

Molluscs were recovered from the Lehner and the Murray Springs sites, although the Lehner Site produced fewer molluscs and did not produce any molluscs from the Graveyard sand, Weik alluvium, or Hargis alluvium. The fossil molluscan assemblages recovered from both sites appear to reveal more accurately changes in the hydrological regime than they do the local vegetational communities (see reconstruction in Mehringer and others 1971). It may be assumed that the molluscan taxa recovered from the Murray Springs and Lehner formations are representative of the immediate (possibly within a 50-m to 100-m radius of the site) local habitats, and the parameters governing their distribution and existence are probably at least local if not valley-wide. It can be concluded that the distribution and occurrence of most of the fossil taxa from the sites are directly related to fluctuations of the water table.

Comparisons of the fossil aquatic taxa to the terrestrial taxa (Fig. 4.10) at the Murray Springs Site indicate that the relative number of aquatic species is directly related to the number of available local aquatic habitats. These habitats may be due to the amount of water, its depth, the amount of shore area, and whether the water is flowing or standing. The period be-

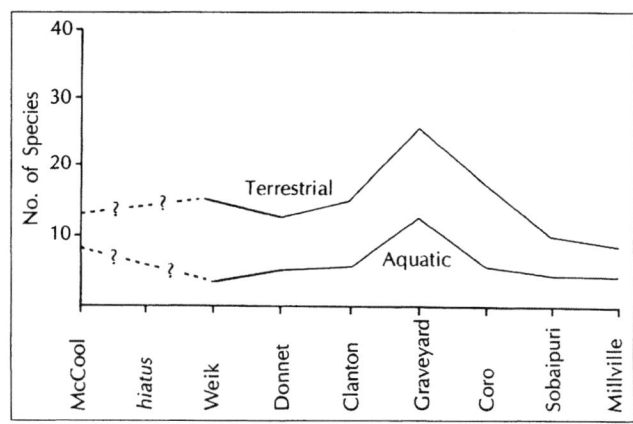

Figure 4.10. Graph illustrating the changes in number of aquatic and terrestrial molluscs for the stratigraphic layers at the Murray Springs Site.

tween the time a spring changes its discharge to the time the local molluscan fauna responds to the point it may be recognized in the fossil record probably depends on how quickly an open pond silts in or dries up and allows the vegetation to take over the former aquatic area. The geochronology indicates that it must be less than the standard deviations of the pertinent radiocarbon ages.

As shown in Figure 4.10, both aquatic and terrestrial species increase in number during the period represented by the Coro marl. Apparently the terrestrial habitats were increasing more rapidly than the aquatic habitats. During a short period within the deposition of the Graveyard sand, there was a vast increase in both aquatic and terrestrial species. The indication is that the site experienced sufficient environmental change to greatly increase the amount of available aquatic and terrestrial habitats. How much of an increase, if any, in spring discharge occurred during this time cannot be estimated from just the change in molluscs. But the molluscs do indicate that there was at least an increase in the amount of available water to the point where new microhabitats were being developed. The molluscs present in the Clanton clay and the Donnet silt indicate that both aquatic and terrestrial habitats were decreasing. What happened during the erosional hiatus after the Donnet silt deposition is not indicated due to the lack of recovered fossils. The period represented by the Weik alluvium is a mixture of events. It was a time when aquatic species were at an all time low, and yet the number of terrestrial species indicates an increase of habitats compared to just prior to the erosional hiatus. The terrestrial species composition alters most significantly during the time represented by the McCool alluvium. However, the number of aquatic species indicates that a brief ponding period due to either groundwater seepage or damming (arroyo wall collapse) occurred. Short term pooling cannot be estimated solely by the mollusc record.

The fossil molluscan habitat reconstructions of both fossil sites do not always correspond directly with the relatively sparse pollen data that have been obtained from southern Arizona (for a review see Mead 1991; Mead and Van Devender 1991; Spaulding and others 1983). Martin (1963a, 1963b; Hevly and Martin 1961) determined that prior to 20,000 B.P., a pine parkland bordered pluvial Lake Cochise (Willcox Playa) at 1,270 m (4,175 feet) elevation (Fig. 4.1). The molluscan assemblages from the Lehner and Murray Springs sites indicate that a pine parkland similar to Martin's Lake Cochise reconstruction did not occur at the Clovis sites, but that an oak woodland to oak woodland-plains grassland did occur, at least locally. There are no well-dated pollen data for southeastern Arizona that represent the time 20,000 to 12,000 B.P. The molluscan assemblages from the two fossil sites indicate that an oak woodland to mixed oak woodland-plains grassland with possible desert grassland occurred at the sites. Plant macrofossils from packrat middens from the Sonoran Desert, less than 100 km (62 miles) northwest of the molluscan sites, suggest that pinyon-juniper-oak woodland existed on rocky substrates (Mead and Van Devender 1991; Spaulding and others 1983; Van Devender 1973; see synthesis of region in Van Devender 1990a, 1990b).

A pollen profile from the Lehner Ranch Arroyo (Mehringer and Haynes 1965) indicates that by 11,200 B.P. at least part, if not all, of the upper San Pedro Valley contained a plains grassland. The molluscan assemblage data from the Murray Springs Site in part supports the pollen data, in that a desert grassland to plains grassland of some sort did occur in the valley. Whereas a pollen profile is a representative of a regional pollen rain, the molluscan assemblage, in this case, is a sample of a local habitat. The molluscs seem to indicate not only that the valley was predominantly a grassland of sorts, but that immediately around isolated spring areas an oak woodland-plains grassland to oak woodland occurred. The valley may have been dominated by grassland but dotted by oases of oak woodland or cienegas.

Mehringer and Haynes (1965) and Mehringer and others (1967) have indicated that pluvial pollen ceases in the Southwestern alluvial record between 13,000 and 12,000 B.P., therefore marking the end of the glacial-age environments. The Murray Springs Site molluscan assemblage would tend to confirm this; however, the Lehner Site does not corroborate it. The woodland molluscs disappear from the Murray Springs Site by about 11,000 B.P., but at the Lehner Site, woodland molluscs stay on-site until sometime during the deposition of the Donnet silt (approximately 9,000 to 8,000 B.P.; Table 4.2). Again, the pollen is representative of the region and would fairly quickly respond to climatic changes, whereas the molluscs in the Murray Springs and Lehner formations are local indicators and respond predominantly to the spring discharge. The Lehner Site today is about 11 km (7 miles) from oak-grassland at the base of the Huachuca Mountains, whereas Murray Springs is about 15 km (9.4 miles) away. A relict Emory oak that occurred as late as 1883 a few miles north of Lewis Springs (Fig. 2.2) was gone by 1960 (Hastings and Turner 1965, Fig. 49*a*).

The overall character of the environments in the upper San Pedro Valley has changed very little during the last 30,000 years. The molluscs from both fossil sites indicate that the upper San Pedro Valley contained a grassland to oak woodland-plains grassland at and immediately around the cienegas in the valley from before 30,000 B.P. to at least 8,000 B.P. and from at least 3000 B.P. to 1000 B.P. A desert grassland to oak woodland-plains grassland almost fills the valley bottom today. An abrupt change does occur with the molluscs that are related to spring discharge, but this is a local change. What has caused the springs to cease discharge at the two fossil sites is not known for certain, but it could be due to a fluctuating water table (Chapter 2; Haynes 1973). Perhaps a climatic change to less precipitation, a switch in seasonality, or both affected the spring recharge. Presumably such a climatic change would have affected other springs in the San Pedro and other adjacent valleys. As mentioned earlier, numerous springs of unknown antiquity still occur in southeastern Arizona. A thorough study of these spring areas might lead to a better understanding of Arizona's late Pleistocene and Holocene environmental changes.

EVALUATION OF THE FAUNAL RECORD

Sedimentary strata were sampled from the Lehner and Murray Springs sites to recover molluscs that could be used in reconstructing the paleoenvironments of the sites and the upper San Pedro Valley. Analysis of the 30,000-year sedimentary record determined that the valley-wide environmental habitats had changed little throughout the late Wisconsin. The major difference from the pre-20th-century habitat seems to be the occurrence of springs with surrounding local oak woodland habitat, similar to extant cienegas near the San Pedro Valley. The fossil molluscan study of these two sites is the first complete study of its kind for Wisconsin-age sediments in southeastern Arizona. The fossil molluscs are instrumental in reconstructing the hydrological history and local environments of the sites. Many questions have been answered, but many new questions have been raised. For example, are the Lehner and Murray Springs sites typical spring localities in the upper San Pedro Valley? Questions such as this and answers such as those within this report can be evaluated by the same multidisciplinary approach used at Lehner and Murray Springs to excavate additional sites within southeastern Arizona. Springs and cienegas such as the St. David Spring, the Knipe Cienega, the Cienega de Agua Fria in Sonora, and a host of smaller, more isolated springs in Arizona, may be useful in future evaluations.

Acknowledgments. I thank the late Joe C. Bequaert who first systematically collected the molluscs at the Murray Springs and Lehner sites and who unselfishly gave me all his field notes and faunal descriptions for the initiation of this report. I especially thank C. Vance Haynes for his encouragement and guidance during my study of the San Pedro Valley molluscs and his helpful editing of this chapter. Helpful comments and discussions from a malacologist's viewpoint and additional shell identifications were amply supplied by Albert R. Mead, Walter B. Miller, Artie L. Metcalf, Carl Christensen, and Richard H. Russell. Additional manuscript comments were supplied by Paul S. Martin, Vera Markgraf, Thomas R. Van Devender, H. Dave Dyer, Karl W. Flessa, Robert S. Thompson, and Karin K. Olsson. Deborah Gaines provided comments on manuscript style and typed earlier editions of the manuscript.

Note: This chapter is based on a manuscript entitled "The Late Pleistocene and Holocene Molluscs of the Murray Springs Clovis Site, Arizona" submitted in lieu of a thesis to the faculty of the Department of Geosciences in partial fulfillment of the requirements for the degree of Master of Science at the University of Arizona in 1979. The chapter was edited and some mollusc terminology revised in 2005 to accord with present usage.

CHAPTER FIVE

Buried Animal Kills and Processing Localities, Areas 1–5

E. Thomas Hemmings

Chapter 5 is compiled from two of Hemmings' unpublished manuscripts (1970, 1975). It has been edited so as to preserve Hemmings' writing style and ideas. To provide readers with current information about the site, results from the 1970 and 1971 field seasons and from more recent work have been added by the volume editors.

Curry Draw was first surveyed for Gila Pueblo in the late 1930s by E. B. Sayles, who found Cochise (Archaic) artifacts eroding out along the arroyo and concentrated in one area. Sayles returned in 1953 and collected a sample of carbonaceous earth from the arroyo wall overlying a mammoth tusk and below the artifacts. The sample (A-69) was subsequently radiocarbon dated 8270 ± 260 years B.P. (Damon and Long 1962). This site (AZ EE:8:13 ASM) was located at a seep spring, marked by dense vegetation and now dissected, known as Murray Springs from an abandoned early 20th-century homesite. This locality was revisited in the early 1960s by Paul S. Martin for palynological and stratigraphic work, and it has particular significance for the nature of the Altithermal climate (Martin 1963c; Mehringer and others 1967), as discussed in Chapter 2.

Aerial photographs taken in 1935 (Fig. 2.9a) show that Sayles had no opportunity to observe Clovis artifacts and extinct animal remains subsequently exposed 1 km (0.6 mile) farther upstream in Curry Draw, for the headcut had not reached their location. The Murray Springs Site (AZ EE:8:25 ASM), was discovered in the spring of 1966 by C. Vance Haynes, Jr., and Peter J. Mehringer, Jr., during reconnaissance of Curry Draw (Chapter 1; Haynes 1968b). It is one of the few Paleoindian sites in the western United States that was not originally discovered and reported by ranchers or amateur archaeologists. Although no artifacts were at first observed, the alluvial stratigraphy, particularly a conspicuous black marker horizon (Stratum F_2; the "black mat") and the occurrence of mammoth bones nearly duplicated conditions at the Lehner Site 17 km (10.5 miles) south (Fig. 1.2). Chapter 2 describes the geological setting of the site.

METHODS OF INVESTIGATION

Four student crews ranging from 8 to 14 persons excavated the buried kill loci (Areas 1–5) at Murray Springs. An additional number of volunteers and specialists in various capacities contributed their efforts frequently during excavations (Appendix G). Summer field seasons ran from 6 June to 30 June 1966, 5 June to 28 July 1967, 3 June to 26 July 1968, and 4 June to 12 July 1969. Jonathan Gell conducted topographic mapping (Fig. 1.3) of the site area during 1966 and 1970. Within the excavated area horizontal control was maintained by a 2-m grid system; east-west rows of stakes were lettered and north-south rows numbered. Each grid square was identified by the letter and number coordinates of the southwest stake. Vertical control was maintained by means of three datum planes: one above the modern terrain of the site area used for topographic mapping, a second slightly above the buried Clovis occupation surface used for convenient stratigraphic recording and vertical measurements to cultural remains, and a third slightly below the Clovis occupation surface used as the datum for contouring that surface at 20 cm intervals.

Of the eight different site areas we defined (Fig. 1.3), seven are described in detail in the following sections of this chapter and Chapter 7. The eighth, consisting of buried spring conduits, is described in Chapter 2. The boundaries of site areas were placed whenever possible where sterile zones intervened between concentrations of cultural remains, but were partially determined by the extent of excavation or the geological removal of deposits as well. Except in a general way the site areas do not represent phases of excavation, but are intended to reflect prehistoric utilization of the site that resulted in discrete concentrations of remains. Areas 1 through 5 have provided evidence of a series of kills of large herbivores and of associated processing activities, Areas 6 and 7 represent the remains of a brief hunting camp (Chapter 7), and Area 8 is a pre-Clovis springhead area (Chapter 2). Area 9 was excavated in 2001 (Appendix E).

Examination of the arroyo exposure showed that overlying sediments were essentially sterile, so this overburden was removed by backhoe to approximately 20 cm above the Clovis level at the base of the black mat. We used shovels down to the top of the black mat, then small tools to remove the mat. An attempt was made to locate every artifact and item of cultural debris in situ and to maintain precise horizontal and vertical proveniences. Excavated earth was continuously screened through one-quarter inch hardware cloth (and in certain cases finer meshes) to recover artifacts. A large part of the site consisted of a clearly marked occupation surface and provided cultural materials in primary archaeological context. The method of excavation and recording was extremely time-consuming but warranted by the use to which the provenience information was applied.

There were three kinds of occurrences of archaeological materials encountered during excavation of Murray Springs: a stream deposit containing contemporaneous materials both laterally and vertically dispersed, an occupation surface or "floor" providing materials in undisturbed or slightly disturbed context, and an old land surface only slightly buried by younger deposits with materials in disturbed (bioturbated) context.

All macroscopic materials resulting from Clovis occupation of the site were collected for laboratory study except some vertebrate remains too poorly preserved to warrant preservation. One objective of this analysis was to discover meaningful variation in cultural materials between and within site areas which, in spatial context, could be related to human activities.

A second objective was to permit empirical comparison of the site assemblage with other site assemblages. Materials collected included (1) flaked stone tools, (2) flaked lithic debris, (3) bone tools, (4) worked bone, (5) manuports (anomalous rocks or rock fragments from occupation floors), (6) vertebrate remains, (7) burned bone, and (8) plant macrofossil (charcoal) remains. Some inferences drawn from initial analysis of these collections are presented in the descriptions of site areas; more detailed analytical treatment is in Chapter 8 and Appendix C. Initial analyses made use of microscopic techniques (Semenov 1964), comparative vertebrate and lithic collections, and expert assistance.

STRATIGRAPHY OF THE CLOVIS OCCUPATION

The stratigraphic context of Clovis occupation at Murray Springs includes a channel fill, a marked erosional surface, and a bioturbated zone at or near the modern surface. The complex sequence of erosional and depositional events and the formation of paleosols, as reflected in this sequence, are discussed in greater detail by Haynes in Chapter 2. Radiocarbon age determinations obtained from the various strata are listed in Appendix A and shown, where possible, on stratigraphic profiles in Chapter 2. The ages are consistent with superposition and with the occurrence of a Rancholabrean vertebrate fauna in the lowermost strata.

The alluvial Millville Formation and lacustrine-paludal Murray Springs Formation were successively deposited within a drainageway coincident with, but larger than, Curry Draw. The latter formation has been attributed to ponds and marshes occupying the upper San Pedro Valley from about 29,000 B.P. to 14,000 years B.P. (Chapter 2). All of the strata were affected by erosion after 14,000 B.P., and the resultant, irregular surface and stream channel were utilized by people and animals.

Several lines of evidence indicate the persistence of wet conditions followed by dry during the Clovis presence at the site. The Graveyard Member of the Murray Springs Formation, Stratum F_1, consists primarily of channel fill deposited by a small stream at the time of occupation. It contains occupational debris and it and the stream margins appear to have been walked upon by large animals. Charcoal from Stratum

F_1 represents wood of riparian species, mainly ash (*Fraxinus*) with some dicotyledon, possibly wild grape (*Vitis*), and less common specimens of maple (*Acer*) and *Juniperus* (Appendix B in Hemmings 1970). The animals from this deposit include a megafauna that must have required a large, dependable, water supply (Saunders 1983). Presumably such a water supply attracted these animals to the site in numbers and provided the opportunity for predation by hunters as drought ensued.

Throughout most of the excavated site area conditions of nondeposition, without significant erosive disturbance, prevailed during Clovis occupation. After the water table dropped to its lowest level, shortly after final deposition of cultural remains on the occupation surface, the local water table rose above the low-lying parts of the site and a black, fine-grained, organic sediment, the Clanton Ranch Member (Stratum F_2 of the Lehner Ranch Formation), was thinly deposited in these areas. A similar event is recorded by the stratigraphy of the Lehner and Escapule sites to the south (Haury and others 1959; Hemmings and Haynes 1969). The origin of this "black mat" is not completely understood, but it may represent a relatively rapid accumulation of organic matter as a result of a series of algal blooms in still water (Rogers in Appendix B). Locally, it is interbedded with a marl or chalk, possibly a spring deposit of related algal origin. The significance of the black mat is that it enhanced preservation by rapid but gentle burial of cultural remains in low-lying occupation areas.

In areas of higher terrain subsequent weathering and erosion acted on the unburied cultural materials. In some areas these materials were eventually covered by the deposition of gray calcareous silt (Stratum F_3), the Donnet Ranch Member, and in others they remain unburied to the present time (Chapter 7). In both cases virtually all organic remains were removed, and lateral and vertical displacement of nonperishable materials has occurred through bioturbation.

Most contacts between Late Quaternary strata (formations and members) at Murray Springs are considered erosional or in part erosional by Haynes (Chapter 2). In most cases minor breaks between conformable strata are represented, except where channel cutting has occurred. The most important of these unconformities (or disconformities) was the result of erosion following the deposition of the Murray Springs Formation and prior to deposition of the Lehner Ranch Formation alluvium. In the early part of this hiatus some of the Millville and Murray Springs formations were eroded away between about 14,000 B.P. and 11,500 B.P., leaving an irregular surface in the site area that became the surface of the land occupied by the Clovis people and their prey. Little weathering of the occupation surface or its contents seems to have taken place during this latter interval. No soil development on underlying strata has been observed. Some exposed bone was slightly weathered, and chert artifacts were occasionally lightly patinated but more often remained remarkably fresh. Shortly after 10,900 B.P. or 13,000 years ago (Chapter 2), the fine-grained black mat Clanton Ranch Member of the Lehner Ranch Formation was deposited over most of the low-lying site area, sealing the cultural materials. Surface corrosion of bones in contact with the acidic black mat as well as chemical alteration and compression damage were common exceptions to otherwise excellent preservation. Thus ideal conditions for preservation of cultural materials in primary archaeological context were present in these areas of the site.

VERTEBRATE REMAINS

Vertebrate remains from Murray Springs (Appendix D) comprise one of the largest and most important collections from the San Pedro Valley (Saunders 1983). Nearly all of these remains are from extinct species of bison, mammoth, and horse, evidently all important food animals. In many cases a number of skeletal elements can be definitely attributed to an individual animal.

The animal remains, in the context of other cultural and natural materials on the site, provide direct evidence for aspects of Clovis subsistence ecology. Therefore, emphasis in the study of the vertebrate remains has been on inferences about the system of knowledge and behavior of this society with respect to animals (ethnozoology), rather than on paleontology. Faunal analysis can contribute to a variety of inferences about an extinct culture beyond the identification of species associated with humans and estimation of numbers of individuals (Wheat 1967). Specifically, such questions as hunting techniques in relation to animal behavior, selection of game by age and sex, butchering techniques and animal physiology, and utilization of animal products are considered in subsequent sections of this chapter. Since Murray Springs, like other excavated kill sites in the San Pedro Valley, primarily reflects the relationship of a hunting society and certain large herbivores, inferences largely concern this aspect of the cultural ecological system. However, many valid, useful inferences in this domain of subsistence ecology can certainly be drawn from the available data.

Bone Preservation

An important requirement for interpretation of these remains was assessment of the adequacy of preservation. All bone uncovered was light and friable until preservative was applied; enamel and dentine components of teeth were usually well preserved, but cement was generally absent. Presumably the loss of indigenous bone organic matter is well advanced as in the case of mammoth bone of comparable age from the Lehner Site (Haynes 1967). Loss of organic substance and calcification have been the dominant processes of fossilization (Cook and others 1962).

Field observations suggested that within the essentially contemporaneous collection of vertebrate remains resulting from occupation there is variation in preservation among species, among skeletal elements, and among areas of the site. Mammoth skeletal elements were relatively well preserved in all parts of the site except at the surface in Area 7, whereas horses were represented almost entirely by teeth. Bison, camel, and other species were intermediate in respect to these extremes of preservation.

Small skeletal elements with thin layers of compact tissue over cancellous structure (such as vertebrae, ribs, carpals, tarsals, phalanges, and epiphyses of long bones) were poorly preserved in all species. The dense, compact tissue of long bones was more resistant, but shafts, especially those with large medullary cavities, were normally flattened and compressed. The periosteal surfaces of most bones were altered to the extent that butchering marks, if ever present, are represented by only a few doubtful examples. Teeth of all species were about equally well preserved.

Preservation of contemporaneous vertebrate remains contrasts sharply among site areas. Specimens from a small stream channel deposit in Areas 1 and 2 were relatively well preserved, but much of the material from occupation floors in Areas 3, 4, and 5 was corroded, compressed, and occasionally comminuted. Except for fragments of a mammoth long bone and a mammoth tooth, no organic material survived in Areas 6 and 7. These surface areas have remained only shallowly buried and partially exposed since the time of Clovis occupation. Presumably differences in preservation among site areas are due to a combination of differential exposure to weathering and corrosion by contact with the acidic black mat.

WOLF CREEK DEPOSITS AREAS 1 AND 2

The two initial excavations at Murray Springs in 1966 were located about 35 m apart on the South and North branches of Curry Draw (Fig. 1.3). These excavations, originally designated Locality 1 and Locality 2, respectively, used identical but separate grid systems and duplicate sets of records. In the course of expanding excavations on the South Branch in 1967 and 1968, other discrete site areas were recognized, and the original locality designations were changed to Areas 1 and 2. Area 1 received additional excavation in 1971, when the area was extended to the south and east.

Areas 1 and 2 were located at points where a fossil stream channel, called Wolf Creek (Chapter 2), intersects the walls of the modern arroyo. These deposits fostered discovery of the site, because the exposed channel fill contained abundant bone, including large mammoth bones. Excavation in Area 1 on the South Branch of Curry Draw covered about 88 square meters and that in Area 2 on the North Branch about 106 square meters. Figure 5.1 shows Area 1 upon completion of excavation in 1966. An intervening section of the stream channel 15 m long between Area 2 and the South Branch remains unexcavated and undoubtedly contains additional vertebrate remains. Another substantial section of the stream deposit and its remains were carried away by headward cutting of the South Branch of Curry Draw after the 1955 aerial photo (Fig. 2.9b) and the discovery of the site in 1966. In addition to bone, charcoal was dispersed through the channel fill in both excavations, but chert and chalcedony flakes were found only in Area 1. On the basis of subsequent excavations we concluded that the remains in the channel fill of Area 1 represented refuse from the activities of Clovis hunters adjacent to the western and eastern banks of the stream.

The Wolf Creek fossil tributary, approximately following the East Swale, contained channel sands of

Figure 5.1. The Murray Springs Clovis Site, June 1966. View across the South Branch of Curry Draw to Area 1; deep overburden removed prior to excavation of the cultural deposit.

Figure 5.2. Mammoth remains in Area 2 include a tusk and fragmentary postcranial elements in the F_1 channel fill.

the Graveyard Gulch Member. The maximum observed depth of the channel deposit of Wolf Creek was about 0.5 m on the axis of the channel in Area 1 and 1 m in Area 2, which may be on the edge of a spring conduit (Chapter 2). The maximum width of the deposit, approximately the distance between banks of the stream, was 6 m upstream in Area 1 and 7 m downstream in Area 2. The course of the fossil stream was north-northeast, leading into Bison Kill Creek beyond the north edge of Area 2 (Plate 8). Bison Kill Creek was a larger, east-draining, buried tributary of the San Pedro River and had approximately the same course as the North Branch of modern Curry Draw. The channel fill consisted of coarse sand over gravel and cobble-sized particles derived primarily as lag from the underlying Millville alluvium.

Bone occurred in concentrations within the channel fill (Fig. 5.2). It was possible to recognize the partial remains of individual animals in both Areas 1 and 2. The skeletal elements of one individual were vertically dispersed through the channel fill, indicating the deposit may have accumulated rapidly. However, with a few exceptions, the vertebrate specimens recovered showed no signs of rolling or abrasion and could not have been transported more than a short distance. Most long bones and other elongated elements occurred in a horizontal position, but some were inclined sharply in various directions, possibly worked into the channel fill by large animals utilizing the stream bed.

Vertebrate Remains

About 220 vertebrate specimens (including groups of elements) were catalogued (Appendix D) and 210 of them were identified in the course of excavation of the Wolf Creek channel deposit in Areas 1 and 2 (Fig. 1.4). The distribution of 170 specimens within the channel fill, believed to represent cultural debris, is evident in Figures 5.3 and 5.4. Most of the vertebrate remains recovered in Areas 1 and 2 came from two mammoths and two bison. Other individuals and other species were represented only by scattered teeth and postcranial elements, including one or more individual bison, horses, camels, and canids.

Preservation of bones and teeth from the channel deposit was superior to that of remains from excavated areas of the occupation surface on the adjacent banks. Bones from the channel may have been less exposed to weathering. Preservation was not sufficient for detecting cutting marks that might be expected to occur

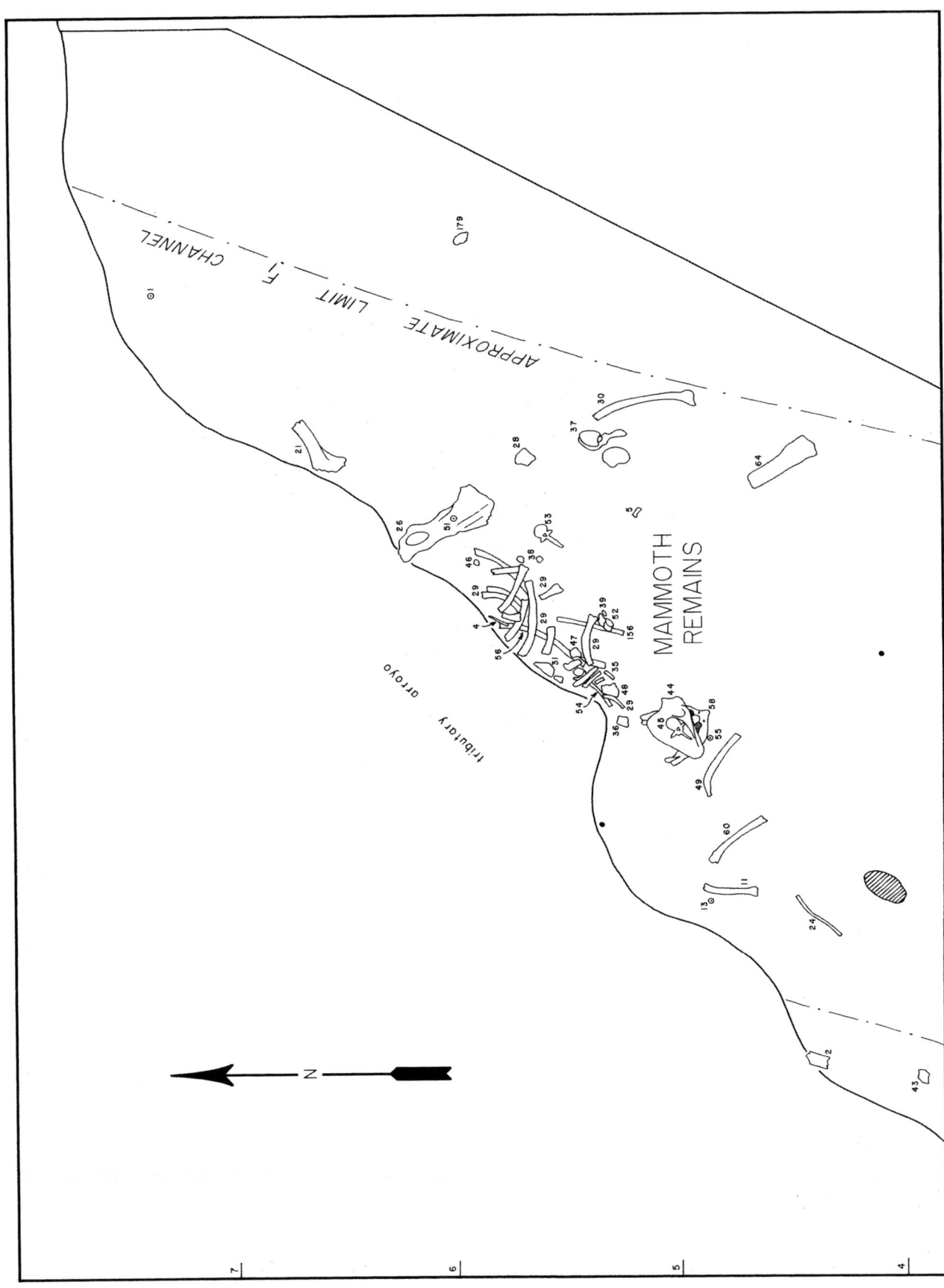

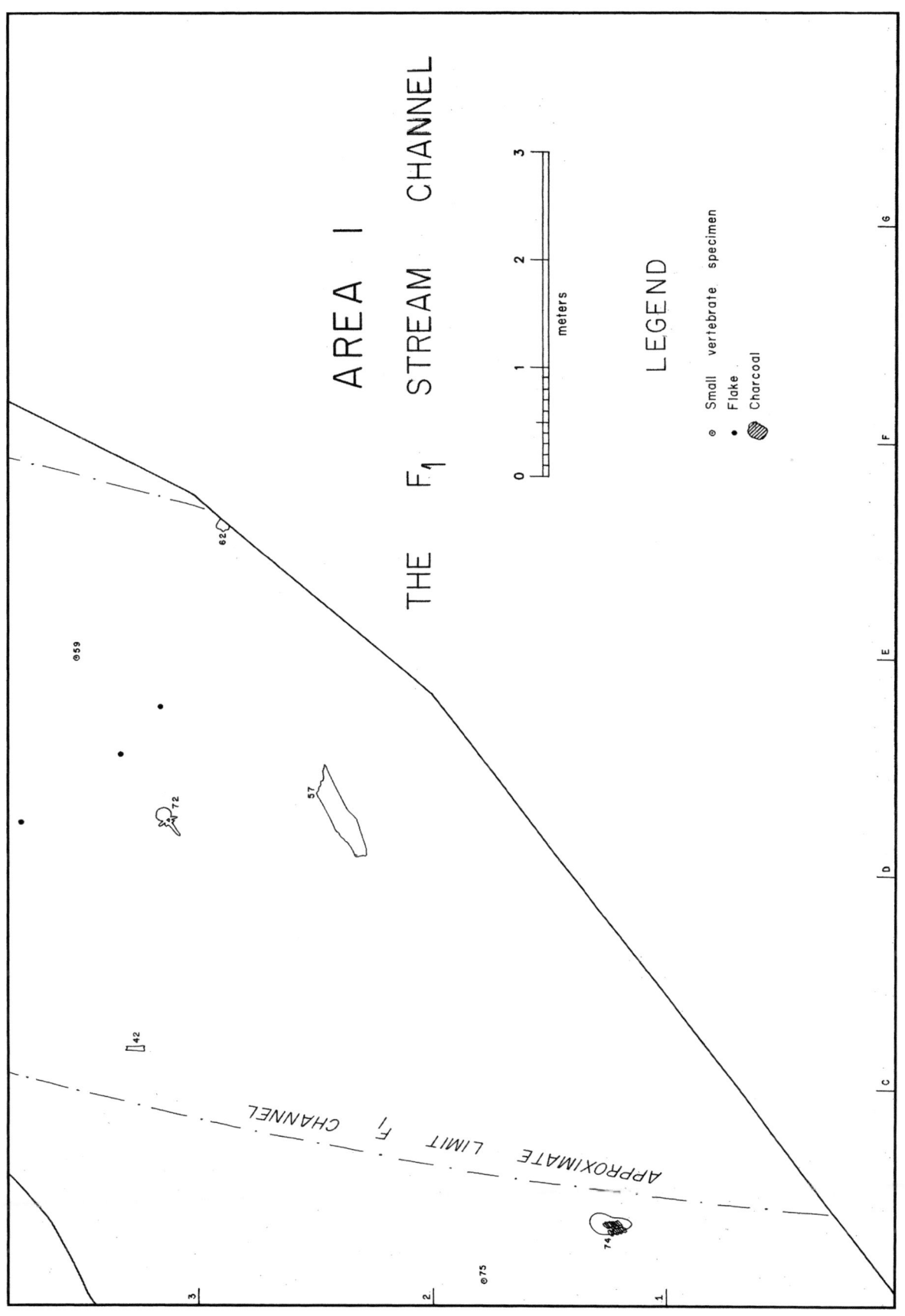

Figure 5.3. Distribution of remains in Area 1.

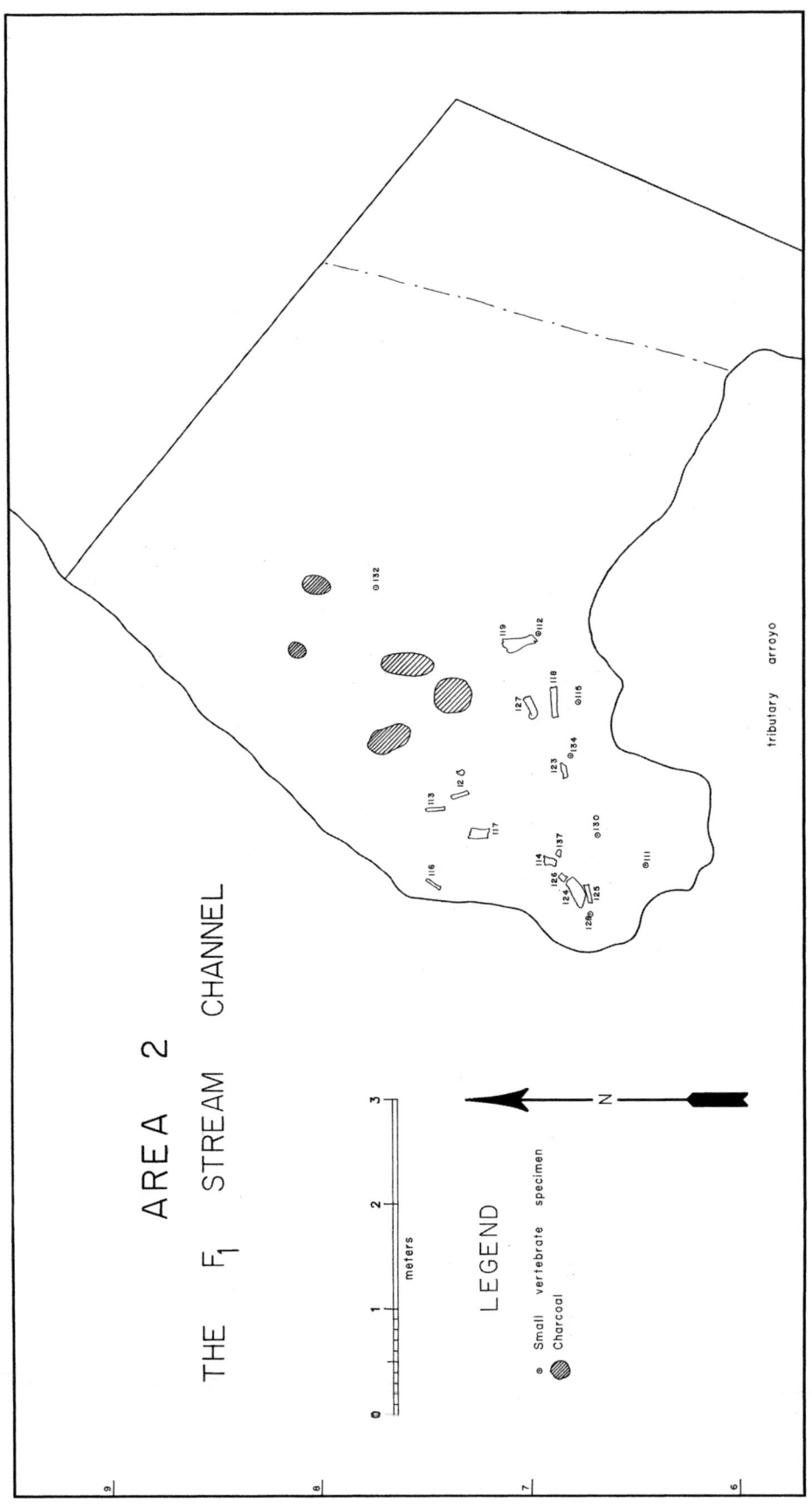

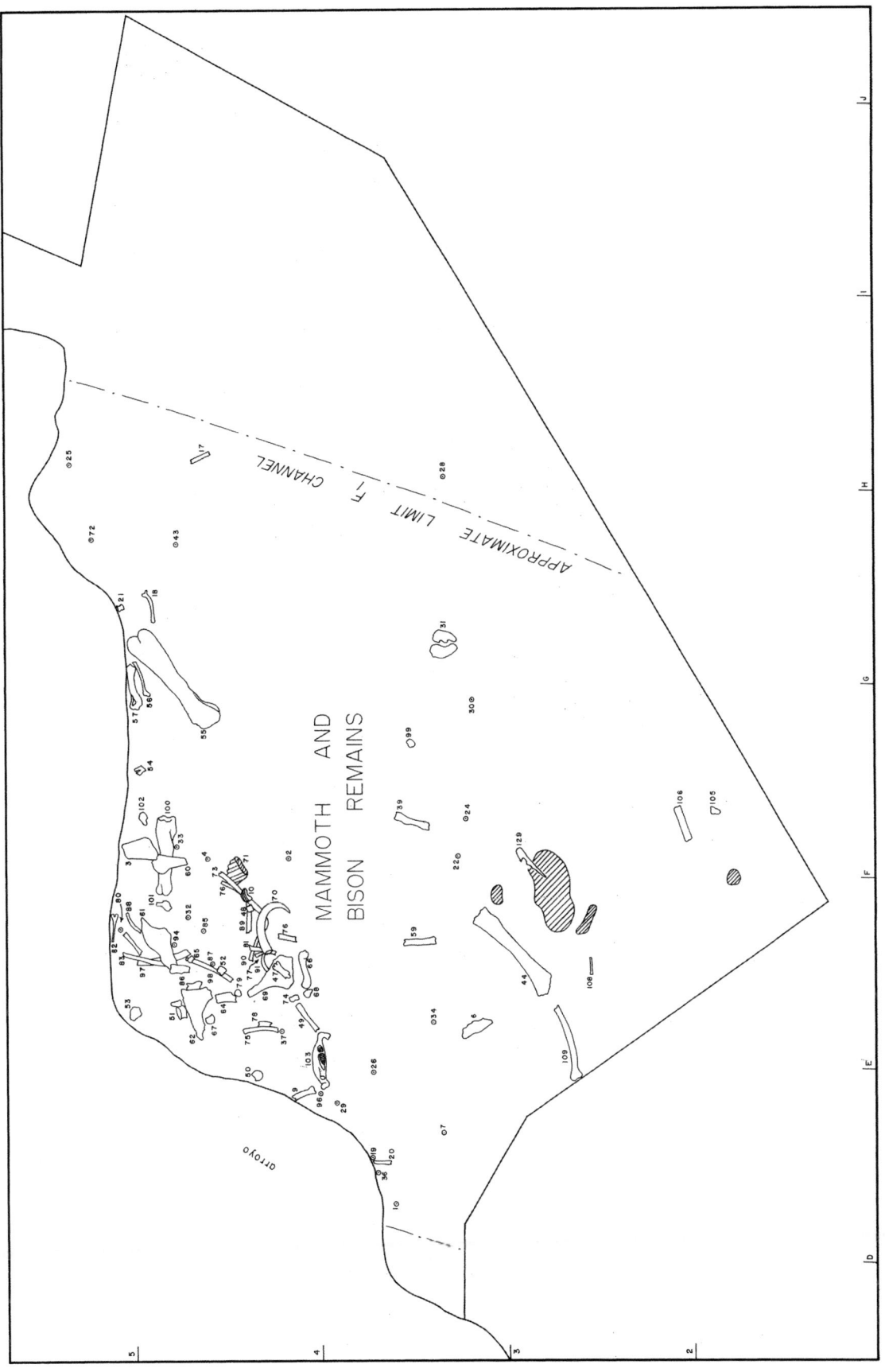

Figure 5.4. Distribution of remains in Area 2.

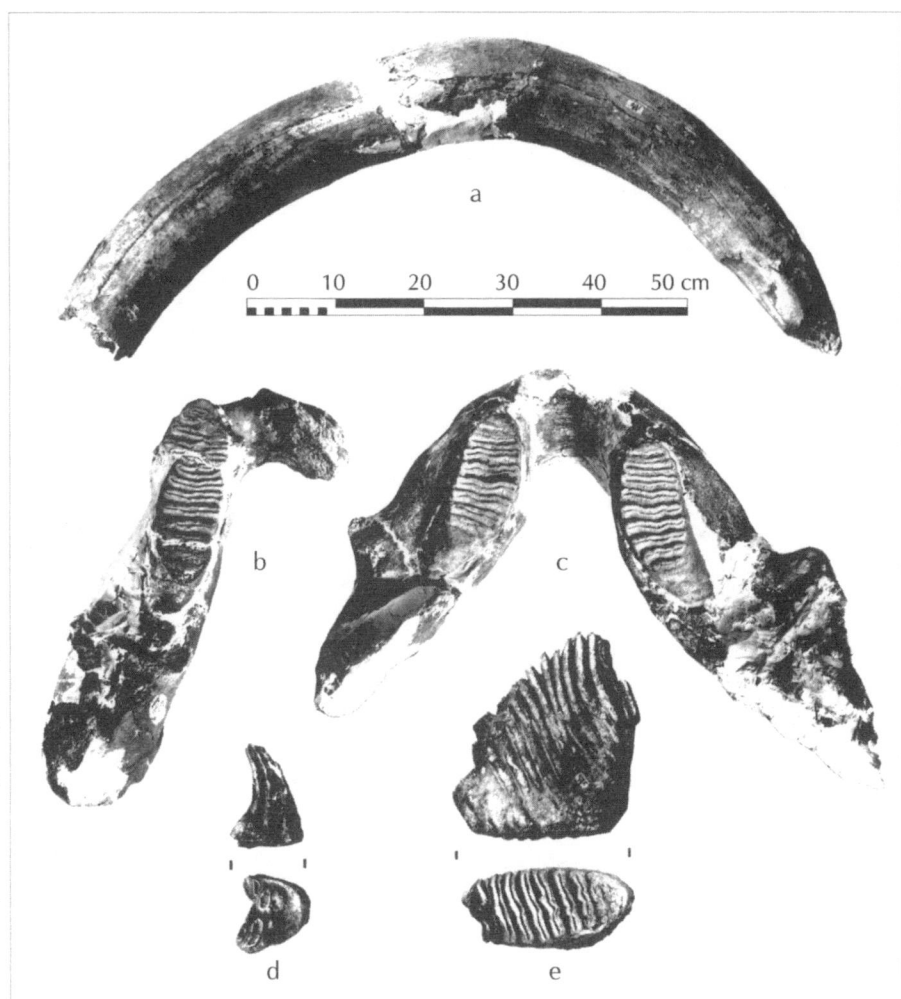

Figure 5.5. Mammoth remains from Areas 1 and 2: *a*, tusk; *b*, occlusal view of left mandibular ramus with M_2 and M_3; *c*, occlusal view of mandible with LM_3 and RM_3; *d*, stub of RM_2, buccal and occlusal views; *e*, RM^3, lingual and occlusal views. All except *c* are from one individual in Area 2; *c* is from Area 1.

on refuse bone from the adjacent occupation surface. Some of the best preserved specimens are shown in Figures 5.5 and 5.6.

Area 1 Mammoths

In Area 1 the incomplete remains of an adult mammoth were concentrated in an area of about 6 square meters in the bed of the channel (Figs. 5.3 and 1.4*d*, *e*). The bone concentration was truncated by the modern arroyo. Although not an articulated carcass, anterior elements (including a mandible and scapula) occurred at the southwest end, and posterior elements (including the pelvis) occurred at the northeast end of the concentration; distributed in between were fragmentary ribs and vertebrae. A tibia and an unidentified long bone shaft were located a few meters to the south.

The lower third molars in the mandible contained 17 to 18 tooth plates with a lamellar frequency (plates per 100 mm) of 6 to 7 (Fig. 5.5*c*). These and other tooth characteristics, such as size, hypsodonty, enamel width, and spacing of plates, are within the range of variation in grinding teeth of *Mammuthus columbi* (Lance 1953: 21, 1959: 36; Osborn 1942: 76; Saunders 1970; Whitmore and others 1967: 1480). The anterior 10 plates of each molar were in wear, suggesting by analogy with living elephants an animal between 41 and 47 years old (Laws 1966: 13, 30). The mandible, scapula, and tibia, the only measurable elements recovered, were relatively small and gracile in comparison to these elements in other adult Columbian mammoths from Murray Springs and other late Quaternary sites in the San Pedro Valley. The remains may thus represent a full-grown, middle-aged cow.

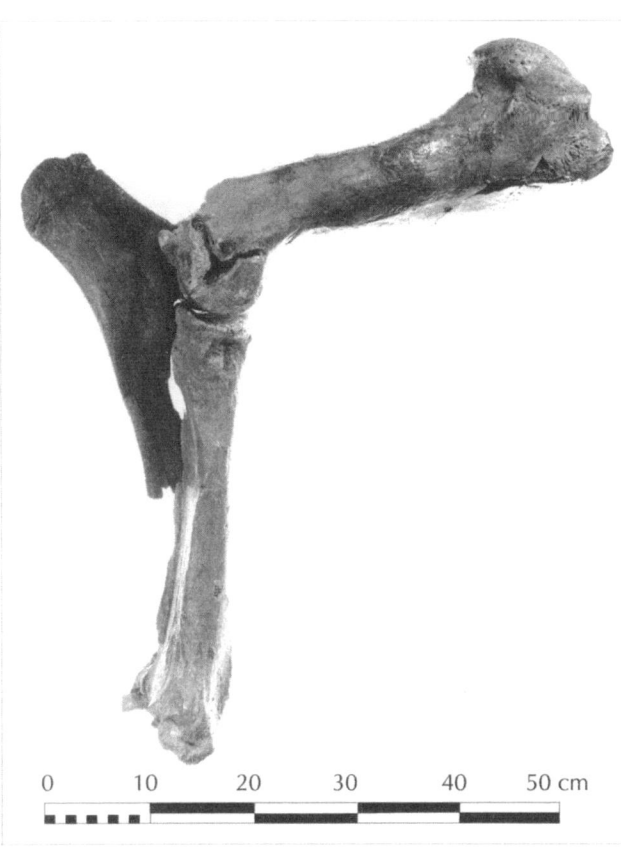

Figure 5.6. Bison upper left forelimb from Area 2. Medial view of humerus, radius, and ulna of a single individual, probably a large bull.

Part of a mammoth skull appeared to be under the Sobaipuri Member between grids F3 and F4 (Chapter 2; Plate 7, Profile D), but may have been against the right bank of Wolf Creek and subsequently pressed into the Sobaipuri mud by overburden pressure. If so, the skull could pertain to the Area 1 mammoth; it could also represent a second, geologically more ancient mammoth.

Area 2 Mammoths

In Area 2 disarticulated elements of two Columbian mammoths of differing size were recovered in an area of about 16 square meters of the channel deposit (Fig. 5.4). Modern arroyo-cutting had removed a part of the bone concentration. One, the smaller individual, was represented by a left mandibular ramus and rostrum with lower second and third molars (Fig. 5.5b), isolated lower second (Fig. 5.5d) and upper third molars (Fig. 5.5e), and a tusk (Fig. 5.5a). Postcranial elements included a humerus, fragmentary ribs and vertebrae, two innominates, and a sacrum. The condition of tooth eruption and wear in the lower dentition is that of a young adult between 34 and 41 years of age (Laws 1966: 13, 30). The small size of the tusk, measuring 1,215 mm on the outside curve, and of the postcranial elements again seem to indicate a female, probably sexually mature and near full growth.

Another mammoth in Area 2 was represented by a number of postcranial elements including a robust humerus and femur, which are distinctly large in comparison to the other Area 2 specimens and probably belonged to a mature bull. The overall length of the humerus exceeds that of the cow from Area 2, but is less than the length of the humerus of the Naco mammoth (Lance 1953).

Bison

The channel deposit in Area 1 produced only a few bison cheek teeth and postcranial elements attributable to the remains of individual animals from the occupation surface in Area 3 to the west (see Fig. 5.7).

In Area 2 the concentration of bone in the bed of the channel contained scattered elements of two bison. A smaller individual was represented by cheek teeth, two humeri, two scapulae, and other fragmentary postcranial elements. A larger animal's remains included heavily worn cheek teeth; a disarticulated, robust left forelimb (Fig. 5.6); and fragmentary postcranial elements. Although diagnostic skulls with horn cores were lacking, the species is presumably that tentatively identified from remains in Area 4 as *Bison antiquus*. The well-preserved long bones of both animals are relatively large, robust, and heavily muscle-scarred when compared to bison remains from Area 4. It seems likely that the remains from Area 2 are those of two mature bison bulls with characteristically heavy forequarters, including one old adult.

Camels

A small number of elements of one or more camels were recovered from the channel deposit in Area 2, including cheek teeth and incisors, an axis vertebra, another cervical vertebra, a thoracic vertebra, a femur, and a navicular. The excellent condition and number of these specimens probably preclude reworking from older sediments and adduce penecontemporaneity with humans at Murray Springs. The femur is that of a juvenile. The size and morphological characters of teeth and skeletal elements, particularly the axis and navicular, compare closely with the large Rancholabrean species *Camelops hesternus* (Webb 1965: 51, 54; but see Saunders 1983 for another view).

Horses

Cheek teeth and incisors of two or more adult horses were scattered in the channel deposit in Areas 1 and 2. No skeletal elements attributable to horse were recovered, although the teeth were excellently preserved and probably not reworked from older strata. The horse teeth have not been studied in detail, but seem to differ little from the living species, *Equus caballus*. They may well belong to the common Rancholabrean horse, *Equus occidentalis*, identified in a stratum of comparable age at Ventana Cave (Colbert 1950).

Canids

A canid metatarsal IV and upper canine were recovered from the channel deposit in Area 2. The length of the metatarsal is below the range of mean lengths for this element in the extinct wolf, *Canis dirus*, from several pits at Rancho la Brea (Nigra and Lance 1947). The metatarsal and canine, if transported by the stream, may have belonged to a wolf whose partial remains were recovered from the occupation surface in Area 3, 40 m southwest. The mandible of this animal, however, has been identified as *C. dirus*.

Artifacts

One chert and four chalcedony flakes were recovered during the first field season from the channel deposit in Area 1 within 3 m of the concentration of mammoth remains (Fig. 5.3). Except for an unworked obsidian nodule no other artifacts were recovered in Area 1 and none at all in Area 2. The raw material of the flakes is identical to chert and chalcedony debitage that occurred in concentrations in knapping areas on the occupation surface to the west and southwest in Area 3. None of the flakes show utilization or effects of rolling or abrasion, although they are relatively large and thin. One flake retains the small striking platform on the interior surface, prior flake removal scars on the exterior surface, and a thin expanding shape typical of flakes of bifacial retouch (Bordes 1961: 6). The edge of the biface had been ground before the flake was detached. Probably all five specimens represent flakes of bifacial retouch produced in knapping activities near the stream margin and inadvertently introduced into the channel deposit.

The obsidian nodule came from the arroyo exposure of the bone bed and could not confidently be said to be contemporary, but obsidian hydration dating subsequently showed it to be the same age as similar material from the Clovis occupation surface in Area 3 (C. W. Meighan, personal communication).

Charcoal

Charcoal occurred frequently as dispersed flecks and concentrated in natural masses up to 40 cm in diameter throughout the channel fill (Figs. 5.3, 5.4). Samples were collected for radiocarbon dating and wood identification (Chapter 2). The first, collected from the Area 1 headcut before excavation began, dated 11,150 ± 450 B.P. (A-805A). Presumably charred wood from occupation surface hearths adjacent to the stream washed in or was otherwise introduced into the F_1 channel deposit. The use of ash (*Fraxinus*) wood as fuel was common, probably because it was readily available in the riparian habitat, but perhaps also because it furnished a relatively hot, smokeless fire. Whenever wood structure was discernible in the charcoal masses, stems of small diameter were represented rather than logs. The wood charcoal seems more likely to be the result of cooking fires than of materials utilized for hunting animals by fire drive.

Area 1 and Area 3 Extensions

Area 1 in 1971 was further expanded to the south and east to investigate a small portion of the Wolf Creek channel as well as the slope deposits on the east bank of the channel. The excavation extended southward from Area 1 all the way to Trench 9 and eastward to the point at which the Clovis occupation surface had been truncated by Stratum G_1 channel erosion during the early Holocene (Area 1 Extension). In addition, Area 3 was extended in 1968 and 1969 (Area 3 Extension). Both extensions are shown in Figure 5.8, under the discussion of Area 3. Altogether the new excavations encompassed approximately 29 square meters of the occupation surface, which consisted of 6 square meters of Wolf Creek channel fill and 23 square meters of F_1 slope deposits east of the channel. This work resulted in the recovery of 66 pieces of flaked lithic debris, one unworked obsidian nodule, and scattered pieces of nondiagnostic bone scrap. In addition, two masses of charcoal were encountered in the channel fill; both produced radiocarbon dates as discussed below.

Charcoal

The two masses of charcoal identified during the 1971 excavation of the channel deposit were in the Area 1 Extension (Fig. 5.8). One in Grid C3S produced a date of 12,940 ± 390 B.P. (Tx-1406) and one in C5S yielded a date of 11,080 ± 180 B.P. (Tx-1413). The older, less precise date appears to be too old for the Clovis occupation of the site, but the younger date is in close agreement with most other assays and is considered an accurate measure of the age of the Clovis use of Murray Springs (Appendix A).

Flaked Lithic Debris

A total of 66 pieces of flaked lithic debitage (waste flakes) was recovered from the 1971 Area 1 Extension. These unmodified flakes and flake fragments were clustered in the northern end of the excavated area (Fig. 5.8), and all but four specimens came from the F_1 slope deposits on the east bank of Wolf Creek. Of this total, 47 were recovered in place or by screening excavated sediments. Another 19 flakes were found between 1986 and 1989 on the surface of the excavated area as it continued to erode after exposure, suggesting that the artifacts deposited on the east bank of the channel were vertically dispersed through several centimeters in and below the F_1 slope deposits. A similar situation was documented for the F_1 slope deposits on the west side of the channel in the Area 3 Extension.

All of the flakes and flake fragments appear to be typical products of the retouching of bifaces. Those that still retain striking platforms exhibit lipping and edge abrasion. Approximately 65 percent of the flakes are of chert, representing three lithologically distinct varieties and hence at least three bifaces. The remaining 35 percent are of chalcedony, similar if not identical to the chalcedony flakes found in the Area 1 channel deposits in 1966.

Also recovered as the excavated area continued to erode was an obsidian nodule. This nodule is unworked, and measures 32 mm long, 25 mm wide, and 18 mm thick. Macroscopically it is similar to obsidian nodules from Areas 1, 3, and 7 in terms of form, cortex characteristics, and translucence. It was found at the northern end of the Area 1 Extension where the bulk of the debitage was concentrated (see Fig. 5.8).

Overview of Areas 1 and 2

The Wolf Creek channel deposit in Areas 1 and 2 was found to contain abundant, relatively well-preserved remains of mammoths and bison and fewer elements of several other large vertebrates. The concentration of remains of individual animals and the condition of bones and teeth indicate that little stream transportation occurred. Thus the coarse nature of the channel sediments may be a result of source rather than of high discharge. Whether the flow was ephemeral, intermittent, or perennial cannot be ascertained, but geologic evidence suggests that the low-lying part of the site intersected the water table shortly before the time of use of the site by humans (see Chapter 2 for a more detailed interpretation of the hydrology). Presumably during at least a part of the year the local water supply attracted large herbivores who in turn attracted predators, including Clovis hunters.

Although the vertebrates recovered from occupation surfaces adjacent to the stream can be assumed to represent kills from their association with projectile points, cutting tools, hearths, and other remains, the animals in the channel deposit lack such a definite cultural association. The possibility that some of these remains are the result of similar events is adduced from several lines of evidence. First, the Wolf Creek channel deposit and its contents are contemporary with the debris of the occupation surface. Stratigraphic observations, radiocarbon chronology, and the sharing of identical knapping materials support this contention. Second, no channel deposits as fossiliferous as the bone concentrations in the Wolf Creek channel fill are known elsewhere in the San Pedro Valley except in archaeological contexts. Third, two of the mammoths and perhaps some of the other animals represented in the deposit died in or near prime times of life when natural mortalities are less likely to occur. Finally, the vertebrate remains in the channel deposit were closely associated with the flakes (in Areas 1 and 3) and charcoal, and like these materials may represent the refuse of cultural activities nearby.

The mammoth remains in Area 1 were attributed to a middle-aged adult, probably a cow. An animal of apparently identical age, size, and sex was excavated on the occupation surface in Area 3, 12 m to the west, associated with tools and debitage. This proximity of stratigraphically contemporary, similar carcasses raises the possibility of a single event, a multiple mammoth kill (see Chapter 2 for an alternative interpretation). Unfortunately, modern arroyo cutting removed a part of the stream channel and margin that could have contained additional evidence of this event.

Bison may also have been killed, utilized, and their remains introduced into the Wolf Creek channel deposit based on a number of elements of two individuals with abundant charcoal in Area 2. Potential occupation surface contiguous to Area 2 was not excavated. Since camels, horses, and wolves are represented by relatively few elements in the channel deposit, their utilization by man is problematical although penecontemporaneity seems certain. It is apparent that the excavation of Areas 1 and 2 has merely sampled the concentration of vertebrate remains in the channel deposit; arroyo-cutting has removed a part of the deposit but more remains to be excavated.

THE MAMMOTH KILL, AREA 3

Area 3 comprises 350 square meters of buried occupation surface (Fig. 5.7) excavated primarily in 1967 and extended to the west and south in 1968 and 1969 (Area 3 Extension; Figs. 1.3, 5.8). This area was a central location for kill and processing activities, based on the density and variety of cultural debris. Area 3 was truncated on the north and northeast by modern arroyo-cutting, which resulted in the removal of an unknown amount of cultural remains. It was bounded on the east by Area 1, the Wolf Creek stream channel, and on the west by an essentially sterile surface where the old terrain sloped up away from the streambed (Fig. 5.9). The southernmost extent of Area 3 has not been defined; cultural remains continued southward as far as excavations were carried in 1968.

Occupation Surface

The erosion surface bearing cultural materials in Area 3 was developed on a sandy gravel of the Millville Formation (Stratum Z) in the low areas along the channel edge, on green clay of the Sobaipuri Member (Stratum D) in areas of intermediate elevation, and on the white Coro Marl Member (Stratum E) on higher slopes to the west. A relief of about 170 cm (1.2–2.9 m below the modern surface) occurred within the excavated area. The average slope was about 9 percent to the east, but considerable microrelief characterized this surface (Fig. 5.7). The black organic mat, Clanton Ranch Member (Stratum F_2), blanketed nearly all of Area 3 in thicknesses of 10 cm or less, but pinched out upslope (westward) slightly above the 260 cm contour. The underlying occupation surface appeared unweathered.

An important natural feature of the occupation surface was a thin mantle of clayey sand and sand, the F_1 slope facies of the Graveyard Gulch Member, which paralleled the western margin of Wolf Creek. This consisted of a wedge of sediment 20 cm to 30 cm thick at the channel margin, where it intergraded with the coarser, poorly sorted channel fill, thinning westward and disappearing no more than 9 m from the channel. In Area 3 west of this deposit cultural remains occurred precisely on a surface marked by the basal contact of the black mat facies of the Clanton Ranch Member (Stratum F_2) with underlying strata. Discrete concentrations of faunal remains and cultural materials appeared to represent an essentially undisturbed context. In contrast, in the eastern half of Area 3 these materials were vertically diffused, usually in the upper 10 cm of the F_1 slope deposit. However, concentrations of lithic debris and bone were again present, indicating that little horizontal dispersion had occurred. In several cases stone or bone specimens showed slightly less weathering on parts located below the surface of the slope deposit than on parts located above it. The tendency of the F_1 slope deposit to parallel the channel edge, even across contours, and the slight vertical dispersion of debris within the sand and clay wedge suggest the disturbance of upper zones of underlying strata D and Z by large animals utilizing the stream. Such reworking does not seem to have been extensive prior to burial by overlying sediments.

A distinctive kind of microrelief was encountered in Area 1 and in the southeastern part of Area 3 adjacent to the F_1 channel (Figs. 5.10 and 1.4f, 1.6c). It consisted of numerous small depressions, 20 cm to 30 cm in diameter and 5 cm to 10 cm deep, occupying an area of approximately 55 square meters below the 180–

cm contour (Fig. 5.7). These depressions, when excavated, had no subsurface structure as might be expected in most geological or pedological features. The best explanation of this phenomenon is that mammoths and perhaps other large animals left tracks in the saturated low ground adjacent to the stream. Since these features were found superposed over the F_1 slope deposit in Area 3 and F_1 channel fill in Area 1, both containing cultural materials, it is likely that the tracks observed were made late in the episode of exposure of the occupation surface, when stream activity had diminished, and just before deposition of the black mat. The best preserved of these features lacked observable impressions of toenails or hooves that could positively identify them, but they appeared similar to tracks made by modern elephants near water holes (G. Haynes 1991, Fig. 4.10).

A different type of microrelief feature occurred on higher ground in the northern part of Area 3. Four anomalous oval depressions were spaced 1 m to 2 m apart (Fig. 5.7). They were generally similar in size and shape, which is more striking when compared to an additional three depressions excavated in Area 4 (described below). The Area 3 depressions were saucer-shaped in section, ranged from 3.9 m to 5.2 m in maximum length, 1.25 m to 2.4 m in maximum width, and extended 0.20 m to 0.25 m below the surrounding terrain. The substrate was sand or sandy clay between 180 cm and 240 cm in elevation. The long axes of the depressions varied around the compass. The easternmost depression was essentially sterile, the next to the west contained debitage, the next revealed bison bone and burned bone, and the westernmost depression contained a number of projectile points and tools (Fig. 5.7). Like the tracks, these features lacked subsurface structure when excavated.

A hypothesis of cultural origin of the depressions was originally considered, but rejected because of the randomness of orientation and the variety of contents. Instead, a natural origin and subsequent adaptation to human use seems more probable. Possibly bison, utilizing the stream as a watering place, made wallows on the adjacent terrain. Such wallows were frequently observed in historic times; small "one-buffalo" depressions and large, circular, wet-ground wallows were well known on the Great Plains. Roe (1951: 103) quoted a description of wallows from the early naturalist, J. A. Allen (1876):

An excavation is made having a diameter of fifteen or twenty feet, and two feet in depth. These wallows thus became characteristic marks of buffalo country, outlasting even the ordinary trails.... The buffaloes, however, do not always choose moist places in which to roll, and are quite content with wallowing in the dust when mud-and-water wallows are not conveniently to hand... hollows formed by their indulgence in this propensity are of very frequent occurrence. These circular depressions, which are also usually called 'wallows', are of smaller size than the water wallows, being from eight to ten or twelve feet or more in diameter, and a few inches to upward of a foot in depth. These also are not effaced by natural agencies for many years, and hence remain a lasting evidence....

Seton (1929: 715) sketched dry wallows of this type in the northern Plains that were used by bison during the summer to gain relief from flies. Hence, the Area 3 and Area 4 depressions may provide some evidence of use of the locale by bison during summer.

Vertebrate Remains

About 120 catalogued vertebrate specimens, comprising many more individual elements, were recovered from Area 3. Approximately 95 identified specimens occurred on the occupation surface or in the F_1 slope deposit (Appendix D) and presumably represent cultural debris, since they were associated with artifacts and charcoal (Fig. 5.7). Skeletal elements of mammoth, bison, canids, and rodents are represented. In most cases elements can be attributed to individual animals because of their location and physical characters.

Mammoth

The partial carcass of a mammoth occupied 9 square meters of the higher terrain of Area 3 (Fig. 5.11), and fragmentary pelvic bone was scattered a few meters downslope (Figs. 1.5, 5.7). The condition of the bone indicated a period of exposure and weathering prior to deposition of Stratum F_2. The loss of indigenous bone organic matter appears well advanced, as in the case of mammoth bone from the Lehner Site (Haynes 1967). The more cancellous elements of the Area 3 mammoth,

98 *Chapter 5, E. Thomas Hemmings*

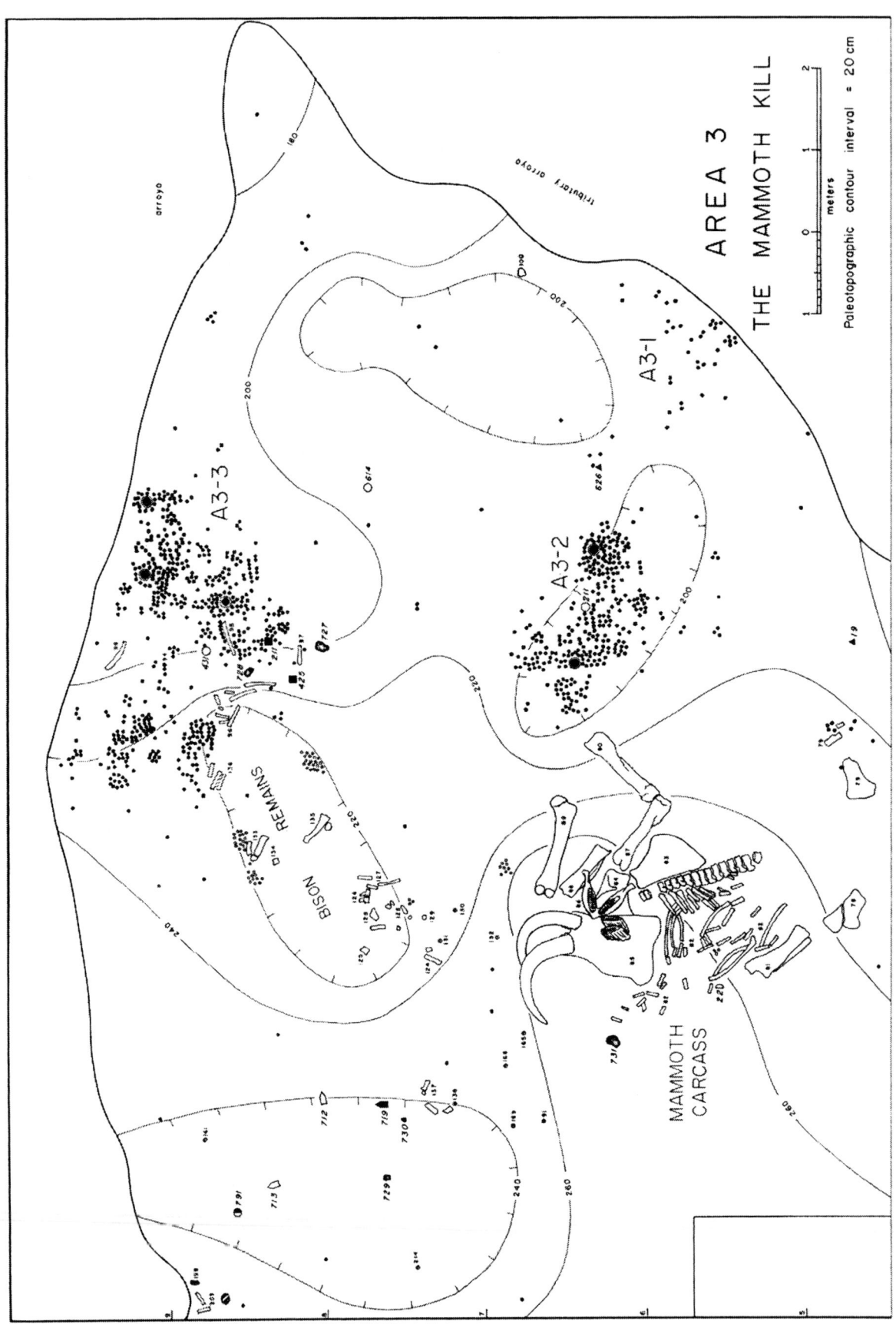

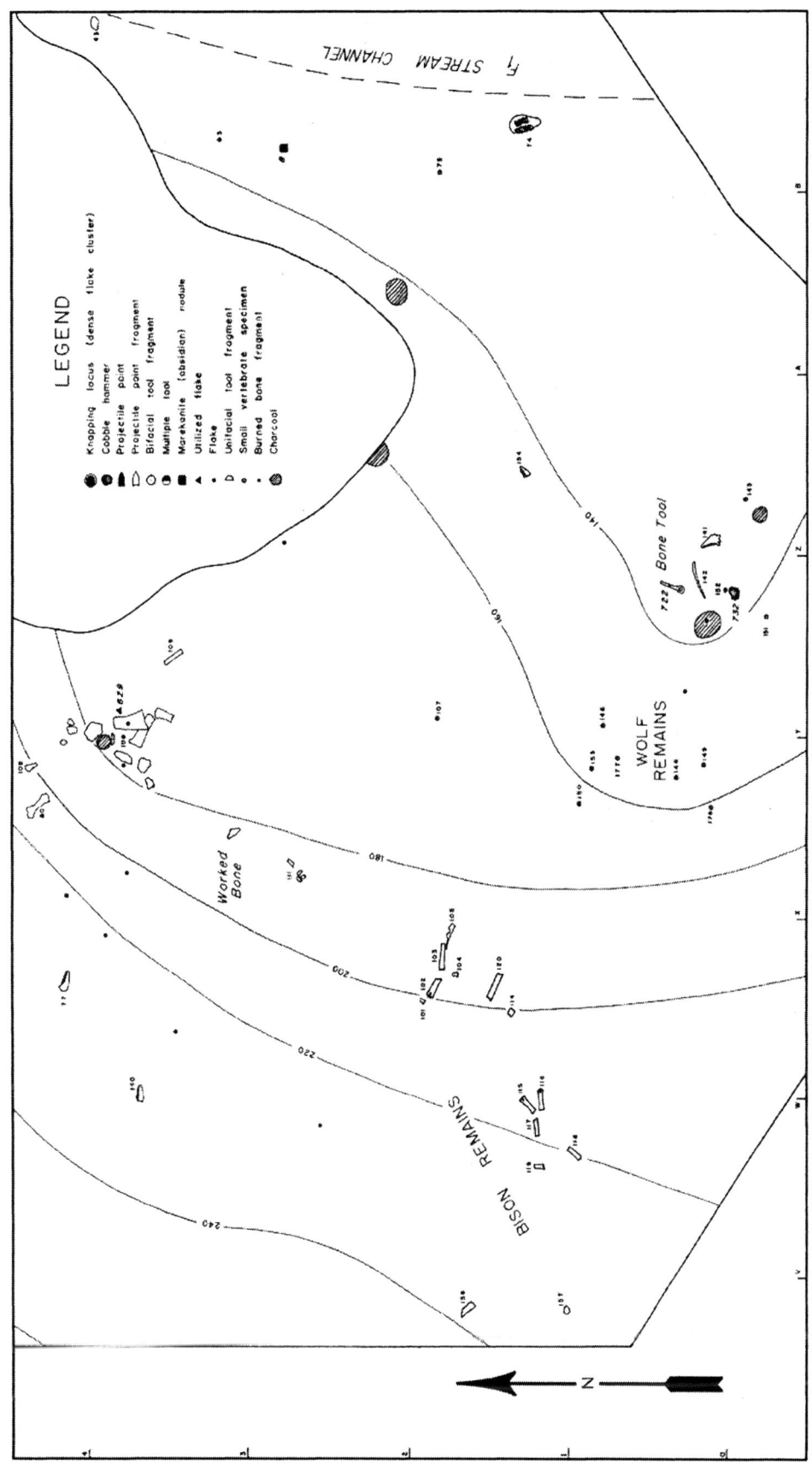

Figure 5.7. Distribution of remains in Area 3.

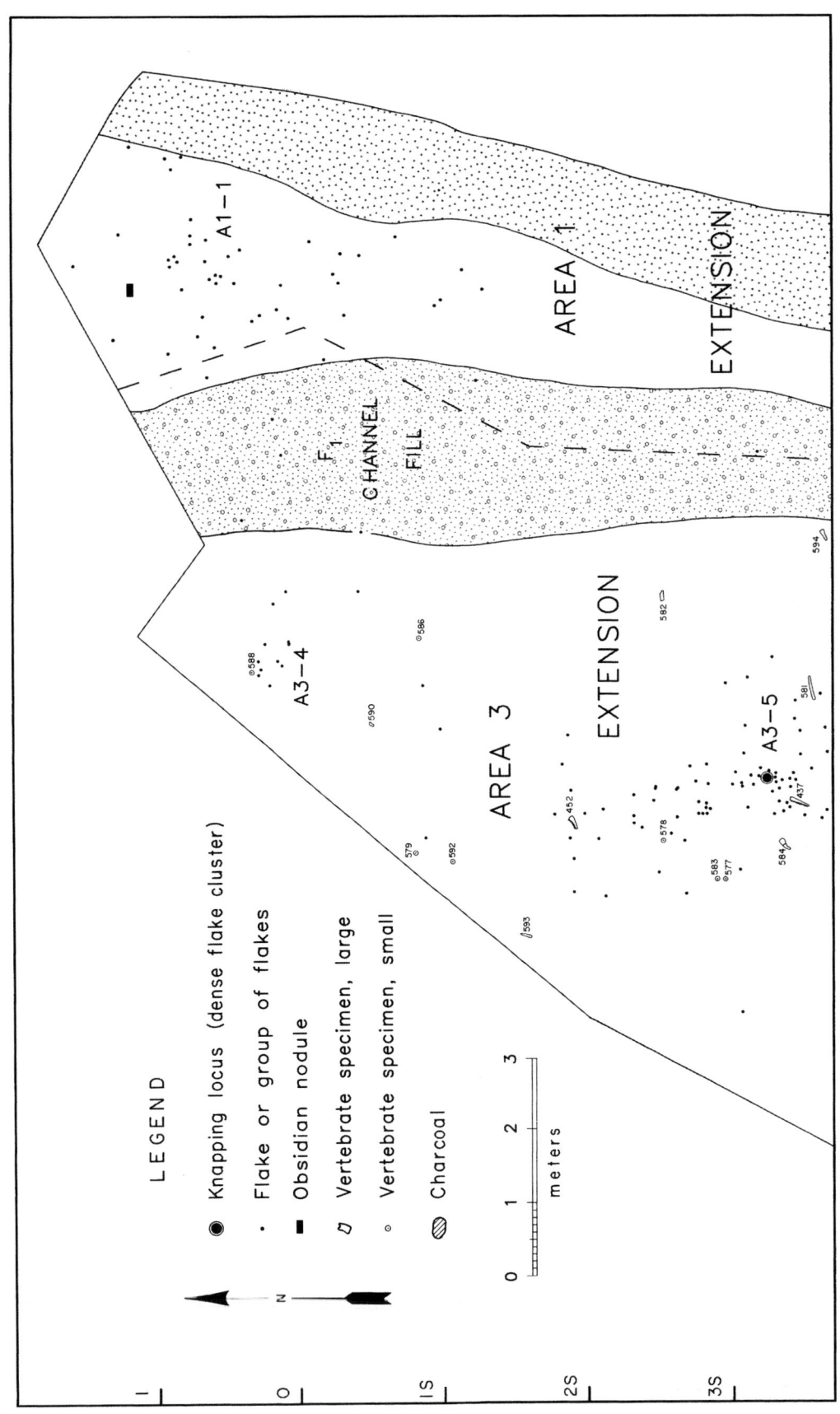

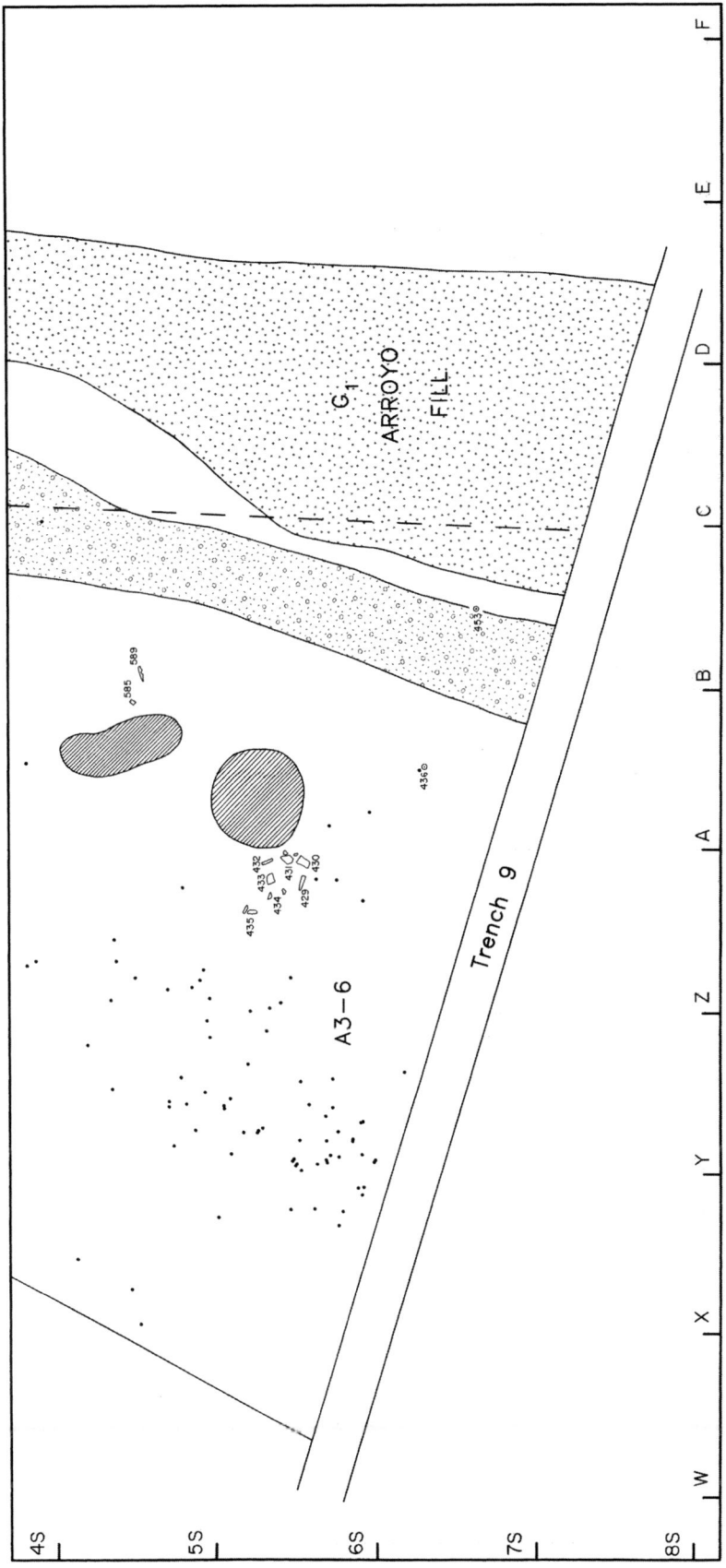

Figure 5.8. Distribution of remains in Area 3 Extension and Area 1 Extension.

Figure 5.9. Excavation of the occupation surface in Area 3, June 1967. Area 1 is at left edge of photo.

Figure 5.10. Mammoth tracks on a low-lying part of the occupation surface in Area 3.

Figure 5.11. Partial carcass of a mammoth on a high part of the occupation surface in Area 3.

observed by Deraniyagala (1955: 78) indicates the sequence of deterioration:

> The tough hide remains more or less unaffected if the weather has been dry and forms a creased and folded covering which remains upon the skeleton for several months. . . . It [the skeleton] is unusually fragile and porous for such a large animal, and disintegrates very rapidly. The tusks being of dentine disintegrate as easily as the bones which crumble into fragments within three years. The cement in the molars begins to split up after about 4 or 5 years, and the enamel folds disintegrate after about 6 or 7 years until nothing remains except a mass of comminuted fragments.

Age and sex. All four third molars are in place in the upper and lower dentition with approximately the anterior 10 plates of each tooth in wear. The condition of the lower dentition suggests a fully grown animal with an estimated age between 41 and 47 years (Laws 1966: 13, 30). The lengths of propodials are less than for comparable specimens from Area 2 and other San Pedro Valley mammoths that may represent large bulls. The tusks also are relatively small and light, measuring about 1,500 mm on the outside curve. Thus, the Area 3 carcass probably represents an adult cow.

including the sacrum and vertebral centra, were partially deteriorated, and no carpals, tarsals, or phalanges were identified. The compact tissue of long bones and the teeth and tusks remained essentially intact. Although not directly comparable because of environmental differences, a Ceylon elephant carcass

Figure 5.12. Mammoth upper molars from Area 3: *left*, buccal view of LM³; *right*, lingual view of RM³; both from one individual.

Species and size. The characters of the grinding teeth are within the range cited for *Mammuthus columbi* (Osborn 1942: 1076, 1480). In the M3s the number of plates is 17 to 18 and the lamellar frequency (plates per 100 mm) is 6 to 7 (Fig. 5.12). Tooth size, hypsodonty, and enamel width support this identification. The size of the forelimb and shoulder girdle, using Osborn's (1942: 1080) comparative data, indicates a shoulder height of about 3.6 m to 3.7 m in the living animal. The live weight is estimated at 5,450 kg (about 6 tons).

Bison

At least two bison were represented on the occupation surface in Area 3 by concentrations of skeletal elements, and an element of a third bison was also found. The condition of this material was uniformly poor although teeth and some limb elements were identifiable. These individuals are ascribed to the species *Bison antiquus*, identified from more complete material in Area 4.

Remains of the first bison, represented by lower cheek teeth and fragmentary postcranial elements, were located in and near a depression about 2 m north of the mammoth carcass (Fig. 5.7). The associated artifacts and debris suggest human breakage of some of the bones in addition to the effects of weathering. The cranium of this animal was located about 16 m southeast of the lower dentition at the margin of the F_1 channel. Tooth eruption and wear in both dentitions are approximately those of a yearling (Kehoe 1967; Skinner and Kaisen 1947). Several unfused epiphyses of long bones recovered separate from shafts tend to corroborate this age estimate.

The second bison was represented in Area 3 some 6 m south of the mammoth carcass by disarticulated mandibular rami and fragmentary forelimb and hindlimb elements. The cranium was not located. The condition of mandibular tooth eruption and wear is that of a four- to six-year-old animal. The remaining limb elements are gracile and probably represent a cow. Presumably the animal was fully grown and in breeding condition as in living bison (Seton 1929).

A third bison was represented in the southern extension of Area 3 by a single left mandibular ramus. It probably also belonged to a four- to six-year-old animal.

Canids

Canid remains from two individuals were recovered in the F_1 slope deposit 9 m south and east of the mammoth carcass (Fig. 5.7). One animal was represented by left and right mandibular rami, cranial fragments, cervical vertebrae, and possibly a rib. The well-preserved right mandibular ramus with P_1–M_2 has been identified as the large extinct Pleistocene dire wolf, *Canis dirus* (Fig. 1.7d). The presence of essentially the head and neck and the association with artifacts and charcoal raise the possibility of human manipulation of a dire wolf carcass. These remains occurred in the area of mammoth tracks and were badly fragmented.

A second canid was represented only by a fragmentary right mandibular ramus similar to the living coyote, *Canis latrans*, but domestic dog cannot be ruled out. [Editors' note: This specimen, consisting of RP_{2-3}, was reexamined by Stanley J. Olsen in 1991. In his view, it may represent either a small *C. lupus* (wolf) or a large *C. latrans*, and is probably best referred to as *C. lupus/latrans*. Saunders and Daeschler (1994: 23) consider the domestic dog a possibility based on the diminutive aspects of dire wolf metapodials from Murray Springs and Lehner Clovis sites (Saunders, personal communication 2005).]

Rodents

A single cheek tooth of a wood rat, *Neotoma*, was recovered on the occupation surface, and incisors, cheek teeth, and postcranial fragments from two or more meadow voles (*Microtus*) were recovered in the F_1 slope deposit in Area 3. Other rodent material was not identifiable. There was no evidence of the use of rodents by humans at Murray Springs.

Hearths

Although no hearths were recognized in Area 3, one may have been present in the depression containing yearling bison bones north of the mammoth carcass, where a relatively large quantity of burned bone fragments was located (Fig. 5.7). Charcoal fragments with woody structure also occurred as dispersed flecks and in small patches in the F_1 slope deposit east and southeast of the mammoth carcass.

Artifacts

Few tools were recovered in Area 3 and most of those found were damaged. Serviceable tools may have been retrieved by their users. On the basis of proximity some tools can be placed in functional context with vertebrate remains, including projectile points and cobble hammers associated with the yearling bison and a flake cutting tool and cobble hammer associated with the mammoth. Concentrations of flaked lithic debris were associated with both these animals and occurred at three other locations in Area 3. The loci of tools and tool fragments tended to be outside bone and lithic debris concentrations. Two unexpected elements of the Area 3 artifact assemblage were a carved bone tool and a fragment of worked bone (Fig. 5.7), which suggest bone tool-making activities in addition to tool kits associated with large animal kills and processing. Tools are described in technological and functional categories deduced from archaeological context as well as tool attributes.

BIFACES

Projectile Points

One whole Clovis projectile point and two tip fragments were located within the northwesternmost depression in Area 3 and adjacent to elements of a yearling bison (Fig. 5.7). Figures 5.13*b-d* and 5.14*b-d* illustrate both surfaces of these specimens.

The whole specimen (Figs. 5.13*d*) is light gray (5Y 7/1) chalcedony with weathered cortex at the tip, 58 mm long, 28 mm in maximum width, and 9 mm in maximum thickness. The basal width is 24 mm, and neither the basal edges nor the basal concavity are ground. The flute length is 18 mm on one surface (Fig. 5.13*d*) and 14 mm on the opposite surface (Fig. 5.14*d*). A projection on one surface near the right hand edge (Fig. 5.14*d*) was left by the knapper after some unsuccessful attempts at thinning. Compared with other Clovis projectile points from the San Pedro Valley, the specimen was poorly made and is without basal edge grinding. It is, therefore, perhaps unfinished.

The larger of the tip fragments (Fig. 5.13*b* and 5.14*b*) is mottled red (10R 4/4), yellow (10YR 5/4), and light purple (5R 6/2) petrified wood, the only piece of such material in the site. The apparent flute on the obverse surface is the scar of a channel flake removed from the direction of the present tip, as shown by the undulations. This flute may indicate the interior surface of the flake blank or reworking of a basal point fragment by creating a new base at what had been the tip. It could also represent an impact "flute" that occurred during an earlier episode of use and was subsequently repaired but not obliterated completely. The smaller tip (Fig. 5.13*c* and 5.14*c*) is a white (5Y 8/2) chalcedony fragment with no distinguishing features.

Both tips were removed by transverse snapping; probably the basal sections were large enough to resharpen and were removed for that purpose. A comparison of the lithologies of the point tips and lithic debris in Area 3 indicates that any subsequent reworking of these specimens was carried out elsewhere.

Bifacial Preforms

Other bifaces were represented in Area 3 by tip fragments and by flakes of bifacial retouch occurring in areas of debitage (Bordes 1961: 6). The minimum number of such bifaces was probably 14; 3 are known from both tips and associated flakes of identical raw material and the remaining 11 are known only from debitage. Bifaces are represented by varying amounts of flake debris that indicate sharpening and thinning. Flakes in seven lithologic groupings of flakes attributed to the working of single bifaces may number in the hundreds; the other seven groupings number fewer than 50 each (Chapter 8).

The inference that biface fragments and most flakes of bifacial retouch from Area 3 do not represent waste from projectile point manufacture is based on several

Figure 5.13. Lithic artifacts from Area 3: *a*, edge-ground biface fragment; *b*, *c*, obverse faces of projectile point tips; *d*, obverse face of projectile point; *e*, exterior surface of utilized blade fragment; *f*, exterior surface of utilized bladelike flake; *g*, flake fragment with utilized concave edge; *h*, unifacially retouched flake tool fragment; *i*, multiple graver; *j*, biface tip fragment. Length of *d* is 58 mm.

Figure 5.14. Reverse sides of lithic artifacts *a–e* in Figure 5.13.

lines of evidence. First, two areas of debitage (A3-2 and A3-3), accounting for 10 of the 14 bifaces, appear to be associated with carcasses where preparation of cutting tools would be expected (Fig. 5.7). Knapping areas of comparable debris occurred in similar relationship to animal remains in Areas 4 and 5 as well. Second, no channel flakes (but see Chapter 8 for a different interpretation) or fragments of projectile points broken during manufacture were recovered in Area 3, and none of the projectile points recovered were worked or reworked locally. The biface tips present, because of their size and shape attributes, do not resemble finished or nearly finished projectile points. Finally, most other tools from Area 3 can be attributed to game processing tool kits.

Bifacial preforms of chert and chalcedony were the source of lithic debris in Area 3. The term "preform" has been used by Crabtree (1967: 63) to indicate a stage in manufacture between quarrying raw material and finishing of a bifacial tool at the occupation site. The exterior margins of the platforms of many flakes of bifacial retouch were ground or dulled. In many cases this was probably intentionally carried out to facilitate thinning and sharpening of cutting tools, since grinding reduces crushing at the edge and permits flakes to "carry" well. In other cases the tool may have been dulled by use and resharpened.

One interesting example of a bifacial preform was recovered in the northeast part of Area 3 (Fig. 5.7). This chert specimen (Fig. 5.13a) with two large flakes refitted (Fig. 5.14a) has a maximum length of 79 mm and maximum thickness of 12 mm. The original length was probably twice as much. The edges were heavily ground (to the roundness of the lip of a drinking glass) and smoothed to an unusual degree. The grinding passes equally around the tip and the striations parallel the edge. Fifteen flakes removed from the biface subsequent to grinding were recovered, most from a small concentration of debitage about 6 m east of the mammoth carcass at the edge of the arroyo (Fig. 5.7, A3-1). Certainly this is the location, now partially lost to erosion, where the biface was worked. Two flakes can be refitted, one on each face of the specimen; thinning was carried out from both edges when, presumably, the biface broke. The remaining part may have been retrieved or carried away by arroyo-cutting.

Two other small chert biface tips were recovered from concentrations of debitage in Area 3 (Fig. 5.7, A3-2 and A3-3). Neither has ground edges and both are irregular in form and flaking, as shown by the single illustrated example (Fig. 5.13j). These appear to represent tips inadvertently broken off during sharpening and thinning of bifacial preforms at these locations. Numerous flakes of bifacial retouch of identical raw material occurred with the tips.

UNIFACES

Unifacial Cutting Tool

A fragmentary chert flake tool with a unifacially retouched edge was recovered among the ribs of the mammoth carcass (Fig. 5.13h). The fragment retains a 31-mm straight edge retouched to an angle of about 30°, considered an optimum edge for meat cutting (Wilmsen 1968a, 1968b). This edge was a lateral margin of the flake blank and shows slight dulling through use. A 3-mm remaining segment of a second unifacially retouched edge on the distal margin shows that at least two edges at about right angles were modified for cutting. Subsequent to modification, the flake was snapped at several points, and potlid spalls and discoloration were caused by heat. Because of these effects, it is difficult to say whether identical chert occurs among the debitage in Area 3, although similar material was present.

Multiple Graving Tool

A small chalcedony flake fragment, notched by abrupt retouch to produce three graverlike spurs, was recovered from a depression 4 m northwest of the mammoth carcass (Fig. 5.13i). The maximum dimension of the fragment is 30 mm. Notching was carried out after the flake blank was fragmented.

UTILIZED FLAKES

Three large chert flakes from Area 3 have traces of utilization on one or more edges in the form of slight irregular spalling. All were found outside the concentrations of debitage. One (Fig. 5.14e) is the 64-mm long proximal end of a true blade of chert. The lateral edges with angles of 35° to 40° show use spalling. It was recovered in two parts, separated by 2 m, and they show slight differential weathering since one part was incorporated in the F_1 slope deposit. The blade was manufactured elsewhere as no similar raw material or blade cores occur in the collection. The striking platform angle is 110° and the platform is smoothed. Notches that may have been intentionally made are located near the broken end of the blade (Fig. 5.13e).

A second utilized flake (Fig. 5.13f) of probable local manufacture is damaged, but has bladelike parallel flake scars on the exterior surface and numerous hinge fractures near the striking platform. A flake fragment found 6 m away subsequently removed from the same core is also bladelike (Fig. 5.15a) and can be fitted to this piece. The utilization scars are preserved on a segment of the distal edge with an edge angle of 30°.

A third utilized flake (Fig. 5.13g) is a chert fragment with use spalling on a concave edge with an edge angle of 26°. Identical raw material occurs among the debitage.

The three utilized flakes from Area 3 seem to have been suitable for several kinds of cutting and scraping tasks related to processing and perhaps other activities. Other flakes may have been utilized in Area 3 that do not bear recognizable traces of wear.

COBBLE HAMMERS AND MANUPORTS

Three cobbles, perhaps used as hammers, were associated with mammoth and bison remains in Area 3 (Fig. 5.7). A quartzite cobble, weighing 1,750 g, with some fragments removed, occurred adjacent to the mammoth carcass on the west. A quartzite cobble fragment and a granite cobble weighing 570 g and 400 g respectively occurred just east of the yearling bison remains. These specimens are slightly weathered, making it difficult to distinguish evidence of use. They were clearly humanly introduced, as cobble-sized particles do not occur naturally in sediments bounding the erosion surface in this area. All were convenient hand-sized tools, perhaps for smashing bone.

Another hammer or chopping tool of black silicified limestone weighing 430 g was associated with wolf remains southeast of the mammoth carcass (Fig. 5.7). It is clearly battered and may have had flakes removed intentionally. The cobble was probably obtained from an outcrop of thermally altered limestone in Lewis Hills 4 km (2.4 miles) east of the site on the axis of the San Pedro Valley.

Other rocks introduced by humans include a limestone pebble and small quartzite cobble fragment from the northwesternmost depression in Area 3, and a weathered limestone cobble and fragments of a quartzite cobble from the area of mammoth tracks. These are termed "manuports" to denote human manipulation, although their use is unknown.

LITHIC DEBRIS

A total of 9,467 flaked lithic items other than tools was excavated in Area 3. About 99 percent of this material was concentrated in five small knapping areas; the remaining 1 percent (93 flakes) was scattered widely across the occupation surface. Three of the knapping areas, A3-1, A3-2, and A3-3, are shown in Figure 5.7. The other three, A3-4, A3-5, and A3-6, lie in the extension of Area 3 (Fig. 5.8). Unfortunately, only three of the knapping areas (A3-2, A3-5, and A3-6) furnished a complete sample. Two others (A3-1 and A3-3) were truncated by modern arroyo-cutting, and one (A3-4) was partially removed by backhoe Trench 9 for geological stratigraphy.

The knapping areas were carefully excavated to maintain precise proveniences insofar as possible. In four areas the lithic debris occurred on a well-marked surface and was collected by peeling back the overlying 5 cm of sediment with small tools, thus locating flakes in situ. One-quarter inch mesh screens were used to check the effectiveness of recovery; less than 1 percent of the collection came from screening. In A3-5 flakes were diffuse through 5 cm of the F_1 slope deposit; the same collecting technique was used with the addition of wet-screening on fine screens.

All lithic debris from Area 3 is considered debitage, that is, waste produced by knapping activities. Thin expanding flakes of bifacial retouch with characteristic soft hammer lipping at the interior edge of the platform are the major component of the collection (Fig. 5.15b-i). Large amounts of flake fragments and irregular debris were also present as a result of the percussion technique. There is no good evidence for any knapping operation, such as scraper retouch, other than thinning and sharpening of bifaces (see Chapter 8 for a different view). The flakes of bifacial retouch and associated fragments are markedly small. Only 16 percent of the collection consists of flakes or fragments with surface areas of about 4 square millimeters or larger. If a standard screening technique only had been used, an estimated 90 percent of the collection would never have been recovered. Evidence of edge grinding

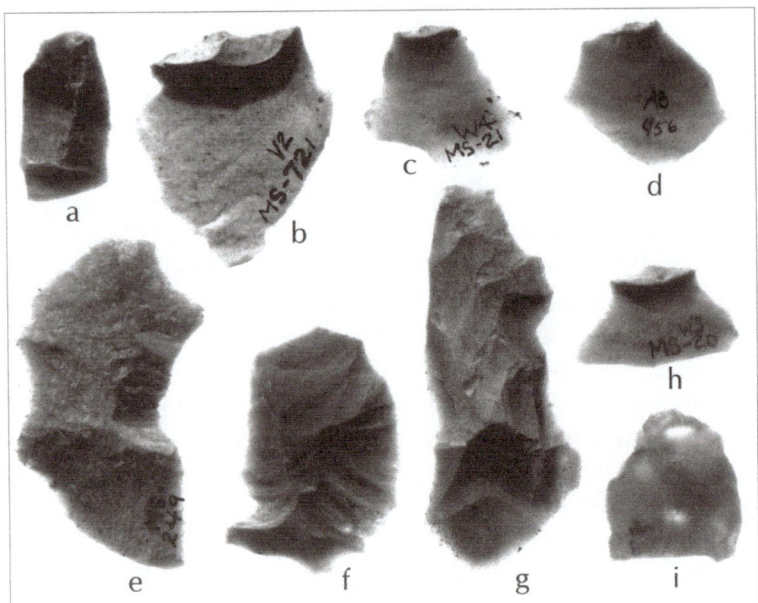

Figure 5.15. Debitage from Area 3: *a*, exterior surface of bladelike flake; *b-d, h*, interior surfaces of flakes of bifacial retouch; *e-g, i*, exterior surfaces of flakes of bifacial retouch. Length of *g* is 57 mm.

of bifaces to facilitate removal of thinning flakes was commonly preserved on the outer edges of the platforms. Some dulling of cutting edges through use may also have been present, but was difficult to distinguish. The output of debitage was a by-product of the preparation of bifacial preforms and perhaps also the resharpening of cutting tools. Two of the knapping areas, A3-2 and A3-3, appear to be associated with mammoth and bison carcasses (Fig. 5.7).

The Area 3 debitage as a whole contains about 77.7 percent chalcedony, 21.7 percent chert, and less than 0.6 percent jasper and basalt. However, one of the knapping areas (A3-5), comprising 78.2 percent of the total collection, contributed most of the chalcedony and an unusual number of small flakes and fragments. A single nodule of chalcedony may have produced nearly the entire content of this knapping area. In the other five knapping areas in Area 3, chert (93.7 percent) was the preferred raw material and the proportion of flakes larger than 4 square millimeters was 50 percent.

The variation between knapping areas and the scattered flakes is summarized in Table 5.1. Each knapping area collection was segregated, and raw materials were sorted by observation of color, luster, microfossils, and inclusions, using primarily the component of flakes and fragments larger than 4 square millimeters. This sorting produced clusters of flakes and fragments that could be attributed to single pieces of raw material. These clusters were studied to ascertain the original form of the raw material and the kinds of flakes and fragments produced. Loci of knapping operations within areas (A3-2 and A3-3) were marked by small dense clusters of hundreds of flakes of identical raw material (Fig. 5.7). The clustering is evidence of the undisturbed nature of the debitage. With the exception of A3-5, the knapping areas and surface collection were technologically and functionally homogeneous. The variation in A3-5 can be attributed to the nodular form of the raw material, the presence of cortex, the use of chalcedony, and, to some extent, the use of fine wet-screening in collection. The scattered flakes from outside the knapping areas represent primarily debris that was scattered during knapping, but some flakes were utilized and discarded. A few discolored, crazed, and pot-lidded flakes were also present, presumably inadvertently altered by heat.

OBSIDIAN NODULES

Three marekanite or obsidian nodules (Apache tears) were recovered from the occupation surface and the F_1 slope deposit in Area 3 (Fig. 5.7). The largest (Fig. 5.16*a*) measures 48 mm in maximum diameter and has had a few small flakes removed. The two smaller nodules (Fig. 5.16*b, c*), measuring 30 mm and 34 mm in maximum diameter, are split. Presumably these were intended for the manufacture of small tools, but must have remained unused since no obsidian flakes were recovered. [Huckell (Chapter 8) considers

Table 5.1. Variation between Knapping Areas and General Surface Collection from Area 3

Collection Designation	No. of Flakes	Sample Studied	Percent raw material			Area of concentration (m²)	Density (Flakes/m²)	No. of Pieces Worked	Portable Form	Faunal Association
			Chert	Chalcedony	Other					
A3–1	56	56	78.8		21.2	1	56	1+	Bifacial preform	
A3–2	818	339	88.2	11.2	0.6	4	204	4	Bifacial preforms	Mammoth
A3–3	1,438	763	95.1	1.2	3.7	8	180	6	Bifacial preforms	Bison
A3–4	129	129	97.8	1.1	1.1	2	64	2	Bifacial preforms	
A3–5	8,710	221	1.5	98.5		2	4,355	1 1	Nodule Bifacial preform	
A3–6	171		90.6	9.4		5	34	2	Bifacial preforms	
General Surface	93	93	67.1	25.3	7.6					
Totals	11,415	1,601				22		17+		

NOTE: Hemmings (1970) examined only the portion of the A3–5 locus that had been sampled by the end of the 1968 season, and none of the A3–6 locus. The A3–5 locus was completely excavated in 1969, and the A3–6 locus was discovered and excavated that same year. The figures in this table have been updated to include final totals for both loci. Because no record exists of which flakes were included in each locus and which were considered to represent the "general surface," the total for the latter has not been updated. These figures can be compared to those presented in Chapter 8.

these objects completely unworked.] The nodules were subjected to obsidian hydration dating as discussed below and in 1986 to X-ray fluorescence for sourcing (Appendix C). A fourth nodule was recovered from the Wolf Creek channel deposit and a fifth was found in the F_1 slope facies, east of the channel in the 1971 area of excavation.

An attempt was made to obtain additional age data from hydration layer measurements on the three obsidian nodules recovered from Area 3. Thin sections were prepared from the possibly flaked surfaces of these specimens by the UCLA obsidian hydration laboratory under the direction of Dr. Clement W. Meighan. Hydration layer thickness in four sections from three specimens ranged from 2.7 to 4.3 microns (average 3.4 microns). Assuming that the radiocarbon age of Clovis occupation is accurate, a lower rate of hydration is indicated by these measurements than has been reported previously (Friedman and Smith 1960; Meighan and Haynes 1968). Inconsistencies, presumably due to geological factors, in obsidian hydration dates characterized a preliminary study in the Southwest where feasibility of this technique for dating remains to be demonstrated (Evans and Meggers 1960).

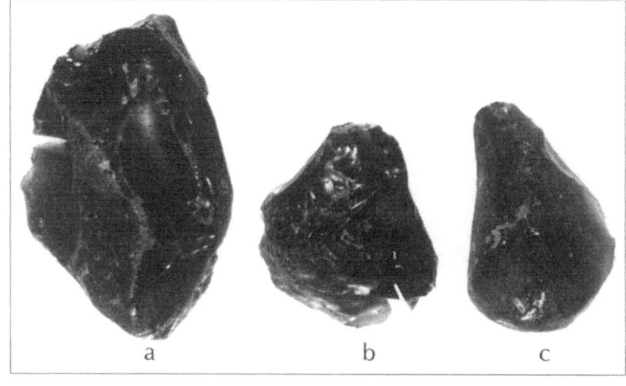

Figure 5.16. Marekanite nodules (Apache tears) from Area 3. Small portions have been removed for obsidian hydration and neutron activation analyses. Length of *a* is 51.4 mm.

BONE TOOL AND WORKED BONE

A carved bone tool (Figs. 5.17 and 1.6*b*) was recovered from the F_1 slope deposit about 10 m southeast of the mammoth carcass in Area 3, closely associated with wolf remains, a battered cobble,

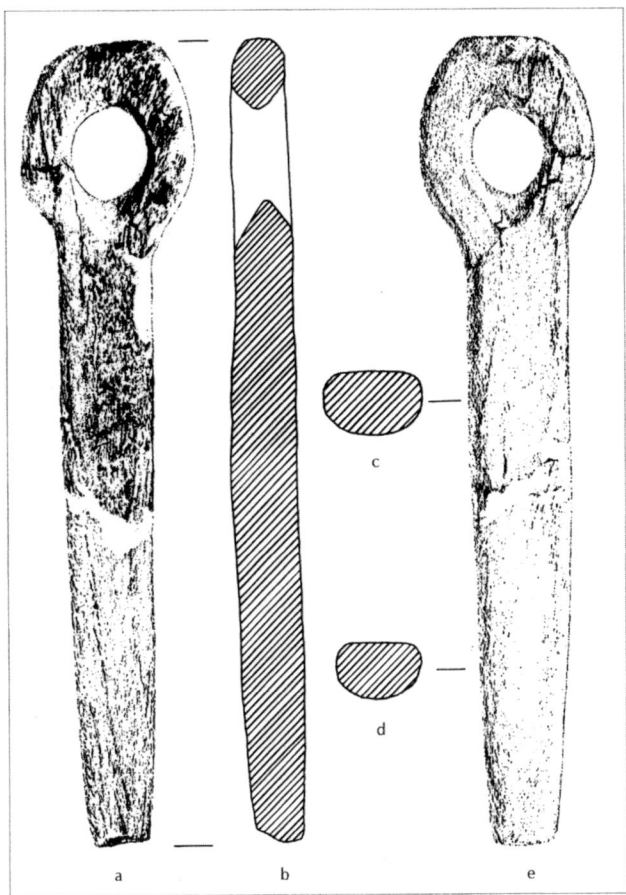

Figure 5.17. Mammoth bone shaft straightener from Area 3: a, obverse face; b, longitudinal section; c, d, transverse sections; e, reverse face. Length is 259 mm.

patches of charcoal, and a few flakes (Fig. 5.7). This area was adjacent to the water hole by the Wolf Creek channel and was thoroughly pitted by mammoth tracks. The tool was broken in two parts; one part lay on the surface of the F_1 deposit and the other, only slightly disassociated at the break, was buried 2 cm below the surface. The upper face of the part that occurred on the surface exhibits slightly more weathering than other parts of the tool (Fig. 5.17a). The jagged, stepped nature of the break suggests fracture when the bone was fresh. Because the two parts were still properly positioned, the breakage probably occurred in situ and may have been caused by the tread of a heavy animal.

The form of this tool has been previously described (Haynes and Hemmings 1968). The length is 259 mm, width at midshaft is 31 mm, and thickness at midshaft is 21 mm. The tool consists of a perforated head on a slightly tapering shaft, the whole resembling a robust eyebolt. The perforation is oval, 25 mm by 30 mm in diameter, and is countersunk or beveled on both faces (Fig. 5.17b). The beveling is pronounced above and below the perforation, seemingly as a result of manufacture rather than of wear.

The texture of the bone resembles the compact outer tissue of mammoth long bone. The dimensions of the tool also indicate mammoth long bone as the source of raw material rather than elements of any smaller species. The flatter surface (Fig. 5.17e) may be the unmodified periosteal surface and the more convex face (Fig. 5.17a) the endosteal surface with cancellous tissue removed. In view of the evidence of bone work described below, the tool may have been manufactured locally from the ample supply of fresh mammoth long bones.

The similarity to Old World Upper Paleolithic *bâtons de commandement* or *bâtons percés*, especially Gravettian and Magdalenian specimens from the Czech Republic and the Ukraine, is striking (Augusta and Burian 1960, Plates 38, 39; Boriskovsky 1958: 213). These have nearly identical form and dimensions, are carved in bone or ivory, and have little or no decoration. Western European *bâtons* are similar in dimensions, but vary in shape, often being carved in reindeer antler, and are frequently engraved. The European *bâtons* are generally believed to have been used as shaft straighteners with possible additional functions in social or religious contexts (Leroi-Gourhan 1957; Oakley 1964). Hardwood or bone shafts, foreshafts, or points were presumably straightened by application of heat or moisture with the mechanical advantage of the straightening tool.

The context of the tool from Area 3 is unenlightening except that the battered hammer or chopperlike cobble found 1 m away was suitable for bone working tasks. Experimentation with casts of the bone tool indicates it would have been highly effective for straightening shafts with diameters between 14 and 17 mm, reasonable hafts for Clovis points known from the San Pedro Valley (Haynes and Hemmings 1968: 187).

A weathered, fragmentary section of worked bone (Fig. 5.18) was recovered on the occupation surface about 4 m southeast of the mammoth carcass (Fig. 5.7). The texture and size of the fragment again indicate the utilization of compact outer tissue of mammoth long bone (or possibly bison as suggested in Chapter 2). The present length of the fragment is 167

Mammoth Processing

The processing of the Area 3 mammoth carcass is inferred primarily from the distribution, presence and absence, and condition of bone, and knowledge of elephant physiology. The processing tool kit is poorly known, but minimally included four bifacial cutting tools sharpened and thinned in knapping area A3-2 northeast of the carcass (Fig. 5.7), a heavy cobble hammer, and a unifacially retouched flake (Fig. 5.13*h*).

Bone Distribution

The precise position of the carcass is indeterminate, but the head lay north of the axial skeleton. The cranium was overturned and collapsed on its left frontal area (Figs. 5.11 and 1.5). The mandible was disarticulated from the cranium and rested upright on the lateral surface of the right scapula. Most post-cranial elements were thoroughly disarticulated and disarranged. At least 14 cervical and thoracic vertebrae were articulated; no lumbar or caudal vertebrae were identified, perhaps due to removal or in part to nonpreservation. The right femur was closely associated with the right tibia and fibula, but this hindlimb was located near the cranium. The left hindlimb was missing. Both humeri and scapulae occurred near the cranium, but only the right shoulder girdle was articulated. The left radius and ulna were located near the sacrum at the hind end of the carcass, and the right radius and ulna were missing. The pelvis and ribs were fragmentary and scattered.

Butchering Sequence and Utilization

The butchering procedure must have been adapted to the position of the animal at death, which could be either on the side or prone with feet splayed, because the carcass would be at first immovable. One of the first operations would have been to remove accessible limbs; relative to the torso, little usable meat was available on them. The forelimbs could have been cut away through soft tissue under the scapula, since the shoulder girdle is free of the axial skeleton. The hind limbs were probably freed by chopping through the pubic symphysis, ossified in the mature animal, and severing the sacroiliac joint. This procedure would help to account for the fragmentary condition of the

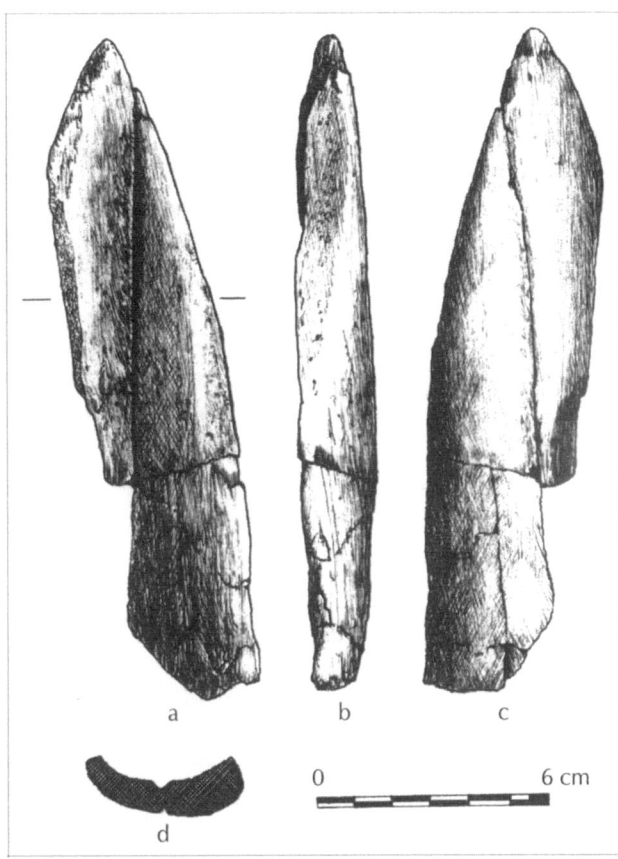

Figure 5.18. Worked bison long bone fragment: *a*, endosteal surface with burin groove; *b*, lateral view showing beveled area; *c*, periosteal surface with shallow burin groove; *d*, transverse section.

mm, the maximum width is 38 mm, and the maximum thickness is 12 mm. The salient features are a beveled or smoothed truncation at one end oblique to the long axis and two V-shaped grooves parallel to the long axis (Fig. 5.18). A shallower groove on the periosteal surface lies directly over a deeper groove on the endosteal surface. Such grooves could have been produced by a burin tool held perpendicular to the length of bone and drawn along the surface to remove shavings. The products of this operation were probably slender bone bars of unknown length, split from one another at the grooves, which could then be worked to a desired shape. One possibility is that the split segments were intended for cylindrical bone points or shaft components such as those from the Clovis level at Blackwater Draw, New Mexico (Cotter 1937, 1954).

Table 5.2. Estimated Weights and Percents of Carcass Weight of Body Parts, Organs, and Contents of a 5,450 kg Mammoth Cow

Body Part	Estimated Weight (kilograms)	Percent of Carcass Weight
Cranium	320	5.87
Brain	16	0.29
Mandible	68	1.25
Shoulder-forelimb units	730	13.39
Hindlimbs	500	9.17
Heart	25	0.46
Kidneys	9	0.17
Liver	48	0.88
Spleen	21	0.39
Stomach	82	1.50
Intestines	175	3.21
Intestinal contents	390	7.16
Blood	55	1.01
Muscle	1,900	34.86
Hide	703	12.90
Other	408	7.49
Total	5,450	

column. Table 5.2 gives the weights of body parts estimated from autopsy data for a smaller, male, African elephant (Benedict 1936: 112). These figures indicate that a thoroughly butchered mammoth might dress out 38 percent or more of live body weight, or in this case 2,075 kg (about 4,565 pounds) of edible products. This amount approaches half of the estimated maximum yield for 11 bison processed in Area 4, as is discussed below.

It could not be determined whether the foramen magnum of the poorly preserved cranium had been enlarged to allow access to the brain, or whether the mandible had been separated to permit removal of the tongue. However, the observed position of these elements was suitable for such operations. The hyoid arch was not recovered.

Bison Processing

The bison remains in Area 3 were poorly preserved, and the identification and distribution of elements are uncertain. Thorough disarticulation of both individuals seems to have occurred as in the case of bison processed in Area 4. The concentration of a large amount of burned bone fragments among the remains of the yearling north of the Area 3 mammoth indicates cooking or rendering or both activities (Kehoe 1967; Leechman 1951). About 100 small fragments ranged from a slightly charred to a highly calcined condition, and both compact and cancellous tissue were represented. Cobble hammers were also present in this area (Fig. 5.7). The second individual, south of the mammoth carcass, was represented primarily by appendicular skeletal elements. The only axial elements identified were the cranium and disassociated mandibular rami. Most of this animal, an adult cow, was probably removed by erosion or humans, but might also remain unexcavated.

Overview of Area 3

Area 3 provides some significant increments to knowledge of Clovis subsistence ecology and technology as well as some problems of interpretation. The presence of tracks and wallows on the occupation surface, if the interpretation of these features is correct, is of paleoecological and paleontological interest. At some time prior to the arrival of hunters the ground adjacent to Wolf Creek was used by bison for wallow-

pelvis. The lower limb segments were separated from humeri and femora, perhaps to facilitate movement of the limbs. Some limb elements were massed near the head and some were removed elsewhere, possibly to the camp (Area 7) where severely weathered fragments were found (Chapter 7). The femur and ulna, among these missing elements, are particularly massive and would not have been carried off by scavengers. The long bones of the mammoth entirely lack medullary cavities, but had marrow disseminated through cancellous tissue surrounded by thick compact tissue. There was no evidence of utilization of marrow locally. In view of the worked bone from Area 3 it may be that missing limb elements were supplying compact bone for tool-making, although the draining of interstitial marrow could have been a concomitant of this activity.

The fragmented, scattered ribs; massing of head, shoulder and limb elements in one area; and separation of the pelvis from the carcass suggest that the torso was of major interest. The potentially useful parts of this area included back and side meat, loins, blood, and various internal organs. To make use of these materials one or more panels of the heavy hide needed to be cut away and the ribs severed from the vertebral

ing, perhaps for dry wallows. Subsequently cultural remains were deposited in the depressions, and one may have sheltered a hearth. Artifacts on low-lying ground adjacent to the stream channel were later trodden into the upper few centimeters of the wet, sandy substrate. Whether these surface conditions were intermittent or perennial is not known. The extent of weathering and preservation of clusters of cultural materials indicate rapid burial of the area after these episodes of utilization by humans and animals.

The chronological relationships between the remains in the stream channel and the several loci of cultural remains on the occupation surface present a problem. In a stratigraphic sense all are contemporary, but finer distinctions are needed. The channel deposit probably contains refuse from the adjacent occupation surface. It is possible that the Area 1 mammoth in the channel deposit represents a kill made simultaneously with that represented by the Area 3 carcass on the occupation surface 12 m due west (see Chapter 2 for a different interpretation). These animals were essentially identical in sex, size, and age so far as I can determine. If a multiple kill was made, one can double the estimates for yield of edible products and sizes of hunting party and processing and transporting task units. The relationship of the mammoths and bison 50 m downstream in Area 2 to this event or events is not clear.

The microchronology of discrete (nonsuperposed) clusters of remains on the occupation surface is similarly a problem. The degree of weathering of faunal remains, artifacts, or lithic debris might indicate relative differences in exposure on the surface, but the same kinds of materials do not recur in each cluster for controlled comparison. No striking differences in weathering were observed. One might speculate that bison kills and associated processing activities were separated in time from mammoth kills, since these animals probably required different tactics for pedestrian hunters.

The technique of hunting the mammoth and two bison represented in Area 3 is not ascertainable from the remaining evidence. These animals were brought down on dry ground within a few meters of a watering area; they apparently were not wounded and pursued over long distances as might be expected. In view of the paucity of weapons recovered, the utilization of carcasses of naturally dead animals is possible but less likely, I think, than the surround method evidently employed in Area 4. One bison was a juvenile, the other a young adult, and the mammoth a middle-aged adult. Could they have been weakened by poisoned water or drought? If not, perhaps 10 or more hunters could contain and dispatch a large mammoth by inflicting an initial mortal wound and repeated disabling wounds.

The processing and utilization of the Area 3 mammoth, adduced from the carcass, is reasonably well known. It was estimated that this animal could have provided 2,075 kg of edible products. About 90 percent of this amount would have been muscle and the remaining 10 percent edible organs and blood. The processors' tool kit inferred from one fragmentary tool and the contents of the associated knapping area (A3-2) numbered no less than five cutting tools. There was no evidence of associated cooking, but some bone-working may have accompanied the primary task. The processing task unit could not easily have moved the heavy limb segments and cranium with fewer than three persons, and it is likely that some such small segment of the hunting party carried out this activity. However, the transportation of food materials must have required a larger group. If reduced by thorough drying, a transporting group of 9 to 16 individuals bearing 25-kg to 45-kg loads could have carried away 415 kg (about 913 pounds), representing thorough utilization of the carcass. Such a group could have constituted a hunting party of the size postulated for accomplishing the surround. But if no drying was employed, a load of 2,075 kg would have required from 46 to 83 individuals for transportation of food materials from the kill.

The debitage and tools from Area 3 provide new information about Clovis lithic technology, although perhaps representing only a facies of that technology. A greater variety of knapping activities would have been carried on in habitation sites, and quarry sites might provide evidence of another aspect of technology. Area 3 lithic debris was produced largely from bifaces, probably entirely by a soft hammer or baton technique. One or more blades produced either by direct or indirect percussion were also present in the collection. The best example (Fig. 5.13*e* and 5.14*e*) was undoubtedly manufactured elsewhere.

The bifacial preform for preparation of cutting tools was an important component of the processing tool kit. Edge grinding seems to be a diagnostic character of the preform and of the sharpening and thinning flakes. Such preforms were readily converted to multipurpose, leaf-shaped, cutting tools that could be used and resharpened until the minimum useful tool size was attained. The bifacial preforms for cutting tools may have differed from those for projectile points primarily in the dimension of thickness, although a generalized preform may also have been used. Specimens that have been interpreted as thin bifacial knives or preforms for bifacial knives are best known from Paleoindian habitation sites at Holcombe Beach, Michigan, and Debert, Nova Scotia (Fitting and others 1966: 62; MacDonald 1966: 62). The type is less well known from western Clovis sites, but is represented by tools, tool fragments, or debris at Blackwater Draw and Mockingbird Gap, New Mexico (Howard 1935, Plate 29; Weber and Agogino 1968). A single edge-ground flake of bifacial retouch, recovered with mammoth bones at the Lehner Site, may represent sharpening of a bifacial cutting tool, whereas primarily unifacial tools were collected there (Haury and others 1959).

The ratio of debitage to tools in Area 3 is approximately 500:1, or 315:1 if bifaces inferred from debitage are included. These ratios reflect the extensive preparation of tools carried on in Area 3, presumably associated with the processing of large animals. Although only three carcasses were discovered here, others are known from the adjacent stream channel deposit and more may have been removed by modern arroyo-cutting, as was a part of the debitage. The debitage:tool ratio probably also reflects the retrieval of serviceable tools. The careful collection of lithic debris at Murray Springs is in part responsible for this high ratio, which far exceeds values reported by Wilmsen (1968b) for eight Paleoindian sites. Debitage:tool ratios are subject to serious sampling errors unless excavation procedures are adapted to standardized recovery of lithic debris, but debitage:tool ratios based on adequate samples should reflect similarities or differences in knapping activity among site areas or sites.

The bone tool and worked bone from Area 3 give some insight into the perishable component of Clovis equipment and techniques for working bone. An Upper Paleolithic groove and splinter method was used to separate sections from mammoth long bones, by-products of the kill, which were then shaped by carving and grinding into finished tools. The shaft straightener may represent a tool finished at the site of the kill or it may have been an item of equipment carried by the hunting party. The context of discovery favors neither one hypothesis nor the other.

THE MULTIPLE BISON KILL, AREA 4

Among the spatially segregated occupation floors excavated at Murray Springs, Area 4 (Fig. 5.19) was in several respects the best preserved. Densely clustered lithic debris, locations of tools and tool fragments, and articulated or near-articulated bison skeletal remains were positive evidence of primary context. The methods of excavation and analysis of remains in Area 4 were thus adapted to three requirements: (1) assessment of preservation or disturbance, (2) exposure of the entire occupation floor, and (3) precise recording and recovery of all nonperishable residue. In this manner internally consistent clusters of remains (activity loci) were defined, permitting comparison with the structure of other sites and site areas.

Occupation Surface

Most of the occupation surface in Area 4 was developed on green mudstone, the Sobaipuri Member (Stratum D), in low areas and on white marl of the Coro Member (Stratum E) in higher areas. A relief of 210 cm occurred within the excavated area, with an average slope of 4.8 percent to the north. The black organic mat, Stratum F_2, covered most of Area 4, thickening to 20 cm in low areas and thinning and disappearing to the south where the old surface rises. There were no slope deposits containing occupational debris as in Area 3, because there are no F_1 channel sands in Area 4. No weathering of the occupation surface itself was observed other than possible sculpturing of the marl surface.

Bison Remains in Area 4

Area 4, excavated in 1968 and 1969, comprises an irregular area of about 390 square meters penetrated by the headcut of the South Branch of Curry Draw (Fig. 5.19). Bison bone was concentrated in a crescent-shaped area of about 120 square meters that was bisected in 1967 by the headcut and thus partly removed. The occupation surface, from 1.4 m to 3.0 m below the modern surface, was characterized by irregular microrelief, including three curious oval depressions, described below. The paleotopography of the occupation surface was mapped at 20–cm contour intervals in Area 4 (as in the other site areas) to

Table 5.3. Comparison of Observed Numbers of Skeletal Elements with Original Numbers in Eleven Bison from Area 4

Element	Observed Left	Observed Right	Observed Unsided	Observed Total (Ob)	Expected Total (Ex)	Frequency (Ob/Ex)
Large Appendicular*						
Scapulae	7	5	5	17	22	.72
Humeri	7	6		13	22	.59
Radii	4	6	1	11	22	.50
Ulnae	1	1	1	3	22	.13
Metacarpals	4	4	3	11	22	.50
Innominates			5	5	22	.23
Femora	2	2	1	5	22	.23
Tibiae	1	1		2	22	.32
Metatarsals	2	3	2	7	22	.32
Small Appendicular*						
Carpals			9	9	88	.10
Tarsals			28	28	88	.32
Patellae			1	1	22	.05
First phalanges			19	19	88	.22
Second phalanges			16	16	88	.18
Terminal phalanges					88	
Axial*						
Sacra				2	11	.18
Hyoid arches					11	
Crania				11	11	1.00
Mandibular rami	10	9		19	22	.86

*Elements not tabulated: fragmentary shafts, sesamoids, sternal and costal elements, vertebrae, ribs.

determine critical slopes or gullies where dispersion of remains could have occurred. Natural dispersion does not seem to have affected any portion, nor are there tracked surfaces within Area 4, although such areas occur in the northwest corner of Area 5 (Fig. 1.9c) and 25 m to the southeast in Area 3 (Fig. 5.10). The inference is that Area 4 was relatively high and dry at the time of the bison kill but adjacent to a muddy swale (see Plate 8 in Chapter 2).

Bone Preservation

In comparison to other reported Paleoindian bison kills, the bone preservation in Area 4 was poor. A selection of relatively well-preserved elements is shown in Figures 5.20 and 5.21. Superior preservation was observed for stratigraphically contemporary bison bones from the Wolf Creek channel fill, especially in Area 2. Presumably, the Area 4 bison bone was exposed and weathered on the occupation floor for some brief period prior to burial. It is also certain that human fragmentation of bones occurred and that deep alluviation of overburden resulted in some compression of bone. Bone was consistently light, soft, and friable, but enamel and dentine components of teeth were well preserved. Every whole or fragmentary specimen was impregnated with preservative as exposed. It is unfortunate that bone periosteal surfaces were altered to the extent that butchering marks (or marks of scavengers or rodents) were not observed except in a few doubtful cases.

About 340 catalogued vertebrate specimens (Appendix D), comprising many more individual elements, were recovered in Area 4. More than 95 percent of this material represents bison remains deposited on the occupation floor as the result of human activity. In spite of poor preservation, the largest part of this collection was scrupulously identified to element, in some cases to sex and, in the case of appendicular elements, to side (Table 5.3), so that the distribution of animal parts is reasonably well known. The variation in preservation among bison skeletal elements may be summarized as follows:

(1) Crania were represented by pairs of petrosals (Fig. 5.20d, e) and groups of upper cheek

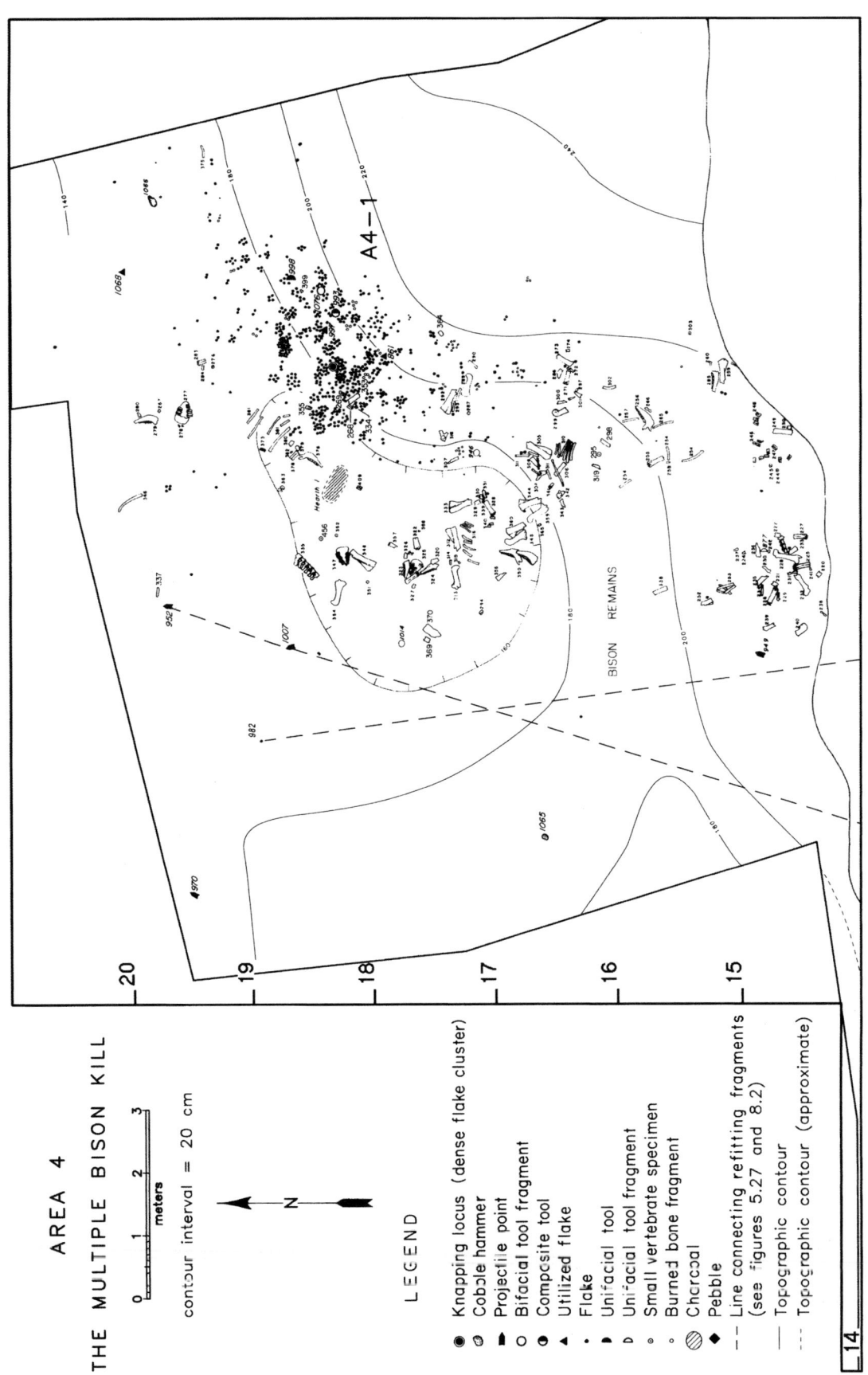

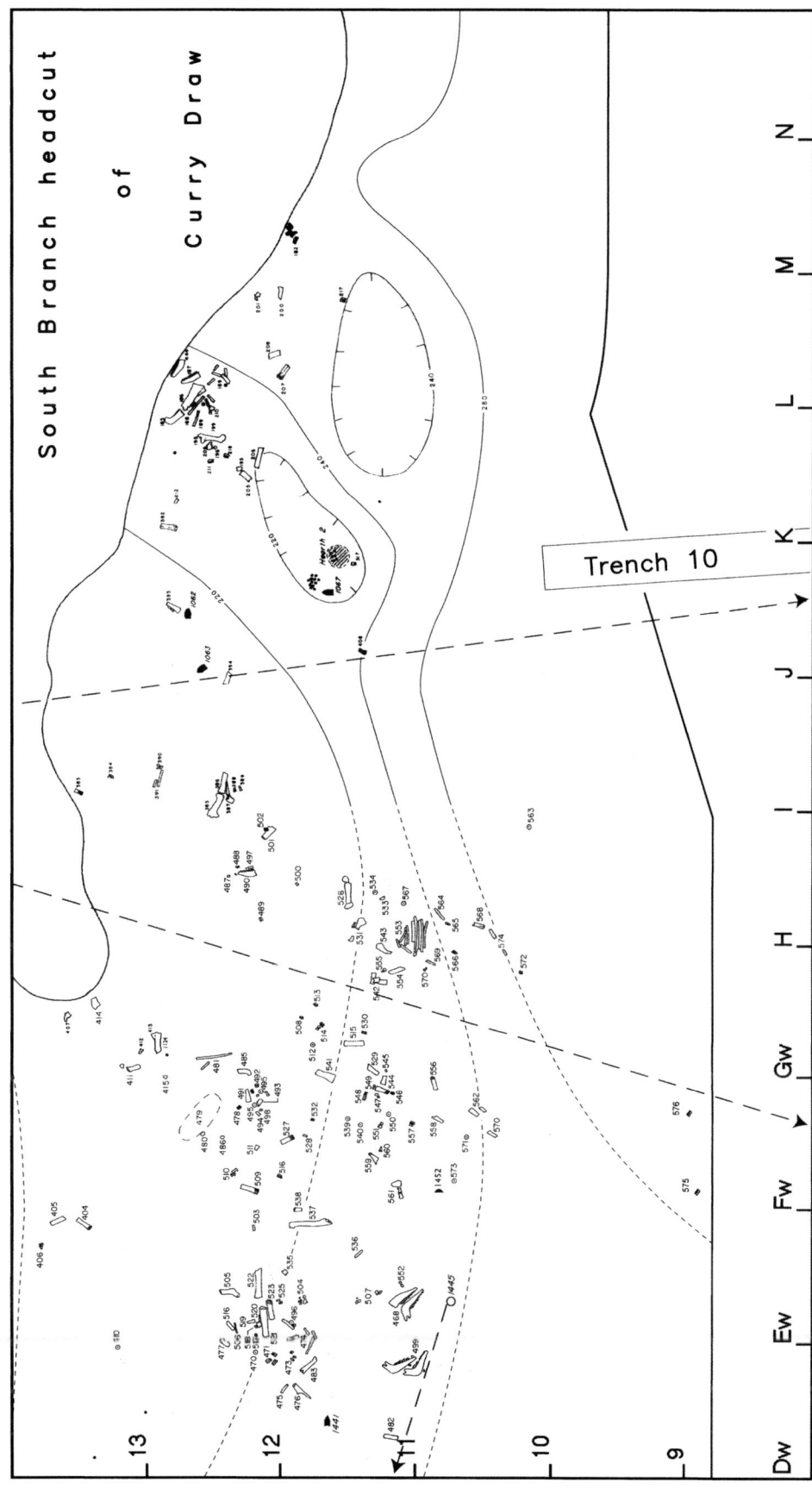

Figure 5.19. Distribution of remains in Area 4.

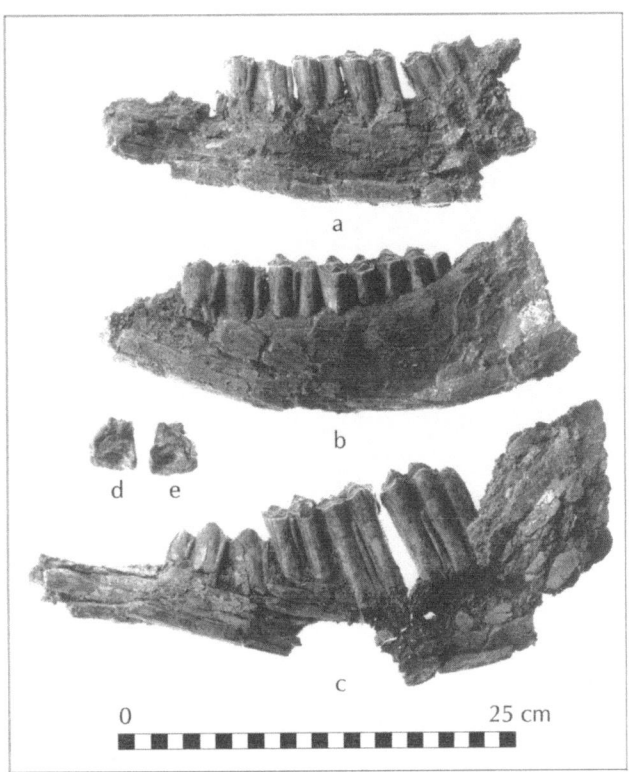

Figure 5.20. Bison skeletal elements from Area 4: *a-c*, mandibular rami; *d*, *e*, petrosals.

Figure 5.21. Bison skeletal material from Area 4: *a*, metatarsal; *b*, metacarpal; *c*, calcaneum; *d*, *e*, phalanges; *f*, astragalus.

teeth; there were no horn cores and only traces of cranial bone remained.

(2) Mandibular rami were moderately well preserved with the cheek tooth rows intact (Fig. 5.20*a–c*).

(3) Vertebral centra, processes, and spines were identifiable, but nearly disintegrated.

(4) Segments of ribs were normally fragmented and compressed (Fig. 1.8*a*).

(5) Large limb bones with medullary cavities were collapsed and epiphyses more or less deteriorated.

(6) Relatively robust metapodials, carpals, and tarsals were moderately well preserved (Fig. 5.21*a, b*).

(7) Pelves and sacra were poorly represented, sometimes as almost shapeless masses of cancellous tissue.

(8) Small appendicular elements, such as patellae, phalanges, and sesamoids, were preserved and identified only in low frequency (Table 5.3; Fig. 5.21*d, e*).

Number of Individuals

The count of bison crania indicates the presence of 11 animals in Area 4 and of mandibular rami at least 10 animals (Table 5.3). No other skeletal elements were sufficiently abundant to corroborate this minimum. Scapulae, normally preserved only as head and neck portions with traces of the blade, indicate a minimum of seven animals. The pattern of thorough dismemberment in Area 4 with scattering of like elements or units rather than sorted concentrations suggest that the strikingly low frequencies in Table 5.3 are not the result of removal of a small portion of bone-bearing area by the arroyo headcut. That is to say, it is unlikely that a "stack" of hind limbs or other infrequent elements was carried away by recent erosion. In the following analysis I assume that the arroyo headcut has not removed any crania, that 11 animals are in fact represented on the occupation floor, and that some unknown number of postcranial elements may have been removed by the headcut. The loss of bone by deterioration and erosion limits but does not prohibit inferences about past human removal or destruction of bone. In conjunction with other positive lines of evidence discussed below, the frequencies of certain skeletal elements permit inferences about the nature of bison processing in Area 4.

Species and Size

Fossil bison taxonomy is based on skulls with horn cores; where these are lacking the investigator has often relied on female metapodial measurements (Bedord 1974; Guthrie 1970; Lorrain 1968; Skinner and Kaisen 1947). The Area 4 sample is too small for entirely positive identification of species, but can certainly suggest the order of size in mature animals. The greatest overall lengths of six mature female metacarpals, which are relatively well preserved and free of distortion, range from 215.0 mm to 231.5 mm with a mean of 219.8 mm. These measurements clearly differentiate the Area 4 bison from the modern species and place them well within the overlapping size range of *Bison antiquus* and *B. occidentalis* (Bedord 1974, Table 5.3; Lorrain 1968, Table 21). In the decreasing size gradient from early (*B. antiquus*) to later (*B. occidentalis*) extinct species (or subspecies of *Bison bison* according to Wilson 1974b), the small Area 4 sample falls near the larger end, as expected.

Since astragali are normally well preserved and are not destroyed in processing of kills, the volume of this element is also used as a size indicator in fossil bison. The sample from Area 4 includes nine astragali, which range in volume from 72.0 cc to 136.0 cc with a mean of 106.1 cc. However, some astragali of animals with immature metacarpals (distal condyles unfused) may be included in the measured sample, and, judging from other postcranial elements, all other astragali may represent females. The interpretation of these volumes is essentially the same as for metacarpal lengths, a large extinct bison in the *B. antiquus-B. occidentalis* range (Lorrain 1968, Table 23; Sellards 1955; Ziemens and Ziemens 1974).

Thus, with two imperfect lines of osteological evidence and the probability of *B. antiquus* in a terminal Rancholabrean fauna, the Area 4 bison are tentatively assigned to that species (Marcus 1960). A mature bull from Rancho la Brea stood about 1.8 m at the shoulder and differed from the living species in greater stature, larger skull and horn cores, and longer vertebral spines, all reflected in heavier body weight (Stock 1963). Wheat (1967, 1972) estimated the body weight of *B. occidentalis* from the Olsen-Chubbuck Site in Colorado as 25 percent greater than the modern species, and presumably the bison population represented at Murray Springs is at least of this order. Body weights are considered below under butchering.

Table 5.4. Age Estimates for Ten Bison Lower Dentitions from Area 4

Field Number	Specimen Description	Tooth Eruption and Wear Group (Reher 1974)	Age Estimate (Years)
393	Left ramus	Group 2	1.0–1.5
575, 576	Incomplete mandible	Group 2	1.0–1.5
499	Mandible	Group 3	2.0–2.5
187, 444	Mandible	Group 4	3.0–3.5
256, 285	Mandible	Group 4	3.0–3.5
323, 324	Mandible	Group 4	3.0–3.5
490, 502	Left ramus	Group 4	3.0–3.5
279, 376	Mandible	Group 5	4.0–4.5
350	Mandible	Group 5	4.0–4.5
468	Mandible	Group 6	Over 5.0

NOTE: An additional animal is represented by a cranium with upper dentition, attributed to Group 4, but no mandible.

Age Composition

The ages and sexes of animals in the Area 4 kill have been determined insofar as sample size and preservation permit. In a preliminary study (Hemmings 1969, 1970), bison mandibles were assigned age estimates in years based on tooth eruption and wear stages for fossil bison from Skinner and Kaisen (1947) and for modern bison from Kehoe (1967). I assumed that life spans, growth rates, and dental changes were essentially comparable in the extinct and living species. A recent study of age groups for a much larger sample of *Bison antiquus* mandibles from Wyoming by Reher (1974, Table 2.1) has been used to refine the Area 4 age estimates with the result presented in Table 5.4. At the Casper Site Reher identified 18 calves of about 0.6 year (seven months), hence the time of that kill was November. The age groups of older Casper site animals were presented in increments of one year (1.6, 2.6, 3.6 years, and so on). No such precision was attained in this study of ten mandibles. The small sample size, variability, and departures from Reher's criteria have resulted in 0.5-year age ranges (in increments of 1 year) assigned to each mandible in Table 5.4.

On the whole the Area 4 mandibles were slightly less mature in tooth eruption and wear characteristics than at the Casper Site, suggesting that the Murray Springs kill was made a few months earlier in the year (probably between early summer and early fall). However, calving times and range conditions were not necessarily comparable in southern Arizona and central Wyoming (about 1,300 km, or more than 800 miles, apart north-south). For example, Seton (1929: 687) places the "running season" of southern herds two months earlier than in recent northern bison herds. It does not seem possible to fix the time of the Area 4 kill precisely by means of lower dentitions, but summer is the best present estimate. (A more recent analysis of the season of the kill is presented in Chapter 6.)

One of the 11 bison in Area 4 is not represented by a mandible. The cranium of this animal is one of five, generally poorly preserved, south of the arroyo headcut (Fig. 5.19). A reasonable age estimate for this individual is Group 4 (3.0–3.5 years) or the predominant age group (Table 5.4).

Age indications from postcranial elements are even more limited by poor bone preservation in Area 4. Two metacarpals, representing different animals, were incompletely fused distally. Presumably, these are from the yearlings or two-year-old in Table 5.4. Fusion of the distal epiphysis at the end of the fourth year (rather than 2.5–3.0 years) as reported by Wilson (1974a: 144) for European bison, is inconsistent with dental age criteria in the Area 4 bison. That is, many more immature metacarpals should have been present with the slower growth rate. Essentially, there were no other usable age indicators among postcranial elements such as pelves, which could supplement age information from dentitions.

Sex determination, again in the absence of skulls and horn cores, was based on observations and measurements of postcranial elements. On this basis, no mature bulls were included among the animals killed. The forelimb elements, which are relatively well represented (Table 5.3), include only small- to moderate-sized long bones. Comparative specimens from large bulls in Area 2 reflect the heavy forequarters of these animals in contrast to the gracile forelimbs from Area 4. Other less characteristic elements of the postcranial skeleton tend to corroborate this contrast. The composition of the group of eleven animals, therefore, is considered to have been two yearlings, a two-year-old, five heifers or young cows, and three mature cows. Breeding condition and full growth was probably reached in the cows at three to five years (Seton 1929).

If the season of the kill, summer, has been correctly inferred, calves of a few months age should have been present and were not. Furthermore, according to Frison (1974: 19), fetal skeletons show up in nearly all bison kills because of normal variation in calving times. Presumably, this variation need not be represented among the few breeding cows in Area 4. However, one or more fetuses as well as several calves may have been transported from the kill site as entire animals. It is unlikely that nonpreservation can account for their complete absence in Area 4.

Other Vertebrate Remains

Partial dentitions of three or more other animals were found on the occupation floor in the vicinity of bison remains and cultural refuse. They include three upper cheek teeth and alveolar bone fragments from an extinct peccary (*Platygonus*); six deciduous upper cheek teeth without any bone from a yearling or two-year-old horse (*Equus*); and scattered upper and lower cheek teeth without bone from one or more adult horses. Presumably these specimens were deposited slightly earlier than the bison kill and were exposed to weathering for a longer period. There is no evidence to suggest that these animals were kills, although they are stratigraphically penecontemporary with human activity at Murray Springs.

Cultural Remains

The cultural remains in Area 4 include two hearths located within depressions on the occupation floor, an assemblage of stone and bone tools associated with the bison bone, and a concentration of flaked lithic debris. A radiocarbon date was obtained from one of the hearths as discussed next.

Hearths and Depressions

The occupation surface in Area 4 was marked by three subtle microrelief features. Two similar, closely spaced, oval depressions were present south of the arroyo headcut and a third, larger, irregular depression occurred to the north (Fig. 5.19). These three features and the four other depressions excavated in Area 3 were relatively homogeneous in shape and dimensions but heterogeneous in compass orientation and contents. The three depressions in Area 4 ranged from 2.4 m to 5.6 m in length, 1.1 m to 4.0 m in width, 0.2 m to 0.4 m in depth (below surrounding terrain) and were oriented with long axes east-west or northeast-southwest. The most southerly depression was sterile, but the remaining two contained shallow hearths, burned and unburned bison bone, stone tools, and lithic debris (Fig. 5.19). All three were dug into underlying sandy clay. The most reasonable hypothesis for the origin of these features assumes they were the result of animal rather than human activity and were subsequently adapted to human use, chiefly in providing shelter for the hearths. Specifically, it is suggested that these are bison wallows, as discussed above for the Area 3 depressions.

The hearths in two of the Area 4 depressions were concentrations of wood charcoal without fire-cracked rock or ash, suggesting transitory use. The larger, Hearth 1, consisted of an oval concentration of charcoal, 26 cm by 62 cm, in the low-lying northeast part of the northernmost depression in Area 4 (Fig. 5.19). A linear pattern of woody stems could still be discerned. The fuel wood was identified by the U.S. Forest Products Laboratory as ash (*Fraxinus* sp.), "apparently rotted and crushed before being charred." Ash is a preferred fuel wood (Gay 1974) and was repeatedly selected for such use by Clovis hunters at Murray Springs. Charcoal from Hearth 1 was dated by the University of Arizona Radiocarbon Laboratory at 10,760 ± 100 years B.P. (A-1045), which is statistically consistent with eight charcoal ages from the F_1 channel (Appendix A) and 20 dates from the Lehner Site. However, as stated in Appendix A, this sample may have been slightly contaminated by crumbs of black mat that were not completely removed during pretreatment, making the age a minimum value. In the vicinity of Hearth 1 were a cluster of heat-spalled chert pieces and a scatter of burned cancellous bone fragments, which may suggest that heat treatment of lithic material and rendering of bone marrow were activities associated with this hearth.

The smaller Hearth 2, located in the low southwest end of the other utilized depression (Fig. 5.19), consisted of a patch of charcoal 35 cm in diameter, mixed with charred fragments of bison long bone. Adjacent charred and calcined fragments of several small bison ribs indicate that "side meat" of one of the yearlings (and probably also limb meat) was cooked here during bison processing. The left mandibular ramus of this animal and two Clovis projectile points were located about 2.5 m north of Hearth 2 (Fig. 5.19). A third Clovis point of obsidian was located about 0.3 m west of the hearth within the depression.

Table 5.5. Illustrated Clovis Lithic Tools and Debitage from Murray Springs, Area 4 and Area 5

Field Number	Specimen Description	Raw Material	Figure Reference
949	Projectile point	Chert	5.22f
952/1007	Projectile point	Chert	5.22b
970	Projectile point	Chalcedony	5.22c
1062	Projectile point tip	Chert	5.22d
1063	Projectile point	Chert	5.22e
1067	Projectile point	Obsidian	5.22g
1441	Projectile point midsection	Chalcedony	5.22a
1400	Projectile point base	Chalcedony	5.29a
1436	Projectile point base	Chert	5.29b
1438	Biface	Chalcedony	5.29d
1014	Biface fragment	Chalcedony	5.22h
1403/1445	Broken biface preform	Chalcedony	5.29c
998	Utilized flake	Chert	5.26a
1452	Unifacially retouched blade	Chert	5.22j
1405	Uniface bladelike flake	Chert	5.29e
786	Utilized blade	Chalcedony	5.26h
861	Utilized flake	Chert	5.26e
997	Utilized flake	Chert	5.26c
1066	Cobble hammer	Sandstone	5.24
993	Composite scraper-burin	Chalcedony	5.22i

Projectile Points and Lithic Tools

The stone tool assemblage associated with bison remains in Area 4 includes Clovis projectile points, bifacial preforms and cutting tools, unifacial edged flake and blade tools, utilized flakes and blades, cobble hammers, and a composite scraper-burin (Table 5.5, Figs. 5.22, 5.23). Presumably these tools represent only a part of the weapons and tool kit employed in Area 4. It is likely that an effort was made to retrieve serviceable tools, and the more heavily damaged ones were discarded on the spot. Metric, typological, and descriptive data for most of these specimens have been reported elsewhere (Hemmings 1970). [They are re-evaluated further in Chapter 8.]

The flaked stone tools in Area 4 were manufactured from materials of superior knapping quality, predominantly cherts and chalcedonies introduced from un-

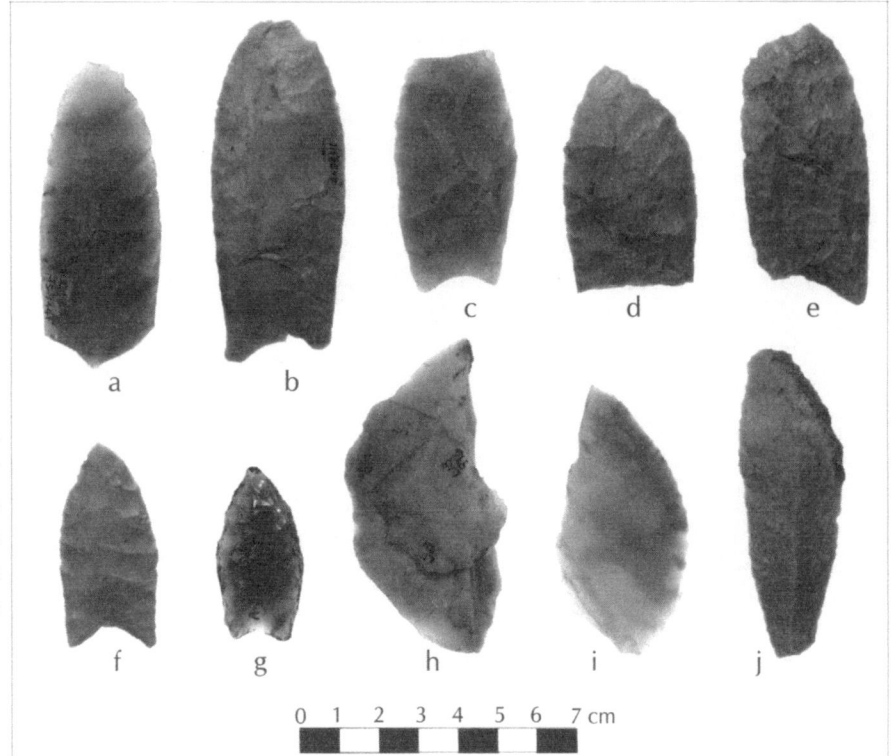

Figure 5.22. Lithic artifacts from Area 4: *a-g*, Clovis fluted projectile points or fragments; *h*, biface fragment with several refitted flakes; *i*, composite burinated tool; *j*, Clovis blade. A flake fits the impact scar on the tip of *b* as shown in Figure 8.8*g*.

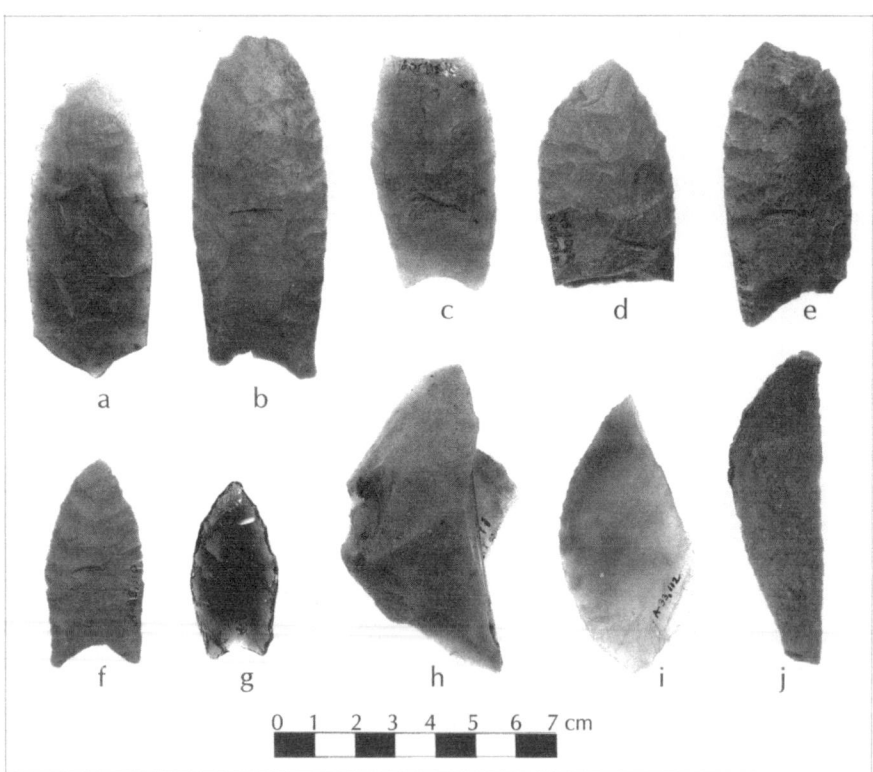

Figure 5.23. Lithic artifacts from Area 4; reverse sides of specimens in Figure 5.22: *a-g*, Clovis fluted projectile points or fragments; *h*, biface fragment with several refitted flakes; *i*, composite burinated tool; *j*, Clovis blade.

known sources possibly outside the San Pedro Valley (see Chapter 8 and Appendix C for more recent evidence of lithic sources). These raw materials occur in projectile points and tools from the Lehner and Naco sites and in projectile points, tools, and debitage from other areas of Murray Springs, but not in collections from later sites in the valley. The chert is lustrous tan or light gray with massed microfossil fragments and the chalcedony is homogeneous matte white or light tan. Presumably the sources for the tan chert were lenses or nodules in outcrops of marine limestones, which are common in southeastern Arizona and northern Sonora. The chalcedony is largely derived from volcanic ash-bearing beds of Pliocene age near Benson (Chapter 8). Petrographic and neutron activation analysis (Wilmsen, personal communication 1970) indicated that the small obsidian Clovis point (Figs. 5.22g) was manufactured from a marekanite (obsidian) nodule ("Apache tear") brought in from perlite deposits at Superior, Arizona, 200 km (124 miles) northwest of Murray Springs (Arizona Bureau of Mines 1969: 360). [Subsequent X-ray fluorescence analysis did not confirm this assessment, and the source now appears to be in east-central Arizona; see Appendix C.] Three slightly modified [or perhaps unmodified, see Chapter 8] marekanite nodules were recovered in Area 3 and a few flakes of obsidian from Area 4; another marekanite nodule, a point base, and more flakes were found in Area 7. The small size of the obsidian Clovis point was probably determined by the form of the raw material.

One of the most interesting aspects of the projectile point series from Area 4 is the extent and kind of damage. Two points are complete, four have impact damage at the tip, three have one or more basal ears snapped, and three are transversely snapped across the blade. It is also of considerable interest that an impact flute flake from the bone concentration in Area 4 can be fitted back on a large point midsection recovered 73 m south in Area 6, near the habitation area. Apparently this point is one of an unknown number employed in the bison kill and retrieved for later use. The basal ear and blade of another projectile point (Fig. 5.22*b*) were found separated by 2.3 m in Area 4. [During subsequent laboratory studies an impact flake found about 140 m to the south in the camp (Area 7) was refitted to the damaged tip of this point, Figs. 8.2, 8.8*g*.] Impact damage was predominant, probably resulting from high velocity casting of projectiles, and transverse snapping was secondary, presumably resulting from thrusting into a vigorously moving animal. This may, in fact, represent the sequence of killing, mortal wounding by repeated dart or spear casts and the *coup de grace* administered by thrusting.

A comparison of the raw materials of projectile points and debitage in Area 4 leads to the conclusion that points were manufactured elsewhere and that local refurbishing cannot have been extensive. One asymmetrical projectile point tip was reworked over impact damage (Fig. 5.22*d*), perhaps locally, as similar raw material is present among the debitage in Area 4.

There are no wear traces on lateral edges of projectile points, as from cutting, and the points were largely found on the periphery of bone concentrations unlike other bifaces and edged tools (Fig. 5.19). Although impressions or remnants of the shaft were sought in the case of each projectile point, no such traces were found anywhere on the occupation floor.

The butchering tool kit in Area 4 appears to have consisted chiefly of sinuous-edged bifaces, generally thicker than projectile points or advanced point preforms, and sharp retouched or unmodified flakes and blades. The bifaces are represented by an asymmetrical chert "fluted" form; a relatively thick chalcedony fragment with edge wear (Fig. 5.22*h*) that was reduced on the spot, resulting in a small amount of debitage; and three other fragments (Table 5.5). At least one biface used in Area 4 is represented by chert debitage alone, and others may have been present but not thinned or sharpened locally. The unifacially retouched flakes and blades, as well as unmodified flakes and blades, have low edge angles (18° to 30°) suitable for meat cutting (Wilmsen 1968a, 1968b).

The majority of cutting tools or presumed cutting tools were found within the bone concentration (Fig. 5.19). Flake tools seem to have been produced expediently during biface sharpening, whereas blades (Fig. 5.22*j*) were fashioned elsewhere from unique raw materials.

Two cobble hammers of sandstone were located on the occupation floor northeast and southwest of Hearth 1 and somewhat distant from other debris (Fig. 5.19). Both specimens are naturally rounded cobbles, convenient for hand-held use and adapted for chopping and smashing, as in dismembering and rendering tasks. The cobble hammer shown (Fig. 5.24) weighs 1.5 kg and is flaked and battered at one end. Sandstone cobbles of this sort were readily available in local

Figure 5.24. Cobble hammer from Area 4.

Figure 5.25. Worked bone gaming(?) piece (*top*) and burned bone with unusual expansion cracks (*bottom*), both from Area 4.

alluvial gravels of both the Millville and Nexpa formations.

The remaining flake implement from Area 4 is a composite tool with three working edges (Fig. 5.22*i*) found 2.5 m east of Hearth 1 (Fig. 5.19). A prominent unifacial scraping edge has edge angles from 42° to 54° degrees, and a second delicate unifacial cutting edge has an edge angle of about 30°. A burin at the distal end of the flake blank constitutes the third edge. Although the most care was expended during manufacture on the scraping edge and burin, only the cutting edge shows slight use. This tool was made elsewhere from unique high quality chalcedony. The sophisticated burin-producing technique is of particular interest: preparation by steep truncation at the platform and notching at the end of the intended burin spall preceded the spall detachment (*Noailles burin*). As described earlier, a section of bison long bone with V-shaped burin grooves (Fig. 5.18), such as this tool would make, was recovered in Area 3.

Bone Tool

Frison (1974) described the modification and use of bison bone itself in processing a mass kill. The condition of preservation unfortunately precludes such observations in Area 4. One fragmentary piece of worked bone was recovered. It is a small, polished and striated, dense bone shaft, oval in section and snapped at both ends (Fig. 5.25). The fragment is 29 mm long, 12 mm in maximum width, and 4.4 mm thick, too thin for a foreshaft or main shaft component. Some other use, such as a gaming or tally piece, may be indicated.

Flaked Lithic Debris

Other than tools, 1,560 lithic items were excavated on the occupation floor in Area 4. About 95.8 percent of this material was concentrated in or near the 4-square-meter flint knapping area (A4-1) just east of Hearth 1; the remaining 66 flakes (4.2 percent) were scattered widely, but associated with the bone concentration (Fig. 5.19). The lithic debris near Hearth 1 includes not only debitage, but also chert spalls produced by heat alone rather than by knapping. The collection from this area ranged from highly heat-altered to apparently unaltered raw material. The Area 4 lithic debris as a whole includes 84 percent chert, 15 percent chalcedony, and 1 percent other materials (obsidian, basalt, silicified limestone, and unidentified flakes or fragments). Some of the debitage pieces are shown in Figure 5.26.

The study of debitage from the knapping area indicates that only a few bifacial cutting tools or preforms were thinned and sharpened at this locus, perhaps one or two of chalcedony and one of chert. Almost all recognizable flakes are typical flakes of bifacial retouch (Bordes 1961: 6). One aspect of the knapping activity is reasonably well known; a relatively large chalcedony biface (Fig. 5.22*h*) with edge wear or platform abrasion was resharpened, producing about 140 flakes, some of which can be replaced on the remaining fragment.

Nearly 800 chert fragments recovered in the knapping area exhibit a range of discoloration, crazing, pot-lidding, and spalling due to heat effects. Much of this chert was recovered in one small locus (Fig. 5.19) and was derived from one piece of nodular chert.

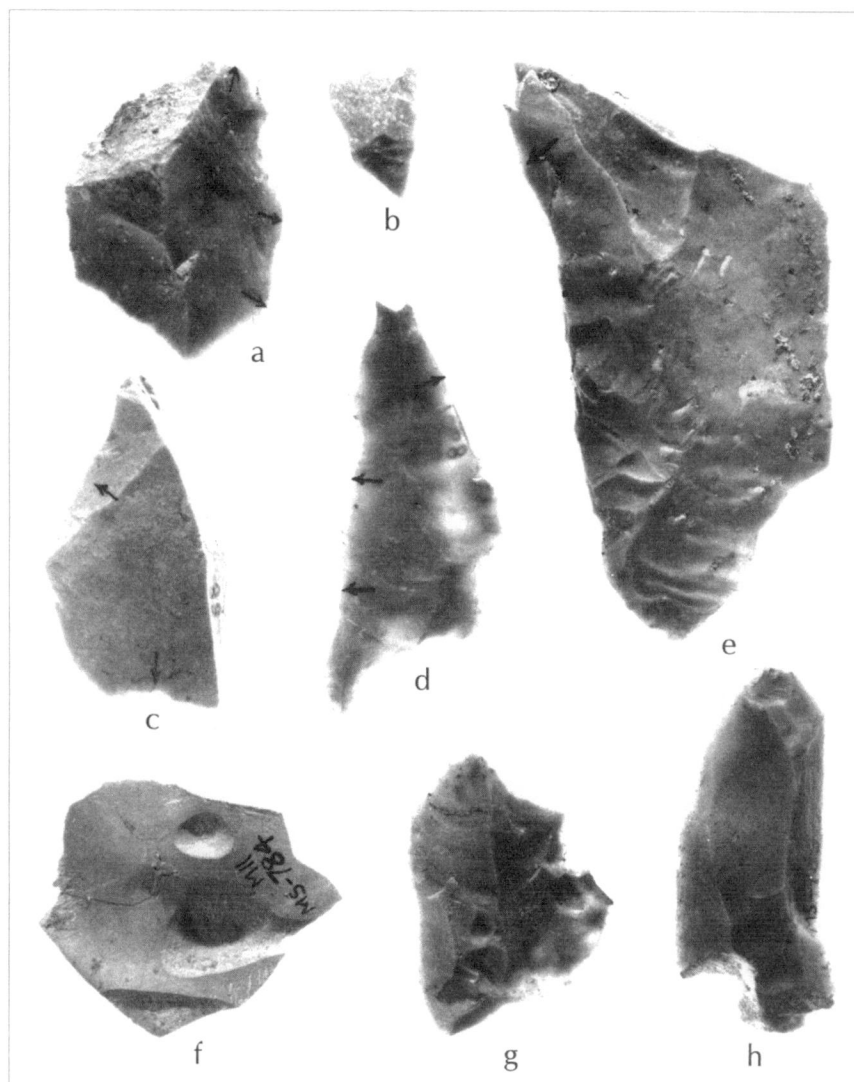

Figure 5.26. Utilized flakes (*a–e, h*) and debitage (*f, g*) from Area 4. Length of *a* is 90 mm.

Because flakes were frequently altered by heat after removal, the intentional heat treatment of the nodule cannot be demonstrated.

The distribution of lithic debris in Area 4, especially within the knapping area and its flake clusters, accurately reflects the nature of knapping operations. Presumably this array of debris was undisturbed (for an alternative view, see Chapter 8), and every effort was made to record it precisely as it was laid down 13,000 years ago.

Bison Processing and Utilization

Bison processing activities in Area 4 are inferred from the distribution of body parts, presence and absence of skeletal elements, the condition of bone, knowledge of bison physiology, and the cultural context of tools, features, and debris. The extensive body of ethnographic and historic data for bison processing, which has been thoroughly reviewed by Wheat (1972), is viewed here as useful in conjunction with empirical evidence.

Bone Distribution and Butchering Sequence

Bone remains in Area 4 were disarticulated and scattered within a 120-square-meter area (Fig. 5.19). Neither recognizable carcasses nor sorted concentrations of like elements were encountered. This distribution is attributed to intensive butchering rather than to erosion, trampling, scavenging, or other natural processes. The pattern or sequence of butchering can be reconstructed with some confidence.

Crania of the 11 animals were distributed essentially along the axis of the bone concentration. Those at the extremes of the bone concentration were about 20 m apart northeast-southwest and the remaining ones irregularly spaced between, a few meters apart, except in one case of two contiguous crania. The positions of these heavy elements may approximate the places where animals fell, as they need not have been moved appreciably during processing. There was no discernible pattern of crania by age except that all three of the youngest animals (two yearlings and a two-year-old), as well as the oldest cow, were located south of the arroyo headcut. It is impossible to say from the condition of crania whether they were opened for brain extraction, but this could have contributed to their deteriorated state.

Mandibles were invariably removed a short distance from crania, and all but two mandibles were separated at the symphysis. The matching rami, however, usually occurred in proximity. Presumably detachment and separation of mandibles and the absence of hyoid arches (Table 5.3) reflect the utilization of tongues in every animal.

Limb elements were widely scattered, although associations (butchering units) of two or more elements from one limb recurred frequently. The most marked of these were nine upper forelimb or scapula-humerus units, six left and three right. In one case the radius and ulna were associated with the shoulder unit, but in other instances the radii were scattered; ulnae were extremely underrepresented (Table 5.3). It appears that the heavy, muscular arm and shoulder were removed by cutting under the scapula, separated from the meatless shank at the wrist, and the upper forelimb stripped of meat as a unit. This upper forelimb was of such great weight and bulk in a mature animal as to be an impractical load. The ulnae may have been snapped at the semilunar notch during this division, or they may have been removed for tool-making purposes. In all but very old animals ulnae were not fused with the radius. One clear example of breaking the humerus at mid-shaft for marrow extraction was observed, and other humeri as well as radii may have been similarly treated, but some were left intact.

The foreshank or metacarpal with carpals and phalanges occurred about equally as articulated or nearly articulated units and as scattered elements. The same was true of hind shanks below the hock, or metatarsals with tarsals and phalanges. These meatless shank units would have been primarily useful as sources of tendon or sinew or as expedient crushing tools. One of the most striking instances of utilization is the absence of the terminal phalanges or hoof elements; not one bone out of an expected 88 was found (Table 5.3). Since the terminal phalanges are as large and robust as other phalanges, differential preservation does not seem to be a plausible explanation for this absence. One possibility is the uniform removal of these elements for glue-making, which was practiced by Plains Indians in historic times. Other possibilities are their destruction through use of the shank and foot as a bone-crushing tool or removal by scavenging animals.

The hind limb was probably removed from the trunk by severing the sacroiliac joint and the pubic symphysis. This chopping operation would result in the fragmentation of innominates and sacra, which were found in low frequency and poor condition (Table 5.3). In two cases axial units consisting of two or more lumbar vertebrae with fragmentary innominates and sacra were observed. The upper hind limb unit or femur-tibia minus the shank was a more reasonable load for transport and comprised two large marrow bones and considerable meat. The low frequency of femora, patellae, and tibiae, therefore, may either be due to carrying away some of the upper hind limb units or to stripping and breaking the large elements for marrow extraction. Only one articulated or nearly articulated upper hind limb unit was observed, representing one of the younger animals. The few other femora and tibiae recovered were scattered and, at least in some cases, intact.

Side meat was obtained by severing the 14 ribs on each side at the neck or nearly at the thoracic vertebrae. The detached sides were then apparently divided again for transport. Although ribs were occasionally scattered, in five instances "half-sides" of six to eight closely grouped ribs were discarded. Since 11 animals would yield 44 such "half-side" units, it would seem that considerable side meat was carried away for use.

The effects of obtaining hump and neck meat from the axial skeleton are not well understood. Dorsal spines were either too deteriorated for identification, or they were removed with the hump meat. The vertebral column was poorly represented and individual vertebrae were often too fragmented or deteriorated to distinguish identifying characteristics. A few cervical, thoracic, and lumbar vertebrae were identified, but no caudals. Although much of this condition is due to poor preservation, some vertebral centra were apparently comminuted and utilized in rendering. Only one segment of six articulated lumbar(?) vertebrae was recorded about 1 m west of Hearth 1 (Fig. 5.19).

A summary of butchering units, those utilized as well as those removed and discarded, includes the following: (1) crania, (2) mandibles, (3) upper forelimbs, (4) foreshanks, (5) upper hind limbs, (6) hindshanks, (7) half-sides, (8) pelvic girdles with lumbars, and (9) segments of vertebral column. This list does not, of course, include the butchering units that are comprised solely of soft or cartilaginous parts; these are discussed below.

The butchering sequence probably began with skinning the animal and dismemberment from the uppermost side. Once the uppermost hide, limbs, and side were removed, the carcass weight was reduced by one quarter; it could then be rolled and the dismemberment repeated. Manipulation of the carcass in a mature bison cow was impractical until dismemberment reduced the weight. Intensive utilization required that the cranium, mandible, and segments of the axial skeleton be separated, and many of the limb and other units subdivided. Whether or not these were highly standardized procedures, the resulting pattern is one of concentrated but fragmented body parts.

Cooking and Rendering

The small sizes and contents of Hearths 1 and 2 do not suggest intensive use in cooking. Hearth 1 contained ash (*Fraxinus*) charcoal and was presumably the source of burned cancellous bone fragments and heat-altered chert scattered to the east and southeast (Fig. 5.19). Hearth 2 was associated with burned limb bone and rib fragments attributed to one of the yearling bison. This material probably represents the cooking of a small amount of choice meat and subsequent discarding of bones in the hearth, perhaps during the processing activity. However, from all indications cooking was not an important aspect of this activity.

Marrow occurs in bison bone in two forms: concentrated in the medullary cavities of the humerus, femur, and tibia, and other long bones and dispersed in the vesicles of cancellous bone such as long bone epiphyses and vertebral centra. Both kinds of marrow were probably extracted in Area 4 on a limited scale. Marrow obtained by smashing the shafts of long bones may have been eaten on the spot. A humerus, for example, contained as much as 900 cc of marrow, but, as was noted above, not all humeri and other marrow bones were exploited.

About 60 fragments of charred to calcined bone from Area 4, including compact bone with cancellous tissue adhering, may be interpreted as the debris of rendering. They could also represent roasting and eating on the spot during butchering. Historically the cancellous fragments were boiled in some suitable container, "bone grease" skimmed from the surface, and the container emptied on or near the hearth (Leechman 1951). In this manner fragments were burned to various degrees. Again, only a limited rendering operation seems to be represented in Area 4.

Meat and By-product Yield

Table 5.6 indicates the prodigious yield of edible parts and by-products that could be obtained from 11 bison, including only cows and juveniles, *under conditions of intensive utilization*. The percents of carcass weight used in Table 5.6, Column 2, are adapted from beef cattle (Ziegler 1954: 97–100, 387). Weaknesses in this comparison are the differences in body part proportions between cattle and bison, between modern and extinct bison, and between older and younger animals. Estimates were made to correct these proportional problems. A yearling may be proportionally deficient in tallow and hide weight, for example. The estimate, however, serves to emphasize apparent maximum yield. The total edible portion alone from 11 animals of "moderate" size constitutes 3,272 kg (about 3.6 tons). Table 5.6 indicates that a thoroughly butchered animal might dress out nearly 55 percent of live body weight in usable meat, viscera, blood, and marrow bone. The usable by-product yield (brains, tallow, and hides) might have added about 14 percent. Less than one-third of carcass weight was "nonusable."

It seems reasonably certain from the distribution of bison remains in Area 4 that processing *was* directed toward intensive utilization, but that the actual yield of edible parts and usable by-products *transported away from the kill* falls short of the potential maximum yield. For the edible parts this is clearly the case; large bones

Table 5.6. Estimated Weights of Body Parts, Organs, and Contents in Eleven Bison from Murray Springs, Area 4

Body Parts	Percentage of Carcass Weight	Body Weight Classes (kg)*				Computed Total†
		Yearling	Two-Year-Old	Heifer/Young Cow	Mature Cow	
Total Carcass Weight	100.0	290.0	460.0	570.0	690.0	5960.0
Upper forelimbs	17.6	51.0	81.0	100.1	121.2	1047.1
Upper hindlimbs	11.8	34.2	54.2	67.2	81.6	703.4
Loins	7.9	22.9	36.4	45.0	54.5	470.7
Plate and brisket	7.4	21.4	34.0	42.2	51.0	440.8
Sides	6.8	19.7	31.2	38.8	46.8	405.0
Blood	1.7	5.0	7.8	9.7	11.8	101.7
Liver	0.9	2.7	4.1	5.2	6.3	54.4
Kidneys	0.6	1.7	2.8	3.5	4.2	36.3
Heart	0.1	0.3	0.5	0.6	0.7	6.2
Tongue	0.1	0.3	0.5	0.6	0.7	6.2
Total Edible Parts	54.9	159.2	252.5	312.9	378.8	3271.8
Hides	10.0	29.0	46.0	57.0	69.0	586.0
Tallow	4.0	11.6	18.4	22.8	27.6	248.4
Brain	0.1	0.3	0.5	0.6	0.7	6.2
Total By-products	14.1	40.9	64.9	80.4	97.3	840.6
Total other (nonusable)	31.0	89.9	142.6	176.7	213.9	1847.6

* Body weight classes estimated for *Bison antiquus*, increasing approximate average weights for modern species by 25 percent.
† Computed totals obtained by multiplying weight class columns by number of animals in each weight class (two yearlings, one two-year-old, five heifers or young cows, and three mature cows).

of upper forelimb and hindlimb units and rib sections representing half-sides were in some cases left behind, although perhaps stripped of meat. Since the habitation area (Areas 6 and 7) was apparently only a few tens of meters away, the task of transporting meat and by-products placed no limit on utilization. From the interpretation of the habitation area at Murray Springs (Chapter 7), we can assume that consumption, preservation, hide-working, and other activity related to bison utilization was carried out locally and on a relatively large scale.

Processing Task Unit

If the bison kills were made during warm weather, the processing task would have been completed rapidly to avoid losses to spoilage. It is likely, therefore, that some segment of the hunting party was recruited for this task. From various lines of evidence the size of the processing task unit was relatively small, perhaps as few as two and probably no more than six people. This evidence includes: (1) the limited number of bifacial cutting tools, retouched or utilized flakes, and cobble or bone hammers that comprise the known tool kit; (2) the small number and size of hearths, apparently used only briefly during processing; and (3) minimal preparation and resharpening of cutting tools, probably by a single flintknapper at a specific location.

Even if the processing of 11 large animal carcasses represents a prodigious task, a few skilled individuals could systematically carry out skinning, dismemberment, stripping, and other immediate tasks in less than a day's time. Wissler (1910: 42) recorded that a single Blackfoot man could butcher 5 to 12 bison in one day with a steel knife, and Turney-High (1937: 119) relates that with almost astonishing skill and speed "a fast [Flathead] worker could butcher a bison carcass in an hour even with a flint knife [but] most men had to take longer." It becomes increasingly clear that the kill-processing sequence, recorded by the remains of Area 4, was a sharply restricted "event."

Procurement

The technique by which 11 bison were contained by pedestrian hunters and brought down within a relatively small, well-defined space can be inferred. Since the paleotopography of the Murray Springs area has been meticulously studied, it is certain that no topographic barrier was available in the vicinity of Area 4, nor was evidence of any artificial enclosure encountered. The surface here was a meter higher than lowlying site areas, and the animals cannot have been mired when killed. From all accounts of the modern species, a group of these large animals was difficult to drive and dangerous to surround and wound (Frison 1974; Roe 1951).

The possibility that the 11 bison were sick, starved, snowbound, blinded, or dying of thirst can probably be ruled out by other evidence. It is more likely the animals were "killed fat," or in prime condition, after the summer rains and before the fall "running season." During this period small summer range "clans" of cows and juveniles, separated from the more dangerous bulls, maintained restricted movements about favored grazing and watering areas. Such small aggregates would have been highly attractive to pedestrian hunters because of their predictable movements and preferred age composition (cows, heifers, juveniles, calves).

At present a surround is the best hypothesis for the technique of containment of the bison in Area 4. The requisite size of the hunting party is mostly a matter of speculation; there are no ethnographic parallels for pedestrian hunters carrying out mass kills of huge animals without the use of pounds, jumps, or traps of some nature. The number of hunters required may have been on the order of two per animal, for a minimum of 22 "armed" males participating in the surround. If some enclosure was used, perhaps fewer hunters would have been required. Presumably the surround was by ambush, and the hunting party did not resort to driving the animals. In this case there was either no "upwind" direction to be avoided on approach or the bison were not sufficiently wary to be startled by an upwind approach. There is some indirect evidence for prevailing northeasterly winds at Murray Springs (Hemmings 1970: 155).

So far as can be determined, the only weapon type used was a light spear tipped by Clovis projectile points. As indicated previously, it probably was both cast (by means of atlatl?) and thrust. Most of the Clovis points were retrieved, a few were lost, and another few damaged beyond further use and discarded at the kill or in the camp.

A reconstruction of the Area 4 bison kill may be hypothesized as follows. Several lookouts were advantageously stationed near the watering place (the now extinct run of Curry Draw). These lookouts sought to avoid alerting watering birds and animals. The large hunting party itself was stationed or encamped at a farther distance, but could be quickly signaled and deployed at the approach of a bison group. All members of this party were thoroughly familiar with animal movements, local terrain and vegetation, wind direction, and other factors related to such predation. The combination of expert hunters, a well-conceived plan, and carefully wrought hunting weapons was a lethal one. Closing rapidly on the watering animals, and inevitably detected, the hunters assaulted the largest animals and those that broke to run. Perhaps not all animals could be contained in the melee, but most of the bison group were soon mortally wounded and brought down, virtually in a "defensive huddle." Wounded cows and juveniles were carefully dispatched by spear thrusts. So great was the skill and organization of the hunting party, that despite the danger of attacking these huge animals, not one hunter came to harm. Only the Herculean processing task remained.

THE HORSE KILL, AREA 5

Near the end of the 1967 field season an attempt was made to locate the western extent of cultural remains at Murray Springs. A test pit was excavated by backhoe (Trench 32) 14 m west of the headcut of the South Branch of the arroyo and 16 m west of the west wall of Area 4. Experience had shown that one-bucket wide backhoe trenches could pass near or even through concentrations of cultural materials without their detection if no large bones or artifacts were exposed. Therefore, the test pit was designed to expose about 30 square meters. When the black mat was removed by hand, the Clovis occupation surface containing both vertebrate remains and lithic debris was again encountered. These materials were indeed sparse enough to have been difficult to detect in narrow trenches. As a result of the new find, the test pit was connected to Area 4 by a trench 2 m to 4 m in width, which proved to be largely sterile. The occupation surface exposed by the test pit was designated Area 5. At the end of the 1969 season Area 5 had been extended to the northwest and eastward to link up with Area 4 (Fig. 5.27).

Area 5, consisting of the test pit and the ground connecting with Area 4, comprised about 100 square meters of occupation surface. Excavation of this area was probably complete, and the materials uncovered

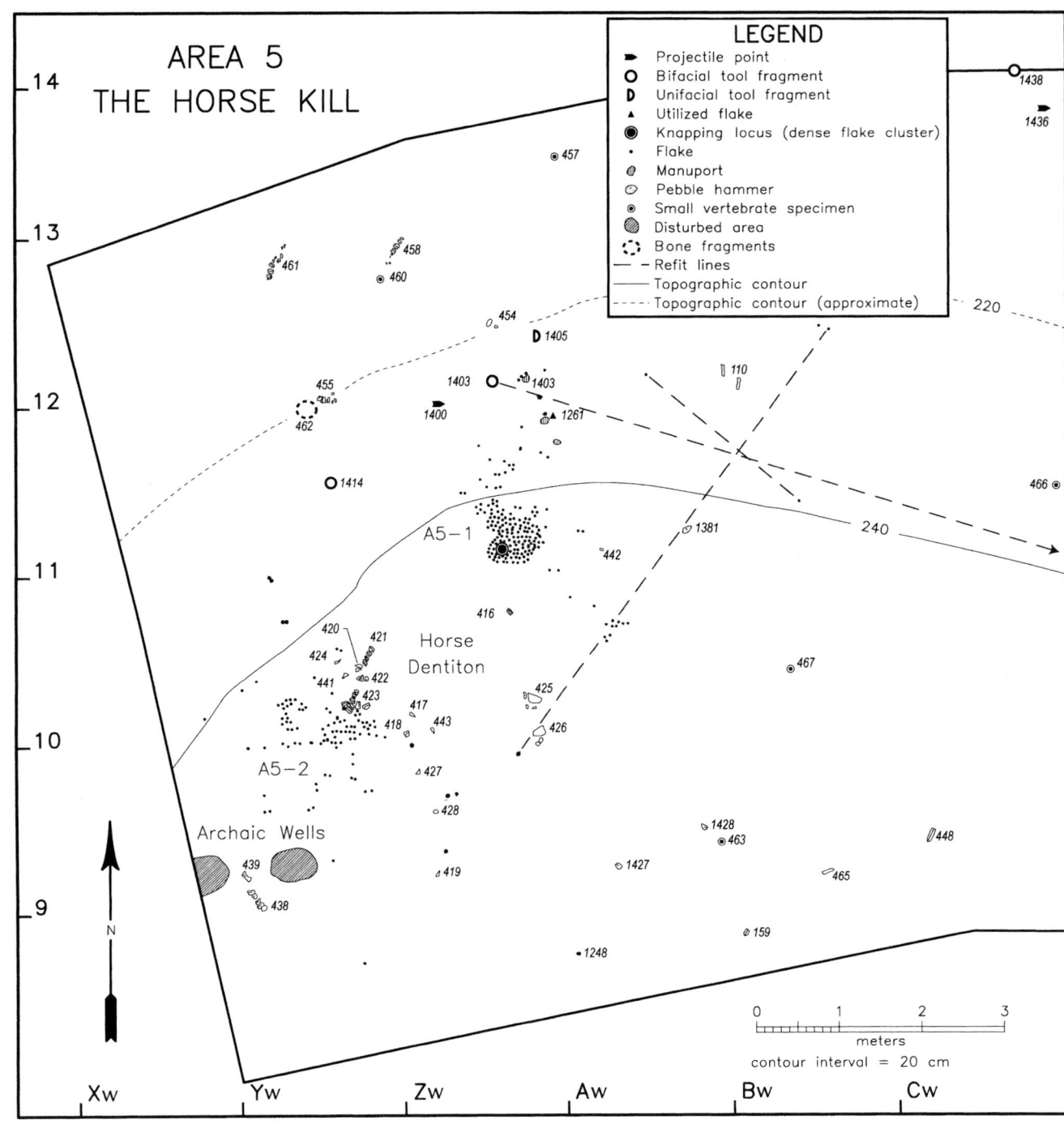

Figure 5.27. Distribution of remains in Area 5. This figure conjoins with Figure 5.19.

are of considerable interest. Remains of a horse (Fig. 5.28) occurred in close association with lithic debris, suggesting the possibility of a kill and utilization of the carcass. Five tools and the bases of two Clovis points were found in Area 5.

Clovis Occupation Surface of Area 5

The portion of the occupation surface uncovered in Area 5 consisted of green Sobaipuri mudstone (Stratum D) with approximately 50 cm of relief. The old surface varied in depth from 2.5 m to 3.0 m below the modern surface. The average slope was about 3.1 percent to the northeast. There was no observable evidence of weathering on or in the upper zone of Stratum D. The black mat (Stratum F_2) blanketed all of Area 5 in thicknesses of 10 cm to 20 cm. Vertebrate remains, especially teeth, and lithic debris were concentrated and juxtaposed in such a manner that little erosional disturbance could have occurred prior to deposition of overlying sediments. It is likely that the array of remains represents essentially undisturbed context.

In the southwest part of Area 5 backhoe excavation revealed two pits of cultural origin (Fig. 5.27) that passed down from younger silts about 1 m above the occupation surface and intersected it (Fig. 2.16f; Foldout 2, Trench 32). Each contained a small amount of charcoal and burned earth in a largely sterile fill and ended about 10 cm below the occupation surface in clay. They could be prehistoric wells, but their actual use is unknown. The time of construction is fixed stratigraphically at roughly 3,000 years ago. They are of primary interest as a cause of disturbance to the Clovis occupation surface. The pits removed only about 0.5 square meter of the surface, but this portion may have included a small number of horse remains.

Vertebrate Remains

In comparison to all other site areas, vertebrate remains in Area 5 were the least well preserved. About 20 catalog numbers were used for vertebrate specimens, including the nearly complete dentition of a horse (Fig. 5.28) and a few unidentifiable postcranial skeletal elements (Appendix D). The enamel and dentine components of the cheek teeth were essentially intact, but the cement had largely disappeared. The remaining bone had weathered to shapeless masses,

Figure 5.28. Lingual view of upper and lower right cheek teeth of the horse from Area 5.

and evidently a considerable amount of bone had completely weathered away. The most satisfactory explanation of this condition is that the bone on the occupation surface in Area 5 was exposed for a sufficient time for thorough deterioration before burial by Stratum F_2. However, the exposure was not so great as to cause disintegration or extensive scattering of teeth.

Horse

The dentition of a horse was concentrated on the occupation surface at two loci about 2 m apart (Fig. 5.27). At one locus the cheek tooth rows of both mandibular rami with a small amount of alveolar bone adhering were largely in place. Scattered about the lower cheek teeth were upper and lower incisors and two upper cheek teeth. At the other locus the right upper cheek teeth were largely in place. Four left upper cheek teeth were missing and the remaining two were recovered 3 m apart. The horse dentition was clearly deposited on the old surface, rather than occurring in either of the bounding strata, and was closely associated with a large amount of lithic debris.

Age and sex. The dentition consisted of the full set of permanent incisors and cheek teeth. According to Cornwall (1957: 227), the last permanent cheek tooth, P4, erupts in living horses at about 3.5 to 4 years.

Simpson's (1961: 17) criteria for aging living horses by incisor wear suggest an animal between 4.5 and 7 years. Cusps are present on all incisors. Neither of the upper canines, which are relatively large in a stallion, was recovered. These are unlikely to have been overlooked in excavation, so the individual may have been a young, fully grown adult mare in breeding condition. It is assumed that the rate of dental development in the extinct and living species is comparable. An alternative is the removal of canines from a stallion's dentition by humans. No postcranial elements were preserved that could corroborate the determination of sex.

Species and size. The dentition is closely comparable to *Equus caballus*, although both incisor and cheek teeth series are relatively large. The teeth have not been studied in detail, but appear to be little different from the living species. The common species contemporary with the Murray Springs horse at Ventana Cave and Rancho la Brea was identified as *E. occidentalis* (Colbert 1950; Marcus 1960). No estimate of the size of the animal is possible with the material available.

Artifacts

Two Clovis point bases, two fragments of the same biface, a small biface, a uniface, a fragment of a utilized flake (Figs. 5.29, 5.30), and a possible pebble hammer were the only tools recovered in Area 5. The scarcity of tools may be due to the retrieval of serviceable ones by users. In addition to the four tools, a large amount of debitage was concentrated in two knapping areas closely associated with the horse remains. Four anomalous rock fragments or manuports also occurred near one of the knapping areas (Fig. 5.27).

Projectile Points

The base of a Clovis point (Fig. 5.29a) was recovered from the occupation surface 1.9 m north-northwest of knapping locus A5-1 (Fig. 5.27). It is made of the same translucent white chalcedony as several other artifacts and many of the flakes from the site. The fragment with ground edges measures 14 mm long by 28 mm wide, and exhibits a maximum thickness of 7 mm; it was broken with a clean transverse snap. Of interest is the presence of pronounced wear on one of the edges of the break, where it intersects the face of the point and creates a nearly right angle edge. Microscopic examination of this polish reveals striations aligned at a slight angle to the broken edge, suggesting that after the point base had broken it was subsequently used as a steep-angled plane.

The second point base (Fig. 5.29b) is of pinkish gray chert and measures 20 mm long by 28 mm wide; the basal corners flare slightly. It was broken by impact in a complex fracture that includes a transverse snap and burinlike impact flakes. The ground edges of the basal concavity and one lateral margin have been blackened by burning, probably after breakage.

Bifaces

The first of the two bifaces is a small, leaf-shaped complete specimen of gray chalcedony (Fig. 5.29d). It measures 63 mm long, 36 mm wide, and 9 mm thick. Although its edges are slightly irregular, they are generally well finished. These attributes suggest that it may have served as a cutting implement that was abandoned because of its small size.

Two fragments of a white chalcedony biface (Fig. 5.29c) were also recovered in Area 5, along with a quantity of debitage produced during its retouching. The two fragments, separated by 7.5 m, were found to the north and east of knapping locus A5-1 (Fig. 5.27); 21 flakes from this biface were present in this knapping locus. Refitting of the fragments reveals a biface 89 mm long, 40 mm wide, and 13 mm thick. It is comparatively thick relative to its width, and was broken by a flake struck from one end that terminated in a reverse hinge (hinge through) break. Several of the flakes can be refitted to the biface. It appears that attempts to thin it from the lateral margins were unsuccessful, and the attempt to thin it from the end resulted in its breakage.

Uniface

A single bladelike flake (Fig. 5.29e) of translucent gray chert with a fine unifacial retouch along a lateral margin was found 1.8 m north of knapping locus A5-1 (Fig. 5.27). The retouch consists of flakes 2 mm to 3 mm long and creates an irregularly convex working edge with an angle of 45° to 55°. The opposite lateral margin is largely cortical. This tool is made on a flake struck from a core, and although bladelike in appear-

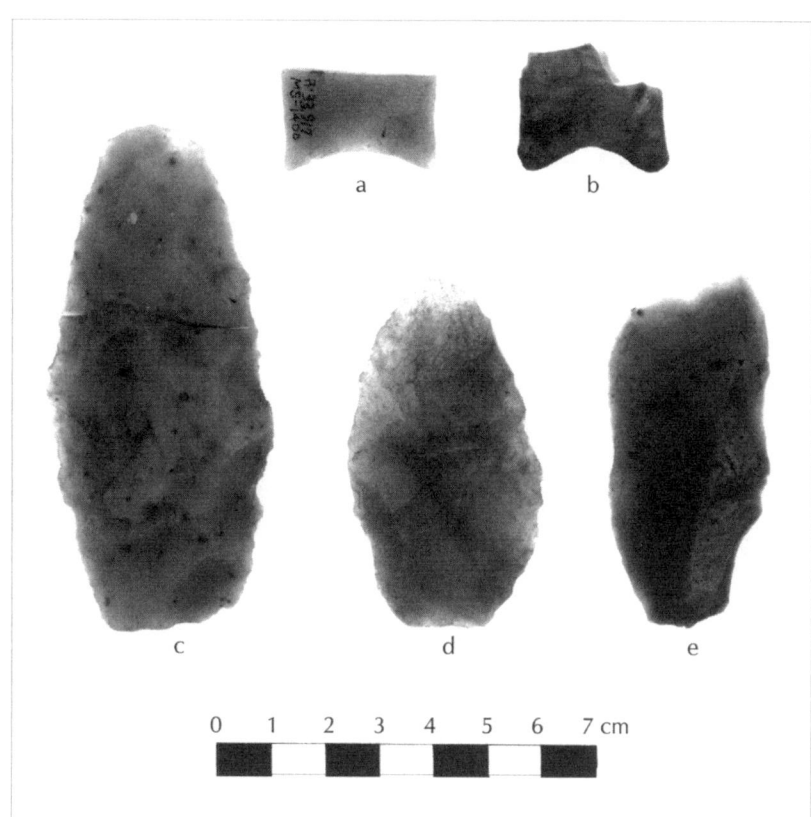

Figure 5.29. Lithic artifacts from Area 5: *a*, chalcedony Clovis point base; *b*, chert Clovis point base; *c*, broken chalcedony biface preform; *d*, chalcedony biface; *e*, unifacially retouched bladelike chert flake.

Figure 5.30. Lithic artifacts from Area 4, reverse sides of artifacts in Figure 5.29: *a*, chalcedony Clovis point base; *b*, chert Clovis point base; *c*, broken chalcedony biface preform; *d*, chalcedony biface; *e*, unifacially retouched bladelike chert flake.

ance it is not necessarily a product of intentional blade manufacture from a prepared core. The tool is 64 mm long, 30 mm wide, and 10 mm thick.

Utilized Flake

A small fragment of a chert flake, probably a cutting tool, retains 18 mm of convex edge with an angle of 31° that has apparent use chipping. The fragment was recovered 3 m northeast of the horse dentition (Fig. 5.27). The material of the flake does not occur among the debitage in Area 5.

Pebble Hammer and Manuports

A sandstone pebble recovered on the occupation surface east of the horse remains and closely associated with a knapping area (Fig. 5.27) may have been used as a hammer, as one end appears battered. Because of its small size and weight (180 g), it was suitable for use as a relatively light percussion hammer. However, it does not exhibit extensive or repeated use, nor is there evidence in the debitage of Area 5 for a hard hammer knapping technique.

Four small, angular fragments of sandstone, weighing between 20 g and 60 g and derived from two naturally rounded pebbles, were recovered on the occupation surface within 1 m of a knapping area (Fig. 5.27). The fragments were clearly introduced by humans, as no such coarse particles occur naturally in sediments bounding the occupation surface. They are weathered and friable in their present condition, but might represent either fire-cracked rock or breakage of two pebble hammers.

Flaked Lithic Debris

About 1,030 flakes and flake fragments were recovered on the occupation surface in Area 5. More than 97 percent of this material was concentrated in two knapping areas, A5-1 and A5-2, located on the occupation surface 2 m northeast of and among the elements of the horse dentition, respectively (Fig. 5.27). The remaining flakes, less than 3 percent of the total, were scattered over the surface at varying distances from the knapping areas.

Essentially all lithic debris in Area 5 was located in situ. Thus, the distribution map (Fig. 5.27) accurately represents the observed array of faunal remains and debitage. It is likely that an essentially complete, undisturbed sample of lithic waste resulting from localized knapping activities was obtained.

All lithic debris from Area 5 was produced as debitage; no component of fragments produced by heat alteration alone was present as in Area 4. Only two flakes exhibited crazing or discoloration. These pieces were distinct from raw materials among the debitage, occurred outside the knapping areas, and presumably are unrelated to the primary activities inferred for Area 5.

The debitage of Area 5 is comparable in most respects to the collections from Areas 3 and 4. About half the flakes and flake fragments are less than 4 square millimeters in greatest surface area. However, the size of the collection permitted smaller as well as larger debris to be studied. The debitage as a whole contains 85.1 percent chalcedony, 10.7 percent chert, and 4.2 percent jasper. Flakes of bifacial retouch produced by a soft hammer technique are predominant in the collection. Frequently, evidence of edge grinding of bifaces or dulling of edges was preserved on the flake platforms. No flake types or fragments were recognized that could not have resulted from preparation and thinning of bifacial preforms. Presumably, bifacial cutting tools were produced and sharpened during processing of a kill, analogous to those activities inferred for Areas 3 and 4.

Knapping area A5-1, located 2 m northeast of the horse lower dentition, contained 916 flakes and flake fragments concentrated in an area of about 2 square meters (Fig. 5.27). Some 816 flakes (89% of debris) were removed from a single large biface of chalcedony. Thin expanding flakes up to 55 mm in length and 45 mm in width had been struck off by a skillful knapper. The locus of preparation of this tool was represented by dense flake clusters of identical raw material (Fig. 5.27). Two other bifaces were represented by 17 chalcedony and 59 chert flakes. An additional 24 flakes of distinct chalcedony and jasper probably represent tools that were worked minimally or for which the locus of knapping remains unexcavated. Certainly one bifacial preform and perhaps two or more others are the sources of debitage concentrated in A5-1. Probably the work of a single knapper is represented by this relatively small, dense concentration of knapping debris.

One flake of chert found 1 m southwest of the center of knapping locus A5-1 appears to be either an impact flake or possibly a channel flake from a projectile point. It was recognized as such during laboratory analysis in the mid-1970s. Because it is of a chert variety not present among the other chert flakes in Area 5, it may well be an impact flake.

Knapping area A5-2, consisting of 104 flakes in an area of about 3 square meters, was closely associated with the horse lower dentition (Fig. 5.27). Two bifacial preforms had been worked in this area by the removal of 49 chert and 44 jasper flakes of bifacial retouch. An additional nine flakes are identical with the extensive chalcedony debitage of A5-1, and two flakes are of exotic chert and chalcedony. The debitage of chert and jasper from the two bifacial preforms comprised 89.4 percent of the total collection from the A5-2 locality.

An interesting attribute of the jasper flakes was slight abrasion of the ridges between flake scars on exterior surfaces. The abrasion was readily observable because of the deep red color and matte surface of the jasper. Ridges on smaller flakes and on parts of larger flakes lacked abrasion. Evidently this bifacial preform had become abraded on high surface areas by contact with other hard materials. Only the first generation of flakes removed subsequent to this wear would show abrasion. One plausible explanation of the cause of facial wear is that preforms were transported in common containers with surfaces in abrasive contact. These preforms would be expected to exhibit facial wear, observable in varying degrees depending on hardness, color, luster, and duration of contact.

Overview of Area 5

The salient interpretive problem of the occupation surface debris in Area 5 is whether these remains represent the kill and processing of a horse. Although the contemporaneity of horse with humans in the New World has been established at a number of sites on both continents, including horse material in the Volcanic Debris Layer at Ventana Cave, Arizona (Colbert 1950), convincing evidence of human exploitation of horses is more limited.

Two partial horse carcasses associated with weapons and tools have been reported from Hueyatlaco, Mexico, and Laguna de Tagua Tagua, Chile (Irwin-Williams 1967; Montané 1968). At Laguna de Tagua Tagua evidence of the use of horse bone for tools was found in addition to evidence of the processing of a carcass for food materials. Burned horse bone and artifacts more than 8000 years old were found by Bird (1938) at Palli Aike and Fells' caves in Chile.

The evidence now at hand indicates with reasonable certainty utilization of a horse carcass in Area 5 at Murray Springs. No skeletal material was preserved to show the position of the carcass, degree of articulation or dismemberment, or removal of body parts, nor was a hearth for cooking or processing tasks uncovered in the area excavated. However, the horse dentition was concentrated at two loci, and debitage, presumably representing sharpening and thinning of bifacial cutting tools, was closely associated.

The juxtaposition of these remains and knapping area A5-1 to the northeast (Fig. 5.27) has apparent parallels in Areas 3 and 4 (Figs. 5.8, 5.19). The relative positions and distances between mammoth, bison, and horse remains and associated knapping areas are essentially identical in the three occupation areas. Perhaps this patterned use of space, which is unlikely to be coincidental, represents the purposeful locating of knapping activity close by and upwind of the kill.

That the horse was a young adult lends plausibility to the hypothesis of a kill, since an animal in the prime of life would be less likely to die from natural causes. Only two projectile point bases were recovered in Area 5, which may be due to the retrieval of serviceable tools or to the limited extent of excavation.

Similarly, the processing tool kit is known directly only from a biface, a unifacially retouched flake, a small fragment of a utilized flake, and a nodule that is possibly a pebble hammer. The analysis of debitage in knapping areas A5-1 and A5-2 suggests that at least five bifacial cutting tools were also used in the processing task and were retrieved or remain unexcavated. It seems probable that no more than one or two individuals produced the Area 5 debitage, and that some such small task unit could have economically processed the carcass in less than a day with the limited, but effective, tool kit.

The debitage:tool ratio in Area 5 is 257:1, or 147:1 if bifacial preforms inferred from debitage alone are also considered. As in the case of other occupation areas, it is probable that serviceable tools were retrieved after use.

If the kill and utilization of a horse occurred, as I have suggested on the basis of available evidence, what was the chronological relationship of this event to kills and processing of large mammals in occupation areas to the east? Although gross stratigraphic contemporaneity can be ascribed to all these areas, their spatially discrete occurrences and the presence of animals of different species suggest a series of temporally close but separate events. As was proposed earlier, the loss of horse bone in Area 5 may indicate exposure and deterioration of the carcass over a longer time prior to deposition of Stratum F_2 than was the case in other site areas. In view of the unweathered and undispersed condition of the horse dentition and debitage, the duration of exposure of Area 5 was perhaps only a few seasons or years more than in Areas 3 and 4. Alternatively, the loss of horse bone could be due to a local post-burial environment more adverse for preservation or to differential susceptibility of horse bone. These are, I think, less likely explanations.

CONCLUSIONS

The two radiocarbon dates for charcoal of cultural origin obtained thus far at Murray Springs are 11,150 ± 450 B.P. (A-805) from Area 1 and 10,760 ± 100 B.P. (A-1045) from Area 4. These dates pertain strictly to the Clovis culture and are stratigraphically contemporary. They are consistent with six other charcoal dates from the F_1 channel that are stratigraphically contemporaneous and probably culturally derived. Statistical averaging produces a mean value of 10,900 ± 50 B.P. (Appendix A; Haynes and others 1984). The time of utilization of Areas 3, 4, and 5, therefore, is most likely between 10,800 B.P. and 11,000 B.P., essentially 13,000 years ago. During perhaps an even shorter period mammoths, bison, and horse were hunted during at least three separate visits to the Murray Springs Site. In any case, the mass kill of bison in Area 4 is remarkably close in time to the more common Folsom bison kills in North America (Frison 1978a; Haynes 1964; Wormington 1957).

The fact that exploitation of bison by various communal techniques persists more or less continuously for 13,000 years in the plains of western North America, ending finally with European disruption of Native American and bison populations, is of considerable interest both from the anthropological and biological points of view. In sub-Arctic areas of North America the only human predation of comparable intensity (over the long run) was directed at white-tailed deer in Eastern North America, where the hunting unit was frequently minimal (the solitary hunter),

the prey was smaller and less gregarious, and intensive predation persisted about 12,000 years (Goodyear 1982). In terms of hunting skill and organization, as well as biomass, the interaction of human predator and bison populations ranks foremost in North America.

Variation in bison procurement systems among Native American cultures can be deduced from a number of discoveries of mass bison kills, including Murray Springs (following Agenbroad 1978; Dibble and Lorrain 1968; Frison 1974, 1978a; Kehoe 1967; Shay 1971; Stanford 1974; Wheat 1972). These studies deal with large controlled samples of bison skeletal remains in cultural and paleoecological context and provide tests for the many hypotheses that can be derived from ethnohistoric accounts of bison procurement. They validate the synthesis of archaeological and ecological approaches (Hester 1967, 1970). It is beyond the scope of this chapter to attempt an analysis of variation in bison procurement systems, although the significance of this problem has been duly emphasized.

In what respects does the 13,000-year-old occupation floor in Area 4 contribute to knowledge of Clovis culture in the San Pedro Valley and western North America? First, by reason of preservation it is a remarkable record of a brief series of behavioral events. The remains of Area 4 may represent *one day's activity by definable social units*, including the mass bison kill and subsequent processing. Second, the interpretations derived from Area 4 supplement and modify in minor, but significant, respects the "traditional" view of Clovis cultural ecology (Stephenson 1965; Wendorf and Hester 1962). Some of these interpretations may be summarized here.

First, Clovis hunters exploited the terminal Rancholabrean megafauna with a repertoire of specialized techniques. Mass kills of "big game" in the San Pedro Valley included small herds of both mammoth and large bison. Female and juvenile animals were frequently selected. The old "Elephant Hunter" and "Bison Hunter" dichotomy must be regarded with some skepticism (Sellards 1952).

Second, selected water holes were favored as "recurrent kill sites" by Clovis hunters. These sites, such as Murray Springs and Lehner, may have been regularly revisited, like stations on a trapline. Other kinds of kills include solitary animals, wounded and pursued, and "unsuccessful" kills (Judge 1974).

Third, Clovis hunters were scrupulous and parsimonious in obtaining raw material and preparing hunting, processing, or maintenance equipment. The basic stone tool kit includes Clovis projectile points (homogeneous in form and variable in size), bifacial preforms and cutting tools, flake and blade cutting tools, end and side scrapers, gravers, and burins, as well as expedient "disposable" tools of local raw material. Chiefly, small tools, rather than heavy duty tools (as might be expected), were employed in processing large animal kills (Clark and Haynes 1970).

Finally, the nature of the bison kill at Murray Springs, as well as the habitation area, renders the concept of a "microband" of 20 to 30 individuals (5 to 8 adult males) improbable for the San Pedro Valley, although such band units may have been optimal in caribou hunting regions (Fitting and others 1966; MacDonald 1968). It seems more likely that Clovis hunters of the Basin and Range area, as well as the Southern Plains, were organized as macrobands of 50 to 100 individuals *year-round*, or at least for much of the year. Models for hunting bands derived from living primitive peoples in marginal northern or arid desert and semidesert areas are a "poor fit" to late pluvial-early postpluvial ecological conditions of the Southwest (Hemmings 1975).

Note: Chapter 5 was compiled from "Early Man in the San Pedro Valley, Arizona," by E. Thomas Hemmings (doctoral dissertation, Department of Anthropology, University of Arizona, Tucson, 1970) and from "Llano Bison Hunters in the San Pedro Valley, Arizona," by E. Thomas Hemmings (1975, an unpublished manuscript on file in the Archives of the Arizona State Museum, Tucson). C. Vance Haynes, Jr., and Bruce B. Huckell have incorporated results from more recent work at the Murray Springs Site.

CHAPTER SIX

Bison Ages from Dentitions at the Murray Springs Clovis Site, Arizona

Michael C. Wilson, Lawrence C. Todd, and George C. Frison

Animal kills comprise an important part of Plains archaeology in general and Paleoindian studies in particular. Whereas the biologist and paleontologist seek the evolutionary history of the different species, the archaeologist wants to know the population structure of the animals that reveals the age, sex, and time of year of the kill event. With this information and a thorough knowledge of animal behavior, the archaeologist stands a better chance of establishing the procurement and processing strategies and the resulting amount of economic products.

At Olsen-Chubbuck, a bison site familiar to all Paleoindian archaeologists, Wheat (1972) relied on the terms immature, juvenile, and adult to establish the age structure of the animals. These divisions have proven to be inadequate and with the influence of University of Wyoming paleontologist Paul McGrew, who introduced several archaeologists to taphonomic analysis of animals in kill sites and the application of the method by Voorhies (1969), the analyses of animal remains in archaeological sites rapidly changed and taphonomy became an indispensable part of faunal analysis. In Chapter 5 Hemmings presents a reasonable case for a summer bison kill, and we concede there could have been a difference in the bison birthing season between the southern and northern Plains. However, in this chapter we now suggest a winter kill on the basis of a more exacting analysis of bison dental characteristics.

There were numerous bison remains from the Clovis component of the Murray Springs Site, dated as 10,900 ± 50 B.P. (Chapter 5, Appendix A; Hemmings 1970). Area 1 of the site yielded scattered bison teeth and bones of two bison were concentrated in Area 2 (Hemmings 1970: 57). The latter differed somewhat in size, and both were viewed as mature bulls (Hemmings 1970: 57–58). Area 3 (the Mammoth Kill) also yielded at least two bison, represented by teeth as well as limb elements. One was a young animal and the other was mature but gracile, probably a female. A possible third individual from this area was about the same age as the female (Hemmings 1970: 73–74).

Area 4 at Murray Springs was designated the Multiple Bison Kill. Excavations during 1968–1969 (Hemmings 1970) recovered a minimum of six completely disarticulated animals, including one juvenile, an immature, and four adults. An absence of large, robust bones suggested that all adults were cows (Hemmings 1970: 110–112); therefore, this was probably a segment of a nursery herd or cow group (McHugh 1958; Reher 1974). Based on the metapodial size, these bison were tentatively assigned to *Bison antiquus* (Hemmings 1970: 113). Crania had been extensively fragmented and were identifiable only as groups of upper cheek teeth and associated petrosals (Hemmings 1970: 107). Excavations in Areas 4 and 5 during 1969 (Chapter 5), which were not reported by Hemmings (1970), recovered additional bison bones and, as discussed below, the minimum number of animals (MNI) based on lower dentitions for the entire excavated area is now eleven.

DENTITIONS

For the present study, we directed attention toward the lower dentitions in the Area 4 sample (Table 6.1) from the 1968–1969 excavations and made inferences relating to morphology and seasonality. Because the upper dentitions constituted a small sample, no detailed examination was made other than to confirm that they did not differ significantly in terms of degree of eruption and wear from tentatively associated lower dentitions. The initial evidence of size and seasonality for Murray Springs has been discussed briefly by Frison (1978a, 1978b).

When possible, lower teeth in the dentary ramus were measured at the alveolus (Table 6.2). We compared eruption and wear with modern aged specimens and with dentitions from other bison kills, particularly the Hawken Site (Frison and others 1976). Attrition of the Murray Springs dentitions was recorded using a combination of descriptions based on wear facets as described for the Hawken Site (Frison and others 1976, Fig. 8) with illustrations of tooth wear stages (TWS) similar to those developed by Grant (1982) for cattle and by Todd and others (1990) for bison from the Lipscomb and Scottsbluff sites. Illustrations of the occlusal surfaces of each Murray Springs specimen showing the pattern of exposed dentine are provided for most of the mandibular dentitions (Figs. 6.1–6.4).

Table 6.1. Bison Lower Dentitions from Murray Springs, Area 4 (1968–1969 Excavations)

Field Specimen Number	Side	Teeth	Age Group	Provenience*
393	L	M_1–M_2	1	J12
576	R	M_1–M_2	2	Fw8
285	R	P_2–M_3	3	L15
256	L	P_2–M_3	3	K15
187	R	M_1–M_3	3	L12
444	L	P_3–M_3	3	L12
323	R	M_1–M_3	3	J17
324	L	P_4–M_3	3	J17
490/502	L	P_2–M_3	3	H12
575	L	M_2	3	Fw8
350	R	P_3–M_3	5	J16
350	L	P_3–M_3	5	J16
499	L	M_1–M_3	5	Dw10/Dw11
499	R	M_2–M_3	5	Dw10/Dw11
376	R	P_2–M_3	6	K19
279	L	P_2–M_3	6	K18
468	L	M_2–M_3	6+	Ew10/Ew11
468	R	M_2–M_3	6+	Ew10/Ew11

* See Hemmings, Chapter 5, Figure 5.19, for specific locations of grids within Area 4.

Group 1 (0.7 to 0.8 Year)

Age Group 0.7 to 0.8 year is represented by dentition *393*, which has two molars, LM_{1-2} (Fig. 6.1) and no dentary bone. Although degree of eruption cannot be determined, presumably the M_2 was still below the alveolus with the enamel not fully formed. The M_1 is complete with wear on facets II and IV and light wear on V and VI (facets I and III are damaged and degree of wear is indeterminate). Facets VII and VIII are unworn. The M_2 is fragmentary; however, the metaconid and protoconid are intact and facets I-IV are unworn. Hemmings' preliminary study (1970) assigned this individual to a "late juvenile: class (I-S) with an approximate age of 1.5 to 2.0 years, and his more recent investigation (Chapter 5), based on Reher's (1974) Casper Site analysis, estimates an age of 1.0 to 1.5 years. Our observations, however indicate that this specimen compares most closely with bison in the University of Wyoming collections in the 0.7- to 0.8-year age range. The M_1s for the Group 1 Hawken Site bison are "erupted with wear on facets I-IV . . . ; wear and facets V and VI light" (Frison and others 1976: 39), which compares favorably with the Murray Springs specimen. Figure 6.1 shows the similarity in wear patterns on dental age Group 1 specimens from Murray Springs and Hawken. The M_3s from Hawken are still below the level of the alveolus and are not illustrated. The MNI for the Murray Springs Group 1 is one.

Group 2 (1.8 Years)

A single specimen (*576*) of Age Group 1.8 years is represented in the Murray Springs sample (Fig. 6.1). The slightly damaged M_1 on *576* is in full wear and the M_2 is erupted and exhibits light wear on facets I, II, and VI. This wear is comparable to the Group 2 specimens from Hawken (Fig. 6.1). The MNI for Group 2 is one.

Group 3 (2.7 to 2.8 Years)

Age Group 2.7 to 2.8 years is composed of eight mandibles or mandible fragments, representing at least five individuals (Table 6.1) based on the number of left M_2s. The M_1–M_2s in the Group 3 dentitions from the Hawken Site are in full wear with the M_1 ectostylid "just beginning to wear. M_3 erupted but with either no

Table 6.2. Measurements of Lower Bison Teeth from the Murray Springs Site, Arizona

No.	Side	Age Group	P_2 AL	P_2 AW	P_3 AL	P_3 AW	P_4 AL	P_4 AW	M_1 AL	M_1 AW	M_1 MH	M_1 EO	M_2 AL	M_2 AW	M_2 MH	M_2 EO	M_3 AL	M_3 AW	M_3 MH	M_3 EO
393	L	1									56.4	12.3			75.4	14.0				
576	R	2									49.3	4.6			66.9	14.8				
285	R	3	15.0	9.0							43.9	2.9			67.2	13.9	50.5	17.3	75.8	21.9
256	L	3			19.4	11.7	26.1	13.0	29.8	18.8	44.8	2.8	36.3	18.4	64.2	9.8			71.0	21.1
187	R	3			21.9	11.0			27.5	17.3	43.7	0.0	35.6	16.9	63.4	8.4	48.0	15.5	70.9	18.3
444	L	3					25.6	13.3	28.7	18.0	42.8	0.0			64.5	11.7			71.2	15.5
323	R	3									42.9	0.0	36.0	16.8	63.7	10.0	48.0	16.1	71.8	17.9
324	L	3																		15.9
490/502	L	3									43.7	3.5			53.5	13.8			69.3	
575	L	3													54.1	11.7				
350	R	5			22.9		26.0		28.8			0.0	36.4	20.8		1.5	47.9	18.4		8.3
350	L	5			23.0	14.3	27.0	15.2	30.2	19.9	(35)	0.0	33.5	20.0	46.7	2.1	50.7	19.2	62.6	11.2
499	L	5									26.4	0.0			45.2	0.0				
499	R	5			18.8	12.6	22.9	14.8	28.0	19.3	24.0		34.1	20.1	(40)	0.0			54.5	4.0
376	R	6	12.9	9.5							23.9				41.3	0.0	40.8	20.0		4.5
279	L	6													17.0	0.0			51.4	0.0
468	L	6+														0.0				0.0
468	R	6+														0.0				0.0

NOTE: AL, alveolar length; AW, alveolar width; MH, metaconid height; EO, distance from top of ectostylid to occlusal surface, approximate distance to ectostylid wear.

wear or light wear on facets I and II" (Frison and others 1976: 39). As indicated by the following descriptions and Figure 6.2, this is similar to the pattern for Group 3 from Murray Springs. Possible paired dentitions include: *285* and *256*; *187* and *444*; *323* and *324*. Two additional left dentitions (*490/502* and *575*) were recovered in 1969.

Dentition *187* is a fragmentary ramus with RM_1–M_3. The ectostylid on the M_1 is in wear but it remains unconnected from the dentine of the rest of the occlusal surface, and those on the M_{2-3} are not yet in wear. The M_3 shows wear on facets I–IV with the anterior portions of facets I and II connected. Specimen *444* consists of LP_3–M_3 and is possibly from the same individual as *187*. Although the P_4 is damaged, it is clearly unworn and just erupting. The pattern of ectostylid wear is the same as on *187*. Facets I and II of the M_3 are in wear and connected; wear is beginning on facets III and IV, which exhibit exposed dentine on only the anterior portions of the facets. Hemmings (1970, Table 6) initially assigned this individual (*187/444*) to "late adolescence (S–1)," based on the age classification of Skinner and Kaisen (1947), with an approximate true age of 3.0–4.0 years. He later revised this estimate to an age of 3.0 to 3.5 years (Chapter 5). As noted above, eruption and wear are more closely comparable to 2.7- or 2.8-year-old bison as exemplified at the Hawken Site (Frison and others 1976).

Dentition *256* includes the LP_2–M_1 and may represent the same individual as *285*, which consists of the RP_3–M_3. The ectostylids on the *256/285* M_1s are nearly in wear and the upper enamel surfaces exhibit a light polish. Ectostylids on the M_2s are unworn, although the M_2s retain a small oval of enamel within the exposed dentine posterior to the postfossetids. Dentine is exposed on M_3 facets I and II and on the anterior portions of III and IV on *256*, with facets I and II unconnected. The M_3 metaconid and the hypoconid on *285* are damaged; wear is present on the intact facets I and III and the wear on facet III is slightly more advanced

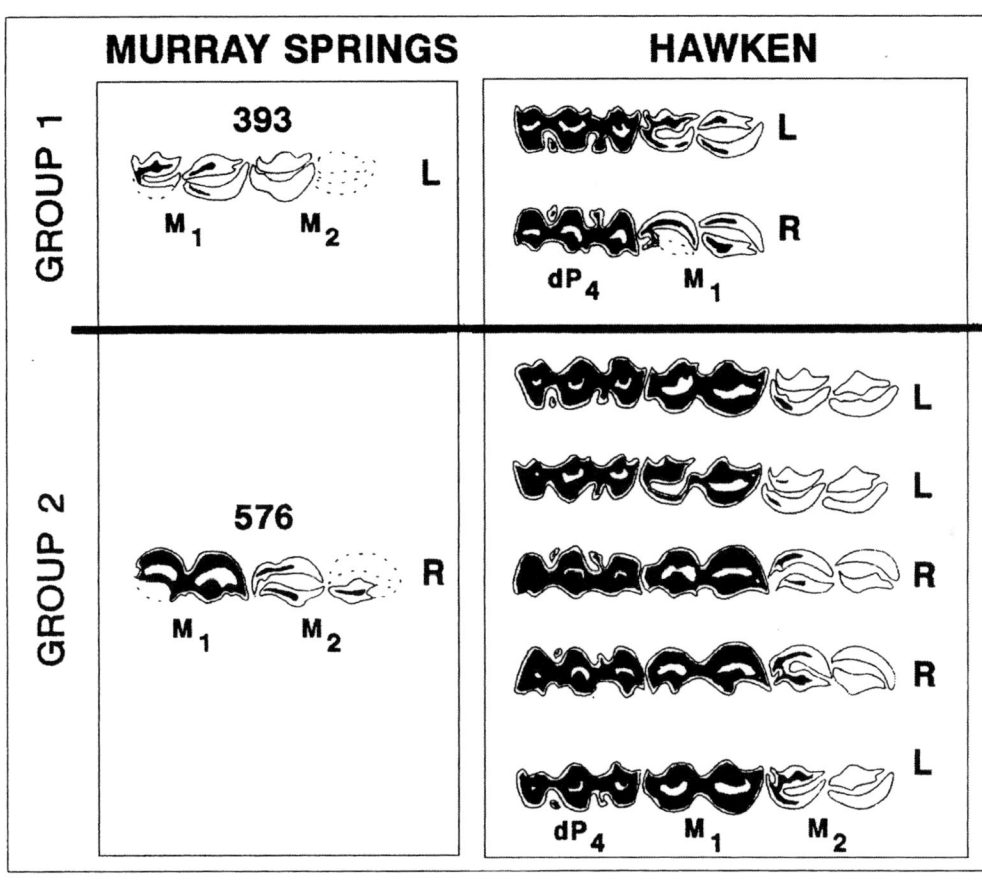

Figure 6.1. Age Group 1 (0.7–0.8 year) and Age Group 2 (1.8 years) bison lower dentitions from the 1968–1969 excavations at Murray Springs, Area 4, compared with Age Groups 1 and 2 from the Hawken Site. "L" and "R" indicate side and are at the distal margin of the tooth rows.

than on *256*. Hemmings (Chapter 5) assigned this individual to Group 4 with an approximate age of 3.0 to 3.5 years, based on the fact that P_4 was just erupting and the M_1 ectostylid was not in wear as compared with the more advanced eruption and wear in *187/444*. However, premolar eruption is highly variable, as is demonstrated by a large modern sample of mandibles from November-killed male bison in the collection of the Department of Anthropology, University of Wyoming. Furthermore, the M_1 ectostylid differences between *256/285* and *187/444* are illusory because the ectostylids in *256/285* are almost in wear and those of *187/444* are only recently in wear. Considering the fact that calving on the northern Plains can extend over a month, plus the possibility that seasonal adaptive constraints were less strongly expressed on the timing of calving seasons in the south, it is quite acceptable for both dentitions to represent the same cohort; hence we assign *256/285* to the 2.7- or 2.8-year-old age class. Comparable specimens are noted in the Hawken Site sample.

Dentition *323* includes a ramus with RM_{1-3} and seems to represent the same individual as *324*, which is a ramus with LP_4-M_3. Ectostylids on the *323/324* M_1s are in early wear and still retain a distinct oval of enamel separating them from the rest of the tooth. Ectostylids on the M_{2-3}s are unworn. Facets I and II are in wear on both M_1s although slightly more dentine is exposed on *323* than on *324*. Hemmings (1970) initially assigned this individual to "late adolescence (S–1)," with an approximate age of 3.0 to 4.0 years, but later revised the estimate to 3.0 to 3.5 years (Chapter 5). P_4 is unworn and is just erupting. The dentitions are therefore virtually identical in characteristics to *187/444*, and *323/324* is assigned an age of 2.7 to 2.8 years.

Specimen *490/502* (not illustrated in Fig. 6.2) is a group of loose left mandibular teeth (P_2-M_3); M_1 is in wear, with the ectostylid not yet worn. M_2 is in a stage of wear very similar to that of specimens *323*, *324*, *285*, and *256* (Fig. 6.2). M_3 facets I and II are in light wear like those of specimens *323* and *324* (Fig. 6.2).

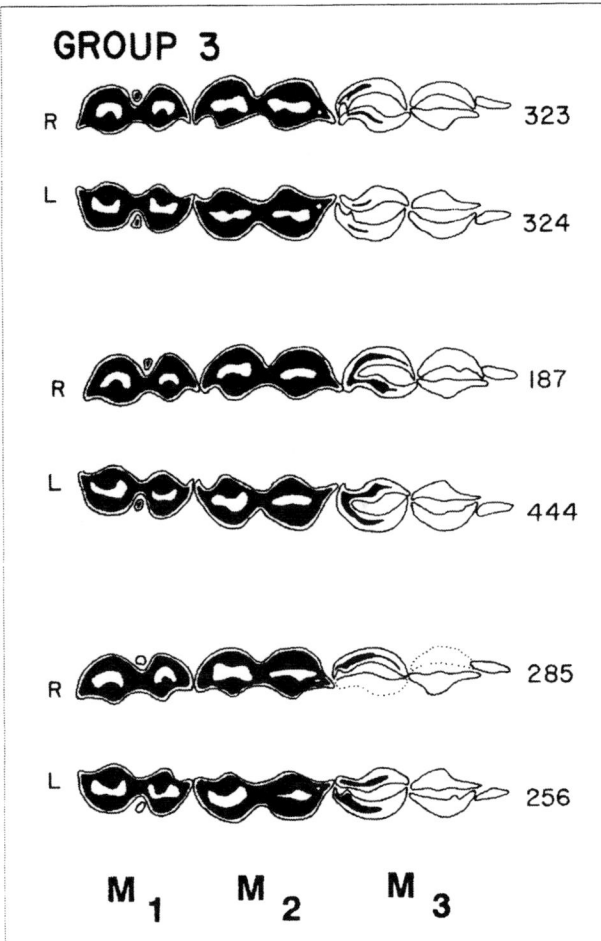

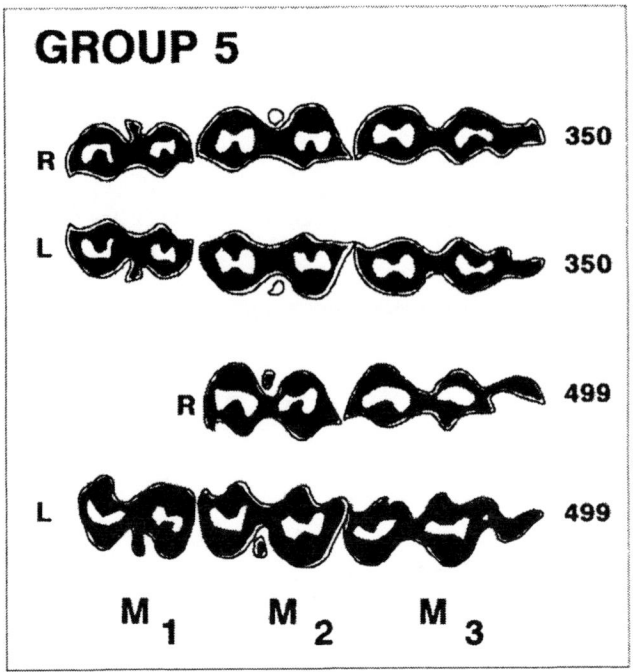

Figure 6.2. Age Group 3 (2.7–2.8 years) bison lower dentitions from the 1968–1969 excavations at Murray Springs, Area 4. "L" and "R" indicate side and are at mesial margin of the tooth row; specimen number is at distal margin.

The final specimen in Group 3, *575*, is a single left M_2 with all facets in full wear, but with the ectostylid well below the occlusal surface (Table 6.2). Although Hemmings (Chapter 5) included this tooth with *576* in Group 2, it exhibits considerably more advanced wear, comparable to that seen on *187* and *444* (Fig. 6.2). The degree of wear on *575* is much more consistent with Group 3 rather than Group 2.

Group 4 (3.7 to 3.8 Years)

No specimens of age group 3.7 to 3.8 years are represented in the Murray Springs sample. The Group 4 specimens from the Hawken Site have the M_1 and M_2 in full wear with "facets I–VIII on M_3 usually in wear;

Figure 6.3. Age Group 5 (4.7–4.8 years) bison lower dentitions from the 1968–1969 excavations at Murray Springs, Area 4 (dentitions oriented as in Fig. 6.2).

wear may be very light or absent on VII and VIII. On two specimens wear is evident on facet VII with none on VIII. Hypoconulid erupted above the alveolus but not yet in wear" (Frison and others 1976: 39).

Group 5 (4.7 to 4.8 Years)

Age Group 4.7 to 4.8 years is represented by two paired mandibles: dentitions *350*, which include both rami with LP_3–M_3 and RP_3–M_3, and specimen *499*, with left and right molars only (Fig. 6.3). The MNI for this group is two. At Hawken the ectostylid on M_2 is "usually in wear. Hypoconulid of M_3 in wear but often the cusp still appears isolated from the remainder of the tooth" (Frison and others 1976: 39).

The M_1 ectostylids on the Murray Springs specimens are in full wear with their dentine connected to that of the rest of the tooth (Fig. 6.3). The teeth are all in wear but are strongly cross-crested. The ectostylids on the *350* M_2 are unworn, but only 1–2 mm from the occlusal surface (Table 6.2). The *499* M_2 ectostylids are in wear, but still surrounded by a distinct enamel ring. Hypoconulid facets IX and IX' of the M_3s are in full wear and connected to the dentine surfaces of the rest of the tooth. Hemmings (1970) initially assigned specimen *350* to "early maturity (S-2)," with an estimated age of 4.0 to 6.0 years. His more recent study (Chapter 5) estimated an age of 4.0 to 4.5 years for specimen *350*, but classified specimen *499* as a dental Age Group 3 individual aged 2.0 to 2.5 years. Because all molars are in wear (Fig. 6.3), *499* is clearly not a Group 3 individual and is judged to compare more favorably with Group 5 specimen *350*.

Group 6 (5.7 to 5.8 Years)

Dentition *279/376* included two rami, possibly a pair, with LP_2-M_3 and RP_2-M_3. Hemmings (1970) assigned this individual to "early maturity (S-2)," with an approximate age of 4.0 to 6.0 years. The teeth are somewhat cross-crested, but not as much as in the case of *350*. Both hypoconulids are in wear and the dentine surface is connected to the main occlusal surfaces of teeth. The M_1 ectostylids are in wear and connected to the body of the tooth as in the ectostylid on *279*, and that on *376* is in wear but separated by a distinct oval of enamel (Fig. 6.4). The M_3 ectostylid on *279* is very slightly worn; the *376* ectostylid is nearly in wear. The *376* M_3, however, is somewhat atypical in formation, with a weak hypoconulid and a large entostylid developed on the entoconid (Fig. 6.4). For this reason, the rate of attrition on *376* M_3 cannot be taken as necessarily normal. The closest match is with 5.7-year-olds of the Hawken Site sample in terms of both general wear attributes (Frison and others 1976: 39) and metaconid heights (Frison 1978b), but the decimal descriptor in this instance can only be inferred on the basis of the remainder of the sample at Murray Springs.

Group 6+

Specimen *468* consists of a left M_2-M_3 and right M_2-M_3 in advanced wear. The differences in M_2 metaconid height between the Group 6 specimens (*376* and *279*) and *468* (Table 6.2) indicate that this specimen may be several years older than *376/279*.

RADIUS

We measured a large mature bison radius from Area 2 of the Murray Springs Site (*39*) and submit this preliminary note; a detailed description has not yet been made. This specimen comes from the F_1 channel

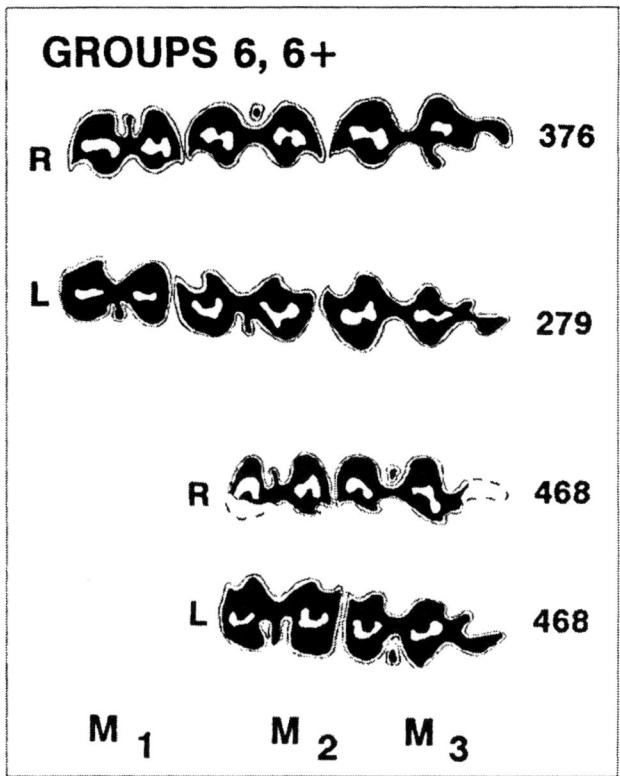

Figure 6.4. Age Group 6 (5.7–5.8 years) and Group 6+ bison lower dentitions from the 1968–1969 excavations at Murray Springs, Area 4 (dentitions oriented as in Fig. 6.2).

deposit in Area 2, and therefore cannot be positively associated with Clovis cultural activity at the site (Chapter 5). However, it must be at least penecontemporaneous with Clovis utilization of Murray Springs.

Measurements of the radius are presented in Table 6.3, along with comparative data from Bonfire Shelter (Lorrain 1968) and the U.P. Site (Wilson 1974b). The U.P. and Murray Springs specimens are considerably larger than those from Bonfire Shelter. It is slowly becoming evident that Clovis-age bison were significantly larger than those present in Folsom and Hell Gap times, decades to a thousand years later.

CONCLUSIONS

The Murray Springs bison sample is not extensive enough to allow detailed cluster analysis of crown heights as conducted by Kurtén (1964) and Voorhies (1969) for paleontological samples, and by Reher (1970, 1974) for Wyoming archaeological bison sam-

Table 6.3. Measurement of Radius from the Murray Springs Site, Arizona

Measurement*	Murray Springs (mm)	U.P. WY (mm)	Bonfire Shelter, Texas		
			Min. (mm)	Av. (mm)	Max. (mm)
1. Length (RD2)	411.0	396.4		383.0	
2. Transverse width, proximal end (RD3)	126.5	129.2	91.0	103.3	124.0
3. Anterior-posterior width, prox. (RD9)	67.0	65.7	46.5	52.4	63.0
4. Transverse width, distal end (RD7)	104+	119.7	86.5	96.0	110.0
5. Transverse width, center of shaft (RD5)	69.5	65.5	50.0	53.8	57.6
6. Anterior-posterior width, center (RD6)	51.0	44.0	29.0	35.4	41.8

* Codes for radius measurements are from Todd (1987).

ples. Nevertheless, metaconid heights show close concordance in the Age Group 3 set, as independently grouped on the basis of dental eruption and wear. Thus the sample exhibits a stepwise progression of metaconid heights, enough to indicate that it is seasonally restricted (following Wilson 1980, 1988). Molar wear facet analysis allows refinement of the season represented, subject to the caveat that birthing seasonality, as suggested by Hemmings (Chapter 5), could have been slightly different in the southwestern United States than on the northern Great Plains.

Isotopic studies of bison and horse teeth from Murray Springs and other late Pleistocene sites in the Southwest indicate that most of the annual rainfall was during the summer (Connin and others 1998). This in turn suggests that birthing seasonality was likely much the same then as in modern times in the north, because weaning of calves occurs at a time when grass shoots are still relatively soft and palatable. Calving thus tends to precede the time of maximum grassland productivity. Hemmings (Chapter 5) cites Seton as authority for the suggestion that calving was earlier on the southern Great Plains than in the north; however, Roe (1970: 9) found Seton's work "the most deficient of all" and decidedly anecdotal. Roe found comparably early calving records on the northern Plains and concluded that calving occurred in all areas over a fairly long span (mid-April to end of June). Within these extremes, others have documented tighter clustering of the majority of births in the first two weeks of May, with a spread of occasional births on either side (McHugh 1972; Meagher 1973). Halloran and Glass (1959) documented late March-early April birthing in the Wichita Mountains herd, Oklahoma, which, if representative, could indicate as much as one month of north-south differential for modern bison.

On the basis of dentitions, bison in Area 4 at the Murray Springs Site fit into an N + 0.7- to 0.8-year seasonal group. If calving times were similar in the southern and northern Plains, we suggest a kill in December or January. Even with differences in calving seasons, the timing of the kill cannot have varied much more than one month earlier or later. Although the sample size is small, the very tight clustering within age group classes and close similarity of dentitions within each age group (particularly Fig. 6.2) indicate that even during the late Pleistocene on the southern Plains, bison calving seasons seem to have been restricted to a single relatively brief birth pulse. A pattern of *winter mortality* for the Murray Springs bison is therefore indicated. The lower dentitions indicate an MNI of 11: one each in Groups 1 and 2, five (based on left M_2s) in Group 3, and two animals each in Groups 5 and 6/6+.

Although the Murray Springs sample size is too small to make definitive statements, there is a tendency for the annual rate of dental attrition (as indicated by metaconid enamel heights) to be less at Murray Springs than for the Altithermal age bison sample from the Hawken Site. Group 1 M_1 metaconid heights in both samples are similar with the Hawken specimens, averaging about 55 mm (Frison 1978b, Fig. 4.5) and the single Murray Springs specimen at 56.4 mm (Table 6.2). In all other dental age groups, there is a trend for the Murray Springs specimens to have a slightly greater metaconid height than corresponding members of the Hawken sample (compare Table 6.2 with Frison 1978b, Fig. 4.5). This characteristic may be indicative of the more extreme Altithermal climatic episode and the resultant increase in the amount of grit incorporated in the diet of the Hawken bison as compared to the animals represented at Murray Springs.

The attrition rate at Murray Springs is similar to or less than rates documented for multiple kills at the Henry Smith Site, Montana (about 1200-940 B.P.), and is lower than that for the Late Prehistoric Garnsey Site, New Mexico (Wilson 1980, 1988). Of course, differences in absolute size and dental robusticity must be taken into account, and that is beyond the scope of our inquiry. Nevertheless, the implication of these findings is that late Pleistocene bison in the Southwest found adequate forage in summer, agreeing with the grassland model deduced by Connin and others (1998) from the isotopic evidence. Whether strong seasonality in grassland productivity led them to be migratory is an open question, still to be addressed, of considerable importance in terms of archaeological modeling of Paleoindian subsistence patterns.

Analysis of late Pleistocene *Bison antiquus* dentitions from Rancho La Brea, California, indicates seasonal clustering and strongly suggests migratory habits (Jefferson and Goldin 1989). A possible pattern of bison wintering in the U.S. Southwest and summering on the open plains to the northeast is plausible and would explain late winter-to-spring mass kills in the Southwest (as also documented at Garnsey), because they would have anticipated the seasonal departure of a key resource (see also Speth 1983). This, however, could also mean that the conclusions of Connin and others (1998) concerning summer rainfall and grassland productivity did not necessarily relate exclusively to the local area.

Acknowledgments. Mr. Paul C. Johnson generously provided lodging, served as a most competent guide to the University of Arizona campus and collections, and shared his knowledge of Arizona archaeology and vertebrate paleontology with M. Wilson during his 1974 visit to Tucson to obtain the Murray Springs dentitions on loan. Dr. Everett H. Lindsay granted access to the vertebrate paleontology collections and readily acceded to the loan of the specimens. Dr. Jeffrey Saunders guided M. Wilson through the Murray Springs collections and helped identify the stratigraphy and contextual parameters of this and other Southwestern sites. We appreciate the helpful suggestions of Stuart Fiedel and comments by an anonymous reviewer. To all of these people, we offer our sincere thanks.

Note. Chapter 6 is a revision of a 1979 report submitted by Michael C. Wilson based on study of a limited number of the Clovis-age bison teeth. The complete collection was evaluated with the collaboration of Lawrence Todd and George Frison in 1991.

CHAPTER SEVEN

The Hunting Camp at Murray Springs

Larry D. Agenbroad and Bruce B. Huckell

In 1968 scattered artifacts were recovered from the surface to the south of excavation Areas 1 and 3 (Fig. 7.1). Hemmings (1968) reported a Clovis point midsection and a double graver from this brush-covered area, which was designated Area 6. During the field season of 1969, Area 6 was cleared of brush, scraped, and swept preparatory to excavations in subsequent field seasons. This operation revealed additional artifacts on the surface to the southwest of Area 6, west and southwest of a large bulldozer backdirt pile from Trench 1. This second locus became Area 7. Together, Areas 6 and 7 comprise a camp occupied by Clovis hunters. It was investigated briefly in 1969 and more intensively during the 1970 and 1971 field seasons (Haynes, Agenbroad, and Kelso 1971).

PRELIMINARY INVESTIGATIONS, 1969

Area 6 is a rectangular area of 448 square meters, encompassing the area where the fragmentary point and double graver were found. The 1969 efforts indicated that the southern two-thirds of Area 6 contained Clovis tools and flakes on the Coro marl (Stratum E) surface, which was interpreted as the Clovis occupation surface by Hemmings (1970). The locality was approximately 1.5 m higher than the Area 3 occupation surface and up to 10 m west of Wolf Creek, the F_1 stream channel formerly occupying the East Swale.

The 1969 surface sweeping of Area 6 produced nine artifacts (five tools, four flakes) attributed to Clovis occupation (Hemmings 1970: 160). A large chert Clovis point midsection (Fig. 7.7a), the first artifact found in Area 6, was linked to Area 4 by an impact flake from the bison bone bed (72 m north and approximately 2.5 m lower) that refitted into the scar on the shattered tip of the fragment (see Figs. 7.4, 8.2, 8.7h).

This association suggested that the point was retrieved from the kill in Area 4 and afterward removed from the spear or foreshaft in Area 6 and that the impact flake remained in the kill area (Hemmings 1970: 161–163). In addition, tool types not present in the kill areas (a composite tool with graver tips and a spurred end scraper) were found in Area 6, again suggesting campsite activity.

The investigation of Area 6 began by extending the grid system from the buried part of the site southward to encompass the area north and east of the spoil pile at the northwest end of Trench 1 (Fig. 7.1). Rather than continuing to extend the original grid system farther west, which would have resulted in some cumbersome grid designations, a new system of 10-m squares was laid out by instrument survey (Fig. 7.2). It began along the west edge of the Area 6 grid and used double letters (beginning with AA at the east and ending with JJ on the west) to designate the east-west axis of the system and single numbers (beginning with 0 at the north and ending with 7 on the south) to designate the north-south axis. Thus a 10-m grid square might be labeled AA4, DD5, EE2, with the stake in the southwest corner acting as the datum. Each 10-m grid was further subdivided into 25 separate 2-m grids. Individual grids were numbered sequentially within each 10-m grid (Fig. 7.2), beginning with 1 in the northeast corner and proceeding from east to west in the first row, then west to east in the second row, ending with the southwest corner square as 25. Two-meter grid designations thus read BB0-10, DD5-24, EE6-7. This system served as the basis for detailed investigation of the camp.

A small area (Area 7) southwest of Area 6 was also brushed, scraped, and swept in 1969 (Fig. 7.2). It yielded two unifacial tools, a utilized flake, and nearly 90 waste flakes.

[146]

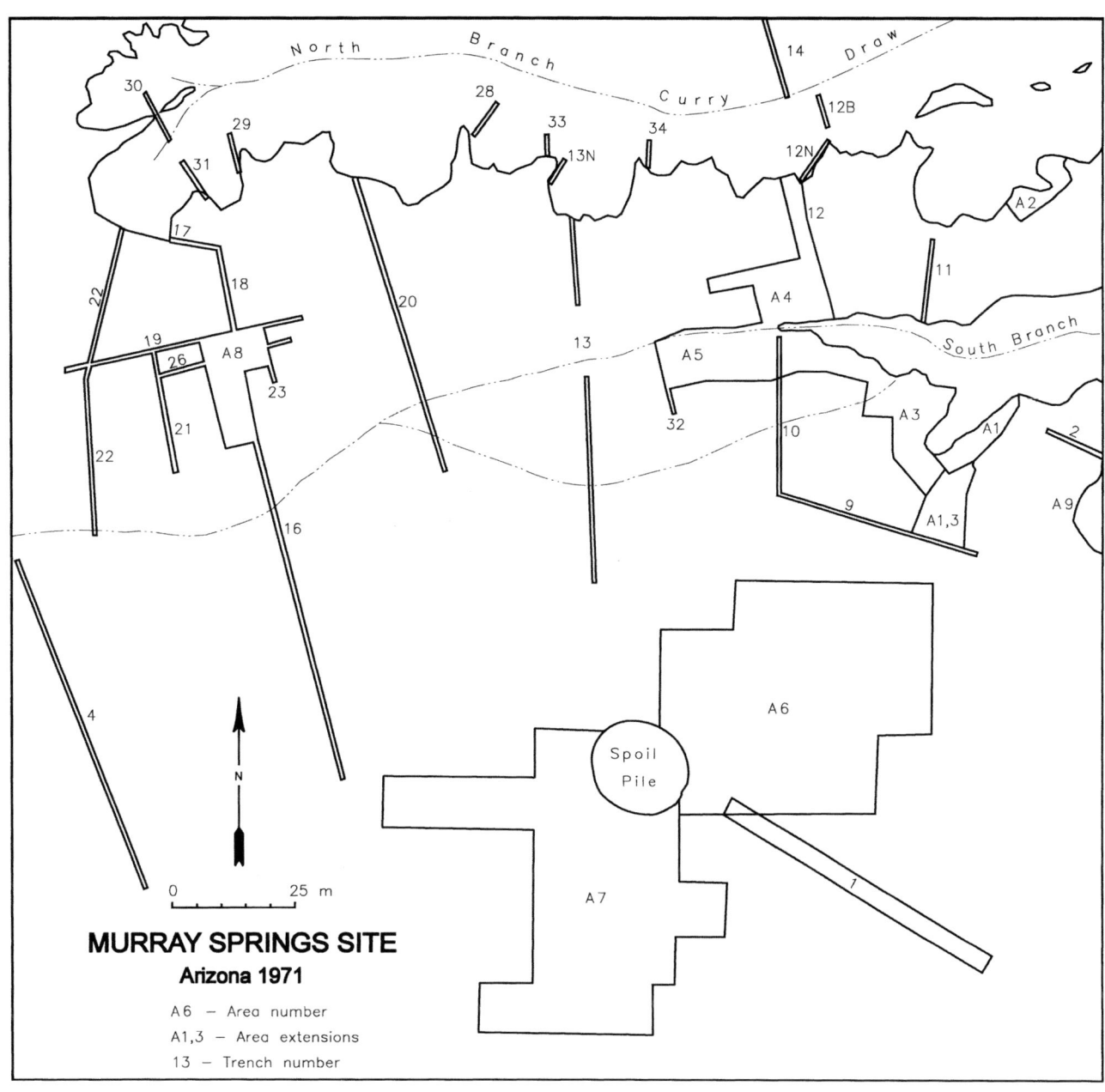

Figure 7.1. Murray Springs Site area, showing locations of Areas 6 and 7.

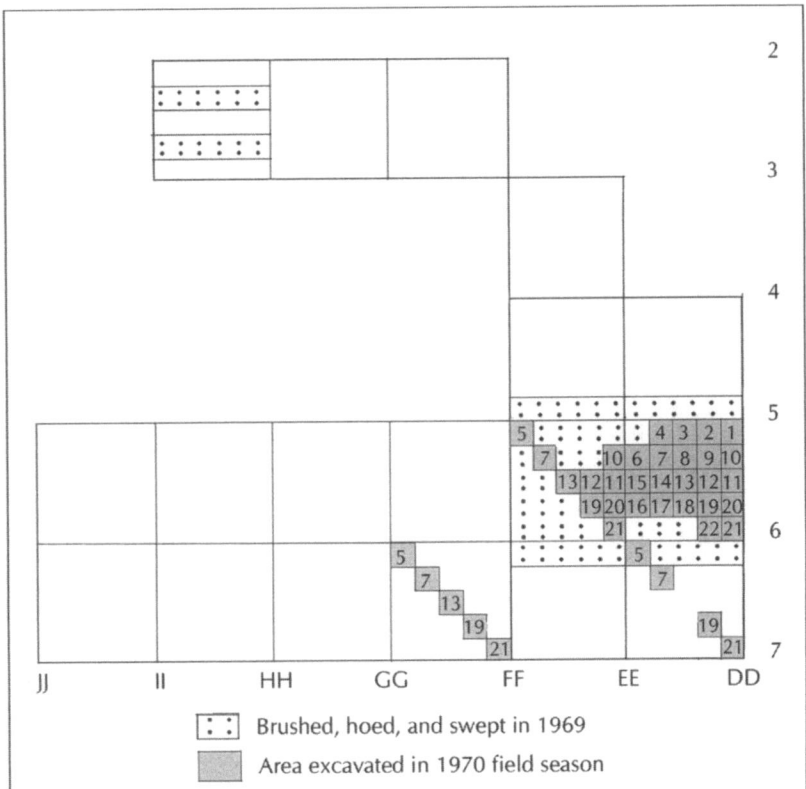

Figure 7.2. Portions of Area 7 cleared, swept, and excavated during the 1969–1970 field seasons showing the grid system and subgrid designations.

AREA 7, 1970

The detailed investigation of Areas 6 and 7 became one of the priorities for the 1970 and 1971 field seasons at Murray Springs. The 1970 season was initiated by removing brush from a large area to the west of the 1969 surface grid (Fig. 7.2). An area of 800 square meters was cleared, giving a total area of 1,400 square meters from which brush had been removed by clipping at the ground surface. To investigate Area 7 we followed a systematic sampling strategy using sample excavation units of 2-m squares (4 square meters) arbitrarily laid out along NW-SE diagonals within the 10-m grids (Fig. 7.2). Almost as soon as excavation began, flakes of Clovis lithic material, a utilized flake, a Clovis scraper, and the base of an obsidian Clovis point were uncovered. As artifacts and flakes were located within the diagonal sampling pattern of 2-m squares, and the NW-SE diagonals were completed, we opened up neighboring 2-m squares. Stratigraphic tests showed loose grayish brown sandy silt slopewash, overlying pale gray clayey Donnet silt, overlying white Coro marl, overlying green Sobaipuri mudstone (all affected by bioturbation; Fig. 2.18), and overlying the Millville alluvium. The pre-occupation Coro marl (Stratum E) served as the stratigraphic control signaling the base of the occupation layer. Depending on local variations in the stratigraphic record, excavations varied in depth from 0 cm to 70 cm, but seldom exceeded 50 cm.

Thirty-nine 2-m squares (156 square meters) were excavated in Area 7 during the 1970 season (Fig. 7.2), yielding artifacts, isolated waste flakes, and three flake concentrations. A cluster of Clovis flakes was found in situ in Square 7 of Block EE6 (EE6-7). As excavation was expanded into the adjacent 2-m grid squares, additional flakes and a Clovis point base were encountered. In one concentration, 305 flakes, dominantly of one lithology, were recovered from the original flake cluster. Additional clusters were found in EE7-5 and EE6-8 (Chapter 8).

Two Clovis point bases, one end scraper, two unifacially retouched flakes and nearly 500 waste flakes were recovered from the excavations. The cultural material occurred in a surface layer of sandy silt with irregular masses of gray clayey silt (Donnet silt,

F_3). The tight flake concentrations were confined mainly to the gray clayey silt.

In a discovery reminiscent of the situation in Area 6, an impact flake recovered from Area 7 was refitted to the impact scar on a point from Area 4, thus tying Area 7 and Area 4. In this case, the flake was found within a flake cluster of a different lithology in Grid EE6-7. The point (A-33,111) was found in two pieces (MS 952 and MS 1007) 143 m to the north-northeast (Fig. 8.8g) in Area 4. The presence of damaged points and impact flakes from both kill and camp areas solidly links Areas 6 and 7 to Area 4 (Fig. 8.2).

The EE6-7 concentration of several hundred Clovis waste flakes of one lithology in an area of less than one square meter within the gray clayey silt clearly demonstrated that the concentration had not dispersed laterally any significant amount during the 13,000 years since the flint knapping was done. However, it is likely that some disorientation of the flakes occurred by insect, rodent, and root bioturbation (Fig. 2.18). The colluvial sandy silt layer has probably been turned over many times by the action of plant roots and burrowing animals and insects. The lack of flake dispersal beyond an area larger than might be expected to be covered by the work of the knapper is surprising, and indicates that the gray clayey silt was not significantly reworked by slopewashing.

Also recovered were artifacts and waste flakes of the Archaic (Cochise) period culture. Two Archaic projectile points had been found on the surface of Area 6 in 1969, and work in Area 7 in 1970 produced numerous flakes of a distinctive black silicified limestone and two manos. The lithology and hard hammer percussion flaking technique were the basis for distinguishing this flaked stone material from the Clovis material, which consisted largely of biface reduction flakes of the same lithologic varieties of chert and chalcedony found in the buried part of the site. Concentrations of small, subrounded cobbles in the silt were probably the remains of hearths of this later period. Clovis artifacts from Area 7 suggest a hunting camp where broken projectile points were discarded and replaced, where biface reduction was performed, and where other knapping activities took place.

AREAS 6 AND 7, 1971

In 1971 excavations were again concentrated in Area 7, expanding on the 1970 investigation. To provide a broader sample and to act as a prospecting technique for cultural material, a 16 percent, stratified, unaligned, random sampling system was adopted (after Haggett 1965). The sample consisted of 2-m squares covering Areas 6 and 7, including the area excavated in 1970 (see Figs. 7.4, 7.5) as a comparison of the efficiency of the sampling methods. Four 2-m squares were randomly chosen from each 10-m grid and were designated by their relative position within the sample; thus the four sample squares in 10-m grid BB0 were labeled BB0, NE; BB0, NW; BB0, SW; and BB0, SE. These designations were necessary because sample squares were chosen in such a manner that they did not utilize the preexisting 2-m grids within the 10-m grids. We found that the stratified, unaligned, random sample would have detected the concentrations identified in 1970 using the systematic approach.

A total of 537 square meters of the hunting camp was excavated, yielding 584 lithic artifacts. Two Clovis point bases, five unifacially retouched tools, four blades and a multiple-use blade tool, three bifaces, and several flake concentrations were recovered. Also found was one obsidian nodule from the Cow Canyon source area near Clifton, Arizona (Appendix C). Clovis artifacts were found within approximately 0.7 vertical meter, ranging from as deep as the contact between the Coro marl and gray silt, within the gray silt, within the brown loose sandy silt, or on the modern surface, but never entirely within the marl. It is believed, therefore, that the original stratigraphic position of the Clovis occupation was at the contact of the gray calcareous clayey silt (which may be a pedogenic facies of basal Stratum F_3 Donnet silt in the kill area) and the Coro marl.

The assemblage of Clovis artifacts from the hunting camp indicates projectile point repair and replacement, reduction of bifaces, and cutting and scraping activities. The presence of a mammoth bone fragment in II3 and a mammoth tooth fragment in FF3, plus the refitting of artifact fragments from kill and camp areas, suggests that these activities were related to making use of the animals killed in Area 4, Area 3, and perhaps other buried parts of the site.

Additional artifacts of the Archaic period were found in the loose silt and on the surface and were generally distinguished from Clovis artifacts by their form, workmanship, and lithology. Excavation of the test grids in Area 7 also produced two hand-dug pits in grids EE4NW and FF2NE (Fig. 7.3). These pits may

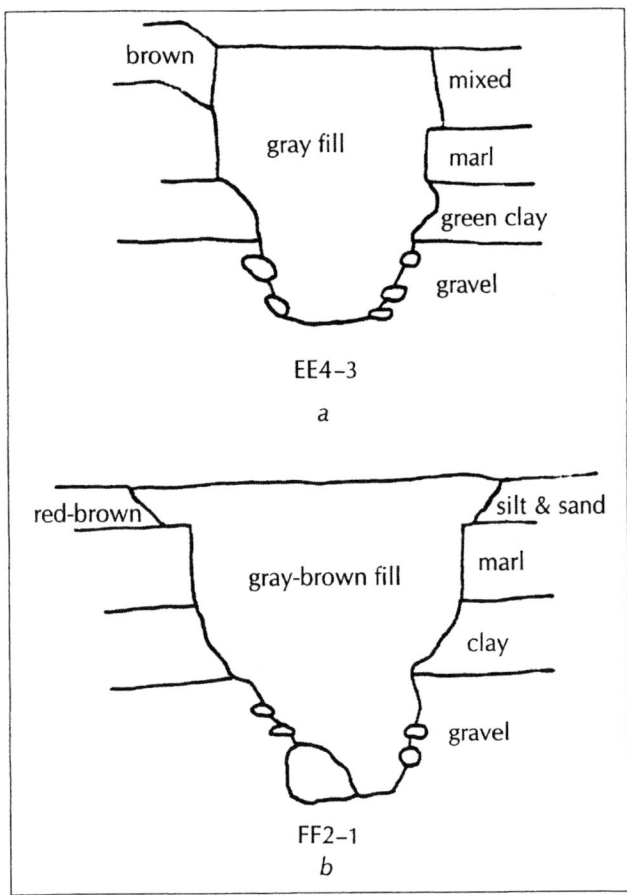

Figure 7.3. Excavated pits that may have been Archaic period wells in Area 7 (not to scale; measurements in text).

Table 7.1. Fire-Cracked Rock Concentrations in Areas 6 and 7

Location	No. of Stones	Depth	Dominant Composition
EE7–4	14		
EE5–22, EE5–21	22	Surface	Quartzite and marl
FF7, NW	11	Surface–20 cm	Quartzite
EE5–1, EE4–21	16	Surface–15 cm	Marl
BB4	18		Quartzite and marl

have been wells and are thought to be Archaic (Cochise culture) features, penetrating all units to the Millville alluvium. The pit in EE4NW was roughly circular in plan, measuring 1.21 m in diameter at the marl and 1.03 m in depth (Fig. 7.3a). The diameter was reduced to 0.95 m in the green Sobaipuri clay and 0.55 m at the bottom of the excavation, in Millville alluvium. The other pit, in the northwest corner of FF2NE, was 1.03 m in diameter at the marl, reducing to 0.70 m in the green clay and 0.50 m in the Millville gravel (Fig. 7.3b). The pit bottomed out on a large boulder at a maximum depth of 1.18 m from the modern surface.

Two similar pits were discovered in Area 5 (Chapter 5). Because they all extend into Millville alluvium under the aquaclude of the Sobaipuri mud, we believe all four pits to be prehistoric wells. Evans (1951) described 13 similar wells from the Clovis type site in a tributary to Blackwater Draw in eastern New Mexico. He concluded they were post-Folsom and represented a dry period in which the water table was dropping from Folsom lake or pond levels. Although he did not refine his conclusions further, it is probable that the wells at the Blackwater Draw Site represent the efforts of Archaic cultures during the Altithermal drought postulated by Antevs (1955). More prehistoric wells were discovered at the Clovis site by Green (1962), and later finds on the Southern High Plains are thought to be related to mid-Holocene drought (Holliday 1989; Meltzer 1991). As stated in Chapter 2, the prehistoric wells in Area 5 are believed to date to about 3000 B.P. based on the stratigraphic positions of their collars.

In addition to the wells, several concentrations of fire-cracked cobbles were encountered in the excavations. Many of these cobbles exhibit oxidation and cracks and are interpreted as hearth stones. Most occurred in the upper 20 cm and are believed to be Archaic period hearths. Table 7.1 lists their locations, contents, and other attributes. A similar feature 100 m to the southeast yielded charcoal that has yet to be radiocarbon dated.

As the excavation of test squares progressed, dark gray basal Donnet silt (Stratum F_3) was also exposed in a number of the excavations. It was decided that enough of the Donnet/Coro contact occurred to allow elevations of the Clovis occupation surface to be determined, permitting the creation of a paleotopographic map of that surface for Areas 6 and 7. The plot (Fig. 7.6) reveals a shallow rill system draining to the northeast toward Area 3. The majority of Clovis artifacts and waste flakes recovered from Areas 6 and 7 occurred within or immediately adjacent to this small drainage system (compare Figs. 7.4 and 7.5 with Fig. 7.6). These data indicate that the Clovis hunting camp was located in and adjacent to a rill drainage system tributary to Wolf Creek of Curry Draw. The highest

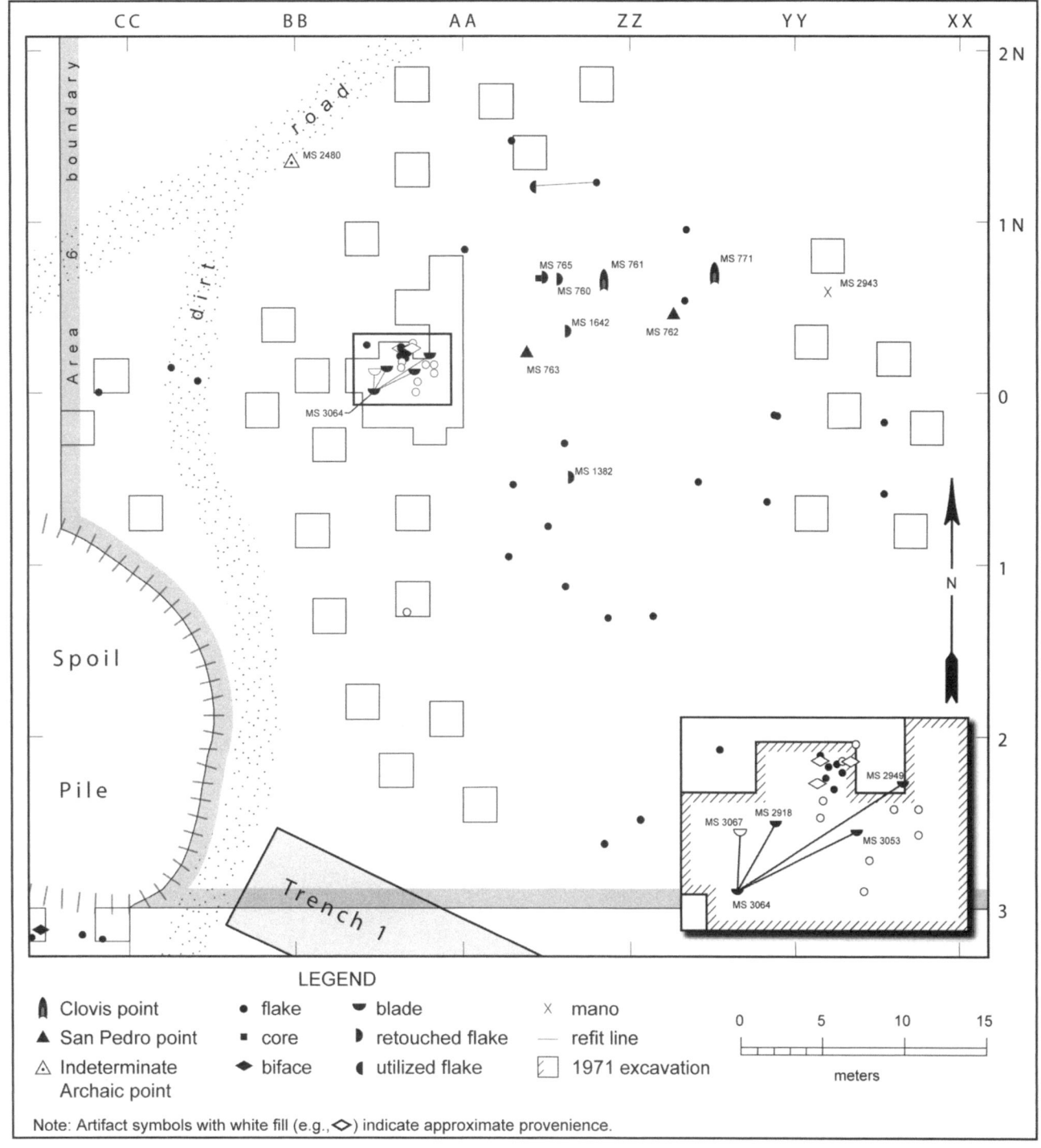

Figure 7.4. Distribution of remains in Area 6.

152   *Chapter 7, Larry D. Agenbroad and Bruce B. Huckell*

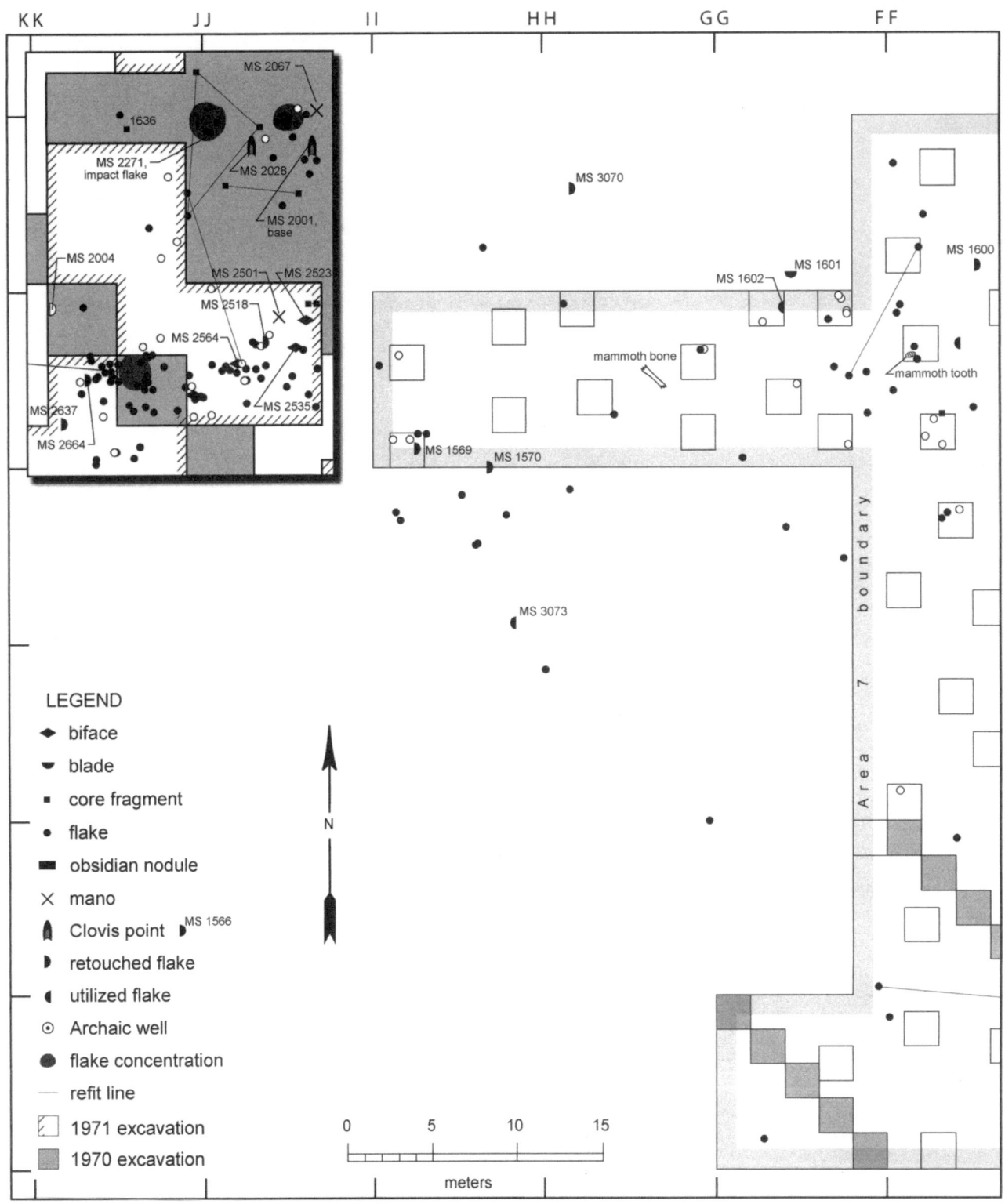

Figure 7.5*a*. Distribution of remains in Area 7.

The Hunting Camp at Murray Springs 153

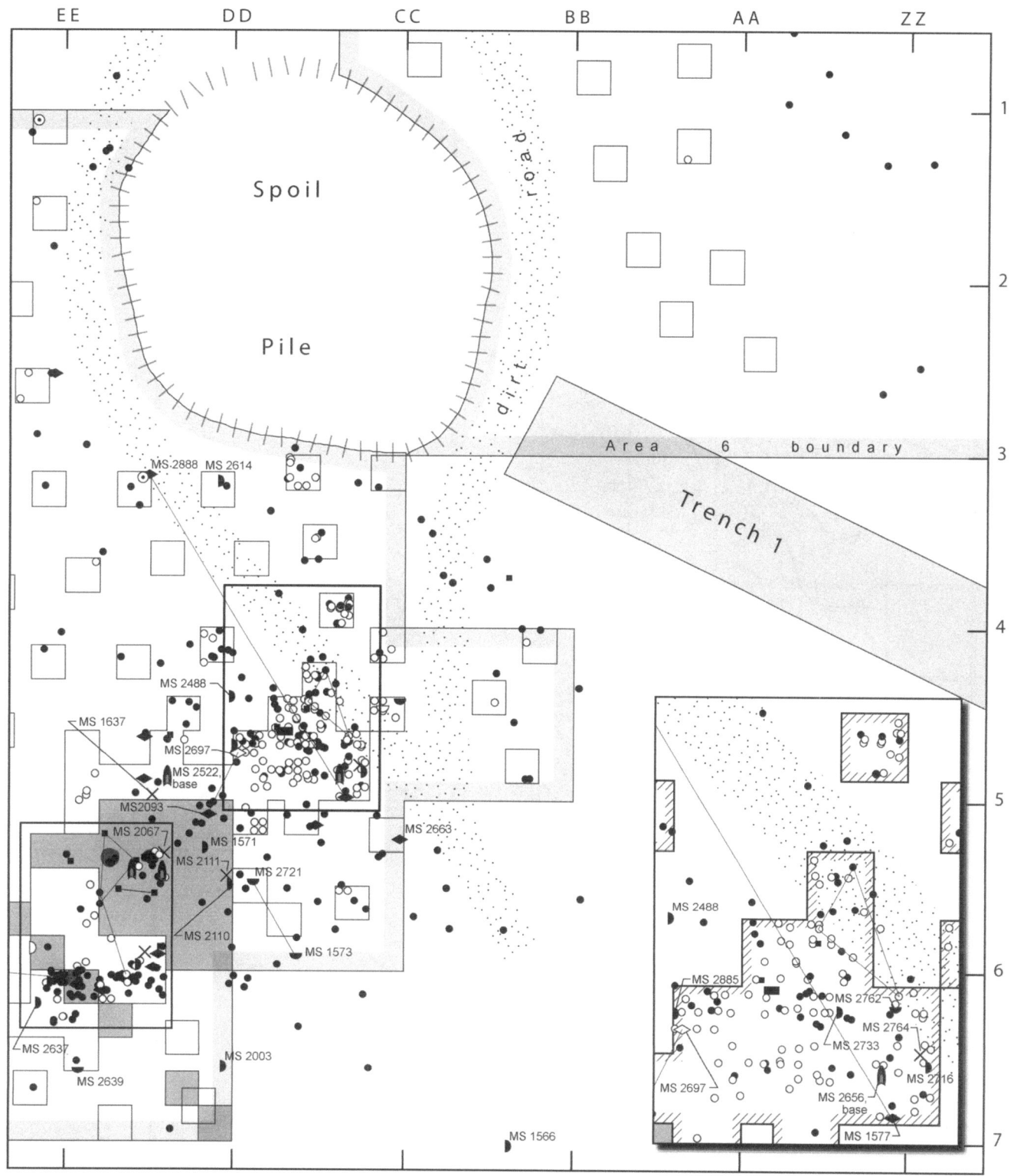

Figure 7.5b. Distribution of remains in Area 7.

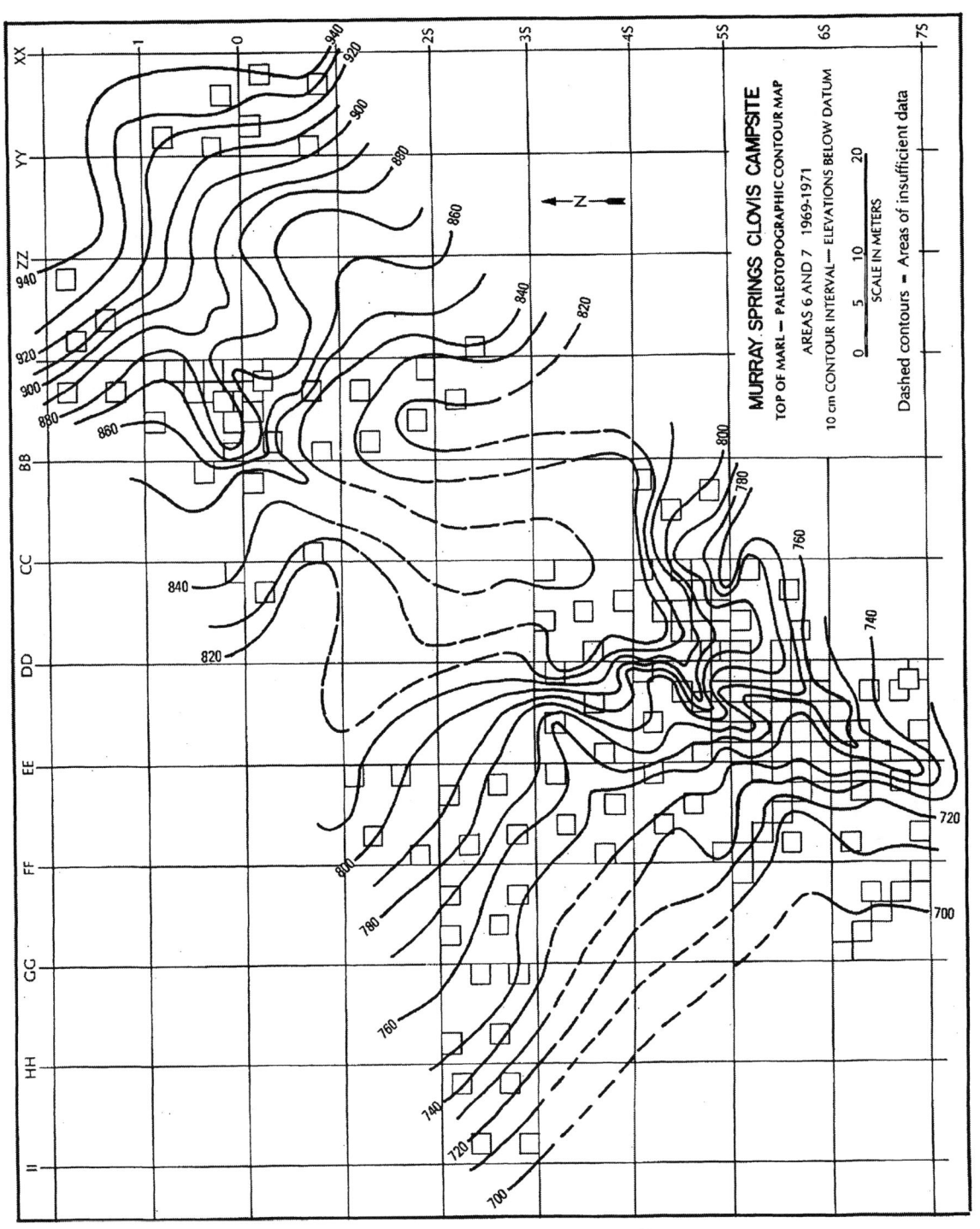

Figure 7.6. Paleotopographic map of Areas 6 and 7.

concentrations of cultural material are coincident with breaks in the profile of the paleowash. This may be interpreted as the hunters selectively locating here for shelter, shade, or concealment. It is improbable that an alternate hypothesis, artificial concentration of remains by redeposition, is tenable in light of the tight monolithic concentrations of waste flakes and the stratigraphic evidence of the two field seasons.

Discussion

Surface collection and excavations in Areas 6 and 7 augmented the artifact inventory taken from the excavations of the kill site areas. More than 1,100 lithic artifacts, the majority of which were waste flakes, were added to the artifact inventory. Importantly, the waste flakes were often recovered from flake clusters, homogeneous in lithic material and tightly massed in horizontal and vertical space.

The 1969–1971 investigations in Areas 6 and 7 produced 33 Clovis tools and 764 waste flakes attributed to Clovis lithic industry. Clovis artifacts were differentiated from the Archaic period artifacts on the basis of knapping technology and lithic material (Chapter 8). The total number of Archaic tools was 18, including 10 flaked stone implements and 8 ground stone tools; 206 pieces of debitage were linked to this occupation. Most of the Archaic materials were made from a dark silicified limestone that was locally available at outcrops in the Lewis Hills (Fig. 2.2). Clovis materials were usually chalcedony, chert, or obsidian. An additional two implements and 47 pieces of debitage could not be assigned to either the Clovis or Archaic occupation.

To support the conclusions made from the lithic raw material and knapping techniques, the stratigraphic position and context serve to substantiate the differentiation of Clovis and Cochise materials. The simplified microstratigraphy presented in Figures 1.9d and 2.18 illustrates the basis for the stratigraphic separation of the cultures. Nearly all the Archaic materials were recovered from the surficial reddish brown sandy silt layer (G_x). The lithic materials attributed to the younger occupation rarely exceeded 20 cm in depth, except in areas of bioturbation. The majority of the Clovis artifacts and debitage was recovered from a marly silt basal F_3, usually gray in color. This mixed zone was heavily reworked by rodents, burrowing carnivores, and especially by ground-dwelling insects such as cicadas. Beneath the mixed zone was a continuous, or remnant, layer of creamy Coro marl (Stratum E) considered to predate the Clovis occupation. Where the marl was missing or present as eroded remnants, it was underlain by the green clay of the Sobaipuri mudstone. Clovis material was recovered throughout the zones overlying the marl and on the surface. This vertical mixing is considered to be due to 13,000 years of bioturbation of the deposits.

CLOVIS ARTIFACTS FROM AREAS 6 AND 7

Some 1,162 artifacts were recovered from the surface and excavated sample of grid squares in the camp area. The majority of these artifacts (889, or 76.5% of the total) can be assigned to the Clovis occupation of the camp; 223 artifacts (19.2% of the total) represent the later Archaic period occupation. Attributes of artifact morphology, material type, and technology have been used to achieve this separation. However, there are two implements and 47 flakes (4.2% of the total sample) that defy easy classification as either Clovis or younger because they are made of materials not immediately recognizable as Clovis, they are extremely small fragments, or they are of unusual form; these items are listed as unclassified in the following descriptions. Finally, a single polychrome sherd constitutes the only definite evidence for ceramic period use of the site area.

Clovis artifacts are described first, followed by those assigned to the Archaic occupation of the camp area, and finally those of uncertain age. Table 7.2 lists Clovis implements from the camp.

Bifacially Flaked Implements

Investigation of the Area 6 and 7 camp yielded six Clovis fluted points and three Clovis bifaces; all but two are fragmentary. Figure 7.7 illustrates all of these artifacts, and descriptive metric data are in Chapter 8.

Projectile Points

One complete point, a large midsection, and four basal fragments were recovered from the camp. The complete point (Fig. 7.7b) and the large midsection (Fig. 7.7a) were found on or just beneath the surface in Area 6. As already indicated, the large midsection can be directly linked to the Area 4 bison kill by virtue

Table 7.2. Clovis Artifacts from the Murray Springs Camp, Areas 6 and 7

ASM Number	MS Number	Area	Grid	Description	Fig. No.
A-32,991	761	6	AA0–10	Clovis point midsection	7.7a
A-32,992	771	6	ZZ0–8	Clovis point	7.7b
A-47,139	2001	7	EE6–13	Clovis point base	7.7d
A-47,140	2028	7	EE6–14	Clovis point base	7.7e
A-47,162	2522	7	EE5–22	Clovis point base	7.7c
A-47,283	2656	7	DD5,SE	Clovis point base	7.7h
A-47,163	2523	7	EE6–23	Biface fragment	7.7f
A-47,199	2564	7	EE7–4	Fits A-47,163	
A-47,170	2535	7	EE6–23	Biface	7.7g
A-46,365	2946	6	BB0–21	Biface fragment	7.7i
A-33,943	1382	6	AA1S–12	End scraper	7.8c
A-33,928	1570	7	II3–22	End scraper with graver	7.8a
A-33,929	1571	7	II4–18	End scraper	7.8b
A-45,615	2004	7	FF6–21	End scraper	7.8d
A-32,990	760	6	AA0–8	Graver	7.8e
A-46,160	2733	7	DD5–18	Graver	
74-52-1	3070	7	HH2–6	Large laterally retouched flake	7.8h
A-46,143	2716	7	DD5,SE	Large laterally retouched flake	7.8i
A-45,614	2003	7	DD7–11	Laterally retouched flake	
A-45,703	2110	7	EE6–11	Laterally retouched flake	7.8g
A-47,158	2518	7	EE6–23	Laterally retouched flake	
A-47,264	2637	7	FF7–1	Laterally retouched flake	7.8j
A-43,026	1611	7	EE6–20	Fits A-47,264	
A-45,694	2101	7	EE6–19	Fits A-47,264	
A-47,291	2664	7	FF7–1	Laterally retouched flake	7.8f
A-33,347	1642	6	AA0–19	Lat. retouched flake frag.	
A-43,022	1600	7	EE2–23	Lat. retouched flake frag.	
A-47,127	2488	7	EE5,SE	Lat. retouched flake frag.	
A-33,927	1569	7	II3,NW	Retouched blade frag.	7.9g
A-33,930	1573	7	DD6–24	Retouched blade frag.	7.9h
A-46,148	2721	7	DD6–15	Fits A-33,930	
A-43,023	1601	7	GG2–23	Retouched blade frag.	7.9e
A-43,024	1602	7	GG3–4	Utilized blade frag.	7.9d
A-46,180	2762	7	DD5–19	Utilized blade	7.9b
A-43,007	765	6	AA0–8	Retouched blade frag.	7.9a
A-47,514	2918	6	BB0,SE	Fits A-43,007	
A-47,514	3053	6	BB0–23	Fits A-43,007	
A-47,514	3067	6	BB0–23	Fits A-43,007	
A-47,513	3064	6	BB0–23	Fits A-43,007	
A-46,368	2949	6	BB0,SE	Utilized blade frag.	7.9c
A-46,292	2871	7	DD5–17	Obsidian nodule	
A-47,266	2639	7	EE7–15	Utilized blade	7.9f

of the refitting of a flake recovered in the kill area to part of the 23-mm long, 16-mm wide impact "flute" extending baseward from the crushed tip (Figs. 7.7a, 8.7h). The point is made of the same pinkish gray chert represented in several of the buried knapping loci in Area 3, although it has developed a yellowish brown patina. Despite its size (87 mm long), this fragment was either lost or not deemed salvageable. The complete point (Fig. 7.7b), found just beneath the surface on Coro marl, is of heavily patinated chert and is short and broad (72 mm long by 34 mm wide) with short (less than 21 mm) flutes on both faces. Its shape and size may reflect a point created by the reworking of a large point blade fragment. The tip exhibits some minor crushing, possibly produced by impact. It appears to be of sufficient size and condition to be serviceable, so the reason for its presence at the northeast edge of the camp is unclear.

From Area 7 came the four basal fragments shown in Figure 7.7c–e and h. Two are of chert, one of obsidian, and one of chalcedony; all but the obsidian specimen exhibit the yellowish brown patina noted for the Area 6 points. The chert basal fragments include one of pinkish gray chert (Fig. 7.7h) and one of tan and gray chert (Fig. 7.7c), both materials represented in the Area 3 knapping loci. The chalcedony base (Fig. 7.7e) is identical to the debitage and artifacts found in all areas of the site and can be traced to a generalized source area near St. David, some 40 km (25 miles) north of Murray Springs in the San Pedro Valley (Chapter 8). Geochemical analysis indicates that the obsidian specimen (Fig. 7.7d) came from near Clifton, Arizona (Appendix C). All four bases display transverse snap breaks, at least three of which occurred within the hafted portion of the point (Fig. 7.7d,e, h); only one (Fig. 7.7c) broke distal of the haft.

Bifaces

Three bifaces of certain Clovis affinity were recovered from the camp. One (Fig. 7.7g) is a complete biface of heavily patinated chalcedony from the St. David area source. It is thick relative to its width and may have been discarded because the thickness prevented it from being effectively resharpened or finished into a projectile point. Another biface of the same material is represented by two refitted pieces (Fig. 7.7f). This biface was severely burned, and both fragments exhibit potlid and arcuate fractures from that

Figure 7.7. Clovis bifacial artifacts from Areas 6 and 7: a–e, h, projectile points; f, i, biface fragments; g, biface. Length of b is 72 mm. Note impact flake scar on a to which flake refits as shown on Figure 8.7h.

event. Whether this burning was caused by a natural fire or a failed attempt to heat treat the biface, or occurred during the younger reoccupation of the camp is impossible to say. Both the complete biface and the burned fragmentary biface were found in Area 7, where abundant chalcedony debitage occurred.

From Area 6 came the short, broad, chert biface fragment shown in Figure 7.7i. It, too, is of tan and gray chert, a material recovered from Area 3 knapping loci. This fragment broke at an inclusion during the reduction process; 25 flakes of the same material were recovered from the immediate vicinity of the fragment, although none refitted to it. Apparently this fragment is but a small piece of a biface considerably larger than either of the chalcedony specimens.

Unifacially Retouched Implements

Unifacially retouched tools were relatively more abundant in the camp than in the buried part of the site

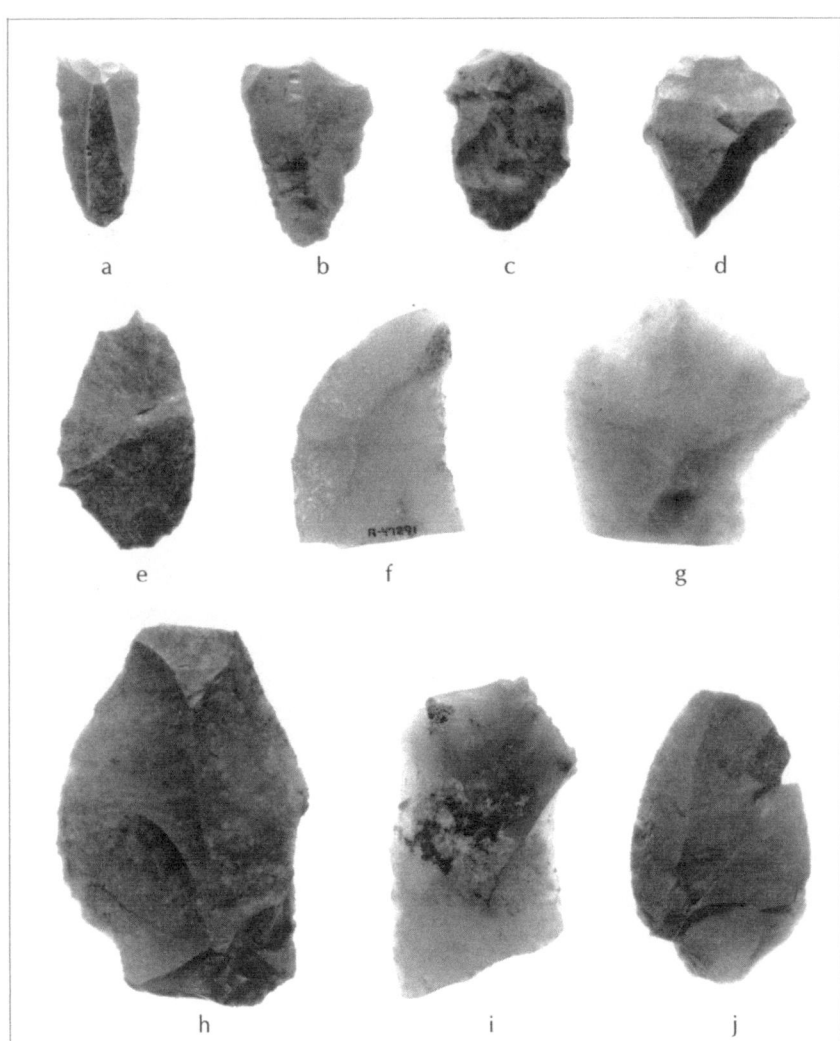

Figure 7.8. Clovis unifacial artifacts from Areas 6 and 7: *a–d*, end scrapers; *e*, graver; *f, g, j*, laterally retouched flakes; *h, i*, large laterally retouched flakes. Length of *h* is 78 mm.

and included tool types unique to the camp. Table 7.2 lists those implements that can be confidently assigned to the Clovis occupation, and Figure 7.8 illustrates a selection of them. The following sections briefly describe the implements, and metric attributes for most of them are presented in Chapter 8.

End Scrapers

Four chert end scrapers, one from Area 6 and three from Area 7, were recovered (Fig. 7.8*a–d*). Three (Fig. 7.8*a–c*) are "classic" end scrapers of the type known from the Blackwater Draw Clovis Site (Hester 1972, Fig. 92*c–j*) and from younger Paleoindian sites (for example, at Lindenmeier; see Wilmsen and Roberts 1978, Fig. 76, second and third rows from the top). All three are made on proximal portions of blades or flakes, triangular to subtriangular in plan view and cross section, with steeply retouched, convex working edges. Note the spur on the scraper shown in Figure 7.8*a*; another spur may have been present on the scraper shown in Figure 7.8*c*, but recent damage has removed this part of the tool.

The fourth end scraper (Fig. 7.8*d*) is somewhat atypical; it was made on a distal blade or flake fragment rather than a proximal one. Although exhibiting the generally triangular form of the other three, this scraper has its convex working edge constructed on a thin distal margin. A portion of the left lateral margin (as it is oriented in Fig. 7.8*d*) has been abruptly retouched to create a nearly vertical edge. The resulting implement is thus formally similar to the other three end scrapers, but the triangular form is the product of intentional retouch instead of the shape provided by the tapered proximal end of the original blade or flake.

Gravers

A pair of gravers was recovered from the camp, one each from Areas 6 and 7. The Area 6 specimen is made on a heavily patinated chert flake derived from biface retouching and bears one spur on its distal margin and another on a lateral margin (Fig. 7.8e). These 2.5-mm to 3.5-mm long spurs were carefully created by unifacially directed pressure retouch. In addition, the lateral margin that does not have a spur bears fine, even, low angle unifacial retouch; a similar but very abrupt retouch occurs on the opposite lateral margin between the spurs.

The graver from Area 7 was constructed on a proximal flake fragment of St. David Chalcedony; it is not illustrated. It bears a single 2-mm long spur constructed on a lateral margin. The tip of the spur appears to have been slightly crushed in antiquity, leaving a comparatively broad, blunt spur in contrast to the long, sharp spurs on the Area 6 graver.

Hester (1972, Fig. 95a–e) illustrates similar Clovis gravers from Blackwater Draw. Area 3 at Murray Springs also yielded a graver (Figs. 5.13i, 8.10f).

Laterally Retouched Flake Tools

This diverse category consists of 10 flake implements grouped together because they all exhibit working edges on their lateral margins created by unifacially directed retouch. However, within this group some distinctions can be made using attributes of overall size and retouch characteristics. The following paragraphs briefly describe three groups, and Figure 7.8f–j illustrates a selection of these implements.

The first group contains one distinctive tool made on a large (78 mm long, 53 mm wide) chert flake that was found on the surface at the western edge of Area 7 (Fig. 7.8h). The left margin of this core flake (as positioned in Fig. 7.8h) displays a series of retouch flakes that create a convex, even working edge. The right margin exhibits bifacial knicking, possibly produced by utilization, and one area of four short, broad flakes detached from the interior surface of the tool. Haury and others (1959, Fig. 14g) illustrate a tool from the Lehner Site that is larger but exhibits the same type and location of retouch; they term it a side scraper. A similar artifact is known from the Clovis type site and is illustrated in Cotter (1937: 12). Because the working edges of the Murray Springs implement are somewhat thin and delicate, it is open to question whether it served for scraping or cutting tasks, but the latter may be more likely.

A slightly smaller laterally retouched flake recovered from Area 7 is shown in Figure 7.8i; it is the sole representative of the second group of laterally retouched flakes. It is made on a 60-mm long by 41-mm wide core flake fragment of St. David Chalcedony and bears a steep retouch that creates a slightly convex working edge along the left margin. The flakes composing the retouch average approximately 5 mm in length, and one is 15 mm long. They create a much more robust edge than that of the tool described above (Fig. 7.8h) and give the implement an appearance perhaps more consistent with what might be expected for a scraper. The Lehner Site produced a tool with similar working edge characteristics (Haury and others 1959, Fig. 14d), and the Clovis component at Blackwater Draw has yielded several tools termed side scrapers by Hester (1972, Fig. 91), some of which (Hester 1972, Fig. 91g, k) appear to be similar to this Murray Springs specimen.

Three other laterally retouched flake implements differ from the preceding ones in that they are made on smaller, thinner flakes and display working edges created by a series of short (less than 4 mm), regular retouch flakes. These comprise the third group of Clovis laterally retouched flakes from Murray Springs. Two of the illustrated specimens (Fig. 7.8f, g) are made on distal fragments of St. David Chalcedony flakes, and the third (Fig. 7.8j) is of chert. All were found in Area 7 and two (Fig. 7.8f, j) were recovered from the same 2-m grid square. The chalcedony specimens may have been made on flakes detached from bifaces, based on the pattern of previous flake scars on their exterior surfaces and the slight curvature in their longitudinal axes, but the chert specimen appears to have been made on a core flake. A single straight to slightly convex working edge is apparent on the left margin of the tool shown in Figure 7.8g. The other two bear retouch on both lateral margins. Two slightly convex working edges are present on one (Fig. 7.8j), whereas one convex and one slightly concave working edge are present on the other (Fig. 7.8f); this latter specimen is fragmentary.

Figure 7.9. Clovis blade tools from Areas 6 and 7: *a, e, g, h*, retouched blade fragments; *b, d, f*, utilized blade and blade fragments; *c*, unmodified blade fragment. Length of *g* is 68 mm.

These three implements may be similar to artifacts termed "flake scrapers" from the Clovis horizon at Blackwater Draw (Hester 1972, Fig. 92*k–r*) and to two tools recovered from the 1974–1975 excavations at the Lehner Site (Agenbroad and Huckell 1981). The Murray Springs examples display generally steep edge angles appropriate for scraping tasks, although their thinness and finely retouched margins imply that they may have served scraping tasks that placed less strain on their edges.

Five other tool fragments bearing similarly fine, even unifacial retouch on a lateral margin were also identified but are not illustrated. Three are of chert, one is of St. David Chalcedony, and one is of pinkish brown silicified siltstone. The St. David Chalcedony specimen was made on a biface reduction flake.

Blades and Blade Tools

Areas 6 and 7 yielded two complete blades and six blade fragments; three were deliberately retouched after being struck from the core and three others bear edge damage but no retouch. All eight specimens are illustrated in Figure 7.9, and their metric attributes are presented in Chapter 8.

Retouched Blades

Two of the retouched blades are particularly noteworthy. One is an 87-mm long blade of gray chalcedony from Area 6 that has an end scraper on its distal end and a pair of notches high on its lateral margins (Fig. 7.9*a*). The blade had been broken into five fragments in antiquity, but all five were recovered. A robust (68 mm long by 42 mm wide) fragmentary blade (Fig. 7.9*g*) made of a fine-grained, pinkish brown silicified siltstone was recovered from Area 7. It also has an end scraper on its distal margin, along with irregular, selective unifacial retouch on its lateral margins. This fragment is strongly triangular in transverse cross section, and bears a series of short flakes removed from the exterior ridge; three helped to straighten the ridge prior to detachment of the blade from the core.

The third retouched blade is a large distal fragment, broken in antiquity, of which two pieces were recovered (Fig. 7.9*h*). It, too, was evidently markedly triangular in cross section, because considerable effort was expended to thin its exterior ridge (after detachment from the core) using longitudinally directed blows from either end. One such blow resulted in the hinge-through break that created the fragments; however, thinning attempts continued on the larger fragment after this break. This larger piece also displays irregular, selective retouch on both margins, including a series of short flakes terminating in broad hinge fractures on the interior surface of one margin. The specimen, also from Area 7, is of the same silicified siltstone as the end scraper in Figure 7.9*g*.

Utilized Blades

Three blades from Area 7, two complete and one fragmentary, display damage to their lateral margins suggestive of utilization without retouching. One of the complete specimens (Fig. 7.9*b*) is of chert, and shows nearly continuous, predominantly unifacial, knicking on both lateral margins composed of scars less than 1 mm long. The other complete blade (Fig. 7.9*f*) is of pinkish brown silicified siltstone and exhibits similar damage along its longer, straighter left margin (as oriented in Fig. 7.9).

The third utilized blade is of pinkish gray chert, but represents a 30–mm long midsection of a blade (Fig. 7.9*d*). Like the other two it has markedly knicked and crushed edges, suggesting heavy utilization. However, this blade midsection shows clear signs that it was intentionally broken at both ends by single blows directed to the exterior central ridge; negative or split bulbs of percussion from this segmentation process are present at both ends. This blade was broken to create an implement of a specific length, perhaps to be hafted in a bone or wood handle as a cutting implement. Such a bone handle was recovered from the Navarrete Site, and the slot in its side is of nearly the same length as the blade segment (Huckell 1981).

Blade Fragments

Two distal blade fragments from the camp are also illustrated in Figure 7.9. One from Area 7 is the distal end of a chert blade that broke at an impurity (Fig. 7.9*e*). It bears a short unifacial retouch series along its right distolateral margin (as oriented in Fig. 7.9) and a vertically snapped extreme distal end. There may once have been a graver spur here, or the blade may simply have been broken in retouching. The other fragment (Fig. 7.9*c*) is the distal end of a gray chalcedony blade, similar but not identical to the material of the notched blade with an end scraper described above. This fragment was found in Area 6 in the same area as the other chalcedony blade, but exhibits no evidence of use or retouching on its margins. However, like the silicified siltstone blade fragment with an end scraper (Fig. 7.9*g*), this blade fragment also has a few flakes removed from the central exterior ridge near its distal end.

Note that three of the illustrated blades (Fig. 7.9*f–h*) are of the same fine-grained, pinkish brown silicified siltstone. An additional three specimens (two of which are illustrated in Chapter 8) may be examples of improperly struck blades of this same material, and several fragments of a burned core of this material were also found in Area 7. A few hundred unmodified flakes, clearly not parts of blades, of this same material were also recovered there. This may be evidence for the manufacture of blades from one or more cores of this material at the site (Chapter 8). Each of the other blades in Figure 7.9*a–e* is of a lithologically distinct chert or chalcedony, representing a minimum of five other blade cores.

As described by Hemmings in Chapter 5, single blades were found in Areas 3 and 4 of the buried portion of Murray Springs. Clovis blades and blade tools are not common, but are known from other sites. Two tools possibly made on distal blade fragments were recovered from the Lehner Site (Haury and others 1959, Fig. 14*a, b*). A cache of blades, recovered under less than ideal circumstances, was reported from Blackwater Draw by Green (1963). A large, utilized, distal blade fragment was recovered from a multicomponent, surface and near-surface site with Clovis and ceramic period occupations near Payson, Arizona (Huckell 1978a, Fig. 28*e*). Despite their contextual problems, these last two occurrences are viewed as reasonable evidence for Clovis blade manufacture and use at other sites. The potential use of blades for side and end scraper manufacture at Blackwater Draw has also been noted by Hester (1972, Figs. 91, 92). Finally, an isolated cache of blades, blade cores, chopping tools, and a biface from near Anadarko, Oklahoma, has been attributed on typological grounds to Clovis (Hammatt 1970). The Murray Springs camp has thus yielded a substantial number of the known and possible Clovis blades so far reported from western sites.

Clovis Cores

Fragments of two cores from Area 7 (not illustrated) were assigned to the Clovis occupation. One of them is a fragment of St. David Chalcedony exhibiting a plain platform surface from which at least two large flakes were struck; parts of these scars and their negative bulbs of percussion are visible on this fragment. Its maximum dimension is slightly less than 60 mm, and its weight is approximately 60 g. The fragment broke at a 20-mm diameter internal impurity.

The other core is represented by 19 small, thermally fractured pieces, several of which can be refitted to create three pieces of a large core of pinkish brown silicified siltstone. Together these three fragments weigh a little over 77 g and appear to represent portions of a bifacial core margin and one piece of the interior of the core. The maximum dimension of the largest reconstructed fragment is 74 mm. The form and extent of fragmentation of this core suggest that it was intentionally burned, though when or for what reason cannot be determined. It is possible that this was a blade core, judging from the limited information provided by the three reconstructed portions and the presence of blades of the same material.

Obsidian Nodule

Also recovered from Area 7 was a single unflaked obsidian nodule or "Apache tear." It is roughly quadrilateral, almost subrectangular in shape, and measures approximately 33 mm long, 28 mm wide, and 25 mm thick. It retains a small amount of patina or cortex on one end and three sides, but shows incipient cones of fracture on the fourth side and an old break with battered edges on the other end. These cones and the battered edges of the break suggest that this nodule was transported some distance in an alluvial environment. It appears to be from the same source in east-central Arizona as the obsidian nodules from Areas 1 and 3 (Chapter 5; Appendix C), and for this reason is assigned to the Clovis component of Area 7.

Clovis Debitage

The investigated portion of the camp area produced a large quantity of debitage, most of which was determined to be of Clovis origin based on material type and flake attributes. As mentioned previously, virtually all of the Clovis artifacts from the camp areas are strongly patinated regardless of material type. Most exhibit a yellow to golden brown patina, but in many cases they are clearly lithologically identical to materials found in unpatinated condition in the buried part of the site. This is true for the chalcedony from the St. David area source and most of the chert; identification of the chert as identical to material from buried contexts was aided by occasional fresh breaks from excavation.

One material poorly represented from the buried part of the site, obsidian, was somewhat more abundant in the camp. Flake type is important in assigning this material to the Clovis occupation. As is the case from the knapping loci in Areas 1, 3, 4, and 5, flakes derived from soft hammer biface reduction were most common in the camp. The obsidian debitage shows the typical features associated with this knapping operation, so this, along with the obsidian Clovis point base from Area 7, support its assignment to the Clovis occupation. Debitage and artifacts of a pinkish brown silicified siltstone from the camp also appear to be of Clovis origin, as discussed above in the sections dealing with blades and blade tools and cores.

Another material, a greenish gray to black silicified limestone, was abundant in Area 7 and is believed to represent one or more Archaic period or younger occupations. Although the material also exhibits patina of varying degrees of development, the flakes are uniformly the product of hard hammer percussion flaking, principally of cores. One artifact of this material was recovered from Area 3, but no debitage; two unifacial implements from the Lehner Site bone bed (Haury and others 1959, Figs. 14*e*, *g*) are the only other definite evidence of Clovis use of this distinctive material. By contrast, it is abundant at Archaic and ceramic period sites throughout the valley, and there is extensive evidence of aboriginal quarrying at its primary source in the Lewis Hills north of Lewis Springs. The few retouched flakes of this silicified limestone from Area 7 are also formally more consistent with Archaic or younger artifacts. Therefore, the debitage of this material has been classified as post-Clovis, although

Table 7.3. Cultural and Material Attributes of Debitage from the Murray Springs Camp, Areas 6 and 7

Material	Number of Flakes		
	Clovis	Archaic	Age Uncertain
Area 6			
Reddish brown chert	54		
Tan and gray chert	32		
Silicified siltstone	2		
Pinkish gray chert	1		
Silicified limestone		2	
Red patinated chert			1
Black chert			4
Gray chalcedony			2
Totals	89	2	7
Area 7			
St. David Chalcedony	374		
Tan and gray chert	130		
Silicified siltstone	85		
Obsidian	50		
Reddish brown chert	26		
Pinkish gray chert	10		
Silicified limestone		204	
Pitchstone*			3
Green quartzite			4
Gray chalcedony			4
Miscellaneous cherts			19
Basalt			1
Miscellaneous quartzites			6
Metasediment			2
Porphyrytic igneous			1
Totals	675	204	40
Areas 6 and 7 Totals	764	206	47

* Opaque obsidian sourced in 1991 by M. S. Shackley to the San Francisco Peaks volcanic field.

the possibility that some of the debitage may be of Clovis age cannot be completely ruled out. Finally, there are several flakes of unique or poorly represented material types that cannot be confidently assigned to the Clovis or the younger occupation.

Table 7.3 lists the materials and quantities of flakes that can be assigned to the Clovis occupation of Areas 6 and 7. Area 6 yielded a far smaller number of pieces of Clovis debitage (89) than did Area 7. Of this number, most (54) are of reddish brown chert and another 32 are of tan and gray chert. Both materials are present in the buried part of the site, and the flakes in Area 6 appear to be the products of biface retouching. The remaining three flakes include two of pinkish brown silicified siltstone and one of pinkish gray chert.

Nine other flakes from the area apparently pertain to younger occupations or cannot be easily assigned to any cultural-temporal position.

Area 7 yielded 675 flakes assignable to the Clovis occupation (Table 7.3). Of this total, 501 (74.2%) occurred as spatially and materially discrete clusters of flakes; seven such clusters were defined within the excavated area. These generally did not exhibit the tight spatial clustering observed in the buried part of the site (Chapters 5, 8) due to slow burial and bioturbation. Some tightly massed clusters were found, however, including a concentration of 305 flakes of the St. David Chalcedony in a 30-cm deep, "wash basin-sized" part of 2-m grid EE6-7 in Area 7. Other concentrations included 77 flakes of tan and gray chert, most from a 1-m by 2-m area at the northwest corner of 10-m grid EE7 and the northeast corner of 10-m grid FF7, and 22 obsidian flakes from an area of similar size at the boundary between 2-m grids EE6-7 and EE6-8. The obsidian Clovis point base (Fig. 7.7d) was found only 1 m southeast of the obsidian flake cluster. Most other defined clusters were spread over larger areas ranging between 8 and 20 square meters. More than one third of the flakes assigned to the Clovis use of the site could not be associated with any spatially distinct cluster, but were simply scattered across the present ground surface or were recovered from 2-m sample grids.

In general the flakes assigned to the Clovis occupation in this area reflect the same emphasis on biface reduction noted among the knapping loci in Areas 1, 3, 4, and 5 (Chapters 5, 8). This inference is based on the abundance of faceted and lipped striking platforms (occasionally ground as well), the pattern of previous flake scars on the exterior surface of the flakes, and the curvature observed in the long axis of the flakes. It appears that at least one biface of tan and gray chert was finished into a projectile point in Area 7, because two fragments of probable channel flakes were identified. The flakes of pinkish brown silicified siltstone include several that appear to have been detached from a core by hard hammer percussion. As described above, several fragments of a badly burned core of this material were recovered, as were three blade tools and three possible misstruck blades. It is therefore conceivable that some or all of these flakes represent the preparation and working of one or more blade cores, a flint knapping activity not represented elsewhere on the site.

ARCHAIC PERIOD AND YOUNGER ARTIFACTS

The camp site was reoccupied at least once and potentially several times during the Archaic period and perhaps in later prehistory as well. Unfortunately, only a few culturally and temporally diagnostic artifacts were found that are of use in dating these younger occupations. However, a few hundred pieces of debitage, several retouched pieces, some ground stone milling equipment, one pot sherd, five clusters of fire-cracked rocks, and two wells indicate that these younger occupations involved a variety of activities, even if they were relatively brief.

The bulk of the artifacts assigned to the younger occupations are probably of Archaic age, based on artifact morphology and patination. Among the specimens of this broad time period are projectile points, bifaces, unifaces, cores, debitage, and ground stone manos and a metate. Table 7.4 lists these specimens and they are described in the following paragraphs.

Archaic Period Bifacially Flaked Artifacts

Three broken or damaged projectile points, two broken but reconstructible bifaces, and a fragment of a third biface represent Archaic period bifacially flaked tools. All of the points were recovered from Area 6, but all of the bifaces came from Area 7.

Projectile Points

Figure 7.10a–c illustrates the Archaic period projectile points from the camp. Two of these, one essentially complete and the other a large basal fragment, appear to be diminutive examples of a corner-notched point style assignable to the Late Archaic period and possibly the early ceramic period as well. Both points are of chert. Often generically referred to as San Pedro points (Sayles and Antevs 1941, Plate 16c, d), these corner-notched points have been found throughout southern and east-central Arizona, as well as southwestern and west-central New Mexico (Dick 1965; Haury 1950, 1957; Martin and others 1952; Sayles 1983; Windmiller 1973). In size and form these two Murray Springs points closely resemble some of the corner-notched points from Tularosa and Cordova caves in west-central New Mexico (Martin and others 1952, Fig. 47). In those two sites this point style

Table 7.4. Archaic Period and Younger Artifacts from the Murray Springs Camp, Areas 6 and 7

ASM No.	MS No.	Area	Grid	Description	Fig. No.
A-33,933	762	6	ZZ0–14	Projectile point frag.	7.10b
A-33,934	763	6	AA0–17	Projectile point	7.10a
A-47,119	2480	6	CC1N–20	Projectile point tip	7.10c
A-44,309	1577	7	DD5-22	Biface fragment	7.10e
A-46,309	2888	7	EE4,NW	Fits A-44,309	
A-45,690	2093	7	EE6-1	Biface fragment	7.10f
A-46,124	2697	7	DD5,SW	Fits A-45,690	
A-47,290	2663	7	DD6,NE	Biface fragment	7.10g
A-47,243	2614	7	EE5-1	Unifacially retouched flake	7.10i
A-46,306	2885	7	DD5-16	Unifacially retouched flake	7.10h
A-47,520	4	7	CC6(?)	Basin metate	
A-33,932	1637	7	EE5-23	Mano	
None*	2067	7	EE6-8	Mano fragment	
None*	2111	7	EE6-11	Mano fragment	
None*	2117	7	EE6-11	Fits MS 2111 to reconstruct whole mano	
None*	2501	7	EE6-23	Mano fragment	
None	2764	7	DD5-19	Mano	
None*	2943	6	None	Mano	
Uncertain Age					
A-43,020	1566	7	KK6	Unifacially retouched flake	
A-43,025	1606	7	II10	Retouched flake fragment	

*Specimen not present in Arizona State Museum collections.

abundant in late preceramic levels but extended into the was most plain ware and later ceramic horizons in diminished numbers.

A chalcedony point tip (Fig. 7.10c) came from the surface of Area 6. Its narrowness at the place where it broke suggests that it was an Archaic period dart point of some undeterminable style and not the tip of a Clovis point.

Mention should be made of another projectile point from the general area of the site. It is a large, stemmed dart point of purplish brown metasediment, found approximately 145 m southeast of Area 7 across the East Swale and on top of a low ridge less than 1 m from where the permanent site datum was established (see Fig. 1.3 for location of datum point D). As shown in Figure 7.10d, it is a nearly complete point missing only a portion of the tip and one of the blade corners. Stylistically it bears affinities to the Pinto point (Campbell and Campbell 1935), and particularly to what Harrington (1957, Fig. 39, third row, third specimen) called the Pinto "square shoulders" subtype at the Stahl

Figure 7.10. Archaic period artifacts from Areas 6 and 7: *a, b*, San Pedro points; *c*, point tip; *d*, stemmed point from surface south of Area 7; *e-g*, bifaces; *h, i*, unifacially retouched tools.

Site in California. Similar points are also known in Arizona from Ventana Cave (Haury 1950, Fig. 61*e–j*), the Lone Hill Site near Redington in the San Pedro Valley (Agenbroad 1970, Fig. 15, third row from the top), and from the McCleary Canyon Site in the Santa Rita Mountains (Huckell 1984, Fig. 5.18*f–i*). This point was a 1986 surface find, and is the only artifact temporally diagnostic of the Middle Archaic period recovered from the Murray Springs Site area.

Bifaces

Three broken bifaces, represented by five fragments, were recovered from Area 7 (Fig. 7.10*e–g*). All are of markedly patinated silicified limestone. As can be seen, two complete bifaces were reconstructed by refitting of fragments (Fig. 7.10*e, f*), but the third biface (Fig. 7.10*g*) is represented by a single large basal fragment. Coincidentally, the fragments that were refitted to reconstruct the two bifaces were 4 m apart from one another in each case. It appears that these bifaces were broken in manufacture, based on their rather irregular shapes, the presence of unfinished portions of the margin with flake scars displaying intact negative bulbs of percussion, and final breakage by diagonal, "perverse" fractures (Crabtree 1972: 82–83) on the two reconstructed specimens. Considering their sizes, it is possible that these bifaces were designed to serve as preforms for projectile points or small hafted knives. The remaining biface fragment (Fig. 7.10g) displays a transverse break similar to what has been called an end shock fracture by Crabtree (1972: 60–61), but like the others it bears extremely irregular, unfinished margins. It, too, probably broke during manufacture.

Archaic Period Unifacially Retouched Pieces

Two pieces of silicified limestone recovered from Area 7 bore unifacial retouch; Figure 7.10h and i illustrate both. One (Fig. 7.10h) is a well patinated flake that bears a series of short (less than 5 mm long) retouch scars on its distal end, creating a nearly straight working edge. One distal corner was broken off in antiquity, taking a portion of the working edge with it.

The second piece (Fig. 7.10i) is a large chunk of slightly patinated black silicified limestone with some irregular bifacial retouch scars around its perimeter. However, one end and part of a contiguous edge exhibit a series of distinctly darker, unpatinated, unifacially directed retouch scars that create an irregular but steep working edge. The difference in patina clearly reflects the passage of some time, several centuries at least, between the initial working of the piece and the creation of the unifacially retouched edges.

Archaic Period Cores

Two complete cores and a core fragment of well-patinated silicified limestone were recovered from Area 7. The larger of the two complete cores is wedge-shaped, weighs approximately 308 g, and measures approximately 76 mm long, 60 mm wide, and 64 mm thick. Flakes have been struck from several plain and bifacial platform areas, and there are two areas where small flakes have been bifacially detached from a platform-core face junction. This feature may suggest use of the core for chopping tasks.

The second core is on an elongated, tabular piece of material, subtriangular in plan view shape. It measures approximately 109 mm long, 57 mm wide, and 32 mm thick; it weighs 189 g. Two cortical edges served as striking platforms for the removal of flakes from the two flat surfaces of the piece. The flake scars on one face are heavily patinated, whereas those on the opposite face are only slightly patinated. It is possible that this core also saw multiple flaking episodes, perhaps several centuries or a few millennia apart.

Finally, a small (57 mm in maximum dimension, 57 g in weight) fragment of a third silicified limestone core was recovered from Area 7. It is well patinated and appears to have been broken from a larger piece along several intersecting, natural fracture planes. Such flaws are common in this material.

Archaic Period Debitage

The only debitage that can be assigned with reasonable certainty to the Archaic or younger occupations of the camp consists of 206 flakes of silicified limestone. These flakes came almost exclusively from Area 7; only two were recovered from Area 6 (Table 7.3). Further, these flakes are large in comparison to the Clovis debitage, ranging in size from 10 mm to 55 mm in maximum dimension and averaging between 25 mm and 30 mm. Those pieces that retain them commonly display prominent, inflated bulbs of percussion usually associated with hard hammer percussion flaking. Although exhibiting varying degrees of patination, the flakes are almost all of gray to black color, typical of the range found in the outcrops of this material approximately 4 km northeast of the site along the San Pedro River north of Lewis Springs (Chapter 8). Nodules, blocks, or large flakes of this material were probably carried from the quarry up Curry Draw to the camp area to be worked into desired products. The production of bifaces such as those described above was clearly one facet of this workshop activity in Area 7. Five flakes of a grayish green silicified limestone were also recovered from Area 7; their specific source is unknown but is probably within the San Pedro Valley.

ARTIFACTS OF UNCERTAIN AGE

Two unifacially retouched implements were recovered from the surface of Area 7 (Table 7.4), but cannot be confidently assigned to either the Clovis or Archaic occupations. One is small, less than 26 mm in maximum dimension, and is made on the distal portion of a well patinated chert flake. It bears an irregular, steeply angled working edge created by unifacial retouch. On a vertical edge, the place at which the original flake was broken, there is some additional steep retouch with associated crushing of the edge.

Both in terms of form and material it does not fit well with the Clovis implements described above, and the development of patina on its surface is similar to that observed on the fragmentary corner-notched point illustrated in Figure 7.10b. The possibility that it is of Archaic period age is thus somewhat stronger than the possibility that it is a Clovis implement, but the evidence is not sufficiently compelling to choose one possibility over the other.

The second implement is made on a fragmentary, small (31 mm in maximum dimension) triangular flake fragment of lightly patinated brown chalcedony. A fine, continuous retouch consisting of flakes 1 mm long is present along a portion of the intact lateral flake margin. This material is not represented elsewhere at Murray Springs, and it is uncertain to which occupation this specimen may pertain.

DEBITAGE OF UNCERTAIN AGE

As may be seen in Table 7.3, 47 flakes (40 from Area 7 and 7 from Area 6) are of materials difficult to assign with confidence to the Clovis or younger occupations. Some are likely part of the post-Clovis occupations, given the fact that they are of locally available cherts, chalcedonies, igneous materials, or quartzites of various colors. Many are also hard hammer, core reduction flakes. Although these attributes are most technologically consistent with Archaic or younger industries and material choices, it must be remembered that a few of the flakes recovered from the buried Clovis occupation surface in Areas 3 and 4 were also produced by hard hammer percussion or were of coarser local materials. The chert debitage assigned to this category includes some heavily patinated flakes and flake fragments, a few of which are probably the products of biface reduction. However, they are so heavily patinated as to prevent their identification with chert varieties from the buried part of the site or are of chert varieties not recognized among the debitage from the buried part of the site. It is perhaps more likely that these are part of the Clovis component, but chert biface reduction flakes are not uncommon on Archaic period sites in southeastern Arizona. Therefore, it seems best not to associate them with any particular time period. Three opaque obsidian flakes ("pitchstone" in Table 7.3) are likely derived from biface manufacture. Steven Shackley (Appendix C) matched these flakes to the Government Mountain source in 1991. Their cultural affinity is uncertain but if Clovis, this material would come from the most distant lithic source represented at the site.

GROUND STONE ARTIFACTS

Area 7 produced one complete metate, three complete manos, and two mano fragments; Area 6 yielded a single complete mano (Table 7.4). These are in all likelihood part of the Archaic period occupations of the camp area; they are typologically well within the range of variation typical for Archaic period ground stone milling equipment in southeastern Arizona (Sayles 1983; Sayles and Antevs 1941).

The metate was recovered in 1966, before the existence of the camp was known. It was found 20 m south of the west end of Trench 1, a bulldozer trench across the East Swale, placing it in Area 7. Made on a small quartzite boulder, this shallow basin metate is only 34 cm long, 22 cm wide, and 9 cm thick. The grinding basin measures 20 cm long, 12 cm wide, and 0.7 cm deep, but shows considerable polish created by use. The boulder is lithologically comparable to locally available quartzites, and given the absence of any intentional shaping it seems probable that the metate was expediently made at or near the site.

Unfortunately, only one of the manos was available for study. It is a bifacial mano of quartzite, well shaped by pecking to create an oval form with convex-sided, subrectangular, transverse and longitudinal cross sections. Measuring 10 cm long, 8 cm wide, and 5 cm thick, the mano exhibits moderate polish on both grinding surfaces. Little can be said about the missing manos (Table 7.4) beyond the descriptions given in the field catalog. A second complete specimen was somewhat larger, measuring 16 cm in length by 11 cm in width; shape, material, and number of grinding surfaces were not noted. The third complete mano was described as unifacial, made on a triangular cobble. The fourth mano, located outside the grid area at the eastern edge of Area 6, was listed as a bifacial mano of red quartzite. Concerning the Area 7 mano fragments, the field catalog indicates that two were found in the same grid square and refitted to form a complete mano. None of the attributes of this mano were recorded. The third fragment was described as representing approximately half of a bifacial mano.

As a final note, two other metates and two more manos were found along Curry Draw where they were exposed by the headcutting arroyo system that revealed the Clovis occupation. One of these is a well-used sandstone basin metate recovered from the floor of the arroyo upstream of Area 2. The second metate is a huge pecked quartzite slab metate from Pollen Profile Locality 1; it has been extensively shaped on both faces and all edges but shows little evidence of grinding. It lay on top of hearth charcoal that provided an age of 1550 ± 90 B.P. (Mehringer and others 1967).

One mano was found approximately 15 m downstream of Area 1 in place in Stratum G_1 above carbonized plant remains that provided a radiocarbon date of 5610 ± 160 B.P. (Plate 7, Profile N). The second mano was recovered from the arroyo bank upstream of Area 2 in Stratum G_2. Both are simple sandstone cobbles used with little or no deliberate shaping. Their stratigraphic positions place them within the Archaic period.

POTTERY

A single pot sherd was recovered from the surface of Area 6, and it provides the only evidence of late prehistoric use of the site area. It is a body sherd from a Gila Polychrome bowl and exhibits the typical black-on-white interior decoration and red-slipped exterior. No other sherds from this vessel were recovered. Gila Polychrome is common in southeastern Arizona, and sites producing it are known from the terraces along the San Pedro River and its tributaries and at the mouths of the major canyons on the east flank of the Huachuca Mountains (Di Peso 1951, 1958; Franklin 1980). Gila Polychrome was probably manufactured between approximately A.D. 1300 and 1450.

OVERVIEW OF AREAS 6 AND 7

In 1969 accidental discovery of artifacts and flakes on the surface to the south of excavation Areas 1–5 led to initial brushing and sweeping of portions of the area in preparation for excavation. The resulting recovery of artifacts and waste flakes warranted continued efforts in the areas designated 6 and 7 in the 1970 and 1971 field seasons. The application of an unaligned random sampling technique successfully detected areas of cultural activity in a large, vegetation-covered surface area. The presence of tools associated with camp activities, such as scrapers, basal fragments of projectile points, and blade and flake tools, led to the definition of a Clovis camp positioned to the south of the main kill and butchering areas. The surface area was definitely linked, culturally and chronologically, to the buried kill loci by the discovery of a broken Clovis point in Area 6 to which an impact flake from the Area 4 bison kill fit perfectly. The lateral separation of 72 m and vertical separation of 2.5 m gave conclusive evidence as to the contemporaneity of the camp and kill/butchering area. An impact fracture scar on a second point from Area 4 was refitted with an impact flake found 143 m to the south in Area 7. Apparently the flake was carried to the camp, in flesh, and the broken point was lost or discarded in the kill area. It may be speculated that the four end scrapers recovered from the camp represent the processing of hides from the Area 4 bison kill. Some of the blade and flake tools may have served for further processing of the meat from this kill.

The lithic debris represents bifacial reduction, point production and replacement, tool use, and manufacture of cutting and scraping implements. Raw materials are varied, some reflecting a nearby source, as well as material transported from as far away as Clifton and the Little Colorado River Valley, Arizona (Chapter 8). Some raw material is from unknown source areas.

The lithic debris has not been moved laterally to any great extent, as attested by large, tight, flake concentrations of specific lithic types. There has, however, been considerable (up to 1 m) vertical disturbance (bioturbation) by roots and burrowing animals and insects. Artifact and activity locations are considered to be in essentially original plan view positions.

The camp occupied the marl surface to the south of the kill and butchering areas, a surface intermediate in elevation between Bison Kill Creek and Wolf Creek, its easterly tributary. The site of most of the cultural activity corresponds to a paleorill system in the marl. Specifically, the highest concentrations of lithic debris are in the slope changes of this rill channel. The conclusion is that the Clovis craftsmen occupied these areas for concealment, shade, shelter, or perhaps the rill edge made a convenient seat. It is not believed that secondary emplacement of the material caused these concentrations, but rather that the flake clusters represent knapping debris in its original position.

The camp area also yielded artifacts of the later Archaic period, but the differences in lithic material and technology allowed nearly complete differentiation of these artifacts and activity areas within the shallow surface deposits. Projectile points from the camp, and from the terrace southeast of the camp, demonstrate Archaic use of the area at intervals during the last 5,000 to 6,000 years. Two wells were also discovered, testifying to attempts by these people to reach the Millville alluvium for ground water.

Murray Springs provides a model for campsite location and activity at Clovis bison and mammoth kill sites. This model helped to structure investigations during the 1974–1975 field seasons at the Lehner Ranch mammoth kill site (Agenbroad and Huckell 1981). Although no Clovis camp was found at the Lehner Site, we believe that the Murray Springs camp provides an important example of Clovis activity organization at a local scale.

Note: This chapter was written in 1981 and revised slightly in 1991.

CHAPTER EIGHT

Clovis Lithic Technology: A View from the Upper San Pedro Valley

Bruce B. Huckell

During the last 30 years, the upper San Pedro Valley has yielded abundant evidence of the Clovis culture. Such sites as Naco (Haury 1953) and Lehner (Haury and others 1959) have been historically important in shaping our understanding of this early hunting society and have provided some of the best examples of the flaked stone artifacts that typify the Clovis industry. However, these sites and the Escapule Site (Hemmings and Haynes 1969) produced only small numbers of artifacts, ranging from two specimens up to the assemblage of 21 specimens recovered from the 1955–1956 excavations at the Lehner Site. This sample of Clovis artifacts has long been known to be highly biased and unrepresentative of the Clovis industry as a whole (Haury and others 1959: 22), and accordingly our knowledge of the variety and complexity of the industry has been limited. Fortunately, the discovery and excavation of the Murray Springs Site has helped to expand our perception of Clovis lithic technology.

Six seasons of excavation at the Murray Springs Site revealed a rich and varied assemblage of flaked stone artifacts in association with the remains of several Pleistocene mammals that had fallen victim to the Clovis hunters. Most of the material came from buried portions of the site (Areas 1, 3, 4, and 5) where it had lain virtually undisturbed from the day it was deposited (Chapter 5). The sample of implements consisted of projectile points, bifaces, blades, and unifaces, a broader range of forms than had been observed at either Naco or Lehner. Also included in this material were several clusters of flaked stone debitage or waste flakes; nearly 14,000 individual flakes or flake fragments were excavated from 10 distinct centers of flint working. Together with additional implements and more than 1,000 flakes from the adjacent hunting camp (Areas 6 and 7; Chapter 7), this assemblage constitutes the largest single sample of Clovis flint knapping activity yet known from the western United States. The size of the sample, the range of implement types, the presence of distinguishable clusters of flakes, each composed of a distinct lithic material, and their preservation on an almost totally undisturbed living floor or occupation surface exposed by painstaking excavation offered a unique chance to study Clovis lithic technology and document the activities of Clovis flint knappers at the Murray Springs Site.

An initial examination of the tools and debitage was completed by E. Thomas Hemmings (1970; Chapter 5) as part of a doctoral dissertation on the first three field seasons at Murray Springs. His studies were used as a point of departure for this investigation, and some of his interpretations were reexamined. Hemmings reported that most of the debitage from Areas 1, 3, 4, and 5 could be attributed to the retouching of bifaces. He further felt that this work could not be interpreted as projectile point manufacture, but was probably related to the retouching of bifacial cutting implements (Hemmings 1970: 174).

In 1974 I began a study of the Murray Springs artifact assemblage, which entailed a reanalysis and mapping of all the knapping loci from the buried and surficial parts of the site and an examination of all the recovered implements. The goals of this study were (1) an interpretation of the knapping operations represented by the individual flake clusters, and (2) the generation of a better understanding of Clovis lithic technology in its entirety, at least as represented at Murray Springs and elsewhere in the San Pedro Valley. To accomplish this second task additional artifacts from the Lehner (Haury and others 1959), Naco (Haury 1953), Escapule (Hemmings and Haynes 1969), and Navarrete (Huckell 1981) sites were also incorporated into the analysis. This chapter was written in 1976, expanded in 1981, and portions of it were revised slightly in 1986. No attempt has been made to update it with more recent developments in either the theoretical realm of lithic artifact analysis or the empirical realm of Clovis lithic technology.

The results of this study are presented in two parts. First is a description and discussion of the debitage from Murray Springs, beginning with a presentation of the methods used to study the debitage as spatially and lithologically discrete clusters that represent, in most cases, the working of a single artifact. I describe each cluster and its characteristics and then summarize Clovis flint knapping activity at the site. The second part of the chapter is a description of the organization of the Clovis industry as reflected by the assemblages from Murray Springs and the other San Pedro Valley Clovis sites. I use data from both the implements and the debitage in this description.

DEBITAGE FROM MURRAY SPRINGS

Methods of Study

To examine the debitage from Murray Springs, I first subdivided the debitage into discrete clusters and material types. An initial sorting of the flakes by material revealed a minimum of twelve major groups of materials that were well represented, and perhaps three times that number of uncommon material types represented by fewer than ten flakes. I made further breakdowns within three of the twelve major groups, based on minor color or textural differences, resulting in two groups with two varieties and one group with three. All flakes of these major groups and their varieties were next plotted on a large scale map of the site area, which resulted in further segregation of material types into distinct, spatially defined clusters. To avoid confusion and make comparisons easier, I retained Hemmings' (1970) system of knapping-area designations (Chapter 5). Each knapping locus is numbered consecutively within a given area of excavation. The area prefix is used, followed by the knapping locus number; designations thus read A3-1, A3-2, A5-1. Since individual clusters of single material types exist within most of these knapping areas, and because they form the basic units of this study, a further breakdown of the designation system was achieved by adding a lower case letter to the knapping area designation (A5-1a, A3-2c) to designate a lithologically distinct cluster of flakes within a locus.

To determine what sort of flint knapping operation each individual cluster represented, I examined each flake or flake fragment, observing the attributes of the striking platform (preparation, lipping, abrasion), the flake scar pattern on the exterior flake surface, the longitudinal curvature of the flake, and its overall size. Most clusters resulted from one of four basic knapping operations: (1) generalized biface retouching or manufacture, (2) projectile point repair or manufacture, (3) unifacial tool retouching or manufacture, or (4) flake production from a core. Several years of flint knapping experience (Huckell 1979, 1982) helped in making these kinds of observations and decisions.

In this collection, biface retouching or manufacture is identified by the presence of flakes or flake fragments exhibiting faceted striking platforms, usually with marked lipping and often with grinding. These flakes vary greatly in size, and most are broken. When complete, they usually display an obvious curvature in the long axis, and their exterior surfaces are characterized by the presence of two or more previous flake scars. The orientation of the axis of flaking of these previous scars often differs from that of the blow used to detach the flake.

The separation of flake clusters produced by projectile point repair or manufacture from clusters derived from generalized biface retouching is based on the presence of channel flake fragments. Channel flake fragments are identified by the presence of several flake scars on the exterior surface with axes of flaking approximately perpendicular to the axis of flaking that detached the flake. These same attributes may also occur on impact flakes detached from projectile points during use or on so-called end thinning flakes (Callahan 1979: 15, 19) detached from bifaces. Channel flake fragments are identified as such only when they occur as part of a lithologically and spatially discrete flake cluster (to differentiate them from impact flakes, which should occur as isolated specimens), and when more than one occurs in a particular cluster. End thinning flakes struck from bifaces at an earlier stage of reduction usually have fewer and larger previous flake scars on their exterior surfaces than do channel flakes, so this attribute is used to discriminate between the two.

Clusters produced by the manufacture or retouching of unifacial tools are identified by the presence of small flakes with plain, featureless striking platforms, a marked curvature in the long axis, and two or more scars on their exterior surface produced by flakes that had been struck previously from the same margin in the same direction (Frison 1968; Jelinek 1966). Core flake production is distinguished by the presence of flakes with plain or faceted striking platforms without lipping, prominent bulbs of percussion, and little or no curvature in the long axis. These flakes tend to show less breakage than biface retouch flakes and are both generally larger and relatively thicker as well.

Because of the fragmentary condition of most of the flakes, I did not attempt a metric analysis. Most of the flakes came from bifaces and a high degree of breakage is usual. Many flakes of bifacial retouch break when they are removed from the biface, and their thinness makes them susceptible to breakage after detachment from causes such as trampling.

Although the material from the buried part of the site is all of Clovis origin, the surface camp was the scene of reoccupation during the Late Archaic period and perhaps later, producing some admixture of Archaic projectile points, bifaces, debitage, and ground stone artifacts with the Clovis camp debris (Chapter 7). Separation of the Archaic material is based on differences in raw material, patina, and flake technological characteristics. Clovis raw materials identified from the buried part of the site were also present in the camp and exhibited a strong patina. Most of these flakes were also produced by biface retouching, as were their buried counterparts. These material and technological features served to assign these clusters to Clovis. What remained were a few hundred flakes of medium-grained to coarse-grained silicified limestone, indurated siltstone, and some unpatinated cherts lithologically distinct from the known cherts used by Clovis artisans. Nearly all of this material was the product of hard hammer reduction of cores and the initial modification of flakes and was assigned to the Archaic period occupation. Forty-seven flakes could not be assigned with confidence to either occupation.

Cluster Descriptions

The flake clusters in Areas 1 and 3 (and their extensions) and Areas 4 and 5 are part of what Hemmings (Chapter 5) emphasizes was a Clovis living

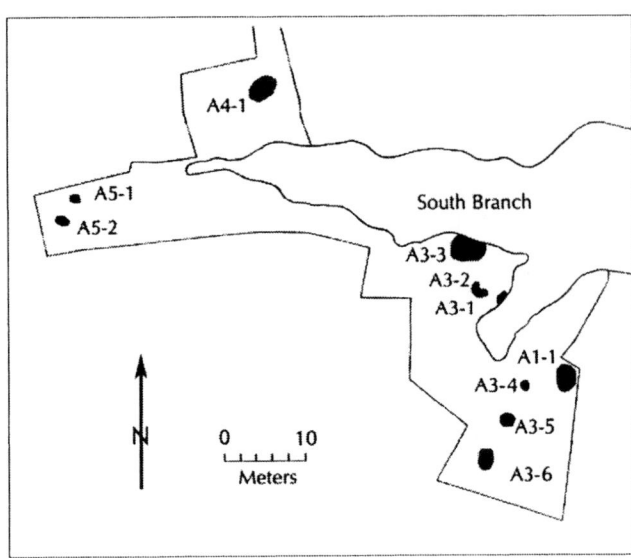

Figure 8.1. Locations of Clovis knapping loci in Areas 3, 4, and 5 and the extensions of Area 1 and Area 3.

surface, where evidence of a series of activities was preserved remarkably intact by rapid burial beneath the black mat of the Clanton clay. In certain respects the preservation of the spatial relationships of individual clusters of flakes within knapping loci is the best evidence of not only the speed but the gentleness with which this surface was buried. It is these flake clusters which produced some of the most specific information regarding Clovis lithic technology. In the surface camp (Areas 6 and 7), 13,000 years of bioturbation had naturally dispersed the clusters to some degree, but even there they remained recognizable as tight concentrations of debitage.

Figure 8.1 is a general plan of the buried portion of the site (Areas 1, 3, 4, 5, Area 1 Extension, and Area 3 Extension) showing the major knapping loci. There are ten distinct flint knapping areas, each containing from two to nine individual clusters. These individual clusters, separated on the basis of lithology and areal extent, represent specific flint knapping operations involving only a single implement in most cases. The following descriptions are organized by excavation area and briefly characterize the raw material, number of flakes (in parentheses), and location of each flake cluster. Descriptions of the raw material types are at the beginning of the section describing the organization of the Clovis industry. Table 8.1 provides summary data on each flake cluster.

Table 8.1. Attributes of the Murray Springs Flake Clusters

Cluster	Material	No. of Flakes	Biface	Point	Tool	Core	Blade	Uncertain
A1–1a	St. David Chalcedony	23	X					
–1b	Pinkish gray chert	30	X					
–1c	Gray chert	11	X					
A3–1a	Red jasper	12	X					
–1b	Mottled blue, green, white chert	17	X					
–1c	Fossiliferous gray chert	5	X					
–1d	Reddish brown chert	10	X					
–1e	Pinkish gray chert	5	X					
A3–2a	Pinkish gray chert	465	X					
–2b	Brown and white chert	277	X					
–2c	Gray chalcedony	42	X					
A3–3a	White and tan banded chert	276		X				
–3b	Pinkish gray chert*	177		X				
–3c	Pinkish gray chert*	112	X					
–3d	Pinkish gray chert*	371	X					
–3e	Tan and gray chert	121	X					
–3f	Fossiliferous gray chert	254	X					
–3g	Basalt	41	X					
–3h	Red jasper	15	X					
–3i	Orange chert	9			X			
–3j	St. David Chalcedony	9						X
A3–4a	St. David Chalcedony	18	X					
–4b	Reddish brown chert	28	X					
A3–5a	St. David Chalcedony	8577	X?			X?		
–5b	Reddish brown chert	133	X					
A3–6a	Reddish brown chert	155	X					
–6b	St. David Chalcedony	16	X					
A4–1a	St. David Chalcedony	152	X					
A4–1b	Reddish brown chert	1364	X					
–1c	Fine gray chalcedony	26	X					
–1d	Basalt	4	X					
–1e	Obsidian	5						X
A5–1a	St. David Chalcedony	836	X					
–1b	Reddish brown chert	46	X					
–1c	Speckled chalcedony	21	X					
A5–2a	Red jasper	45	X					
–2b	Reddish brown chert	46	X					
–2c	St. David Chalcedony	8	X					
A6–1a	Reddish brown chert†		X					
–1b	Tan and gray chert††	25	X					
A7–1	St. David Chalcedony†	305	X					
–2	St. David Chalcedony†	16	X					
–3	Tan and gray chert††	77		X				
–4	Obsidian	22	X					
–5	Obsidian	12	X					
–6	Black silicified limestone†	175	X					X
–7	Silicified siltstone†	49					X	
–8	Silicified siltstone†	20					X	
TOTAL		14,513	40	3	1	1	2	3

* Although spatially separated, these three clusters may represent the flaking of one biface to produce a Clovis point.
† Patinated or stained, see text.

Area 1 and Area 1 Extension

The first area of excavation was explored initially in 1966 and extended in 1971; it was centered on and east of the F_1 channel (Chapter 2). Three small clusters of flakes in a single knapping locus were recovered during the 1971 work, and five scattered flakes were recovered from the F_1 channel in 1966. It is probable that at least one cluster (A1-1a) is related to the large cluster of the same material (A3-5a) in the Area 3 Extension located some 6 m to the southwest (Fig. 8.1). Flakes of the three material types were mixed together in an area measuring approximately 4.0 m northeast-southwest by 2.8 m northwest-southeast.

A1-1a (23), Grids D1S and D2S (St. David Chalcedony)

Mixed flake types, perhaps representing mixed flint knapping activities, characterize this cluster of St. David Chalcedony flakes. One flake fragment refits with a flake fragment from the A3-5a cluster, indicating a close relationship between these clusters. Debitage size range is 15-50 mm in maximum dimension, with an average of approximately 25 mm.

A1-1b (30) Grid D1S (Pinkish gray chert)

A single flake type is represented by this cluster of pinkish gray chert, suggesting the retouching of a single biface. This group of flakes may be related to cluster A3-2a. Average debitage size is about 15 mm in maximum dimension; range is 10-20 mm.

A1-1c (11) Grids D1S and D2S (Gray chert)

A scatter of small pieces of debitage (average maximum dimension less than 10 mm) consists of gray chert derived from a single biface. Two flakes of this same material were found at the northern edge of Area 4.

Area 2

Excavated in 1966, Area 2 was characterized by faunal remains in association with the F_1 channel but yielded no flaked stone artifacts (Chapter 5).

Area 3

Excavated in 1967, Area 3, along with the contiguous Area 3 Extension investigated in 1968 and 1969, was apparently a preferred workshop locus for Clovis flint knappers. This area produced more debitage than any part of the site excavated thus far. Three separate knapping loci containing 18 distinct clusters were identified (Fig. 8.1, Table 8.1).

Area 3-1

Unlike the other Area 3 loci, the A3-1 knapping locus is a mixture of five different materials in a small area with no spatial separation of flakes of the various lithologies. It is situated in Grids A5 and Z5, and an unknown part of it was removed by the cutting of a short headcut into the South Branch of Curry Draw (Fig. 8.1). Locus A3-1 covers an area measuring approximately 1.6 m east-west by 1.5 m north-south and is 1.5 m southeast of the A3-2 knapping locus.

A3-1a (12) Grid Z5 (Red jasper)

Derived from a biface, this debitage is the same red jasper found in clusters A3-3h and A5-2a. Four of the flakes are banded and slightly coarser in texture; they may represent an impurity in the implement or may be from a separate tool. The flakes average about 8 mm in maximum dimension; range is 5-15 mm.

A3-1b (17) Grids Z5 and A5 (Mottled chert)

This group of small pieces of debitage (less than 10 mm in average maximum dimension) is of mottled blue, green, and white chert from a single biface, a large fragment of which was located in Grid Z7. Another small part of this cluster consists of 5 flakes of this material in Grids Y5 and Y6. Two large flakes that can be refitted to the biface fragment were found in Grids T6 and Y4. The largest complete flake is about 35 mm long.

A3-1c (5) Grid A5 (Fossiliferous gray chert)

These flakes are almost all small and fragmentary and are derived from a biface of fossiliferous gray chert. The same material was found in cluster A3-3f. The debitage averages approximately 10 mm in maximum dimension.

A3-1d (10) Grid A5 (Reddish brown chert)

This debitage comes from a biface and is mostly small. It represents the same reddish brown chert as clusters A3-4b, A3-5b, A4-1b, A5-1b, and A5-2b. Average maximum dimension of the flakes is approximately 12 mm; range is 5-20 mm.

A3-1e (5) Grid Z5 (Pinkish gray chert)

These small fragmentary flakes are from a biface of the same pinkish gray chert as A1-1b, A3-2a and A3-3b. Average size is approximately 10 mm.

Area 3-2

Situated just over 1.5 m to the northwest of A3-1 (Fig. 8.1), the A3-2 knapping locus is predominantly composed of three material types. It is also the most highly concentrated knapping locus, with more than 90 percent of the flakes of all three large clusters lying within the confines of the 2-m by 2-m area of Grid Y6 (Plate 9). This cluster is immediately east of the mammoth carcass, which is the most prominent feature of Area 3 (Chapter 5).

A3-2a (465) SE ¼ of Grid Y6
(Pinkish gray chert)

This is a large cluster of debitage from a single biface, with flakes ranging in size from 4 mm to 55 mm in maximum dimension and averaging about 15 mm. Several of the flakes were refitted, permitting an estimate of the size of the biface. A tip fragment of this biface was also recovered with the cluster. This same pinkish gray chert is represented in knapping loci A1-1b, A3-1e, and A3-3b-d.

A3-2b (277) W ⅓ of Grid Y6, E ½ of Grid X6
(Brown and white chert)

Except for a few scattered flakes, this brown and white chert occurs only in this cluster. The debitage is derived from a large biface, the size of which can be estimated by the refitting of laterally and distally overlapping groups of flakes. Debitage size averages approximately 15 mm in maximum dimension; range is 5-40 mm.

A3-2c (42) SW ¼ of Grid Y6 (Gray chalcedony)

This cluster of gray chalcedony flakes is also derived from a biface but is composed of smaller flakes than the other A3-2 clusters; an average piece of debitage measures approximately 10 mm in maximum dimension. No refitting flake groups were discovered.

Area 3-3

Although it is located at the extreme northern edge of Area 3 and has certainly lost some material to the cutting of the South Branch of Curry Draw, the A3-3 knapping locus shows more diversity of material types than any other knapping locus. It is 3 m north of locus A3-2 (Fig. 8.1) and covers an area approximately 4.0 m northwest-southeast by 2.4 m northeast-southwest.

Ten separate clusters representing eight different materials were identified during analysis; these are shown on the map of the A3-3 locus (Plate 10).

A3-3a (276) Grid Y8
(White and tan banded chert)

This cluster represents the repair or, more likely, the manufacture of a Clovis point, as evidenced by three channel flake fragments. This white and tan banded chert occurs only in this knapping locus, although one of the Clovis points recovered from the Area 4 bison kill is made of it. A small (7 mm long by 11 mm wide) biface tip or corner fragment of this material was found with the debitage. Average debitage size is approximately 10 mm in maximum dimension; range is 2-35 mm.

A3-3b (177) S ½ of Grid X9 (Pinkish gray chert)

This cluster is of the same pinkish gray chert as A3-2a, A3-3c and A3-3d; these flakes may in fact be derived from the same biface as those in clusters A3-3c and A3-3d. Two channel flake fragments are present, again suggesting projectile point manufacture or repair. Average debitage size is about 10 mm; range is 2-25 mm in maximum dimension.

A3-3c (112) N ½ of Grid X8
(Pinkish gray chert)

Though slightly separated from cluster A3-3b, this cluster is probably from the same large biface of pinkish gray chert. Three channel flake fragments were identified, suggesting point manufacture and a possible relationship with A3-3b. Additionally, a flake from A3-3c refits with two from A3-3d, proving that these two clusters are closely related and making it possible to estimate the width of the biface or point preform. Debitage size range is 2-30 mm in maximum dimension, with an average of 10 mm.

A3-3d (371) SE ¼ of Grid Y9, NE ¼ of Grid Y8
(Pinkish gray chert)

As noted above, this cluster is clearly from the same biface as A3-3c and perhaps also A3-3b. Debitage size range is 2-50 mm and flakes average about 12 mm in maximum dimension.

A3-3e (121) SE ¼ of Grid Y9 (Tan and gray chert)

This tan and gray chert is probably a variety of the reddish brown chert also found in Areas 1, 4, 5, and

6. One very large flake (65 mm long) and fragments of two others suggest that the implement from which the flakes were struck was a large biface at an early stage of reduction. Average debitage size reflects this, exceeding 15 mm in maximum dimension.

A3-3f (254) NE ¼ of Grid Y8, SW ¼ of Grid Z9, NW ¼ of Grid Z8, and SE ¼ of Grid Y9 (Fossiliferous gray chert)

Some overlapping flakes were refitted and suggest that the biface from which the flakes came was a large one. This fossiliferous gray chert is only found in the A3-3 locus and in small numbers of the A3-1 locus; in both cases it occurs with red jasper. The largest flake is approximately 50 mm long and average maximum dimension of the debitage exceeds 10 mm.

A3-3g (41) N ½ of Grid Y8 (Basalt)

These flakes of basalt are apparently derived from a biface and represent one of the few noncryptocrystalline chert materials that can be associated with the Clovis occupation at Murray Springs. Average debitage size is about 10 mm in maximum dimension, but range is 5–35 mm. The same material is present in cluster A4-1d.

A3-3h (15) SE ¼ of Grid X9 (Red jasper)

This cluster is of the same red jasper as cluster A5-2a and A3-1a. Only small debitage from a biface is present here; average size is less than 10 mm in maximum dimension, and none exceeds 15 mm.

A3-3i (9) NE ¼ / NE ¼ / NE ¼ of Grid Y8 (Orange chert)

Nine pieces of debitage appear to represent the retouching of a unifacial tool. The orange chert is unique to this knapping locus, and the tool from which these flakes were struck was not recovered. Average debitage size is less than 8 mm in maximum dimension.

A3-3j (9) Grids Y8 and Y9 (St. David Chalcedony)

These pieces of debitage of St. David Chalcedony are of interest largely because the same material occurs in other areas of the site. The flakes in this cluster are small, averaging less than 10 mm in maximum dimension. They probably do not represent a single implement, but just what sort of tools they were derived from cannot be established with certainty.

Also present in Grid X4 of Area 3 was a small cluster of nine dark grayish green quartzite flakes. It was not associated with any of the Area 3 knapping loci but was approximately 3 m south-southwest of locus A3-2 (Fig. 8.1). This cluster represents one of the coarser materials worked by the Clovis flint knappers at Murray Springs. The flakes appear to have been detached by hard hammer direct percussion from a large cobble or core tool. All of the flakes are fragmentary, very irregular in shape, and range between 5 mm and 40 mm in maximum dimension. Finally, three unworked obsidian nodules occurred within this knapping locus as well.

Area 3 Extension

In 1968 and 1969 Area 3 was extended southward approximately 12 m, with Trench 9 forming the southern boundary. This work revealed three more flint knapping loci designated A3-4, A3-5, and A3-6 (Fig. 8.1). All three loci contain the same two materials, but differ dramatically in the numbers of flakes they contain. The A3-4 locus yielded fewer than 50 flakes, and the A3-6 locus had fewer than 175; however, the A3-5 locus contained more than 8,700 flakes.

Area 3-4

Located at the northern edge of the Area 3 Extension, locus A3-4 consists of a small number of flakes clustered in a small area approximately 1 m in diameter, but a few scattered flakes recovered from up to 4 m away are included. It is at the west edge of the F_1 stream channel and is adjacent to Area 1.

A3-4a (18) SE ¼ of Grid A0; also Grids B1, C1, B0, and B1S (St. David Chalcedony)

With the exception of one very large flake approximately 90 mm long, this cluster consists of small pieces of debitage (average maximum dimension approximately 12 mm) probably derived from a single biface of St. David Chalcedony. The large flake, which has been slightly burned, did not come from the same implement, based on its different textural properties.

A3-4b (28) Grid A0 (Reddish brown chert)

This cluster is derived from a biface of reddish brown chert, but contains morphologically atypical flakes. The flakes exhibit bifacially prepared, lipped striking platforms but are relatively short in length and thick in cross section. They are probably derived from some sort of biface at a relatively early stage of manufacture or from the retouching of a thick, steeply angled biface margin. Average debitage size is slightly less than 15 mm in maximum dimension; range is 2–40 mm.

Area 3-5

Approximately 4 m southwest of locus A3-4 is knapping locus A3-5 (Fig. 8.1). It measures approximately 3.8 m north-south by 2.5 m east-west. Though it contains only two material types, one of these clusters accounts for more than half of all the debitage recovered from the Murray Springs Site.

A3–5a (8,577) Grids Z4S and A4S
(St. David Chalcedony)

The large quantity of flakes (8,577) is due to the recovery of several thousand extremely small (less than 5 mm in maximum dimension) pieces of debitage of St. David Chalcedony; wet screening alone produced 4,238 of these tiny flakes. Another small provenience area yielded 1,426 flakes. The larger flakes are different from the flake types that compose the other St. David Chalcedony clusters; lipped, soft hammer biface thinning-type striking platforms are rare. It seems that either some process other than biface retouching was being pursued here, or the cluster may represent a mixture of hard and soft hammer reduction of one or more large, incipient bifaces. Debitage size varies from 1 mm to 90 mm in maximum dimension, and averages between 5 mm and 10 mm.

A3–5b (133) Grid Z3S (Reddish brown chert)

This is the same reddish brown chert as in clusters A3-4b, A3-6a, and A4-1b, though the debitage that makes up this cluster is smaller, averaging approximately 10 mm in maximum dimension. The flakes are probably derived from a biface.

Area 3-6

Some 3.5 m southwest of the A3-5 locus is a rather scattered knapping locus centered in Grid Y6S (Fig. 8.1). Designated A3-6, it is composed primarily of flakes from one or two bifaces of chert but it also has a few chalcedony flakes. This locus measures approximately 4.6 m northeast-southwest by 4.6 m northwest-southeast.

A3–6a (155) Grids Y6S and Y5S
(Reddish brown chert)

This cluster may be composed of flakes from two separate bifaces of nearly identical reddish brown chert. Seventy-two flakes are redder in color and of a slightly finer texture than the rest. However, it is almost impossible to completely separate the two groups of flakes on this basis due to the amount of intergradation they exhibit. The slightly coarser, less red material is similar to the flakes composing the A5-2b cluster. All the debitage in this cluster is derived from one or more bifaces. Average debitage size is approximately 10 mm; range is 2–20 mm in maximum dimension.

A3–6b (16) Grids Z5S, Z6S, Y5S, Y6S, A6S, and A7S
(St. David Chalcedony)

This scatter of flakes may be related to the large concentration of St. David Chalcedony in Grid Z3S, cluster A3-5a. Most of the flakes are large and apparently from two different bifaces. Some of the flakes are burned and display arcuate and potlid fractures. The debitage averages approximately 20 mm in maximum dimension; range is approximately 10–45 mm.

Area 4

Area 4 is the scene of a multiple bison kill and an associated area of flint knapping activities. The single major area of debitage was present in the northeastern quarter of Area 4 (Fig. 8.1) and contained flakes of five material types. The flakes were scattered across portions of eight 2-m grid squares, and no tight clusterings of individual material types such as those in Area 3 were in evidence. This scattering, coupled with the fact that more than 40 percent of the chert flakes were badly burned, suggests that this locus was disturbed by some agency after its creation.

A4–1a (152) Grids L18 and K18
(St. David Chalcedony)

These flakes are derived from a single large biface of St. David Chalcedony; the base of it was found in Grid L17 nearly 2.5 m west-southwest of the flake cluster. Five flakes were fitted back onto this biface end fragment (Fig. 5.22) and a group of three flakes was refitted to provide an estimate of its width near the midpoint of its length. Average debitage size is greater than 10 mm in maximum dimension; range is 2-60 mm.

A4-1b (1,364) Grids L18, L17, K18, K17, and parts of 14 other grids (Reddish brown chert)

Despite the large number of flakes recovered in this cluster, no refitting groups of flakes could be reconstructed. The presence of 759 burned flakes and the high degree of breakage were largely responsible for the lack of success at this task. It is likely, though difficult to prove, that more than one implement of this reddish brown chert is represented in this knapping locus. Almost all of the flakes are probably derived from one or more bifaces, though a small number may come from a core or other large piece of material. The debitage averages more than 15 mm in maximum dimension; range is 2-50 mm.

A4-1c (26) Grids L18 and L19 (Fine gray chalcedony)

Though somewhat similar to the finer grades of St. David Chalcedony, these chalcedony flakes are more likely from a separate source. These small pieces of debitage average approximately 10 mm in maximum dimension and are from a single biface.

A4-1d (4) Grids L18 and K15 (Basalt)

This basalt is the same as that from cluster A3-3g, and all four flakes are from a biface. The debitage averages approximately 15 mm in maximum dimension; range is from 15-35 mm.

A4-1e (5) Grid L18 (Obsidian)

Five tiny flake fragments (all less than 5 mm in maximum dimension) of nearly transparent obsidian comprised this cluster. They were removed from an unknown type of implement.

Also from knapping locus A4-1 came six pieces of heavily burned chert, fragments of a single biface that was nearly totally destroyed by fire. These fragments, which include one piece of the margin of the biface, display cracking and crazing to such an extent that probably many pieces of this biface crumbled upon discovery and went unrecognized. The material has been altered to an opaque white color, making it impossible to compare it with other raw material types from the site. Original exterior surfaces of the biface are burned black. Finally, an impact flake was found in Grid I18 that refits to a point recovered from the northern edge of Area 6 (see Fig. 8.2).

Area 5

Originally excavated in 1968 and later expanded in 1969, Area 5 was interpreted as probably a horse kill (Hemmings 1970). The dental remains of a single horse were in association with two distinct knapping loci approximately 3 m apart (Fig. 8.1).

Area 5-1

The first of these loci, A5-1, consists of debitage of three different material types concentrated tightly in an area slightly more than one square meter in extent.

A5-1a (836) SE ¼ of Grid Zw11 (St. David Chalcedony)

This cluster contains several very large flakes derived from the reduction of at least one large biface. Two distinct textural varieties of St. David Chalcedony may imply that more than one biface was being flaked here. However, specimens of a texture intermediate between the two extremes prevent precise separation of the flakes into two groups. Possibly only a single biface is represented, made on a piece of chalcedony with variable textural qualities. Several pairs or groups of refitting flakes were discovered, along with one large reconstructed overshot or *outre passe* flake. Debitage size exceeds 10 mm on average; range is 2-60 mm in maximum dimension.

A5-1b (46) SE ¼ of Grid Zw11, NW ¼ of Grid Aw10 (Reddish brown chert)

This cluster is of the same reddish brown chert as A4-1b and A3-5b. All of the debitage in this cluster is from a single biface. Debitage size averages slightly more than 10 mm; range is 2-45 mm in maximum dimension.

A5-1c (21) E ½ of Grid Zw11, NW ¼ of Grid Aw10 (Speckled chalcedony)

This cluster is of interest for two reasons; first, it is from a biface of reddish brown speckled chalcedony that was probably heat-treated, and second, the biface was broken in half during flaking and the halves were found 9 m apart north and east of the cluster. Three flakes refit to the biface. Average debitage size is approximately 10 mm in maximum dimension; range is 5–30 mm.

Area 5–2

The A5–2 knapping locus is 3 m southwest of A5–1 (Fig. 8.1). It contains fewer flakes than the first locus and is also larger, extending across an area measuring approximately 1.4 m east–west by 1.2 m north–south. Two of the three material types present in the A5–2 locus are present in the A5–1 locus but the third material is represented only in Area 3.

A5–2a (45) Grid Yw10 (Red jasper)

This cluster of debitage is of the same red jasper as A3–3h. It is derived from a biface, with three pairs of refitting flakes. One flake of red jasper occurred in locus A5–1, but it probably came from this cluster. Average debitage size is greater than 10 mm; range is 2–25 mm in maximum dimension.

A5–2b (46) Grids Yw10 and Yw9 (Reddish brown chert)

This debitage is also derived from a biface. The reddish brown chert is slightly different from the reddish brown chert found in Area 4 and the A3–4b cluster, but is similar to the lighter-colored, coarser variety noted in the A3–6a cluster. All the reddish brown chert probably comes from a single source area. The debitage averages about 10 mm; range is 5–35 mm in maximum dimension.

A5–2c (8) Grids Yw10 and Yw9 (St. David Chalcedony)

These flakes of St. David Chalcedony are similar in texture and may have come from the same biface or bifaces as the flakes of cluster A5-1a, although no refitting flakes were found to definitely link the two clusters.

Flakes Not Assigned To Clusters

In addition to these spatially discrete knapping loci and flake clusters, there were 168 flakes that could not be confidently assigned to any cluster. Some were completely isolated, others only separated from loci by two or three meters; nearly all were of the same material types represented in the major knapping loci. There were, however, 20 flakes that could not be assigned to the material types already described, and

Table 8.2. Flakes Not Assigned to Clusters in Areas 1, 3, 4, and 5

Material	Number	Predominant Flake Type
St. David Chalcedony	41	Biface reduction
Reddish brown chert	18*	Biface reduction
Pinkish gray chert	25	Biface reduction
Fossiliferous gray chert	7	Biface reduction
Green quartzite	9	Decortication?
Red Jasper	4	Biface reduction
Brown and white chert	4	Biface reduction
White and tan banded chert	3	Biface reduction
Mottled chert	3	Biface reduction
Gray green limestone	3	Decortication?
Tan and gray chert	2	Biface reduction
Gray chert	2	Biface reduction
Gray chalcedony	1	Biface reduction
Fine gray chalcedony	1	Biface reduction
Basalt	2	Biface reduction
Unassigned materials	20	Biface reduction
Too small	23	Indeterminate
TOTAL	168	

*6 burned

these were classified as unassigned, unique material types. In addition, 23 flakes were too small to be assigned to particular lithologic varieties of material. All of the isolated flakes, flakes of unassigned materials, and flakes too small to identify are listed in Table 8.2. The predominant flake type represented among the flakes of each material is also indicated.

Discussion

Considering the buried portion of the site as a whole, Area 3 contained the most interesting and in many ways the most informative knapping loci; particularly remarkable were loci A3–2 and A3–3. Locus A3–2 contained three lithologically, and to a large extent, spatially discrete flake clusters (Plate 9). These were in an area only 2.30 m long by 1.75 m wide that contained 784 complete and fragmentary flakes. All three materials represented the reduction of bifaces. Just 3 m to the north lay locus A3–3, composed of eight lithologically distinct raw materials segregated into ten tightly massed clusters across an area approximately 4.05 m long by 2.10 m wide (Plate 10). The cluster may originally have continued somewhat farther to the north, but the south headcut of Curry Draw truncated the Clovis living surface at this spot. Within the remaining portion of the locus there were 1,385 flakes, three unworked obsidian nodules (marekanites), as well as a few flakes of miscellaneous materials not pertaining to the identified flake clusters. Flint knapping operations represented here included generalized biface reduction (7 clusters), projectile point repair or manufacture (2 clusters), and uniface tool retouching (1 cluster). The A3-1 knapping locus was just 1.5 m to the east of A3-2 (Figs. 8.1, 8.2), but it had been seriously impacted by a small portion of the Curry Draw tributary headcut. This cluster yielded flakes of five distinct materials, but no single material was represented by more than 17 flakes. One of the materials in this locus was a distinctively mottled chert; in addition to debitage it was represented by a large biface fragment to which several flakes could be refitted. This fragment was 4.3 m north of the knapping locus.

The Area 3 Extension was also informative but somewhat puzzling in terms of the types of flint knapping that took place there. The A3-5 knapping locus contained more flakes than any other: 8,710, representing only two materials. The cluster was extremely dense and consisted principally of more than 8,500 flakes of St. David Chalcedony produced by both hard and soft hammer flaking. Most of the debitage was small. An area approximately 3.9 m long by 2.0 m wide contained the knapping locus, but the bulk of it lay in an area only 1.0 m by 0.6 m. The chalcedony flakes may have been derived from the early stages of reduction of more than one piece of this material, but the accompanying chert flakes represent generalized biface retouching. Approximately 4.0 m to the northeast of A3-5 was the A3-4 knapping locus, which contained only 46 flakes of two materials in an area measuring approximately 0.8 m by 0.7 m. The final Area 3 locus, A3-6, was approximately 3.4 m southwest of A3-5. It was composed primarily of chert flakes and a small number of St. David Chalcedony flakes scattered over an area measuring 4.8 m northeast-southwest by 4.0 m northwest-southeast.

Area 4 was the location of a single very large knapping locus covering an area measuring approximately 5 m north-south by 3 m east-west. Five separate materials, totaling 1,551 flakes and flake fragments, and a few pieces of miscellaneous other materials occurred within its bounds. Approximately 44 percent of the 1,364 chert flakes here had been burned after their deposition on the living floor. This factor, and the position of the cluster on the slope of a low topographic mound, suggest that the flakes were not buried as rapidly as at the Area 3 or Area 5 loci. The lack of tight, lithologically discrete clustering like that in the A3-2, A3-5, and A5-1 loci is evident. Generalized biface retouching appears to be the function represented here. Also present was a large biface fragment of St. David Chalcedony to which several flakes could be refitted (Figs. 5.22, 5.23).

Two knapping loci about 3 m apart from one another occurred in Area 5. The three materials present in each locus all represented biface reduction. The A5-1 locus covered an area measuring about 3.2 m north-south by 1.3 m east-west with all three materials largely mixed together. Most of the flakes here were recovered from a highly concentrated area measuring only 0.6 m by 0.4 m. Area 5-1 also contained flakes of a distinctive speckled chalcedony that could be refitted to a broken biface of the same material found in two pieces nearby. To the southwest, the A5-2 knapping locus occupied an area 2.2 m north-south by 1.4 m east-west; it contained only 99 flakes, in contrast to the 903 flakes in locus A5-1.

Several instances were recorded of flake clusters of the same material in different knapping loci and in different areas of excavation. Considerable effort was made to find refitting flakes among these spatially separate clusters, but no such refits were found.

Area 6 and Area 7

Attention was first drawn to an area approximately 20 m southwest of Area 3 when a fragmentary Clovis point was discovered on the surface there in 1968 (Chapter 7). Close examination of the surface disclosed the presence of debitage, tools, and a second Clovis point. The following season a grid of 10-m squares was placed here; the area was mapped, then hoed, swept, and screened to recover as much material as possible. Further inspection revealed additional artifacts scattered across the surface at distances up to 135 m south and west of Area 3. Two new areas of excavation were defined, separated by a bulldozer trench and backdirt (spoil) pile: Area 6, northeast of the backdirt pile, and Area 7, southwest of the backdirt pile (Fig. 8.2). Test excavations revealed the presence of artifacts at depth, and the 1970 and 1971 seasons were devoted to testing a sample of 2-m grid squares within the original 10-m squares in both Areas 6 and 7. A surprising amount of material was encountered and a number of small clusters of flakes were found

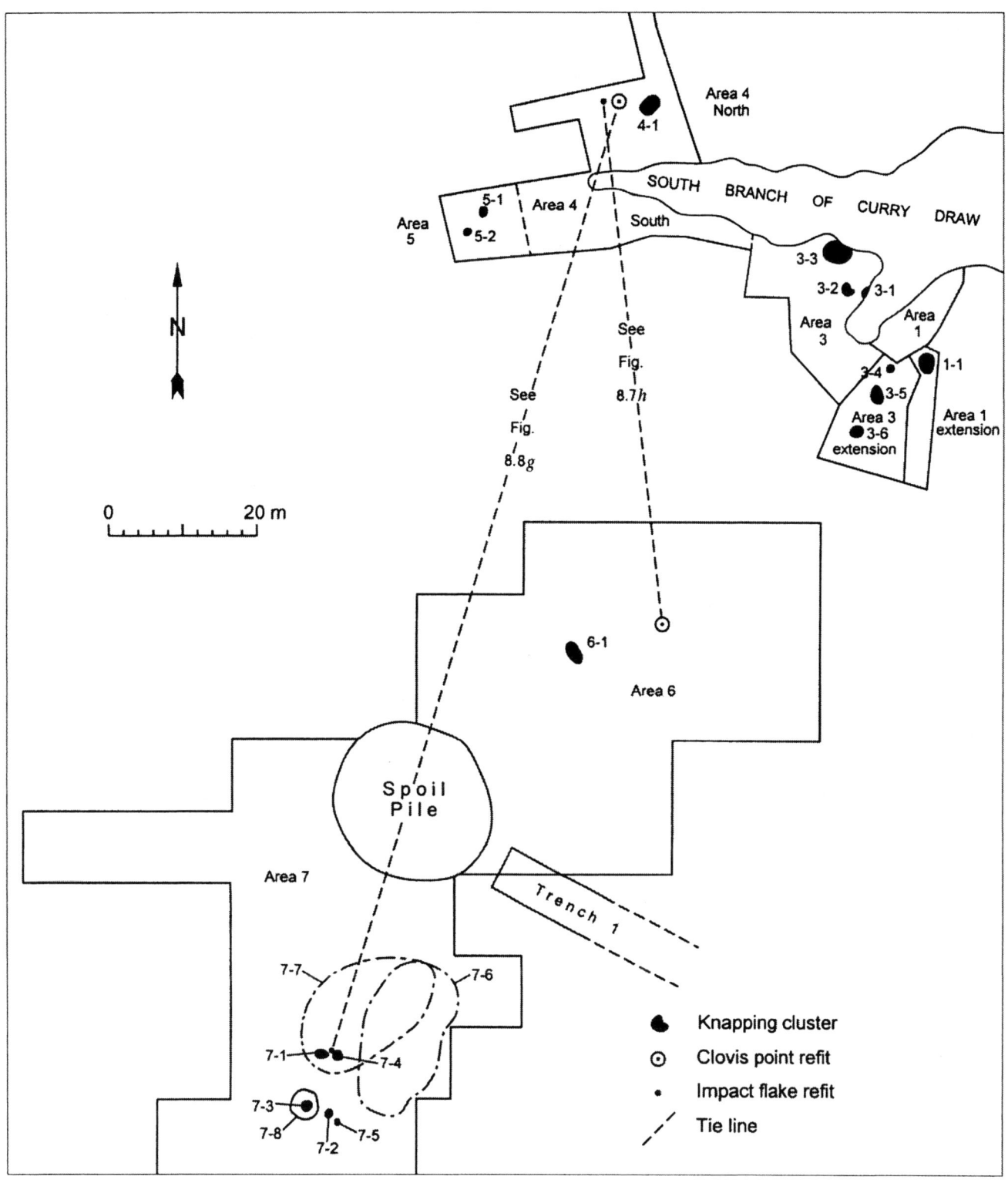

Figure 8.2. Locations of Clovis and Archaic knapping loci in Areas 6 and 7.

particularly in Area 7. Investigations also showed that a prominent Archaic period component was present in both areas, usually to some extent mixed stratigraphically with the Clovis component. Fortunately, almost complete separation of the two components was possible by means of lithology and technology.

Area 6

Area 6 yielded only one definable knapping locus, composed of flakes from two separate implements; this locus is designated A6-1 (Fig. 8.2, Table 8.1). A thin scatter of isolated flakes was also present throughout the area. Retouched tools, mostly scrapers or light-duty cutting tools, occurred in larger numbers in this area than in Areas 1, 3, 4, and 5. An end scraper made on a blade came from this knapping locus.

A6–1a (50) SW ¼ / SE ¼ of 10–m Grid BB0 (Reddish brown chert)

This cluster is of the same reddish brown chert that was recovered from the buried portion of the site in clusters A4-1b, A5-1b, A5-2b, and A3-6a, but it has a yellowish brown patina or stain. The debitage in this cluster averages slightly less than 10 mm in maximum dimension; range is 2–20 mm. All debitage is derived from a single biface.

A6–1b (25) SW ¼ / SE ¼ of 10–m Grid BB0 (Tan and gray chert)

This small group of flakes was derived from a single large biface, a fragment of which was recovered approximately 1 m southeast of the cluster. This tan and gray chert is identical to that recovered in cluster A3-3e, but it has a yellowish brown patina or stain. Average debitage size exceeds 10 mm in maximum dimension; range is 5–30 mm.

Area 7

Far more prolific evidence of Clovis (and Archaic period) flint knapping activity appeared in Area 7. This area produced several artifacts such as Clovis point bases, blades, and retouched tools, as well as nearly 1,000 pieces of debitage. Most of this material was in a square area of concentrated excavation that measured nearly 20 m on a side. Within it were eight clusters of flakes designated A7-1 through A7-8 (Fig. 8.2, Table 8.1). A second area of artifacts composed primarily of isolated flakes and artifacts spread out west–southwestward in a shallow arc from the bulldozer backdirt pile. No distinct clusters of flakes were found in this locus, which essentially parallels the northern limits of the silt-capped Coro marl surface on which the Clovis hunters camped.

Area 7 has been heavily bioturbated during the 13,000 years since the Clovis people camped here (Chapter 2). Both burrowing animals and plant roots have caused the flakes of many of the clusters to be dispersed; however, much of this dispersal has taken place in a vertical, rather than a horizontal, plane. Several of the clusters of Clovis debitage were concentrated in areas of restricted lateral extent, even though individual flakes of the clusters were located from the modern surface down to a depth of 50 cm below surface. Thus, despite the disturbance, in most cases it is still possible to treat these flake clusters in the same fashion as those from the buried part of the site.

A7–1 (305) SE ¼ / NW ¼ of 10–m Grid EE6 (St. David Chalcedony)

This cluster of St. David Chalcedony (stained yellow) debitage was found in a "wash basin–sized" part of a 2-m grid square from the surface to a depth of about 30 cm. Most of the flakes are fragmentary, but some complete flakes were reconstructed. Indications are that all these flakes were derived from a single large biface. Debitage size averages between 15 and 20 mm; range is 5–50 mm in maximum dimension. Also recovered was a chert impact flake that refit to a point found in Area 4 (Figs. 8.2, 8.8g).

A7–2 (16) NE ¼ / NW ¼ of 10–m Grid EE7 (St. David Chalcedony)

Though small in size, this cluster consists of a series of flakes probably all removed from a single biface of St. David Chalcedony (with yellow stain) of a slightly different texture than that represented in cluster A7-1. One of the biface thinning flakes from this cluster is large, measuring at least 52 mm in length (it is incomplete); the remaining debitage is mostly fragmentary but much smaller in size, averaging 10 to 15 mm in maximum dimension.

A7–3 (77) NW ¼ / NW ¼ / NW ¼ of 10–m Grid EE7 (Tan and gray chert)

This tan and gray chert is identical to that of clusters A6-1b and A3-3e, but it has a yellowish brown patina or stain. Most of the debitage is small (slightly less than 15 mm in average maximum dimension, none larger than 25 mm) in comparison to the A7-1 cluster. However, despite the amount of flake breakage, some refitting groups of flakes were reconstructed. Two channel flake fragments recovered in this cluster demonstrate that it represents projectile point manufacture or repair.

A7-4 (22) 1.5 m N of center
of 10-m Grid EE6
(Obsidian)

This translucent obsidian debitage is indistinguishable from an obsidian Clovis point base located 1.0 m southwest of the flake cluster. Both the point base and flakes are in turn identical lithologically to the complete obsidian Clovis point from Area 4. As discussed in Appendix C, the lithic source is the Cow Canyon marekanite locality. The A7-4 cluster is approximately 1.75 m east of cluster A7-1 and consists entirely of fragmentary flakes averaging less than 10 mm in maximum dimension. Most of the debitage exhibits typical soft hammer striking platform characteristics.

A7-5 (12) NE ¼ / NW ¼ / NW ¼
of 10-m Grid EE7
(Obsidian)

Cow Canyon obsidian and the same type of biface reduction flakes are present in this cluster as in A7-4. The A7-5 cluster is only 1.0 m southeast of flake cluster A7-2. The debitage here averages less than 15 mm in maximum dimension and is generally of uniform size.

A7-6 (175) 10-m Grids DD4, DD5, DD6,
EE5, and EE6 (Black silicified limestone)

This scatter of black silicified limestone flakes (stained reddish gray) apparently represents an Archaic period lithic workshop where several different flint knapping activities were being performed. Primary among these activities was flake production, followed by biface manufacture and tool production. There were three cores. Fragments of many large flakes of variable grades of silicified limestone indicate that multiple large pieces of this material were present. Five fragments representing three separate bifaces were recovered; all exhibited manufacture breaks and were only incipiently flaked by hard hammer percussion techniques (Fig. 7.10*e–g*). Two large scrapers were in the cluster. All of the unmodified flakes exhibited features typical of hard hammer percussion products. The debitage averages between 25 and 30 mm; range is 10–55 mm in maximum dimension.

This material appears to be of Archaic period derivation for three reasons. First, there is little evidence to suggest that the Clovis people were extensively exploiting this material either at Murray Springs or at any of the other Clovis sites in the upper San Pedro Valley. One expedient core tool of it was recovered from Area 3. Second, almost every Archaic site in the valley is characterized by extensive use of this silicified limestone; the primary source area, about 4.0 km (2.5 miles) east-northeast of Murray Springs (Fig. 2.2), was heavily exploited. Finally, the dominant flint knapping technique (hard hammer percussion) shown on this debitage is unlike the soft hammer biface reduction used by the Clovis flint knappers at the site.

A7-7 (49) Most in 10-m Grid EE6,
but also in10-m Grids DD5, DD6,
DD7, EE5, FF5, and FF6
(Silicified brownish yellow siltstone)

This scatter of silicified siltstone (with brownish yellow staining) is similar in its distribution to A7-6, the black silicified limestone. Several squares in Grid EE6 yielded small fragments of a burned core; some of the fragments could be refitted, but the complete core could not be reconstructed. The majority of the debitage of this material consists of hard hammer percussion flakes with plain or cortical striking platforms ranging in size from 10 mm to 45 mm in length. Five flakes could be classified as blades or blade fragments. These flakes, the blades, and the burned core may all be derived from blade production and are interpreted here as being of Clovis origin. A single burned flake of this material from Area 4 (Hemmings 1970, Fig. 27*f*) may further support a Clovis association.

A7-8 (20) 2-m Grids EE7-5 and FF7-1
(Silicified brownish yellow siltstone)

This cluster displays the same types of silicified siltstone flakes as A7-7, but it is differentiated from that group by the degree of concentration of flakes in these two grid squares. The scatter of flakes between the two groups makes it impossible to completely separate them. The discussion of the debitage composing the A7-7 cluster applies to this one as well.

Table 8.3. Flakes Not Assigned to Clusters in Area 7

Material	Number	Affiliation	Predominant Flake Type
St. David Chalcedony	53	Clovis	Biface reduction
Tan and gray chert	53	Clovis	Biface reduction
Black silicified limestone	24	Archaic	Decortication
Green silicified limestone	5	Archaic	Decortication
Obsidian[1]	16	Clovis	Biface reduction
Obsidian[2]	3	Clovis?	Indeterminate
Reddish brown chert	26	Clovis	Biface reduction
Silicified siltstone	16	Clovis	Decortication
Pinkish gray chert	10	Clovis	Biface reduction
Green quartzite	4	Clovis?	Decortication
TOTAL	210		

1. Cow Canyon source
2. Government Mountain source

Flakes Not Assigned to Clusters

Only 676 flakes described above were found in such positions so as to permit their assignment to one of the eight clusters described for Area 7. Another 210 flakes, many of the same material types, were found scattered throughout the area; a listing of these flakes by material type and quantity is provided in Table 8.3.

Discussion

In Areas 6 and 7 there were identifiable flake clusters, but they were more vertically and horizontally dispersed than their buried counterparts. A single knapping locus in Area 6, covering an area measuring approximately 2.5 m by 2.0 m, contained 75 flakes and flake fragments representing two different materials, and a biface fragment of one of these materials was also found within the locus. Further, one blade tool and a blade fragment were recovered from this locus, although both were of materials not represented by any debitage.

Area 7 was more difficult to characterize, due to a broad scattering of flakes across an area measuring approximately 28 m northeast-southwest by 15 m northwest-southeast. Within this area were eight lithologically or spatially separable groupings of flakes, some in fairly confined loci. In the northwest quadrant of Grid EE7 were three clusters: one of 77 complete and fragmentary chert flakes, one of 16 chalcedony flakes and flake fragments, and one of 12 obsidian flakes and flake fragments. The chert cluster represented the manufacture or repair of a projectile point, and the two others derived from generalized biface retouching. Six meters to the northeast in Grid EE6 were two clusters: one of 305 chalcedony flakes and flake fragments, and one of 22 pieces of obsidian debitage, both representing generalized biface retouching. The remaining materials were broadly spread over the large area noted above, including 175 flakes of black silicified limestone believed to represent Archaic period tool manufacture and the 69 flakes of silicified siltstone that are probably Clovis. In addition, other flakes of the same materials represented in the Clovis surface knapping loci or in the ones found in the buried part of the site were recovered as isolated specimens from various portions of the camp area.

CLOVIS FLINT KNAPPING AT MURRAY SPRINGS

It is probable that not all of the flint knapping activity described above occurred during a single occupational episode, but rather from periodic, closely spaced utilizations of the site area. The manufacture or repair of implements occurred in both the buried kill and butchering section of the site (Areas 1, 3, 4, and 5) and at the surface campsite (Areas 6 and 7). In a few cases the knapping loci that have been identified may be coeval with one another, but others are probably not. Each locus, however, is assumed to be the product of a single occupational episode. In any case, whether coeval or not, some indications concerning the organization of flint knapping activities within the site may be obtained from these clusters.

First and most obviously, flint knapping appears to have been a highly localized activity. With the exception of virtually isolated flakes scattered very thinly across the buried living surface, stone tool manufacture or repair occurred only in small, concentrated areas. The presence of such tightly massed concentrations of debitage separated by areas nearly completely devoid of debitage suggests that flint knapping tasks were carried out only in areas specifically chosen for that purpose. Although we do not know what factors may have been operative in the selection of space for flint knapping, it is apparent that this phenomenon is not accidental. The same pattern is present in limited form at the Lehner Site (Agenbroad and Huckell 1981), where the only concentration of debitage on the occupation surface was found in an area measuring approximately 3.00 m by 4.25 m.

Hemmings (Chapter 5) has interpreted these clusters as representing the resharpening of bifaces used in the processing of elephant, bison, and horse carcasses in Areas 3, 4, and 5. This may well be the case for certain of the generalized bifaces, but does not adequately explain the presence of flake clusters representing projectile point repair or manufacture, uniface retouching, or more intensive reduction of large pieces of material. It seems possible that the knapping loci may also represent the manufacture or refurbishing of hunting gear following a kill and butchering event. The presence of knapping loci of identical composition and type in the Area 6 and 7 camp away from the kill areas lends further support to this proposition.

One possible interpretation of the inferred activities within the knapping loci may be that the flake clusters generally represent flaking operations of short duration, primarily biface reduction. With the exception of large flake clusters like A3-5a, A4-1b, and A5-1a (Table 8.1), these operations could easily have been performed in periods of time ranging from a few seconds to perhaps 20 minutes. Most of the work is not extensive in nature. Another interpretation is that the separate clusters within a locus may, in most cases, be the work of a single knapper working on a single implement. By extension, the spatial separation of the clusters implies that more than one individual was at work in most of the knapping loci. It is conceivable, for example, that three individuals were flaking together in a group in knapping locus A3-2, based on the three spatially and lithologically identifiable clusters within it. The presence of three tiny flake clusters in locus A3-3 confuses the picture to some extent (Table 8.1), but it is possible that six or seven individuals were at work there. Were these knapping loci occupied by only a single individual, it would seem unlikely to encounter such discrete separation of individual flake clusters and raw material types. A locus showing spatial mixing of flakes of different lithologies would be expected in such a case. Such a situation is observed in a few knapping loci, most notably A3-1, A5-1, and A5-2, where flakes of two or more materials are found mixed together across a small area. Clusters of this kind imply the retouching of more than a single implement by one person. It seems probable, therefore, that the Clovis flint knappers at Murray Springs preferred to work together in groups at specific locations, probably enjoying conversation as they worked.

THE CLOVIS INDUSTRY

To determine the composition and nature of the Clovis flaked stone industry in the San Pedro Valley, I studied finished artifacts from the Murray Springs, Lehner, Naco, Escapule, Leikem, and Navarrete (Huckell 1981) sites. These specimens were classified into a series of general typological categories, based on mode of production, size, shape, working edge configuration and angle, and presumed function. The finished implements, together with the debitage from Murray Springs, make it possible to reconstruct the organization and content of the Clovis industry as it was expressed in southeastern Arizona, both in terms of its characteristic artifact forms and the manufacturing processes used by the Clovis flint knappers in this area.

Before discussing the specific aspects of the Clovis industry in the San Pedro Valley it is necessary to consider the organization of the industry in general terms; Figure 8.3 presents the hypothesized organization of this industry in diagrammatic form. Because this diagram is designed to present only the general flow paths of the industry, some of the complexities that have been observed in certain portions of it have been omitted. The presentation of these details appears in later sections of the text.

The system (Fig. 8.3) is divided into four technological subsystems or modes of production: the biface mode, the flake mode, the expediency mode, and the blade mode. Each is characterized by a specific reduction sequence and a specific set of products, though some overlap or exchange among modes is apparent. Cross-cutting these production modes are three arbitrary stages of reduction that have been included for greater clarity: initial products, intermediate products, and final products. Debitage and other by-products, which naturally occur in all these modes and at all three stages of reduction, have not been included in the diagram.

All four modes are initiated by raw material procurement, an activity for which no direct evidence exists at Murray Springs. Some scant information is present on raw material sources, but the specific techniques used in the generation of the initial products

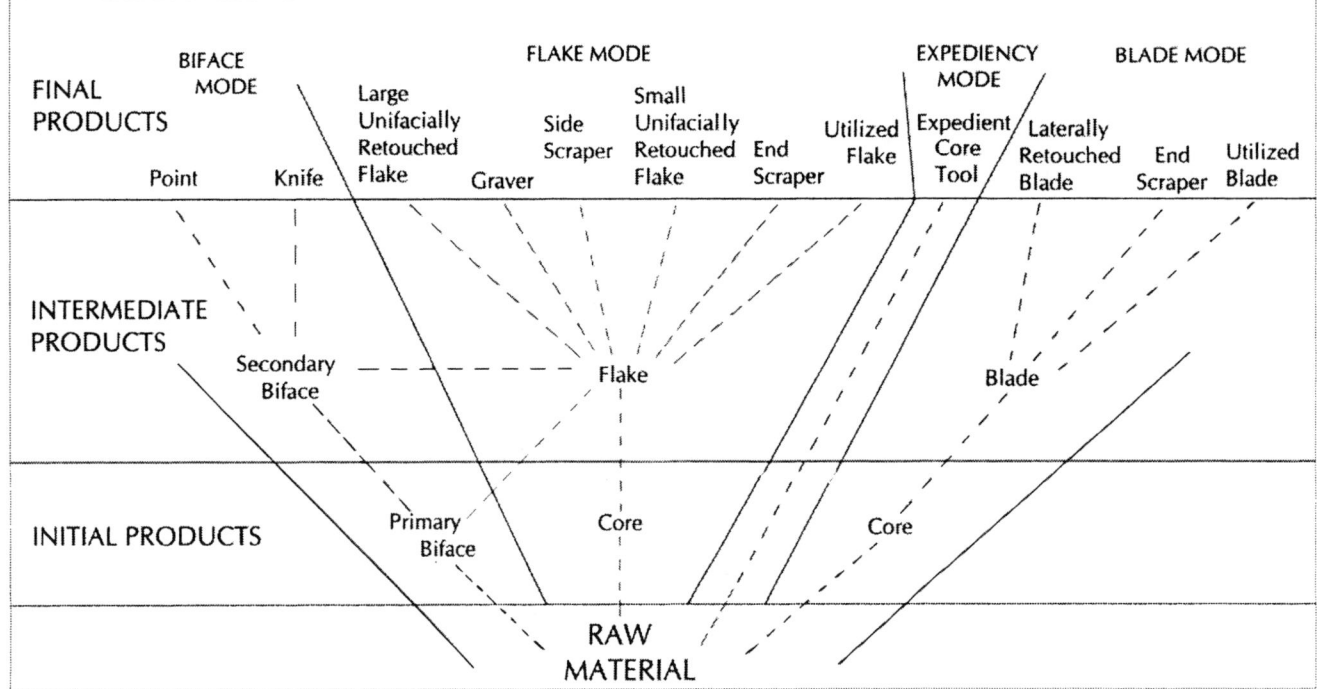

Figure 8.3. Schematic diagram showing Clovis lithic technological organization.

may only be inferred. However, it is at this stage that the three major production modes (biface, flake, and blade) are started and differentiated. It is proposed that core preparation was the initial modification of the raw materials for both the flake and blade modes, and preliminary bifacial preparation was performed in the biface mode. Because no complete flake or blade cores were recovered, these initial products are hypothetical; however, direct evidence exists for primary bifaces, the initial products of the biface production mode. Following the completion of this stage, the initial products might either be transported or further reduced to generate intermediate products. In the case of the flake and blade production modes, these products were the flake and blade respectively, and the primary biface was further reduced to a secondary biface. All of these products may be utilized without further modification or may be finished by further reduction into retouched final products recognizable as specific implement types or forms. Those forms listed as final products are general categories only.

Figure 8.3 covers only the initial production of implements; the use, damage, repair or modification, and discard or loss of a given artifact may be viewed as another component of each mode. The importance of use and repair must not be overlooked, for it is the use of an implement, or its "life history," that often determines its appearance when it is finally included in the archaeological record. This is particularly true of artifacts that are used in high stress operations, such as projectile points, and those implements that are resharpened frequently. It is more difficult to generalize concerning these changes through use, for they tend to be individualistic and variable from specimen to specimen and may be difficult to interpret with assurance. Therefore, these have not been included in Figure 8.3. When possible, however, aspects of artifact use and modification are presented and discussed in detail for specific implements and production modes.

Raw Material Sources

A selection of 20 distinct varieties of stone may be identified from clusters of flakes assignable to the Clovis occupation at Murray Springs. Of this number nine are fine-grained cherts, four are chalcedonies, and the remaining six include jasper, obsidian, fine-grained basalt, silicified siltstone, silicified limestone, and quartzite. Table 8.4 presents a description of each

Table 8.4. Major Raw Materials Identified from Knapping Loci at Murray Springs

No.	Description	Color	Number*	%
1	St. David Chalcedony[1]	5Y 8/1 white–7/3 pale yellow	10,047	67.30
2	Reddish brown chert[2]	7.5YR 6/2 pinkish gray–5/4 brown	1,879	12.59
3	Pinkish gray chert[3]	7.5YR 7/2 pinkish gray–6/4 light brown	1,182	7.92
4	Tan and gray chert[2]	7.5YR 6/2 pinkish gray–5YR 6/4 light reddish	285	1.91
5	Brown and white chert	5Y 8/1 white–7.5YR 7/4 pink	281	1.88
6	White and tan chert	5Y 8/1 white–7/1 light gray	278	1.86
7	Fossiliferous gray chert[2]	5YR 6–7/1 light gray	261	1.75
8	Silicified limestone[4]	2.5YR 2/0 black (fresh surface)	204	1.37
9	Silicified siltstone	5YR 6/3 light reddish brown	104	0.70
10	Red jasper	2.5YR 4–5/2 weak red	76	0.51
11	Obsidian	10YR 2.1 black (translucent)	58	0.39
12	Basalt	2.5Y 3/1 very dark gray	47	0.31
13	Gray chalcedony	10YR 5/1 gray–10R 5/1 reddish gray	43	0.29
14	Fine gray chalcedony	10YR 5/1 gray (translucent)	27	0.18
15	Mottled chert	5Y 7/1 light gray–6/3 pale olive	20	0.13
16	Speckled chalcedony	2.5Y 6/1 gray with 7.5YR 5/6 strong brown inclusions	19	0.13
17	Dark green quartzite	5Y 4/1 dark gray	13	0.08
18	Gray chert	2.5Y 6/2 light brownish gray	10	0.07
19	Orange chert	5YR 6/8 reddish yellow	9	0.06
20	Miscellaneous[5]		85	0.57
	TOTAL		14,928	100.00

NOTE: Color readings from Munsell Color Company (1975).
* Number of artifacts, including flakes.
1. Same material present at Navarette Site.
2. Contains microfossils.
3. Same material present at Naco, Lehner, and Leikem sites.
4. Attributed to Archaic occupation.
5. Mixed Clovis and Archaic materials.

material as well as some numerical expressions of its relative abundance in the debitage. Additional materials, represented by finished artifacts or debitage, are present but not included in this table because they comprise less than 1 percent of the total assemblage.

As noted by Hemmings (1970: 173–174), none of the Clovis lithic materials of the San Pedro Valley may be attributed to any of the more famous source areas such as Alibates, and attempting to identify specific sources has proved difficult. The mountains that border the upper San Pedro Valley contain abundant exposures of Paleozoic sedimentary rocks, many of which contain massive beds or nodules of chert (Bryant 1968; Burnette 1957; Gilluly and others 1954; Hayes and Landis 1965). Exposures of these chert deposits tend to be localized but are abundantly scattered through the Huachuca and Whetstone Mountains on the west side of the valley and in the Tombstone Hills, Mule Mountains, and Naco Hills on the east side. Variability in color and inclusions in the cherts, coupled with a paucity of systematic investigation, make it difficult to determine whether the cherts used at Murray Springs and the other Clovis sites in the valley are of local origin or were imported from outside the valley. Much of the chert that has been observed during visits to these mountain ranges is badly fractured into small pieces; rarely are pieces larger than 10 cm found that are free of flaws. However, both the Whetstones and the Naco Hills contain some cherts lithologically similar to those found at the sites. It is conceivable that some or even most of the cherts are of nonlocal origin, but the identification of specific source areas must await a great deal more work.

One distinctive chert variety present at Murray Springs, Lehner, and Naco is pinkish gray with occasional cream-colored bands and reddish brown bands and spots; its source remains unknown. Two points from the Naco Site (Haury 1953, Fig. 6b, e) and two from the Lehner Site (Haury and others 1959, Fig. 12j, k) are of this chert, as are several Murray Springs flake clusters in Area 3 and projectile points, other tools, and debitage from Areas 1, 4, 6, and 7. Nearly 1,200 flakes (approximately 8% of the debitage) are of this pinkish gray chert (Table 8.4). Whether the source area is within the San Pedro Valley or outside it, the material was the second most abundant chert in the Murray Springs debitage.

The most abundant lithic material used at Murray Springs, however, has been traced to a generalized, local source area. St. David Chalcedony is variable, ranging from very fine-grained and nearly translucent to quartzitic in texture and nearly opaque; however, it is easily worked by both percussion and pressure techniques. It is typically white to light gray and tends to be stained to a pale yellow or yellowish brown in near-surface contexts. It occurs as large primary nodules in the Plio-Pleistocene St. David Formation (R. Gray 1965), where several minor, pocketlike outcrops of this material have been located in the eroded badlands west of the town of St. David, between the San Pedro River and State Route 90. Typically these outcrops are associated with tuffs or tuffaceous limestones (R. Gray 1965: 75), and I have observed evidence of aboriginal quarrying activity in these areas. Because the material comes from a distinctive source, it has been named St. David Chalcedony. Although so far identified only from the area west of St. David, other outcrops of the chalcedony may be found in areas where the St. David Formation is well exposed and eroded. Also occurring with the chalcedony is a white to pale yellow opal-like material. Although it is fine-grained and is available in nodules up to 50 cm in maximum dimension, it is extremely light in weight and brittle. No evidence of Clovis utilization of this material has been observed.

One other raw material only rarely used by the Clovis artisans outcrops in close proximity to Murray Springs on the east side of the San Pedro River and approximately 4 km (2.5 miles) northeast of the site. This material is a greenish gray to black silicified limestone that appears in massive exposures in the Lewis Hills north of Lewis Springs on the San Pedro River. Occurring as ledges and boulders and forming the 140-m high hills east of the river, the silicified limestone varies widely in grain size and quality. Most of it is medium grained, contains crystalline inclusions and fracture planes, is light to dark gray in color, and notably tough. The best grade is black, free of inclusions and flaws, and responds well to both soft hammer direct percussion and pressure techniques. Both the hill and surrounding exposures bear extensive evidence of quarrying, and the observed variation in patina suggests some time depth for the use of the exposure. Three Clovis butchering tools of this material were found at the Lehner Site (Haury and others 1959, Fig. 14c, e, g), and one battered cobble of it came from Area 3 of Murray Springs. However, the most extensive exploitation of this source appears to have occurred during the Archaic period; the Archaic component from Areas 6 and 7 at Murray Springs is typical in this regard. That the Clovis people all but ignored such an obvious and nearby raw material source may imply that it was not deemed a particularly desirable material for stone tool production.

Two other rarely used lithic materials provide evidence of nonlocal procurement. One Clovis point tip fragment from Murray Springs is of a distinctive light purple to brownish red petrified wood. The nearest known occurrences of such material are north of the Mogollon Rim in areas around Holbrook and St. Johns, approximately 225 km (140 miles) north of the site. Petrified wood is widely distributed in northeastern Arizona in the Triassic Chinle Formation and other secondary contexts, so it is not possible to identify a particular source within that portion of the state.

Murray Springs also yielded two projectile points, a small quantity of debitage, and four small unmodified nodules of obsidian (marekanite) of the "Apache tear" variety. Recent X-ray fluorescence study of these artifacts suggests that all represent a single source in the far east-central part of Arizona, about 27.5 km (17 miles) north of Clifton. The source, known as Cow Canyon (Appendix C), yields nodules of sufficient size to permit production of small Clovis points. Three flakes of opaque obsidian from Area 7 (not certainly Clovis) have been sourced to Government Mountain.

Work at the Lehner Site yielded three Clovis points made of clear quartz. The small size of the points, coupled with the relative purity and quality of the quartz, suggests that they were probably manufactured from large crystals. Localized deposits of these crystals occur in portions of the Huachuca Mountains such as Carr Canyon (Haury and others 1959: 15), but whether the three points are from this local source is not known.

The general locations of three of the material sources may indicate a line of movement of this group of Clovis hunters prior to their arrival at Murray Springs. The petrified wood point tip implies use of the area of the upper Little Colorado River basin; movement south from that area for 175 km to 250 km (109–155 miles) might take them into the area of the Cow Canyon obsidian source near Safford. Chert-bearing limestone formations might have been encountered and exploited along such a route. Continued movement to the south and west, perhaps westward along the Gila River for 140 km (87 miles) and then southward up the San Pedro for 135 km (84 miles), or perhaps southwestward from Safford up the San Simon Valley, past Willcox Playa, and into the San Pedro Valley near Benson, would bring them to the St. David area where the chalcedony was procured. Judging from the abundance of St. David Chalcedony debitage at Murray Springs, this was the last quarry visited by them before arriving at the site.

In summary, the sources of the lithic materials utilized by the Clovis flint knappers in the San Pedro Valley are largely unknown. There is clear evidence, however, that both materials local to the valley and materials from outside of it were used. Almost all are evidence of careful selection of only those materials of sufficient quality that the large bifaces and flakes on which the Clovis industry was based could be fashioned from them. The majority of these materials are also aesthetically pleasing, though to what extent such a consideration figured into the selection of the materials cannot be ascertained. It does seem generally true that Clovis flint knappers had a predilection for choosing high quality, visually appealing materials for tool manufacture, both in southern Arizona and other parts of North America (Haynes 1980b: 118).

When necessary, other lithic materials of lesser quality were used to produce expedient tools. Quartzites, metasandstones, limestones (silicified or not), and poor quality cherts were all represented at Murray Springs and Lehner in the form of flakes and implements. Such materials probably reflect occasional needs for heavy duty cutting or chopping tools, needs that could be satisfied by the use of cobbles from stream beds or lag gravels local to the sites.

The Biface Mode

The retouching of bifaces apparently occupied the Clovis flint knappers' time more than any other manufacturing activity at Murray Springs. Of the 48 clusters of debitage identified at the site, 42 are interpreted as the result of biface retouching, mute testimony to the importance of this mode in the industry. These flake clusters are typified by thin, expanding flakes with faceted striking platforms, often strongly lipped and abraded. The exterior surfaces of the flakes tend to display a gentle curvature in the long axis. In addition to the clusters, three complete non-projectile point bifaces and fragments of four others were recovered from various portions of the site.

Table 8.5. Biface Widths from Distally Overlapping Flake Groups

Cluster	Material	No. of Flakes in Group	Biface Width (mm)	Fig. No.
A3–2a	Pinkish gray chert	6	46.5	8.4a
A3–2b	Brown and white chert	4	54.0	8.4b
A3–3c, d	Pinkish gray chert	3	44.5	8.4c
A4–1a	St. David Chalcedony	3	89.5	8.4d
A5–1a	St. David Chalcedony	1*	68.0†	8.4e

* Overshot flake.
† Estimate; probably not maximum width.

Bifaces

It is clear that bifaces were a vital part of the Clovis lithic technological system, but the range in their relative size, shape, and degree of refinement is not readily ascertained from the seven complete and fragmentary bifaces from the site. To obtain a better idea of the nature of the bifaces that were being retouched at Murray Springs, I focused on the individual flake clusters in an effort to find pairs or groups of flakes within single clusters that overlapped (refitted) with one another. The most common type of refitting is termed *lateral overlap*, in which flakes were removed sequentially from the same face and same margin of a biface and thus overlap lateral side to lateral side. Less common is *distal overlap*, in which flakes have been removed from opposite margins on the same face and thus overlap distal end to distal end (Fig. 8.4).

For purposes of determining the relative sizes of bifaces represented by the various clusters, groups of flakes that overlap distally are most useful. If the individual flakes composing the group are complete (or reconstructed) and have intact striking platforms, the width dimension of the biface can be obtained. Four clusters contained such flake groups (A3–2a, A3–2b, A3–3c and 3d, and A4–1a) and provide exact widths, and a fifth biface width was estimated by a reconstructed overshot or *outre passe* flake from cluster A5–1a (Fig. 8.4e). Table 8.5 presents the width measurements obtained for each group. Table 8.6 provides measurements for the seven whole and fragmentary bifaces recovered from all parts of the site.

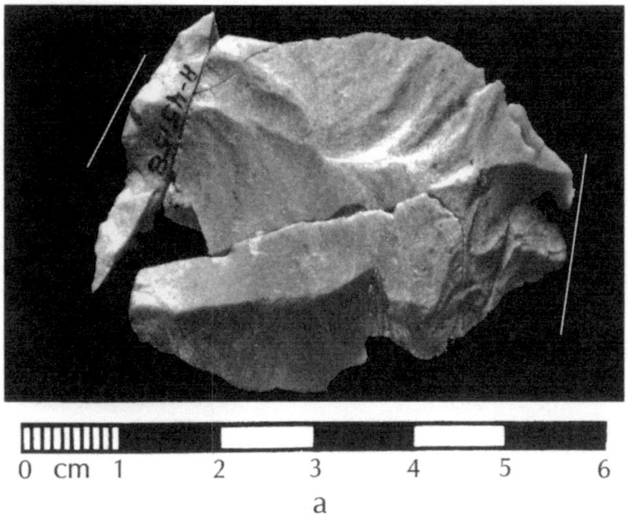

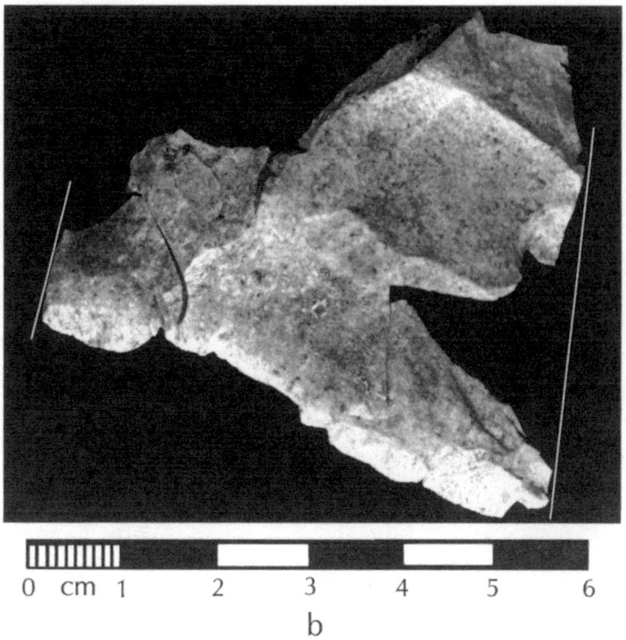

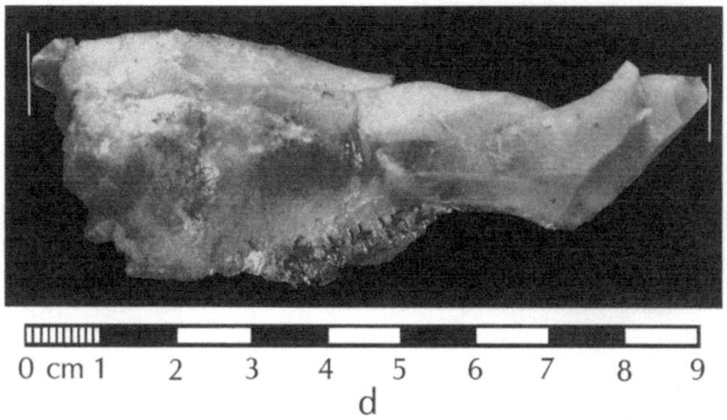

Figure 8.4. Refitted flake groups that allow measurement of biface widths: *a*, Cluster A3-2a; *b*, A3-2b; *c*, A3-3c and d; *d*, A4-1a; *e*, A5-1a (*e* is a single reconstructed overshot flake). White lines indicate the edges of the bifaces.

Table 8.6. Measurements of Bifaces and Biface Fragments from Murray Springs

ASM No.	Area	Material	Condition	Length (mm)	Width (mm)	Thick. (mm)	Fig. No.
A-32,715	3	Mottled chert	F	48	36	11	8.6c
A-33,923	5	Gray chalcedony	C	63	36	9	8.6d
A-33,918	5	Speckled chalcedony	C[1]	89	42	13	8.6f
A-47,170	7	St. David Chalcedony	C	95	42	14	8.6e
A-46,365	6	Tan and gray chert	F	27	66	11	8.6b
A-33,113	4	St. David Chalcedony	F	31	78	23	8.6a
A-47,163/ A-47,199	7	St. David Chalcedony	F[2]	36	33*	9*	

NOTE: ASM, Arizona State Museum
F, fragmentary; C, complete.
1. Two fragments refit to form a complete specimen.
2. Burned.
* Minimum measurement.

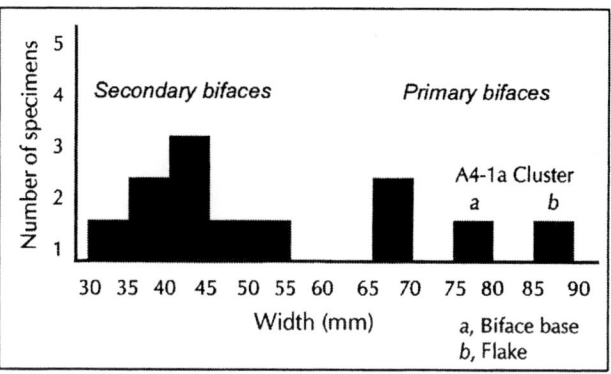

Figure 8.5. Histogram of biface widths from refitted flake groups and biface fragments.

As Tables 8.5 and 8.6 demonstrate, the Murray Springs bifaces display a range of widths, as determined from both the reconstructed biface flake groups and the whole and fragmentary bifaces. If widths of both flake groups and bifaces are plotted on a histogram, two broad groups result (Fig. 8.5). These groups may be interpreted as the first two product stages in the biface mode in Figure 8.3 that ultimately leads to the production of a Clovis fluted point or a knife. The *primary biface* grouping is composed of three representatives: the A4-1a cluster (flake group and biface base), the A5-1a overshot flake, and the A6-1b biface base. Figure 8.6a and b illustrate the Area 4 biface base and the Area 6 biface base respectively, both of which display transverse bend breaks that reflect errors in manufacture such as end shock (Crabtree 1972: 60-61). Figure 8.4d illustrates a reconstructed distally overlapping flake group derived from the same flake cluster (A4-1a) that yielded the biface end fragment (Fig. 8.6a), and Figure 8.4e presents a reconstructed overshot flake recovered from the A5-1a flake cluster. Although both the A4-1a flake group and the A5-1a overshot flake permit an approximation of the widths of two large bifaces, the overshot flake also demonstrates what is probably an important aspect of the biface manufacturing approach used by Clovis flint knappers: the removal of large, single flakes that terminate near the opposite margin of the biface or remove part of it. These fragments and flake groups represent bifaces in an early stage of reduction hereafter termed *primary bifaces*. Based on characteristics displayed by these specimens and debitage, a typical primary biface exhibits several large, expanding scars of flakes removed in a selective fashion; some irregularities in shape and thickness; possibly some cortex; and probably a generalized, elongated oval shape with little or no differentiation of the tip and basal ends. Specimens from the Simon Site cache in Idaho have an appearance similar to complete primary bifaces; they illustrate well a selective, large flake removal reduction strategy (Butler 1963, Figs. 4, 5a-c, f, 6a-b, 7). Size ranges of primary bifaces are based on limited knowledge, but it is estimated that these bifaces were at least 150 mm in length, with widths of 65 mm to 90 mm. The loss of the fragments illustrated in Figure 8.6a and 8.6b apparently did not cause the remainder of the biface to be discarded.

The *secondary biface* grouping shown on the width histogram (Fig. 8.5) encompasses bifaces ranging in width from 33 mm to 54 mm and includes specimens that have received more thinning and shaping than the primary bifaces. Figure 8.4a-c illustrates some of the flake groups that represent reconstructed portions of secondary bifaces, and Figure 8.6c-f shows examples of broken or discarded secondary bifaces. It is possible that most of the debitage clusters resulted from the flaking of such bifaces, but neither distally overlapping flake groups nor biface fragments were recovered to corroborate this interpretation. Secondary bifaces, based on the known examples, are typified by

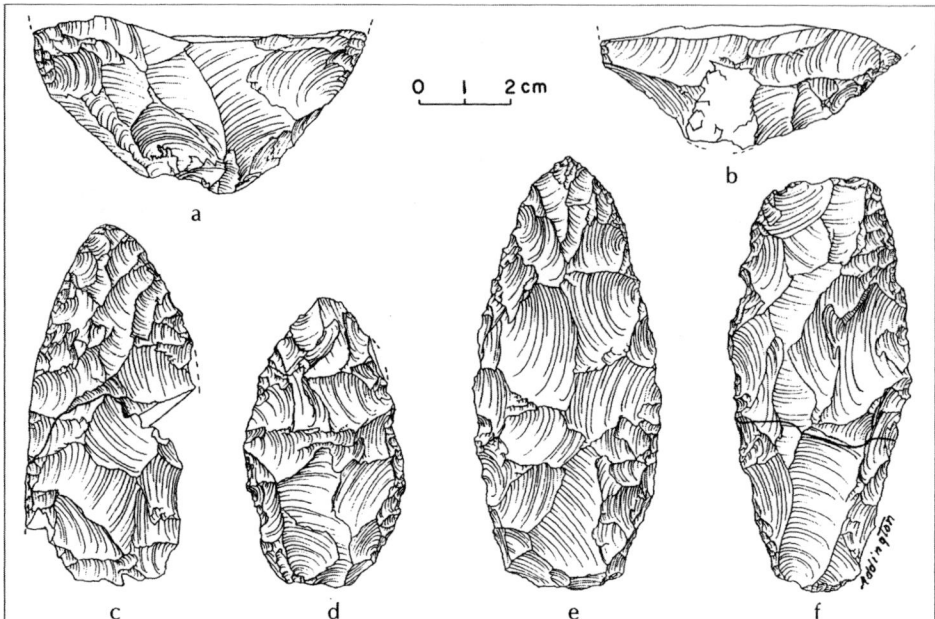

Figure 8.6. Complete and fragmentary bifaces from Murray Springs.

smaller, more closely spaced flake scars often removed in serial fashion, fewer irregularities in shape and thickness, and a more elongate shape; the tip and basal ends of the biface may have been established by this stage as well. Again, certain specimens from the Simon Site are good approximations of the configuration of complete secondary bifaces (Butler 1963, Fig. 3*f–i*).

The four illustrated secondary bifaces are all rejects or discards. Two of them (Figs. 8.6*d, e*) are complete but for various reasons were not deemed worthy of further effort. In all likelihood the specimen in Figure 8.6*d* was regarded as too small to be of further use, and the larger biface (Fig. 8.6*e*) contains two areas of excessive thickness on opposite faces that could not be removed without greatly reducing the width and destroying the shape of the biface. If, as suggested in Figure 8.3, one of the final products of the biface reduction sequence is a projectile point, neither of these two specimens offers much chance for successful completion of the sequence. Efforts to correct the problem of excessive thickness relative to width are likely the cause of failure and breakage of the bifaces illustrated in Figure 8.6*c* and 8.6*f*. In the case of the specimen in Figure 8.6*f*, lateral thinning had failed to adequately reduce the thickness of the biface, so the flint knapper attempted end thinning by establishing a strongly prepared striking platform at one end and delivering a longitudinally directed percussion blow. Unfortunately for the flint knapper, this action resulted in a hinge-through break, destroying the biface. I stress that although this action may appear to resemble fluting, it is distinct from that specialized process. This biface was not at a stage to be fluted, and neither the surface nor the base of the biface had been prepared for a true flute removal (Callahan 1979: 15, 152–153, 164–165); end thinning was simply a last resort to salvage the biface. The biface in Figure 8.6*c* may represent another attempt to salvage a biface with excessive thickness relative to width, this time by the use of lateral thinning. Both margins of the biface were heavily abraded, apparently to create a strong striking platform, and efforts were made to remove large, single flakes that would carry well beyond the midline of the biface and radically thin it. At least one was successfully detached, but the removal of the flake (illustrated with the biface fragment in Figure 8.6*c*) initiated a perverse fracture (Crabtree 1972: 82) that broke the biface in half.

Primary bifaces and secondary bifaces represent stages in a single reduction continuum, but their differentiation is supported by technological data. Part of this evidence is in the form of differences in flake scar patterns between primary and secondary bifaces. These flake scar patterns reveal major differences in reduction strategies and techniques. In the manufacture of primary bifaces, it was apparently advantageous to remove large, single flakes that expanded and carried beyond the midline of the piece almost to or off the opposite margin. These flakes may measure up to 60 mm in length by 50 mm in width and 2 mm in thickness and almost always exhibit ground striking platforms. Such an approach is useful in that it permits quick and easy removal of areas of cortex and flaws, but most importantly it enables the flint knapper to thin the biface quickly with minimum loss in the width and length dimensions.

The Clovis artisans used this strategy in the reduction of primary bifaces, as exemplified in clusters A5-1a and A4-1a. Large flakes, both whole and fragmentary, probably produced by a heavy antler or bone hammer, are common to both clusters. The small number of overlapping flakes in these clusters is due to the fact that the removal of these large flakes was carried out on a selective, rather than serial, basis. Single, well-prepared and abraded striking platforms were created at points along the margin from which it would be possible to obtain a flake that would remove a specific, desired area of biface surface. Striking platform preparation was accomplished by bifacial reduction and isolation, followed by generally heavy abrasion. Only when a single flake was impossible to generate or did not do the job was a second flake necessary. It might be removed from an adjacent striking platform or from one on a different margin; the distally overlapping flake group from cluster A4-1a is an example of this type of situation (Fig. 8.4d).

Bradley (1982: 203-208) has described a similar reduction strategy used by Clovis flint knappers at the Sheaman Locality of the Agate Basin Site in Wyoming; he terms it "alternating opposed biface thinning." It resembles the technique described above, but Bradley suggested that the removal of the large, single flakes was performed in a patterned sequence of blows removing flakes in alternate fashion from the lateral margins (Bradley 1982, Fig. 3.10a). He suggested that this strategy was employed in the majority of cases and may constitute a specifically Clovis biface production process. My own handling of Clovis bifaces suggests that such regularity in the removal of large single flakes is not apparent and that a less patterned, more selective approach predominates.

Secondary bifaces are characterized by a change in the reduction strategy, and it is this change that marks the end of a primary biface and the inception of the secondary biface. The goal of this work was apparently to generate an evenly thinned biface with slightly convex surfaces and relatively uniform lateral and longitudinal cross sections. Rather than relying on large single flakes to do the thinning, smaller flakes were removed in closely spaced, often serial groups. At Murray Springs these flakes range from 20 mm to 40 mm long, 10 mm to 25 mm wide, and approximately 1 mm to 2 mm thick. More often than not, their striking platforms are not abraded. It is likely that a somewhat smaller, lighter, antler or bone hammer was employed for this work. Thus two or three smaller flakes do the job of a single large one and in a slightly more controlled fashion. A number of clusters contained laterally overlapping flake groups that demonstrate this approach to biface thinning. In general the flakes removed during the reduction of a secondary biface carry only slightly beyond the midline of the biface. However, if a biface were deemed too thick relative to its width at this stage, the Clovis flint knappers did not hesitate to return to the strategy of removing large flakes, as shown by the specimen illustrated in Figure 8.6c. The A3-2a flake group (Fig. 8.4a) also reflects an attempt to quickly thin a biface and still conserve width. This flake group began with a large overshot (*outre passe*) flake that removed a portion of one margin, the distal end of which is visible at the left edge of the reconstructed flake group. Two large flakes were detached from the opposite face using the termination of this overshot flake as a striking platform. Happily for the Clovis flint knapper, this effort apparently successfully thinned the biface, because it was not found along with the debitage. Bradley (1982: 207) has also noted this same shift in biface reduction strategy at the Sheaman Locality, and has labeled the latter approach "opposed diving biface thinning" flake removal.

Although the evidence does support the distinction of primary bifaces from secondary bifaces, it must be kept in mind that they are still parts of a single reduction continuum. The small size of the sample of bifaces from Murray Springs probably makes the distinction more apparent than real. As shown by the flakes of the various clusters, this reduction continuum extends from large primary bifaces to Clovis points. The indications are, however, that this reduction sequence was not accomplished in a single session of flint knapping; rather it was drawn out through a long period of time.

In the 42 flake clusters from Murray Springs, few bifaces were being finished into projectile points; only three clusters contain channel flakes indicative of Clovis point manufacture. The other 39 clusters show only that the bifaces were being thinned or resharpened, not "finished." This limited flaking of material is a key to understanding the Clovis system of lithic resource exploitation and utilization. As Hemmings (1970) noted, despite the large numbers of flakes at the site, Clovis use of raw material must be considered parsimonious. In fact, he saw no evidence of projectile point manufacture after the first three seasons' work. Based on the amount of biface thinning debitage at the site, it is possible to propose that bifaces were the mainstay of the Clovis lithic industry in the San Pedro Valley. Further, it is proposed that the most important feature of this industry is that the biface was not viewed simply as a "blank" or "preform," but as a fully functional implement.

The manner in which the biface filled this role can be sketched. The reduction sequence was initiated with the production of a primary biface, perhaps at a quarry. Either large flakes or naturally suited pieces of raw material were reduced there, an operation that probably entailed a relatively minor amount of work with either a hammerstone or large antler or bone hammer. The resulting primary biface was ready for transport, and in this form could have been an excellent tool for cutting tasks (Huckell 1979) and was easily resharpened. As it was sharpened it was reduced in width, but not necessarily in thickness. Sharpening can be accomplished without the removal of large biface thinning flakes (Huckell 1979, Fig. 3); however, when sharpened the thickness of the biface increases relative to its width until it becomes necessary to thin the biface in order to maintain its usefulness as a butchering implement. Clusters such as A5-1a and A4-1a are examples of concentrated thinning operations performed on primary bifaces. The largest biface thinning flakes are also useful for the manufacture of unifacially retouched tools; in essence the primary biface may also be viewed in part as a core for the production of these flake blanks. The repetition of periodic thinning, along with the change in the thinning strategy, gradually reduced the size of the primary biface to that of a secondary biface. It continued to serve as a cutting implement until either it was reduced to a particular minimum size or it became necessary to replace projectile points lost or damaged beyond repair (Huckell 1979: 183-184). As long as the biface had been reduced in the fashion described and the thickness-to-width ratio maintained at a proper level, it could have been fluted and finished into a Clovis point. This final stage of the reduction sequence is discussed below. Callahan (1979) has also stressed the importance of the thickness-to-width ratio in the preparation of Clovis bifacial preforms.

A system of this sort is nothing more than a prolonged reduction or manufacturing sequence, but this strategy has several benefits for the people who use it. Bifaces are easier to transport than cores, nodules, or unmodified large flakes. For mobile, pedestrian hunter-gatherers, lightening the load is an important consideration. Some of the flakes from one cluster of red jasper, A5-2a, exhibit abrasion and rounding of the ridges between the flake scars that Hemmings (1970: 253-254) interpreted as transport wear caused by implements rubbing against one another in bags or other containers. A second advantage is that prolonged periodic reduction can confer a long functional life on a biface. Outside of the occasional necessity to remove larger thinning flakes, simple resharpening can be accomplished with little loss of material. Third, bifaces have a long useable cutting edge. Essentially their entire perimeters can be used if they are not hafted, thus eliminating the need for resharpening as frequently as would be necessary for a single-edged unifacially retouched tool. Further, this conservation of material would support a group through an extended period of time during which no suitable lithic raw material sources might be encountered, an important asset for a group entering a region unfamiliar to them or one they knew to be poor in suitable materials. Finally, at the end of the reduction sequence, the biface could be fashioned into a projectile point, essentially giving it a new and different function. The evidence from Murray Springs demonstrates a concern on the part of Clovis flint knappers that they obtain maximum utility from every piece of raw material. Thus the biface, rather than being considered simply as a "blank" or "preform," must be viewed as a functional implement in its own right for the Clovis inhabitants of the San Pedro Valley.

Projectile Points

Murray Springs has yielded a total of 18 complete and fragmentary Clovis points and a tiny fragment of

Table 8.7. Attributes of Nineteen Murray Springs Clovis Points

ASM No.	Area	Condition	Material	Max. Length (mm)	Max. Width (mm)	Max. Thick. (mm)	LF1 (mm)	LF2 (mm)	LMG1 (mm)	LMG2 (mm)	Min. Basal Width (mm)	Depth of Basal Concavity (mm)	Fig. No.
A–32,718	3	Complete	St. David Chalcedony	55	30	9	14	18	a	a	24	2	8.7k
A–32,716	3	Tip frag.	Petrified wood	26	26	6							8.7g
A–32,719	3	Tip frag.	St. David Chalcedony	13	14	4							8.7f
A–33,116	4	Complete	Obsidian	37	22	6	14	28	21	23	16	3	8.8c
A–33,110	4	Complete	White chert	45	25	6	20	10	24	20	23	5	8.8a
A–33,111	4	Nearly comp.	Tan and gray chert	78	34	10	23	37	39	38	26	5†	8.8g
A–33,924	4	Nearly comp.	Gray chalcedony	75	31	9	29	27	24*	25*	28*		8.8d
A–33,115	4	Nearly comp.	Reddish brown chert	69	31	9	32	23	34†	33	27†	5†	8.8e
A–33,109	4	Nearly comp.	Light gray chert	53	31	9	15	19	34	23	21	3	8.8f
A–33,114	4	Blade portion	Pinkish gray chert	55	34	8							8.8b
A–33,925	4	Tip frag.?	Reddish brown chert	5	13	4							
A–33,917	5	Basal frag.	St. David Chalcedony	15	28	7					27	4	8.7c
A–33,922	5	Basal frag.	Pinkish gray chert	20	28	6					28	5	8.7d
A–33,992	6	Complete	Pinkish gray chert	67	34	10	14	21	31	35	31	5	8.7i
A–32,991	6	Midsection	Pinkish gray chert	87	33	10							8.7h
A–47,162	7	Basal frag.	Pinkish gray chert	45	33	11	27	42	28	30	27	4	8.7j
A–47,283	7	Basal frag.	Pinkish gray chert	17	33	7					31	5	8.7b
A–47,140	7	Basal frag.	St. David Chalcedony	12	30	6					28	2	8.7a
A–47,139	7	Basal frag.	Obsidian	7	20	5					20	3	8.7e

NOTE: ASM, Arizona State Museum.
    LF1, Length of first flute; LF2, Length of second flute.
    LMG1, Length of grinding along one margin; LMG2, Length of grinding along second margin.
   a, specimen not basally ground.
* Incomplete measurement.
† Estimate.

what may be another point tip. All but the last specimen are illustrated in Figures 8.7 and 8.8 and some of their basic attributes are presented in Table 8.7. In addition, three clusters of debitage are interpreted as representing the manufacture of Clovis points. The Murray Springs specimens exhibit extensive damage and breakage, far more than the Clovis points recovered from Naco (Haury 1953) or Lehner (Haury and others 1959). To address the technological characteristics of Clovis points, I added the Naco, Lehner, Leikem (Johnson and Haynes 1967), Escapule (Hemmings and Haynes 1969), and Navarrete (Huckell 1981) projectile points to those from Murray Springs to create a larger, more representative sample. The 43 specimens available for study included 27 complete or nearly complete specimens that exhibit only minor damage, 6 tip fragments, 2 large midsection fragments, and 8 basal fragments. As noted by Haury (1953: 7–11) in discussing the Naco Site, a high degree of formal variation may exist even in an assemblage of points recovered from a single animal carcass; excavations at other sites in the valley have continued to support this observation. However, it is certain that these artifacts were the products of craftsmen working

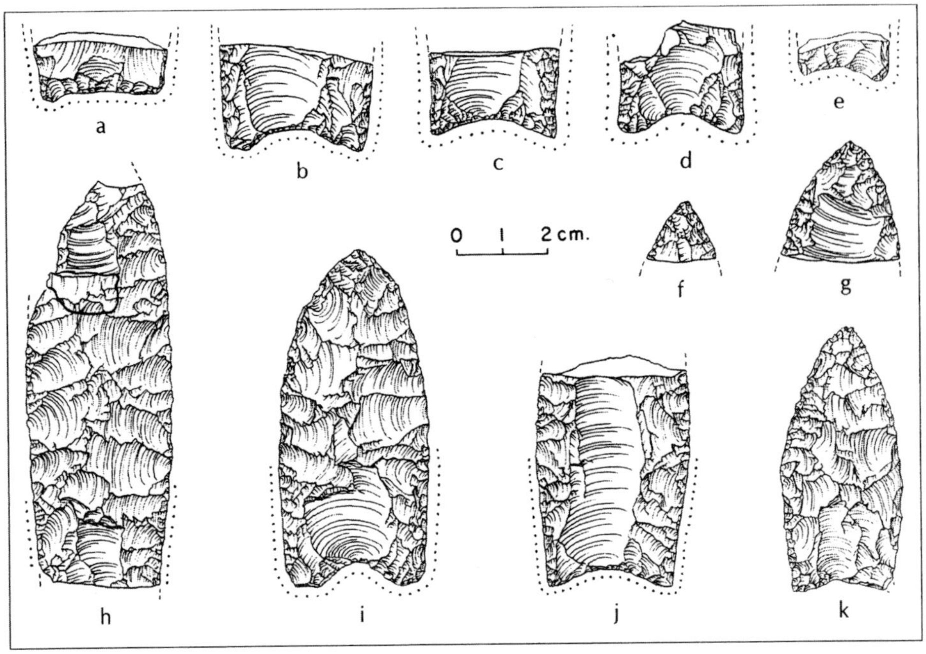

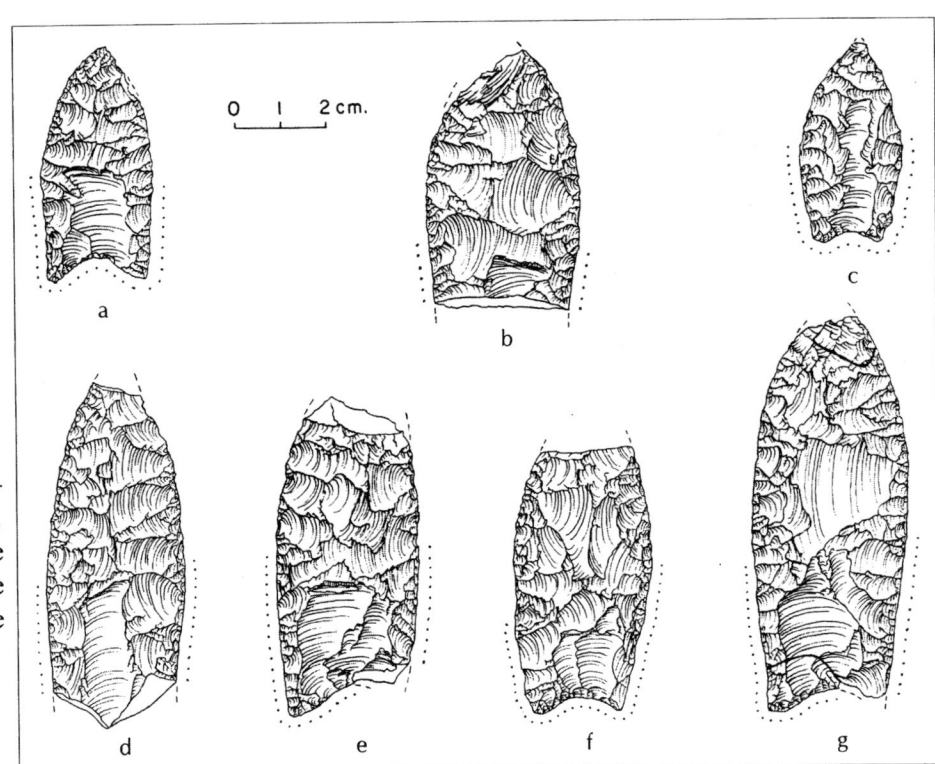

Figure 8.7. Clovis points and fragments from Murray Springs: *a–e, j*, basal fragments; *f, g*, tip fragments; *h*, midsection fragment; *i, k*, complete points. Note refitted impact flake on *h*. Compare with Figure 7.7.

Figure 8.8. Clovis points and fragments from Murray Springs: *a, c, d–g*, complete and nearly complete Clovis points; *b*, blade portion. Note refitted impact flake on *g*. Compare with Figure 5.22b.

within a single tradition, and, in many cases, most likely within a single social unit. The technological consistencies that may be observed among the 43 projectile points from the San Pedro Valley sites are a reflection of this tradition, but what forces led to the high degree of formal variation?

Two distinct but closely related technological processes are considered in an analysis of projectile point variability. The first is the initial manufacture of a point, here termed the *production process*. Second is the reconstruction of a point in response to damage caused during use, here termed the *repair process*. In many cases both of these processes have affected the configuration and appearance of Clovis points that have been recovered from archaeological sites. In rarer instances, points may be identified that bear no evidence of any repair; their appearance has been determined purely by the production process.

In all likelihood the same basic techniques are used for both processes. The differentiation of the two processes must rely on the identification of the intent of the flint knapper during each operation and the constraints imposed by the physical and social conditions that form the environment in which the processes occur. It is assumed that the goal of the production process is the creation of a projectile point that conforms to a culturally determined concept and set of standards, subject to minor individual variation introduced by the artisan. Constraints placed on the artisan during this process are largely those that lie within the piece of raw material (size, shape, flaws, textural qualities), societal norms, and his own abilities and skills. In the repair process it is assumed that the goal is to repair the projectile point as simply as possible; that is, effecting the needed repairs with the smallest necessary loss of point size and shape characteristics so as to restore it to functional condition. Constraints in this case are much more closely defined and are determined by the nature of the damage to the point. Thus, in the production process there is a wider range of variables that influence or determine the final appearance of the point; in the repair process the situation is much more limited and the artisan does not have the same degree of latitude in determining point size and shape that was present in the production process.

Clovis Point Production

The production of Clovis points and fluted points in general has been studied and discussed by a number of archaeologists and lithic technologists. A variety of experimental techniques for and approaches to the production of the known types of fluted points exist; Callahan (1979: 8-24) has identified and summarized these studies as they apply to Clovis technology. The following description is intended specifically for the San Pedro Valley Clovis points and is based on close examination of these specimens, my own replicative experiments, and the work of other technologists. This is not designed to be an exhaustive description, but rather a generalized one in keeping with the level of a technological overview of the San Pedro Valley Clovis industry.

The production of a Clovis point is integrally linked to biface manufacture. The biface reduction sequence is a complex one, and this description of point manufacture deals only with the final stages of the biface reduction sequence. The secondary biface may be used as a knife either until it reaches the critical size at which it must be finished, or until it becomes necessary to use it to replace a projectile point. Depending on its size, configuration, and width-to-thickness ratio at that time, the final projectile point manufacture sequence probably begins with soft hammer percussion thinning and shaping. The three clusters of debitage from Murray Springs that are interpreted as representing projectile point manufacture or repair are composed primarily of fragments of smaller, soft hammer biface thinning flakes that probably originally ranged in size from approximately 15 mm to 25 mm in length by 10 mm to 20 mm in width. Interestingly, almost no abraded striking platforms are observed on any of these flakes; platform preparation consists of careful bifacial reduction with a final unifacial bevel in the direction opposite the face from which the major flake is to be removed. The striking platforms are only slightly convex, not particularly well isolated from the surrounding margin. However, they tend to be well centered on ridges or convexities that serve to guide the flake. During this process there is a tendency for small groups of flakes to be removed in serial fashion from a margin, as demonstrated by reconstructed flake groups from Murray Springs in which flakes overlap one another laterally. Presumably this final percussion retouch readied the biface for fluting.

The importance of establishing appropriate lateral and longitudinal cross sections to facilitate fluting has been discussed elsewhere (Crabtree 1966: 18-19); it need only be emphasized that proper cross sectional and surficial configurations must be created to enable channel flakes to be removed successfully. Some of the consequences of improper preparation include hinge-through flute terminations, short flutes, or the inability to remove flutes at all. Striking platform preparation is also critical in this process; unfortunately none of the channel flake fragments from Murray Springs retained the striking platform, so the San Pedro Valley Clovis preparation technique remains unknown. However, in all likelihood it was constructed in much the same manner as a biface thinning flake striking platform. Experiments have shown that it is necessary to isolate the channel flake striking platform from the surrounding basal margin, establish the proper angle for the platform, position the platform correctly relative to the longitudinal section of the point, and grind or abrade the platform (Crabtree 1967: 19). Such adjustments will vary slightly depending on the texture and fracturing characteristics of the raw material. The Murray Springs channel flake fragments range from 8 mm to 17 mm in width; flute lengths cannot be reconstructed from these fragments. The completed points from the San Pedro Valley show a wide range in flute length, with extant flute remnants on the points measuring from approximately 20 mm to 60 mm. Typically the longest flute remnant will not exceed half of the length of the point, and normally will be closer to one third the overall point length.

After the first face was fluted, the base was reworked to establish a striking platform for the opposite face. Depending on the characteristics of the first channel scar and the thickness of the preform at the base, it might be necessary to shorten the overall length dimension of the point markedly in order to establish an adequate second striking platform. Such work rarely results in the removal of less than 5 mm, and may entail the loss of as much as 10 mm to 15 mm of length. To thin the base, the major goal of the fluting operation, it may be necessary to reflute one or both sides of the point. Multiple fluting is identifiable on some of the San Pedro Valley Clovis points (for examples see Haury 1953, Fig. 7*f*; Haury and others 1959, Fig. 13*h*, *l*).

The method used by the Clovis flint knappers to remove the channel flakes has not been identified; any one of three might have been used: direct percussion, indirect percussion, and some form of massive pressure, such as chest pressure with a crutch. I have obtained good results with the first two methods and have seen others produce good Clovis points with the pressure method. Massive pressure, however, seems to be more useful for producing points such as the Cumberland variety, with long, narrow flutes running the length of the point. Until more debitage and bifaces broken during fluting are recovered, it is not possible to choose among these methods for the San Pedro Valley Clovis industry.

After fluting was completed, the final finishing of the point was accomplished by pressure flaking. Normally this entailed selective (rather than patterned) pressure flaking, a process by which flakes were removed only at intervals along the margins of the point where it was necessary to either thin or shape it. Virtually all of the San Pedro Valley Clovis points display such work, particularly around the tip, the basal margins, and the basal concavity. On all of the Clovis points that have not had major reworking, it is possible to identify partial remnants of from three to seven percussion flake scars on and near the midline of each face of the specimen; these are truncated nearer the margins by the subsequent pressure work. In addition, pressure scars from the lateral margins that invade the channel scars are equally common. One feature that is fairly consistent and deserves mention is the use of pressure flakes to remove the terminations of the channel flakes. Usually these channel flakes will terminate in a low hinge or step fracture; it is relatively simple to remove such a flute termination using one or more pressure flakes from the lateral margins opposite the termination. One or both terminations had been removed on all but three of the 33 points complete enough to evaluate for this feature. This action may have been taken to further facilitate hafting.

The final step in finishing the point was to abrade the lateral margins and basal concavity. This practice dulls the lateral margins to prevent them from cutting the bindings on the haft and may help keep the basal concavity from splitting or cutting into the spear shaft on impact. The lateral edge abrasion commonly extends as far as either the termination of the longest flute or until the point of maximum width is reached. At Murray Springs the points display a mean lateral grinding length of 29.5 mm. The points from Naco exhibit a mean lateral grinding length of 30.9 mm, and those from Lehner exclusive of the three quartz specimens average 30.4 mm of edge abrasion. Although the range observed in grinding length is on the order of 15 mm and may vary on opposite margins of the same point as much as 5 mm, the close correspondence among points from the three sites in mean lateral grinding length is notable.

Finished Clovis points that do not display evidence of breakage and subsequent repairs are few in the assemblage presently available for study; one point from Lehner is probably the best example. It embodies the characteristics described in the preceding paragraphs and best typifies the San Pedro Valley Clovis point style (Haury and others 1959, Figs. 12*j*, 13*j*).

Exactly how much work might be required to produce a finished point from a secondary biface is difficult to evaluate and doubtlessly varied considerably. One way in which to measure this is by the amount of debitage that remains after the completion of the point. Few figures are available at present, but three experiments I conducted yielded 10.5 g, 27.6 g, and 30.5 g of debitage. All three entailed the finishing of a biface in a late stage of reduction into a Clovis point, using percussion flake removals for fluting and occasional thinning but relying largely on pressure flaking. The weights reported here consist of all debitage, including the channel flakes. How typical such figures are is unknown, but the debitage that composes the three clusters identified as representing projectile point manufacture at Murray Springs, A7-3, A3-3a, and A3-3b and c, weighs 19.9 g, 21.6 g, and 27.4 g, respectively. Of the three clusters, A7-3 has probably been affected by loss of flakes through nearly 13,000 years of bioturbation and the use of a quarter-inch mesh screen during excavation. Although obviously not conclusive, these experimental and archaeological data at least help to define a range of figures for the weight of debitage that might be expected to result from this process.

Another experiment concerning the sizes and quantities of debitage produced by the manufacture of a Clovis point from a flake was conducted by Henry and his colleagues (1976). The debitage in this experiment was segregated by technique and type of flaking tool used rather than by stage of reduction, so direct comparisons with the Murray Springs data are not possible.

Clovis Point Repair

It was probably an exceptional event when a Clovis projectile point bearing no flake scars other than those generated during the production process was deposited in an archaeological context; the life of a flaked stone projectile point is a difficult one. Personal experience using stone-tipped spears on fresh elephant and bison carcasses suggests that breakage, both minor and major, is frequent when spears are thrown or thrust into animals (Huckell 1982). If the damage sustained by the point is sufficiently minor, repairs may be effected, and indications are that repair occurred frequently in the sample of Clovis points from the San Pedro Valley sites. This sample includes both repaired points and broken, unrepaired fragments, and is thus helpful in understanding the range of variability. In particular, Murray Springs has yielded a large sample of broken and damaged points.

The repair process likely began with an assessment of the type of break sustained by a point and weighing the chances of successful repair of the damage. Figure 8.9 illustrates the types of breaks that have been observed on the San Pedro Valley Clovis points. There are four basic categories of damage: tip damage, basal damage, lateral damage, and various combinations of the three. Tip damage is common, judging from extant unrepaired specimens and experiments (Huckell 1982). It may vary from the minor crushing (Hemmings and Haynes 1969, Fig. 6b-b') and simple snaps (Fig. 8.7f; Hemmings and Haynes 1969, Fig. 6a-a') visible on points from the Murray Springs and Escapule sites to impact "flutes" (Figs. 8.7g-h, 8.8g; Haury and others 1959, Fig. 12m) observed on Lehner and Murray Springs points to the loss of a large part of the point tip by transverse snap or bend breaks on three Murray Springs specimens (Figs. 8.7j, 8.8e, f). The response to such damage was the repointing of the tip if sufficient length remained. This reshaping may result in the creation of markedly shorter, broader points in extreme cases (Haury 1953, Figs. 6c, 7c; Haury and others 1959, Figs. 12e, h and 13e, h), but in minor cases repairs might not be detectable at all. Such work was apparently accomplished largely if not totally by pressure flaking.

Basal damage is also common (Huckell 1982) and may or may not involve major repairs. If a small part of a basal corner is crushed or snapped the repair might be done without regard to restoring symmetry, thus creating one shorter basal corner (Di Peso 1953a). However, if one or both basal corners were removed by bend breaks (Fig. 8.8d, e, g; Haury 1953, Figs. 6e, f, h and 7e, f, h), a new basal concavity would need to be created. Such a repair might also involve refluting the point. A major basal snap break (Figs. 8.7a-e; 8.8b; Haury and others 1959, Figs. 12k, l and 13k, l) would certainly necessitate refluting and lateral thinning as well. Figure 8.7i represents a point from Murray Springs that was probably repaired after such a break. With the exception of refluting and perhaps the removal of the vertically broken edge, pressure flaking would suffice for most of this work.

Broken bases may have served secondary functions. The basal fragment illustrated in Figure 8.7c was

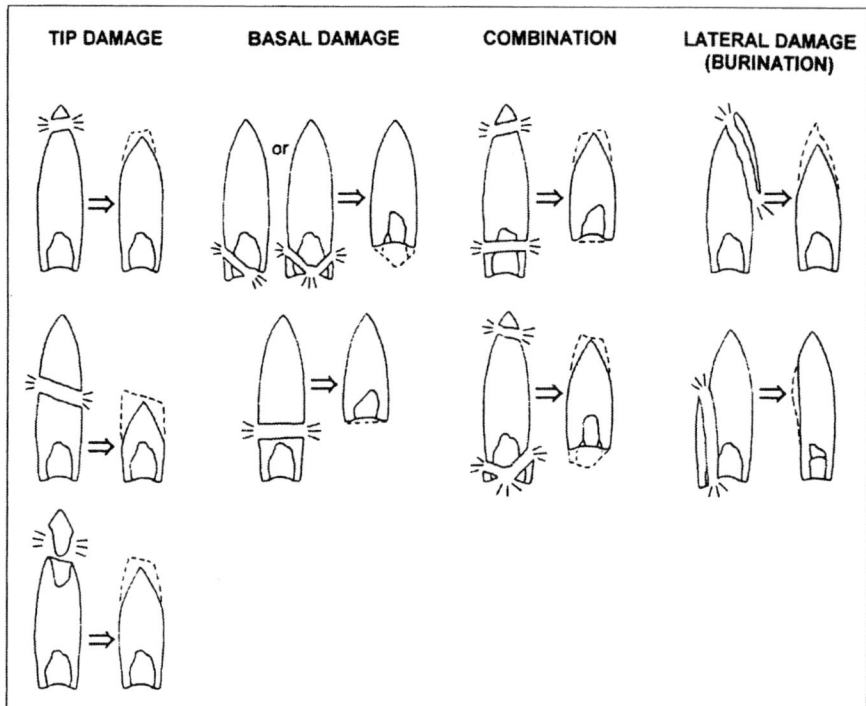

Figure 8.9. Clovis point breakage and repair options, based on specimens from the San Pedro Valley.

reused as a scraper or plane, as witnessed by the polish and striations transverse to the broken edge on one face of the point fragment.

Damage to the lateral margins of Clovis points from the San Pedro Valley sites is rare, but is still observed in the collection. In its simplest form lateral damage may occur as crushing near the tip, often in conjunction with simple tip damage (Fig. 8.8b; Haury and others 1959, Figs. 12b, 13b); pressure flaking may be used to resharpen the margin and restore symmetry if desired. However, one point from Naco and one from Lehner (Haury 1953, Figs. 6d and 7d; Haury and others 1959, Figs. 12f, 13f) show the repair of major burin breaks originating at the base and traveling up one margin toward the tip. In both cases as much of the burin scar as possible was removed by bifacial pressure flaking, and a new base was created by recentering the concavity and refluting the point.

Combinations of tip, basal, and lateral damage may be identified in the Murray Springs assemblage; such breakage appears to be the result of particularly violent impacts and is likely to damage the point beyond repair. Nevertheless, in some cases salvage may have been achieved. Figure 8.7h presents a point apparently damaged beyond repair recovered from Area 6 of Murray Springs. It displays a snapped base, a snapped, crushed, and impact-fluted tip, and some lateral burin breakage along the margins near the tip. A point from Area 4 with similar but not quite so extreme damage is shown in Figure 8.8g. Note the short impact flute (the flake has been replaced) at the tip, and the snapped basal corners (one of which was recovered and has been refitted). Figure 8.8d and e show other Murray Springs points with both tip damage and basal corner removal. The repair of such heavily damaged points would entail much more extensive work than that discussed previously.

Many of the projectile points from Areas 4 and 5 (Figs. 8.8a–g, 8.7c–d) and the Area 6 specimen linked to them by the refitted impact flake (Figs. 8.2, 8.7h) display more extensive and more complex damage and breakage than do any of the points from Naco or Lehner. To what can this greater damage be attributed? It may be speculated that it is due to use of the Area 4 points in killing bison, whereas those from Naco and Lehner are from elephant kills. However, for what specific reason that should be the case is not immediately clear. It may be because bison are smaller than elephants, thus offering less vital target area between ribs or other bones. With their larger size, elephants may be more easily speared in areas unprotected or less well protected by bones. Further, elephants are

Table 8.8. Attributes of Twenty-three Unifacially Retouched Flake Tools from Murray Springs

ASM No.	Area	Type	Material	Max. Length (mm)	Max. Width (mm)	Max. Thick. (mm)	WE 1L (mm)	WE 1A	WE 2L (mm)	WE 2A	Fig. No.
74-52-1	7	Large lat. ret. flake	Cream chert	78	53	13	73	35°†	63	70°	8.10*l*
A-46,143	7	Side scraper	St. David Chalcedony	60	41	13	60	85°			8.10*i*
A-47,264-x	7	Thin lat. ret. flake	Pinkish gray chert	61	38	7	53	70°	46	60°	8.10*j*
A-47,291	7	Thin lat. ret. flake	St. David Chalcedony	45	35	5	47*	90°	29	(a)	
A-45,703	7	Thin lat. ret. flake	St. David Chalcedony	53	52	9	39*	40°			
A-32,717	3	Thin lat. ret. flake	Tan and gray chert	28	32	3	31*	25°			8.10*h*
A-33,919	5	Thin lat. ret. flake	Gray chalcedony	60	29	10	50	40°			
A-47,158	7	Fine lat. ret. flake	St. David Chalcedony	28	32	4	16*	65°			8.10*g*
A-45,614	7	Fine lat. ret. flake	Tan and gray chert	40	31	7	19*	90°	30*	70°†	8.10*k*
A-33,347	6	Fine lat. ret. flake	Pinkish gray chert?	24	26	4	16*	70°†			
A-32,990	6	Double graver	Pinkish gray chert?	51	30	5	3		2		8.10*e*
A-33,935	3	Triple graver	St. David Chalcedony	29	14	3	3		3		8.10*f*
A-46,160	7	Single graver	St. David Chalcedony	24	25	6	2*				
A-33,112	4	Composite tool	Banded chalcedony	67	34	8	67	40°	34	40°	8.11
A-33,929	7	End scraper	Pinkish gray chert	42	28	10	26	80°			8.10*a*
A-33,928	7	End scraper/graver	Pinkish gray chert	37	18	8	17	100°			8.10*c*
A-33,943	6	End scraper	Tan and gray chert	39	28	10	25	(a)			8.10*b*
A-45,615	7	End scraper	Tan and gray chert	40	30	7	28	60°			8.10*d*
A-33,936	4	Lat. ret. flake frag.	Light gray chert	21	14	4	21*	30°			
A-47,127	7	Lat. ret. flake frag.	Pinkish gray chert	18	13	5	10*	90°			
A-43,053-x	3	Lat. ret. flake frag.?	Reddish brown chert	17	8	4	15*	70°			
A-45,088-x	3	Lat. ret. flake frag.?	Pinkish gray chert	28	9	4	12	50°			
A-43,022	7	Lat. ret. flake frag.	Silicified siltstone	25	17	4	21*	30°			

NOTE: ASM, Arizona State Museum.
WE1L, Length of one working edge; WE1A, Angle of one working edge.
WE2L, Length of second working edge; WE2A, Angle of second working edge.
(a), No measurement possible.
* Incomplete measurement due to breakage; † Estimated measurement.

taller, perhaps affording a hunter more direct access to preferred target areas. This may suggest that different procurement methods were used, with bison perhaps hunted with throwing spears and elephants with thrusting spears. The lower accuracy resulting from a throwing spear, coupled with a smaller, better protected target area, may be responsible for the more extensive damage to the Clovis points from the Area 4 bison kill.

Clearly, damage to a point and subsequent repair of it can alter the formal attributes of a Clovis point or any other type of flaked stone projectile point (Bradley 1974; Huckell 1978b). If a group of hunters were operating away from suitable raw material sources, the recovery and repair of damaged projectile points would likely be of importance and a high incidence of such repairs might be expected. That such a situation might have prevailed in the San Pedro Valley has been noted above in the discussion of the conservative approach to raw material consumption observed at Murray Springs. Provided that no specimens were lost on the site, it is probable that none of the fragments illustrated in Figures 8.7 and 8.8 were viewed as having the potential to be successfully reworked. It is argued, therefore, that much of the variability in projectile point form in the San Pedro Valley is a consequence of the need to achieve the maximum amount of use possible from every biface or other tool requiring a large piece of raw material.

The Flake and Flake Tool Mode

The second major production mode in the Clovis technological system involves nonspecialized flakes derived from cores or bifaces, retouched to produce working edges needed for specific tasks (Fig. 8.3). Murray Springs yielded 23 of these tools (Table 8.8). By combining the specimens from the Lehner Site with the Murray Springs assemblage, we can reach a fuller understanding of this category of implements, identify a few consistent types of flake tools, and obtain a

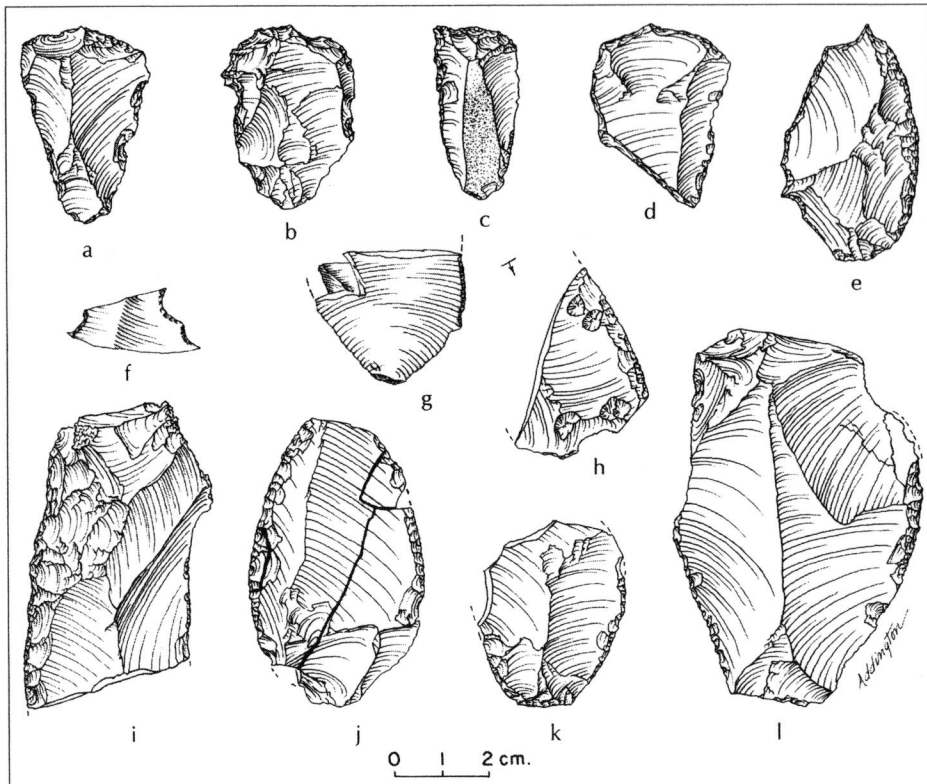

Figure 8.10. Unifacially retouched flake tools from Murray Springs: *a–d*, end scrapers; *e, f*, gravers; *g, k*, fine laterally retouched flake fragments; *h, j*, thin laterally retouched flake fragments; *i*, side scraper; *l*, large laterally retouched flake.

better sense of the ranges within which certain types may vary. One flake cluster from Murray Springs (A3–3i) and two flake clusters from Lehner (Agenbroad and Huckell 1981) represent the manufacture or sharpening of unifacially retouched flake tools.

This portion of the Clovis lithic technological system is perhaps the least completely understood. Unfortunately, because no complete cores have been found at any of the Clovis sites in the San Pedro Valley, basic flake production strategies cannot be fully outlined. A fragment of what might have been a flake core was found in Area 7 of Murray Springs but is too incomplete to permit any reconstruction of its size or shape, let alone technical attributes. Thus, this portion of the flake tool production sequence can only be reconstructed from flake attributes. Evidence provided by tools made on flakes that retain the bulb of percussion and striking platform permits identification of some of the attributes of the flake production process. Striking platforms are usually faceted, though they may also be plain. Platform construction normally consisted of singling out a prominent ridge to guide the flake and then preparing the platform by reducing it. Normally the flake was detached by hard hammer direct percussion, an inference based on prominent, well-focused bulbs of percussion and little or no lipping.

Biface reduction flakes also were used for tool production. Identifiable characteristics include bifacially prepared, lipped, and abraded striking platforms; relative thinness; and relatively greater curvature in the long axis. The size range of these flakes suggests that they were probably derived from primary bifaces; thus the primary biface may also have functioned as a core, to a limited degree.

Unifacially retouched tools produced on flakes (Fig. 8.10) are an important part of the Clovis industry, but to date only 30 have been recovered from Murray Springs and the other sites in the San Pedro Valley. The small size of this sample makes it inadvisable to attempt too fine a typological breakdown. Therefore the classification of the unifacially retouched flake tools has tended toward lumping rather than splitting, and the descriptions of the various groupings of implements are somewhat generalized. The eight categories used to classify the assemblage of flake tools from Murray Springs and Lehner include four varieties of laterally retouched flakes, a single composite tool, gravers, end scrapers, and utilized flakes. When possible, comparisons are made with Clovis implements from other sites in the West; the Blackwater Draw assemblage is the most useful of these.

Laterally Retouched Flakes

Four groups of laterally retouched flake tools are defined, based on the attributes of overall implement size and type of retouch. The first of these groups is present at both Murray Springs and Lehner and is termed the large laterally retouched flake. The three known specimens all exhibit an even unifacial retouch along one lateral margin that creates a convex working edge with an angle of 30° to 50°. These tools range from 78 mm to 130 mm long and from 53 mm to 73 mm wide. It is probable that all three represent butchering tools, despite the steepness of their working edges. The two Lehner specimens (Haury and others 1959, Fig. 14*f, g*) come from an elephant butchering and kill context and the Murray Springs example (Fig. 8.10*l*) is from the Area 7 camp. A fourth smaller implement from Lehner (Haury and others 1959, Fig. 14*e*) is similar in form but far less extensively retouched and has a much lower edge angle of 10°. It may represent a tool at an earlier stage in the wear cycle. Directly comparable specimens from other sites are difficult to find; however, Blackwater Draw has yielded at least two implements with generally similar size and working edge configurations (Cotter 1937: 12; Hester 1972, Fig. 94*i*).

Laterally retouched flake tools in the second group are somewhat similar in size but steeper in edge angle and most closely resemble side scrapers. The Area 7 camp at Murray Springs produced a single slightly convex-edged tool made on a large flake fragment, with an edge angle of 85° (Fig. 8.10*i*). Its working edge configuration is most similar to a tool from the Lehner Site (Haury and others 1959, Fig. 14*d*), though the latter specimen exhibits a more markedly convex edge. The context of the Lehner tool is a kill/butchering area, which raises the question of whether the tool is in fact a scraper or simply a butchering tool that was deemed unserviceable after the last attempted retouch. The same question may be applied to the Murray Springs tool as well; under low power magnification neither specimen shows any obvious wear patterns. Side scrapers are known from Blackwater Draw and some of them appear similar to the Murray Springs specimen (Hester 1972, Fig. 91*g–k*; Warnica 1966, Fig. 5*b–g*).

The third group of laterally retouched flakes consists of seven flake tools, five from Murray Springs and two from Lehner, that also bear retouch along one or both lateral margins. Made on thin (3–10 mm) flakes or flake fragments, these implements are characterized by slightly convex working edges with average angles of 20° to 45° on six of the seven. The height of the retouch on these tools ranges from 2 mm to 4 mm, noticeably less than on either of the preceding two groups. Figure 8.10*j* illustrates one specimen from Area 7 at Murray Springs that is retouched on both lateral margins; one other fragmentary implement of this group from Murray Springs is also bilaterally retouched. Figure 8.10*h* presents a fragmentary specimen, from within the skeleton of the Area 3 mammoth, bearing a low angle retouch on one margin, and Haury and others (1959, Fig. 14*c*) illustrate what appears to be another fragment of one of these tools. The functions that these implements served are not immediately apparent; they would perform well either as knives for light cutting tasks or as scrapers. Hester (1972, Fig. 94*a, d, e, f, i*) classified similar specimens from Blackwater Draw as unifacial knives, though no edge angle measurements were given.

The fourth group of laterally retouched flakes contains three implements from Murray Springs grouped together because they all bear a fine retouch on one or both lateral margins. This retouch is even and averages approximately 1 mm in height; Figure 8.10*g* and *k* illustrate two examples. All three of these tools are to some extent fragmentary or damaged, and all come from Areas 6 and 7. It is certain that the two illustrated specimens are constructed on large biface reduction flakes; it is possible that the third is as well. With edge angles measuring from 65° to 90°, it is possible that these fine flake tools served as scrapers. There are resemblances to some implements termed flake scrapers at Blackwater Draw (Hester 1972, Fig. 92*q, r*).

The 1974 season at the Lehner Site produced a small tool that is similar to these finely retouched flakes, but differs in that it is made on a relatively thick fragment of a core flake and bears a less regular retouch (Agenbroad and Huckell 1981). This retouch varies in height from 1 mm to 3 mm and forms an edge angle of approximately 50°, suggesting a scraping function.

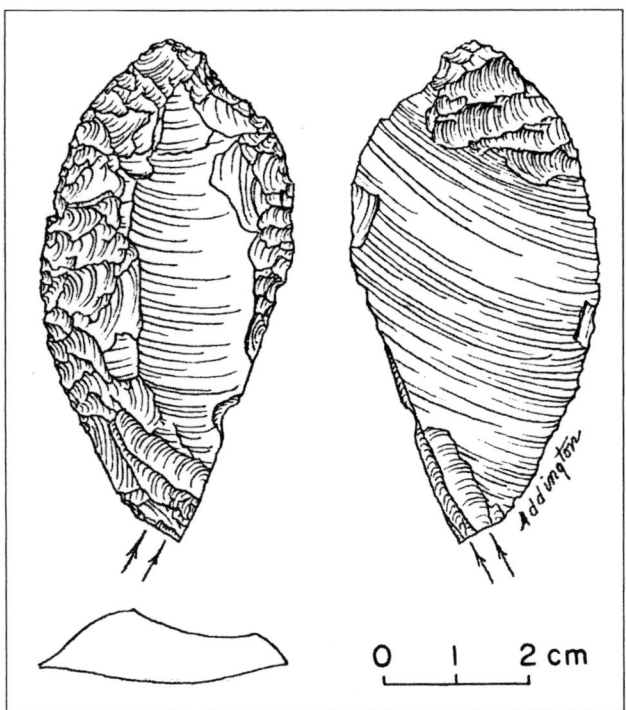

Figure 8.11. Composite flake tool from Murray Springs.

Five small fragments of laterally retouched flake tools were recovered from Areas 3, 4, and 7 at Murray Springs (Table 8.8). All were too fragmentary to classify more specifically.

Composite Flake Tool

A unique composite tool of banded chalcedony that has unifacial retouch on two convex, lateral margins and a multiple burin at one end was recovered from Area 4 at Murray Springs (Fig. 8.11). The more extensively retouched lateral margin bears an edge angle of 40° to 50°, and the opposite lateral margin shows less retouch and has an edge angle of approximately 40°. At the distal end of this second margin is a multiple burin, formed by two blows that were stopped by an intentionally placed notch. As Figure 8.11 indicates, the interior surface of the flake on which the tool was constructed displays a series of at least four flakes that removed the bulb of percussion. Removal of the bulb may have helped to create a flatter, more uniform interior flake surface; in turn this would have enabled the construction of a more consistent edge angle along the major lateral working edge.

Gravers

Four gravers, three from Murray Springs and one from Lehner, have been identified. The Lehner specimen was recovered during the 1955–1956 work at the site but not recognized until recently in the collections at the Arizona State Museum. This graver is made on a small hard hammer percussion flake and bears a single spur slightly less than 2 mm in length. All three of the Murray Springs gravers are made on biface reduction flakes or flake fragments and exhibit from one to three spurs, each 2 mm to 3 mm in length. The most complete Murray Springs specimen is from Area 6 and has two spurs; it is illustrated in Figure 8.10e. Blackwater Draw has also produced gravers similar in form to this Murray Springs specimen (Hester 1972, Fig. 95a–e; Warnica 1966, Fig. 3a–f). An unusual graver was recovered from Area 3. It was constructed on a midsection fragment of a flake and bears three separate spurs (Fig. 8.10f). Each of the spurs was produced by notching just inside the broken edge of the original flake, and so each spur incorporates a portion of the vertically broken edges of the flake fragment.

End Scrapers

Four end scrapers of the type commonly associated with Paleoindian sites were recovered from Areas 6 and 7 at Murray Springs. One of these (Fig. 8.10c) and possibly one other (Fig. 8.10b) are spurred and the other two (Fig. 8.10a and d) appear to be simple, unelaborated end scrapers. Virtually identical specimens are known from Blackwater Draw (Hester 1972, Fig. 92a–j). Although classified here as flake tools, it is conceivable that at least three of the Murray Springs examples were made on typical blades or blade fragments. This possibility is based on the bifacially prepared and ground striking platforms still in evidence on the three specimens (Fig. 8.10a–c), as well as on their triangular or trapezoidal cross section and exterior flake scar pattern. All four end scrapers are of similar length (Table 8.8), which may indicate that they were considered worn out and discarded. Use of a blade or bladelike flake for a distally retouched tool such as an end scraper would be advantageous, in that it could be resharpened numerous times through a relatively long use life. The fourth end scraper (Fig. 8.10d) is made on the distal end of a flake or perhaps a blade; it also bears an abrupt, 90° retouch on the

Table 8.9. Attributes of Thirteen Blades and Blade Tools from Murray Springs

ASM No.	Area	Type	Material	Max. Length (mm)	Max. Width (mm)	Max. Thick. (mm)	WE 1L (mm)	WE 1A	WE 2L (mm)	WE 2A	DW EW (mm)	DW EA	Fig. No.
A-32,720	3	Utilized blade frag.	Grayish brown chert	64	27	10	55*	40°	63*	40°			8.12d
A-33,926	4	Retouched blade	Grayish brown chert	74	26	7	57	30°	41	35°			8.12b
A-43,024	7	Utilized blade frag.	Pinkish gray chert	30	27	8	28	20°	32	35°			8.12a
A-43,023	6	Retouched blade frag.	Grayish brown chert	36	19	12					18	60°	
A-46,180	7	Utilized blade	Grayish brown chert	67	24	9	60	30°	63	45°			8.12e
A-43,007	6	Retouched blade	Dark gray chalcedony	87	29	6					15	35°	8.12c
A-46,368	6	Blade frag.	Dark gray chalcedony	41	18	6			42	15°			
A-47,266	7	Utilized blade	Silicified siltstone	61	27	12			66	40°			8.13a
A-46,187	7	Misstruck blade?	Silicified siltstone	30	20	5							8.13b
A-46,179	7	Primary blade?	Silicified siltstone	65	42	15							8.13c
A-33,927	7	Retouched blade frag.	Silicified siltstone	68	42	22	64	40°	64	55°	29	90°	8.13d
A-33,930	7	Retouched blade frag.	Silicified siltstone	113	45	20							8.13e
A-45,647	7	Blade? frag.	Silicified siltstone	29	15	4							

NOTE: ASM, Arizona State Museum.
WE1L, Length of one lateral working edge; WE1A, Angle of one lateral working edge.
WE2L, Length of second lateral working edge; WE2A, Angle of second lateral working edge.
DWEW, Width of distal working edge; DWEA, Angle of distal working edge.
* Incomplete measurement due to breakage.

margin opposite the working edge. This retouch may have been designed to serve as backing or blunting. The lateral edges of all four end scrapers show irregular unifacial retouch, perhaps to dull the margins or adjust their shapes to fit into bone, antler, or wooden tool handles similar to those known from Plains sites (G. Metcalf 1970; Wedel 1970).

Unretouched Implements

Both Lehner and Murray Springs have yielded flakes that were utilized for tasks without any post-detachment modification of their margins. A single utilized core flake was recovered from Lehner in 1974 (Agenbroad and Huckell 1981), and five utilized flakes came from Murray Springs. Three of the latter specimens are from the Area 4 bison kill (Hemmings 1970, Fig. 27c–e), and two are from Area 3 (Hemmings 1970, Fig. 16f–g); three of them are fragmentary, hard hammer flakes detached from cores and two are biface reduction flakes. The three Area 4 specimens, one from Area 3, and the Lehner artifact exhibit edge damage in the form of nicking and microspalling along straight to convex margins with edge angles in the 10° to 30° range. Such edge angles imply a cutting function. The fifth Murray Springs tool displays damage in a natural concavity on one margin of a flake fragment; it may have been used as a spokeshave. It is highly probable that these specimens represent only a small part of the actual quantity of flakes that might be expected in this class of implements. More unretouched but utilized flakes may have existed in Areas 6 and 7 at Murray Springs, but recent edge damage and thousands of years of exposure have served to make their identification less than certain.

The Blade and Blade Tool Mode

There exists at Murray Springs positive evidence for Clovis blade technology, both in the form of several blade tools and perhaps on-the-spot blade manufacture. The site has yielded 13 artifacts, not including the end scrapers described above, that are classifiable as blades or tools made on blades. Eight of these are blades or blade fragments that do not bear any intentional post-detachment retouch, although five display edge damage that is probably attributable to use. The remaining five include two that exhibit retouch on the distal end, one laterally retouched blade, and one with distal retouch and paired lateral notches. Table 8.9 presents the basic attributes of the blades, and Figures 8.12 and 8.13 illustrate a selection of them.

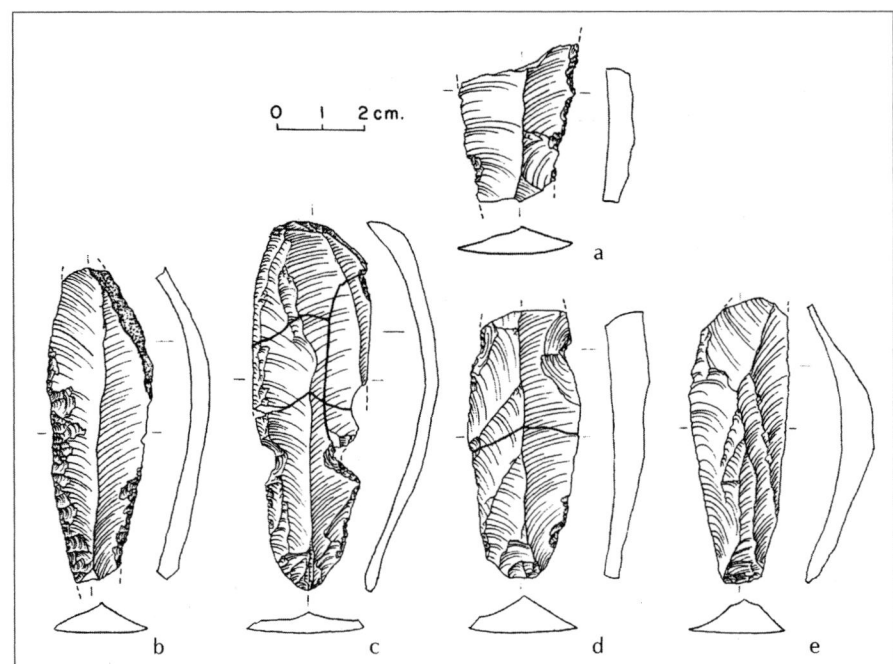

Figure 8.12. Clovis retouched and utilized blade tools from Murray Springs: *a*, utilized blade fragment; *b*, *c*, retouched blades; *d*, *e*, utilized blades.

All but two of the blades from the site are termed *typical blades* (Fig. 8.12). These typical blades are all true blades produced from prepared cores, not simply fortuitous, bladelike flakes; they conform to the definition of a blade proposed by Bordes and Crabtree (1969: 1). Those that are sufficiently complete to permit measurement (5) average 62.5 mm in length by 25.0 mm in width by 8.8 mm in thickness and are single ridge blades with triangular cross-sections. All but one of those blades that retain them display striking platforms that were carefully prepared in bifacial fashion and then heavily ground. One blade (Fig. 8.12c) has a featureless, plain striking platform. Three of the complete or nearly complete blades display a marked curvature in longitudinal section (Fig. 8.12*b*, *c*, and *e*). Three major raw materials are represented: a gray chalcedony, a light brownish gray fossiliferous chert, and a pink silicified siltstone. However, it is probable that these blades were derived from a minimum of seven different pieces of raw material among these major groups.

A second variety of blade is represented by two extremely large, massive specimens that are termed *large blades* (Fig. 8.13*d* and *e*). One (Fig. 8.13*d*) bears an end scraper on its distal end and the other displays retouch on its lateral margins and exterior surface; both are of pink silicified siltstone and may be from the same core. Although they lack striking platforms and display less curvature in their longitudinal sections, they appear to be technologically identical to the typical blades. Two fragmentary pointed tools from Lehner with converging retouched margins (Haury and others 1959, Fig. 14*a*, *b*) may also have been manufactured from large blades.

Under low power magnification, five typical blades show nicking and microspalling along their lateral margins suggestive of utilization. Two of the utilized specimens are illustrated in Figure 8.12*d* and *e*; a third utilized blade fragment (Fig. 8.12*a*) was recovered from the surface of Area 7. The last specimen is a segment of an intentionally broken blade that bears prominent nicking, spalling, and polish along both lateral margins; on the vertical face at the distal end there is an obvious negative bulb of percussion that represents the place where a blow was delivered to the exterior surface to segment the blade. A corresponding area of crushing on the interior surface of that broken distal end may indicate that the blade was resting on an anvil when it was segmented. The proximal end of the segment also exhibits evidence of an intentional break in the form of a negative bulb of percussion on the vertically broken edge. The two working edges of the implement measure 28 mm and 32 mm in length. It is conceivable that this blade segment was designed to be

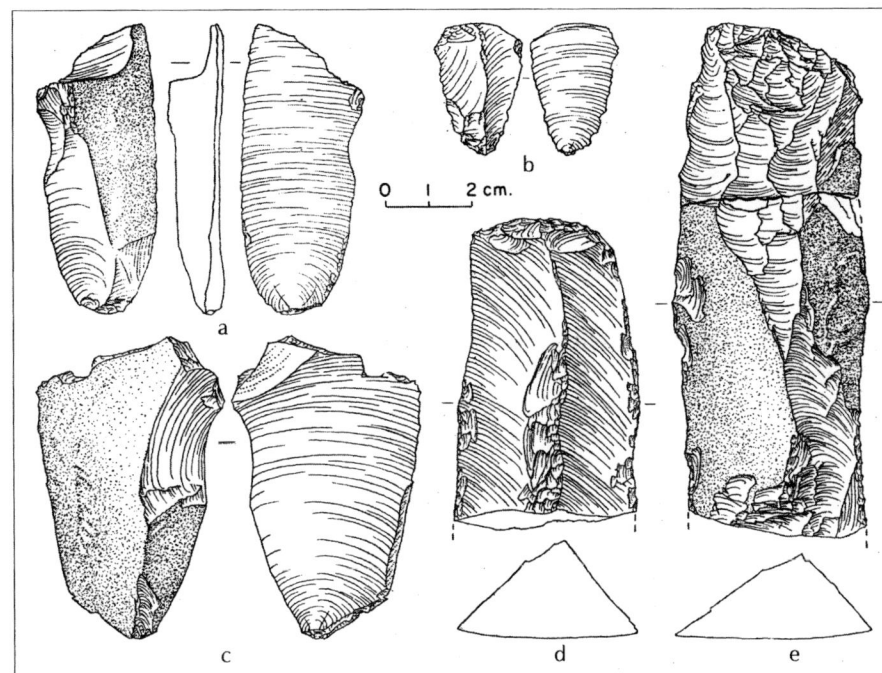

Figure 8.13. Clovis large blade tools and possible blades from Murray Springs: *a*, hinge fracture recovery blade; *b*, misstruck blade(?); *c*, misstruck primary blade(?); *d*, large blade fragment with end scraper; *e*, large retouched blade fragment.

used in a slotted bone haft similar to those from Upper Paleolithic Ukrainian sites (Klein 1973, Fig. 13) and later prehistoric North American Plains sites (Caldwell and Jensen 1969, Plate 31*a–d*; Lehmer and Jones 1968, Plate 15*a–c*). A possible bone tool handle of this type has been recovered from the Navarrete Site (Huckell 1981).

Two of the remaining three typical blades are interpreted as examples of "missed" or improperly struck blades (Fig. 8.13*b–c*), and the third appears to be a hinge fracture recovery blade (Fig. 8.13*a*) struck from one end of the core to help clear a hinge fracture termination. These blade artifacts all come from two clusters of silicified siltstone debitage in the surface camp (A7-7, A7-8) and are discussed in more detail below.

The five retouched blades or blade fragments include three well formed implements and two that may have been broken during retouching. A laterally retouched typical blade from Area 4 (Fig. 8.12*b*) bears a fine, even, unifacial retouch along most of one lateral margin and approximately half of the opposite margin, creating two relatively acute working edges. Such an implement likely served in a cutting capacity. Other possible examples of blades or blade fragments bearing lateral retouch have been described from Blackwater Draw (Warnica 1966, Fig. 4*h–k*). A second retouched typical blade from Area 6 (Fig. 8.12*c*) bears retouch on its distal end, apparently designed to construct an end scraper, and has two notches positioned opposite one another on the lateral margins one-third the distance from the striking platform to the distal end of the blade. These notches may have been designed to aid in hafting the implement, although it is also possible that they were intended to serve some other purpose. This specimen was reconstructed from five fragments and appears to be a unique Clovis tool form at this time.

A distal fragment of a probable typical blade (Fig. 7.9*e*) was found in Area 6 that bears a steep, unifacial retouch apparently designed to remove the hinge fracture termination in which the blade ended. It is conceivable that this operation was unsuccessful; part of the hinge fracture remains and the blade is broken at a large impurity in the material 38 mm above the hinge termination. Possibly the retouching operation caused sufficient shock to initiate the break at the weak point caused by the impurity.

The two final retouched blade implements from Murray Springs are both on large blades with thick triangular cross sections. One is an end scraper constructed on the distal end of a distal large blade fragment. The working edge is evenly retouched (Fig. 8.13*d*), and both lateral margins bear an irregular series of small unifacial flakes. In addition, an obvious retouch series has been removed from the exterior ridge and is believed to relate to the manufacture of the blade and not the function of the tool.

The second implement (Fig. 8.13e) is a laterally retouched fragment of a large blade that also bears obvious scars along its exterior ridge; although the scars are mostly directed longitudinally instead of transversely, they apparently were an attempt to thin the blade segment from the ends. One of these flakes caused a hinge-through break, but both of the resulting fragments appear to have been worked further after the break. Occasional flake scars along the lateral margins of the larger fragment do not create a uniform working edge.

Two fragmentary pointed tools from Lehner may have been made on large blades (Haury and others 1959, Fig. 14a, b), based on their size and marked degree of curvature in the longitudinal axis; in this regard they differ noticeably from the large laterally retouched flake tools. Both bear extensive lateral retouch and were recovered from a mammoth kill and butchering context.

Blade Technology

Although it is not appropriate to speak of Clovis as a blade industry, it is nevertheless clear that the Clovis flint knappers in Arizona had the technical knowledge to produce these specialized flakes consistently and at will. Further, this skill was not limited to one geographic area; Clovis blades technologically identical to those at Murray Springs were first recognized at Blackwater Draw (Green 1963), and are also reported from central Arizona (Huckell 1978a: 66–68), Virginia (Callahan 1979: 88–89; Haynes 1972, Fig. 4b, c), and the Northeast (Byers 1954, Fig. 92h; Witthoft 1952: 473–476). In addition, Hammatt (1970) has reported an isolated cache of 26 blades, two blade cores, two core choppers, and two large bifaces inferred to be of Paleoindian, possibly Clovis, age. The cache was found near Anadarko, Oklahoma. Stoltman (1971) has described eight blades and an end scraper, apparently from a cache and possibly of Paleoindian age, found in northern Minnesota.

The blades from Murray Springs and casts of the blades from Blackwater Draw are the only ones that I have personally examined, but they display consistent technical features that indicate Clovis expertise in blade manufacture. First and most obvious is the method of striking platform construction. The knapper first selected a ridge on the core face to guide the blade, then removed a few small flakes down the core face from the striking platform, thus eliminating the "overhang" caused by negative bulbs of percussion from previous blade removals. Second, he removed a series of small flakes across the striking platform surface from the core face, principally from the areas immediately adjacent to the ridge on the core face, thus creating a markedly convex, bifacially prepared striking platform that was well isolated from the remaining core platform perimeter. At Murray Springs, the striking platform was then ground, completing its preparation; judging from the casts, the Blackwater Draw blades apparently also exhibit this platform abrasion.

One other feature that is present on several of the Clovis blades from both Murray Springs and Blackwater Draw is core face or ridge preparation. The ridges left by previous blade removals were used to guide subsequent blades down the core face; due to slight variations in applied force and raw material texture, it is not uncommon for these ridges to be slightly irregular, curving from side to side or having places of greater or lesser height. To produce blades that are reasonably straight in the long dimension and to insure a clean, even fracture in blade removal, these ridges may be straightened and evened by percussion. This ridge preparation creates a small series of flakes removed from the ridge in a direction perpendicular to the axis of blade removal; Figure 8.13a and d illustrate examples of such ridge preparation on typical and large blades, as does the blade fragment illustrated in Figure 7.9c. Four blades from Murray Springs and four blades from Blackwater Draw exhibit this feature. Green (1963: 156) also noted this feature on the Blackwater Draw blades, although he interpreted it as resulting from use.

Such care in core preparation is clear evidence of in-depth knowledge of blade manufacture, but several aspects of Clovis blade manufacture remain unknown. One aspect is the form or forms of the cores from which the blades were struck. A single blade core, possibly of Clovis age, comes from the surface of the Williamson Site (Haynes 1972, Fig. 4b); it conforms technologically to what an exhausted Clovis blade core could be expected to look like. Other blade cores that could also approximate Clovis cores in appearance are the two reported from Anadarko, Oklahoma (Hammatt 1970, Fig. 2a), though these are not precisely dated.

Of interest is the presence of both bifacial and plain or cortical striking platforms on these cores.

The method by which Clovis flint knappers detached the blades from the core remains unknown, though experimental work suggests two possibilities: indirect percussion with a punch, or direct percussion with a soft hammer. Indirect percussion is usually cited as the manufacturing method for Clovis blades (Green 1963; Hammatt 1970), and it is possible to produce blades within the range of the Blackwater Draw and Murray Springs specimens using either the Corbiac blade technique (Bordes and Crabtree 1969) or the *sous le pied* method advanced by Tixier (1972). However, it is also possible to produce blades indistinguishable from the known Clovis specimens by direct percussion with a heavier antler hammer (Newcomer 1975). On the basis of the experimentation that has been done thus far there does not seem to be sufficient evidence on which to base a decision as to which method was used by the Clovis artisans; both indirect percussion and soft hammer direct percussion remain possibilities.

It is possible that blade production was being undertaken in Area 7 at Murray Springs (Fig. 8.2). This area yielded two dispersed clusters of silicified siltstone flakes (A7-7 and A7-8) that consisted largely of percussion flakes; however, several fragments of a burned core and four blades of the same material were also recovered here. Three of the four blades are interpreted as errors in manufacture, and the fourth was designed to remove the effects of another manufacturing error from the core. The three misstruck blades include one that terminated in a hinge fracture 29 mm down the core face (Fig. 8.13*b*); one that was struck too near the edge of the platform, resulting in a shallow, narrow blade; and one in which the platform was not sufficiently isolated from the edge of the core, thus causing the blade to expand excessively (Fig. 8.13*c*). All three of these misstruck blades exhibit the same platform preparation as do the more successfully detached blades. The fourth blade (Fig. 8.13*a*) was struck to remove a hinge fracture termination created by an apparently unsuccessful effort to detach a blade. Removal of the hinge termination was achieved by creating a bifacially prepared, heavily ground striking platform at the opposite end of the core and using it to drive a blade in the opposite direction, toward the original striking platform from which the hinge-terminated blade had been detached. The nonblade flakes all appear to be percussion, though some display the platform and bulbar characteristics of hard hammer flakes and others seem to be more typical of soft hammer flakes. It is emphasized that these are not the normal biface thinning and retouching flakes most common at Murray Springs, although bifacial (faceted) striking platforms are dominant among them.

Unfortunately, the possible blade core from Area 7 has been badly burned and fractured into small pieces; no estimate of its original size or configuration could be obtained from the 19 fragments of it that were recovered. Two portions of it reconstructed from fragments indicate that it was bifacial in part, though it is not possible to determine what part of the core these portions represent. One portion could represent the striking platform/core face juncture, and the other fragment could represent part of the core face on which a ridge was being prepared bifacially. The core may have been still functional or it may represent an exhausted or aborted effort at blade production.

Considering the A7-7 and A7-8 clusters together, I propose that this assemblage of debitage, core fragments, and blades represents the on-the-spot preparation and shaping of one or more cores and the removal of blades. Because the core has been so badly fragmented and because only a sample of the area producing the siltstone flakes has been excavated, it is not possible at this time to further support this proposal.

The point to be stressed is that there is accumulating evidence that the Clovis industry includes the manufacture of true blades from prepared cores. Although these are definitely not the central feature or basis of the industry, neither are they flakes "...incidentally removed from bifaces during the normal course of reduction" (Callahan 1979: 89). Additional data are needed to permit a more complete understanding of this mode, but there should be no doubt as to the existence of blade manufacture as part of the Clovis industry in the western United States.

The Expediency Mode

A minor but nonetheless important aspect of the Clovis lithic repertoire is the production of what may be termed expediency tools. This term has been applied to bone implements in the past (Johnson 1985), but is equally applicable to stone tools. These expediency tools are produced quickly from materials at

Figure 8.14. Clovis expedient tools from Murray Springs: *a*, retouched silicified limestone nodule; *b*, broken and retouched metasandstone cobble; *c*, unmodified metasandstone cobble. Length of *b* is 17.5 cm.

hand, and in the case of Murray Springs and the other San Pedro Valley sites, they consist of modified cobbles. The cobbles were obtained either from nearby deposits of lag gravels or from exposures of buried cobble deposits (Nexpa or Millville gravels), and were either modified by a few percussion blows or used as they were found. Three specimens are known from Murray Springs and one from Lehner.

The first Murray Springs tool is an elongated, cylindrical cobble (Fig. 8.14*b*) of metasandstone from Area 4, measuring 17.5 cm in length by approximately 7.0 cm in average diameter, and weighing 1532 g. One end has been broken off either intentionally or naturally, and the resulting broken edge has been sharpened by the removal of a few percussion flakes. A second quartzite or metasandstone cobble (Fig. 8.14*c*) was found in Area 3. It measures 18.0 cm in maximum dimension and weighs 1745 g; it does not appear to have been modified prior to utilization but displays a slightly rounded and battered end. A broken silicified limestone cobble (Fig. 8.14*a*) weighing 430 g and bearing what appear to be intentionally retouched margins was recovered from Area 3. This retouch occurs on three separate positions, in each case creating a steep (nearly 90°) working edge; the function of this tool is unknown.

From Lehner comes a smaller quartzite cobble measuring 12 cm long, 11 cm wide, and 4 cm thick. One lateral margin has been irregularly flaked, partly bifacially, by a series of percussion blows (Haury and others 1959, Fig. 14*h*).

It is probable that these tools were designed to aid in butchering tasks such as dismemberment or the severing of muscle origins and insertions. Similar tools have been reported from the Colby Site in Wyoming (Frison 1977: 105–106, 1978a, Fig. 3.12), including at least one cobble that was used as a hammer without any modification.

DISCUSSION

Perhaps the greatest value of the flaked stone assemblage from the Murray Springs Site is the broader view that it permits of the technological richness and sophistication of the Clovis industry. The high quality workmanship and beauty of the few artifacts recovered from kill sites such as Naco and Lehner have long been recognized, but they are only glimpses into what is without question the most technologically sophisticated flaked stone industry known from the prehistoric Southwest. With the addition of the Murray Springs tools and particularly the debitage, we can finally see much, if not all, of the range of implement forms and technological approaches used by a people whose not-so-distant ancestors were born in the Old World.

The most outstanding aspect of the Murray Springs assemblage is undoubtedly the documentation it provides of the key role filled by the biface in the Clovis industry. Although the Clovis emphasis on bifaces has been recognized as a technological factor that separates it from both Eurasian Paleolithic and putatively older New World industries, the specific manner in which the biface was used by Clovis flint knappers has not been so clear.

With the Murray Springs data it becomes possible to infer the existence of a range of biface sizes; the existence of two different stages of biface reduction based on size, configuration, and reduction strategy; and the uses to which bifaces were put. Undoubtedly bifaces were used as functional implements, as cores for useful flakes, and as an easily transported supply of raw material to serve anticipated needs, as shown not only by complete and fragmentary bifaces but by the many clusters of waste flakes and the flakes that were modified for other purposes.

The knapping loci reveal that when used, bifaces seem to have been retouched sparingly; when in need of major refurbishing, the work was done carefully to remove only what was necessary to thin and shape the piece. Apparently they left the quarry as large primary bifaces, roughly ovate in shape and thinned to remove most of the cortex, irregularities, and flaws. They were subsequently flaked by the selective removal of large, single flakes that not only radically thinned them but also yielded flakes of sufficient size to be modified into other implements. At some point, perhaps when they reached the desired thinness and a size of 65 mm wide and 150 mm long or thereabouts, they were flaked into keen-edged, probably leaf-shaped secondary bifaces designed to serve primarily as knives. From this stage on they were probably resharpened as needed, and when necessary they were worked by the removal of smaller flakes, often removed in serial fashion, to maintain the desired ratio of width to thickness. In this form and manner they could serve for a long time, until they became too small or a new projectile point was needed. Then, with a relative minimum of effort, they were finished into projectile points.

The role of bifaces in the technology is obviously pivotal in the San Pedro Valley, but to what extent it is the product of local conditions or preferences and to what extent it is "typical" of Clovis as a whole is difficult to assess. As careful and waste-conscious as the pattern of biface reduction seems to be, is it possible that it is due to raw material constraints, a reflection of a group operating in a region where they were not certain of finding lithic material sources for replenishment? Clearly their last stop at a quarry had been at a source of St. David Chalcedony, probably somewhere in the vicinity of the present town of St. David about 40 km (25 miles) north of Murray Springs. Most of the debitage, two of the three primary bifaces, a core fragment, and a number of larger flakes (both from cores and bifaces) are of this material, indicating that they took the opportunity to replenish a dwindling stock of material at that quarry. Without being able to assign the other raw materials to particular sources it is not possible to ascertain the size of the area across which this particular group was operating. It may be significant that other western United States Clovis sites show this same strategy of parsimonious material use, for example the large primary and secondary bifaces from the Simon Site (Butler 1963), those from the Anzick Site (Lahren and Bonnichsen 1974), and the few from the Sheaman Locality at Agate Basin (Bradley 1982). It thus seems that similar strategies of biface use were followed by Clovis hunters on the northern Plains as well. This pattern may reflect their attempt to deal with the problems posed by covering large "territories" with relatively great distances between known sources of high quality materials. If the model of rapid spread of Clovis hunters is accurate (Mosimann and Martin 1975), the strategy may also be viewed as a response to movement into areas where the existence of suitable raw materials was completely unknown. In any case, there was an apparent concern with the efficiency of taking along lithic material in the form or forms that would at once answer the needs of tool use and manufacture, and yet maximize ease of transport. Relatively high group mobility can be inferred from such a pattern.

Another important aspect of the Murray Springs assemblage is the presence of blades and blade tools in the Clovis industry. These are true blades removed from prepared cores, not by-products of the biface reduction process. They were used either just as they came from the core or were retouched on the lateral or distal margins to produce a variety of tool forms. Certain technological features bespeak sophisticated understanding of the production of blades, including the detailed attention to platform preparation, the straightening (when necessary) of the ridge that would guide the blade, and the knowledge of how to recover from errors of manufacture. It is interesting and perhaps significant that blades do not appear widely in western or eastern Clovis assemblages. The blades reported by Green (1963) and the apparent retouched blade tools reported by Warnica (1966, Fig. 4), all from Blackwater Draw, are the only other well-documented Clovis blades. No securely associated Clovis blade cores are known, although one may have been present in Area 7 at Murray Springs. Specimens of cores such as the one from the Williamson Site, Virginia, illustrated by Haynes (1972), and the two reported by Hammatt (1970) from near Anadarko, Oklahoma, provide examples of the forms Clovis blade cores may have taken.

The absence of blade cores at sites such as Murray Springs and Blackwater Draw is significant in understanding the functioning of blade tools in the Clovis system. Blades representing a minimum of five cores were recovered from Murray Springs, but there was only one questionable core, suggesting that two possible approaches to blade manufacture may have existed: either blades were produced at a quarry and those deemed useful were carefully packaged and carried away with the group, or the cores themselves were carried along and blades were struck from them as the need arose. If the badly burned specimen present in Area 7 was a blade core, the latter approach to blade manufacture may be indicated; certainly the misstruck blade and hinge fracture recovery blade from Area 7 do not represent examples of blades likely to be carried away from a quarry. However, carrying along a large, preformed blade core would seem to violate the apparent attempt by Clovis artisans to minimize the weight of transported lithic material. One might ask whether the Area 7 silicified siltstone blades and core could represent an attempt to manufacture blades from a piece of material that was obtained nearby; unfortunately that cannot be ascertained because the source of the material has not been positively identified. There is other evidence to suggest blade manufacture at a quarry and transportation of selected blades for later use. The blades reported by Green (1963) from Blackwater Draw were apparently deposited as a cache and represent a minimum of seven separate nodules. The Murray Springs blades represent at least five cores. Such data argue more strongly for the first approach and would also be more consistent with transport constraints. On the other hand, the possibly Clovis blade cache reported by Hammatt (1970) contained two blade cores and 26 blades of gray flint, along with two large bifaces and two chopping tools. The bifaces and chopping tools included one specimen each of gray flint and Alibates flint. In this case the blade cores had been previously flaked but were still transported from the quarry, perhaps a distance of 320 km (199 miles). Clearly more information is needed before it will be possible to understand which of these two strategies, or perhaps both, may have been followed.

As a final note on blades, I see no basis for the argument that Clovis is a blade-based industry. I cannot agree with West's (1981: 187) assertion that Clovis is a core and blade industry, or his characterization of the Clovis point as "little more than a pointed, face-faceted blade core." Certainly the bulk of Clovis tool forms were not constructed on blades like the classic European Upper Paleolithic industries, nor can blades even remotely be described as common. Rather, they seem to form a relatively less important facet of the lithic technological repertoire. Not only is this suggested by their comparative rarity, but by the fact that slightly younger Paleoindian sites do not produce them at all, although flakes of bladelike appearance may be recognized. These facts may suggest that with the Clovis industry we are seeing the last vestiges of blade manufacture and use, the passing of a technology no longer central to the industry as a whole.

Murray Springs has also expanded significantly the range of flake tools known from the San Pedro Valley and helps show the importance of this aspect of the technological system. A variety of forms of laterally retouched flakes, in a range of sizes suitable for many kinds of tasks, and made on both core flakes and biface reduction flakes, can be documented. These specimens are still too few in number to permit more than a tentative classificatory typology, but they clearly served in butchering contexts, functioned as scraping tools, and fulfilled roles that seem to include piercing and detailed finishing of bone or wood implements or hides. Large flakes were struck from cores with prepared striking platforms and perhaps prepared faces, although the Murray Springs assemblage is lacking in examples of these cores. The same approaches discussed for blade manufacture also apply in this situation; the large flakes may be quarry products carried in that form or may have been produced from transported cores as needed. There are clusters of debitage at the site that include hard hammer flakes, particularly in the A3–5a cluster, but they are mixed with soft hammer flakes. Such clusters may represent core preparation and reduction or incipient modification of large flakes into bifaces using a hammerstone. Aside from one core fragment of St. David Chalcedony from Area 7, we have no knowledge of the form or forms that such cores took, nor of the flake production strategy or strategies. It is certain that we have much to learn about this aspect of Clovis lithic technology.

The final facet of the Clovis industry is that represented by expediency tools. These implements take the form of large cobbles, simply flaked to produce a working edge, or in some cases used as found. They seem to have served principally for heavy duty butchering work and were produced as needed from whatever large cobbles were available on the spot, with little regard to material. They served the necessary task and were left where they were dropped; there was nothing to be gained by transporting them, for they were easily obtained and made.

The Murray Springs Site, in conjunction with other San Pedro Valley sites, has allowed a detailed view of the basics of the Clovis lithic technological system as it was manifested in this particular valley. More specific information can yet be obtained from this collection of material by investigating the sources of the materials and the details of the debitage itself. I hope that this treatment of the assemblage from Murray Springs will be of value in furthering understanding of these early hunters and their flaked stone industry and in stimulating further research.

Note: Chapter 8 is based on an analysis of the Murray Springs tools and debitage conducted by Huckell while serving as a Research Assistant to Vance Haynes from 1974 through 1976. He expanded the study in 1981 by incorporating data from the lithic assemblages recovered from other Clovis sites in the San Pedro Valley and using those data to explore Clovis lithic technology more broadly. He revised the chapter in 1986.

CHAPTER NINE

Clovis Paleoecology as Viewed from Murray Springs, Arizona

Bruce B. Huckell and C. Vance Haynes, Jr.

Murray Springs is the most remarkable site recorded in a valley long known for its stunning concentration of Clovis sites. Of all the San Pedro Valley sites, it possesses the most extensive, detailed record of Clovis hunting, butchering, and camp activity; of the lithic tool assemblage; and of technological organization and land use, all in a stratigraphic record documenting late Pleistocene and early Holocene environmental change. We estimate that more than 98 percent of the artifacts and debitage recovered from Areas 1, 3, 4, and 5 were recorded in situ, attesting to the incredible integrity of the site. The kill in Area 3 adds to the chronicle of mammoth hunting so well represented in the valley, and the multiple bison kill in Area 4 provides a new dimension to our understanding of Clovis subsistence and hunting capability.

The camp in Areas 6 and 7 is unique in the San Pedro Valley and affords an unprecedented look at a short-term residential locus adjacent to a kill site. No place in the valley has yielded such a large and varied sample of Clovis implements and debitage or offered such a detailed look at Clovis technological organization as well as patterns of land use and mobility. Capping it all, the incredible detail of the alluvial stratigraphic context affords new insights into late Pleistocene-early Holocene climate, environment, and faunal change both within the valley and across the Southwest.

Of the three mammoths at Murray Springs, only two (in Area 1 and Area 3) were likely acted upon by Clovis people. On the basis of the stratigraphic position of the bones, the Area 1 mammoth died before the Area 3 mammoth. We cannot tell if it was killed or scavenged. A scapula resting on the mandible and a thoracic vertebra on top of that suggests the work of humans. The lack of associated artifacts, other than four flakes that could be a part of the Area 3 scatter, indicates that the Area 1 mammoth probably had a natural death that occurred on the streambed when the sand and gravel bedload was saturated. The penetration of bones deep into the streambed may be due to subsequent mammoth traffic as indicated by footprints.

The Area 3 mammoth was more intact and had artifacts in clear association. Of the three projectile points, two are tip fragments that were produced by breakage upon impact. The third is a complete Clovis point but it lacks basal grinding and appears unfinished. All three were found 2 m to 4 m northeast of the mammoth's skull and roughly equal distances west of a few bison elements. Further evidence of human interaction with the mammoth is a missing hind leg and the occurrence of a mammoth long bone in the Clovis camp. Most of the other hind leg had been moved up by the skull. All of the foot bones were missing. Some may have been carried off by scavengers but parts of the feet may have been eaten by the hunters. Historically, some native hunters of the African elephant considered the foot pads to be delicacies (Sikes 1971b: 17). We conclude that the Area 3 mammoth was killed by Clovis hunters. A less likely alternative is that they scavenged the carcass, in which case the projectile points might have been a part of the bison kill.

The evidence for the killing of at least 11 bison by Clovis people is the direct association of at least six Clovis points with the bison skeletal remains, or seven if one point just into Area 5 is included. Add to this the associated flake concentrations, the scatter of butchering tools and hammerstones, at least two hearths, and the impact flakes and scars, and the evidence becomes compelling.

The Area 6 and 7 camp is thus far unique to Murray Springs in the San Pedro Valley, and only the recently excavated camps at the Aubrey Site (Ferring 2001) and Gault (Collins 2002) are comparable to it. Much of the activity in the camp appears to center around the processing of meat and hides derived from the Area 4 bison kill. Tip replacement on weapons and other tool maintenance tasks occurred there, perhaps again relating to the Area 4 bison kill but possibly associated with some other occupational episode at the site.

Thirty-five years have passed since the final field season at Murray Springs, an interval during which considerable change has occurred in the theoretical and empirical landscape of Clovis and Paleoindian research. Debates have arisen over these three and a half decades, including the nature of Clovis ecology and land use, the timing and course of human colonization of the New World, the human role (or lack thereof) in megafaunal extinction, and the environmental dynamics of the late glacial and postglacial periods. These topics are closely related and discussion of any one typically entails aspects of the others. Theoretical sophistication has grown rapidly in the treatment of hunter-gatherer ecology, based in large part on developments in ecological theory for the study of human and nonhuman foraging. In the empirical realm, Clovis sites in the western United States that were discovered and excavated since the end of the Murray Springs project have contributed considerable new information about these issues but have done little to promote consensus about, let alone resolve, most of the debated topics. These sites include Aubrey (Ferring 2001), Colby (Frison and Todd 1986), East Wenatchee (Mehringer 1988; Gramly 1993), Fenn (Frison and Bradley 1999), Gault (Collins 2002), Keven Davis (Collins 1999), Lange-Ferguson (Hannus 1990), Navarrete (Huckell 1981), and Pavo Real (Collins and others 2003). Our purpose in this closing chapter is to examine how the knowledge gained from the six seasons of work at Murray Springs can contribute to discussions of Clovis diet, Clovis land use, and human involvement in megafaunal extinction.

CLOVIS DIET: SPECIALISTS, GENERALISTS, OR OTHER?

Debates concerning Clovis diet have spanned more than 40 years and reflect different readings of the empirical data and applications of ethnologic research as well as ecological and anthropological theoretical perspectives. The empirical record, which is the basis for the early perspective of Clovis as elephant-hunters (Haynes 1966; Sellards 1952), has more recently been called into question (Meltzer 1993) as a reliable source of information on Clovis diet, both in the western United States where most of the known kill sites were excavated from the 1930s through the 1970s and in the eastern part of the country where preservation is poor and the environment is different. Views of subsistence have changed accordingly, shifting from early portrayals of Clovis people as mammoth-hunting specialists who disdained both small mammals and most things vegetal, to more recent characterizations of them as generalist hunter-gatherers who managed an occasional large mammal kill. Today, supporters of the specialist view point to the evidence from excavated large mammal kill sites, whereas those comfortable with the generalist interpretation suggest that those few kill-butchery sites only provide a biased sampling of the archaeological record. Those supporting the generalist model offer the testimony of the ethnological record of hunter-gatherer diet breadth; the specialist camp counters with arguments of a lack of analogous environmental and demographic conditions among recent foraging societies. Interestingly, both groups support their positions using arguments founded in behavioral ecology, albeit emphasizing slightly different perspectives within that general body of theory and research (Bettinger 1991: 83–111; Kelly 1995: 50–110).

Theoretical Perspectives on Large Mammal Hunting

Arguably the best known and most influential of the recent treatments of Early Paleoindian (essentially Clovis, Folsom, and other fluted point makers) foraging is that of Kelly and Todd (1988), who proposed that Clovis hunters were focused on hunting large mammals, although they were not exclusively hunting large game. They based this conclusion on the existing archaeological record, suggesting that the energetic returns from this strategy were high in relation to costs as long as there was an abundance of large mammals and that the foragers had the technology to support the procurement and processing of these animals. Human population densities across North America were low, and when preferred large mammal species became scarce in a particular area due to hunting-related animal population declines, the foragers simply moved to a new area that contained the same large mammals and continued their basic pattern of hunting. This subsistence was facilitated by a technology that supported exploitation of large mammals and by detailed knowledge of the behavior and ecology of those mammals. Because this strategy was successful and the distribution of key large mammal species such as proboscideans and bison was continent-wide, there was little need to remain in areas of declining resource returns and reorder or broaden the diet to include other, lower-ranked resources. Kelly and Todd argued that Early Paleoindians were technology-oriented rather than place-oriented, and therefore the archaeological record of their behavior is generally similar across huge areas of the North American continent. Only after megafaunal extinction and human population growth were they forced to devise new strategies; therefore, the use of ethnographic analogy with contemporary or recent foragers is inappropriate. Early Paleoindians existed under environmental and demographic conditions that have no Holocene equivalents. Waguespack and Surovell (2003) have examined the empirical record of kill sites and interpret it to support the Kelly and Todd model of relative specialization in large animal prey species. Buchanan (2005) has evaluated the technological and chronological similarities among Early Paleoindian projectile points and tool assemblages across the continent and found them to be closely similar, in accord with predicted rapid spread and technological consistency elements of the model.

Meltzer (1993, 2002, 2004; also see Cannon and Meltzer 2004; Grayson and Meltzer 2002) has argued that what he terms large mammal specialization is rare among recent hunting-gathering societies and has suggested that it can only exist in restricted environmental settings characterized by large or abundant prey species with high reproductive rates, high energy content per unit weight, reliable and predictable distributions, and if those species can be exploited at low levels of risk. In his view, late Pleistocene environments, often consisting of biotic communities without contemporary equivalents, were species-rich, although whether open, treeless environments supported large animal herds like those known historically is uncertain. He offered the possibility that late Pleistocene bison were not present in herds as large as those represented by the much greater numbers of animals in post-Folsom kills. Meltzer suggested that the varied late Pleistocene environments of North America would have promoted diversity in Clovis and later (post-megafaunal extinction) subsistence practices and he supported this interpretation by pointing to the existence of distinct regional styles of projectile points and lithic tool assemblages. He also argued that mammoth and mastodon kill sites are overrepresented in the archaeological record due to their comparative ease of discovery. Large mammal bones protruding from arroyo banks or inadvertently discovered in lacustrine settings are hard to miss, and so archaeological attention is drawn to such locales. Finding associated Clovis artifacts effectively biases the record in favor of large mammal kills, whereas the subtle signatures of campsites or less spectacular manifestations are more easily overlooked. Finally, he suggested that large mammal (especially proboscidean) hunting was too risky to be a viable strategy as a subsistence base (also see Byers and Ugan 2005).

More recently, Gary Haynes (2002) has presented a different perspective on Clovis large mammal hunting, particularly of mammoth and mastodon, again based in the realm of behavioral ecological theory. He observed that more recent investigators have rejected the notion that resources are harvested by foragers in proportion to their abundances in the environment, and that instead diets are the product of conscious forager choice. The application of diet breadth models, those that examine the choice and ranking of items that compose the diet, permits an understanding of the factors that encourage foragers to choose how to structure their subsistence. Particular foods may be high-ranked (always taken when encountered) or low-ranked (taken only when higher-ranked resources are unavailable or under conditions of risk aversion on the part of the forager). Rank is generally modeled as being predicted by the relative energy expended in search time and handling time. Diet breadth (the number of ranked items within the diet) may be narrow, consisting of a few items that have high return rates (calories gained versus calories expended in pursuit, capture, and processing) or are easily harvested. Conversely, diet breadth may be broad, incorporating many items of varying rank but often relying heavily on lower-ranked foods (such as plant foods, possibly abundant but necessitating increased handling). The diet breadth model predicts that high-ranked resources will always be taken when encountered, even under conditions of high risk, and G. Haynes (2002: 215–229) developed a scenario in which mammoths would have been a high-ranked resource for Clovis hunters. He suggested that as late Pleistocene environments changed in structure and distribution, mammoths may have become restricted to but abundant in refugia, patches that contained the water and food resources they needed to survive. If this were the case, hunters familiar with mammoth ecology and behavior would have known how to recognize such patches; the signs of contemporary elephant presence within a particular environmental patch (trails and dung boluses) are not subtle (G. Haynes 2002, Fig. 5.3). In addition, G. Haynes stressed that changes in diet breadth are unlikely to occur until populations are forced to make them. That is, if proboscideans (and other large mammals) are highly ranked, they will remain so, and foragers will not cease to target them until forced to do so by extinction. Thus, Clovis foraging would continue to be dominated by the search for those refugia that contained proboscideans.

In writings following his 1993 paper, Meltzer (2002, 2004) emphasized the importance of landscape learning, the development of specific knowledge of available resources, to foraging success and subsistence stability. His concern is with explaining why colonizing populations might behave differently than later occupants of the same region. Colonizing populations, such as Clovis, were at some disadvantage because they lacked familiarity with the nature and distribution of resources in particular areas. For them, developing a subsistence strategy involved resolving five competing demands: (1) maintaining resource returns; (2) minimizing group size; (3) maximizing mobility; (4) staying as long as possible in resource-rich habitats; and (5) maintaining contact among dispersed social groups. Meltzer proposed a model he feels is an optimal solution to these competing demands, the "minimizing-uncertainty-and-demographic-risk" (MUDR) model.

The primary differences between the MUDR model and the models of G. Haynes and Kelly and Todd are that with the former, settling into megapatches and diversification or reorganization of subsistence resources would be expected. In the G. Haynes and Kelly and Todd models, large mammals remain the top-ranked resource choices, and only when the return rates for them drop below a satisfactory level (which could be zero) will the hunters move to a new patch to continue hunting the same high-ranked large mammals. This process continues as long as movement is possible and large mammals remain to be hunted. Certainly at the point when those conditions change new subsistence strategies, presumably tailored to smaller geographic scales, must have developed. It is important to recognize that Early Paleoindian fluted point industries span nearly 1,000 years, an interval that encompasses extinction of the megafauna. As proboscideans and other large mammals dwindled in numbers and disappeared, humans were ultimately faced with the need to adapt their subsistence practices. By at least 10,700 B.P. across North America, this process was underway, with evidence of changes in diet breadth and patch choice. Detailed understanding of the dynamics of the late Pleistocene environment across North America as it was found by Clovis people is poor, but is critical to all these models. Specific knowledge of the numbers, density, and availability of animal prey species is of crucial importance if we are to understand the framework within which Clovis people made subsistence choices. Were animals already reduced in numbers by the termimal Pleistocene environmental changes (V. Haynes 1991), or were they abundant and widely distributed (Waguespack and Surovell 2003)? This is a difficult question to answer with assurance because the paleontological record is not sufficiently fine-grained with respect to time. To understand Clovis diet choice, better control of biogeographic data on potential prey species is crucial.

Clovis Subsistence in the San Pedro Valley

Research at Murray Springs indicates that we can attribute with some confidence one mammoth kill (possibly more?) to Clovis hunters and without question a successful kill of at least 11 bison. These kill events are probably separated in time by an unknown but likely very short period. Horse remains in Area 5 were identified, although questions remain about human involvement in the death of that animal. A second horse excavated in Area 9 in 2001 was similarly represented primarily by dental remains, but lacked any cultural association. Were horses already extinct in the San Pedro Valley by the time of Clovis occupation? Similarly, it is difficult to associate the scattered remains of other late Pleistocene animals such as dire wolf with human activity. The paleontological "background" of other animals at many Clovis sites creates interpretive problems in attempts to reconstruct diet breadth; are the remains of other animals there because of natural deaths in an environment favorable for preservation or do those remains represent victims of Clovis predation?

If we broaden our view to include the other San Pedro Valley sites, we can add several mammoths from Lehner (perhaps as many as 13; Agenbroad and Huckell 1981; Haury and others 1959), two each from both Leikem (Johnson and Haynes 1967) and Navarrete (Huckell 1981), and one each from Naco (Haury 1953) and Escapule (Hemmings and Haynes 1969). The latter two may represent animals that survived attacks by Clovis hunters, at least briefly, only to succumb at a distance from them. In fact, the San Pedro Valley sites are key localities in providing evidence that mammoth hunting was not simply a rare practice.

Evidence of bison hunting at Murray Springs is not replicated at the other San Pedro Valley sites, although scattered bison remains occur on the eroded surface that forms the Clovis occupation floor at the Lehner Site (Agenbroad and Huckell 1981; Haury and others 1959; Saunders 1983). Horse and camel remains were also scattered across that surface, along with dire wolf and black bear. None were in direct association with stone tools or other artifacts, although black bear teeth were burned and were found in a roasting pit that contained a highly fragmented and calcined mammoth cranium. Whether these are incidental occurrences or victims of Clovis predation is debatable. The idea that a partly charred tapir mandible from near Hearth 1 at the Lehner Site reflected hunting of that animal (Haury and others 1959) cannot be supported. Reexamination showed the specimen was stained rather than burned.

Some writers note that the discovery of large mammal bones protruding from the walls of arroyos or resting in pond sediments has biased interpretation of Clovis subsistence by overemphasizing the hunting of mammoths and bison. By implication, more subtle manifestations of Clovis occupation have gone unrecognized or at least underappreciated. The Aubrey Site, with its small quantity of large mammal (mammoth and bison) remains but abundance of small (turtle, rabbit, rodent, fish) and medium (deer) fauna (Ferring 2001; Yates and Lundelius 2001), is cited as an example of this overlooked but implicitly typical evidence of a broad, unspecialized diet. In the eastern United States, the recovery of small animal and even plant food remains from Shawnee Minisink (McNett 1985) also adds to this view.

Supporters of this "generalist" position point out that no more than 14 (Grayson and Meltzer 2002) sites with clear association of Clovis human activity with proboscidean remains are known, a number that they suggest is paltry evidence on which to base arguments of large mammal dietary specialization. A more extreme aspect of this view suggests that Clovis people more likely scavenged rather than killed mammoths, or killed one mammoth in their lifetimes and never stopped talking about it (Meltzer 1993). From a gender theory perspective, Chilton (2004) also supports a generalist subsistence model, with women providing significant quantities of gathered resources to the diet.

The other reading of the empirical record is that Clovis people were skilled hunters of mammoths and other large game and that the sites with evidence of such predation are not unrepresentative of their diet (G. Haynes 2002). Gary Haynes identifies 22 sites with definite or possible Clovis-mammoth or mastodont associations. The number of North American mammoth or mastodon kill-butchery sites is not small but rather impressively large in comparison to the numbers known from the Old World, and that number is all the more impressive when the narrow time frame, spanning only a few centuries, of Clovis-proboscidean associations is considered. The fact that at least 14 such sites have been discovered may suggest that mammoth, and to perhaps a lesser degree mastodon, hunting was an integral part of Clovis subsistence. At the local scale, the occurrence of four of these 14 sites within the San Pedro Valley would suggest that in southeastern Arizona mammoths were significant targets of Clovis hunters, and that these people were intimately acquainted with mammoth ecology and ethology. Obviously, however, this strategy was viable only as long as there were mammoths to hunt.

African Elephant Behavior and Implications for Mammoth Hunting

Studies of the behavior of the African elephant (*Loxodonta africana*) can serve as proxies for mammoth behavior, which can in turn permit insights into Clovis mammoth hunting (G. Haynes 1991; Moss 1988; Olivier 1982; Sikes 1971a). Observations by Douglas-Hamilton and Douglas-Hamilton (1975: 90–261) provide indications of how some of the features uncovered at Murray Springs may have formed.

Elephants form family units led by a matriarch that move about three miles each day within their range. After about three days or so, the matriarch will move the family about ten miles to a new range (p. 90). In good times, family units band together in herds of up to 200 or more elephants. During drought, families disperse and family units may split into subgroups of three to five animals. Some elephants, including matriarchs, die during times of extreme drought. Upon the return of a good wet season, families will band together (pp. 214–215). Group size depends on a balance between spacing for competition and clustering for mutual protection. Coordinated group defense has been a significant factor in elephant survival for hundreds of thousands of years (p. 259).

Specific springs appear to be favored for the mineral content of the water. In sandy areas of shallow ground water, usually bulls or old cows will dig water holes. "Using their feet as shovels to loosen the earth, they kicked the sand backwards and forwards, until a wide hole was formed. At times they would dig down three feet or more with their trunks and feet, their toenails acting like a spade. They would push the sand with the side of a foot on to the curved end of the trunk, which they used like a cupped hand to throw the sand to one side. When the sand got damp and the water began to seep into the hole, they used the tips of their trunks, like fingers, to dig a deep, narrow, clean hole.... Within about a quarter of an hour little wells had been dug all over the place, some only a few feet away from each other" (p. 165).

Elephants are well known for their attention to carcasses of dead animals, especially of their own. In describing a family encounter with a decomposed elephant carcass, touching and feeling each bared bone, Douglas-Hamilton and Douglas-Hamilton (1975: 236–237) write: "Tusks excited special interest. Pieces were picked up, twiddled and tossed aside." Some tusks were reportedly carried off up to a mile and some bones were reportedly carried back to the place of death if the carcass had been moved. Such behaviors might help account for the scattering of mammoth elements at Murray Springs and other sites.

A family member held in low esteem usually trails along behind the family at several hundred yards. One named Isabelle and her three calves formed a subunit within Boadicia's family unit and was found all alone browsing and drinking without competition from elderly cows (pp. 212–213). Perhaps such an outcast could be a less risky target for hunters. However, "Family units within kinship groups were almost always within earshot of each other and would swiftly combine to beat off any attack by a predator" (p. 213). Survivors from culling operations became extremely aware of danger from humans.

When walking along elephant paths, one "could smell and track elephants long before" seeing them. "It was incredibly easy to creep down-wind to within a few feet of them" (p. 174). Their studies show that individual elephants have their own threat behavior in that one may charge to within a few meters of a person and turn away, perhaps stomping a tree or breaking a branch to show its anger and what it had the potential to do. Others may do no more than trumpet, flap their ears, and turn away, whereas a few will carry through an attack if the threat has crossed an imaginary threshold and invaded the critical distance whereupon the elephant feels it must fight for its life (pp. 102–104). All observers agree that prediction of elephant behavior is not always accurate because of exceptions to rules and generalities. Regarding cycles of vegetation changes, "The very adaptability of elephants makes accurate predictions impossible" (p. 261).

In time of drought, as we propose for the Clovis presence in the San Pedro Valley, mammoths would be in smaller groups, and favored watering places, such as Murray Springs must have been, would be visited frequently by mammoths as well as bison and other animals. The well-making activity Iain and Oria Douglas-Hamilton described explains the scatter of the F_1 channel sand over the surface of Area 3 away from the channel of Wolf Creek and the water hole. Their description of bone manipulation may also help explain the scattering or piling of mammoth elements within and near the F_1 channel.

Weaponry Design and Technological Organization

Additional light can be shed on the question of the relative importance of large mammal hunting in the subsistence strategy of Clovis from an examination of their technological organization. As proposed by Kelly and Todd (1988), Clovis can be viewed as "high technology foragers" with a basic, uniform technology that brought them success in large mammal hunting in multiple environments. This technology enabled them to spread rapidly across North America, continuing to target the same suite of large mammal species.

Clovis technological organization (see Nelson 1991 for an overview of technological organization) in the

San Pedro Valley appears centered on the need to conserve weapons and to provide Clovis projectile points. Hunting large mammals is an expensive proposition, particularly in terms of the potential for damage to or loss of the projectile points that tip the spears used in hunting. The Naco mammoth skeleton had eight complete points associated with it, and yet there were no signs of butchery (Haury 1953). One interpretation is that the animal escaped from its attackers and died beyond their reach; the cost to the hunters, in this case, was eight spear points and the foreshafts or shafts to which they were attached. Two more points were found at the Escapule Site, again in an animal that likely carried two spears away with it (Hemmings and Haynes 1969).

At the Lehner Site (Haury and others 1959) there were 13 points among the remains of a dozen mammoths, along with butchering tools. A minimum of eight points were irreparably damaged or at least unretrieved from the Area 4 bison kill at Murray Springs; the camp in Areas 6 and 7 yielded another 5 broken or lost points. From this short list it is obvious that demands on this component of the lithic assemblage were significant.

Huckell (1999, 2003) has proposed that Clovis hunters in the San Pedro Valley and elsewhere in the Plains and Southwest must have been concerned with meeting this demand for point repair and replacement. When possible, points were probably retrieved from successful kills and repaired for additional use. Clovis points usually are sufficiently robust to survive impact damage and clear examples of repaired points are known from San Pedro Valley sites (Chapter 8).

Loss or irreparable damage of points (after one use or more) is another outcome of hunting that would necessitate the transportation of a sufficient supply of lithic raw material to enable replacement of points. At Murray Springs the overwhelming dominance of biface reduction debitage, including at least three instances of projectile point manufacture, indicates that large bifaces were being transported. Most pieces were reduced only slightly, suggesting that they served as multifunctional implements that included bifacial cores for flake production, knives for butchering, and, ultimately, preforms for projectile points. When sufficient care is taken during reduction, large bifaces can fulfill all three roles sequentially through time.

An assessment of the Anzick cache artifacts led Wilke and his colleagues (1991) to the same conclusion. Comparative analysis of the widths of bifaces in the Anzick, Simon, and East Wenatchee caches with the widths of refitted flakes and bifaces from Murray Springs (Tables 8.5 and 8.6; Fig. 8.7) revealed no statistically significant differences in that dimension among the sites (Huckell 1999). The occupants of Murray Springs and those of the Plains adopted similar conservation strategies to supply themselves with the stone needed to pursue the hunting of large mammals in areas where no sources of high quality lithic material were known or anticipated.

A final consideration is that of all the known Paleoindian cultures, the caching of bifaces, projectile points, blades, and other tools is nearly unique to Clovis. Several caches are known, including those that contain a variety of different kinds of implements such as Anzick (Lahren and Bonnichsen 1974; Wilke and others 1991), Simon (Butler 1963; Butler and Fitzwater 1965; Woods and Titmouse 1985), and East Wenatchee (Mehringer and Foit 1990; Gramly 1993). Other caches contained only a single type of implement such as Drake (Stanford and Jodry 1988), which contained only Clovis points, and the Blackwater Draw (Green 1963) and Keven Davis (Collins 1999) caches, which consisted of blades.

The purposes of such caches are debated, but they appear to be the products of both utilitarian concerns for the positioning of stores of lithic materials in already reduced form for anticipated future needs in particular regions as well as for more esoteric, perhaps ritual purposes. Meltzer (2002), taking a slightly different perspective, has linked caches to exploration of unknown regions by Clovis people. In his view, they provided a means to overcome uncertainty about the availability of suitable stone in areas new to the explorers.

Whatever the reasons, these caches provide convincing evidence of the forms in which Clovis flint knappers transported supplies of material and of the quantities of material being carried to meet the demands of hunting. Later Paleoindians seemingly did not cache raw material to the same extent, although rare later caches such as at the Ryans Site (a Plainview point and biface cache) have been reported (Hartwell 1995). Meltzer suggests that as knowledge of lithic material sources and other environmental variables increased, caching became less necessary. It is noteworthy that post-Clovis projectile points are typically smaller and lighter than Clovis points, as are the other bifaces.

Further, blades, which make up an important aspect of the Clovis industry (Collins 1999), disappear from later Paleoindian industries. Blades were a way to get maximum cutting edge from a volume of material and would seem to reflect conservation of material. Perhaps the redesign of weaponry to target bison, the sole survivor of the late Pleistocene extinction event, included the deliberate shift to smaller points and the reorganization of other aspects of the technology that supported carcass processing, wood-working, and other tasks. The net effect may have been a lessening need to carry as much lithic material as earlier Clovis hunters (Huckell 2003).

Subsistence Strategies

Attempts to characterize Clovis diet as "specialist" or "generalist" are unproductive and polarizing (Waguespack and Surovell 2003) and mask what must have been considerable flexibility in subsistence strategies. At Murray Springs and in the San Pedro Valley, the record indicates that the overwhelming percentage of calories was likely derived from hunting, and more specifically from the hunting of two species of large mammals (mammoth and bison). From the theoretical perspective of behavioral ecology and diet breadth models, we agree with G. Haynes (2002) that these two species were likely highly ranked in Clovis diet. Evidence from lithic technological organization, especially that available from Murray Springs, is consistent with this theoretical perspective and with the empirical record, including the Clovis type site in Blackwater Draw, New Mexico where Sellards (1952) was the first to report a Clovis multiple bison kill (Hester 1972). More recently Bement and Carter (2003, 2004) have reported a Clovis multiple bison kill at Jake Bluff, Oklahoma.

Viewing the West and North America more broadly, we agree that diet must have changed as local environmental patches, their particular resource structures, and human population numbers varied across space and changed through time. A focus on large mammals is only viable in those places and times when those resources are present in sufficient quantities to support a diet dominated by hunting. With declining numbers of proboscideans as their extinction played out, this adaptation would have become increasingly problematic to sustain. The consumption of other, lower-ranked resources was undoubtedly important when the higher-ranked ones were difficult to find or unavailable in particular areas. Ultimately, later Paleoindian populations in the West had to reorganize their subsistence strategies to include both open plains bison-focused hunting and a mountains-foothills economy featuring medium-sized mammal hunting (Frison 1992). At the same time, the Murray Springs and Lehner sites represent some of the chronologically most recent mammoth kills, indicating that the targeting of that animal as a high-ranked resource endured as a centerpiece of Clovis adaptation for several centuries. Bison were already a high-ranked resource, as shown by the Area 4 bison kill at Murray Springs and the ones excavated by Sellards in 1955 from the Clovis type site in Blackwater Draw, New Mexico (Hester 1972: 46–47).

CLOVIS LAND USE AND MOBILITY

Clovis people are viewed as perhaps the first successful colonists of North America, people who devoted considerable effort to exploration of a landscape that was new to them (Barton and others 2004; Kelly 2002; Meltzer 2001, 2002, 2003). The nature of the exploration process, the rate at which they spread, and subsequent "settling in" are all aspects of colonization that have been discussed. Murray Springs and the other San Pedro Valley sites contribute to this discussion by providing insights into Clovis land use in Arizona. Whether they were the initial explorers and colonists of the valley (which we believe to be the case) or not, they left a comparatively full record of their activities there. However, the sequence of events that led to site creation, the temporal span over which those events occurred, and how they may fit into the larger picture of Clovis use of the landscape, remain difficult to assess. Do the Clovis sites in the San Pedro reflect a rapid, once-through sweep of the valley, or is there evidence for multiple occupations at particular sites? The former would be consistent with a rapid spread in a particular direction with little or no reoccupation. The latter would have been a slower process, perhaps with some repetitive use of portions of the landscape.

Hemmings (1970) observed that the entire Clovis occupation of the San Pedro Valley most likely spanned a few years at most and may represent the activities of a single social unit; the pooled averages of radiocarbon dates from Murray Springs and Lehner support the idea of a short span of time. Examining the occupational structure of the Murray Springs and Lehner sites and the similarities and differences of the lithic materials recovered at the San Pedro Valley sites helps to clarify the nature of the occupation.

Clovis Site Structure in the San Pedro Valley

The five known Clovis sites in the San Pedro Valley differ from one another significantly with respect to the nature of the occupations in each. Naco and Escapule each contain the remains of a single mammoth and projectile points, but no evidence of butchering tools or debitage from tool resharpening or manufacture. Both may represent unsuccessful kill attempts that resulted in the ultimate death of the animal away from the hunters. We do not know whether they reflect escapees from hunts that targeted multiple mammoths, or represent single animals that were hunted and lost. Greenbush Draw, in addition to Naco, contains the Leikem and Navarrete sites. At Leikem the remains of two mammoths were recovered; unfortunately the single Clovis point recovered was found out of context, but with strong circumstantial evidence of association with one of the mammoths. The Navarrete Site, only 50 m upstream of the Naco Site, contained portions of two mammoths associated with one broken, reworked Clovis point blade fragment and a slotted bone tool handle that might indicate butchering (Huckell 1981). The small exposures excavated at the three Greenbush Draw sites produced no evidence of any associated campsites.

The Lehner Site with its 13 mammoths, 13 projectile points, and a half dozen butchering tools represents at least one successful hunt and perhaps repeated hunts. Saunders (1977, 1980), comparing the age structure of the mammoths to that of contemporary African elephant matriarchal family units, proposed that Clovis hunters eliminated an entire mammoth matriarchal family unit. An alternative reading of the evidence is that the site was the scene of multiple hunts and that perhaps not all of the animals there were killed by human hunters. The remains of one mammoth, excavated in 1974, was associated with a hearth or roasting pit and some 70 pieces of debitage resulting from uniface and biface tool resharpening. The remains of other fauna on the Clovis occupation surface are difficult to attribute to Clovis activity. A 1974–1975 research project was unsuccessful in attempting to locate an associated camp.

Murray Springs reflects two (or perhaps more) episodes of use. The Area 4 bison kill and much of the activity in Areas 6 and 7 may represent one event. The Area 3 cultural debris and knapping loci may be associated with the probable mammoth kill in that area. It seems unlikely that a mammoth would be killed on the heels of a successful bison hunt, or vice versa, but there is no way to ascertain which occurred first.

Lithic Raw Material Evidence

A second line of evidence for Clovis land use practices is derived from studying the sources of lithic materials used for tool manufacture. If one assumes that in the course of their movements Clovis knappers obtained their lithic materials directly, rather than through trade (Ingbar 1994; Meltzer 1989), the positions of those sources, as well as the relative abundance and types of artifacts made from each different material, help to identify the areas they visited prior to their arrival in the San Pedro Valley and possibly the relative order in which they had been visited.

With one important exception, the few materials that can be assigned with confidence to source areas all occur north of the San Pedro Valley (Chapter 8; Huckell and Haynes 2004). At least one of these materials, the pinkish gray chert, is found in the form of projectile points at Naco, Leikem, Lehner, and Murray Springs. Other tool forms and debitage of this chert are present at Murray Springs. Furthermore, what appears to be matching banding between a large overshot flake from Area 3 and the largest Clovis point from the Naco mammoth suggests the manufacture of at least one of the Naco points at Murray Springs. However, attempts to refit pinkish gray chert channel flakes from Murray Springs to Naco and Lehner points were unsuccessful. Although its source is not known with certainty, we suspect that it is to the north, perhaps in the Paleozoic limestones that are well exposed along the Mogollon Rim.

Obsidian from the Cow Canyon source (Appendix C) is unique to Murray Springs and was clearly used by the people who occupied that site. Three flakes of Government Mountain obsidian from Area 7 remain impossible to conclusively associate with the Clovis occupation of Murray Springs.

Another important element of the lithic material story is St. David Chalcedony. It is local to the San Pedro Valley, available from the St. David Formation, and is the single most abundant lithic material at Murray Springs. It is present at only one other Clovis site, Navarrete, where a large (6.5 cm long) reworked point fragment was found (Huckell 1981). Its absence at Lehner is striking, considering the size of the artifact assemblage. Although not wishing to place too much emphasis on evidence of absence, it appears that the occupants of the Lehner Site were unaware of the source at the time or times they were there. Similarly, the absence of obsidian points and debitage at Lehner and their occurrence at Murray Springs may be significant as well. Recently what is perhaps another local material source was found by Jesse Ballenger during his survey of the upper San Pedro Valley in 2005. It is an outcrop of silicified mudstone north of the ruins of the Boquillas railroad station northwest of Fairbank and about 20 km (12.3 miles) north of the site and resembles the material from which the blades in Area 7 are made. Only one tool of the silicifed limestone near the Lewis Hills is clearly affiliated with the Clovis occupation of Murray Springs, along with expedient use of local metasandstone (Chapter 8).

The geographic locations of these sources provide a sketch of a general route of movement across Arizona (Chapter 8; Huckell and Haynes 2004) to Murray Springs. A single point tip of petrified wood from the Petrified Forest (Table 8.4), provides a starting point. Cow Canyon obsidian, eleventh in abundance and represented by points, debitage, and unworked nodules, is derived from a specific source 26 km (16 miles) north of the Clifton-Morenci area. The most abundant material, St. David Chalcedony, is derived from a local source in the San Pedro Valley, approximately 40 km (25 miles) north of Murray Springs.

From Area 7 there are three obsidian biface reduction flakes of material from Government Mountain in the San Francisco Peaks volcanic field, about 190 km (118 miles) west of the Petrified Forest (Huckell and Haynes 2004). The flakes cannot be assigned to the Clovis occupation with certainty at this time. If we knew the source of either the reddish brown chert or the pinkish gray chert, second and third in abundance respectively (Table 8.4), it could change the scenario significantly. It is noteworthy that the other lithic materials of the rest of the points and tools cannot presently be assigned to particular sources; they seem to be unique to the sites from which they were recovered. The considerable diversity in lithic material sources reflects a large geographic area from which they were procured. However, it is likely that a trip down the Mogollon Rim would have brought people into contact with a wide array of lithic materials of multiple ages exposed in the formations of Paleozoic age along the crown and rugged face of the Rim. Until specific materials can be assigned to specific sources, the diversity of raw materials will remain difficult to interpret.

Based on these observations, we hypothesize that there were repeated Clovis visits to the San Pedro Valley. The site structural and lithic material evidence seems to indicate at least two visits to the valley, which may be thought of as "pre-St. David Chalcedony discovery" and "post-St. David Chalcedony discovery." Lehner, Naco, and possibly Leikem represent one (probably the earlier) occupational episode and Murray Springs (at least the bison kill) represents another, probably later use of the valley. The Navarrete Site may be temporally related to the occupation at Murray Springs. The alternative hypothesis is that of a single, longer occupation, during which time the Clovis hunters foraged intensively within the valley. Ignorant of the St. David Chalcedony source at first, they eventually discovered the location of that source and made use of it as stocks of nonlocal material dwindled.

The implications of these two alternative hypotheses for understanding Clovis land use and the colonization process are important. The single longer occupation view is consistent with aspects of G. Haynes' (2002) foraging model for the exploitation of mammoth, wherein the San Pedro Valley might be viewed as a patch, or refugium, in which mammoths still roamed, and the Clovis hunters who entered it may have extirpated that population before moving on. The sourcing of lithic raw material indicates movement in a general southward direction, and the absence of evidence for subsequent occupation of the valley for several centuries is consistent with rapid expansion across the continent. The hypothesis of repeated visits is perhaps more akin to Meltzer's (2004) MUDR model, although we note that there is little evidence to support extended occupation of the San Pedro Valley at the scale of decades or longer or a subsistence shift to game other than mammoth or bison. Still, landscape learning and perhaps the establishment of recurrent patterns of foraging within a region may be implied by both the site structural data and the lithic source data.

EXTINCTION AND MURRAY SPRINGS

One of the most debated aspects of the Clovis period is whether, or how, Clovis hunters played a role in the megafaunal extinction. From the outset, Paul Martin's (1967; also see Martin 1984, 1990, 2005; Mosimann and Martin 1975) "overkill" theory has been controversial among archaeologists, ecologists, and Native Americans, and it continues to be so to this day. Martin observed that the terminal Pleistocene extinction event is unusual in that it was differentially manifested among large mammals (those weighing more than 45 kg). Smaller animals went virtually untouched. He further observed that the principal difference between the Pleistocene-Holocene glacial-interglacial transition and extinction of 34 genera of large mammals and those that occurred earlier in the Pleistocene but were unaccompanied by large mammal extinction events involved a single factor: humans first appeared in North America some 13,000 or 14,000 calendar years ago. He proposed that this was not a coincidence and that humans were the cause of Pleistocene extinction. Clovis large mammal kill sites and the fact that they represented a predominantly hunting culture, exploiting large prey species unfamiliar with human hunters, were critical to the hypothesis.

Both prior to Martin's overkill hypothesis and during the past four decades since he proposed it, others have placed the cause of extinction on end-Pleistocene climate and environmental change, with humans playing either no role or a limited one (Graham and Lundelius 1984; Grayson 1984; Hester 1967; Slaughter 1967). Other causes such as "hyperdisease" (MacPhee and Marx 1997) have been proposed but remain difficult to support (Lyons, Smith, and Brown 2004). A principal criticism of Martin's model is that for most of the extinct animals, no definite archaeological associations are known. Archaeologists (Hester 1967; Grayson 1984, 2001; Grayson and Meltzer 2002, 2003) have been skeptical of the model to varying degrees for this reason, because only mammoth, mastodon, and bison are clearly associated with humans in archaeological contexts. Martin (2005) has generally responded that the extinction event played out too rapidly for many kill sites to have been created, preserved, and discovered. With respect to environmental change, recent documentation of the nature and speed of postglacial environmental change has been obtained from ice and deep ocean cores. The ice core data demonstrate that warming occurred incredibly rapidly in the Northern Hemisphere shortly after 15,000 B.P. (Alley 2000; Bradley 1999: 158–166), which has led to speculation that such rapid change may have been unlike previous glacial-interglacial changes. These same cores suggest, however, that the Pleistocene-Holocene change was not obviously different in magnitude or rapidity than previous glacial-interglacial changes.

Apart from the empirical realm, recent quantitative modeling analyses by biologists and ecologists have offered new support for human involvement in the late Pleistocene extinction, both in North America and elsewhere. One of the models (Alroy 1999, 2001) demonstrates that adding human hunting to the environmental changes at the end of the Pleistocene results in a high fidelity representation of how the extinction process seems to have occurred. Of some concern is the way in which initial conditions for models are set; that is, assumptions about animal numbers, environmental carrying capacity, human foraging success, human population growth rates and the mathematics of the models may predestine the outcome in favor of a human role in the extinction.

A recent review of the literature and the status of thinking on late Pleistocene extinction in North America and the rest of the globe is by Barnosky and his colleagues (2004; also see Lyons, Smith, Wagner and others 2004; MacPhee 1999). For North America, an emerging consensus pins extinction on a combination of environmental change and human predation (Haynes 1991; Mehringer 1967; but see Grayson and Meltzer 2003 for a dissenting view).

Evidence from the San Pedro Valley

There is evidence of human predation of mammoths at Murray Springs and stronger evidence at the other San Pedro Valley sites. Mammoths are perhaps the species that is the easiest to accommodate in the overkill model. It is clear that these animals were hunted by Clovis people (G. Haynes and Eiselt 1999; Lyons, Smith, and Brown 2004; Surovell and others 2005). As the largest of North American land mammals, with considerable needs for forage and water, they were likely never present in large numbers. Like their close kin the Indian and African elephants, they probably had low reproductive rates and took many years to reach reproductive age (G. Haynes 1991). With environmental deterioration at the close of the Pleistocene (G. Haynes 2002; C. V. Haynes 1991), their populations could have been significantly reduced and geographically restricted. Reductions in carrying capacity and range fragmentation can threaten the long-term viability of a species, as is known today for elephant populations in Africa and India. It may not have taken much hunting pressure to reduce their numbers across broad geographic ranges to levels that made extinction inevitable. In the San Pedro Valley alone, the deaths of as many as 19 mammoths may have resulted from Clovis hunting.

Did Clovis hunters cause the extinction of the horse? Strong evidence of horse hunting is lacking at Murray Springs, although horses must have been penecontemporaneous with humans there and elsewhere in the San Pedro Valley. There is recent evidence that points toward Clovis exploitation of horse in Saskatchewan (Kooyman and others 2006), but it consists of direct evidence of nondiagnostic stone tools with horse skeletons. There is little evidence for the hunting of camel (*Camelops*), although again their remains occur on the Clovis-age occupation surface at the Lehner Site and Frison (2000) now suggests the Clovis point at the Casper Site is probably associated with the camel remains that date $11,190 \pm 50$ B.P. A tapir, formerly believed to be associated with the Clovis occupation at the Lehner Site, is now considered unlikely to have been killed by hunters. Concerning these and other animals, detailed taphonomic analyses are necessary to determine how their bones came to rest on the same geomorphic surface on which we find Clovis occupations.

Extinction and the Black Mat

The stratigraphic record in the San Pedro Valley provides one of the best temporal and ecological contexts of the extinction event that is known in North America (Haynes 1991). The remarkable circumstances of the termination of the Rancholabrean fauna occurring on the Clovis landscape immediately before deposition of the F_2 black mat and the total absence of mammoth, mastodon, horse, camel, dire wolf, American lion, tapir, and other elements of the Rancholabrean fauna, as well as Clovis people, above the contact lend strength to Martin's (1967) hypothesis that Clovis people caused the Pleistocene extinction. However, the basal black mat contact marks a major climatic change from the warm dry climate of the terminal Allerød to the glacially cold Younger Dryas, so climate change cannot be ruled out as a contributing factor. The association of this event ("the Clovis drought") with diminished spring flow and surface water availability at Murray Springs indicates that it is ultimately associated with a climatic shift toward decreased or at least less effective precipitation that likely resulted in changes in plant species abundance and perhaps plant community composition. Such shifts would have negatively impacted San Pedro Valley animal populations and, if regional in scope, populations across western North America. Murray Springs and the other San Pedro Valley Clovis sites thus appear to be a microcosm of the extinction event in North America, providing evidence of an apparent decline in environmental productivity and carrying capacity at about the time of Clovis arrival. With the addition of a new, highly effective human predator, mammoth and perhaps other megafauna disappeared from the Valley and the rest of North America.

There are at least 40 other localities in the United States with Younger Dryas age black mat deposits in one form or another (Haynes 1998b, 2003). Many of them overlie terminal Pleistocene fauna remains, a few with Clovis artifacts. The Rancholabrean termination everywhere appears to have occurred as rapidly and at the same time as the termination in the San Pedro Valley. Could drought, deep freeze, and Clovis predation have occurred at all of these places at the same time? Probably not. With regard to the cause of the Pleistocene termination, something happened 13,000 years ago that we have yet to fully understand.

AFTERWORD

Does the Past have a Future at Murray Springs?

C. Vance Haynes, Jr.

What does the future hold for the Murray Springs Clovis Site? Since the end of excavations in 1971, the site has continued to yield information of interest to science. For several years flakes and artifacts have turned up on the surface in the Area 1 Extension and in Area 7, and we were able to tie most of them into existing grid stakes. Although today all but a few of the metal stakes have been removed, presumably by souvenir collectors or vandals, the few remaining stakes would allow the grid to be reestablished.

There have been many field trips to Murray Springs since 1966 conducted for the benefit of geologists, archaeologists, and other scientists from all over the world. Annually, University of Arizona geoarchaeology classes are taken to the site. The Bureau of Land Management has done a superb job of signing the site for self-guided tours. Geochronological investigations continue to the present in order to better refine the chronology. Sampling for Optically Stimulated Luminescence (OSL) dating has been conducted by Oxford University. The results of radiocarbon dating using accelerator mass spectrometry (AMS), a technique for better precision not available during the excavations, are on-going. Several visits have been made to the site to continue study and sampling of the black mat (F_{2a}) and its facies (F_{2b}) and to better understand their origin. The site will be important for scientific study and education for years to come provided it is adequately protected. And the tourism potential for displaying San Pedro Valley sites of perhaps the earliest Americans is unequaled.

Much of the site remains to be excavated. Probably 80 percent of Areas 6 and 7 remains unexcavated. Whereas we did uncover the main activity areas, all of the unexcavated ground between the randomly spaced squares remains, and other activity areas could lie outside of these locations, particularly between them and Areas 1, 3, 4, and 5. Also, it is obvious that the spoil pile from Trench 1 covers part of the campsite. It is in these unexplored areas that we may find missing parts of the broken artifacts on hand. The base of the Clovis point tip in Area 3 of petrified wood from the Petrified Forest National Monument area has yet to be found, as does the base of the chalcedony tip also found in Area 3. South of the Clovis camp in Area 7, fragments of tufa have been found on the surface near the lone mesquite tree just across the boundary fence with Section 35 (Fig. 1.9a). Tufa is usually associated with spring discharge, and its presence raises the possibility that Clovis people interacted with a spring in that area.

The area between the east end of Area 4 at Trench 12 and Area 2 is a buried swale that extends westward to the bison tracks in Area 5 (Fig. 2.3). Even though we found no cultural remains in expanded Trench 12 north of Area 4, the area eastward from the Clovis hearth and knapping locus A4–1 has a high potential for additional Clovis materials. Furthermore, keeping in mind the water-gathering activity in Area 8, the area west of Area 4 to Area 8 needs to be explored not only for Clovis artifacts but for water collecting features such as wells and water holes.

Evidence of a possible pre-Clovis presence at Murray Springs includes abraded and faceted bone fragments from Stratum D_1 in the spring conduits of Area 8 and a large chipped cobble from Stratum D in Trench 1. It is similar to the cobble hammer from Area 4 (Fig. 5.24). On the other hand, the faceted bone fragments are probably the result of natural fracturing by animal trampling and faceting due to natural abrasion by sand in a roiling spring, as found at the Tule

Springs Site in Nevada in 1963 (Shutler 1967). The chipped rock could be a natural geofact or a Clovis or later age artifact that sank into the Sobaipuri mud at a much later date. Equivocal evidence of this type will never be adequate for proving pre-Clovis presence.

Of significant interest in this regard, both archaeologically and geologically, is the untested area between Area 2 and the north wall of the South Branch across from Area 1. Are there buried spring conduits there as suggested in Chapter 2? Archaeological remains in association with bones in Strata E_1, E, D, D_1, and D_2 would be in excess of 13,000 years old, making the site a worthwhile place to search for pre-Clovis evidence.

If the presence of pre-Clovis cultures in North America is to be proven beyond any reasonable doubt, a site will have to be discovered that has the artifactual evidence and integrity of a location like the Murray Springs kills, that is, multiple artifacts, debitage, and features in a well-defined stratigraphic context. A tool or a few flakes under bones of an extinct animal in shallow context, or equivocal lithics in pre late glacial stratigraphic context, or unequivocal artifacts in equivocal stratigraphic contexts will always leave an element of doubt in the minds of objective scientists. If Curry Draw has evidence of pre-Clovis human presence, archaeological excavation should reveal it as unequivocal artifacts in clear patterned association with features and fauna in conjunction with the well-defined and radiocarbon dated stratigraphic framework. We maintain that all faunal remains in pre-Clovis strata should be treated as archaeological sites until proven otherwise.

The greatest single threat to the site is erosion. The site is intimately associated with the arroyo environment and is in constant danger of being destroyed by arroyo expansion. Whereas arroyo cutting exposed the site, we were fortunate in finding it before very much was lost. However, there remains a considerable area of significant potential for further evidence of Clovis activities as well as areas for pre-Clovis investigation.

There has been significant erosion in Curry Draw since the end of excavations. Trench 22 was only partly backfilled with the idea that it would eventually be flushed out and thereby divert most, if not all, subsequent flow to the North Branch of Curry Draw. Before this happened, a significant summer rainfall in 1983 caused enough discharge to enter the south headcut so that it cut headward beyond Trench 32.

Subsequent high discharge events have been diverted to the North Branch via Trench 22 such that very little runoff enters the south headcut (Figs. 2.3, 2.9). However, streams do not like a right-angle bend, so as time goes by Trench 22 will not only widen but the water course will change from a straight reach to a meandering one. At the south end the meander bend will cut eastward toward Area 8 and remove potential Clovis activity areas. It will cut westward at the north end where there will be less loss because the west wall is mostly Stratum G_2 except for a remnant of Strata F_1, F_2, and F_3 at the north end (Fig. 2.26). This meandering has already started.

Since the beginning of the 21st century, the water table below Curry Draw has risen. Sometime before December 2005 it had emerged in the headcut of the South Branch causing ponding in the upper South Branch where cattails (*Typha* sp.) are growing in several places. A few pools of open water are covered with duckweed (*Lemna* sp.) and bull frogs are living there. Now perennial flow persists down stream. At the same time, the water table in the North Branch emerges as a saturated streambed a short distance above Area 2 and is 2 cm to 5 cm deep where the two branches merge. Perennial flow continues all the way to the San Pedro River as a shallow 2 cm to 20 cm deep stream with a sandy bed. At the site proper, bank collapse has already begun.

These drastic changes continue in spite of the past decade being one of the driest on record. The cause appears to be the infiltration of treated water from the Sierra Vista wastewater treatment plant about 2 km upstream in the catchment of Curry Draw (Fig. 2.2). Instead of recharging to the deep aquifer of the San Pedro, the water appears to be encountering a shallow aquaclude, thus forming a perched aquifer that discharges to Curry Draw at the Murray Springs archaeological site. Further proof of this model is the fact that neither Moson Wash to the north nor Horsethief Draw to the south has perennial flow; both have dry stream beds except during times of local rainfall.

The solution for preserving the Murray Springs archaeological site and its arroyo environment is to prevent the discharge of the shallow aquifer by injecting the treated wastewater into the deep aquifer below the treatment plant and stabilizing the arroyo walls and headcut with reinforced concrete as proposed to the Bureau of Land Management (Haynes 1997, 2001). In doing the latter procedure, the archaeological excavations could be reproduced in colored concrete that exactly duplicates the geological strata as exposed at the end of the 1971 excavations. With an on-site interpretive center, the site would become a permanent world class showplace for students, scientists, and the public where, like chapters in the book of time, the last 50,000 years of earth history and at least 13,000 years of human history, if not more, could be read from the strata and from the Ice Age fauna and archaeology that they contain.

APPENDIX A

Radiocarbon Dating at Murray Springs and Curry Draw

C. Vance Haynes, Jr.

Radiocarbon dating is an important part of the Murray Springs project, and all four aspects of the method, collection, pretreatment, conversion, and age measurement were carried out under careful supervision. Sample *collection* requires an accurate stratigraphic framework for proper geochronological positioning and an interpretable context. This was accurately accomplished by geologic mapping and stratigraphic profiling (Chapter 2). *Pretreatment* requires stringent mechanical and chemical treatment to remove physical and chemical contaminants, after which the sample is *converted* to either carbon dioxide (CO_2) for gas proportional counting of beta (β) emissions, benzene for liquid scintillation counting, or graphite for accelerator mass spectrometric (AMS) measurement of carbon 14 (^{14}C). The ^{14}C *measurement* is then compared to that of a standard (equivalent to the atmosphere of A.D. 1950) to determine its age in years B.P. (before present, present being 1950).

Sample collecting in Curry Draw began in 1953 when E. B. Sayles collected "carbonaceous earth" from above "elephant" bones (Wise and Shutler 1958, A-69). In 1959 Paul Martin (1963a) and James Schoenwetter collected two charcoal-bearing "earth" samples in 1959 from their pollen-sampling profile (Pollen Profile 1) downstream from the Murray Place (Chapter 1) and submitted the samples to Austin Long of the radiocarbon laboratory of the Geochronology Laboratories, University of Arizona, for age determination (Damon and others 1963). In 1964 Peter Mehringer and I resampled Pollen Profile 1 for both pollen and ^{14}C (Mehringer and Haynes 1965). This was before the discovery of the Murray Springs Clovis site in 1966. What follows will serve as a good introduction to sample pretreatment and some of the problems that can be encountered.

STANDARD A-B-A PRETREATMENT

The standard sample pretreatment at most radiocarbon laboratories is to subject the sample to a treatment with acid followed by a basic solution and a final acid bath before final washing and drying. It is referred to as the acid-base-acid (A-B-A) pretreatment.

Before measurement by accelerator mass spectrometry (AMS), at least a gram of carbon was required for accurate ^{14}C analysis by gas proportional counting or liquid scintillation. Charcoal samples are routinely inspected for physical contaminants such as rootlets, insect parts, and anything not a part of the charcoal. Under magnification these are mechanically removed by picking with tweezers.

Charcoal samples are then immersed in pure water and agitated to promote the flotation of plant contaminants too small for hand picking. In this way much of the fine contaminates are removed by decantation. In some cases the charcoal starts to break up in water. If it does so to a strong degree, it is an indication that it may not be charcoal but naturally oxidized wood or plant matter instead, as described later.

Diluted hydrochloric acid ($\sim 3N$ HCl) is added next to chemically remove calcium carbonate ($CaCO_3$) which, in most cases, is a secondary source of carbon and therefore a contaminant. The acid bath is digested near the boiling point for about 30 minutes to insure complete removal of CO_2 derived from the carbonates. More fine grained contaminants that float may be removed in this step by decantation as before.

After a thorough washing in water the sample is next treated with a strong base solution, usually sodium hydroxide ($\sim 1\%$ NaOH), and again digested. In this stage soluble organic contaminants, mainly humic and fulvic acids, are extracted as sodium humates and the like and usually discarded. Finally, charcoal is washed in weakly acidified water to insure removal of any remaining hydroxyl ions that could absorb CO_2 from the atmosphere.

A preliminary test of a fragment of Martin's 1959 Murray Springs sample (Damon and others 1963: 292) showed Austin Long that it was highly soluble in the strong base solution, so much so that he feared most of it would be lost to the base treatment. In such cases, in those days, it was common practice in radiocarbon laboratories to skip the base treatment in order to have enough sample for analysis. Fearing such loss, two of the samples (Table A.1, A-186 and A-187) were not subjected to the base treatment.

When Peter Mehringer and I resampled Pollen Profile I (Chapter 1) in 1964, I personally pretreated the carbon samples, having understudied Austin Long before he took over operation of the Smithsonian Institution's laboratory. Under Paul Damon's guidance, I had replaced Austin in the Arizona lab. Having decided to include the base treatment in the newly collected Murray Springs samples, I discovered that they (Table A.1, A-696 and A-697) were so soluble in NaOH that only one of the two samples (Table A.1, A-696) yielded enough residual carbon for a radiocarbon age. This is a strong indication that the samples were not charcoal produced by fire but naturally oxidized wood or plant matter. Charcoal per se is essentially elemental carbon and not normally attacked by strong acids or bases.

The problem with omitting the base extraction is that, although much of the humic and fulvic acids may be derived from natural decay of the sample itself, extraneous humic and fulvic acids are derived from soil formation and usually younger contaminants or from groundwater and possibly older. There is no practical way to separate indigenous from extraneous humic acids. Therefore, my preference in the base pretreatment step is to let as much of the sample as possible go into solution. If most or all of it dissolves in base solution one knows it was not charcoal. The humic acids can then be recovered from solution by acidification to pH 1 or less resulting in flocculation of the humates, which, after washing and drying, can be combusted and analyzed for ^{14}C. It is evident from Table A.1 that my results (A-696A and B and A-697 B1; Haynes and others 1967: 5) essentially duplicated Austin Long's (A-187 and A-186 respectively) earlier results.

Later resampling of Pollen Profile I produced wood (A-879) that duplicated the previous results (Haynes, Grey, and Long 1971) and indicated that in this case all of the humic acids were most likely derived from the natural oxidation of wood. All ages are accurate within the standard errors (1 sigma) and correlate with similar samples collected from stratigraphic Profile N at the Murray Springs Site (Plate 7; Table A.1, A-905A and B).

DATING THE CLOVIS OCCUPATION

At the time of the discovery of the Murray Springs Area 1 mammoth, the first associated charcoal sample was collected from the top of stratum F_1, the Graveyard sand, in the head wall of the tributary headcut and provided an age of 11,150 ± 450 B.P. (Table A.1, A-805A), whereas the humates extracted from the charcoal were 11,300 ± 500 B.P. (Table A.1, A-805B), essentially the same age within one standard error (1 sigma). Most of the Clovis-age charcoal collected from the site has been identified as ash (*Fraxinus* sp.) by either R. C. Koeppen, Forest Products Laboratory, Madison, Wisconsin (personal communications 1967 and 1969) or Vorsila L. Bohrer, then with the Botany Department, University of Arizona (personal communications 1966, 1967, 1968). Later James E. King (personal communication 1972) identified other charcoal samples from the Clovis occupation as *Fraxinus* sp., probably *F. velutina*, as Vorsila Bohrer had suggested earlier. Regarding the apparently consistent use of ash wood (*Fraxinus*) by Clovis, R. C. Koeppen said in a letter dated 29 September 1969: "Ash wood is one of the better woods for campfires, having much better fuel properties than any of the softwoods, willows, or cottonwood."

We were fortunate that Clovis age charcoal was abundant in the F_1 channel sand and on the Clovis occupation surface. These samples were readily pretreated by the standard A-B-A procedure. In most cases the humates from these charcoals were discarded because of the similarity in age shown by A-805B.

Eight Clovis charcoal ages deemed most accurate were averaged using the procedure presented by Long and Rippeteau (1974). In Table A.1 these are indicated by + as a superscript and produced an average age for the Clovis occupation of 10,900 ± 50 B.P. At least two visits were made by Clovis people to Murray Springs, all probably within a brief period of a year or less as explained in Chapter 2. An earlier visit is implied if the horse kill is valid. The testing of mammoth bone for indigenous collagen amino acids by T. W. Stafford and others (1991) revealed none suitable for reliable ^{14}C dating of bone from Murray Springs. However, Surovell (2000) has demonstrated that the radiocarbon dating of tusk apatite by step heating shows promise. Six results at six temperatures between 642° C and 1130° C ranged between 10,605 ± 95 B.P. and 10,815 ± 85 B.P.

MULTIPLE FRACTION RADIOCARBON DATING OF THE BLACK MAT (F_2)

As covered in Chapters 1 and 2 and in Appendix B, Stratum F_2 is a black organic silty clay of algal origin that directly overlies the Clovis occupation surface. Radiocarbon dating of the black mat (F_2) has been difficult because it was necessary to use bulk sediment samples. Before AMS technology, it required as much as several hundred grams of sediments to yield enough carbon for dating. Whereas the standard A-B-A pretreatment is applied to bulk samples, they are considerably more difficult to deal with than charcoal because of their size and the common presence of clays that typically clog filters. The Clanton clay (F_2) was no exception (Appendix B). However, it contained abundant carbon and usually yielded two, and sometimes three, humate extractions. This procedure involved subjecting the insoluble residue of the first pretreatment to another acid-base cycle to yield a second humic acid extraction. The results indicated that the residue contained humins, which are those molecules of soil or sediment organic matter that are soluble only upon repeated acid-base treatment. In a few cases a third humic acid extraction could be obtained. Insoluble carbon may still remain in the residue.

At the time we were excavating the Murray Springs Site I pretreated the black mat samples at a new radiocarbon dating laboratory I had established at Southern Methodist University in Dallas, Texas (Haynes and Haas 1974). Before our liquid scintillation counter was up and running, I sent pretreated samples to Sam Velastro and Mott Davis for counting at the University of Texas radiocarbon dating laboratory. Therefore, all such sample lab numbers are preceded by Tx (Table A.1) and are reported in the journal *Radiocarbon* (Velastro and others 1975).

When I discovered that two and sometimes three, separate humate extractions could be obtained I thought perhaps the first extraction would be the most contaminated and the last one the least contaminated. However, the humate radiocarbon ages have all been within one or two sigmas (δ) of each other with no systematic trend as to which is older. Because of the practical inability to remove all microscopic particulate contaminants during the standard pretreatment, one can assume that the residue ages are minimum values but hopefully within 2 sigma.

Typically the Clanton clay is 2 cm to 10 cm thick and probably mixed from top to bottom by bioturbation, so it is difficult to collect the earliest (bottom) and latest (top) increments for obtaining the oldest and youngest radiocarbon ages. However, in places where the black Clanton clay (F_{2a}) disperses into stringers separated by thicknesses of white Earp marl (F_{2b}) facies there is an opportunity to collect samples in fine stratigraphic increments. Trench 13N provided an excellent opportunity for this microstratigraphic sampling because here there are up to seven thin (1–5 mm) black stringers separated by 2 cm to 8 cm thicknesses of white marl, except where the stringers come together to form thicknesses of up to 5 cm (Fig. A.1a, b). The origin of this boudinagelike sedimentary structure is not clear but may be due to post-depositional compaction. In any case, multifraction radiocarbon dating was performed on nine samples, four black stringers and five marls (Table A.2).

Unfortunately, none of the fractions show any particular trend with the stratigraphic order in part due to the large standard errors. The well defined microstratigraphy in Stratum F_2 of Trench 13N precludes bioturbation. The younger than expected age for sample 44 at the base of F_2 suggests redeposition but this can be ruled out because of the ^{14}C ages of basal black mat elsewhere in Curry Draw that are consistent with the ages of strata above and below F_2 (Table A.1). Therefore, contamination appears to be the problem. The fact that all three fractions of sample 44 are within one sigma of each other indicates that all are about equally contaminated.

Possible sources of contamination include soil organics translocated by rainwater, ground water carrying younger organic matter, and nuclear age carbon derived from the testing of atomic weapons (Haas and others 1986). At Trench 13N, Stratum F_2 lay far enough above the water table to be free of

Table A.1. Curry Draw Radiocarbon Ages Arranged Stratigraphically by Locality

Locality	Sample Number	Radiocarbon age (Lab. No.) Years Before Present (1950)	Material*	Stratum	Radiocarbon or other reference
		Historic bison skeleton			
North headcut	7MS66	103.5 ± 3.0% Mod. (A–819A)	Collagen	H/G_{2b} contact	1971 13(1): 5
North headcut	7MS66	102.4 ± 2.8% Mod. (A–819B)	Humates	H/G_{2b} contact	1971 13(1): 5
North headcut	7MS66	124.9 ± 4.6% Mod. (A–819C)	Secondary CO_2	H/G_{2b} contact	1971 13(1): 5
North headcut	18MS66	100.9 ± 2.4% Mod. (A–819D)	Soluble organics	H/G_{2b} contact	1975 17(1): 53
North headcut	7MS66	98.8 ± 6.7% Mod. (A–819E)	Fulvic acid	H/G_{2b} contact	1971 13(1): 5
North headcut	18MS66	340 ± 370 (Tx–1174)	Apatite CO_2	H/G_{2b} contact	1975 17(1): 53
		Bakarich Alluvium (G_{3b})			
Murray Place	23–2	500 ± 80 (SMU–39)	Charcoal	G_{2b}	1974 16(3): 372
		Surface and Soils			
North side surface hearth	8MS66	840 ± 60 (Tx–937)	Charcoal	G_{2a} surface	1975 17(1): 54
Profile Y	14–54	1340 ± 120 (Tx–1196)	Residue	H/E contact	1975 17(1): 53
Profile Y	14–54	1570 ± 80 (Tx–1197)	Humates	H/E contact	1975 17(1): 53
		McCool Alluvium (G_{2b})			
Profile 30 (Pollen Profile I)	2MS65	1550 ± 90 (A–617)	Charcoal	G_{2b}	1967 9(1): 5
		Hargis Alluvium (G_{2a})			
Draw mouth hearth	———	3190 ± 80 (SMU–40)	Charcoal	G_{2a}	1974 16(3): 372
S.P. milepost 1060.8	24–13A	4000 ± 130 (SMU–154)	Carbonized plants	G_1	No listing
		Weik Alluvium (G_1)			
Trench 27	23–31	4850 ± 110 (SMU–156)+	Charcoal	G_1	No listing
Trench 27	23–31	4910 ± 70 (SMU–157)+	Humates	G_1	No listing
		4890 ± 60 (Average of 2)			
East Swale Headcut 3	24–15	6400 ± 100 (SMU–139)	Humates	G_1	No listing
Profile 30	———	4120 ± 490 (A–186)	Carbonized plants	G_1	1963 5: 292
Profile 30	4MS65	4230 ± 290 (A–697B:1)	Humates	G_1	1967 9(1): 5
Profile 30	5MS65	5500 ± 400 (A–879)	Wood (*Salix* sp.)	G_1	1971 13(1): 9
Profile 30	———	5280 ± 330 (A–187)	Carbonized plants	G_{1a}	1963 5: 292
Profile 30	3MS65	5890 ± 270 (A–696B)	Humates	G_{1a}	1967 9(1): 5
Profile 30	3MS65	4340 ± 250 (A–696A)	Residue	G_{1a}	1967 9(1): 5
Profile 30	1MS65	8270 ± 180 (A–580B)	Humates	Redeposited	1967 9(1): 5
Area 1	6MS66	5630 ± 130 (Tx–936)	Humates	G_{1a}	1975 7(1): 54
Profile N	12MS66	5750 ± 250 (A–905A)	Charcoal	G_{1a}	1971 13(1): 10
Profile N	12MS66	5520 ± 200 (A–905B)	Humates	G_{1a}	1971 13(1): 10
		Donnet Member (F_3)			
Area 1	4–26	7920 ± 150 (Tx–971)	Carbonate CO_2	F_3	1975 17(1): 54
Area 1	4–26	8160 ± 130 (Tx–972)	Carbonate CO_2	F_3	1975 17(1): 54
Trench 17	14–23	9100 ± 290 (Tx–1173)	Humates	F_3	1975 17(1): 54
Trench 13	53A70	10,800 ± 1700 (Tx–1245)	Residue	F_3	1975 17(1): 57
Trench 13	53A70	8820 ± 250 (Tx–1246)	Humates	F_3	1975 17(1): 57
Trench 13	53A70	8980 ± 140 (Tx–1244)	Carbonate CO_2	F_3	1975 17(1): 57
Trench 13	58A70	9200 ± 440 (Tx–1192)	Residue	F_3	1975 17(1): 58
Trench 13	58A70	8090 ± 130 (Ix–1193)	Humates	F_3	1975 17(1): 58
Trench 13	57A70	7410 ± 610 (Tx–1249)	Residue	F_3	1975 17(1): 57
Trench 13	57A70	9320 ± 200 (Tx–1250)	Humates (1st)	F_3	1975 17(1): 57

Table A.1. Curry Draw Radiocarbon Ages Arranged Stratigraphically by Locality (Continued)

Locality	Sample Number	Radiocarbon age (Lab. No.) Years Before Present (1950)	Material*	Stratum	Radiocarbon or other reference
Trench 13	57A70	9020 ± 190 (Tx–1251)	Humates (2nd)	F_3	1975 17(1): 57
Trench 13	55A70	9640 ± 180 (Tx–1189)	Residue	F_3	1975 17(1): 57
Trench 13	55A70	9630 ± 310 (Tx–1190)	Humates (1st)	F_3	1975 17(1): 57
Trench 13	55A70	9450 ± 180 (Tx–1191)	Humates (2nd)	F_3	1975 17(1): 57
Area 8	24A70	7430 ± 100 (Tx–1178A)	Residue	F_3	1975 17(1): 55
Area 8	24A70	7110 ± 140 (Tx–1178B)	Humates (1st)	F_3	1975 17(1): 55
Area 8	24A70	6980 ± 180 (Tx–1179)	Humates (2nd)	F_3	1975 17(1): 55
Area 8	25A70	8200 ± 70 (SMU–160)	Humates (1st)	F_3	No listing
Area 8	25A70	8330 ± 130 (SMU–165)	Humates (2nd)	F_3	No listing
Trench 12	4–28	8620 ± 160 (Tx–1046)	Humates (2nd)	F_3	1975 17(1): 53
		Clanton Member (F_2)			
Area 1	16MS67A	8900 ± 400 (A–969A)+	Residue	F_{2c}	1971 13(1): 10
Area 1	16MS67B	9270 ± 800 (A–969B)+	Humates	F_{2c}	1971 13(1): 10
		9020 ± 360 (Average of 2)			
Area 1	17MS67C	10,250 ± 170 (A–977)	Carbonate CO_2	F_{2b}	1971 13(1): 10
Area 1	15MS67B	10,360 ± 90 (A–989B)	Humates	F_{2a}	1971 13(1): 11
Trench 13N	51A70	10,200 ± 680 (Tx–1241)	Residue	F_2	1975 17(1): 56
Trench 13N	51A70	8600 ± 240 (Tx–1242)	Humates (1st)	F_2	1975 17(1): 56
Trench 13N	51A70	8940 ± 210 (Tx–1243)	Humates (2nd)	F_2	1975 17(1): 56
Trench 13N	51A70	9240 ± 140 (Tx–1240)	Carbonate CO_2	F_2	1975 17(1): 55
Trench 13N	52A70	10,580 ± 3500 (Tx–1186)	Residue	F_2	1975 17(1): 57
Trench 13N	52A70	8870 ± 140 (Tx–1187)	Humates (1st)	F_2	1975 17(1): 57
Trench 13N	52A70	8580 ± 240 (Tx–1188)	Humates (2nd)	F_2	1975 17(1): 57
Trench 13N	50A70	5050 ± 2030 (Tx–1247)	Residue	F_2	1975 17(1): 56
Trench 13N	50A70	9820 ± 160 (Tx–1248)	Humates	F_2	1975 17(1): 56
Trench 13N	49A70	9310 ± 150 (Tx–1239)	Carbonate CO_2	F_2	1975 17(1): 56
Trench 13N	48A70	10,480 ± 960 (Tx–1252)+	Residue	F_2	1975 17(1): 56
Trench 13N	48A70	9560 ± 150 (Tx–1253)+	Humates	F_2	1975 17(1): 56
		9600 ± 150 (Average of 2)			
Trench 13N	47A70	9810 ± 150 (Tx–1238)	Carbonate CO_2	F_2	1975 17(1): 56
Trench 13N	46A70	9660 ± 150 (Tx–1237)	Cabonate CO_2	F_2	1975 17(1): 56
Trench 13N	44A70	9810 ± 570 (Tx–1183)	Residue	F_2	1975 17(1): 56
Trench 13N	44A70	9570 ± 370 (Tx–1184)+	Humates (1st)	F_2	1975 17(1): 56
Trench 13N	44A70	9980 ± 360 (Tx–1185)+	Humates (2nd)	F_2	1975 17(1): 56
		9820 ± 100 (Average of 2)			
Profile B	———	8830 ± 170 (I–4566)	Carbonate CO_2	F_2	No listing
Profile B	———	9823 ± 46 (AA–26210)	Residue	F_{2a4}	Jull et al. 1999
Profile B	———	10,325 ± 44 (AA–26211)	Residue	F_2	Jull et al. 1999
Profile B	———	10,628 ± 60 (AA–26212)	Residue	F_{2a1}	Jull et al. 1999
North of RR	2A70	10,680 ± 140 (SMU–109)	Residue	F_2	1975 17(3): 355
North of RR	2A70	9420 ± 80 (SMU–130)+	Humates (1st)	F_2	1975 17(3): 355
North of RR	2A70	9190 ± 250 (SMU–133)+	Humates (2nd)	F_2	1975 17(3): 355
		9400 ± 30 (Average of 2)			
Area 8	28A70	10,260 ± 430 (Tx–1180)	Residue	F_2	1975 17(1): 55
Area 8	28A70	9410 ± 160 (Tx–1181)+	Humates (1st)	F_2	1975 17(1): 55

Table A.1. Curry Draw Radiocarbon Ages Arranged Stratigraphically by Locality (Continued)

Locality	Sample Number	Radiocarbon age (Lab. No.) Years Before Present (1950)	Material*	Stratum (Square)	Radiocarbon or other reference
Area 8	28A70	9240 ± 270 (Tx–1182)+ 9370 ± 140 (Average of 2)	Humates (2nd)	F_2	1975 17(1): 55
Trench 28	23–21	9790 ± 160 (Tx–1460)+	Humates (1st)	F_2	1975 17(1): 55
Trench 28	23–21	9850 ± 160 (Tx–1461)+ 9820 ± 110 (Average of 2)	Humates (2nd)	F_2	1975 17(1): 55
Sayles sample	———	8270 ± 260 (A–69 bis.)	Residue	F_2 or F_3	1962 4: 245
		Clovis Surface (Basal F_2 contact)			
Area 4 hearth	H–7	10,760 ± 100 (A–1045)	Charcoal + F_2	F_2/D contact (K18)	1981 23(2): 209
Area 4 hearth	4–29	12,600 ± 2440 (Tx–1044)	Charcoal + F_2	F_2/D contact (K18)	1975 17(1): 54
Area 4 hearth	4–29	10,260 ± 140 (Tx–1045)	Humates + F_2	F_2/D contact (K18)	1975 17(1): 54
Trench 28	23–20	10,740 ± 190 (SMU–19)	Humates	F_2/F_1 contact	1974 16(3): 371
		Graveyard Member (F_1)			
Trench 28	23–28	10,790 ± 150 (SMU–29)	Humates	F_1	1974 16(3): 371
Trench 28	23–21	9790 ± 160 (Tx–1460)	Humates (1st)	F_1	1975 17(1): 55
Trench 28	23–21	9850 ± 160 (Tx–1461)	Humates (2nd)	F_1	1975 17(1): 55
Trench 28	23–19	10,930 ± 170 (Tx–1462)+	Charcoal	F_1	1975 17(1): 55
Trench 28	23–19	10,900 ± 200 (Tx–1463)	Humates	F_1	1975 17(1): 55
Discovery site (Area 1)	1MS66	11,150 ± 450 (A–805A)+	Charcoal	F_1	1967 9(1): 11
	1MS66	11,300 ± 500 (A–805B)	Humates	F_1	1967 9(1): 11
Area 1	4–32	8770 ± 80 (SMU–17)	Charcoal (*Fraxinus* sp.)	F_1 (C4)	1974 16(3): 370
Area 1 Extension	23–15	12,940 ± 390 (Tx–1406)	Charcoal	F_1 (C3S)	1974 17(1): 55
Area 1	23–17	11,080 ± 180 (TX–1413)+	Charcoal	F_1 (C5S)	1975 17(1): 55
Area 1	MSS–10	12,820 ± 450 (SMU–190)	Snail shell CO_2	Marl lens in F_1	No listing
Area 2	———	10,840 ± 140 (SMU–42)+	Charcoal	F_1 (E1)	1974 16(3): 371
Area 2	4–2	11,190 ± 180 (SMU–18)+	Charcoal (*Fraxinus* sp.)	F_1 (F2)	1974 16(3): 370
Area 2	4–35A	10,840 ± 70 (SMU–41)+	Charcoal	F_1 (E3)	1974 16(3): 371
Area 2	4–35B	11,160 ± 110 (SMU–43)	Humates	F_1	1974 16(3): 371
Profile B	23–26	10,710 ± 160 (Tx–1459)+	Charcoal	F_1	1975 17(1): 55
Trench 20	23–22	10,890 ± 180 (SMU–27)+	Charcoal	F_1	1974 16(3): 371
Trench 20	23–22	11,210 ± 200 (SMU–28) 10,900 ± 50 (Average of 8)	Humates	F_1	1974 16(3): 371
		Coro Marl (E)			
Profile A	4–24	10,430 ± 160 (I–4565)	Carbonate CO_2	E	No listing
Profile A	26MS66	9780 ± 140 (I–4563)	Carbonate CO_2	E	No listing
Profile A	25MS66	12,310 ± 170 (I–4562)	Carbonate CO_2	E	No listing
Profile A	24MS66	19,620 ± 380 (I–4564)	Carbonate CO_2	E	No listing
Profile A	23MS66	21,200 ± 500 (A–897)	Carbonate CO_2	E	1971 13(1): 10
Profile Y	23–55	11,880 ± 250 (SMU–33)	Marl Residue	E	1974 16(3): 371
Profile Y	23–57	13,980 ± 190 (SMU–34)	Marl Residue	E	1974 16(3): 371
Profile Y	23–59	18,060 ± 150 (SMU–35)	Marl Residue	E	1974 16(3): 371
Profile Y	23–61	16,810 ± 420 (SMU–36)	Marl Residue	E	1974 16(3): 371
Profile Y	23–63	27,560 ± 2300 (SMU–37)	Marl Residue	E	1974 16(3): 371
Profile Y	23–64	19,650 ± 1400 (SMU–38)	Marl Residue	E	1974 16(3): 371
Trench 1	14–51	10,480 ± 200 (Tx 1234)	Carbonate CO_2	E	1975 17(1): 54
Trench 1	14–52	13,310 ± 190 (Tx–1235)	Carbonate CO_2	E	1975 17(1): 54
Tributary	14–53	10,750 ± 170 (Tx–1236)	Carbonate CO_2	E	1975 17(1): 60

Table A.1. Curry Draw Radiocarbon Ages Arranged Stratigraphically by Locality (Continued)

Locality	Sample Number	Radiocarbon age (Lab. No.) Years Before Present (1950)	Material*	Stratum	Radiocarbon or other reference
		Sobaipuri Mud (D)			
Trench 12N	2MS66	29,000 ± 2000 (A–896A)	Residue	D	1971 13(1): 10
	2MS66	19,200 ± 1600 (A–896B)	Humates	D	1971 13(1): 10
Profile A	27MS66	9450 ± 270 (SMU– ?)	Humates	D	No listing

* Residue refers to soil or sediment organic residue remaining after standard acid-base-acid chemical pretreatments. Humates are the humic acids extracted by the standard pretreatment and precipitated at low pH as sodium humates. Residue plus humates refers to a recombination of the two. Humates (2nd) refers to a second extraction after repeating the acid-base treatment a second time. Two or more fractions from the same sample are isolated by spaces in the table, and in some cases letters following the laboratory numbers designate residue (A), humates (B), and carbonate (C).
+ Values used in determining the average, using the procedure of Long and Rippeteau (1974).

Table A.2. Multifraction Radiocarbon Ages of Clanton Clay (F_{2a}) and Earp Marl (F_{2b}) Microstrata in Trench 13 North and Trench 18, Area 8 in Stratigraphic Order as shown in Figure A.1

Sample No.*	Stratum	Residue	Lab. No.†	Chemical Fraction 1st Humate	Lab No.	2nd Humate	Lab No.	Carbonate	Lab. No.
				Trench 13 North					
58	F_{3a5}	9200 ± 440	Tx–1192	8090 ± 130	Tx–1193				
54	F_{3b1}								
57	F_{3a2}	7410 ± 610	Tx–1249	9320 ± 200	Tx–1250	9020 ± 190	Tx–1251		
56	F_{3a2}								
55	F_{3a2}	9640 ± 180	Tx–1189	9630 ± 310	Tx–1190	9450 ± 180	Tx–1191		
				(Disconformity)					
53	F_{3a2}	10,800 ± 1700	Tx–1245	8820 ± 250	Tx–1246			8980 ± 140	Tx–1244
52	F_{2a4}	10,580 ± 3500	Tx–1186	8870 ± 140	Tx–1187	8580 ± 240	Tx–1188		
51	F_{2b3}	10,200 ± 680	Tx–1241	8600 ± 240	Tx–1242	8940 ± 210	Tx–1243	9240 ± 140	Tx–1240
50	F_{2a3}	5050 ± 2030	Tx–1247	9820 ± 160	Tx–1248				
49	F_{2b2}							9310 ± 150	Tx–1239
48	F_{2a2}	10,480 ± 960	Tx–1252	9560 ± 100	Tx–1253				
47	F_{2b1}							9810 ± 150	Tx–1238
46	F_{2b1}							9660 ± 150	Tx–1237
45	F_{2b1}								
44	F_{2a1}	9810 ± 570	Tx–1183	9570 ± 370	Tx–1184	9980 ± 360	Tx–1185		
				Trench 18, Area 8					
24		7430 ± 100	Tx–1178A	7110 ± 140	Tx–1178B	6980 ± 180	Tx–1179		
25									
26				8200 ± 70	SMU–160	8330 ± 130	SMU–165		
27									
28	F_{2a}	10,260 ± 430	Tx–1180	9410 ± 160	Tx–1181	9240 ± 270	Tx–1182		

* All sample field numbers are succeeded by AZ70 for the state and year of collection.
† University of Texas laboratory number as reported in 1975 *Radiocarbon* 17(1): 55–58.

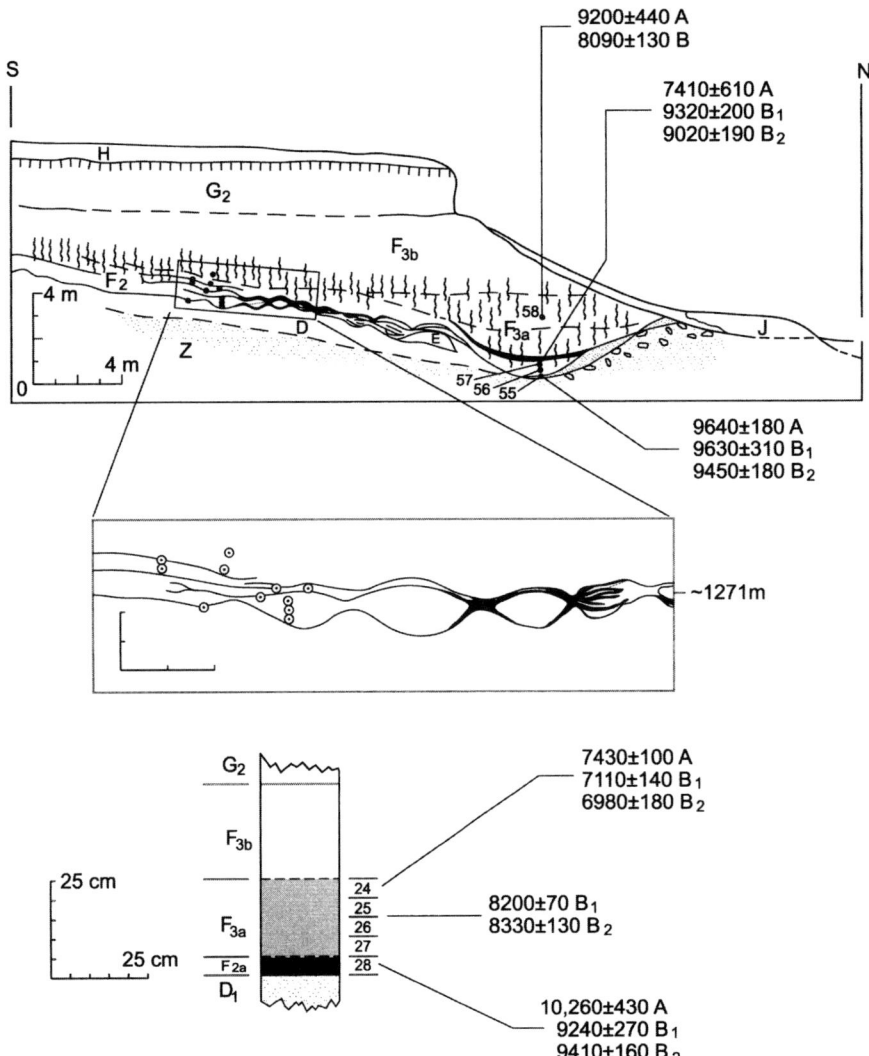

Figure A.1. Detailed stratigraphy of interbedded Clanton clay stringers and Earp marl at Trench 13N and Trench 18 in Area 8: *a*, stratigraphic profile of Trench 13N (radiocarbon dates in Table A.2, A = carbonaceous residue; B = humic acids); *b*, detailed stratigraphy of interbedded Clanton clay (F_{2a}) stringers and Earp marl (F_{2b}) at Trench 13N where sampled for multifraction radiocarbon dating in 1970 (numbers in *b* refer to F_2 and F_3 sample numbers followed by A70 in Table A.1); *c*, multifraction radiocarbon dating of sample sequence through Clanton clay (F_{2a}) and basal Donnet silt (F_{3a}) in Trench 18 in Area 8.

contamination from this source. Whereas it lay about 6.5 m below the pre-dissection floor of the valley, it was practically exposed in the arroyo wall except for a relatively thin cover of colluvium.

On 26 June 1970 we cut a fresh face in the wall with a backhoe to facilitate mapping and profiling the wall designated Trench 13N (13 North), an extension of Trench 13. We cut approximately 50 cm back into the wall and straightened up the profile with a trench shovel and troweling before extending the level line from Trench 13. After completing the stratigraphic profile, we collected samples on 30 June 1970. At this time, due to nuclear testing, the ^{14}C content of the atmosphere was about 152 percent of Modern (that of the 1950 troposphere) according to Nydal and Lövseth (1983).

There was no rainfall on this site during the four days the profile was exposed before sampling. However, it is possible that rain had penetrated the 50 cm or so of cover since the beginning of the thermonuclear age in 1955. In 1962 and 1963, due to two 50-megaton tests by the Soviet Union, the ^{14}C content of the atmosphere nearly doubled the natural amount (Nydal and Lövseth 1983). If rainfall at Murray Springs during this time penetrated to the level of samples collected in 1970, it is possible that this could account for the anomalously young ages in all fractions in Table A.2 and to a lesser extent for those from Trench 18 in Area 8.

Trench 18, as explained in Chapter 2, exposed a buried spring conduit covered by the black mat. Here the black mat consisted of 5 cm of truly black F_2 overlain by about 20 cm of dark brownish gray F_3 about 2 m below the surface. This occurrence was sampled in 5-cm increments (Fig. A.1c), the bulk sediment pretreated, and the fractions dated as shown in Table A.2. The basal age for the residue fraction of 10,260 ± 430 B.P. is within one sigma of other basal ages for the Clanton clay but definitely on the young side. These ages include a date of 10,680 ± 140 B.P. (Table A.1) from a natural exposure north of the railroad bed at Murray Springs and an AMS value of 10,630 ± 60 B.P. from a black stringer (Figs. 2.12, 2.13) resting on the Graveyard channel sand (F_1) at the north wall exposure in the South Branch of the draw (Jull and others 1999). At the Lehner Site the oldest ages obtained on the Clanton Member are 11,000 ± 100 B.P. in Trench 25 and 10,410 ± 190 B.P. in Area 2.

Radiocarbon ages of the top of the black mat vary widely due to bioturbation, possible nuclear ^{14}C contamination, and humic acid mobility, but a deposit with a date of 9900 ± 80 B.P. at the Lehner Site is overlain by a basal Donnet silt (F_3) with a date of 9530 ± 100 B.P. This, plus a 9640 ± 180 B.P. age for a basal F_{3a} channel at Murray Springs Trench 12N (Table A.1) and the three fraction ages for sample 55 from Trench 13N, suggest an age of about 9800 B.P. for the end of F_2 deposition. This is supported by an AMS age of 9820 ± 45 B.P. for the upper of four F_{2a} stringers (Figs. 2.12, 2.13) at the north wall of the South Branch of Curry Draw (Jull and others 1999).

Overall the results indicate that the Clanton clay probably began to form at about 10,800 B.P. and ended about 9800 B.P. This age range corresponds to that of the Younger Dryas climate reversal, a glacially cold period that reversed the warming trend of deglaciation during the Bølling-Allerød chronozones (Nilsson 1983: 267).

DATING THE CORO MARL

The white Coro marl is a late glacial-age lake or pond deposit that underlies the Clovis occupation surface (Chapter 2). It consists of relatively soft calcium carbonate (calcite) and clay with dispersed sand and silt grains. Up to five relatively thick marl beds are separated by relatively thin light olive green clay partings (Figs. A.2, 2.11).

In radiocarbon dating carbonates, one is faced with two problems. One is that during initial precipitation in water the bicarbonate ion can include carbon derived from older sources such as limestone or caliche (the "hard water" effect), thus making ^{14}C ages too old. The other problem is that calcium carbonate of the porous marl is subject to chemical exchange such that atmospheric CO_2, particularly in rainwater carrying nuclear ^{14}C, can invade the marl, thus making ^{14}C ages too young. To avoid this problem samples were collected about a meter back from the arroyo wall from an exposure made with a backhoe at the location of Profile A (Figs. A.2, 1.3, and 2.11). Radiocarbon dating of the marl carbonate produced ages ranging from 9780 ± 140 B.P. near the top to 21,200 ± 500 B.P. near the bottom (Table A.1, Figs. A.2, 2.11).

Another way to avoid the exchange problem is to date the organic fraction of the marl. This was accomplished by pyrolysing blocks of marl in a closed electric furnace at ~600°C, which caused a color change from white to various shades of gray depending on the amount of organic carbon in the sample. By hydrolysing the sample in hydrochloric acid, a black carbon residue was obtained and radiocarbon dated. At the locality of Profile Y (Fig. A.2) on the right bank nearly opposite Profile A, six samples provided ages ranging from 11,880 ± 250 B.P. to 19,650 ± 1400 B.P. and, apparently, an anomalous value of 27,560 ± 2300 B.P. (Table A.1). On the other hand, considering the large standard errors, the lowest two values could be approximate ages with the stratigraphically lowest sample possibly being contaminated by rainwater conveyed into the arroyo wall on top of the less permeable Sobaipuri mudstone, an aquatard.

DATING THE SOBAIPURI MEMBER

As stated in Chapter 2, the Coro marl is conformably underlain by the light olive green Sobaipuri Mem-

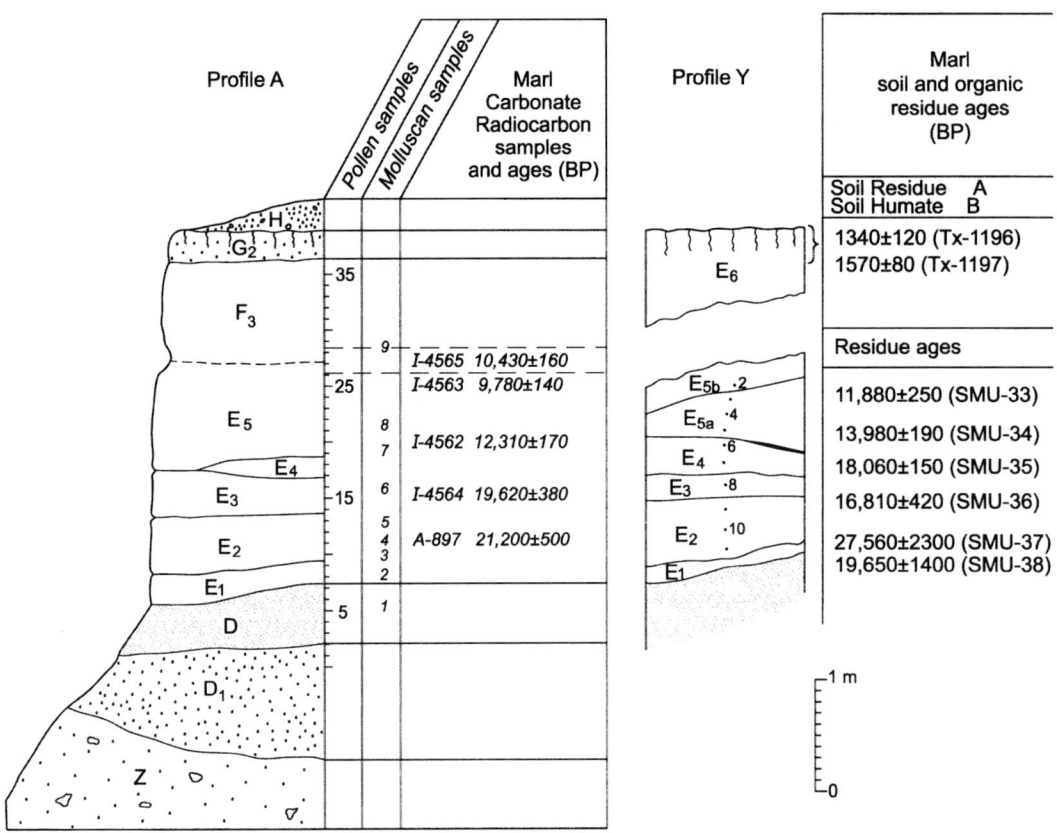

Figure A.2. Type section of the Coro Member at Profile A (Mehringer Pollen Profile 6; Fig. 2.19) at the north bank of the South Branch of Curry Draw at Murray Springs (Figs. 1.3 and 2.10), showing locations of molluscan samples taken by Jim I. Mead (Chapter 4), carbonate radiocarbon ages, and Profile Y on the south bank that shows the organic fraction radiocarbon ages of the marl.

ber (Stratum D) of the Murray Springs Formation. This is a clay or mudstone that varies in thickness from less than 10 cm to more than 1 m. In its thicker occurrences, it contains a dark brown to dark gray layer 5 cm to 10 cm thick that on cursory examination is similar to the Clanton Member (F_{2a}). However, it is not as black and is more clayey. A bulk sample from Trench 12N, pretreated the same way as the black mat samples, provided radiocarbon ages of 29,000 ± 2000 B.P. on the residue fraction and a humate age of 19,200 ± 1600 B.P. (Table A.1), the latter being highly contaminated with younger humates. Another bulk sample from Profile A, collected several years later from the surface of the cut wall, was highly contaminated and provided a very erroneous age of 9450 ± 270 B.P. (Table A.1), probably due to nuclear ^{14}C (Haas and others 1986).

This sample exemplifies the problem of nuclear age contamination. As stated above, in the early 1960s the atmospheric content of radiocarbon nearly doubled the prebomb level. Therefore, surface or near surface samples, such as this one, become highly contaminated as rainwater carries thermonuclear bomb-produced ^{14}C into permeable sediments. The backhoe trench at Profile A was cut to avoid this problem by exposing sediments at least a meter back from the arroyo wall. However, the Stratum D bulk sample was collected many years after the exposure was made. In spite of the decades since the Nuclear Test Ban Treaty, the atmosphere currently still contains an excess of about 10 percent nuclear ^{14}C.

The problem of nuclear contamination is particularly bad for bulk sediment and soil samples because of the complex organic content and the presence of clays that form complexes with organic molecules. Also, the permeability and large surface areas in these materials enhance the opportunity for absorption of contaminants. Furthermore, this contamination of bulk samples is a very inconsistent phenomenon. It depends mostly on the accessibility of the sampled section to vadose water that percolates downward from the surface. If organic soil horizons are encountered they can contribute soluble humic and fulvic acids to the translocation of contaminants, including nuclear ^{14}C. Pathways from the surface can be highly variable due to inhomogeneities, including cracks and rodent burrows (krotovinas). Also, as with Trench 13N, rainwater can penetrate laterally from side walls of exposures. These are the variables that probably account for the anomalous variations in the radiocarbon results (Table A.2) seen in Trench 13N and Trench 18.

These factors are much less of a significant problem with charcoal and oxidized wood because they do not form complex molecules with contaminants as long as all clays are removed. During normal A-B-A pretreatment, as stated above, the sample is subjected to many washings as well as the acid and base treatments. These repeated washings should adequately flush away such contaminants from charcoal and oxidized wood.

Recent investigations by Pigati have shown that some species of terrestrial gastropods incorporate carbon in their shells that is in equilibrium with the contemporaneous atmosphere and, therefore, potentially very useful for radiocarbon dating. Samples of *Succinea, Pupilla muscorum,* and *Enconulus fulvus* collected from the Coro marl in the headcut southwest of Profile Y (Fig. 1.3) yielded ages from ~25,000 B.P. to 13,000 B.P., essentially duplicating the carbonate and organic fraction ages but with greater precision and less contamination (Pigati and others 2004). Also, they are less likely to be penetrated by water because of their greater density than the marl. Furthermore, the shell surfaces are acid etched to remove any surface contamination.

CONCLUSIONS

The pretreatment of charcoals from the Murray Springs Clovis level reveals they are indeed charcoals that provide reliable ages for the Clovis occupation. Was this ash (*Fraxinus* sp.) wood selected by the Clovis people for its high heat value or was it simply the most readily available firewood? We may never know for certain but if the typical riparian mix today of cottonwood (*Populus* sp.), walnut (*Juglans* sp.) and ash was the same during Clovis time, the near 100 percent use of ash suggests deliberate selection.

The maximum life span of desert ash (*F. velutina*) today is about 75 years, but it is fast growing in well-watered riparian habitats where it would reach its maximum size and die considerably earlier (J. Betancourt, personal communication). Therefore, the dated charcoals could have an inherited age of perhaps 50 years or less at the time of Clovis use. If it had been dead for a decade, another ten years could be added. However, Hemmings (Chapter 5) mentions that charcoal from the Clovis hearth in Area 4 appeared to be of small twig sizes and therefore would have little or no age inherited from older tree rings. As the average of eight Clovis charcoals is 10,900 ± 50 B.P., the latest probable age for the Clovis occupation is 10,850 B.P.

The fact that all of the charcoals yielded humic acids of essentially the same age upon pretreatment suggests that at least some of the samples (each sample consisted of many fragments) contained partially burned wood that on decay converted to humic acids. It seems unlikely that a secondary source would yield dates of the same age as the charcoal.

Bulk sediment radiocarbon dating of the black mat (Stratum F_2) organic matter, although more subject to contamination and not as stratigraphically specific as the Clovis charcoal, suggests an age range of 10,800 B.P. to 9,800 B.P., essentially a Younger Dryas correlative. Ages obtained on the carbonate fractions appear to be about a millennium too young, indicating contamination but no hard water effect, suggesting the surface water ^{14}C was in equilibrium with the atmosphere at the time of precipitation.

Absence of the hard water effect can be assumed for the Coro marl where carbonate, organic fraction, and snail ages were all similar except where carbonates in the upper and lower strata were contaminated by later pedogenic carbonates or nuclear age carbon. The snail dates are certainly the most precise ages and probably the most accurate. Therefore, the Coro marl was deposited throughout the entire late glacial period.

The redating of Murray Springs strata by AMS analysis, including analysis of single charcoal grains, is in progress. We expect this new assessment to eventually provide better precision by reducing the standard errors.

APPENDIX B

Nature and Origin of the Black Mat, Stratum F_2

C. Vance Haynes, Jr.

Contributors
Michael J. Holdaway, Southern Methodist University, Dallas, Texas
James L. Bischoff, U.S. Geological Survey, Menlo Park, California
Raymond N. Rogers, Los Alamos National Laboratory, New Mexico
Artur Stankiewicz, Shell International
Erik Tegelaar, Baseline Resolution, Inc.
Jerry A. Leenheer, U.S. Geological Survey, Denver, Colorado
Jesse A. M. Ballenger, Department of Anthropology, University of Arizona

The Clanton Ranch Member (Stratum F_2) of the Lehner Ranch Formation is commonly referred to as the black mat (Chapter 2). In its simplest form it is a black organic clayey silt up to 10 cm thick in the low areas, thins up slope, and pinches out between one and two meters above the lowest areas (thalwegs). In breaking into aggregates it shows a strong fine angular blocky structure (Fig. 2.19). At an early date it was referred to as an azonal A horizon, but it is not a soil per se. It has a distinct, sharp, basal contact across variable lithologies and usually breaks cleanly away from the underlying surface, which allowed most of the Clovis artifacts to be exposed in situ exactly as they had been deposited 13,000 years ago. In the lowest areas of the site, the black mat splits into stringers (thin bands) 1 mm to 10 mm thick (F_{2a}) separated by white marl facies, the Earp Member (F_{2b}), up to 20 cm or more thick (Fig. 2.16). The marl contains a mixture of aquatic and terrestrial gastropods (Chapter 4). The black mat is clearly water laid, perhaps with wet meadow soil facies around the edges.

As reported by Abelson and Hare (1970), the black mat is essentially kerogen, which is described by McIver (1967: 26) as follows.

> The kerogen considered herein is not simple unaltered detritus incorporated into the sediment; it has no counterpart in nature, but is formed from varying mixtures of simple organic precursors. At or near the sediment-water interface in the Recent environment, the carbohydrates, proteins, lipids, etc. are attacked and altered in varying degrees by the microbial population, and then some of the products probably undergo a condensation or polymerization to form the kerogen which resists bacterial attack, but which is subject to the effects of temperature and pressure. Therefore, the composition of kerogen is just as varied as the precursors that may combine to form it. As Breger and Brown (1962) suggest, the end members may be primarily humic or sapropelic, or as this paper prefers, carbohydrate and lignin-rich or lipid-rich.

Whereas in the field it is commonly referred to as the black mat, the Clanton clay is actually a clayey sandy silt (Table B.1). Chemically it contains up to 10 percent organic carbon, ≤ 0.3 percent nitrogen, and typically less than 1 percent $CaCO_3$. A marl facies contained nearly 50 percent $CaCO_3$. The samples in Table B.1 are from a microstratigraphic sequence exposed in 2001 by backhoe trench 13N (Appendix E; Figs. E.1, E.3).

In 1971 Dr. Michael J. Holdaway of Southern Methodist University, Dallas, Texas, ran atomic absorption and X-ray analysis of a basal portion of the

Table B.1. Analyisis of Black Mat (F_2) Samples from Trench 13N
(by J. Ballenger)

	\multicolumn{6}{c}{AZ01 No.}					
	23	25	26	27	39a	39b
Initial weight**	6.68	7.47	8.58	7.21	3.02	9.84
% Coarse sand				3.60	6.38	
% Medium sand	10.58	13.27	23.37	24.39	5.63	1.73
% Silt	40.58	30.30	36.71	36.64	62.24	19.11
% Clay†	22.67	16.44	11.23	9.97	8.08	2.48
% Humates	26.17	39.98	25.07	22.62	24.05	7.38
	100.00	99.99	99.98	100.00	100.00	
% $CaCO_3$*	0.02	0.08	0.49	5.96	49.53	
% Carbon	2.84	9.71	0.80	0.96	5.51	1.69
C/N ratio	22.9	30.3	14.6	15.77	29.71	

NOTE: Sample 39b percentages based on initial marl weight of 9.835 g before hydrolysis.
* Determined by Chittick apparatus.
** Residue weight (g) after Chittick hydrolysis.
† Contains some fine silt

Table B.2. Atomic Absorption Analysis of Black Mat (F_2)
(by M. J. Holdaway)

Compound	Black Mat	Residue*
% SiO_2	67.79**	64.88
% Al_2O_3	16.44	15.77
% Fe_2O_3	3.79	3.07
% MgO	1.33	1.24
% CaO	2.45	0.43
% Na_2O	1.14	1.55
% K_2O	3.42	4.56
	96.36†	91.50

* Insoluble residue from HCl hydrolysis.
** Accuracy is about ± 2% of amount present.
† Remainder is probably mostly H_2O.

Table B.3. Chemical Composition of the Acid-soluble Component of the Black Mat (F_2)
(by J. L. Bischoff)

Compound	Black Mat
% SiO_2	5.00
% Al_2O_3	6.37
% Fe_2O_3	1.10
% MgO	0.50
% CaO	3.43
% Na_2O	0.13
% K_2O	0.37
% CO_2 inorganic	2.30
% CO_2 organic	24.39
% LOI*	<0.01
% Insoluble residue	55.04
	98.99

* Loss on ignition at 900° C corrected for organic carbon and carbonate as volatile CO_2.

black mat from Area 8. The X-ray pattern is mostly that of the clay montmorillonite plus quartz. The results of the atomic absorption analysis are shown in Table B.2. The chemical composition of the acid-soluble component of the black mat from Area 4 was determined by Dr. James Bischoff of the U.S. Geological Survey, Menlo Park, California, and is shown in Table B.3

An early organic analysis on black mat, unfortunately, was not from the Murray Springs Site. In 1970 Dr. Philip Abelson of the Geophysical Laboratory of the Carnegie Institution of Washington, D.C, visited the Department of Geosciences at the University of Arizona. After I explained the mystery of the origin of the black mat, he asked if he could take a sample for analysis. Not having any Murray Springs samples on hand, I happily gave him about 400 g from the Boquillas arroyo locality about 21 km (13 miles) north of Murray Springs where the same age black mat overlies the Sopaipuri mudstone. At Carnegie, this sample was analyzed by Dr. P. E. Hare and reported in the Carnegie annual report as kerogen with a carbon-nitrogen (C/N) ratio of 37 (Abelson and Hare 1970). Samples were incubated with amino acids at various temperatures for comparisons to other kerogens under both oxidizing and reducing conditions. The authors offer no conclusions as to the origin of the black mat other than stating that humic substances can derive from lignin and leaf litter as well as algae, lichens, and mosses that do not contain lignin.

During the 1968 excavation at Murray Springs, we were fortunate in having the late Dr. Raymond N. Rogers as a volunteer crew member. Ray was an organic chemist and thermal analyst from the Los Alamos National Laboratory and was visiting the Geochronology Laboratories of the University of Arizona when he volunteered his services. In addition to personally discovering one of the Clovis points in the bison kill area (Area 4), he took a keen interest in the origin and nature of the black mat and offered to analyze some of the F_2 black mat. He analyzed several other black mat samples as well as those from Murray Springs, but his main sample came from Area 4 where he was excavating.

CHEMICAL EVALUATION OF THE BLACK MAT DEPOSIT AT MURRAY SPRINGS
Raymond N. Rogers

Several hypotheses have been advanced for the genesis of the black mat (F_2), the Clanton Ranch Member of the Lehner Ranch Formation. It has been suggested that the black mat could be the result of the decay of the large amount of animal tissue indicated by the local concentrations of bones found in the areas observed. It is also possible that the layer could contain residues of shallow-water plants, mosses, and grasses. Another possibility is that the organic fraction of "moorwasser" (water that has percolated through high humic or active organic regions) could have been precipitated by a high calcium-ion concentration near the inorganic surface. Finally, the black mat could be the result of a heavy deposition of algae. This chemical study of the black mat was designed to furnish observations that could be used to test these hypotheses. Morphological and chemical evidence taken together strongly suggest an algal origin for the organic material of the black mat.

Morphological Observations

The black mat is characterized by (1) sharp contacts; (2) variations in thickness, the thickest parts appearing in low areas; (3) deposition on quite different lithologic units forming a buried topography; (4) the absence of visible plant structures; (5) fine angular blocky to granular structure; (6) a waxy, sticky consistence; and (7) interfingering with lacustrine marl facies in the lowest area (Fig. 2.16).

The black mat covers the surface of pond clays (Stratum D) in many places at the Murray Springs Site, and when carefully removed from its contact with the clay, the surface shows shrinkage cracks (Fig. B.1) and an undisturbed surface. The clay at contact surfaces with thick black mat tends to have a superficial green color.

Chemical Observations

A sample from the center of the black mat taken at a fresh, unweathered location at Murray Springs was treated with 2N HCl to remove all carbonates. The washed and dried residue was analyzed for carbon (C),

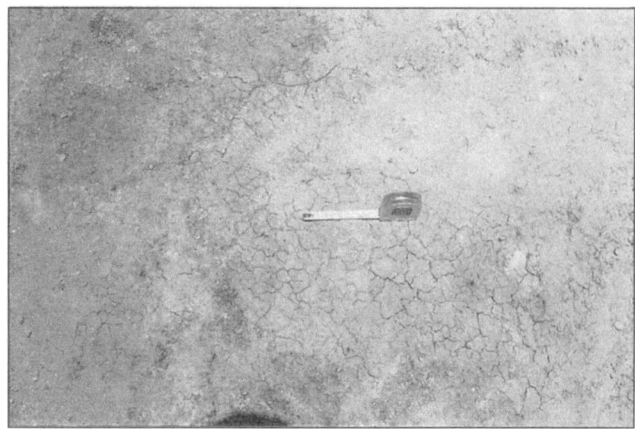

Figure B.1. Pond clays just under the black mat, showing shrinkage cracks on the Clovis surface.

hydrogen (H), and nitrogen (N) by standard combustion techniques, yielding the following results: C = 4.6 percent, H = 1.3 percent, and N = trace.

When normal soils are analyzed, the organic content can be approximated as 1.72 times the percent C; therefore, the black mat sample should be about 7.9 percent organic material. Similar samples gave weight losses of 8–11 percent by cold-oxygen-plasma combustion, and weight losses as high as 22 percent have been observed after heating in oxygen. The weight loss observed on heating black mat samples includes considerable water and some carbon dioxide from different inorganic sources.

Inorganic components comprise by far the larger fraction of the black mat. Spectrographic analysis showed that the inorganic fraction is composed largely of silica (Si), iron (Fe), and aluminum (Al) with smaller amounts of magnesium (Mg), potassium (K), and calcium (Ca). X-ray diffraction analysis detected significant amounts of montmorillonite. Chemical and microscopic analyses showed that a representative sample of the black mat contains about 11 percent calcite; however, microscopic observations proved that the calcite was largely localized between the peds. A representative sample contains about 0.19 percent phosphorus, no gypsum, and only a faint trace of sulfate by standard analytical methods (U.S. Regional Salinity Laboratory 1947). The hydrolytic pH of a sample selected to be free of calcium carbonate($CaCO_3$) is slightly acid (pH = 6.7).

Attempts were made to extract organic material from rich black mat samples with both acid and base.

After prolonged room-temperature extraction and desalting by dialysis against distilled water, yields of largely ash-free organic material were the following: from extraction with 2N HCl, 0.2 percent; from extraction with 0.2N NaOH, 0.025 percent.

The largest part of the organic material of the black mat cannot be extracted without reaction, it is exceedingly stable to hydrolysis, and it appears to dehydrate and char rather than decouple on dry pyrolysis. The organic fraction largely has the properties of a kerogen as found independently by Abelson and Hare (1970) on black mat from 21 km north of the site.

As received, air-dried samples of black mat and both the acid and alkaline extracts showed barely detectable traces of nitrogen. The important organic components of the black mat appear to be composed only of C, H, and O.

Samples of the black mat were studied by combined pyrolysis and thin-layer chromatography (Rogers 1967; Rogers and Smith 1970). The black mat was found to be essentially free of aromatic constituents. No polynuclear aromatic compounds were found in any mat samples, but traces of aromatic aldehydes and hydroxy compounds could be detected. A fresh sample from Murray Springs showed the lowest concentration of aromatic compounds; however, samples from Boquillas, Lehner, and Moson showed only traces. No vanillin could be found in the pyrolysis products of any of the samples.

Black mat samples did not give strong tests for carbohydrates by direct pyrolysis at any temperature; however, a very strong test was obtained when the sample was wetted with syrupy phosphoric acid before pyrolysis. Furfural (and occasionally hydroxymethyl furfural) was detected between 140° C and approximately 250° C.

Animal materials but not plant materials contain hydroxyproline units that produce pyrrole on pyrolysis. The specificity of a test based on the pyrolytic production of pyrrole for the detection of animal matter has been demonstrated (Feigl 1934). The pyrrole can be detected with great sensitivity with p-dimethylaminobenzaldehyde (Fischer and Meyer-Betz 1911). Only faint tests for animal matter could be obtained from some fresh samples of black mat.

Benzene, acetone, ethanol, 1N HCl, methanol, and water extracts of the black mat were analyzed by thin-layer chromatography. An activated silica gel substrate and 95/5–benzene/methanol solvent system gave useful separations. Terpenes and other hydrocarbon pigments could be separated from "fulvic acids." Benzene was the most useful extractant, and easily detectable amounts of terpenes were recovered. Small amounts of the unoxidized carotene isomers and xanthophylls were identified. No attempt was made to identify all of the remaining terpenes and pigments.

It is recognized that differences exist among different samples of the black mat. There may have been local variations in the proportions to which various materials contributed to the formation of the system; however, there certainly were major differences in preservation. Common characteristics among different locations must be considered first in identifying the primary source of the black mat.

Interpretation of Chemical Observations

The organic material of the black mat is significantly different from that of a normal mature soil (Mortensen and Himes 1964). Whether soil humates are derived from lignin and proteins (Lyon and Buckman 1949) or fungi acting on carbohydrates and lignin (Kononova 1961; Kumada and Hurst 1967), it is well established that aromatic compounds are characteristic of humates. Vanillin is a characteristic degradation product of humates (Christman and Oglesby 1966) and unmodified lignin, and it can be detected and identified with good sensitivity and specificity. Very stable humates are high in polynuclear aromatic compounds (Kononova 1961), and they can be detected with good sensitivity by their intense fluorescence on pyrolysis-TLC plates. The absence of significant amounts of vanillin in the black mat indicates an organic source free of lignin. The absence of polynuclear aromatic compounds indicates preservation of the lignin-free source with relatively little fungal activity.

The presence of the carotene and xanthophyll pigments proves that photosynthetic organisms were contributors to the deposit. The green clay surface in contact with the black mat suggests chlorophyll-derived porphyrins, but no concerted attempt was made to identify porphyrins.

Testing of Hypotheses

In order for an organic layer to persist in the soil, three conditions must be met: (1) it must be sterilized (Nikiforoff 1943), (2) it must be covered and protected soon after production, and (3) hydrolysis products must be rendered insoluble (or hydrolysis must be extremely slow). These conditions, morphological observations, and chemical observations form the basis for testing the possible hypotheses for the formation of the black mat.

Animal tissue (the "mammoth meat hypothesis") could not have provided a significant contribution to the black mat. Pyrrole could be detected in large amounts in the pyrolysis products of bone associated with Clovis artifacts at the Murray Springs Site. No significant amount of pyrrole was detected in the pyrolysis products of the black mat.

Lignin and chemical compounds derived from it were not present in a significant concentration in any black mat sample. All higher plants contain lignin; therefore, water plants, mosses, and grasses could not have been important in the formation of the deposit.

Moorwasser precipitates can be eliminated on the basis of low aromatic content as well as the absence of hydrocarbons in the pyrolyzates. Alkali and alkaline earth salts of organic acids produce hydrocarbons on pyrolysis (the Dumas reaction).

Algae, however, are important photosynthetic sources of organic material free of lignin. The polysaccharides of algal cell walls are extremely resistant to hydrolysis and enzymatic attack (Shefner and others 1962). Algae are usually 14–24 percent carbohydrate, and the cell-wall material consists largely of protein and polysaccharides (Dunn and Wolk 1970). The polysaccharides of algal cells contain significant amounts of pentose units (Shnyukova and Pirozhenko 1974). Algal residues have a saccharide-type structure nearly free of aromatic components and heterocycles, but kerogens contain heterocycles and some unsaturation and aromatic structures (Tissot and others 1974). A hydrolytically stable organic deposit low in aromatic fractions but rich in polysaccharides containing photosynthetic pigments strongly suggests an algal origin.

Carotenoids have recently been used as stratigraphic indicators of eutrophication in a lake, and it was stated that myxoxanthin is characteristic of blue-green algae (Gorham and Sanger 1976). A detailed separation of the xanthophyll pigments in the black mat might enable identification of a specific algal type with a specific deposit.

Pentose sugars and pentosans when decomposed in strong sulfuric acid or heated slowly to the beginning of thermal pyrolysis produce pure furfural (2-furaldehyde). Hexose sugars and their polymers (for example, starch and cellulose) are much more difficult to decompose, and they produce a complex mixture of compounds, including hydroxymethylfurfural. There is no furfural in the primary decomposition products of hexoses; however, a minor amount of furfural is found in products that have been heated for a significant amount of time. Hydroxymethylfurfural deformylates (loses formaldehyde) slowly as it is heated. A small amount of furfural does not indicate the presence of pentosans, but a complete absence of hydroxymethylfurfural proves the absence of hexoses in the black mat.

Woody plants and grasses contain a large amount of cellulose (a polymer of hexose units), hemicelluloses, pectins, and lignin. After burial, the less stable saccharides decompose rapidly, leaving lignin and cellulose. The cellulose decomposes relatively slowly, and the lignin decomposes more slowly yet. Any polyhexose deposit that showed rapid colonization by fungi would produce significant hydroxymethylfurfural on pyrolysis. The black mat does not.

The large amount of furfural obtained from the black mat on acid-catalyzed pyrolysis proves that the deposit is rich in pentosans. The same pyrolysis products are obtained from modern algal tissues that were dried in direct sunlight. Pentosans can provide a relatively easy carbon source for fungal metabolism. Humates and true kerogens do not.

Analysis of vacuum-dried *Chlorella* cells gave a phosphorus content of 8.75 percent; however, Arizona soils have phosphorus contents between about 400 (McClellan, cultivated) and 1600 ppm (Pima, virgin). Straw has a phosphorus content of about 0.008 percent (Rogers 1951). A sample from the thickest area of the black mat contained 0.19 percent phosphorus, a surprisingly high amount. Algae are characteristically high in phosphorus; normal plant materials are not. The composition of the black mat is consistent with an algal source.

Algae develop rapidly in soils and water (Stevenson 1964), and they are even found in reasonable concentrations in rain crusts of desert soils (Fletcher and Martin 1948). The bottom of a sewage lagoon is quickly covered and cemented by an algal deposit, and thick algal deposits are observed on the bottom of drained sewage lagoons (W. H. Stein, personal communication). Very large amounts of blue-green algae are known to have been obtained from lake surfaces in

Mexico. The material was cured in the sun and used by the Aztecs to form a stable foodstuff (*tecuitlatl*) with the consistency of cheese (Toribio de Motolina 1541). Such large amounts were produced that it was used as a trade item, and it was carried by the *pochtecas* (long distance traders) as a travel ration.

A continuous algal surface layer extending onto the moist soil at the pond margin was produced in three hours on an experimental pond. The pond was prepared at Tucson, Arizona, and it was inoculated with *Chlorella* at 9:00 A.M. during the summer. The algal layer quickly coated the pond bottom, and a dried surface could be rewetted without damage. The algal deposit preserved the fine structure of surface features under it. A series of wet/dry cycles of the pond produced a laminar structure of algal deposits that might help explain some of the gross laminar features observed in the black mat at Murray Springs. A dried algal surface can be sterilized by the sun to such an extent that little or no oxygen or carbon dioxide is produced by or from the material on rewetting, new algal activity being observed first in the water.

Conclusions and Discussion

Morphological, chemical, and experimental observations of black mat and algal deposits strongly suggest an algal origin for the deposit. Assuming that the black mat has a predominantly algal origin, different species may be expected in different locations. Different species of algae are known to prefer unique combinations of temperature and salinity. Differences in preservation involving oxidation and fungal activity confuse interpretations of some analytical results; however, a comprehensive study of polysaccharide and pigment composition might be of considerable interest. Temporal variations in water temperature and composition might be identified.

Kerogens yield aliphatic and alicyclic hydrocarbons and a significant amount of heterocyclic and/or bridged compounds on pyrolysis. This is the process used to recover fuels from oil shales. Humates yield significant amounts of phenolic and polycyclicaromatic compounds. The black mat is unique. The organic phase of the black mat dehydrates and chars without the evolution of volatile organic products on dry pyrolysis. This type of action is characteristic of polysaccharides (Lewellen and others 1977), as can be demonstrated by caramelizing and charring sugar.

The fact that a relatively large amount of a blue-green alga (*tecuitlatl*) could be tolerated in the diet of the Aztecs suggests that the "black-mat" alga of Murray Springs could have provided a food source for the fauna of the area. [End of report]

From Rogers' report it is clear that because of a near absence of aromatic hydrocarbons, vanillin, and pyrrole and the presence of pentosans and photosynthetic indicators, an algal origin is indicated. Apparently all of Rogers' samples yielded similar findings.

Additional organic analyses on two black mat samples (6AZ90 and 18AZ94) were conducted in 1999 by Dr. B. Artur Stankiewicz, Shell International, and Dr. Erik Tegelaar, Baseline Resolution, Inc. Their report follows.

PYROLYTIC GAS CHROMATOGRAPHIC MASS SPECTROMETRY ANALYSIS (Py-GC/MS)
Artur Stankiewicz and Erik Tegelaar

Methods

1. Pyrolysis conditions: Analyses of the dichloromethane extracted samples were performed using a CDS 120 pyroprobe (CDS Analytical, Inc., Oxford, Pennsylvania) coupled to an HP 5890 gas chromatograph (Hewlett-Packard, Palo Alto, California), with an HP 5970 mass selective detector and a 50 m HP-1 GC column (0.2 mm i.d., film thickness 0.33 μm). The samples were pyrolyzed in a flow of He for 10 sec. in a platinum coil at 800°C (Fig. B.2).

2. Microscopic observations were carried out on the two samples. A Leitz MPV-II microscope was used for all the analyses, with magnification of the objective 50x and the ocular 10x. After initial observation of the samples, two petrographic analyses were carried out on each sample: one in reflected white light, and one in fluorescent light.

Results and Discussion

Petrography. Both samples are dominantly inorganic and have ~1–2% (by volume) of organic fragments. Organic fragments in the sample 6AZ90 are composed of vitrinite (coaly material) and fragments of spores. Organic matter in sample 18AZ94 is mainly algal and spore origin. *Pyrolysis-gas chromatography/mass spectrometry.* Both samples were pyrolyzed in similar conditions and yielded similar products.

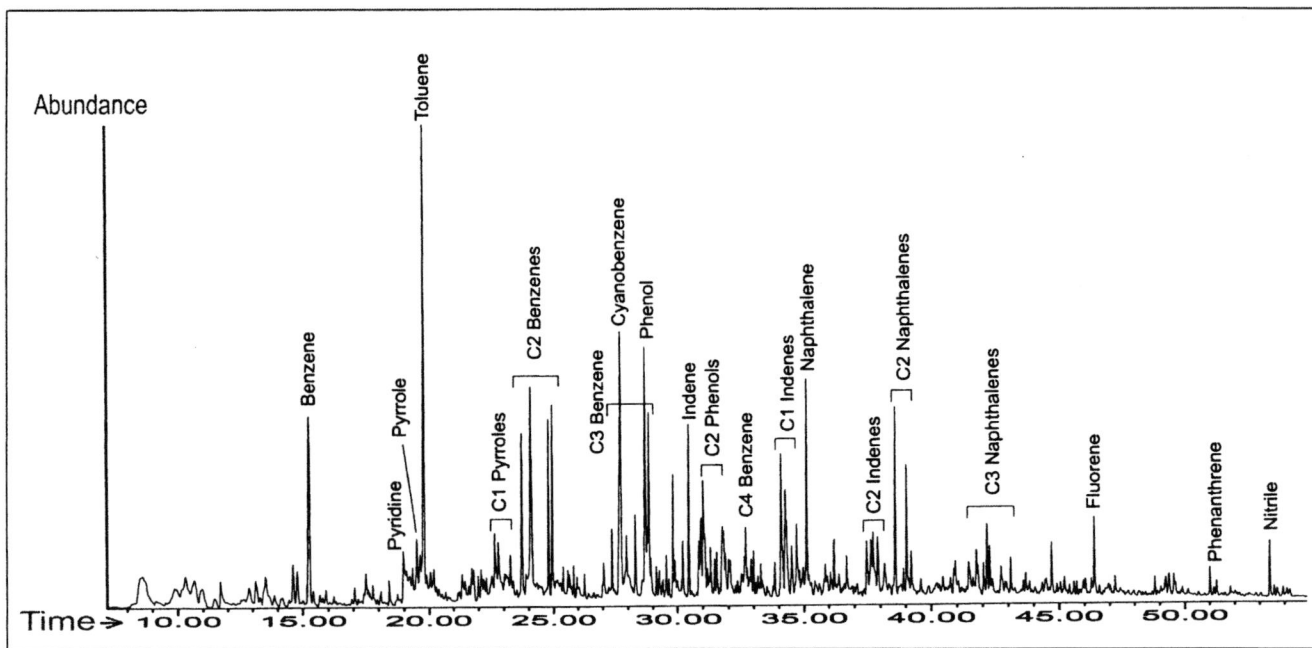

Figure B.2. Sample 18AZ94, 14 mg of material pyrolysed at 800° C for 10 seconds.

Major compounds released upon pyrolysis are aromatics, such as homologue series of benzene and Cl–C4 alkylated benzenes, naphthalene and Cl–C3 alkylated naphthalenes, fluorene and methylfluorenes, phenanthrene and anthracene, as well as indenes and phenols. This type of signature is characteristic for highly mature coals or burned wood fragments. Other minor pyrolysis components observed in the samples were pyrroles, pyridine, cyanobenzenes and nitriles, which can be attributed to the presence of bacterial or fungal fragments (these compounds are often present in pyrolysates of soil). Presence of n-alkenes and n-alkanes is attributed to a pyrolytical fragmentation of aliphatic molecules common in algae or spores.

Conclusions

1. Petrography and Py-GC/MS techniques showed that the organic matter present in both samples is scarce and mainly derived from very aromatic molecules (which can be derived from burned wood). Nitrogen compounds common in pyrolysates of soil are most probably of bacterial and/or fungal origin. Aliphatic compounds are derived from algae or spores present in both samples.

2. Since the organic matter is scarce in both samples, it is suggested that in the future HCl and HF treatment will be first employed to remove inorganics, thus concentrating the organic matter. This step will allow for much more reliable analysis.
[End of report]

Stankiewicz and Tegelaar conclude that the organic matter present in both samples is mainly derived from "very aromatic molecules" possibly derived from burned wood. Lesser amounts of aliphatic compounds are probably derived from algae or spores. They add that more reliable analyses could be made by first removing the inorganic fraction with hydrofluoric and hydrochloric acids, thus concentrating the organics. It appears that the algal component indicated by aliphatic compounds is minor compared to organic matter indicated by aromatic compounds, presumably the decay products of burned wood fragments. These results are somewhat in conflict with those of Rogers, who finds the absence of phenolics and the large component of pentosans as evidence for algae. These differences could be due to differences in black mats from different places in the Murray Springs Site.

Sample 6AZ90 is from a solid black band about 15 mm thick overlying Sobaipuri mud that is about 9 m west of 18AZ94, which is a 1.5-mm black band resting directly on Graveyard sand of the Clovis age channel and overlain by ~3 cm of white soft marl of the Earp Member. Whereas both samples are treated and reported as the same in their reports, Tegelaar, in an earlier telephone conversation, said that the pyrolysis pattern of sample 18AZ94 was unlike anything he had seen. Unfortunately, their report does not elaborate on this characterization.

However, their petrographic analyses indicated that 18AZ94 "is mainly [of] algal and spore origin" whereas organic fragments in 6AZ90 "are composed of vitrinite (coaly material) and fragments of spores." It is possible that what has been identified petrographically as vitrinite is actually charcoal or vitreous carbon as suggested later by Rogers. This would be concordant with Stankiewicz and Tegellar's later statement regarding results of pyrolysis-gas chromatography/mass spectrometry that "this type of signature is characteristic for highly mature coals or burned wood fragments." In this case, the lowland environment of 18AZ94 in the Clovis age stream channel (Stratum F_1) would contain more degradation products of algae than 6AZ90 on higher ground that is richer in burned wood fragments, some of which could be from the Clovis occupation surface where ash-wood charcoal has provided the numerous radiocarbon ages.

In 2002 a sample (7MS75-5) of black mat from a 5-cm thick band exposed by Trench 12 in Area 4 was submitted to Dr. Jerry A. Leenheer of the U.S. Geological Survey, Denver, for analysis by ^{13}C nuclear magnetic resonance (^{13}C-NMR). The reader will see that, independent of the suggestions of the other analysts, Leenheer concentrated the organic matter before subjecting it to ^{13}C-NMR. Below is his letter report of 17 January 2003.

^{13}C-NMR Spectral Analyses of the Black Mat Samples
Jerry A. Leenheer

I have completed the ^{13}C-NMR spectral analyses of organic matter isolated from the "black mat" sample you sent to me. A copy of the spectrum is enclosed (Fig. B.3). I isolated the organic matter as follows: 400 g of sample were gently crushed in a mortar and sieved through a 32 mesh sieve. As the sample was very fine grained, all of the sample passed through the sieve. To remove carbonates, the sample was split into four 100 g portions that were placed in four 14,000 dalton dialysis bags and dialyzed against 4-L of 10 percent acetic acid for 7 days. To remove salts and acetic acid, the samples were exhaustively dialyzed against deionized water for 7 days. Next, to remove metal sesquioxides and silica coatings that bind organic matter to clay minerals, the samples were dialyzed against 3 to 4 liter portions of 0.25 M HF over a seven day period. To remove HF and its reaction products, the samples were exhaustively dialyzed against distilled water for 7 days. The samples were then removed from the dialysis bag and freeze-dried. The dried samples were extracted with 500 mL of methylene chloride to remove any resins that might bind organic matter such as charcoal to the sediments. The samples were air dried and split into two equal weight portions and 150 mL of sodium polytungstate solution, density 2.3 was added to the samples in polyethylene centrifuge bottles. The samples were sonified in the centrifuge bottles with a sonic probe at a high power setting to disaggregate the organic matter from the sediment. The samples were then centrifuged at 5,000 rpm for one hour to float off the organic matter from the sediment. The floating organic matter was decanted and filtered from solution using a 1-μm glass fiber filter. The filter was washed with deionized water, and the sample was scraped off the filter and freeze dried. A total of 430 mg of organic matter was isolated. The color was black like charcoal and the material was very fine grained. There was no evidence of undegraded plant material such as wood or roots. The yield is not quantitative as one dialysis bag burst during processing, and one sample foamed out of the centrifuge bottle during sonication. A solid state ^{13}C-NMR spectrum was obtained under conditions known to give reasonably quantitative results for the different types of carbon (including charcoal) found in soil. The spectrum indicates only a small amount of aromatic carbon (peak at 129) that may or may not be charcoal. The major peak is aliphatic carbon near 30 ppm that is indicative of kerogen likely derived from algae and bacteria. If I had to guess, this type of organic matter is typical for a lake bed sediment kerogen. This is a disappointing result, but I do not know of any alternative explanation. I will save the isolated organic matter for the time being. Let me know if you want it back. [End of report; sample was returned to Haynes.]

OVERVIEW

In a 2004 letter to me, Rogers commented that "Leenheer's method for extracting the organic material was probably the best that has ever been done on

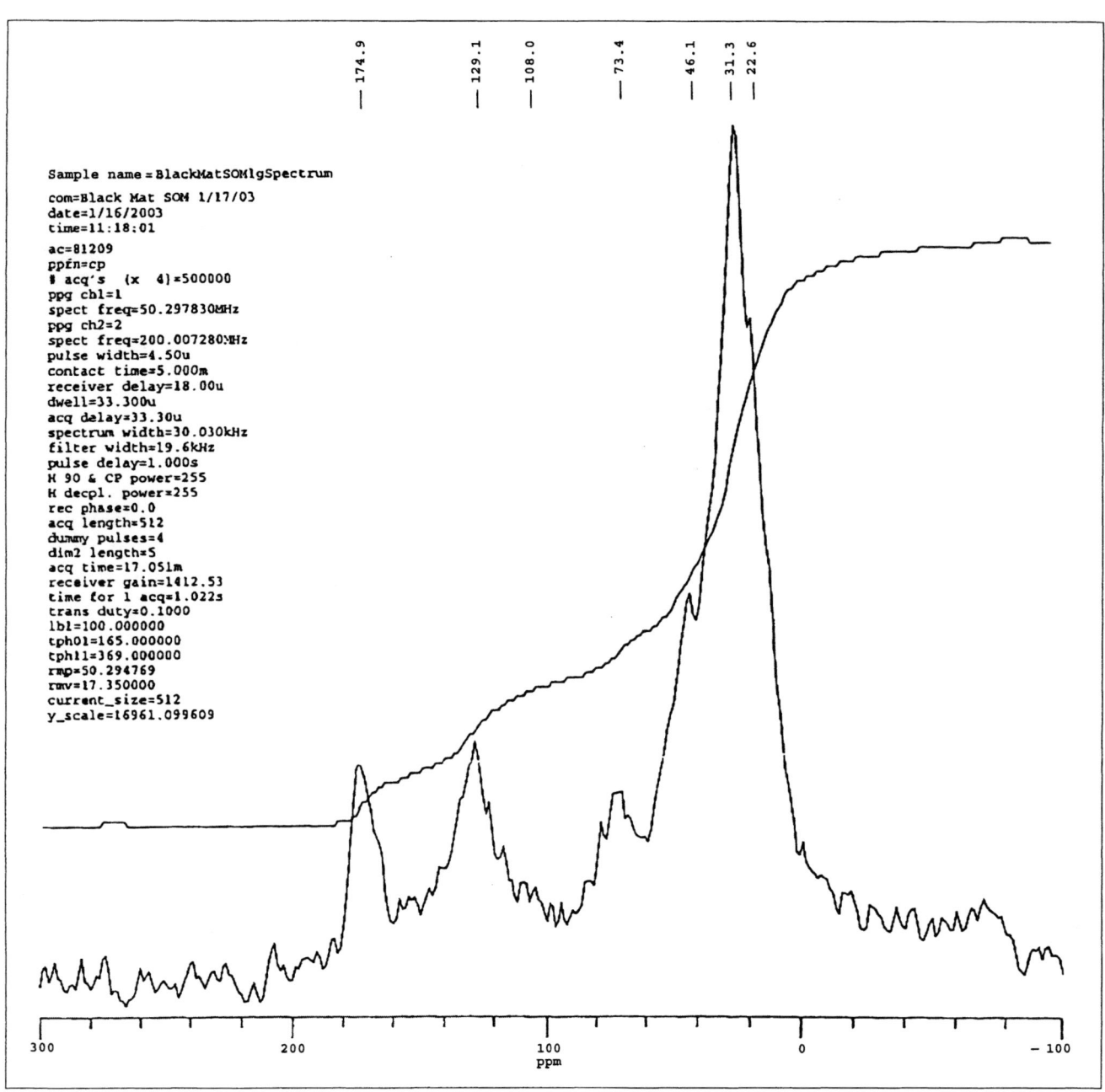

Figure B.3. ^{13}C-NMR Spectrum of the black mat.

Stratum F_2, but the 0.25 M HF may have hydrolized some polysaccharide chains." Leenheer concentrated the black mat organics by removing the inorganic sediments by a combination of dissolution in HF and heavy liquid gravimetric separation. His findings of only a small amount of aromatic carbon and a major amount of aliphatic carbon suggest kerogens likely derived from algae and bacteria. This finding is in accord with that of Rogers and somewhat opposite that of Stankiewicz and Tegelaar. These differences must be due to the different sampling locations. Leenheer's sample 7MS75-5 comes from an elevation of about 1271.4 m in Area 4, only about 7 m from Rogers' sample and about half a meter higher in the same area. Stankiewicz and Tegelaar sample 18AZ94 comes from about 38 m east of 7MS75-5 and at an elevation of

1270.6 m or 0.8 m lower. Their sample 6AZ90 comes from 9 m west of 18AZ94 and about 0.8 m higher, therefore at essentially the same elevation as 7MS75-5 but directly upslope of 18AZ94.

Apparently organic matter of basal black mat on the Clovis age channel is derived mostly from algae, as is organic matter of 7MS75-5, which included the total thickness of the black mat at the sample locality. Sample 6AZ90 from higher ground appears to be derived mostly from burned wood. For his sample from nearby, Rogers believes the absence of phenolics and the large component of pentosans in the organic phase indicates mostly algae as the organic precursor of the black mat's organic matter, essentially in agreement with Leenheer's findings. However, Rogers (personal communication, 2004) adds that the high component of polysaccharides in the San Pedro black mat is unique to his experience and likely is what the white fungus, mentioned earlier, is metabolizing. The fact that these sugars have survived nearly 13,000 years without degrading is another odd fact regarding the black mat.

Rigid pretreatment of black mat grain-size fractions from a microstratigraphic sequence exposed by Trench 13N (Fig. E.3) by Jesse Ballenger and me revealed both humates and insoluble organic matter in all fractions. Microscopic examination of the sand and silt fractions revealed black specks that are too small to positively identify optically but are probably charcoal. However, recently Rogers (personal communication, 2004) stated that furfural polymerizes to "vitreous carbon," a high-density, amorphous carbon (Rogers 1980).

Perhaps this "vitreous carbon" is the source of the black particles that we found in the sand fraction and of the "vitrinite" reported by Stankiewicz and Tegelaar. Therefore, in the pretreatment of the San Pedro black mat for radiocarbon dating, it is possible that the insoluble organic residue is vitreous carbon derived from polymerization of furfural in turn derived from algae, whereas the soluble humates come from the metabolism of pentosans largely by fungi and bacteria.

Whereas the exact origin of the black mat remains an enigma, it is clear that very soon after the Clovis occupation, during a dry period, the low areas of the Murray Springs site went underwater due to a rise in the water table. Pond and marsh conditions prevailed in the low areas for the next millennium.

Sources of Obsidian at the Murray Springs Clovis Site

A Semiquantitative X-Ray Fluorescence Analysis

M. Steven Shackley

Chemical characterization to determine the source provenience of obsidian from early hunter-gatherer contexts in the Southwest is gaining acceptance because of its utility for inferences concerning range and mobility, exchange, and interaction (Hughes 1988; Lesko 1989; Shackley 1986, 1988, 1990, 1992; Stevenson and Klimkiewicz 1990). The X-ray fluorescence analysis of 11 obsidian artifacts from the Murray Springs Site in southeastern Arizona indicates that all the material is from a single source in east-central Arizona (Cow Canyon), more than 200 km (124 miles) north of the site rather than closer sources such as Antelope Wells, New Mexico, or Los Vidrios, Sonora, or the newly discovered small marekanite source region near Safford, Arizona (Fig. C.1; Shackley 1988, 1990, 1992, 2005).

The data presented here are the results of an analysis performed in 1986 using what was then a somewhat outdated semiquantitative XRF technique with the wavelength X-ray spectrometer at Arizona State University. Although the data are not quantitative and not directly comparable to other analyses with different instruments, the results are "internally" valid using this instrument for both the analyses of the source and archaeological obsidian (Hughes 1984; Shackley 1990).

Since this analysis, Cow Canyon obsidian has been extensively quantitatively analyzed. Although the artifacts specific to Murray Springs have not been reanalyzed quantitatively, all of the previously semi-quantitatively assigned Cow Canyon artifacts from other sites have remained assigned to that source. This certainly would be the case at Murray Springs. Further information is available at http://www.swxrflab.net or Shackley (2005).

INSTRUMENT METHODOLOGY AND SOURCE DESCRIPTION

A sample of Murray Springs obsidian artifacts, including debitage, unmodified nodules, and projectile points (Table C.1), was subjected to the same analytic conditions. Melt incompatible trace elements were used to determine the source.

The samples were analyzed for rubidium (Rb), strontium (Sr), zirconium (Zr), and niobium (Nb) using the semiquantitative rapid scan method (Jack and Carmichael 1969) on a manual Philips PW 1410 wavelength X-ray spectrometer with a Philips power supply, ratemeter, and teletype in the Chemistry Department at Arizona State University. A tungsten (W) X-ray tube, scintillation counter and LiF (200) crystal were used, operated in a vacuum path at 45Kv and 45mA for 80 live-seconds per element. The intensity values for all elements were computed for ratios of $RbK\alpha$, $SrK\alpha$, $ZrK\alpha$, and $NbK\alpha$ radiation lines. The data were reduced through specific programs with a Zenith Z-161 Data Systems microprocessor. The elemental proportions are divided by the rubidium peak intensity and summed. These results are then divided by the summed intensities and the resulting element proportions are plotted in a ternary system or bivariate plots of relevant elements for comparison to known obsidian sources in the Southwest (Figs.

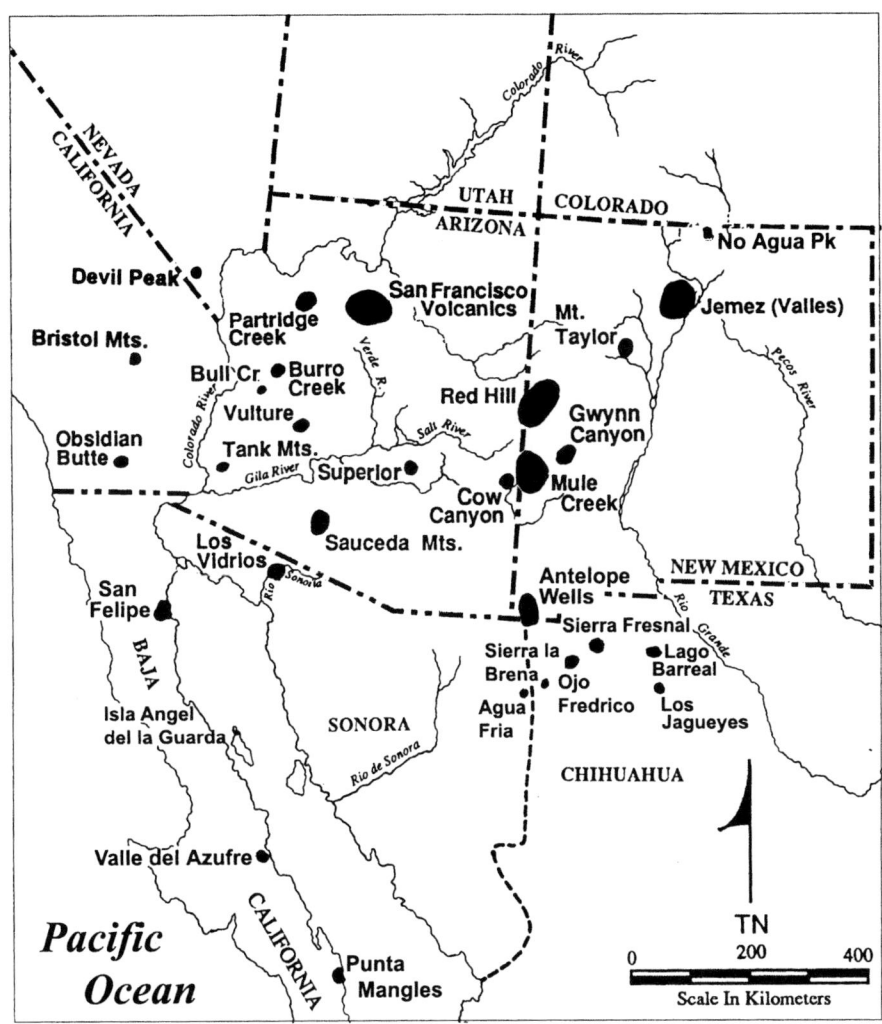

Figure C.1. Archaeological obsidian sources in the Southwest (revised from Shackley 1990).

C.2, C.3). The solid incompatible elements Rb, Sr, Zr, and Nb are quite sensitive in separating rhyolite glass sources (Cann 1983; Shackley 1990; Zielinski and others 1977). Niobium (Nb) is normally utilized when strontium values are low, especially in peralkaline lavas. In this study, niobium was analyzed to increase confidence in the source assignment, given the earlier assignment to the Picketpost Mountain (Superior) source discussed below.

The glass itself is megascopically consistent. Gray-brown flow banding was common in many specimens, and some of the flakes and the projectile points exhibit nearly transparent matrix. Many perlite-derived obsidian sources in the Southwest display these attributes, although Superior is consistently nearly transparent and rarely exhibits banding (Shackley 1988, 1990).

The Cow Canyon Source

The Cow Canyon source proper has been reported previously in the archaeological literature (Shackley 1988). The source is located in sections 34 and 35, T1S/R29E of the 1977 Apache-Sitgreaves National Forest Map. The material was found as secondary deposits as far as 14 km (8.7 miles) to the east in the Blue River Drainage. The obsidian occurs as nodules within a Quaternary rhyolite regolith/ash deposit as well as within the associated alluvium. The greatest density of nodules greater in size than 2 cm is less than two per 5 square meters. The source was surveyed on foot in four cardinal directions until the obsidian disappeared for 50 meters or more. The density of the nodules decreased gradually toward the periphery. X-

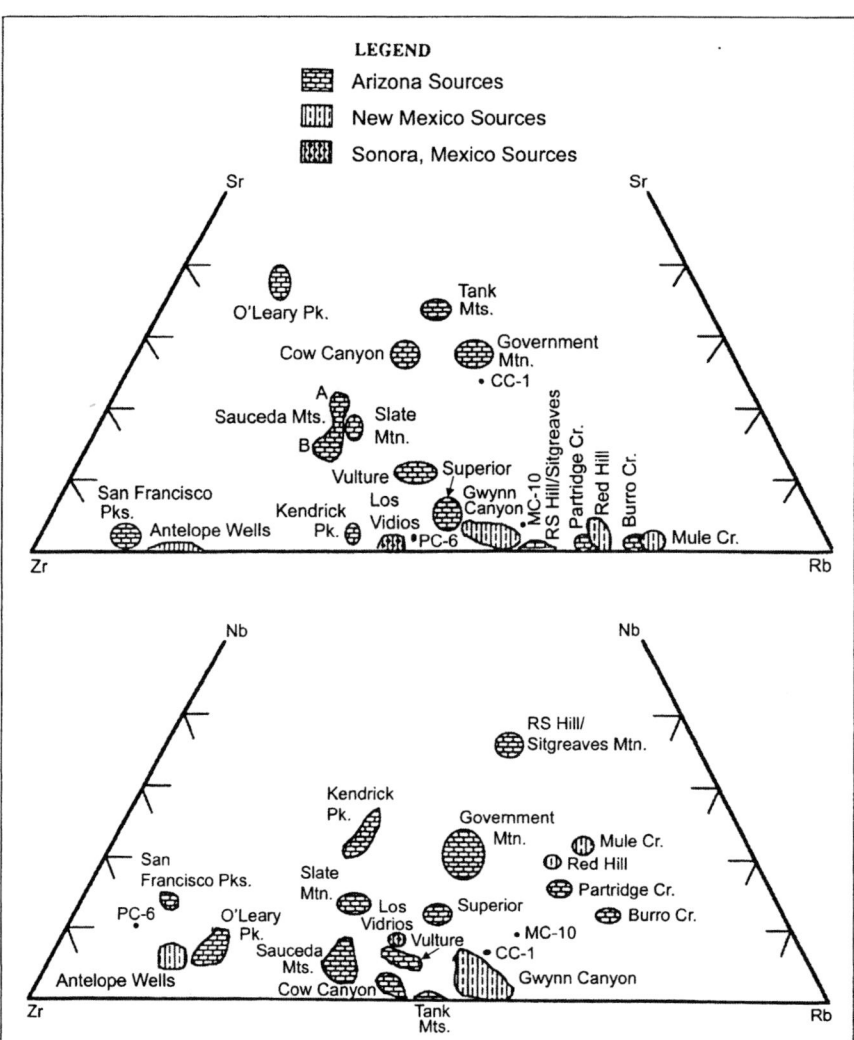

Figure C.2. Ternary plot for Southwestern net intensity obsidian data (revised from Shackley 1990).

ray samples were selected from peripheral samples and samples in the geographic center of the source to examine potential intrasource variability. Perlite is present, but in small nodule sizes (10 cm or less). The present environment includes a piñon-juniper woodland with associated grasses. The character of this source is discussed at length in Shackley (1990).

DISCUSSION

Previous analyses of some of the Murray Springs obsidian using only sodium (Na) and manganese (Mn) ratios suggested that the material was derived from the Superior (Picketpost Mountain) source (Hemmings 1970; C. Vance Haynes, personal communication 1986). The present analysis using the previously discussed four elements indicates that Superior is not the source of the obsidian from Murray Springs (Tables C.1, C.2; Figs. C.2, C.3). Both sodium (Na) and manganese (Mn) used in the instrumental neutron activation analyses are solid compatible elements and may be differentially absorbed into minerals before extrusion. Unlike the incompatible elements used here, they can exhibit quite similar concentrations between separate sources (Cox and others 1979). The Superior source designation could be considered correct using just these two compatible elements, since the concentrations are probably similar in many rhyolite glass sources. This is essentially why the compatible elements were not used in this XRF analysis. The Rb, Sr, Zr and Rb, Nb, Zr analyses both indicate the Cow Canyon source as the original provenience of the raw

Table C.1. X-Ray Fluorescence Data for Obsidian Specimens from the Murray Springs Clovis Site

Artifact	Sample No.	Rb/Rb	Sr/Rb	Zr/Rb	Σ	Rb%	Sr%	Zr%
Nodule	A-31611	1.00	0.8756	1.2837	3.1593	0.3165	0.2771	0.4063
Point	A-33116	1.00	0.8371	1.2462	3.0833	0.3243	0.2715	0.4042
Nodule	A-33948	1.00	0.8699	1.2633	3.1332	0.3192	0.2776	0.4032
Nodule	A-33949	1.00	0.8830	1.3059	3.1889	0.3136	0.2769	0.4095
Flake	A-44343	1.00	0.8413	1.3582	3.1995	0.3126	0.2629	0.4245
Flake	A-45632	1.00	0.8463	1.3392	3.1855	0.3139	0.2657	0.4204
Point base	A-47139	1.00	0.8365	1.2355	3.0721	0.3255	0.2723	0.4022
Flake	A-47143	1.00	0.8688	1.2674	3.1362	0.3189	0.2770	0.4041
Flake	A-47194	1.00	0.8567	1.3718	3.2285	0.3097	0.2654	0.4249
Flake	A-47244	1.00	0.9204	1.4132	3.3337	0.3000	0.2761	0.4239
Flake	A-47270	1.00	0.8919	1.4231	3.3150	0.3017	0.2690	0.4293

Artifact	Sample No.	Rb/Rb	Nb/Rb	Zr/Rb	Σ	Rb%	Nb%	Zr%
Nodule	A-31611	1.00	0.0844	1.2475	2.3319	0.4288	0.0362	0.5350
Point	A-33116	1.00	0.0805	1.1731	2.2536	0.4437	0.0357	0.5205
Nodule	A-33948	1.00	0.0737	1.1615	2.2352	0.4474	0.0330	0.5196
Nodule	A-33949	1.00	0.0000	1.2639	2.2639	0.4417	0.0000	0.5583
Flake	A-44343	1.00	0.0000	1.4797	2.4797	0.4033	0.0000	0.5967
Flake	A-45632	1.00	0.0976	1.4342	2.5319	0.3950	0.0386	0.5665
Point base	A-47139	1.00	0.0000	1.2355	2.2355	0.4473	0.0000	0.5527
Flake	A-47143	1.00	0.0734	1.3135	2.3869	0.4190	0.0307	0.5503
Flake	A-47194	1.00	0.0641	1.3266	2.3907	0.4183	0.0268	0.5549
Flake	A-47244	1.00	0.1123	1.2576	2.3700	0.4219	0.0474	0.5307
Flake	A-47270	1.00	0.0372	1.2328	2.2699	0.4405	0.0164	0.5431

Table C.2. Rb, Sr, Zr and Rb, Nb, Zr X-Ray Fluorescence Data for the Cow Canyon Obsidian Source, Greenlee County, Arizona

Sample No.	Rb/Rb	Sr/Rb	Zr/Rb	Σ	Rb%	Sr%	Zr%
CC-2	1.00	0.9203	1.2330	3.1533	0.3171	0.2918	0.3910
CC-3	1.00	0.8748	1.1521	3.0268	0.3304	0.2890	0.3806
CC-4	1.00	0.8462	1.1507	2.9969	0.3337	0.2824	0.3840
CC-5	1.00	0.9108	1.2376	3.1483	0.3176	0.2893	0.3931
CC-6	1.00	0.8630	1.1671	3.0301	0.3300	0.2848	0.3852
CC-7	1.00	0.8028	1.0971	2.8999	0.3448	0.2768	0.3783
CC-8	1.00	0.9083	1.2047	3.1131	0.3212	0.2918	0.3870
CC-9	1.00	0.8800	1.1816	3.0616	0.3266	0.2874	0.3860
CC-10	1.00	0.9061	1.2962	3.2024	0.3123	0.2830	0.4048

Sample No.	Rb/Rb	Nb/Rb	Zr/Rb	Σ	Rb%	Nb%	Zr%
CC-2	1.00	0.0718	1.2330	2.3048	0.4339	0.0311	0.5350
CC-3	1.00	0.0683	1.1521	2.2204	0.4504	0.0308	0.5189
CC-4		Nb not analyzed for this sample					
CC-5	1.00	0.0750	1.2376	2.3126	0.4324	0.0324	0.5352
CC-6	1.00	0.0099	1.1671	2.1770	0.4593	0.0046	0.5361
CC-7	1.00	0.0348	1.0971	2.1319	0.4691	0.0163	0.5146
CC-8	1.00	0.0466	1.2047	2.2514	0.4442	0.0207	0.5351
CC-9	1.00	0.0514	1.1816	2.2330	0.4478	0.0230	0.5292
CC-10	1.00	0.0780	1.2962	2.3742	0.4212	0.0329	0.5460

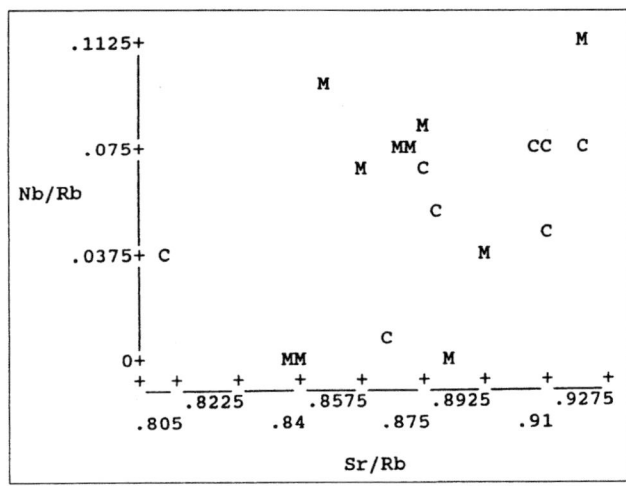

Figure C.3. Net intensity peak count bivariate plot of Cow Canyon source material (C) and Murray Springs obsidian artifacts (M).

material. The Rb, Sr, Zr and Rb, Nb, Zr ternary positions of all known Southwestern obsidian sources in Arizona, New Mexico, Sonora, and Chihuahua are shown on Figure C.2. As evident in Tables C.1 and C.2 and Figures C.2 and C.3, there is a close correspondence with the Cow Canyon material.

Importantly, this study suggests that all the artifacts, including the projectile points, were derived from the same source. To produce a biface the size of the complete Murray Springs Clovis point (37 mm long by 22 mm wide), a nodule slightly larger than the biface would be required. This is significant in light of the predominance of small perlite-derived marekanite nodules (Apache tears) that are generally available in the Southwest (Vulture, Superior, Antelope Wells), outside the Valles Caldera region in New Mexico, and the San Francisco Volcanic Field in northern Arizona (Findlow and Bolognese 1982; Jack 1971; Newman and Nielsen 1985; Shackley 1988, 1990, 2005). Although 3 cm to 5 cm is most common today, the Cow Canyon source produces nodules up to 7 cm in diameter, quite adequate for the production of a Clovis point the size of the one recovered from Murray Springs. The nodule sizes suggest that bipolar reduction of the obsidian may have been the reduction technology employed at Murray Springs (Shackley 1990; Shott 1989).

Without the benefit of a comprehensive source data base, earlier attempts to determine the source of the obsidian at Murray Springs suggested Superior (Picketpost Mountain) or Vulture in central and western Arizona (Hemmings 1970: 48). As indicated above all the obsidian recovered from Murray Springs was procured from the Cow Canyon source approximately 210 km (130 miles) north in the Mogollon Highlands. The chemistry of this source is so unique there can be little doubt of the origin (Shackley 1990). The source is essentially on the way to or from the San Augustin Plains and the southern Plains area, by way of the river valleys (San Pedro to Gila to San Francisco and then Blue River (Fig. C.1). According to Hemmings (1970), the silicified wood recovered from the site was identified as coming from the Petrified Forest area in northern Arizona. Although the silicified wood assignment is based on megascopic comparison, the obsidian is certainly from Cow Canyon to the north. It is quite possible that the group that inhabited the site just arrived from the north (that is, the San Augustin Plains or Mogollon Highlands). The kills in Area 3 and Area 4 may represent the earlier portions of the site, or at least a portion of the site inhabited after the descent from the uplands. All this obsidian was probably the result of the reduction of a half a dozen or so nodules carried to the site in the personal gear. More obsidian would likely have been recovered if smaller screen sizes were used, but it would still probably represent the same amount of original material.

APPENDIX D

Vertebrate Specimens from Murray Springs Areas 1–5

E. Thomas Hemmings

Areas 1, 3, 4, and 5

Field No.	Taxon	Specimen Description	Map Location	Stratigraphic Unit
1	Bison	RP^4	F7	F_1 channel fill
2	Mammuthus	Long bone fragments	C4	F_1 slope deposit
3	Canis	Right lower canine	B3	F_1 slope deposit
4	Mammuthus	Fibula shaft	E5	F_1 channel fill
5	Bison	First phalanx	E5	F_1 channel fill
6	Camelops	LM_1; RM_1	F4	D
7	Camelops	Cheek tooth fragments	F4	D
8	Bison	Tooth scraps	B3	F_1 channel fill
9	Camelops	Right scapula	F6	E
10	Camelops	Right femur	F6	E
11	Mammuthus	Proximal end of rib	C4	F_1 channel fill
13	Microtus	M_1; incisor	C4	F_1 channel fill
15	Camelops	Thoracic vertebra; shaft of left femur	F6	E
16	Equus	RM_3; 2 incisors	E6	E
17	Equus	Upper cheek tooth	F5	D
18	Camelops	Vertebral fragment	F6	E
21	Mammuthus	Pelvic fragment	E6, F6	F_1 channel fill
22	Equus	Right upper molar	F6	E
23	Camelops	2 lower cheek teeth	E6	E
24	Bison	Rib	C4	F_1 channel fill
26	Mammuthus	Right innominate	E5, E6	F_1 channel fill
28	Mammuthus	Fragment of pelvis	E5	F_1 channel fill
29	Mammuthus	12 sections of rib	E5, D5	F_1 channel fill
30	Mammuthus	Proximal end of rib	F4, F5	F_1 channel fill
31	Mammuthus	Fragments of pelvis	D5	F_1 channel fill
35	Bison	Long bone fragments	D5	F_1 channel fill
36	Mammuthus	Vertebral fragments	D5	F_1 channel fill
37	Mammuthus	Vertebra	E5	F_1 channel fill
38	Mammuthus	Vertebral fragments	E5	F_1 channel fill
39	Mammuthus	Vertebral fragments	E5	F_1 channel fill
42	Bison	Long bone fragments	C3	F_1 channel fill
43	Mammuthus	Vertebral centrum	B3	F_1 slope deposit
44	Mammuthus	Left scapula	D4, D5	F_1 channel fill

Field No.	Taxon	Specimen Description	Map Location	Stratigraphic Unit
45	*Mammuthus*	Thoracic vertebra	D4, D5	F_1 slope deposit
46	*Camelops*	Right navicular	E5	F_1 slope deposit
47	*Mammuthus*	Fragment of pelvis	D5	F_1 channel fill
48	*Mammuthus*	Fragment of pelvis	D4, D5	F_1 channel fill
49	*Mammuthus*	Rib section	E5	F_1 channel fill
51	*Bison*	Thoracic vertebra	E6	F_1 channel fill
52	*Mammuthus*	Vertebral centrum	E5	F_1 channel fill
53	*Mammuthus*	Vertebra	E5	F_1 channel fill
54	*Mammuthus*	Thoracic vertebra	D5	F_1 channel fill
55	*Equus*	LM_1	D5	F_1 channel fill
56	*Mammuthus*	Rib	D5, E5	F_1 channel fill
57	*Mammuthus*	Long bone fragments	D2	F_1 channel fill
58	*Mammuthus*	Mandible with LM_3 and RM_3	D4, D5	F_1 channel fill
59	*Equus*	Right upper premolar	E3	F_1 channel fill
60	*Mammuthus*	Rib section	C4, D4	F_1 channel fill
61	*Mammuthus*	Cheek tooth fragment	E3	D
62	*Mammuthus*	Long bone fragment	E2	F_1 channel fill
63	*Mammuthus*	Long bone fragment	E2	F_1 channel fill
64	*Mammuthus*	Tibia	E4	F_1 channel fill
65	*Mammuthus*	Occipital cranial fragment	E3	D
66	*Camelops*	Upper cheek teeth fragments	F4	D
67	*Equus*	LM_3	A2	Z
68	*Equus*	Upper cheek tooth	A2	Z
69	*Camelops*	Lower cheek tooth	B2	Z
70	*Equus*	LM_2	A2	Z
71	*Mammuthus*	Long bone fragment	A2	Z
72	*Mammuthus*	Vertebra	D3	F_1 channel fill
73	*Equus*	Left lower premolar	D4	F_1 channel fill
74	*Bison*	Fragmentary cranium with left and right dP^{2-4} and M^{1-2}	B1	F_1 channel fill
75	*Canis*	Right mandibular ramus with P_2-M_1	B1	F_1 slope deposit
76	Rodentia	Bone fragments	W4	Occupation surface
77	*Bison*	Right mandibular ramus with P_2-M_3	W4	Occupation surface
78	*Mammuthus*	Fragmentary sacrum	W4	Occupation surface
79	*Mammuthus*	Fragments of ilium	X4	Occupation surface
80	*Mammuthus*	Fragment of pubis	X4	Occupation surface
81	*Mammuthus*	Left ulna and radius	W5	Occupation surface
82	*Mammuthus*	Ribs and rib sections	W5	Occupation surface
83	*Mammuthus*	Left scapula	W5	Occupation surface
84	*Mammuthus*	Right scapula	W6	Occupation surface
85	*Mammuthus*	Cranium with RM^3 and LM^3; 2 tusks	V6, W6	Occupation surface
86	*Mammuthus*	Mandible with RM_3 and LM_3	W6	Occupation surface
87	*Mammuthus*	Right humerus	W6, X5	Occupation surface
88	*Mammuthus*	Right tibia and fibula	W6	Occupation surface
89	*Mammuthus*	Right femur	W6, X6	Occupation surface
90	*Mammuthus*	Right humerus	X6	Occupation surface
91	*Bison*	Lower cheek tooth fragments	V6	Occupation surface
92	*Mammuthus*	12 or more vertebral dorsal spines	W5	Occupation surface

Field No.	Taxon	Specimen Description	Map Location	Stratigraphic Unit
93	*Mammuthus*	14 thoracic and cervical vertebral centra	W5	Occupation surface
94	Rodentia	Cheek tooth fragments	X9	Occupation surface
96	*Bison*	Rib sections	X8	Occupation surface
97	*Bison*	Rib section	Y8	Occupation surface
98	*Bison*	Rib section	Y8	Occupation surface
99	*Bison*	Rib section	Y9	Occupation surface
100	*Mammuthus*	Vertebral centrum	A6	Occupation surface
101	*Bison*	Second phalanx	W1	Occupation surface
102	*Bison*	Distal end of metapodial	W1	Occupation surface
103	*Bison*	Long bone shaft	W1	Occupation surface
104	*Bison*	Second phalanx	W1	Occupation surface
105	*Bison*	Ulna	W1	Occupation surface
107	*Bison*	Cheek tooth fragments	Y1	F_1 slope deposit
108	*Mammuthus*	Fragments of pelvis	X3, Y3	F_1 slope deposit
109	*Mammuthus*	Rib section	Y3	F_1 slope deposit
111	*Bison*	Long bone fragments	X2	F_1 slope deposit
114	*Bison*	Astragalus	W1	Occupation surface
115	*Bison*	Metapodial	V1	Occupation surface
116	*Bison*	Metapodial	V1, W1	Occupation surface
117	*Bison*	Long bone shaft	V1	Occupation surface
118	*Bison*	Long bone shaft	V0	Occupation surface
119	*Bison*	Long bone fragments	V1	Occupation surface
120	*Bison*	Long bone shaft	W1	Occupation surface
124	*Bison*	Long bone shaft; vertebral fragments	W7	Occupation surface
125	*Bison*	Distal end of metapodial	W7	Occupation surface
126	*Bison*	2 vertebrae	W7	Occupation surface
127	*Bison*	Rib sections; vertebral fragments	W7	Occupation surface
128	*Bison*	Distal end of calcaneum; vertebral fragments	W7	Occupation surface
129	*Bison*	Head of femur	W7	Occupation surface
130-132	*Mammuthus*	Tusk fragments	W7	Occupation surface
133	*Bison*	Long bone shaft	W8	Occupation surface
134	*Bison*	Astragalus	W8	Occupation surface
135	*Bison*	Right tibia	W8, X8	Occupation surface
136	*Bison*	Rib sections	X8	Occupation surface
137	*Bison*	Long bone fragments	V7	Occupation surface
138	*Bison*	Lower cheek tooth	V7	Occupation surface
140	*Bison*	Left mandibular ramus with M_{1-3}	W3	Occupation surface
141	*Canis*	Right mandibular ramus with P_1-M_2	Z0	F_1 slope deposit
142	*Canis*	Rib	Y0	F_1 slope deposit
143	*Canis*	Left lower canine	Z1S	F_1 slope deposit
144	*Canis*	Cranial fragments	X0	F_1 slope deposit
146	*Canis*	Cranial fragments	Y0	F_1 slope deposit
149	*Canis*	Petrosal	X0	F_1 slope deposit
150	*Canis*	Cervical vertebra	X0	F_1 slope deposit
151	*Canis*	Incisor	Y1S	F_1 slope deposit
152	*Canis*	Vertebral fragment	Y1S	F_1 slope deposit
153	*Canis*	Cervical vertebra	Y1S	F_1 slope deposit

Field No.	Taxon	Specimen Description	Map Location	Stratigraphic Unit
154	Canis	Left mandibular ramus with P_4, M_1	Z1S	F_1 slope deposit
156	Mammuthus	Rib section	E5	F_1 slope deposit
157	Bison	Head of humerus	U1	Occupation surface
158	Bison	Long bone shaft	U1	Occupation surface
159	Camelops	Lower cheek tooth	V2	D
160	Bison	Cheek tooth fragments	X2S	F_1 slope deposit
161	Bison	Cheek tooth fragments	V8	D
162	Mammuthus	Vertebral fragments	Y3	F_1 slope deposit
164	Equus	Upper cheek tooth	Z8	D
165	Bison	Lower cheek tooth fragments	V6	Occupation surface
168	Bison	Unerupted P_3; lower cheek tooth	V6	Occupation surface
169	Bison	M_1 or M_2	V6	Occupation surface
171	Rodentia	Incisors; bone fragments	W4	F_2
172	Rodentia	Incisor	V6	F_2
173	Rodentia	Incisor	W1	F_2
174	Microtus	Incisors; cheek teeth; bone fragments	Y3	F_1 slope deposit
175	Neotoma	M_1	V0	Occupation surface
176	Rodentia	Incisor	W1	F_2
177	Microtus	Cheek teeth	X0	F_1 slope deposit
178	Microtus	Incisor	X0	F_1 slope deposit
179	Mammuthus	Proximal epiphysis of tibia	F5	F_1 slope deposit
180	Camelops	Unerupted M_3	T9	D
181	Bison	Left petrosal	P11	Occupation surface
182	Equus	5 lower cheek teeth	M11	D/F_2 contact
183	Bison	Long bone fragment	Q10	Occupation surface
184	Bison	Long bone shaft; scapula fragment	Q10, Q11	Occupation surface
185	Bison	Distal end of right humerus	K12	Occupation surface
186	Bison	Right scapula	L12	Occupation surface
187	Bison	Right mandibular ramus with M_{1-3}	L12	Occupation surface
188	Bison	First phalanx	L12	Occupation surface
189	Bison	Rib sections	K12, L12	Occupation surface
190	Bison	Rib section	O11	Occupation surface
191	Bison	Long bone shaft	P10	Occupation surface
192	Bison	Long bone fragments	O11	Occupation surface
193	Bison	Left astragalus	K12	Occupation surface
194	Bison	Rib section	P10	Occupation surface
195	Bison	Left femur	K12	Occupation surface
196	Bison	Right petrosal	K12	Occupation surface
197	Rodentia	Incisor	K14	F_2
198	Equus	Left upper molar	U8	Occupation surface
199	Bison	Left petrosal	K12	Occupation surface
200	Bison	Right radius	L12	Occupation surface
201	Bison	Vertebral fragment	L12	Occupation surface
203	Bison	Rib sections	U8	Occupation surface
204	Bison	Long bone fragment	T8, U8	Occupation surface
205	Bison	Metapodial	K12	Occupation surface
206	Bison	Long bone shaft	K12	Occupation surface
207	Bison	Left metacarpal	L11, L12	Occupation surface

Field No.	Taxon	Specimen Description	Map Location	Stratigraphic Unit
208	*Bison*	Long bone fragment	L12	Occupation surface
209	*Bison*	Vertebral fragment	K12	Occupation surface
210	*Bison*	Vertebral fragment	K12	Occupation surface
211	*Bison*	LP^4	K12	Occupation surface
212	*Bison*	First phalanx	K12	Occupation surface
214	*Bison*	Left petrosal	U7	Occupation surface
216	*Bison*	Upper cheek tooth; teeth and bone fragments	T8	Occupation surface
217	*Bison*	Right upper premolar	L11, L12	Occupation surface
218	*Bison*	Upper cheek tooth	K12	Occupation surface
219	*Mammuthus*	Long bone fragment	T6	Occupation surface
220	*Bison*	Left astragalus	J14	Occupation surface
221	*Bison*	Right astragalus	J14	Occupation surface
222	*Bison*	Right astragalus	J14	Occupation surface
223	*Bison*	3 lumbar vertebrae; anterior portion of sacrum	J14	Occupation surface
224	*Bison*	Second phalanx	J14	Occupation surface
225	*Bison*	Left metatarsal	J14	Occupation surface
226	*Bison*	Left metatarsal; left ectocuneiform	J14	Occupation surface
227	*Bison*	Immature right metacarpal	J14	Occupation surface
228	*Bison*	Right femur	J14	Occupation surface
229	*Bison*	Right calcaneum	J14	Occupation surface
230	*Bison*	Right calcaneum	J14	Occupation surface
231	*Bison*	First phalanx; second phalanx	J14	Occupation surface
232	*Bison*	Femur shaft	J14	Occupation surface
233	*Bison*	Right radius	J14	Occupation surface
234	*Bison*	Rib section	J14	Occupation surface
235	*Bison*	Long bone fragment	J14	Occupation surface
236	*Bison*	Long bone fragment	J14	Occupation surface
237	*Bison*	First phalanx	J14	Occupation surface
238	*Bison*	Right calcaneum	J14	Occupation surface
239	*Bison*	Long bone fragment	J14	Occupation surface
240	*Bison*	Distal end of right humerus	J14	Occupation surface
241	*Bison*	Left ectocuneiform	J14	Occupation surface
242	*Bison*	Right ectocuneiform	J14	Occupation surface
244	*Bison*	Left petrosal	K14	Occupation surface
245	*Bison*	Right petrosal	K14	Occupation surface
246	*Bison*	Right petrosal	K14	Occupation surface
247-248	*Bison*	LM^{1-3}; RM^{1-3}; LM^{1-2}; RM^{1-2}; premolar fragments	K14	Occupation surface
249	*Bison*	Long bone shaft	K14	Occupation surface
250	*Bison*	Right astragalus	K14	Occupation surface
251	*Bison*	Long bone fragment	K14	Occupation surface
252	*Bison*	Neck portion of scapula	J15	Occupation surface
253	*Bison*	4 rib sections	J15	Occupation surface
254	*Bison*	3 rib sections	K15	Occupation surface
255	*Bison*	Metacarpal	K15	Occupation surface
256	*Bison*	Left mandibular ramus with P_2-M_3	K15	Occupation surface

Field No.	Taxon	Specimen Description	Map Location	Stratigraphic Unit
257	*Bison*	Rib section	K15	Occupation surface
258	*Bison*	Magnum	K15	Occupation surface
259	*Bison*	Proximal end of right scapula	L15	Occupation surface
260	*Bison*	First phalanx	L15	Occupation surface
261	*Bison*	Left petrosal	K14	Occupation surface
265	*Bison*	Rib section	K15	Occupation surface
266	*Bison*	Right calcaneum	K15	Occupation surface
267	*Bison*	2 incisors	K19	Occupation surface
268-269	*Bison*	2 left deciduous upper molars	K18	Occupation surface
271	*Bison*	Left metacarpal	L16	Occupation surface
272	*Bison*	First phalanx; left magnum	L16	Occupation surface
273	*Bison*	Left radius	L16	Occupation surface
274	*Bison*	Second phalanx	L16	Occupation surface
276	*Platygonus*	3 fragmentary upper cheek teeth	L19	Occupation surface
277-278	*Bison*	Cranial fragments with P^3, LdP^4, LM^{1-2}, RM^{1-2}, and left petrosal; right petrosal	K19	Occupation surface
279	*Bison*	Left mandibular ramus with P_2-M_3	K19	Occupation surface
280	*Bison*	First phalanx	K19	Occupation surface
283	*Bison*	Distal end of metapodial	L19	Occupation surface
284	*Bison*	First phalanx	L19	Occupation surface
285	*Bison*	Right mandibular ramus with P_3-M_3	L15	Occupation surface
286	*Bison*	Proximal end of radius	L16	Occupation surface
287	*Bison*	Patella	K17	Occupation surface
289	*Bison*	Left humerus	K17, L17	Occupation surface
290	*Bison*	Rib section	L17	Occupation surface
292	*Bison*	Left scapula	K17	Occupation surface
293	*Bison*	2 rib sections	K17	Occupation surface
294	*Bison*	Upper cheek tooth	J17	Occupation surface
297	*Bison*	Second phalanx	K16	Occupation surface
298	*Bison*	Long bone fragment	K16	Occupation surface
299	*Bison*	Distal end of left humerus; fragment of head	K16	Occupation surface
300	*Bison*	Long bone fragments	K16	Occupation surface
301	*Bison*	Long bone fragments	K16	Occupation surface
302	*Bison*	Rib section	K16	Occupation surface
305	*Bison*	Left scapula	K16	Occupation surface
306	*Bison*	Long bone shaft	K16	Occupation surface
307	*Bison*	Long bone fragments	K17	Occupation surface
308	*Bison*	Ulna	K16	Occupation surface
309	*Bison*	Long bone fragment	K16	Occupation surface
310	*Bison*	6 parallel rib sections	K16	Occupation surface
311	*Bison*	5 rib sections	K16	Occupation surface
312	*Bison*	Proximal end of left scapula	J17	Occupation surface
313	*Bison*	Left humerus	J17	Occupation surface
314	*Bison*	First phalanx	J17	Occupation surface
315	*Bison*	Second phalanx	J17	Occupation surface
316	*Bison*	8 or more rib sections	J17	Occupation surface
317	*Bison*	3 incisors	J17	Occupation surface
318	*Bison*	Pelvic fragment	K17	Occupation surface

Field No.	Taxon	Specimen Description	Map Location	Stratigraphic Unit
319	*Bison*	Long bone fragment	K16	Occupation surface
320	*Bison*	Proximal end of metapodial	J17	Occupation surface
321	*Bison*	Metatarsal	J17	Occupation surface
322	*Bison*	Distal end of metapodial	J17	Occupation surface
323	*Bison*	Right mandibular ramus with M_{1-3}	J17	Occupation surface
324	*Bison*	Left mandibular ramus with P_4-M_3	J17	Occupation surface
325	*Bison*	8 upper cheek teeth; cranial fragments	J17	Occupation surface
326	*Bison*	Astragalus	J17	Occupation surface
327	*Bison*	Second phalanx	J17	Occupation surface
328	*Bison*	Right metatarsal	J17, K17	Occupation surface
329	*Bison*	Right astragalus	K17	Occupation surface
330	*Bison*	Proximal end of scapula	K17	Occupation surface
331	*Bison*	Right calcaneum	K17	Occupation surface
332	*Bison*	Left petrosal	K17	Occupation surface
333	*Bison*	Scapula	K17	Occupation surface
334	*Equus*	LdM^3	K18	Occupation surface
335	*Bison*	6 vertebrae	J18	Occupation surface
337	*Bison*	Rib section	J19	Occupation surface
338	*Bison*	Long bone shaft	J15	Occupation surface
339	*Bison*	Right ectocuneiform	K17	Occupation surface
340	*Bison*	2 first phalanges; second phalanx	J17	Occupation surface
341	*Equus*	RdM_1	K16	Occupation surface
342	*Bison*	Pelvic fragment	K16	Occupation surface
343	*Bison*	Long bone fragment	K16	Occupation surface
344	*Bison*	Right scapula	K16	Occupation surface
345	*Bison*	Left humerus	J16	Occupation surface
346	*Bison*	Rib section	K19, K20	Occupation surface
347	*Bison*	Cranium with RP_3-M_3, LP_3-M_3	J18	Occupation surface
348	*Bison*	Right scapula	J18	Occupation surface
349	*Bison*	3 incisors	J18	Occupation surface
350	*Bison*	Right and left mandibular rami with P_3-M_3	J16	Occupation surface
351-352	*Bison*	Right and left petrosals	J18	Occupation surface
353	*Bison*	Long bone shaft	K18	Occupation surface
354	*Bison*	Right humerus	J18	Occupation surface
355	*Equus*	RdP^3	K18	Occupation surface
356	*Bison*	Long bone fragment	J16	Occupation surface
357	*Bison*	Proximal end of right radius	J17	Occupation surface
358	*Bison*	Podial	J17	Occupation surface
359	*Bison*	Right humerus	J16, K16	Occupation surface
360	*Bison*	Proximal end of left scapula	J16	Occupation surface
363	*Bison*	RP^3; LP^4; incisor	K18	Occupation surface
365	*Bison*	Second phalanx	J16	Occupation surface
369	*Bison*	Left astragalus	I17	Occupation surface
373	*Equus*	Right upper molar	K17	Occupation surface
375	*Bison*	Rib section	M19	Occupation surface
376	*Bison*	Right mandibular ramus with P_2-M_3	K18	Occupation surface
378	*Bison*	Proximal end of right metatarsal	K18	Occupation surface
379	*Bison*	Right naviculocuboid	K18	Occupation surface

Field No.	Taxon	Specimen Description	Map Location	Stratigraphic Unit
380	Bison	Right astragalus	K18	Occupation surface
381	Bison	6 rib sections	K18	Occupation surface
382	Bison	Right ectocuneiform	K18	Occupation surface
383	Equus	Right upper molar	I13	Occupation surface
384	Bison	Cheek tooth fragments	I13	Occupation surface
385-387	Bison	Left humerus; left radius; left ulna	H12, I12	Occupation surface
388	Bison	Second phalanx	I12	Occupation surface
389	Bison	First phalanx	I12	Occupation surface
390	Bison	Left scaphoid; left lunar; left magnum	I12	Occupation surface
391	Bison	2 rib sections	I12	Occupation surface
392	Bison	Metacarpal	K12	Occupation surface
393	Bison	Left mandibular ramus with M_{1-2}	J12	Occupation surface
394	Bison	Long bone fragment	I12, J12	Occupation surface
397	Bison	Upper premolar	J11	Occupation surface
398	Camelops	M_3	M15	E/F_3 contact
399	Bison	Second phalanx	L18	Occupation surface
404	Bison	Left metacarpal	Ew13	Occupation surface
405	Bison	Left radius	Ew13	Occupation surface
406	Bison	2 rib sections	Ew13	Occupation surface
407	Bison	Vertebra	Ew13	Occupation surface
408	Equus	Left upper molar	J11	Occupation surface
409	Bison	LP^4	K18	Occupation surface
410	Bison	RM^1	Dw13	Occupation surface
411	Bison	Left humerus	Gw13	Occupation surface
412	Bison	First phalanx	Gw13	Occupation surface
413	Bison	Left scapula fragment	Gw12	Occupation surface
415	Bison	Left scaphoid	Fw12	Occupation surface
416-424, 427, 438-439, 441, 443	Equus	Left and right mandibular rami with P_2-M_3; right maxilla with P^2-M^2; left upper cheek teeth; 12 incisors	Yw9, Yw10 Zw9, Zw10	Occupation surface
428	Bison	Cheek tooth fragments	Zw9	Occupation surface
429	Mammuthus	Vertebral dorsal spine	Z6S	Occupation surface
430	Mammuthus	Rib section	Z6S	Occupation surface
431	Mammuthus	Vertebral fragments	Z6S	Occupation surface
432	Mammuthus	Fibula shaft(?)	Z6S	Occupation surface
433	Mammuthus	Vertebral dorsal spine	Z6S	Occupation surface
434	Mammuthus	Vertebral fragments	Z6S	Occupation surface
435	Mammuthus	Rib sections	Z6S	Occupation surface
436	Rodentia	Incisor; bone fragments	A7S	Occupation surface
437	Bison	Left mandibular ramus with P_2-M_3	Z4S	F_1 slope deposit
440	Bison	Long bone fragments	Aw12, Bw12	Occupation surface
444	Bison	Left mandibular ramus with P_4-M_3	L12	Occupation surface
445	Carnivora	Phalanx	K18	F_3

Area 2

Field No.	Taxon	Specimen Description	Map Location	Stratigraphic Unit
1	*Equus*	Right lower cheek tooth	D3	F_1 channel fill
2	*Equus*	RM_3	F4	F_1 channel fill
3	*Mammuthus*	Pelvic fragment	F4, F5	F_1 channel fill
4	*Equus*	Lower cheek tooth	F4	F_1 channel fill
6	*Mammuthus*	Long bone fragment	E3	F_1 channel fill
7	*Camelops*	Upper cheek tooth	D3	F_1 channel fill
9	*Mammuthus*	Proximal end of rib	D4	F_1 channel fill
10	*Mammuthus*	RM_2 stub	E4	F_1 channel fill
12	*Mammuthus*	Rib section	D5	F_1 slope deposit
13	*Mammuthus*	Vertebral centrum	D5	F_1 slope deposit
14	*Mammuthus*	Rib section	D4	F_1 slope deposit
15	*Mammuthus*	Molar fragments	D4	F_1 slope deposit
17	*Bison*	Rib section	H4	F_1 channel fill
18	*Bison*	Proximal end of rib	G4	F_1 channel fill
19	*Equus*	Incisor	D3	F_1 channel fill
20	*Bison*	Rib section	D3	F_1 channel fill
21	*Bison*	Thoracic vertebra	G5	F_1 channel fill
22	*Equus*	LM_3	F3	F_1 channel fill
24	*Equus*	Right upper cheek tooth	F3	F_1 channel fill
25	*Equus*	Cheek tooth fragments	H5	F_1 channel fill
26	*Equus*	Cheek tooth fragments	D3	F_1 channel fill
28	*Equus*	Right lower cheek tooth	H3	F_1 channel fill
29	*Equus*	Cheek tooth fragments	D3	F_1 channel fill
30	*Equus*	RM_3	F3	F_1 channel fill
31	*Mammuthus*	Pelvic fragments	G3	F_1 channel fill
32	*Equus*	Left lower cheek tooth	E4	F_1 channel fill
33	*Bison*	Worn incisor	F4	F_1 channel fill
34	*Bison*	LP_2	F4	F_1 channel fill
36	*Bison*	Femoral condyle	D3	F_1 channel fill
37	*Equus*	Incisor	E4	F_1 channel fill
39	*Bison*	Left radius	F3	F_1 channel fill
40	*Mammuthus*	Long bone fragment	D3	F_1 channel fill
41	*Equus*	Left lower cheek tooth	B6	D
42	*Bison*	Left lower molar	B6	D
43	*Bison*	2 lower cheek teeth	G4	F_1 channel fill
44	*Mammuthus*	Left femur	E2, E3	F_1 channel fill
46	Rodentia	Long bone fragment	E3	F_1 channel fill
47	*Camelops*	Axis	E4	F_1 channel fill
48	*Bison*	Lumbar vertebra	E4	F_1 channel fill
49	*Mammuthus*	Rib section	E4	F_1 channel fill
50	*Mammuthus*	Vertebral centrum	D4	F_1 channel fill
51	*Mammuthus*	Vertebra	E4	F_1 channel fill
52	*Bison*	Vertebral centrum	E4	F_1 channel fill
53	*Mammuthus*	Patella	E4, E5	F_1 channel fill
54	*Bison*	Distal end of metapodial	F4	F_1 channel fill
55	*Mammuthus*	Left humerus	F4, G4	F_1 channel fill
56	*Bison*	Proximal end of rib	F4, G4	F_1 channel fill

Field No.	Taxon	Specimen Description	Map Location	Stratigraphic Unit
57	Bison	Left humerus	F4, G5	F_1 channel fill
59	Bison	Long bone shaft	E3	F_1 channel fill
60	Mammuthus	Pelvic fragment	F4	F_1 channel fill
61	Mammuthus	Ilium	E4	F_1 channel fill
62	Mammuthus	Ilium fragment	E4	F_1 channel fill
63	Mammuthus	Ilium fragment	E4	F_1 channel fill
64	Mammuthus	Long bone fragment	E4	F_1 channel fill
65	Bison	Lumbar vertebra	E4	F_1 channel fill
66	Bison	Left humerus	E4	F_1 channel fill
67	Mammuthus	Carpal or tarsal element	E4	F_1 channel fill
68	Mammuthus	Patella	E4	F_1 channel fill
69	Mammuthus	Ilium	E4	F_1 channel fill
70	Mammuthus	Tusk	E4	F_1 channel fill
71	Mammuthus	RM_3	F4	F_1 channel fill
72	Equus	Right upper cheek tooth	G5	F_1 channel fill
73	Mammuthus	Rib section	E4, F4	F_1 channel fill
74	Mammuthus	Phalanx	E4	F_1 channel fill
75	Mammuthus	Rib section	E4	F_1 channel fill
76	Bison	2 rib sections	E4	F_1 channel fill
77	Camelops	Left femur shaft	E4	F_1 channel fill
78	Mammuthus	Vertebral centrum	E4	F_1 channel fill
79	Bison	Lumbar vertebra	E4	F_1 channel fill
80	Equus	Unerupted right lower premolar	E5	F_1 channel fill
81	Bison	Rib section	E4	F_1 channel fill
82	Bison	Vertebral dorsal spine	E5	F_1 channel fill
83	Bison	2 rib sections	E4, E5	F_1 channel fill
84	Mammuthus	Long bone fragment	E5	F_1 channel fill
85	Camelops	Vertebral dorsal spine	E4	F_1 channel fill
86	Mammuthus	Sacrum	E4	F_1 channel fill
87	Mammuthus	Cranial fragments	E4	F_1 channel fill
88	Bison	Rib section	E4, E5	F_1 channel fill
89	Mammuthus	Rib section	E4	F_1 channel fill
90	Bison	Rib section	E4	F_1 channel fill
91	Bison	Rib section	E4	F_1 channel fill
92	Mammuthus	Rib section	C5	F_1 channel fill
93	Mammuthus	Rib section	C5	F_1 channel fill
94	Mammuthus	Maxillary and molar fragments	E4	F_1 channel fill
96	Canis	Right metatarsal IV	D4	F_1 channel fill
97	Mammuthus	Rib section	E4	F_1 channel fill
98	Mammuthus	Rib section	E4	F_1 channel fill
99	Bison	Thoracic vertebra	F3	F_1 channel fill
100	Mammuthus	Right humerus	D4, F4	F_1 channel fill
101	Mammuthus	Pelvic fragment	E4	F_1 channel fill
102	Mammuthus	Molar fragments	F4	F_1 channel fill
103	Mammuthus	Left mandibular ramus and rostrum with LM_2 stub and LM_3	D3, E3, F4	F_1 channel fill
105	Mammuthus	Cranial fragments	F_1	F_1 channel fill
106	Mammuthus	Rib section	F2	F_1 channel fill

Field No.	Taxon	Specimen Description	Map Location	Stratigraphic Unit
108	Bison	Rib section	E2, E3	F_1 channel fill
109	Mammuthus	Proximal end of rib	D2, E2	F_1 channel fill
111	Equus	Left upper cheek tooth	F6	F_1 channel fill
112	Bison	Upper cheek tooth	G6	F_1 channel fill
113	Bison	Rib section	F7	F_1 channel fill
114	Bison	Proximal end of right scapula	F6	F_1 channel fill
115	Mammuthus	Molar fragments	G6	F_1 channel fill
116	Bison	Rib section	F7	F_1 channel fill
117	Mammuthus	Long bone fragment	F7	F_1 channel fill
118	Bison	Long bone shaft	G6	F_1 channel fill
119	Bison	Right scapula	G6, G7	F_1 channel fill
120	Bison	Rib section	F7	F_1 channel fill
121	Bison	Long bone fragment; upper cheek tooth	H6	F_1 channel fill
123	Mammuthus	Long bone fragment	F6	F_1 channel fill
124	Mammuthus	Long bone fragment	F6	F_1 channel fill
125	Bison	Scapula fragment	F6	F_1 channel fill
126	Bison	Thoracic vertebra	F6	F_1 channel fill
127	Bison	Distal end of humerus	G6, G7	F_1 channel fill
128	Bison	LM_3	F6	F_1 channel fill
129	Bison	Left ulna	F2	F_1 channel fill
130	Bison	LM_3	F6	F_1 channel fill
131	Equus	Incisor	G9	F_1 channel fill
132	Equus	Lower cheek tooth	G7	F_1 channel fill
133	Canis	Upper canine fragment	F7	F_1 channel fill
134	Bison	RP_2	F6	F_1 channel fill
135	Lagomorpha	3 lower cheek teeth	F8	F_2 (?)
136	Lagomorpha	Postcranial skeletal fragments	G8	F_2
137	Camelops	Head of femur	F6	F_1 channel fill
138	Mammuthus	Rib tubercle	E4	F_1 channel fill
139	Equus	Lower cheek tooth	E4	F_1 channel fill
140	Mammuthus	Rib tubercle	E4	F_1 channel fill
141	Equus	Cheek tooth fragment	C3	F_1 channel fill
142	Camelops	2 incisor fragments	B2	F_1 channel fill
143	Equus	Upper cheek tooth fragments	B6	F_1 channel fill
144	Camelops	Lower cheek tooth fragments	A2	F_1 channel fill

APPENDIX E

Geological and Archaeological Investigations at Murray Springs, Area 9 and Trench 13N

Bruce B. Huckell and C. Vance Haynes, Jr.

From May 14–17, 2001, archaeological test excavations were conducted at the Murray Springs Clovis Site in the headcut of the East Swale of the South Branch of Curry Draw. At the same time, stratigraphic investigations were undertaken along the south wall of the north headcut of Curry Draw; Figure E.1 shows the locations of both areas. This report, submitted to the Bureau of Land Management in fulfillment of Cultural Resource Use Permit AZ–000219 in 2002, briefly describes the background to the work, the research methods employed, and the results obtained.

BACKGROUND TO THE RESEARCH

As the South Branch of Curry Draw eroded headward up the main swale in the 1950s and 1960s, it revealed the principal archaeological loci at the Murray Springs Clovis Site. Beginning with the easternmost locus, Area 1, and continuing west through Areas 3, 4, and 5, this South Branch of the draw was intensively excavated from 1966 through 1971. It has been carefully monitored during the 35 years since the last excavation season. A comparatively minor part of the South Branch has slowly cut its way to the southwest, up the unentrenched East Swale of Curry Draw (Fig. E.1). Beginning in the late 1980s and early 1990s, the headcut began to expose the distinctive black mat or Clanton clay, at the base of which Clovis artifacts and the bones of the animals they hunted were known to occur. In the year 2000 fragments of large mammal bone were discovered eroding from the west wall of the headcut at the base of the black mat. Because the west wall of the headcut was within about 20 m of the east edge of Area 1, there was clearly the potential for these bones to be associated with evidence of human activity. Further, because the headcut continues to erode, the faunal remains and possibly cultural material were in danger of being lost. A complicating factor is the presence of a buried early Holocene arroyo channel (the G_1 channel) in the area. The west wall of this northeast-southwest aligned channel formed the eastern edge of Area 1, but how wide the arroyo channel might be was unknown. Thus, as little as one meter or as many as several meters of undisturbed late Pleistocene stratigraphy might be present between the west wall of the modern arroyo headcut and the eastern edge of the early Holocene arroyo. It seemed prudent to undertake limited archaeological test investigations to determine whether the area contained additional evidence of Clovis activity that might be lost to continuing erosion. Accordingly, a cultural resources use permit application and research design were filed by C. Vance Haynes, Jr., and Bruce B. Huckell with the San Pedro Riparian National Conservation Area Office of the Bureau of Land Management in April, 2001. BLM granted a permit (AZ–000219) and offered their full support of test investigations. The goals of the work, as specified in the research design, were two: (1) was there evidence of Clovis cultural activity in this area and (2) how wide was the early Holocene G_1 arroyo channel in this area?

In addition, there was a second objective of the investigations. Some questions remained about the complexity of the depositional history of the black mat and how that complexity might have links to paleoclimatic fluctuations during the Younger Dryas climatic interval some 10,000 to 11,000 years ago. In one area along the south bank of the North Branch of

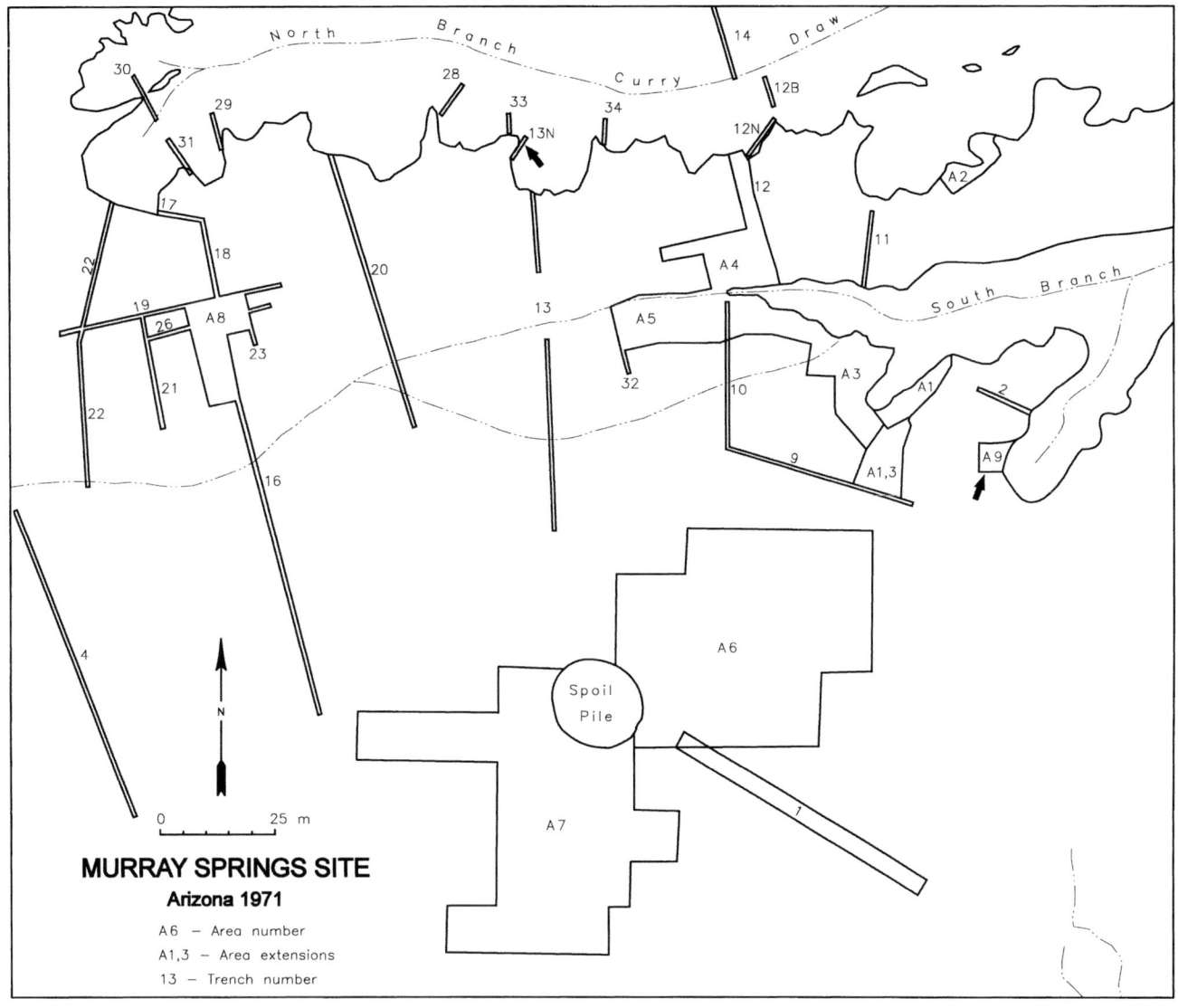

Figure E.1. Arrows indicate the locations of Area 9 and the Trench 13N black mat sampling area.

Curry Draw, the mat displays a complex differentiation into several facies. These facies include bands of the standard highly organic black clay separated by bands of marl. This area is located at the north end of Trench 13N (the more northerly section of Trench 13 depicted on Fig. E.1). Plans were made to reexpose the mat in this area and to precisely record and sample the internal stratigraphy of the mat.

TESTING IN AREA 9

Work in the East Swale headcut began with the profiling of the stratigraphy in the northwestern part of the headcut, both upstream and downstream of the exposed bone fragments. Next, with assistance of BLM, a backhoe was used to open up an area approximately 5.0 m north-south by 4.5 m east-west to be hand excavated. The goal was to mechanically remove as much overburden as possible down to within approximately 10 cm of the top of the black mat. Because the eastern edge of Area 1 was marked by the western edge of the 6,000 to 8,000-year old G_1 channel, it was considered likely that the excavations would encounter the eastern edge of this early Holocene arroyo. Therefore, the excavations by the backhoe were carefully monitored to avoid cutting through the black mat and

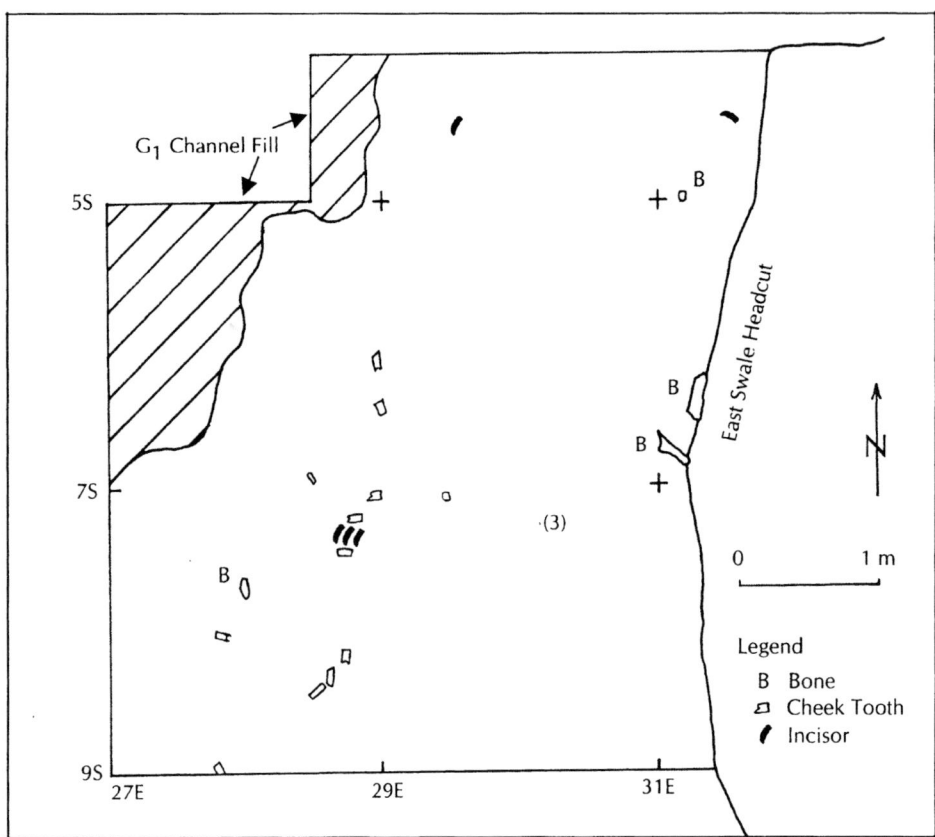

Figure E.2. Distribution of horse teeth and bone fragments in Area 9. Eastern margin of the G_1 channel truncates the late Pleistocene surface along the northwestern portion of the excavated area.

to attempt to locate where the eastern margin of the G_1 channel might be; the latter task proved the more difficult of the two. The backhoe quickly removed most of the overburden; hand excavation with picks and shovels succeeded in getting most of the area down to the top of the black mat. The mat could not be located at the northwestern edge of the excavation area, and it was ultimately determined that only in this area did the eastern margin of the G_1 channel appear. For the sake of continuity with previous work at the site, this new area was designated Area 9.

Once the area was excavated to the top of the black mat, it was sectioned into a system of 2-m grid squares. Figure E.2 presents a map of Area 9 showing the grid area, which covered 4.5 m north-south and 4.0 m east-west. The grid system was aligned identically to the 1966-1971 grid but employed a different system of designation. In essence, the Area 9 grids were designated in relation to the old grid point Z8, which was chosen because it was one of the few grid stakes that was still in position in Area 3 to the west (Fig. E.1). Working south and east from Z8, the southwestern corner of the grid area within Area 9 is 17 m south and 27 m east of that point.

A crew of four University of New Mexico graduate students, one University of Arizona graduate student, and one volunteer performed the excavations under the direction of the authors. Standard excavation procedure was to remove the black mat with trowels, awls, or other small tools to the underlying contact with either Coro marl or older strata of the ancient erosion surface buried by the black mat. Any bone or tooth fragments larger in size than 5 cm were left in place, and all excavated black mat was passed through ¼-inch mesh screen to ensure that any small artifacts or bone fragments would be recovered. The excavation was documented with 35 mm slides, field notes, and maps of individual excavation units.

The excavation revealed that no other bones were present to the west of the pair of large bone fragments that were exposed in the headcut. However, the scattered incisor and cheek teeth from what appears to be a single horse (*Equus* sp.) mandible were found on the erosional surface at the base of the mat. The teeth were concentrated in the southwestern portion of the excavated area, although two incisors were found along the northern edge of the area. Figure E.2 is a map of Area 9 showing the locations of the two large bone fragments and the scattered teeth. Aside from a few small scraps, mandibular bone was not in evidence; the condition of the teeth ranged from very poor to very good. In total, 10 cheek teeth were recognized from either complete specimens or large fragments, and at least 5 nearly complete incisors were recovered. Missing altogether were both lower third molars (although both P_2 were found), and all but one of the incisors was recovered. The relatively small size of the teeth suggests that this particular horse was not a large individual.

The two bones that were exposed along the arroyo wall were in extremely poor condition and had been badly crushed by the weight of the overlying sediment. Neither could be identified as to element or taxon, except to say that they represented limb elements from an animal in the horse-bison-camel size range. No artifacts were encountered in the excavations, so there is no direct evidence to suggest that Clovis hunters had anything to do with the demise of this horse.

After excavation was completed, a contour map of the paleotopography at the base of the black mat was prepared by EDM survey. In general, the entire topography shows a marked slope from south to north, with a particularly prominent rise at the southeastern corner. It also reveals that the teeth are located around the margins of a topographic high between approximately 7.50–8.50 m south and 28.0–28.75 m east. It is possible that the poor preservation of mandibular bone and the scattering of the teeth is due to the fact that the mandible was slowly buried by the black mat. The top of the topographic high is some 18 cm above the lowest portion of the excavated area.

As shown on Figure E.2, the eastern margin of the G_1 arroyo channel was encountered in the northwestern portion of the Area 9 excavations. Although short, the exposure revealed that the ancient arroyo bank in this area had a southwest-northeast orientation and was fairly sinuous. Thus, from this portion of Area 9 west to Area 1, a distance of approximately 20 m, the G_1 channel has probably removed all of the latest Pleistocene-earliest Holocene Lehner Ranch Formation and all or most of the older late Pleistocene Murray Springs Formation. Clovis artifacts extended right up to the western edge of the G_1 channel in Area 1, which strongly suggests that some part of the Clovis occupation surface was lost to the early Holocene arroyo. It is difficult to draw with confidence any inferences from the lack of Clovis artifacts in Area 9 because of the small area that was excavated, but it is possible that Clovis activities did not extend that far to the east from Area 1. The eastern edge of the buried Clovis component of the site may have been somewhere in the 20 m between Areas 1 and 9.

BLACK MAT TESTING AT TRENCH 13N AND AREA 9

Excavation of Trench 13N (Tr. 13N) in June 1970 showed that the about 10–cm thick black mat or Clanton clay (Stratum F_{2a}) interfingered with the white marl (Stratum F_{2b}) as it reached the lowest areas of the ancient valley of Curry Draw (Appendix A, Fig. A.1*a, b*). Up to five stringers of black organic clay ranging in thickness from less than 1 cm to approximately 10 cm are separated by marl lenses from 2 cm to 20 cm thick. This provided an exceptional opportunity to conduct microstratigraphic sampling for radiocarbon and stable isotope analyses to better age date the microstrata and to evaluate $\delta^{13}C$ changes in relation to changes in plant photosynthetic pathways during the Younger Dryas paleoclimatic chronozone (Chapter 2, p. 47). However, in the late 1960s much larger samples were required for radiocarbon dating prior to the advent of accelerator mass spectrometry (AMS) measurement of ^{14}C. Results also left much to be desired at that time (Appendix A, Table A.2). Now, with AMS, a new opportunity to resample is at hand.

In May of 2001 sampling was accomplished by BLM using a backhoe to open a 1.15–m by 3.0–m trench against the natural exposure of the modern arroyo bank in the North Branch of Curry Draw. This trench was at the north end of Trench 13N. Unfortunately, the exact strata of Fig. A.1 were not found due either to bank erosion since 1970 or placement of the present exposure too far north. The subject strata, buried by talus at the foot of the arroyo wall, were exposed and the fresh exposure was cleaned and

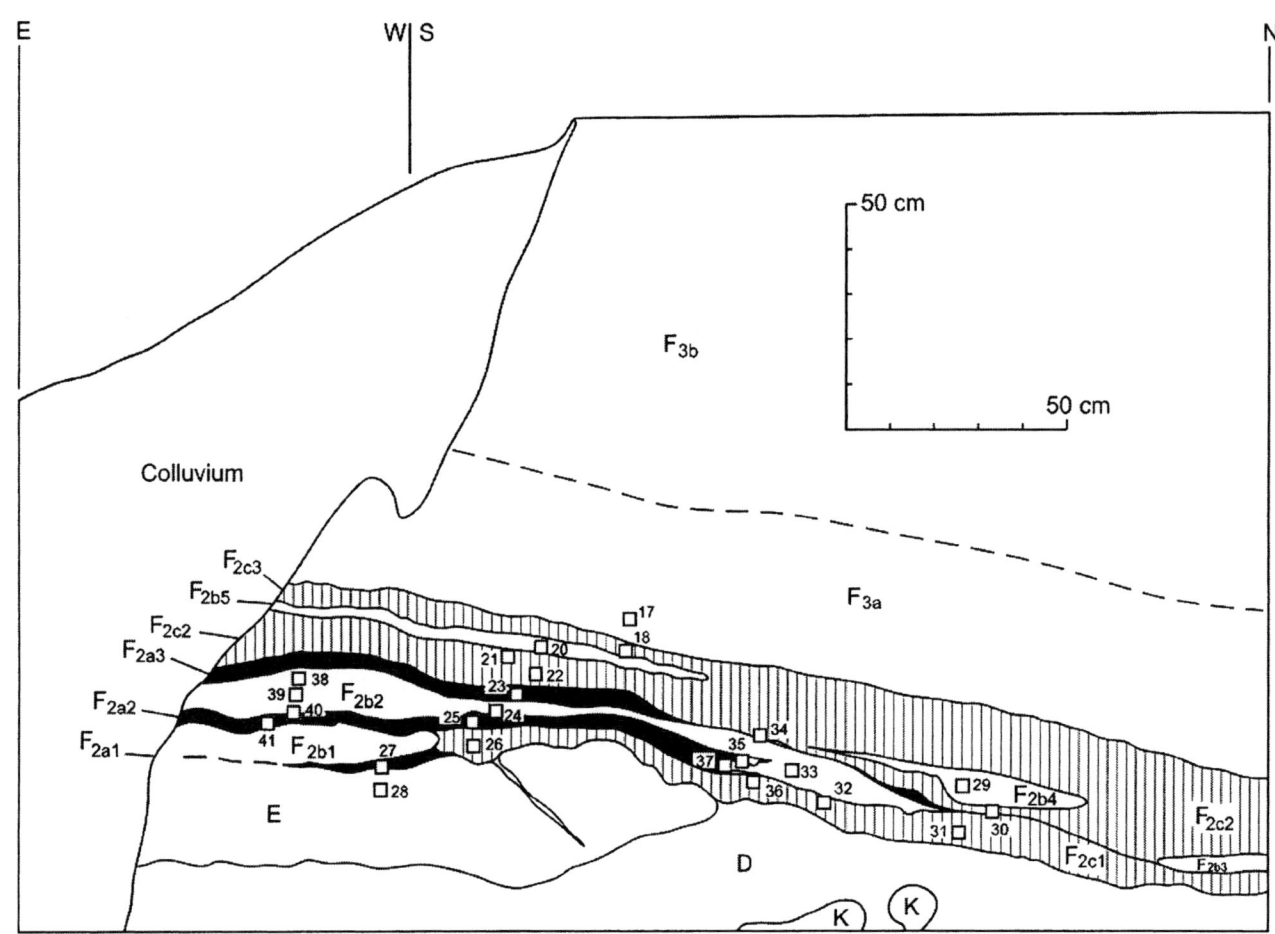

Figure E.3. Murray Springs Trench 13N stratigraphic profile with ^{14}C sample locations numbered. Strata F_{2a} are black mat, F_{2b} are white marl, and F_{2c} are dark gray mat.

straightened by trench-shovel scraping and troweling. Detailed stratigraphic mapping was undertaken (Fig. E.3). We collected 24 bulk sediment, thin-increment samples from less than 2-cm thicknesses of each stratum in several locations on the stratigraphic profile. The exposure was photographed as well and then backfilled.

During the archaeological testing of Area 9, the natural exposure of strata in the headcut of the East Swale was recorded by plotting from a level line with 1-m spacing marked with vinyl tape flagging (Fig. E.4). Detailed microstratigraphic profiling was done at two places (Fig. E.4 sample columns A and B) on the line where thin-increment (less than 2 cm) bulk sediment sampling was done for radiocarbon, stable isotope, and chemical analyses. Thirteen samples were collected for this purpose. Substratum F_o is a 5-cm thick brown lens between the base of the black mat (Stratum F_2) and the Coro marl (Stratum E) that may represent local clay deposition during the Allerød chronozone.

In addition, two charcoal or carbonized wood samples were collected from the stratum G_1 (Weik alluvium) channel exposure in the south wall of Curry Draw at Area 1, and a thin-increment bulk sample was collected from the basal black mat stringer (about 4 mm thick) exposed in the east wall of the Area 1 excavations at the bulge between the 1969 and 1971 excavations. These samples are now curated in the Geoarchaeology Laboratory of the Department of Geosciences, University of Arizona, Tucson.

SUMMARY AND CONCLUSIONS

The testing program was successful in reaching its two basic goals. Work in Area 9 demonstrated that the

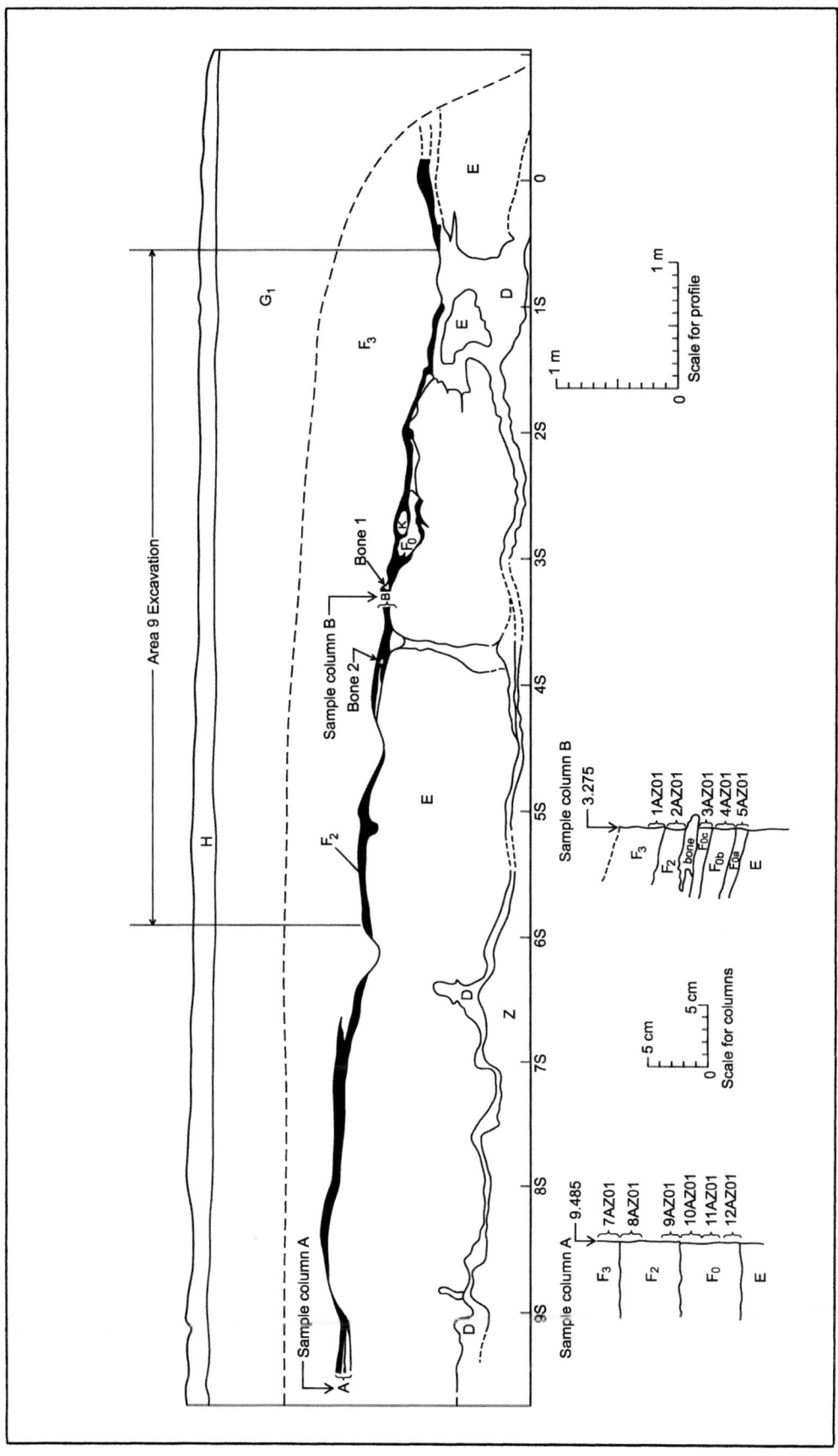

Figure E.4. Murray Springs Area 9 headcut stratigraphic profile and microstratigraphic columns A and B for sediment sampling.

scattered mandibular dentition of a horse and the two unidentified postcranial elements were apparently deposited independently of Clovis activity. Further, the investigations located a small portion of the eastern margin of the early Holocene G_1 arroyo channel, positioned along the northwestern margin of the excavated area. This portion provides an indication of the width of the G_1 channel that borders Area 1 on the east and demonstrates that the arroyo removed a swath of the late Pleistocene deposits approximately 20 m wide in the Area 1/Area 9 region. In the area of Trench 13N and along the headcut of the East Swale, the microstratigraphic complexities of the black mat were exposed, mapped, and sampled. These samples, when analyzed, should provide valuable new data concerning the chronology and environmental characteristics of the Younger Dryas in the San Pedro Valley.

With respect to the future, it is important to recognize that as the headcut of the East Swale of Curry Draw continues to erode to the south, new exposures of late Pleistocene and early Holocene stratigraphy will be created. It is certainly possible that additional vertebrate fossils will be exposed and the potential for new evidence of Clovis occupation will remain high. The lack of Clovis artifacts in the Area 9 test excavations should not be generalized beyond the small space actually excavated. Therefore, the East Swale headcut area should be monitored frequently after major storms and floods in the site area.

Also, the reexamination of the black mat microstratigraphy at the north end of Trench 13N and elsewhere should underscore the research potential of Murray Springs. The site remains an incredible resource for the study of late Quaternary environments and human adaptations to the rapid environmental changes before, during, and after the Younger Dryas. As new investigative methods are developed and new questions are posed, Murray Springs will continue to serve Quaternary scientists as an excellent laboratory.

Acknowledgments

We greatly appreciate the efforts of our volunteer excavators: Jesse Ballenger, Marcus Hamilton, David Kilby, Leon Lorentzen, Armand Mijares, and Susan Ruth. In addition, we are indebted to Jane Pike-Childress and the rest of the Bureau of Land Management San Pedro Project personnel for facilitating and supporting our research by allowing us to stay at the Boquillas Ranch and providing the services of a backhoe.

APPENDIX F

Identification Numbers of Illustrated Artifacts from Murray Springs

C. Vance Haynes, Jr.

Figure No.		Artifact	Arizona State Museum Catalogue No.	Field Number
5.13	a	Biface fragment	A–32,715	MS–614
	b	Clovis point tip	A–32,716	MS–712
	c	Clovis point tip	A–32,719	MS–713
	d	Clovis point	A–32,718	MS–719
	e	Blade fragment	A–32,720a	MS–19
		Blade refit	A–32,720b	MS–629
	f	Utilized flake	A–43,006	MS–626
	g	Utilized flake	A–43,005	MS–91
	h	Flake tool	A–32,717	MS–22
	i	Multiple graver	A–33,935	MS–791
	j	Biface tip	A–33,947	MS–211
5.14	a	Biface fragment	A–32,715	MS–614
		Refit flake	A–43,009	MS–811
		Refit flake	A–43,004	MS–18
	b	Clovis point tip	A–32,716	MS–712
	c	Clovis point tip	A–32,719	MS–713
	d	Clovis point	A–32,718	MS–719
	e	Blade fragment	A–32,720a	MS–19
		Blade refit	A–32,720b	MS–629
5.15	a	Bladelike flake	A–43,052	MS–373
	b	Thinning flake	A–43,058	MS–721
	c	Thinning flake	A–43,049	MS–21
	d	Thinning flake	A–43,055	MS–456
	e	Thinning flake	A–43,051	MS–249
	f	Thinning flake	?	?
	g	Thinning flake	A–43,056-x	MS–569
	h	Thinning flake	A–43,048	MS–20
	i	Thinning flake	?	?
5.16	a	Marekanite nodule	A–31,611	MS–8
	b	Marekanite nodule	A–33,949	MS–425
	c	Marekanite nodule	A–33,948	MS–221

Figure No.		Artifact	Arizona State Museum Catalogue No.	Field Number
5.17		Bone shaft wrench	A–32,640	MS–722
5.18		Worked bone	A–33,955	MS–110
5.22,	a	Clovis point	A–33,924	MS–1441
5.23	b	Clovis point	A–33,111	MS–1007,
(Not shown)		Impact flake	A–45,781	MS–2271
		Refit ear	A–33,111	MS–952
	c	Clovis point	A–33,109	MS–970
	d	Clovis point	A–33,114	MS–1062
	e	Clovis point	A–33,115	MS–1063
	f	Clovis point	A–33,110	MS–949
	g	Clovis point	A–33,116	MS–1067
	h	Biface fragment	A–33,113	MS–1014
		Refit flake	A–44,122	MS–996
		Refit flake	A–43,011	MS–911
		Refit flake	A–43,391	MS–959
		Refit flake	A–43,015	MS–824
	i	Scraper-burin	A–33,112	MS–993
	j	Clovis blade	A–33,926	MS–1452
5.24		Cobble hammer	A–33,940	MS–1066
5.25	a	Worked bone	A–33,946	MS–534
	b	Burned rib fragment	A–33,944	MS–275
5.26	a	Utilized flake	A–43,245	MS–784
	b	Small flake	A–33,936	MS–877
	c	Utilized flake	A–43,012	MS–997
	d	Utilized flake	A–44,172	MS–1068
	e	Utilized flake	A–43,010	MS–861
	f	Burned flake	A–43,245	MS–784
	g	Flake	A–44,146	MS–1029

274   Appendix F, C. Vance Haynes, Jr.

Figure No.		Artifact	Arizona State Museum Catalogue No.	Field Number
5.26	h	Utilized bladelike flake	A–43,008	MS–786
5.29, 5.30	a	Clovis point base	A–33,917	MS–1400
	b	Clovis point base	A–33,922	MS–1436
	c	Bifacial preform	A–33,918	MS–1445
		Refit piece	A–33,918	MS–1403
	d	Biface	A–33,923	MS–1438
	e	Bladelike flake	A–33,919	MS–1405
7.7	a	Clovis point	A–32,991	MS–761
(Not shown)		Impact flake	A–33,938	MS–982
	b	Clovis point	A–32,992	MS–771
	c	Clovis point base	A–47,162	MS–2522
	d	Clovis point base	A–47,139	MS–2001
	e	Clovis point base	A–47,140	MS–2028
	f	Biface fragment	A–47,163	MS–2523
		Refit piece	A–47,199	MS–2564
	g	Biface	A–47,170	MS–2535
	h	Clovis point base	A–47,283	MS–2656
	i	Biface fragment	A–46,365	MS–2946
7.8	a	End scraper	A–33,928	MS–1570
	b	End scraper	A–33,929	MS–1571
	c	End scraper	A–33,943	MS–1382
	d	End scraper	A–45,615	MS–2004
	e	Graver	A–32,990	MS–760
	f	Lat. ret. flake	A–47,291	MS–2664
	g	Lat. ret. flake	A–45,703	MS–2110
	h	Lat. ret. flake	74–52–1	MS–3070
	i	Lat. ret. flake	A–46,143	MS–2716
	j	Lat. ret. flake	A–47,264-x	MS–2637a, b
		Refit piece	A–45,694	MS–2101
		Refit piece	A–43,026	MS–1611
7.9	a	Ret. blade frag.	A–43,007	MS–765
		Refit piece	A–47,513	MS–2918
		Refit piece	A–47,514	MS–3053
		Refit piece	A–47,514	MS–3067
		Refit piece	A–47,513	MS–3064
	b	Utilized blade	A–46,180	MS–2762
	c	Blade fragment	A–46,368	MS–2949
	d	Utilized blade	A–43,024	MS–1602
	e	Ret. blade frag.	A–43,023	MS–1601
	f	Utilized blade	A–47,266	MS–2639
	g	Ret. blade frag.	A–33,927	MS–1569
	h	Ret. blade frag.	A–33,930	MS–1573
		Refit piece	A–46,148	MS–2721

Figure No.		Artifact	Arizona State Museum Catalogue No.	Field Number
7.10	a	San Pedro point	A–33,934	MS–763
	b	San Pedro point frag.	A–33,933	MS–762
	c	Point tip	A–47,119	MS–2480
	d	Stemmed point		MS–3097
	e	Biface frag.	A–46,309	MS–2888
		Refit piece	A–44,309	MS–1577
	f	Biface	A–45,690	MS–2093
		Refit piece	A–46,124	MS–2697
	g	Biface fragment	A–47,290	MS–2663
	h	Unifacially ret. tool	A–46,306	MS–2885
	i	Unifacially ret. tool	A–47,243	MS–2614
8.6	a	Biface fragment	A–33,113	MS–1014
	b	Biface fragment	A–46,365	MS–2946
	c	Biface fragment	A–32,715	MS–614
		Refit flake	A–43,004	MS–18
	d	Biface	A–33,923	MS–1438
	e	Biface	A–47,170	MS–2535
	f	Biface fragment	A–33,918	MS–1445
		Biface fragment	A–33,918	MS–1403
8.7	a	Clovis point base	A–47,140	MS–2028
	b	Clovis point base	A–47,283	MS–2656
	c	Clovis point base	A–33,917	MS–1400
	d	Clovis point base	A–33,922	MS–1436
	e	Clovis point base	A–47,139	MS–2001
	f	Clovis point tip	A–32,719	MS–713
	g	Clovis point tip	A–32,716	MS–712
	h	Clovis point midsec.	A–32,991	MS–761
		Refit flake	A–33,938	MS–982
	i	Clovis point	A–32,992	MS–771
	j	Clovis point base	A–47,162	MS–2522
	k	Clovis point	A–32,718	MS–719
8.8	a	Clovis point	A–33,110	MS–949
	b	Clovis point blade portion	A–33,114	MS–1062
	c	Clovis point	A–33,116	MS–1067
	d	Clovis point	A–33,924	MS–1441
	e	Clovis point	A–33,115	MS–1063
	f	Clovis point w/o tip	A–33,109	MS–970
	g	Clovis point	A–33,111	MS–1007
		Impact flake	A–45,781	MS–227
		Refit ear	A–33,111	MS–952
8.10	a	End scraper	A–33,929	MS–1571
	b	End scraper	A–33,943	MS–1382
	c	End scraper/graver	A–33,928	MS–1570

Identification Numbers of Illustrated Artifacts from Murray Springs

Figure No.		Artifact	Arizona State Museum Catalogue No.	Field Number
8.10	d	End scraper	A–45,615	MS–2004
	e	Multiple graver	A–32,990	MS–760
	f	Multiple graver	A–33,935	MS–791
	g	Lat. ret. flake	A–47,158	MS–2518
	h	Flake tool	A–32,717	MS–22
	i	Side scraper	A–46,143	MS–2716
	j	Lat. ret. flake	A–47,264	MS–2637
		Refit piece	A–45,694	MS–2101
		Refit piece	A–43,026	MS–1611
	k	Lat. ret. flake	A–45,614	MS–2003
	l	Large lat. ret. flake	74–52–1	MS–3070
8.11		Scraper-burin	A–33,112	MS–993
8.12	a	Utilized blade frag.	A–43,024	MS–1602
	b	Retouched blade	A–33,926	MS–1452
	c	Ret. blade frag.	A–47,513	MS–3064
		Refit piece	A–43,007	MS–765

Figure No.		Artifact	Arizona State Museum Catalogue No.	Field Number
		Refit piece	A–47,513	MS–3064
		Refit piece	A–47,514	MS–3067
		Refit piece	A–47,514	MS–3053
		Refit piece	A–47,514	MS–2918
	d	Utilized blade frag.	A–32,720a	MS–19
		Blade refit	A–32,720b	MS–629
	e	Utilized blade	A–46,180	MS–2762
8.13	a	Utilized blade	A–47,266	MS–2639
	b	Misstruck blade	A–46,187	MS–2759
	c	Misstruck primary blade	A–46,179	MS–2752
	d	Ret. large blade	A–33,927	MS–1569
	e	Ret. blade frag.	A–33,930	MS–1573
		Refit blade	A–46,148	MS–2721
8.14	a	Ret. nodule	A–33,954	MS–732
	b	Ret. cobble	A–33,940	MS–1066
	c	Utilized cobble	A–33,953	MS–731

NOTE: Lat. Ret. = Laterally retouched; Ret. = Retouched

APPENDIX G

Murray Springs Project Field Personnel, Volunteers, and Site Visitors

C. Vance Haynes, Jr.

1966
Director   C. Vance Haynes, Jr.
Foremen   E. Thomas Hemmings, Gerald K. Kelso
Crew
    Darrell Clark   William Daniel
    Peggy E. Davis   Timothy Farrell
    Steve Hardin   David Libbey
    Beth Walton
Specialists
    Peter J. Mehringer, Jr., Palynology
    Jeffrey J. Saunders, Paleontology
    Susan Woodward, Ecology
    Jonathan Gell, Surveyor
    Larry D. Agenbroad, Geology
Advisors
    Paul E. Damon, Radiocarbon
    Emil W. Haury, Archaeology
    John F. Lance, Paleontology
    Paul S. Martin, Palynology
    Terah L. Smiley, UA Geochronology Laboratories
    Raymond H. Thompson, Arizona State Museum
Volunteers, part-time
    George Batchelder
    Allen Gottefeldt
    James West
Visitors
    Elizabeth H. Haynes
    Lisa A. Haynes
    Mary Ann Mehringer
    G. E. Freeman
    J. H. Burk
    W. A. Dick-Peddie
    David Rea
    Donald C. Gray
    Col. Bud Morris, Fort Huachuca

1967
Director   C. Vance Haynes, Jr.
Foremen   E. Thomas Hemmings, Barney T. Burns
Crew
    Peter Banks   William Barrera
    Morris Eckhardt   Frederick Gorman
    Donald Graybill   Judy Green
    Wes Jernigan   Virginia Kosarko
    Peter M. Laudeman   Susanne Rothstein
    Jeffrey J. Saunders   Dennis J. Stanford
    Beth Walton
Advisors
    Paul E. Damon, Radiocarbon
    Emil W. Haury, Archaeology
    Everett H. Lindsay, Paleontology
    Terah S. Smiley, UA Geochronology Laboratories
    Raymond H. Thompson, Arizona State Museum
Volunteers, full time
    Father Norman Whalen, Tombstone
Volunteers, part-time
    Louis and Jackie Escapule
    Ursula Hurley
    Ernie and Judy Kuncel
    Kathy Moore
Visitors
    Sam Abel, NGS photographer
    Mr. Arnold, Soil Conservation Service, Bisbee
    George Bratsonas
    Roy Christiansen, Ft. Huachuca Security
    Robert DuBois, Paleomagnetist
    Vicki Grafstrom
    Dr. and Mrs. Emil W. Haury
    Elizabeth H. Haynes
    Lisa A. Haynes
    Charles Hoffman and family (NAU archaeologist)

1967 (continued)
  CWO Stanley Hurley, Ft. Huachuca
  Lt. Hutchinson, Ft. Huachuca
  Albert Johnson, Archaeologist
  Ed and Lyn Lehner (Lehner Site)
  Anne Lehner (Lehner Site)
  Larry and Ellie Manire
  Don Matheson, Sierra Vista
  Richard Meyers, Archaeologist
  Leon Smelzer, Bella Vista Ranch
  Helga Teiwes, Arizona State Museum Photographer
  Mark Winters, Graduate Student
  Sgt. Zangmeister, Ft. Huachuca

1968
Director C. Vance Haynes, Jr.
Asst. Director E. Thomas Hemmings
Foreman Barney T. Burns
Crew
  Steven Armesbury
  Darrell Drew
  Peter M. Laudeman
  Geraldine Moreno
  Gene Paul
  Beth Walton
  William Barrera
  Steven Greenberg
  Jean Martin
  Tom Naylor
  Catherine Ungar
Specialists
  Jeffrey J. Saunders, Paleontology
  Susan Woodward, Ecology
Advisors
  Paul E. Damon, Radiocarbon
  Emil W. Haury, Archaeology
  Everett H. Lindsay, Paleontology
  Terah S. Smiley, UA Geochronology Laboratories
  Raymond H. Thompson, Arizona State Museum
Volunteers, full time
  Raymond N. Rogers, Los Alamos
  Father Norman Whalen, Tombstone
Volunteers, part-time
  Mitchel Cantwell, Paleontologist
  Earl Dunkerson, Cochise County
  Louis and Jackie Escapule
  Carol Hemmings
  Judy Kuncel
  Scott Rogers
  Ginny Smyer
Visitors
  Claude C. Albritton, Southern Methodist University, and 16 SMU students
  Keith Anderson, National Park Service, Southwest Archaeological Center, Globe, Arizona
  Bernard C. Arms, UA Geochronology Laboratories
  Robert Baker, Arizona State Museum
  Mr. Bennett, Sierra Vista radio station
  Henry and Pamala Bollweg
  Mr. and Mrs. George Bredt, Elgin teachers
  Robert Buettner, University of Arizona student
  Jill Cantwell
  Paul E. Damon, UA Radiocarbon Laboratory
  Fred Davidson, Coronado National Monument
  Charles C. Di Peso, Amerind Foundation
  Mr. and Mrs. Hugh Downs, NBC News
  Bruce Duke, Arizona Game and Fish
  Craig B. Fisher, NBC News and crew
  Jonathan and Elizabeth Gell and two sons
  Bruce Harrell, University of Arizona student
  Noye M. Johnson, Dartmouth College
  Ernie Kuncel, Coronado National Monument
  Ed and Lyn Lehner (Lehner Site)
  Austin Long, UA Radiocarbon Laboratory
  Paul S. Martin, UA Geosciences Department
  Maurice Powers, Coronado Ranger
  Tom Quick, University of Arizona student
  Richard Reeves and 11 University of Arizona students, Geography Department
  Larry Roush and family, Superintendent, Coronado National Monument
  E. B. Sayles, Arizona State Museum
  Terah L. Smiley and daughters
  Chris Stone
  Paul Swartzlert
  Fred Wendorf, Southern Methodist University and 16 SMU students

1969
Director C. Vance Haynes, Jr.
Asst. Director E. Thomas Hemmings
Foreman Gerald K. Kelso
Crew
  Martha Ames
  John R. F. Bower
  Afifa Hassan
  Donald O. Henry
  Geraldine Moreno
  Robert Pardee
  Byron Sudbury
  John Barthelme
  Cathleen Burke
  Fekri Hassan
  Louis McNaughton
  Tom Naylor
  Gene Paul
Specialist Jeffrey J. Saunders, Paleontology
Advisors
  Paul E. Damon, Radiocarbon

1969 (continued)
    Emil W. Haury, Archaeology
    Everett H. Lindsay, Paleontology
    Terah L. Smiley, UA Geochronology Laboratories
    Raymond H. Thompson, Arizona State Museum
Volunteers, part-time
    Stuart Aitchison
    Louis and Jackie Escapule
    Edie Hopper
    Ursula Hurley
    Ernie and Judy Kuncel
Visitors
    Bernard C. Arms
    Steve Barrett
    François Bordes, Université de Bordeaux, France
    Andrea Carrachiolo, Bella Vista properties
    Donald Crabtree, Idaho State Museum
    Cam Greenleaf, Arizona State Museum
    Laurens and Nancy Hammack
    Stanley Hurley
    Jamie Lytle
    Terah L. Smiley and two daughters
    Bob Thomas and son, *Arizona Republic*
    Jacques Tixier, CNRS, Paris, France
    William W. Wasley, Arizona State Museum

1970
Director   C. Vance Haynes, Jr.
Asst. Director   Larry D. Agenbroad
Foreman   Gerald K. Kelso
Crew
    Martha H. Ames   Garcia B. Berry, Jr.
    Peggy Jean Corman   Steven E. Haney
    David T. Hughes   Rosa Portell-Ferrer
Specialists
    Jonathan Gell, Cartography
    Robert L. Laury, Stratigraphy
    Jeffrey J. Saunders, Paleontology
Advisors
    Paul E. Damon, Radiocarbon
    Emil W. Haury, Archaeology
    Everett H. Lindsay, Paleontology
    Terah L. Smiley, UA Geochronology Laboratories
    Raymond H. Thompson, Arizona State Museum

Volunteers
    Emma Lou Davis
    Judy Kuncel
Visitors
    Adrien Anderson, Arizona State Museum
    Bernard C. Arms, UA Geochronology Laboratories
    James Ayres, Arizona State Museum
    Bryant Bannister, UA Tree-Ring Laboratory
    Steve and Jill Cassells
    Louis Escapule
    Jim Garboni, UA Geosciences Department
    William Haney (father of Steve Haney)
    Mr. Hunsacker, Coronado National Monument
    Everett H. Lindsay, UA Geosciences Department
    William Robinson, UA Tree-Ring Laboratory
    Norm Tessman, UA Geosciences Department

1971
Director   C. Vance Haynes, Jr.
Asst. Director   Larry D. Agenbroad
Foremen   Gerald K. Kelso, Jeffrey J. Saunders
Crew
    Martha H. Ames   E. Steven Cassells
    Steven E. Haney   Donald O. Henry
    Bruce B. Huckell   Donna K. La Rocca
    Peter M. Laudeman   Jamie Laverne Lytle
    Marian E. McIntyre   Kenneth G. McIntyre
    Barbara Ann Purdy
Specialists
    Herbert Haas, Radiocarbon dating
    Robert L. Laury, Stratigraphy
    Jeffry J. Saunders, Paleontology
Volunteers, part-time
    Barney T. Burns
    Mary Rainey
Visitors
    Charles Hoffman, Northern Arizona University
    Austin Long, UA Geosciences

1972
Director   C. Vance Haynes, Jr.
Specialists
    Gerald K. Kelso, Palynologist
    James E. King, Palynologist

References

Abelson, P. H., and P. E. Hare
- 1970 Reactions of Amino Acids with Natural and Artificial Humus and Kerogens. *Carnegie Institution of Washington 1969 Yearbook*, pp. 327–337. Washington.

Adam, David P.
- 1970 Some Palynological Applications of Multivariate Statistics. Doctoral dissertation, Department of Geosciences, University of Arizona, Tucson.

Agenbroad, Larry D.
- 1967 Cenozoic Stratigraphy and Paleohydrology of the Redington–San Manuel Area, San Pedro Valley, Arizona. Doctoral dissertation, Department of Geosciences, University of Arizona, Tucson.
- 1970 Cultural Implications from the Statistical Analysis of a Prehistoric Lithic Site in Arizona. Master's thesis, Department of Geosciences, University of Arizona, Tucson.
- 1978 [Editor] *The Hudson-Meng Site: An Alberta Bison Kill in the Nebraska High Plains.* University Press of America, Washington, D.C.

Agenbroad, Larry D., and Bruce B. Huckell
- 1981 New Discoveries at the Lehner Site: 1974–75 and 1980. Manuscript on file, Arizona State Museum Archives, University of Arizona, Tucson.

Allen, Joel A.
- 1876 The American Bisons, Living and Extinct. *Memoirs of the Museum of Comparative Zoology* 4(10). Harvard University Press, Cambridge.

Alley, Richard B.
- 2000 The Younger Dryas Cold Interval as Viewed from Central Greenland. *Quaternary Science Reviews* 19: 213–226.

Alroy, John
- 1999 Putting North America's End-Pleistocene Megafauna Extinction in Context: Large-Scale Analyses of Spatial Patterns, Extinction Rates, and Size Distributions. *Extinctions in Near Time: Causes, Contexts, and Consequences*, edited by Ross D. E. MacPhee, pp. 105–143. Kluwer Academic/Plenum Publishers, New York.
- 2001 A Multispecies Overkill Simulation at the End-Pleistocene Megafaunal Mass Extinction. *Science* 292(5523): 1893–1896.

Anderson, David G., and Michael K. Faught
- 2000 Paleoindian Artefact Distributions: Evidence and Implications. *Antiquity* 74(285): 507–513.

Antevs, Ernst
- 1941 Age of the Cochise Culture Stages. In "The Cochise Culture," by E. B. Sayles and Ernst Antevs, pp. 31–56. *Medallion Papers* 29. Gila Pueblo, Globe, Arizona.
- 1948 The Great Basin, with Emphasis on Glacial and Postglacial Times. III. Climatic Changes and Pre-White Man. *University of Utah Bulletin* 38(20): 168–191.
- 1955 Geologic–Climatic Dating in the West. *American Antiquity* 20(4): 317–335.
- 1959 Geological Age of the Lehner Mammoth Site. *American Antiquity* 25(1): 31–34.
- 1962 Late Quaternary Climates in Arizona. *American Antiquity* 28(2): 193–198.

Augusta, Josef, and Zdenek Burian
- 1960 *Prehistoric Man.* Paul Hamlyn, London.

Bahre, Conrad J., and Donald E. Bradbury
- 1978 Vegetation Change along the Arizona–Sonora Boundary. *Annals of the Association of American Geographers* 68: 145–165.

Bailey, L. R.
- 1998 *Henry Clay Hooker and the Sierra Bonita.* Western Lore Press, Tucson.

Bandelier, Adolph F.
- 1929 The Discovery of New Mexico by Fray Marcos of Nizza. *The New Mexico Historical Review* 4(1): 28–44.

Barnosky, Anthony D., Paul L. Koch, Robert S. Feranec, Scott L. Wing, and Alan B. Shabel
- 2004 Assessing the Causes of Late Pleistocene Extinctions on the Continents. *Science* 306 (5693): 70–75.

Barton, C. Michael, Geoffrey A. Clark, David R. Yesner, and Georges A. Pearson, Editors
- 2004 *The Settlement of the American Continents, A Multidisciplinary Approach to Human Biogeography.* University of Arizona Press, Tucson.

Bedord, Jean N.
- 1974 Morphological Variation in Bison Metacarpals and Metatarsals. *The Casper Site: A Hell Gap Bison Kill on the High Plains*, edited by George C. Frison, pp. 199–240. Academic Press, New York.

Bell, C. J., E. L. Lundelius, A. D. Barnosky, R. W. Graham, and E. H. Lindsay
- 2004 The Blancan, Irvingtonian, and Rancholabrean

Bell, C. J., E. L. Lundelius, A. D. Barnosky, R. W. Graham, and E. H. Lindsay (*continued*)
Mammal Ages. *Late Cretaceous and Cenezoic Mammals of North America*, edited by M. Woodburne, Fig. 7.1. Columbia University Press, New York.

Bement, Leland C., and Brian J. Carter
2003 Clovis Bison Hunting at the Jake Bluff Site, NW Oklahoma. *Current Research in the Pleistocene* 20: 5-7.
2004 The Jake Bluff Site: Clovis Bison Hunting Adaptations at the Brink of Mammoth Extinction on the Southern Plains of North America. *Guidebook for Field Trips, 18th Biennial Meeting of the American Quaternary Association*, compiled by Rolfe D. Mandel, Open File Report 2004-33. Kansas Geological Survey, Lawrence.

Benedict, F. G.
1936 The Physiology of the Elephant. *Carnegie Institution of Washington Publication* 474. Washington.

Bequaert, Joseph C., and Walter B. Miller
1973 *The Mollusks of the Arid Southwest*. University of Arizona Press, Tucson.

Berger, W. H.
1990 The Younger Dryas Cold Spell–A Quest for Causes. *Palaeogeography, Palaeoclimatology, Palaeoecology* 89: 219-237.

Bettinger, Robert L.
1991 *Hunter-Gatherers, Archaeological and Evolutionary Theory*. Plenum Press, New York.

Binney, W. G.
1885 A Manual of American Land Shells. *Bulletin of the United States National Museum* 28: 1-528.

Bird, Junius B.
1938 Antiquity and Migrations of the Early Inhabitants of Patagonia. *Geographical Review* 28: 250-275.

Bock, C. E., J. H. Bock, K. L. Jepson, and J. C. Ortega
1986 Ecological Effects of Planting African Lovegrasses in Arizona. *National Geographic Research Reports* 2(4): 456-463.

Bordes, François
1961 Typologie du Paléolithique ancien et moyen. *Publications de l'Institut de Prehistoire, Université de Bordeaux, Mémoire* 1. Université de Bordeaux, Bordeaux.

Bordes, François, and Don E. Crabtree
1969 The Corbiac Blade Technique and Other Experiments. *Tebiwa* 12(2): 1-21.

Boriskovsky, P. I.
1958 Le Paléolithique de L'Ukraine. *Annales du Service d'Information Géologique du Bureau de Recherches Géologiques, Geophysiques et Minieres* 27. Bureau de Recherches Geologiques, Geophysiques et Minieres, Paris.

Bradbury, David E.
1969 Vegetation as an Indicator of Rock Types in the Northern Swisshelm Mountains, Southeastern Arizona. Master's thesis, Department of Geography and Area Development, University of Arizona, Tucson.

Bradley, Bruce A.
1974 Comments on the Lithic Technology of the Casper Site Materials. *The Casper Site, A Hell Gap Bison Kill on the High Plains*, edited by George C. Frison, pp. 191-197. Academic Press, New York.
1982 Lithic Technology. *The Agate Basin Site*, edited by George C. Frison and Dennis J. Stanford, pp. 181-208. Academic Press, New York.

Bradley, Raymond S.
1999 *Paleoclimatology, Reconstructing Climates of the Quaternary*. 2nd edition. Harcourt Academic Press, San Diego.

Breger, Irving A., and Andrew Brown
1962 Kerogen in the Chattanooga Shale. *Science* 137(3525): 221-224.

Broecker, W. S., and W. R. Farrand
1963 Radiocarbon Age of the Two Creeks Forest Bed, Wisconsin. *Geological Society of America Bulletin* 74: 795-802.

Brown, David E., and Charles H. Lowe
1974 The Arizona System for Natural and Potential Vegetation–Illustrated Summary through the Fifth Digit for the North American Southwest. *Journal of the Arizona Academy of Science* 9 (Supplement 3): 1-56.

Brown, David E., Neil B. Carmony, and Raymond M. Turner
1981 Drainage Map of Arizona Showing Perennial Streams and Some Important Wetlands. Arizona Game and Fish Department, Phoenix.

Bryan, Kirk
1926 San Pedro Valley, Arizona, and the Geographic Cycle. [Abstract] *Geological Society of America Bulletin* 37: 169-170. New York.
1928a Change in Plant Associations by Change in Ground Water Level. *Ecology* 9(4): 474-478.
1928b Historic Evidence on Changes in the Channel of the Rio Puerco, a Tributary of the Rio Grande in New Mexico. *Journal of Geology* 36: 265-282.
1941 Pre-Columbian Agriculture in the Southwest as Conditioned by Periods of Alluviation. *Annals of the Association of American Geographers Annals* 31(4): 219-242.

Bryant, Donald L.
1968 Diagnostic Characteristics of the Paleozoic Formations of Southeastern Arizona. *Southern Arizona Guidebook* III, edited by S. R. Titley, pp. 33-47. Arizona Geological Society, Tucson.

Buchanan, Briggs
  2005 *Cultural Transmission and Stone Tools: A Study of Early Paleoindian Technology in North America.* Doctoral dissertation, Department of Anthropology, University of New Mexico, Albuquerque. University Microfilms, Inc., Ann Arbor.

Bull, William B.
  1991 *Geomorphic Responses to Climate Change.* Oxford University Press, Oxford.

Burnette, Charles R.
  1957 Geology of the Middle Canyon, Whetstone Mountains, Cochise County, Arizona. Master's thesis, Department of Geosciences, University of Arizona, Tucson.

Butler, B. Robert
  1963 An Early Man Site at Big Camas Prairie, South-central Idaho. *Tebiwa* 6(1): 22–33.

Butler, B. Robert, and R. J. Fitzwater
  1965 A Further Note on the Clovis Site at Big Camas Prairie, South-central Idaho. *Tebiwa* 8: 38–39.

Byers, David A., and Andrew Ugan
  2005 Should We Expect Large Game Specialization in the Late Pleistocene? An Optimal Foraging Perspective on Early Paleoindian Prey Choice. *Journal of Archaeological Science* 32: 1624–1640.

Byers, Douglas S.
  1954 Bull Brook, A Fluted Point Site in Ipswich, Massachusetts. *American Antiquity* 19(4): 343–351.

Caldwell, Warren W., and Richard E. Jensen
  1969 Grand Detour Phase. *Smithsonian Institution River Basin Surveys Publications in Salvage Archeology* 13. Lincoln.

Callahan, Errett
  1979 The Basics of Biface Knapping in the Eastern Fluted Point Tradition: A Manual for Flint-knappers and Lithic Analysts. *Archaeology of Eastern North America* 7(1): 1–180.

Campbell, Elizabeth W. C., and William H. Campbell
  1935 The Pinto Basin Site. *Southwest Museum Papers* 9. Southwest Museum, Los Angeles.

Cann, J. R.
  1983 Petrology of Obsidian Artefacts. *Petrology of Archaeological Artefacts*, edited by D. R. C. Kempe and A. P. Harvey, pp. 227–255. Clarendon Press, Oxford.

Cannon, Michael D., and David J. Meltzer
  2004 Early Paleoindian Foraging: Examining the Faunal Evidence for Large Mammal Specialization and Regional Variability in Prey Choice. *Quaternary Science Reviews* 23: 1955–1987.

Carmony, Neil B.
  1995 *Next Stop: Tombstone, George Hand's Contention City Diary, 1882.* Transcribed and edited by Neil B. Carmony. Trail to Yesterday Books, Tucson.

Chilton, Elizabeth S.
  2004 Beyond "Big": Gender, Age, and Subsistence Diversity in Paleoindian Societies. *The Settlement of the American Continents*, edited by C. Michael Barton, Geoffrey A. Clark, David R. Yesner, and Georges A. Pearson, pp. 162–172. University of Arizona Press, Tucson.

Christman, R. F., and R. T. Oglesby
  1966 The Microbiological Degradation of Lignin and the Formation of Humus. *Lignin–Chemistry and Utilization*, edited by K. V. Sarkanen. Interscience, New York.

Clark, J. Desmond, and C. Vance Haynes, Jr.
  1970 An Elephant Butchery Site at Mwanganda's Village, Karonga, Malawi, and Its Relevance for Paleolithic Archaeology. *World Archaeology* 1(3): 389–411.

Colbert, Edwin H.
  1950 The Fossil Vertebrates. *The Stratigraphy and Archaeology of Ventana Cave, Arizona*, by Emil W. Haury, pp. 126–148. University of Arizona Press and University of New Mexico Press, Tucson and Albuquerque.

Collins, Michael B.
  1999 *Clovis Blade Technology.* University of Texas Press, Austin.
  2002 The Gault Site, Texas, and Clovis Research. *Athena Review* 3(2): 24–36.

Collins, Michael B., Dale B. Hudler, and Stephen L. Black
  2003 Pavo Real (41BX52): A Paleoindian and Archaic Camp and Workshop on the Balcones Escarpment, South-Central Texas. *Studies in Archeology* 41. Texas Archeological Research Laboratory, University of Texas, Austin.

Connin, S. L., Julio L. Betancourt, and J. Quade
  1998 Late Pleistocene C_4 Plant Dominance and Summer Rainfall in the Southwestern United States from Isotopic Study of Herbivore Teeth. *Quaternary Research* 50: 179–193.

Cook, S. F., S. T. Brooks, and H. E. Ezra-Cohn
  1962 Histological Studies on Fossil Bone. *Journal of Paleontology* 36(3): 483–494.

Cooke, Ronald U., and Richard W. Reeves
  1976 *Arroyos and Environmental Change in the American Southwest.* Clarendon Press, Oxford.

Cornwall, I. W.
  1957 *Bones for the Archaeologist.* Macmillan, New York.

Cotter, John L.
  1937 The Occurrence of Flints and Extinct Animals in Pluvial Deposits near Clovis, New Mexico. Part IV, Report on Excavation at the Gravel Pit, 1936. *Proceedings of the Academy of Natural Sciences* 89: 1–16. Academy of Natural Sciences, Philadelphia.

Cotter, John L. (*continued*)
   1954   Indications of a Paleo-Indian Co-tradition for North America. *American Antiquity* 20(1): 64–67.

Cox, K. G., J. D. Bell, and R. J. Pankhurst
   1979   *The Interpretation of Igneous Rocks*. George Allen & Unwin, London.

Crabtree, Don E.
   1966   A Stoneworker's Approach to Analyzing and Replicating the Lindenmeier Folsom. *Tebiwa* 9(1): 3–39.
   1967   Notes on Experiments in Flintflaking: 4. Tools Used for Making Stone Artifacts. *Tebiwa* 10(1): 60–73.
   1972   An Introduction to Flintworking. *Occasional Papers of the Idaho State University Museum* 28. Idaho State University, Pocatello.

Damon, Paul E., and Austin Long
   1962   Arizona Radiocarbon Dates III. *Radiocarbon* 4: 239–249.

Damon, Paul E., C. Vance Haynes, Jr., and Austin Long
   1964   Arizona Radiocarbon Dates V. *Radiocarbon* 6: 101, A–481.

Damon, Paul E., Austin Long, and Joel J. Sigalove
   1963   Arizona Radiocarbon Dates IV. *Radiocarbon* 5: 283–301.

Davis, J. R.
   1975   Late Quaternary Sedimentation in the San Pedro Valley, Southeastern Arizona. Master's thesis, Department of Geological Sciences, Southern Methodist University, Dallas.

Deraniyagala, P. E. P.
   1955   *Some Extinct Elephants, Their Relatives and the Two Living Species*. Ceylon National Museum, Colombo.

Dibble, David S., and Dessamae Lorrain
   1968   Bonfire Shelter: A Stratified Bison Kill Site in Val Verde County, Texas. *Texas Memorial Museum Miscellaneous Papers* 3. University of Texas, Austin.

Dick, Herbert W.
   1965   Bat Cave. *School of American Research Monograph* 27. School of American Research, Santa Fe.

Di Peso, Charles C.
   1951   The Babocomari Village Site on the Babocomari River, Southeastern Arizona. *The Amerind Foundation* 5. The Amerind Foundation, Dragoon, Arizona.
   1953a   Clovis Fluted Points from Southeastern Arizona. *American Antiquity* 19(1): 82–85.
   1953b   The Sobaipuri Indians of the Upper San Pedro Valley, Southeastern Arizona. *The Amerind Foundation* 6. The Amerind Foundation, Dragoon, Arizona.
   1958   The Reeve Ruin of Southeastern Arizona: A Study of a Prehistoric Western Pueblo Migration into the Middle San Pedro Valley. *The Amerind Foundation* 8. The Amerind Foundation, Dragoon, Arizona.

Douglas-Hamilton, Iain, and Oria Douglas-Hamilton
   1975   *Among the Elephants*. The Viking Press, New York.

Du Buois, Susan M., and A. W. Smith
   1980   The 1887 Earthquake in San Bernardino Valley, Sonora: Historic Accounts and Intensity Patterns in Arizona. *Bureau of Geology and Mineral Technology Special Paper* 3. University of Arizona, Tucson.

Dunn, J. H., and P. C. Wolk
   1970   Composition of the Cellular Envelopes of *Anabena cylindrica*. *Journal of Bacteriology* 103: 153.

Evans, Clifford, and Betty J. Meggars
   1960   A New Dating Method Using Obsidian. Part II, An Archaeological Evaluation of the Method. *American Antiquity* 25(4): 523–537.

Evans, Glen L.
   1951   Prehistoric Wells in Eastern New Mexico. *American Antiquity* 17(1): 1–9.

Fallaw, W. C.
   1977   Trends in Trans-North Atlantic Commonality among Phanerozoic Invertebrates, and Plate Tectonic Events. *Geological Society of America Bulletin* 88(1): 62–66.
   1978   Reply. *Geological Society of America Bulletin* 89(3): 478–480.

Feigl, F.
   1934   Differentiation of Animal and Vegetable Fibers. *Mikrochemie* 15: 7.

Ferring, C. Reid
   2001   *The Archaeology and Paleoecology of the Aubrey Clovis Site (41DN479), Denton County, Texas*. Center for Environmental Archaeology, Department of Geography, University of North Texas, Denton.

Figgins, Jesse D.
   1933   A Further Contribution to the Antiquity of Man in America. *Proceedings of the Colorado Museum of Natural History* 12(2): 4–10.

Findlow, Frank J., and Marisa Bolognese
   1982   Regional Modeling of Obsidian Procurement in the American Southwest. *Contexts for Prehistoric Exchange*, edited by Jonathan E. Ericson and Timothy K. Earle, pp. 53–81. Academic Press, New York.

Fischer, H., and F. Meyer-Betz
   1911   Detection of Pyrrole and Pyrrole Derivatives. *Zeitschrift für Physiologisch Chemie* 75: 232.

Fitting, James E., Jerry DeVisscher, and Edward J. Wahla
   1966   The Paleo-Indian Occupation of the Holcombe

Beach. *Museum of Anthropology Anthropological Papers* 27. University of Michigan, Ann Arbor.

Flessa, Karl W., J. M. Miyazaki, and W. C. Fallaw
 1978 Trends in Trans-North Atlantic Commonality among Phanerozoic Invertebrates, and Plate Tectonic Events: Discussion. *Geological Society of America Bulletin* 89(3): 476–480.

Fletcher, Joel E., and W. P. Martin
 1948 Some Effects of Algae and Molds in the Rain-crust of Desert Soils. *Ecology* 29(1): 95.

Franklin, Hayward H.
 1980 Excavations at Second Canyon Ruin, San Pedro Valley, Arizona. *Arizona State Museum Contribution to Highway Salvage Archaeology in Arizona* 60. University of Arizona, Tucson.

Friedman, Irving, and Robert L. Smith
 1960 A New Dating Method Using Obsidian. Part I, The Development of the Method. *American Antiquity* 25(4): 476–493.

Frison, George C.
 1968 A Functional Analysis of Certain Chipped Stone Tools. *American Antiquity* 33(2): 149–155.
 1974 [Editor] *The Casper Site: A Hell Gap Bison Kill on the High Plains*. Academic Press, New York.
 1977 Paleoindian Sites and Economic Orientations in the Big Horn Basin. In "Paleoindian Life-ways," edited by Eileen Johnson, pp. 97–116. *The Museum Journal* 27. Texas Tech University, Lubbock.
 1978a *Prehistoric Hunters on the High Plains*. Academic Press, New York.
 1978b Animal Population Studies and Cultural Inference. In "Bison Procurement and Utilization: A Symposium," edited by Leslie B. Davis and Michael Wilson, pp. 44–52. *Plains Anthropologist Memoir* 14.
 1992 The Foothills-Mountains and the Open Plains: The Dichotomy in Paleoindian Subsistence Strategies Between Two Ecosystems. *Ice Age Hunters of the Rockies*, edited by Dennis J. Stanford and Jane S. Day, pp. 323–342. Denver Museum of Natural History and University Press of Colorado, Denver.
 2000 A ^{14}C Date on a Late Pleistocene *Camelops* at the Casper-Hell Gap Site, Wyoming. *Current Research in the Pleistocene* 17: 28–29.

Frison, George C., and Bruce A. Bradley
 1999 *The Fenn Cache, Clovis Weapons and Tools*. One Horse Land and Cattle Co., Santa Fe.

Frison, George C., and Lawrence C. Todd
 1986 *The Colby Mammoth Site, Taphonomy and Archaeology of a Clovis Kill in Northern Wyoming*. University of New Mexico Press, Albuquerque.

Frison, George C., Michael Wilson, and D. J. Wilson
 1976 Fossil Bison and Artifacts from an Early Altithermal Period Arroyo Trap in Wyoming. *American Antiquity* 41(1): 28–57.

Gardner, J. L.
 1951 Vegetation of the Creosotebush Area of the Rio Grande Valley in New Mexico. *Ecological Monographs* 21: 379–403.

Gay, Larry
 1974 *The Complete Book of Heating with Wood*. Garden Way Publishing, Charlotte, Vermont.

Gile, L. H., F. F. Peterson, and R. B. Grossman
 1966 Morphological and Genetic Sequences of Carbonate Accumulation in Desert Soils. *Soil Science* 101: 347–360.

Gilluly, James
 1956 General Geology of Central Cochise County, Arizona. *U.S. Geological Survey Professional Paper* 281. Washington.

Gilluly, James, John R. Cooper, and James S. Williams
 1954 Late Paleozoic Stratigraphy of Central Cochise County, Arizona. *U.S. Geological Survey Professional Paper* 266. Washington.

Goodyear, Albert C.
 1982 The Chronological Position of the Dalton Horizon in the Southeastern United States. *American Antiquity* 47(2): 382–395.

Gorham, E., and J. E. Sanger
 1976 Fossilized Pigments as Stratigraphic Indicators of Cultural Eutrophication in Shagawa Lake, Northeastern Minnesota. *Geological Society of America Bulletin* 87(11): 1638–1642.

Graham, Russell W., and Ernest L. Lundelius
 1984 Coevolutionary Disequilibrium and Pleistocene Extinctions. *Quaternary Extinctions: A Prehistoric Revolution*, edited by Paul S. Martin and Richard G. Klein, pp. 223–249. University of Arizona Press, Tucson.

Gramly, R. Michael
 1993 The Richey Clovis Cache: Earliest Americans Along the Columbia River. *Monographs in Archaeology*. Persimmon Press, Buffalo.

Grant, A.
 1982 The Use of Tooth Wear as a Guide to the Age of Domestic Ungulates. In "Aging and Sexing Animal Bones from Archaeological Sites," edited by B. Wilson, C. Grigson, and S. Payne, pp. 91–108. *British Archaeological Reports* 109. Oxford.

Gray, Robert S.
 1965 Late Cenozoic Sediments in the San Pedro Valley near St. David, Arizona. Doctoral dissertation, Department of Geosciences, University of Arizona, Tucson.

Gray, Robert S. (*continued*)
1967 Petrography of the Upper Cenozoic Non-Marine Sediments in the San Pedro Valley, Arizona. *Journal of Sedimentary Petrography* 37(3): 774–789.

Grayson, Donald K.
1984 Explaining Pleistocene Extinctiions: Thoughts on the Structure of a Debate. *Quaternary Extinctions: A Prehistoric Revolution*, edited by Paul S. Martin and Richard G. Klein, pp. 807–823. University of Arizona Press, Tucson.
2001 The Archaeological Record of Human Impacts on Animal Populations. *Journal of World Prehistory* 15: 1–68.

Grayson, Donald K., and David J. Meltzer
2002 Clovis Hunting and Large Mammal Extinction: A Critical Review of the Evidence. *Journal of World Prehistory* 16: 313–359.
2003 A Requiem for North American Overkill. *Journal of Archaeological Science* 30: 585–593.

Green, Christine R., and William D. Sellers
1964 *Arizona Climate*. University of Arizona Press, Tucson.

Green, F. Earl
1962 Additional Notes on Prehistoric Wells at the Clovis Site. *American Antiquity* 28(2): 230–234.
1963 The Clovis Blades: An Important Addition to the Llano Complex. *American Antiquity* 29(2): 145–165.

Guthrie, R. D.
1970 Bison Evolution and Zoogeography in North America During the Pleistocene. *Quarterly Review of Biology* 45(1): 1–15.

Haas, Herbert, and C. Vance Haynes, Jr.
1975 Southern Methodist University Radiocarbon Date List II. *Radiocarbon* 17(3): 354–363.

Haas, Herbert, Vance Holliday, and R. Stuckenrath
1986 Dating of Holocene Stratigraphy with Soluble and Insoluble Organic Fractions at the Lubbock Lake Archaeological Site, Texas: An Ideal Case Study. *Radiocarbon* 28(2A): 473–485.

Haggett, Peter
1965 *Locational Analysis in Human Geography*. Edward Arnold, Ltd., London.

Halloran, Arthur F., and Bryan P. Glass
1959 The Carnivores and Ungulates of the Wichita Mountains Wildlife Refuge, Oklahoma. *Journal of Mammalogy* 40(3): 360–370.

Hammatt, Hallett H.
1970 A Paleo-Indian Butchering Kit. *American Antiquity* 35(2): 141–152.

Hannus, L. Adrien
1990 The Lange-Ferguson Site: A Case for Mammoth Bone Butchering Tools. In "Megafauna and Man, Discovery of America's Heartland," edited by Larry D. Agenbroad, Jim I. Mead, and Lisa W. Nelson, pp. 86–99. *Scientific Papers* 1, The Mammoth Site of South Dakota, Inc., Hot Springs.

Harrington, Mark R.
1957 A Pinto Site at Little Lake, California. *Southwest Museum Papers* 17. Southwest Museum, Los Angeles.

Harris, David R.
1966 Recent Plant Invasions in the Arid and Semi-arid Southwest. *Annals of the Association of American Geographers* 56(3): 408–422.

Harrison, Jessica A.
1978 Mammals of the Wolfe Ranch Local Fauna, Pliocene of the San Pedro Valley, Arizona. *University of Kansas Museum of Natural History Occasional Papers* 73: 1–18. University of Kansas, Lawrence.

Hart, Herbert M.
1980 *Tour Guide to Old Western Forts*. The Old Army Press, Fort Collins, Colorado.

Hartwell, William T.
1995 The Ryan's Site Cache: Comparisons to Plainview. *Plains Anthropologist* 40: 165–184.

Hastings, James R.
1959 Vegetation Change and Arroyo-cutting in Southeast Arizona. *Journal of the Arizona Academy of Science* 1(2): 60–67.

Hastings, James R., and Raymond M. Turner
1965 *The Changing Mile*. University of Arizona Press, Tucson.

Haury, Emil W.
1950 *The Stratigraphy and Archaeology of Ventana Cave*. University of Arizona Press and University of New Mexico Press, Tucson and Albuquerque.
1953 Artifacts with Mammoth Remains, Naco, Arizona: I. Discovery of the Naco Mammoth and Associated Projectile Points. *American Antiquity* 19(1): 1–14.
1957 An Alluvial Site on the San Carlos Indian Reservation, Arizona. *American Antiquity* 23(1): 2–27.

Haury, Emil W., Ernst Antevs,
and John F. Lance
1953 Artifacts with Mammoth Remains, Naco, Arizona. *American Antiquity* 19(1): 1–24.

Haury, Emil W., E. B. Sayles,
and William W. Wasley
1959 The Lehner Mammoth Site, Southeastern Arizona. *American Antiquity* 25(1): 2–30.

Hayes, Philip T., and Edwin R. Landis
1965 Paleozoic Stratigraphy of the Southern Part of the Mule Mountains, Arizona. *U.S. Geological Survey Bulletin* 1201-F. Washington.

Haynes, C. Vance, Jr.
1964 Fluted Projectile Points: Their Age and Dispersion. *Science* 145(3639): 1408–1413.
1966 Elephant Hunting in North America. *Scientific American* 214(6): 104–112.
1967 Bone Organic Matter and Radiocarbon Dating. *Radioactive Dating and Methods of Low-Level Counting*, editorial staff of the International Atomic Energy Agency, pp. 163–168. International Atomic Energy Agency, Vienna.
1968a Geochronology of Late Quaternary Alluvium. *Means of Correlation of Quaternary Successions*, edited by Roger B. Morrison and Herbert E. Wright, Jr., pp. 591–631. University of Utah Press, Salt Lake City.
1968b Preliminary Report on the Late Quaternary Geology of the San Pedro Valley, Arizona. *Southern Arizona Guidebook III*, edited by S. R. Titley, pp. 79–96. Arizona Geological Society, Tucson.
1969 The Earliest Americans. *Science* 166(3906): 709–715.
1970 Geochronology of Man-Mammoth Sites and Their Bearing Upon the Origin of the Llano Complex. *Pleistocene and Recent Environments of the Central Plains*, edited by W. Dart and J. Knox Jones, pp. 77–92. University of Kansas Press, Lawrence.
1971 Time, Environment, and Early Man. *Arctic Anthropology* 8: 3–14.
1972 Stratigraphic Investigations at the Williamson Site, Dinwiddie County, Virginia. *The Chesopiean* 10(4): 107–114.
1973 Exploration of a Mammoth-kill Site in Arizona. *National Geographic Society Research Reports 1966 Projects*, pp. 125–126.
1974 Archaeological Excavations at the Clovis Site at Murray Springs, Arizona, 1967. *National Geographic Society Research Reports, 1967 Projects*, pp. 145–147.
1976 Archaeological Investigation at the Murray Springs Site, Arizona 1968. *National Geographic Society Research Reports, 1968 Projects*, pp. 165–171.
1978 Archaeological Investigations at the Murray Springs Site, 1969. *National Geographic Society Research Reports, 1969 Projects*, pp. 239–242.
1979 Archaeological Investigations at the Murray Springs Clovis Site, Arizona, 1970. *National Geographic Society Research Reports, 1970 Projects*, pp. 261–267.
1980a Archaeological Investigations at the Murray Springs Clovis Site, 1971. *National Geographic Society Research Reports* 12: 347–353.
1980b The Clovis Culture. *Canadian Journal of Anthropology* 1(1): 115–121.
1981 Geochronology and Paleoenvironments of the Murray Springs Clovis Site, Arizona. *National Geographic Society Research Reports* 13: 243–251.
1982a Pleistocene-Holocene Boundary in the United States: Alluvial Stratigraphy and Geochronology. *Program and Abstracts, Seventh Biennial Conference of American Quaternary Association*, p. 97. University of Washington, Seattle.
1982b Were Clovis Progenitors in Beringia? *Paleoecology of Beringia*, edited by D. M. Hopkins, J. V. Mathews, Jr., C. E. Schweger, and S. B. Young, pp. 383–398. New York, Academic Press.
1982c Archaeological Investigations at the Lehner Site, Arizona, 1974–1975. *National Geographic Society Research Reports* 14: 325–334.
1984 Stratigraphy and Late Pleistocene Extinction in the United States. *Quaternary Extinctions: A Prehistoric Revolution*, edited by Paul S. Martin and Richard G. Klein, pp. 345–353. University of Arizona Press, Tucson.
1986 Alluvial Cycles and Water Table Fluctuations. Paper presented at the Penrose Conference of the Geological Society of America, Lake Havasu, Arizona, 1985. Unpublished Abstract No. 1000057, Geological Society of America Abstracts.
1987 Curry Draw, Cochise County, Arizona: A Late Quaternary Stratigraphic Record of Pleistocene Extinction and Paleoindian Activities. *Geological Society of America Centennial Field Guide, Cordilleran Section*, pp. 23–28.
1991 Geoarchaeological and Paleohydrological Evidence for a Clovis Age Drought in North America and Its Bearing on Extinction. *Quaternary Research* 35(3): 438–450.
1997 A Proposal for the Public Display and Preservation of the San Pedro Valley Clovis Sites. MS submitted to the Tucson Office of the Bureau of Land Management, 17 November 1997. Manuscript on file, Arizona State Museum Archives, University of Arizona, Tucson.
1998a The Rancholabrean Termination: Sudden Extinction in the San Pedro Valley, Arizona, 11,000 B.C. *Abstracts of the International Conference on Mammoth Site Studies*, edited by Anta Montet-White and D. L. West, p. 6. Lawrence, Kansas.
1998b Stratigraphic Manifestations of Paleoclimatic Events at Paleoindian Sites: Geochronology of the Pleistocene-Holocene Transition and Megafauna Extinction. *Abstracts of the 63rd Annual Meeting, Society for American Archaeology, 25–29 March*, p. 138.

Haynes, C. Vance, Jr. (*continued*)
   2001   A Proposal for the Public Display of Curry Draw and the Murray Springs Clovis Site, Upper San Pedro Valley, Arizona. University of Arizona Department of Anthropology Proposal for Campaign Arizona, 2001. Manuscript on file, Arizona State Museum Archives, University of Arizona, Tucson.
   2003   Younger Dryas "Black Mats" and Other Stratigraphic Manifestations of Climate Change in North America. *Abstracts of the XVI INQUA Congress*. Reno, 29 July.

Haynes, C. Vance, Jr., and Herbert Haas
   1974   Southern Methodist University Radiocarbon Date List 1. *Radiocarbon* 16(3): 368–380.

Haynes, C. Vance, Jr., and E. Thomas Hemmings
   1968   Mammoth-bone Shaft Wrench from Murray Springs, Arizona. *Science* 159(3811):186–187.
   1970   Preliminary Report on the 1969 Murray Springs Project. Paper presented at the 35th Annual Meeting of the Society for American Archaeology, Mexico City.

Haynes, C. Vance, Jr., Larry D. Agenbroad, and Gerald Kelso
   1971   The Clovis Hunting Camp at Murray Springs. Paper presented at the 36th Annual Meeting of the Society for American Archaeology, Norman.

Haynes, C. Vance, Jr., Donald C. Grey, and Austin Long
   1971   Arizona Radiocarbon Dates VIII. *Radiocarbon* 13(1): 9.

Haynes, C. Vance, Jr., D. J. Donahue, A. J. T. Jull, and T. H. Zabel
   1984   Application of Accelerator Dating to Fluted Point Paleoindian Sites. *Archaeology of Eastern North America* 12: 184–191.

Haynes, C. Vance, Jr., Donald C. Grey, Paul E. Damon, and Richard Bennett
   1967   Arizona Radiocarbon Dates VII. *Radiocarbon* 9(1): 5.

Haynes, C. Vance, Jr., Dennis J. Stanford, Margaret Jodry, Joanne Dickinson, J. L. Montgomery, P. H. Shelley, Irwin Rovner, and George A. Agogino
   1999   A Clovis Well at the Type Site, 11,500 B.C.: The Oldest Well in America. *Geoarchaeology* 14(5): 455–470.

Haynes, Gary
   1991   *Mammoths, Mastodonts, and Elephants: Biology, Behavior, and the Fossil Record*. Cámbridge University Press, Cambridge.
   2002   *The Early Settlement of America: The Clovis Era*. Cambridge University Press, Cambridge.

Haynes, Gary, and B. Sunday Eiselt
   1999   The Power of Pleistocene Hunter-Gatherers: Forward and Backward Searching for Evidence about Mammoth Extinction. *Extinctions in Near Time: Causes, Contexts, and Consequences*, edited by Ross D. E. MacPhee, pp. 71–93. Kluwer Academic/Plenum Publishers, New York.

Hemmings, E. Thomas
   1968   Preliminary Archaeological Report on the Murray Springs Clovis Site, Arizona. Paper presented at the 33rd Annual Meeting of the Society for American Archaeology, Santa Fe, New Mexico.
   1969   Analysis of a Clovis Bison Kill Site and Processing Area. Paper presented at the 34th Annual Meeting of the Society for American Archaeology, Milwaukee, Wisconsin.
   1970   Early Man in the San Pedro Valley, Arizona. Doctoral dissertation, Department of Anthropology, University of Arizona, Tucson.
   1975   Llano Bison Hunters in the San Pedro Valley, Arizona. MS on file, Arizona State Museum Archives, University of Arizona, Tucson.

Hemmings, E. Thomas, and C. Vance Haynes, Jr.
   1969   The Escapule Mammoth and Associated Projectile Points, San Pedro Valley, Arizona. *Journal of the Arizona Academy of Science* 5(3): 184–188.

Henderson, J.
   1928   Molluscan Provinces in the Western United States. *Nautilus* 41: 85–91.
   1931   Molluscan Provinces in the Western United States. *University of Colorado Studies* 18: 177–186.

Hendrickson, David A., and William L. Minckley
   1984   Cienegas–Vanishing Climax Communities of the American Southwest. *Desert Plants* 6: 130–175.

Henry, Donald O., C. Vance Haynes, Jr., and Bruce Bradley
   1976   Quantitative Variation in Flaked Stone Debitage. *Plains Anthropologist* 21(71): 57–61.

Hereford, Richard
   1991   Geomorphic Evolution of the San Pedro River Channel Since 1900 in the San Pedro River Riparian National Conservation Area, Southeastern Arizona. *USGS Open-File Report* 91.
   1993   Entrenchment and Widening of the Upper San Pedro River. *Geological Society of America Special Paper* 282.

Hereford, Richard, and Julio L. Betancourt
   In preparation   Historic Geomorphology of the San Pedro River: Archival and Physical Evidence. MS prepared for *Riparian Area Conservation in a Semi-Arid Region*, edited by Juliet Stromberg and Barbara Tellman.

Herrington, H. B.
   1962   A Revision of the Sphaeriidae of North America. *Miscellaneous Publication of the Museum of Zoology, University of Michigan* 118: 1–74. University of Michigan, Ann Arbor.

Hester, James J.
- 1967 The Agency of Man in Animal Extinctions. *Pleistocene Extinctions: The Search for a Cause*, edited by Paul S. Martin and Herbert E. Wright, Jr., pp. 169-192. Yale University Press, New Haven.
- 1970 Ecology of the North American Paleo-Indian. *BioScience* 20(4): 213-217.
- 1972 Blackwater Locality No. 1: A Stratified, Early Man Site in Eastern New Mexico. *Publication of the Fort Burgwin Research Center* 8. Southern Methodist University, Dallas.

Hevly, Richard H., and Paul S. Martin
- 1961 Geochronology of Pluvial Lake Cochise, Southern Arizona. I: Pollen Analysis of Shore Deposits. *Journal of the Arizona Academy of Science* 2(1): 24-31.

Holliday, Vance T.
- 1989 Middle Holocene Drought on the Southern High Plains. *Quaternary Research* 31(1): 74-82.

Howard, Edgar B.
- 1935 Evidence of Early Man in North America. *The Museum Journal* 24(2-3). The University Museum, Philadelphia.
- 1943 The Finley Site. Discovery of Yuma Points, in situ, near Eden, Wyoming. *American Antiquity* 8(3): 224-234.

Huckell, Bruce B.
- 1978a The Oxbow Hill-Payson Project: Archaeological Excavations South of Payson, Arizona. *Arizona State Museum Contribution to Highway Salvage Archaeology in Arizona* 44. University of Arizona, Tucson.
- 1978b Hudson-Meng Chipped Stone. *The Hudson-Meng Site: An Alberta Bison Kill in the Nebraska High Plains*, by Larry D. Agenbroad, pp. 153-191. University Press of America, Washington.
- 1979 Of Chipped Stone Tools, Elephants, and the Clovis Hunters: An Experiment. *Plains Anthropologist* 24(85): 177-189.
- 1981 The Navarrete Site: A Third Clovis Locality on Greenbush Draw, Arizona. Manuscript on file, Arizona State Museum Archives, University of Arizona, Tucson.
- 1982 The Denver Elephant Project: A Report on Experimentation with Thrusting Spears. *Plains Anthropologist* 27(87): 217-224.
- 1984 The Archaic Occupation of the Rosemont Area, Northern Santa Rita Mountains, Southeastern Arizona. *Arizona State Museum Archaeological Series* 147(1). University of Arizona, Tucson.
- 1999 Camps, Kills, and Caches: Reconstructing Clovis Lithic Technological Organization in the Western United States. Paper presented at the Conference to Honor C. Vance Haynes, Jr., University of Arizona, Tucson.
- 2003 Paleoindian Traditions and Adaptations Before and During the Younger Dryas in Western North America. Paper presented in the symposium "Paleoindian Western North America: Climate and Life at the Last Glacial Termination," at the XVI INQUA Congress, Reno, Nevada.

Huckell, Bruce B., and C. Vance Haynes, Jr.
- 2004 Clovis Lithic Technological Organization in the San Pedro Valley, Southeastern Arizona. Paper presented in the symposium "The Clovis Age Continent: Early Paleoindian Foragers in North America," at the 69th Annual Meeting of the Society for American Archaeology, Montreal, Canada.

Hughes, Richard E.
- 1984 Obsidian Sourcing Studies in the Great Basin: Problems and Prospects. In "Obsidian Studies in the Great Basin," edited by Richard E. Hughes, pp. 1-19. *Contributions of the University of California Archaeological Research Facility* 45. University of California, Berkeley.
- 1988 Archaeological Significance of Geochemical Contrasts among Southwestern New Mexico Obsidians. *The Texas Journal of Science* 40(3): 297-307.

Ingbar, Eric E.
- 1994 Lithic Material Selection and Technological Organization. In "The Organization of North American Prehistoric Chipped Stone Tool Technologies," edited by Philip J. Carr, pp. 45-56. *International Monographs in Prehistory Archaeological Series* 7. Ann Arbor.

Irwin-Williams, Cynthia
- 1967 Associations of Early Man with Horse, Camel and Mastodon at Hueyatlaco, Valsequillo (Puebla, Mexico). *Pleistocene Extinctions: The Search for a Cause*, edited by Paul S. Martin and Herbert E. Wright, Jr., pp. 337-347. Yale University Press, New Haven.

Irwin, Cynthia, Henry Irwin, and George A. Agogino
- 1962 Ice-Age Man vs. Mammoth in Wyoming. *National Geographic* 121(6): 828-837.

Jack, Robert N.
- 1971 The Source of Obsidian Artifacts in Northern Arizona. *Plateau* 43(1): 103-114.

Jack, Robert N., and I. S. E. Carmichael
- 1969 The Chemical "Fingerprinting" of Acid Volcanic Rocks. *California Division of Mines and Geology Special Report* 100: 17-32.

Jaehnig, M. E. W.
- 1971 The Study of Gastropods: Methodology. *Plains Anthropologist* 16(54, Part 1): 289-297.

Jefferson, George T., and Judith L. Goldin
   1989   Seasonal Migration of *Bison antiquus* from Rancho La Brea, Califonia. *Quaternary Research* 31: 107–112.

Jelinek, Arthur J.
   1966   Some Distinctive Flakes and Flake Tools from the Llano Estacado. *Papers of the Michigan Academy of Science, Arts, and Letters* 51: 399–405.
   1971   Early Man in the New World: A Technological Perspective. *Arctic Anthropology* 8(2): 15–21.

Johnson, Alfred E., and C. Vance Haynes, Jr.
   1967   The Leikem Mammoth Site, Arizona, and a Probable Clovis Association. Manuscript on file, Arizona State Museum Archives, University of Arizona, Tucson.

Johnson, Eileen
   1985   Current Developments in Bone Technology. *Advances in Archaeological Method and Theory* 8, edited by Michael B. Schiffer, pp. 157–235. Academic Press, New York.

Johnson, N. M., N. D. Opdyke, and Everett H. Lindsay
   1975   Magnetic Polarity Stratigraphy of Pliocene-Pleistocene Terrestrial Deposits and Vertebrate Faunas, San Pedro Valley, Arizona. *Geological Society of America Bulletin* 86: 5–12.

Johnston, W. A.
   1933   Quaternary Geology of North America in Relation to the Migration of Man. *The American Aborigines: Their Origin and Antiquity*, edited by D. Jenness, pp. 9–45. University of Toronto Press, Toronto.

Judge, W. James
   1974   An Evaluation of the Overkill Model. Paper presented at the 39th Annual Meeting of the Society for American Archaeology, Washington, D.C.

Jull, A. J. T., C. Vance Haynes, Jr., D. J. Donahue, G. S. Burr, and J. W. Beck
   1999   Radiocarbon Ages of Early Man in the New World and the Influence of Climate Change. Third International Conference "Archaeologie et ^{14}C," edited by J. Ervin and others, Lyon, France, 1998. *Revue d'Archaeometrie, Supplement* 1999 et *Soc. Préhis. Fr, Mémoire* 26, pp. 339–343.

Karlstrom, T. N. V.
   1988   Alluvial Chronology and Hydrologic Change of Black Mesa and Nearby Regions. *The Anasazi in a Changing Environment*, edited by George J. Gumerman, pp. 45–91. Cambridge University Press, Cambridge.

Kehoe, Thomas F.
   1967   The Boarding School Bison Drive Site. *Plains Anthropologist Memoir* 4.

Kelly, Robert L.
   1995   *The Foraging Spectrum, Diversity in Hunter-Gatherer Lifeways*. Smithsonian Institution Press, Washington, D.C.
   2002   Maybe We Do Know When People First Came to North America; and What Does It Mean if We Do? *Quaternary International* 109–110: 133–145.

Kelly, Robert L., and Lawrence C. Todd
   1988   Coming into the Country: Early Paleoindian Hunting and Mobility. *American Antiquity* 53(2): 231–244.

Klein, Richard G.
   1973   *Ice-Age Hunters of the Ukraine*. University of Chicago Press, Chicago.

Kononova, M. M.
   1961   *Soil Organic Matter*. Pergamon Press, New York.

Kooyman, Brian P., L. V. Hills, Paul McNeil, and M. Shayne Tolman
   2006   Late Pleistocene Horse Hunting at the Wally's Beach Site (DhPg-8), Canada. *American Antiquity* 71(1): 101–121.

Kumada, K., and H. M. Hurst
   1967   Green Humic Acid and Its Possible Origin as a Fungal Metabolite. *Nature* 214: 631.

Kurtén, Bjorn
   1964   Population Structure in Paleoecology. *Approaches to Paleoecology*, edited by J. Imbrie and N. D. Newell, pp. 91–106. John Wiley and Sons, New York.

Lahren, Larry A.
   2001   The On-going Odyssey of the Anzick Clovis Burial in Park County, Montana (24PA506): Part I. *Archaeology in Montana* 42(1): 55–59.

Lahren, Larry A., and Robson Bonnichsen
   1974   Bone Foreshafts from a Clovis Burial in Southwestern Montana. *Science* 186(4159): 147–150.

Lance, John F.
   1953   Artifacts with Mammoth Remains, Naco, Arizona. III. Description of the Naco Mammoth. *American Antiquity* 19(1): 18–22.
   1959   Faunal Remains from the Lehner Mammoth Site. *American Antiquity* 25(1): 35–39.

Lanphere, M. A., D. E. Champion, R. L. Christiansen, G. A. Izatt, and J. D. Obradovich
   2002   Revised Ages for Tuffs of the Yellowstone Plateau Volcanic Field: Assignment of the Huckleberry Ridge Tuff to a New Geomagnetic Polarity Event. *Geological Society of America Bulletin* 114(5): 559–568.

LaRocque, A.
   1966   Pleistocene Molluscs of Ohio, Part I. *Division of Geological Survey Bulletin* 62. Ohio Department of Natural Resources.
   1970   Pleistocene Molluscs of Ohio, Part IV. *Division of Geological Survey Bulletin* 62. Ohio Department of Natural Resources.

Laury, R. L., and C. Vance Haynes, Jr.
1977 Late Quaternary Sedimentation in the San Pedro Valley, Southeastern Arizona. *Geological Society of America Abstracts with Programs* 9(7): 57.

Laws, R. M.
1966 Age Criteria for the African Elephant, *Loxodonta a. africana*. *East African Wildlife Journal* 4(1): 1–37.

Leechman, Douglas
1951 Bone Grease. *American Antiquity* 16(4): 355–356.

Lehmer, Donald H., and David T. Jones
1968 Arikara Archeology: The Bad River Phase. *Smithsonian Institution River Basin Surveys Publications in Salvage Archeology* 7. Lincoln.

Leonhardy, Frank C., Editor
1966 Domebo: A Paleo-Indian Mammoth Kill in the Prairie-Plains. *Great Plains Historical Association Contribution* 1. Museum of the Great Plains, Lawton, Oklahoma.

Leopold, L. B.
1951 Rainfall Frequency, An Aspect of Climatic Variation. *American Geophysical Union Transactions* 32(3): 347–357.

Leopold, L. B., M. G. Wolman, and J. P. Miller
1964 *Fluvial Processes in Geomorphology*. W. H. Freeman, San Francisco.

Leroi-Gourhan, A.
1957 *Prehistoric Man*. Philosophical Library, New York.

Lesko, Lawrence M.
1989 A Reexamination of Northern Arizona Obsidians. *The Kiva* 54(4): 385–399.

Lewellen, P. C., W. A. Peters, and J. B. Howard
1977 Cellulose Pyrolysis Kinetics and Char Formation Mechanism. *Sixteenth Symposium (International) on Combustion*, pp. 1471–1480. The Combustion Institute, Pittsburg.

Lindsay, Alexander J., Jr.
1958 Fossil Pollen and Its Bearing on the Archaeology of the Lehner Mammoth Site. Master's thesis, Department of Anthropology, University of Arizona, Tucson.

Lindsay, Everett H.
1978 Late Cenozoic Vertebrate Faunas, Southeastern Arizona. *New Mexico Geological Society Guidebook, 29th Field Conference, Land of Cochise*. Albuquerque.
1984 Windows to the Past: Fossils of the San Pedro Valley. *Field Notes from the Arizona Bureau of Geology and Mineral Technology* 14(4): 1–12.

Lindsay, Everett H., N. M. Johnson, and N. D. Opdyke
1975 Preliminary Correlation of North American Land Mammal Ages and Geomagnetic Chronology. In "Studies on Cenezoic Paleontology and Stratigraphy in Honor of C. W. Hibbard." *Michigan Papers on Paleontology* 12: 111–119.

Lindsay, Everett H., G. A. Smith, C. Vance Haynes, Jr., and N. D. Opdyke
1990 Sediments, Geomorphology, Magnetostratigraphy, and Vertebrate Paleontology in the San Pedro Valley, Arizona. *Journal of Geology* 98: 605–619.

Long, Austin, and Bruce Rippeteau
1974 Testing Contemporaneity and Averaging Radiocarbon Dates. *American Antiquity* 39(2, Part 1): 205–215.

Lorrain, Dessamae
1968 Analysis of the Bison Bones from Bonfire Shelter. In "Bonfire Shelter: A Stratified Bison Kill Site, Val Verde County, Texas," by David S. Dibble and Dessamae Lorrain, pp. 77–132. *Texas Memorial Museum Miscellaneous Papers* 1. Texas Memorial Museum, Austin.

Lowe, Charles H., Editor
1964 *The Vertebrates of Arizona*. University of Arizona Press, Tucson.

Lyon, T. L., and H. O. Buckman
1949 *The Nature and Properties of Soils*. Macmillan, New York.

Lyons, S. Kathleen, Felisa A. Smith, and James H. Brown
2004 Of Mice, Mastodons and Men: Human-Mediated Extinctions on Four Continents. *Evolutionary Ecology Research* 6: 339–358.

Lyons, S. Kathleen, Felisa A. Smith, Peter J. Wagner, Ethan P. White, and James H., Brown
2004 Was "Hyperdisease" Responsible for the Late Pleistocene Extinction? *Ecology Letters* 7: 859–868.

MacDonald, George F.
1966 The Technology and Settlement Pattern of a Paleo-Indian Site at Debert, Nova Scotia. *Quaternaria* 8: 59–74. Rome.
1968 Debert: A Paleo-Indian Site in Central Nova Scotia. *National Museums of Canada Anthropology Paper* 16. National Museums of Canada, Ottawa.

MacPhee, Ross D. E., Editor
1999 *Extinctions in Near Time: Causes, Contexts, and Consequences*. Kluwer Academic/Plenum Publishers, New York.

MacPhee, Ross D. E., and Preston A. Marx
1997 The 40,000-year Plague: Humans, Hyperdisease, and First-Contact Extinctions. *Natural Change and Human Impact in Madagascar*, edited by S. M. Goodman and B. D. Patterson, pp. 169–217. Smithsonian Institution Press, Washington, D.C.

Madsen, David B., Editor
- 2004 *Entering America: Northeast Asia and Beringia Before the Last Glacial Maximum*. University of Utah Press, Salt Lake City.

Marcus, L. F.
- 1960 A Census of the Abundant Large Pleistocene Mammals from Rancho la Brea. *Los Angeles County Museum Contributions to Science* 38: 1–11.

Martin, Paul Schultz
- 1963a Early Man in Arizona: The Pollen Evidence. *American Antiquity* 29(1): 67–73.
- 1963b Geochronology of Pluvial Lake Cochise, Southern Arizona. II. Pollen Analysis of a 42-Meter Core. *Ecology* 44(3): 436–444.
- 1963c *The Last 10,000 Years: A Fossil Pollen Record of the American Southwest*. University of Arizona Press, Tucson.
- 1967 Prehistoric Overkill. *Pleistocene Extinctions: The Search for a Cause*, edited by Paul S. Martin and Herbert E. Wright, Jr., pp. 75–120. Yale University Press, New Haven.
- 1984 Prehistoric Overkill: The Global Model. *Quaternary Extinctions: A Prehistoric Revolution*, edited by Paul S. Martin and Richard G. Klein, pp. 354–403. University of Arizona Press, Tucson.
- 1990 Forty Thousand Years of Extinctions on the "Planet of Doom." *Palaeogeography, Palaeoclimatology, Palaeoecology* 82: 187–201.
- 2005 *Twilight of the Mammoths, Ice Age Extinctions and the Rewilding of America*. University of California Press, Berkeley.

Martin, Paul Schultz, and Richard G. Klein, Editors
- 1984 *Quaternary Extinctions: A Prehistoric Revolution*. University of Arizona Press, Tucson.

Martin, Paul Schultz, and Peter J. Mehringer, Jr.
- 1965 Pleistocene Pollen Analysis and Biogeography of the Southwest. *The Quaternary of the United States*, edited by Herbert E. Wright, Jr., and D. G. Frey. Princeton University Press, Princeton.

Martin, Paul Sidney, John B. Rinaldo, Elaine Bluhm, Hugh C. Cutler, and Roger Grange, Jr.
- 1952 Mogollon Cultural Continuity and Change, The Stratigraphic Analysis of Tularosa and Cordova Caves. *Fieldiana: Anthropology* 40. Chicago Natural History Museum, Chicago.

McCool, Grace B.
- 1967 *Sunday Trails in Old Cochise*. Tombstone Epitaph, Tombstone.

McDonald, James E.
- 1956 Variability of Precipitation in an Arid Region: A Survey of Characteristics for Arizona. *Institute of Atmospheric Physics Technical Reports on the Meteorology and Climatology of Arid Regions* 1. University of Arizona, Tucson.

McHugh, Tom
- 1958 Social Behavior of the American Buffalo (*Bison bison bison* L.). *Zoologica* 43: 1–40.
- 1972 *The Time of the Buffalo*. Alfred A. Knopf, New York.

McIver, R. D.
- 1967 Composition of Kerogen: Clue to Its Role in the Origin of Petroleum. *7th World Petroleum Congress Proceedings* 2: 25–36.

McNett, Charles W., Jr., Editor
- 1985 *Shawnee Minisink*. Academic Press, Orlando.

Mead, Jim I.
- 1979 The Late Pleistocene and Holocene Mollusks of the Murray Springs Clovis Site, Arizona. Master's thesis, Department of Geosciences, University of Arizona, Tucson.
- 1991 Late Pleistocene and Holocene Molluscan Faunas and Environmental Changes in Southeastern Arizona. In "Beamers, Bobwhites, and Blue-Points: Tributes to the Career of Paul W. Parmalee," edited by J. R. Purdue, W. E. Klippel, and B. W. Styles, pp. 215–226. *Illinois State Museum Scientific Papers* 23. Springfield.

Mead, Jim I., and Thomas R. Van Devender
- 1991 Late Quaternary *Chaenaxis tuba* (Pupillidae) from the Sonoran Desert, South-Central Arizona. *The Veliger* 34(3): 259–263.

Meagher, M. M.
- 1973 The Bison of Yellowstone National Park. *National Park Service Scientific Monograph Series* 1. Washington.

Mehringer, Peter J., Jr.
- 1967 The Environment of Extinction of the Late Pleistocene Megafauna in the Arid Southwestern United States. *Pleistocene Extinctions: The Search for a Cause*, edited by Paul S. Martin and Herbert E. Wright, Jr., pp. 247–266. Yale University Press, New Haven.
- 1988 Clovis Cache Found: Weapons of Ancient Americans. *National Geographic* 174: 500–503.

Mehringer, Peter J., Jr., and Franklin F. Foit
- 1990 Volcanic Ash Dating of the Clovis Cache at East Wenatchee, Washington. *National Geographic Research* 6: 495–503.

Mehringer, Peter J., Jr., and C. Vance Haynes, Jr.
- 1965 The Pollen Evidence for the Environment of Early Man and Extinct Mammals at the Lehner Mammoth Site, Southeastern Arizona. *American Antiquity* 31(1): 17–23.

Mehringer, Peter J., Jr., David P. Adam, and Paul S. Martin
- 1966 Pollen Analysis of the Lehner Site, Southeastern Arizona. Manuscript on file, Arizona State Museum Archives, University of Arizona, Tucson.
- 1971 Pollen Analysis at Lehner Ranch Arroyo. In "American Association of Stratigraphic Paly-

nologists Field Trip Guide: Lehner Early Man-Mammoth Site." *Department of Geosciences Contribution* 23: 10–26. University of Arizona, Tucson.

Mehringer, Peter J., Jr., Paul S. Martin, and C. Vance Haynes, Jr.
1967   Murray Springs, A Mid-Postglacial Pollen Record from Southern Arizona. *American Journal of Science* 265: 786–797.

Meighan, Clement W., and C. Vance Haynes, Jr.
1968   New Studies in the Age of the Borax Lake Site. *The Masterkey* 42(1): 4–9.

Meltzer, David J.
1989   Was Stone Exchanged Among Eastern North American Paleoindians? *Eastern Paleoindian Lithic Resource Use*, edited by Christopher J. Ellis and Jonathan C. Lothrop, pp. 11–39. Westview Press, New York.
1991   Altithermal Archaeology and Paleoecology at Mustang Springs, on the Southern High Plains of Texas. *American Antiquity* 56(2): 236–267.
1993   Is There a Clovis Adaptation? *From Kostenki to Clovis: Upper Paleolithic-Paleo-Indian Adaptations*, edited by Olga Soffer and N. D. Praslov, pp. 293–310. Plenum Press, New York.
2001   Why We Still Don't Know When the First People Came to North America. In "On Being First: Cultural Innovation and Environmental Consequences of First Peoplings," edited by J. Gillespie, S. Tupakka, and C. De Mille, pp. 1–25. *Proceedings of the 31st Annual Chacmool Conference*. Archaeological Association of the University of Calgary, Calgary, Alberta.
2002   What Do You Do When No One's Been There Before? Thoughts on the Exploration and Colonization of New Lands. In "The First Americans, The Pleistocene Colonization of the New World," edited by Nina G. Jablonski, pp. 27–58. *Memoirs of the California Academy of Sciences* 27. California Academy of Sciences, San Francisco.
2003   Lessons in Landscape Learning. *Colonization of Unfamiliar Landscapes: The Archaeology of Adaptation*, edited by M. Rockman and J. Stele, pp. 222–241. Routledge, London.
2004   Modeling the Initial Colonization of the Americas: Issues of Scale, Demography, and Landscape Learning. *The Settlement of the American Continents*, edited by C. Michael Barton, Geoffrey A. Clark, David R. Yesner, and Georges A. Pearson, pp. 123–137. University of Arizona Press, Tucson.

Metcalf, A. L.
1962   Gastropods of Cowley County, Kansas. *Transactions of the Kansas Academy of Science* 65: 275–289. Washburn University, Topeka.
1967   Late Quaternary Mollusks of the Rio Grande Valley, Caballo Dam, New Mexico to El Paso, Texas. *Science Series* 1. University of Texas at El Paso.
1970   Late Pleistocene (Woodfordian) Gastropods from Dry Cave, Eddy County, New Mexico. *Texas Journal of Science* 22: 41–46.

Metcalf, A. L., and R. A. Smartt
1997   Land Snails of New Mexico. *New Mexico Museum of Natural History and Science Bulletin* 10: 1–145.

Metcalf, George
1970   Some Wooden Scraper Handles from the Great Plains and the Southwest. *Plains Anthropologist* 15(47): 46–53.

Montané, Julio
1968   Paleo-Indian Remains from Laguna de Tagua Tagua, Central Chile. *Science* 161(3846): 1137–1138.

Morrison, R. B.
1985   Pliocene/Quaternary Geology, Geomorphology, and Tectonics of Arizona. In "Soils and Quaternary Geology of the Southwestern United States," edited by David L. Weide, pp. 123–146. *Geological Society of America Special Paper* 203.
1991   Quaternary Geology of the Southern Basin and Range Province. In "Quaternary Nonglacial Geology, Conterminous U.S.," edited by R. B. Morrison, pp. 353–371. *The Geology of North America*, K-2. Geological Society of America, Boulder.

Mortensen, J. L., and F. L. Himes
1964   Soil Organic Matter. *Chemistry of the Soil*, edited by F. E. Bear, pp. 206–241. Reinhold Publishing, New York.

Mosimann, James E., and Paul S. Martin
1975   Simulating Overkill by Paleoindians. *American Scientist* 63(3): 304–313.

Moss, Cynthia
1988   *Elephant Memories: Thirteen Years in the Life of an Elephant Family*. William Morrow, New York.

Muller, C. H.
1947   Vegetation and Climate of Coahuila, Mexico. *Madroño* 9: 33–57.

Munsell Color Company
1975   *Munsell Soil Color Charts*. Munsell Color Company, Baltimore.

Nations, J. Dale, and J. J. Landye
1984   Cenozoic Plant and Animal Fossils in Arizona. *Landscapes of Arizona: The Geological Story*, edited by Terah L. Smiley, J. Dale Nations, Troy L. Pewe, and J. P. Schafer, pp. 2–35. University Press of America, Lanham, MD.

Nelson, Margaret C.
    1991   The Study of Technological Organization. *Advances in Archaeological Method and Theory* 3, edited by Michael B. Schiffer, pp. 55–100. University of Arizona Press, Tucson.

Newcomer, M. H.
    1975   "Punch Technique" and Upper Paleolithic Blades. *Lithic Technology: Making and Using Stone Tools*, edited by Earl Swanson, pp. 97–102. Mouton Publishers, The Hague.

Newman, Jay R., and Roger L. Nielsen
    1985   Initial Notes on the X-ray Fluorescence Sourcing of Northern New Mexico Obsidians. *Journal of Field Archaeology* 12: 377–383.

Nigra, J. O., and John F. Lance
    1947   A Statistical Study of the Metapodials of the Dire Wolf Group from the Pleistocene of Rancho la Brea. *Bulletin of the Southern California Academy of Sciences* 46(Part 1): 26–34.

Nikiforoff, C. C.
    1943   Introduction to Paleopedology. *American Journal of Science* 241: 194.

Nilsson, Tage
    1983   *The Pleistocene. Geology and Life in the Quaternary Ice Age*. D. Reidel, Boston.

North American Commission on Stratigraphic Nomenclature
    1983   North American Stratigraphic Code. *American Association of Petroleum Geologists Bulletin* 67(5): 864–869.

Nydal, R., and K. Lövseth
    1983   Tracing Bomb ^{14}C in the Atmosphere 1962–1980. *Journal of Geophysical Research* 88(66): 3621–3642.

Oakley, Kenneth P.
    1964   *Man the Tool-Maker*. University of Chicago Press, Chicago.

Olivier, Robert C. D.
    1982   Ecology and Behavior of Living Elephants: Bases for Assumptions Concerning the Extinction of the Wooly Mammoth. *Paleoecology of Beringia*, edited by D. M. Hopkins, J. V. Mathews, Jr., C. E. Schweger, and S. B. Young, pp. 291–305. Academic Press, New York.

Osborn, Henry F.
    1942   *Proboscidea. II. Stegodontoidea, Elephantoidea*. American Museum of Natural History, New York.

Packard, Frank A.
    1974   The Hydraulic Geometry of a Discontinuous Ephemeral Stream on a Bajada near Tucson, Arizona. Doctoral dissertation, Department of Geosciences, University of Arizona, Tucson.

Pattie, James O.
    1905   The Personal Narrative of James O. Pattie. *Early Western Travels, 1748–1846*. Vol. 18, edited by R. G. Thwaites. Arthur H. Clarke, Cleveland.

Pierce, H. G.
    1975   Diversity of Late Cenozoic Gastropods of the Southern High Plains. Doctoral dissertation, Department of Geology, Texas Tech University, Lubbock.

Pigati, J. S., J. Quade, T. M. Shahanan, and C. Vance Haynes, Jr.
    2004   Radiocarbon Dating of Minute Gastropods and New Constraints on the Timing of Late Quaternary Spring-discharge Deposits in Southern Arizona. *Palaeogeography, Palaeoclimatology, Palaeoecology* 204: 33–45.

Pilsbry, Henry A.
    1939–1948   Land Mollusca of North America (North of Mexico). *Academy of Natural Sciences of Philadelphia Monograph* 3. Philadelphia.

Reher, Charles A.
    1970   Population Dynamics of the Glenrock *Bison bison* Population. In "The Glenrock Buffalo Jump, 48CO304: Late Prehistoric Period Buffalo Procurement and Butchering on the Northwestern Plains," edited by George C. Frison, pp. 51–55. *Plains Anthropologist Memoir* 7.
    1974   Population Study of the Casper Site Bison. *The Casper Site: A Hell Gap Bison Kill on the High Plains*, edited by George C. Frison, pp. 113–124. Academic Press, New York.

Rodgers, William M.
    1965   Historical Land Occupance of the Upper San Pedro River Valley Since 1870. Master's thesis, Department of History, University of Arizona, Tucson.

Roe, Frank Gilbert
    1951   *The North American Buffalo: A Critical Study of the Species in its Wild State*. University of Toronto Press, Toronto.
    1970   *The North American Buffalo: A Critical Study of the Species in its Wild State*. University of Toronto Press, Toronto. Second Edition

Roeske, R. A., and W. L. Werrell
    1973   Hydrologic Conditions in the San Pedro River Valley, Arizona. *Arizona Water Commission Bulletin* 4: 1–76.

Rogers, Raymond N.
    1951   The Rate of Utilization of the Phosphorus of Algal Cells by Barley Plants. Master's thesis, Department of Agricultural Chemistry and Soils, University of Arizona, Tucson.
    1967   Combined Pyrolysis and Thin Layer Chromatography. *Analytical Chemistry* 39: 370.
    1980   The Chemistry of Pottery Smudging. *Pottery Southwest* 7(2): 1–4.

Rogers, Raymond N., and L. C. Smith
　1970　Application of Combined Pyrolysis–TLC to the Study of Chemical Kinetics. *Journal of Chromatography* 48: 268.

Russell, R. H.
　1970　Zoogeography of Late Cenozoic Mollusca from the San Pedro Valley, Southeastern Arizona. *Journal of the Arizona Academy of Science Supplement* 6. Abstracts from the 14th meeting, April 17–18.
　1971　The Pleistocene Molluscan History of the San Pedro Valley, Southeastern Arizona. *The Echo, Abstract Proceedings of the 4th Annual Meeting of the Western Society of Malacologists*, p. 29.

Saunders, Jeffrey J.
　1970　The Distribution and Taxonomy of *Mammuthus* in Arizona. Master's thesis, Department of Geosciences, University of Arizona, Tucson.
　1974　Additions to the Lehner Site (UALP 14) Fauna, 1974 Field Season, May 20–June 29. Report on File at the Laboratory of Paleontology, University of Arizona, Tucson.
　1977　Lehner Ranch Revisited. In "Paleoindian Lifeways," edited by Eileen Johnson, pp. 48–64. *The Museum Journal* 17. Texas Tech University, Lubbock.
　1980　A Model for Man-Mammoth Relationships in Late Pleistocene North America. In "The Ice-Free Corridor and Peopling of the New World," edited by N. W. Rutter and C. E. Schweger, pp. 87–89. *Canadian Journal of Anthropology* 1(1).
　1983　Late Pleistocene Vertebrates of the San Pedro Valley, Arizona. Manuscript on file, Arizona State Museum Archives, University of Arizona, Tucson.

Saunders, Jeffrey J., and Edward B. Daeschler
　1994　Descriptive Analyses and Taphonomical Observations of Culturally-Modified Mammoths Excavated at "The Gravel Pit," Near Clovis, New Mexico in 1936. *Proceedings of the Academy of Natural Sciences of Philadelphia* 145: 1–28.

Saunders, Jeffrey J., and Gerald K. Kelso
　1971　Fossil Mammals in a Spring Conduit, Cochise County, Arizona. *Program of the 47th Annual Meeting of the Southwestern and Rocky Mountain Division, American Association for the Advancement of Science and the 15th Annual Meeting of the Arizona Academy of Science*, p. 27. Tempe.

Sayles, E. B.
　1983　The Cochise Cultural Sequence in Southeastern Arizona. *Anthropological Papers of the University of Arizona* 42. University of Arizona Press, Tucson.

Sayles, E. B., and Ernst Antevs
　1941　The Cochise Culture. *Medallion Papers* 29. Gila Pueblo, Globe, Arizona.

Schmidt, R. H., Jr.
　1979　A Climatic Delineation of the "Real" Chihuahuan Desert. *Journal of Arid Environments* 2: 243–250.

Schumm, S. A.
　1973　Geomorphic Thresholds and Complex Response of Drainage Systems. *Fluvial Geomorphology, Publications in Geomorphology*, edited by M. Morisawa, pp. 299–310. State University of New York, Binghamton.

Sellards, E. H.
　1952　*Early Man in America*. University of Texas Press, Austin.
　1955　Fossil Bison and Associated Artifacts from Milnesand, New Mexico. *American Antiquity* 20(4): 336–344.

Semenov, S. A.
　1964　*Prehistoric Technology*. Cory, Adams and Mackay, London.

Seton, Ernest Thompson
　1929　*Lives of Game Animals*. Doubleday, Doran and Co., New York

Shackley, M. Steven
　1986　Obsidian Geochemistry and Lithic Technology: Inferences for Archaic Hunter-Gatherer Procurement Ranges. In "Prehistoric Hunter-Gatherers of South Central Arizona: The Picacho Reservoir Archaic Project," edited by Frank E. Bayham, Donald H. Morris, and M. Steven Shackley. *Anthropological Field Studies* 13. Arizona State University, Tempe.
　1988　Sources of Archaeological Obsidian in the Southwest: An Archaeological, Petrological, and Geochemical Study. *American Antiquity* 53(4): 752–772.
　1990　*Early Hunter-Gatherer Procurement Ranges in the Southwest: Evidence from Obsidian Geochemistry and Lithic Technology*. Doctoral dissertation, Department of Anthropology, Arizona State University, Tempe. University Microfilms, Ann Arbor.
　1992　The Upper Gila River Gravels as an Archaeological Obsidian Source Region: Implications for Models of Exchange and Interaction. *Geoarchaeology* 7(4): 315–326.
　2005　*Obsidian: Geology and Archaeology in the North America Southwest*. University of Arizona Press, Tucson.

Shay, C. Thomas
　1971　*The Itasca Bison Kill: An Ecological Analysis*. Minnesota Historical Society, St. Paul.

Shefner, A. M., M. E. King, and B. Kohn
　1962　Biologistics for Space Systems Symposium. Wright-Patterson Air Force Base, 6570th Medi-

Shefner, A. M., M. E. King,
and B. Kohn (*continued*)
    cal Research Laboratories Documentary Report AMRL-TDR-62-116, p. 391.

Shnyukova, E. I., and S. U. Pirozhenko
    1974   Monosaccharide Composition of Some Blue-green Algae Polysaccharides. Ukr. Bot. Zh. 31(4): 499. *Chemical Abstracts* 82: 82639v.

Shott, Michael J.
    1989   Bipolar Industries: Ethnographic Evidence and Archaeological Implications. *North American Archaeologist* 10(1): 1–24.

Shutler, Richard, Jr.
    1967   Archaeology of Tule Springs. In "Pleistocene Studies in Southern Nevada," edited by H. Marie Wormington and Dorothy Ellis, pp. 298-203. *Nevada State Museum Anthropology Papers* 13. University of Nevada, Carson City, Nevada.

Sikes, Sylvia K.
    1971a   The African Elephant, *Loxodonta africana*: A Field Method for the Estimation of Age. *Journal of Zoology (London)* 150: 279-295.
    1971b   *The Natural History of the African Elephant*. Weidenfeld and Nicolson, London.

Simpson, George Gaylord
    1961   *Horses*. American Museum of Natural History, New York.
    1965   *The Geography of Evolution*. Chilton Books, Philadelphia.

Skinner, Morris F., and O. C. Kaisen
    1947   The Fossil Bison of Alaska and Preliminary Revision of the Genus. *Bulletin of the American Museum of Natural History* 89 (Article 3): 123-256.

Slaughter, Bob H.
    1967   Animal Ranges as a Clue to Late-Pleistocene Extinction. *Pleistocene Extinctions: The Search for a Cause*, edited by Paul S. Martin and Herbert E. Wright, Jr., pp. 155-167. Yale University Press, New Haven.

Smith, G. A.
    1994   Climatic Influences on Continental Deposition during Late-stage Filling of an Extensional Basin, Southeastern Arizona. *Geological Society of America Bulletin* 106: 1212-1228.

Sneath, Peter H. A., and Robert R. Sokal
    1973   *Numerical Taxonomy: The Principles and Practice of Numerical Classification*. W. H. Freeman, San Francisco.

Sonnichsen, C. L.
    1974   *Colonel Greene and the Copper Skyrocket*. University of Arizona Press, Tucson.

Spaulding, W. Geofrey, E. B. Leopold,
and Thomas R. Van Devender
    1983   Late Wisconsin Paleoecology of the American Southwest. *Late Quaternary Environments of the United States*, edited by Herbert E. Wright, Jr. Vol. 1, *The Late Pleistocene*, edited by Stephen C. Porter, pp. 259-293. University of Minnesota Press, Minneapolis.

Speth, John D.
    1983   *Bison Kills and Bone Counts: Decision Making by Ancient Hunters*. University of Chicago Press, Chicago.

Stafford, T. W., Jr., P. E. Hare, L. A. Currie,
A. J. T. Jull, and D. Donahue
    1991   Accelerator Radiocarbon Dating at the Molecular Level. *Journal of Archaeological Sciences* 18: 35-72.

Stanford, Dennis J.
    1974   Progress Report of the Archeological Investigation at the Jones-Miller Paleo-Indian Site in Northeastern Colorado. Manuscript on file, Smithsonian Institution, Washington.
    1999   Paleoindian Archaeology and Late Pleistocene Environments in the Plains and Southwestern United States. *Ice Age People of North America: Environments, Origins, and Adaptations*, edited by Robson Bonnichsen and K. L. Turnmire, pp. 281-339. Oregon State University Press, Corvallis.

Stanford, Dennis J., and Margaret A. Jodry
    1988   The Drake Clovis Cache. *Current Research in the Pleistocene* 5: 21-22.

Stephenson, Robert L.
    1965   Quaternary Human Occupation of the Plains. *The Quaternary of the United States*, edited by Herbert E. Wright, Jr., and David G. Frey, pp. 685-696. Princeton University Press, Princeton.

Stevenson, Christopher, and Maria Klimkiewicz
    1990   X-Ray Fluorescence Analysis of Obsidian Sources in Arizona and New Mexico. *Kiva* 55(3): 235-243.

Stevenson, I. L.
    1964   Biochemistry of the Soil. *Chemistry of the Soil*, edited by Firman E. Bear, pp. 242-291. Reinhold Publishing, New York.

Stock, Chester
    1963   Rancho la Brea: A Record of Pleistocene Life in California. *Los Angeles County Museum Science Series* 20.

Stoltman, James B.
    1971   Prismatic Blades from Northern Minnesota. *Plains Anthropologist* 16: 105-109.

Stuiver, M., P. J. Reimer, E. Bard, W. J. Beck, G. S. Burr, K. A. Hughen, B. Kromer, G. McCormac, J. Van de Plicht, and M. Spurk
    1998   INTCAL 98 Radiocarbon Age Calibration, 24,000-0 cal B.P. *Radiocarbon* 40(3): 1041-1083.

Surovell, Todd, Nicole Waguespack,
and P. Jeffrey Brantingham
    2005   Global Evidence for Proboscidean Overkill. *Proceedings of the National Academy of Sciences* 102: 6231-6236.

Tahirkheli, R. A. K., and C. N. Naeser
    1975   Zircon Fission Track Age of Post Ranch Ash Bed near Benson, Arizona. *Journal of the Arizona Academy of Science* 10: 111-113.

Taylor, Dwight W.
    1958   Geologic Range and Relationships of the Freshwater Snail *Anisus pattersoni*. *Journal of Paleontology* 32(6): 1149-1153.
    1960   Late Cenozoic Molluscan Faunas from the High Plains. *U.S. Geological Survey Professional Paper* 337.
    1966   Summary of North American Blancan Nonmarine Molluscs. *Malacologia* 4: 1-172.
    1967   Late Pleistocene Molluscan Shells from the Tule Springs Area. In " Pleistocene Studies in Southern Nevada," edited by H. Marie Wormington and Dorothy Ellis, pp. 395-399. *Nevada State Museum Anthropological Papers* 13. Carson City.

Taylor, R. E., C. Vance Haynes, Jr., and M. Stuiver
    1996   Clovis and Folsom Age Estimates: Stratigraphic Context and Radiocarbon Calibration. *Antiquity* 70(269): 515-525.

Tissot, B., B. Durand, J. Espitale, and A. Combaz
    1974   Influence of Nature and Diagenesis of Organic Matter in Formation of Petroleum. *American Association of Petroleum Geologists Bulletin* 58: 499-506.

Tixier, Jacques
    1972   Obtention de lames par debitage "sous de pied." *Bulletin de la Societé Préhistorique Française* 69: 134-139.

Todd, Lawrence C.
    1987   Bison Bone Measurements. *The Horner Site: The Type Site of the Cody Cultural Complex*, edited by George C. Frison and Lawrence C. Todd, pp. 371-403. Academic Press, Orlando.

Todd, Lawrence C., Jack L. Hofman,
and C. Bertrand Schultz
    1990   Seasonality of the Scottsbluff and Lipscomb Bison Bonebeds: Implications for Modeling Paleoindian Subsistence. *American Antiquity* 55(4): 813-827.

Toribio de Motolina, Fray
    1541   Memoriales. *Documentos Historicos de Mejico* 1: 327 (1903).

Turgeon, D. D., J. F. Quinn, A. E. Bogan,
E. V. Coan and others
    1998   Common and Scientific Names of Aquatic Invertebrates from the United States and Canada: Mollusks. *American Fisheries Society Special Publication* 26. Bethesda.

Turney-High, Harry H.
    1937   The Flathead Indians of Montana. *American Anthropological Association Memoir* 48.

United States Regional Salinity Laboratory
    1947   Diagnosis and Improvement of Saline and Alkali Soils. MS, U.S. Department of Agriculture, Riverside, California.

Van Devender, Thomas R.
    1973   Late Pleistocene Plants and Animals of the Sonoran Desert: A Survey of Ancient Packrat Middens in Southwestern Arizona. Doctoral dissertation, Department of Geosciences, University of Arizona, Tucson.
    1990a   Late Quaternary Vegetation and Climate of the Chihuahuan Desert, United States and Mexico. *Packrat Middens: The Last 40,000 Years of Biotic Change*, edited by Julio L. Betancourt, Thomas R. Van Devender, and Paul S. Martin, pp. 104-133. University of Arizona Press, Tucson.
    1990b   Late Quaternary Vegetation and Climate of the Sonoran Desert, United States and Mexico. *Packrat Middens: The Last 40,000 Years of Biotic Change*, edited by Julio L. Betancourt, Thomas R. Van Devender, and Paul S. Martin, pp. 134-165. University of Arizona Press, Tucson.

Van Devender, Thomas R., and W. Geoffrey Spaulding
    1979   Development of Vegetation and Climate in the Southwestern United States. *Science* 204(4394): 701-710.

Velastro, S., Jr., E. Mott Davis, and Alejandra G. Varela
    1975   University of Texas at Austin Radiocarbon Dates X. *Radiocarbon* 17(1): 52-98.

Voorhies, M. R.
    1969   Taphonomy and Population Dynamics of an Early Pliocene Vertebrate Fauna, Knox County, Nebraska. *University of Wyoming Contributions to Geology Special Paper* 1. University of Wyoming, Laramie.

Waguespack, Nicole M., and Todd A. Surovell
    2003   Clovis Hunting Strategies, or How to Make Out on Plentiful Resources. *American Antiquity* 68(2): 333-352.

Wallmo, O. C.
    1955   Vegetation of the Huachuca Mountains, Arizona. *American Midland Naturalist* 54(2): 466-480.

Warnica, James M.
    1966   New Discoveries at the Clovis Site. *American Antiquity* 31(3): 345-357.

Waters, Michael R.
    1985   Late Quaternary Alluvial Stratigraphy of Whitewater Draw, Arizona: Implications for Regional Correlation of Fluvial Deposits in the American Southwest. *Geology* 13(10): 705-708.

Waters, Michael R. (*continued*)
1986 The Geoarchaeology of Whitewater Draw, Arizona. *Anthropological Papers of the University of Arizona* 45. University of Arizona Press, Tucson.

Waters, Michael R., and C. Vance Haynes, Jr.
2001 Late Quaternary Arroyo Formation and Climate Change in the American Southwest. *Geology* 29(5): 399–402.

Webb, S. David
1965 The Osteology of *Camelops*. *Los Angeles County Museum of Science Bulletin* 1: 1–54.

Weber, Robert H., and George A. Agogino
1968 Mockingbird Gap Paleo-Indian Site: Excavations in 1967. Paper presented at the 33rd Annual Meeting of the Society for American Archaeology, Santa Fe, New Mexico.

Wedel, Waldo R.
1970 Antler Tine Scraper Handles in the Central Plains. *Plains Anthropologist* 15(47): 36–45.

Wendorf, Fred, and James J. Hester
1962 Early Man's Utilization of the Great Plains Environment. *American Antiquity* 28(2): 159–171.

Wentworth, T. R.
1981 Vegetation on Limestone and Granite in the Mule Mountains, Arizona. *Ecology* 62(2): 469–482.
1983 Vegetation and Flora of the Mule Mountains. *Journal of the Arizona–Nevada Academy of Science* 17: 29–44.

West, Frederick Hadleigh
1981 *The Archaeology of Beringia*. Columbia University Press, New York.

Wheat, Joe Ben
1967 A Paleo-Indian Bison Kill. *Scientific American* 216(1): 44–52.
1972 The Olsen-Chubbock Site: A Paleo-Indian Bison Kill. *Society for American Archaeology Memoir* 26.

Whitfield, Charles J., and Hugh L. Anderson
1938 Secondary Succession of the Desert Plains Grassland. *Ecology* 19(2): 171–180.

Whitmore, Frank C., Jr., K. O. Emery, H. B. S. Cooke, and Donald P. J. Swift
1967 Elephant Teeth from the Atlantic Continental Shelf. *Science* 156(3781): 1477–1481.

Whittaker, R. H., and W. A. Niering
1968 Vegetation of the Santa Catalina Mountains, Arizona. IV, Limestone and Acid Soils. *Journal of Ecology* 56(2): 523–544.

Wilke, Philip J., Jeffrey J. Flenniken, and Terry L. Ozbun
1991 Clovis Technology at the Anzick Site, Montana. *Journal of California and Great Basin Anthropology* 10: 3–31.

Wilmsen, Edwin N.
1968a Functional Analysis of Flaked Stone Artifacts. *American Antiquity* 33(2): 156–161.
1968b Lithic Analysis in Paleoanthropology. *Science* 161(3845): 982–987.

Wilmsen, Edwin N., and Frank H. H. Roberts
1978 Lindenmeier, 1934–1974. *Smithsonian Institution Contributions to Anthropology* 24. Washington.

Wilson, Michael C.
1974a The Casper Site Local Fauna and Its Fossil Bison. *The Casper Site: A Hell Gap Bison Kill on the High Plains*, edited by George C. Frison, pp. 125–171. Academic Press, New York.
1974b History of the Bison in Wyoming, with Particular Reference to the Early Holocene Forms. In "Applied Geology and Archaeology: The Holocene History of Wyoming," edited by Michael Wilson, pp. 91–99. *Geological Survey of Wyoming Report of Investigations* 10. Laramie.
1980 Population Dynamics of the Garnsey Site Bison. In "Late Prehistoric Bison Procurement in Southeastern New Mexico: The 1978 Season at the Garnsey Site (LA-18399)," edited by John D. Speth and W. J. Parry, pp. 88–129. *Museum of Anthropology Technical Report* 12. University of Michigan, Ann Arbor.
1988 Bison Dentitions from the Henry Smith Site, Montana: Evidence for Seasonality and Paleoenvironments at an Avonlea Bison Kill. *Avonlea Yesterday and Today: Archaeology and Prehistory*, edited by L. B. Davis, pp. 203–225. Saskatchewan Archaeological Society, Saskatoon, SK.

Windmiller, Ric
1973 The Late Cochise Culture in the Sulphur Spring Valley, Southeastern Arizona: Archaeology of the Fairchild Site. *The Kiva* 39(2): 131–169.

Wise, Edward N., and Richard Shutler, Jr.
1958 University of Arizona Radiocarbon Dates. *Science* 127(3289): 72–74.

Wissler, Clark
1910 Material Culture of the Blackfoot Indians. *Anthropological Papers of the American Museum of Natural History* 5 (Part 1). American Museum of Natural History, New York.

Witthoft, John
1952 A Paleo-Indian Site in Eastern Pennsylvania: An Early Hunting Culture. *Proceedings of the American Philosophical Society* 96(4): 464–495.

Woods, James C., and Gene L. Titmus
1985 A Review of the Simon Clovis Collection. *Idaho Archaeologist* 8: 3–8.

Woodward, Susan L.
1969 Vegetation of the Murray Springs Area, Cochise County, Arizona. Master's thesis, Department of Geography and Area Development, University of Arizona, Tucson.

1972 The Spontaneous Vegetation of the Murray Springs Area, San Pedro Valley, Arizona. *Journal of the Arizona Academy of Science* 7(1): 12-16.

Wormington, H. Marie
1957 Ancient Man in North America (4th ed.). *Denver Museum of Natural History Popular Series* 4.

Yang, T. W.
1970 Major Chromosome Races of *Larrea divaricata* in North America. *Journal of the Arizona Academy of Science* 6: 41-45.

Yates, Bonnie C., and Ernest L. Lundelius, Jr.
2001 Vertebrate Faunal Remains from the Aubry Clovis Site. *The Archaeology and Paleoecology of the Aubrey Clovis Site (41DN479) Denton County, Texas*, by C. Reid Ferring, pp. 103-119. Center for Environmental Archaeology, Department of Geography, University of North Texas, Denton.

Ziegler, P. T.
1954 *The Meat We Eat*. Interstate Printers and Publishers, Danville.

Zielinski, R. A., P. W. Lipman, and H. T. Millard
1977 Minor Element Abundances in Obsidian, Perlite and Felsite of Calc-alkalic Rhyolites. *American Mineralogist* 62: 426-437.

Ziemens, George, and Sandy Ziemens
1974 Volumes of Bison Astragali. *The Casper Site: A Hell Gap Bison Kill on the High Plains*, edited by George C. Frison, pp. 245-246. Academic Press, New York.

Index

Abbott, Jim, xv
Abelson, Philip, 241
Adam, David P., xii, xiii, xiv, xv
Addington, Lucille R., xv
Agate Basin Site, WY, 193, 211
Albritton, Claude C., xiv
Alder, 40
Allerød chronozone, 54, 225, 237
Alluvial deposits, at Murray Springs.
    See Bakarich Ranch Member;
    Curry Draw Member; Hargis
    Ranch Member; McCool Ranch
    Member; Millville Formation;
    Teviston Member; Weik Ranch
    Member.
Altithermal
    climate of, 5-6, 55, 83, 144, 150
    lack of alluvial pollen record
        during, 6
American lions
    extinction of, 55, 225
    remains of, 14, 32, 40
Anadarko, OK, lithic cache near,
    161-162, 210, 212
Antevs, Ernst, 1, 5, 51, 55, 150
Anzick Clovis Site, MT, 5, 211, 220
Archaic period
    artifacts of, 149, 155, 162-166,
        172, 182, 183, 184, 187, 188.
        See also Cochise culture.
    evidence of, 5, 44, 56, 83, 149,
        150, 155, 162-166
Arizona State Museum, xiii
Arizona State University, 250
Artillery range, xiv
Ash (*Fraxinus*), 8, 36, 40, 54, 58, 85,
    94, 121, 127, 230, 239
Atlatl, xiv
Aubrey Site, TX, 42, 214, 215, 218

Babocomari Cienega, 25, 34, 47, 63,
    64, 77

Bajadas (pediments), in San Pedro
    Valley, 16, 19, 60
Bakarich Ranch Member (Stratum G_3,
    alluvium), 24, 53, 56, 232
Ballenger, Jesse, xiv, 241, 249
Basalt
    debitage of, 108, 173, 176, 178,
        179, 187
    sources and artifact abundance of,
        188-191
Bear remains
    at Lehner Site, 1, 218
    at Murray Springs Site, 32
Beaver, 51
Beckwith, Ron, xv
Bella Vista Ranch, xiv
Bequaert, Joseph C., 64, 68, 82
Betancourt, Julio, xiii
Biface edge grinding, 94, 105, 106,
    107-108, 113, 132, 134, 171, 194,
    200
Bifaces, Archaic period, 164-166,
    172
Bifaces, Clovis
    at Lehner Site, 222
    at Murray Springs Site, 8, 12, 42,
        94, 95, 104-108, 111, 113-
        114, 121-124, 132, 133, 134,
        149, 155-157, 163, 170-184,
        189-213, 220, *See also* Clovis
        projectile points.
    role in Clovis industry, 210-213
Big Bend, of Curry Draw, 28, 29, 30,
    31, 50, 52, 53, 68
Bioturbation, at Murray Springs, 11,
    12, 44, 48, 50, 53, 84, 148, 149,
    155, 163, 172, 182, 199, 231, 237
Bischoff, James L., xiv, 241
Bison (*Bison antiquus*)
    age composition of, 93, 103, 113,
        119-120, 126, 127, 129, 136,
        138-145

birthing season of, 144
dentitions of, 138-145
gender of, 93, 103, 112, 120, 136,
    138
processing of, 112, 121, 125-129
season (time) of killing of, 119-
    120, 128, 138-145
Bison Kill Creek, 15, 24, 39, 40, 41,
    42, 44, 47, 48, 54, 87, 168
Bison remains
    at Lehner Site, 1, 218
    at Murray Springs Site, 1, 11, 14,
        32, 41, 42, 55, 87, 93, 103, 108,
        114-120, 214, 218, 255-265
Bison tracks, 12-13, 42. *See also*
    Mammoth tracks.
Black mat (Stratum F_2)
    and extinction events, 225
    as ideal Pleistocene-Holocene
        boundary, 40, 225
    at Escapule Site, 3
    at Lehner Site, 1, 3, 6
    at Murray Springs Site, 1, 10, 18,
        29, 36, 40-44, 45-47, 48, 50,
        52, 55, 56, 84, 85, 96, 114, 131,
        172, 231-237, 240-249, 269-
        272. *See also* Clanton Ranch
        Member
    chemical evaluation of, 242-245
    C-NMR spectral analyses of,
        247-248
    climate change signaled by, 225
    continuation of studies on, 226
    dating of, 229-239
    deposition of, 24, 45-46, 55
    derivation (origin) of, 45, 231,
        240-249
    in Curry Draw, 6, 46, 266, 269-272
    occupation above (post-Clovis), 5
    pyrolytic gas chromatographic mass
        spectrometry analysis of, 245-
        247, 248-249

[299]

Black mat (*continued*)
  widespread distribution of, 225
Blackwater Draw Site, NM, xi, 42, 111, 114, 150, 158, 159, 160, 161, 203, 204, 207, 208, 209, 212, 221
Blade (lithic) technology, 204, 208–209
Blades (lithic)
  at Murray Springs, 12, 44, 105, 113, 121, 123, 137, 149, 160–162, 182, 183, 184, 204, 205–209, 212–213, 223
  disappearance of, 220
  in caches, 220
Bohrer, Vorsila L., xv
Bølling chronozone, 54, 237
Bone
  burned, 112, 121. *See also* Heat alteration, of bone
  preservation of, 86–88, 97–103, 115, 119, 120, 126–127, 131
Bone artifacts
  at Naco, 222
  at Navarrete Site, 3–4, 207
  at Murray Springs Site, 9, 109–110, 114
  gaming(?) piece, 124
  shaft wrench, 9, 109–110, 114
  slotted tool, 3–4, 207
Bones, of animals
  human(?) manipulation of, 8, 40, 103, 115, 119, 212–213. *See also* Bison, processing of; Mammoths, processing of
Bonfire Shelter, TX, 143, 144
Boquillas Land and Cattle Co., 24
Brady, Ray, xiv
Brickell bush, 58
"Buffalo wallows," at Murray Springs, 42, 97, 112–113, 120–121
Bureau of Land Management, xiv, 16, 226, 227, 266
Burin. *See* Scrapers, scraper-burin
Bush muhly, 57
Butchering. *See* Bison, processing of; Mammoth, processing of

C-NMR nuclear magnetic resonance of black mat, 45, 247–248
Caches
  at Anadarko, OK, 161–162, 208, 214
  at Anzick Site, 220
  at Blackwater Draw Site, 161, 212, 220
  at Drake Site, 220
  at East Wenatchee, 220
  at Keven Davis Site, 220
  at Ryan's Site, 220
  at Simon Site, 191, 220
Camel remains
  at Casper Site, WY, 225
  at Lehner Site, 1, 218, 225
  at Murray Springs Site, 1, 14, 32, 40, 87, 93–94, 96, 255, 256, 258, 262–265
Camels, extinction of, 55, 225
Camp locality. *See* Murray Springs Site, camp locality at
Camp Newell, at Naco, AZ, 53–54
Cananea, Mexico, 16
Canid (*Canis*) remains, 87, 94, 103, 255, 256, 258
Carbonate blebs, coating bones and lithics, 3
Carmichael, Leonard, xiii
Carnivora remains, 262
Casper Site, WY, 119, 139, 225
Ceramics
  appearance of, 56
  Gila Polychrome, 168
Cerros Negros, AZ, 46
Chalcedony
  artifacts of, 94, 95, 104–108, 121–124, 132, 133, 134, 135, 149, 155–167, 173, 175, 176, 178–179, 184, 204, 205, 206. *See also* St. David Chalcedony
  sources and artifact abundance of, 188–191
Charcoal, 36, 39, 40, 42, 50, 51, 52, 53, 84–85, 86, 94, 95, 103, 104, 110, 121, 127, 131, 136, 168, 230, 239, 270. *See also* Dating, by ^{14}C
Charleston, AZ, 35
Charleston Hills, 48
Cheno-ams, 40, 45
Chert
  artifacts of, 94, 95, 106, 107, 121–124, 132, 133, 134, 135, 146, 149, 155–167, 173–184, 186–209, 222
  sources and artifact abundance of, 188–191, 222

Chihuahuan Desert, 57, 59–61, 63
Childress, Jane Pike, xiv
Childress, William, xiv
Christensen, Carl, 82
Clanton Ranch house, 10
Clanton Ranch Member (Stratum F_{2a}, clay), 10, 18, 38, 39, 41, 42, 44, 45–47, 56, 68, 70–76, 81, 85, 96, 172, 231, 233–238, 240–249, 266, 269. *See also* Black Mat
Climate during Clovis times, reconstructions of, 5–6, 54–56, 62–82
Clovis culture
  age of, xi. *See also* Radiocarbon ages
  description of, xi
  limited perishable artifacts of, 5
Clovis diet, 215–221
Clovis lithic industry, 185–213. *See also* Knapping techniques
Clovis occupation surface
  dating of, 95
  paleogeology of, 40–44, Plate 8, 49, 150
  undisturbed condition of, 9, 10, 11, 96, 114, 131, 168, 172, 240
  weathering of remains on, 113, 115
  worked bone on, 110–111
Clovis paleoecology, 214–225
Clovis people
  as initial New World colonists?, 221
  as skilled hunters, 5. *See also* Hunting techniques
  attempts to find water by, 13, 14, 15, 42
  disappearance of, 55, 56, 225
  limited skeletal remains of, 5
  population densities of, 215–216, 221
  subsistence strategies of, 215–221
  travel route of, 188–189, 223
Clovis projectile points
  associated with bison remains, 121–123, 201, 214
  associated with mammoth remains, 1, 3, 41, 195, 214, 219, 222
  at Escapule Site, 3, 8
  at Lehner Site, 1, 195, 198, 200
  at Leikem Site, 3
  at Murray Springs, 9, 11–13, 44, 104, 121–123, 132, 133, 137, 146, 148, 149, 155–156, 162,

163, 171, 175, 181, 182, 183, 186, 187, 188, 194–201
at Naco Site, 1, 195, 198, 200
at Navarrete Site, 3
description of, xi
distribution of, xi
fluting technology of, 197–200
impact damage to, 123, 168
of obsidian, 121, 123, 148, 156, 163, 254
of petrified wood, 104, 188, 195, 223, 226, 254
repair or manufacture of, 175, 180, 183, 184, 185, 194–201, 220
technological characteristics of, 194–201
Cobbles, at Murray Springs Site, 107, 110, 111, 121, 123–124, 149, 150, 164, 176, 188, 209–210, 213. *See also* Expedient tools
Cochise culture, evidence of, 5, 44, 56, 83, 149, 150. *See also* Archaic period
Colby Site, WY, 210, 215
Composite flake tool, 204
Composites (plants), 40, 45
Conduits, at Murray Springs, 13, 14, 15, 32, 42, 43, 227, 237
Contzen, Philip, 8, 23, 24
Cooking of meat, evidence of, 112, 121, 127
Cordova Cave, NM, 164
Cores
 Archaic period, 164, 166, 183
 Clovis, 162, 163, 176, 178, 183, 202–204, 208–209, 211, 212, 213
Coro Marl Member (Stratum E), 29, 30, 32–34, 40, 42, 44, 45–46, 48, 49, 50, 51, 54, 59, 68, 70–76, 77, 78, 79, 81, 96, 114, 146, 148, 149, 150, 155, 182, 234, 237, 238, 239, 268
Cottonwood trees, 24, 46, 52, 54, 58, 59, 64
Cow Canyon, source of obsidian at, 40, 149, 183, 188, 222, 223, 250–254
Cracchiolo, Andrea, xiv
Cracchiolo, Joseph, xiv
Cramer, Joseph L., xv
Cramer, Ruth, xv

Creosotebush, 27, 57, 59, 60
Curry, Joe, 21
Curry Draw
 black mat in, 6, 46, 266, 269–272. *See also* Black mat
 erosion of archaeological features by, 174, 175, 176, 180, 227, 266
 explorations in, 6, 83–84
 geology of, 16–56
 modern environment of, 57–61
 stratigraphy of, 28–40
Curry Draw Member (Stratum J, alluvium), 27, 29, 54, 56

Damon, Paul E., xiii
Dating
 by ^{14}C, 226, 229–239
 by OSL, 226
 See also Radiocarbon ages
Debert Site, Nova Scotia, 114
Debitage. *See* Lithic debitage
Dent Clovis Site, CO, xi
Desert grassland, 59, 60, 64, 79, 80
Desertscrub, Chihuahuan, 21, 22, 27, 48, 49, 54, 56, 60–61, 80
Diet breadth models, 216–217, 221
Dire wolf
 at Lehner Site, 218
 at Murray Springs Site, 10, 39, 40, 94, 103, 217
 extinction of, 55, 225
Domebo Clovis Site, OK xii
Donnet Ranch Member (Stratum F_3, silt), 22, 24, 29, 33, 38, 42, 44, 45, 46, 47–49, 55, 56, 68, 70–76, 80, 81, 85, 148, 149, 150, 232–233, 236, 237
Donnet Site, AZ, xiii, 8
Downs, Hugh, xiv
Drake cache, 220
Drought of 11,000 B.P., 10, 15, 41, 54, 55, 113, 219
Dyer, H. D., 64

Earp Member (Stratum F_{2b}, marl), 10, 36, 38, 45, 46, 47, 231, 235, 236, 240, 246
East Wenatchee Site, WA, 215, 220
Edge angles, of lithic tools, 106, 107, 123, 124, 132, 134, 160, 203–205
Eichenberger, Allen, xv
Elephant behavior, 218–219

Empire Cienega, 47
End scrapers, 182, 202, 203, 204, 206, 207, 208. *See also* Scrapers
Environmental history of southeastern Arizona, 59–61. *See also* Paleo-environmental reconstructions
Escapule, Ernest B., 24
Escapule, Louis W., xii, 3, 8
Escapule Ranch Formation, 19, 29, 46, 49–54, 56
Escapule Site
 artifacts at, 170, 171, 195, 199, 219, 222
 excavations at, 3, 8
 mammoth at, 217, 219, 222
 stratigraphy at, 85
Expedient tools (lithic), 187, 209–210, 213. *See also* Cobbles
Extinction, Pleistocene
 and the black mat, 225. *See also* Black mat
 bison survivor of, 220
 environmental change as cause of, 224
 of Rancholabrean megafauna, 5, 55, 56, 84, 223–225
 "overkill" theory of, 223–225

Fells' Cave, Chile, 135
Fenn cache, WY(?), 215
Ferg, Alan, xv
Fire-cracked cobbles or rocks, 150, 164. *See also* Heat alteration, of lithics
Fisher, Craig, xiv
Flake clusters (concentrations), 148, 155, 163, 201–204. *See also* Knapping loci
Folsom points, xi
Folsom Site, NM, xi
Foote, L. J., xv
Fossil molluscan fauna, 69–82
Fregoso, Barbara, xv
Fry Ranch Member (Stratum D_2), 34

Garnsey Site, NM, 144
Gault Site, TX, 214, 215
Gell, Jonathan, xiv, 83
Geochronological investigations at Murray Springs, continuation of, 226
Geochronology Laboratories, xiii

Gila Polychrome pottery, 168
Gila Pueblo Archaeological
  Foundation, 83
Gila River, 2
Gordus, A. A., xv
Government Draw, 25, 35, 40
Government Mountain, source of
  obsidian at, 167, 188, 222, 223. See
  also Obsidian, sources of
Granite cobble, 107
Granite Wash alluvium, 16, 17
"Grass circles," 18, 19, 48, 51, 57, 60
Grasses, grassland, 40, 49, 54, 56, 57,
  59–61, 64, 78, 79, 80, 81, 82,
  144–145
  deer grass, 27, 54
  Lehman's lovegrass, 20, 22, 27
Gravers, lithic, 105, 135, 146, 159,
  202, 204
Graveyard Gulch Member (Stratum
  F_1, sand), 12, 32, 33, 34, 35–40,
  41, 45, 47, 54, 55, 56, 68, 70–76,
  77, 78–79, 81, 84, 87, 96, 230,
  234, 246
Green, Col. W. C., 24
Greenbush Draw, 1, 3, 53–54, 222

Haas, Herbert, xiv
Haas, Wm. Randy, xv
Hackberry trees, 40, 54, 58
Hafting, evidence of, 161, 166, 198,
  205, 207, 209
Hammer, antler, 193
Hammerstones, 107, 110, 111, 121,
  123–124, 134, 213, 214. See also
  Cobbles
Hargis Ranch Member (Stratum G_{2a},
  alluvium), 29, 38, 49, 50, 51–52,
  53, 55, 56, 80, 232
Haury, Emil W., xiii, 1, 3, 5, 39
Haver, Bozman, xiv
Hawken Site, bison dentition
  comparisons with, 139–142, 144
Hearths
  at Lehner Site, 1, 218, 222
  at Murray Springs (Clovis), 12, 42,
    104, 113, 120–121, 124, 127,
    214, 226, 239
  post-Clovis, 5, 50, 150, 168
Heat alteration
  of bones, 112, 121, 127, 218
  of lithics, 124–125, 132, 156–157,
    161, 162, 163, 176, 177, 178,
    183, 209, 212
  of rocks (cobbles), 150, 164
Hell Gap Site, WY, 6
Henry Smith Site, MT, 144
Hereford, Richard, xiii
Herron, John, xiv
Hinge fractures, of lithic tools, 107,
  132, 161, 192, 197, 200, 207, 208,
  209, 212
Holcombe Beach Site, MI, 114
Holdaway, Michael J., xiv, 240–241
Holocene arroyo in Area 9, 266–272
Holocene sediments, 19, 28, 30, 51,
  54, 55, 56
Holmlund, James P., xv
Horse (*Equus*) remains
  at Lehner Site, 218
  at Murray Springs Site, 1, 11, 14,
    32, 40, 42, 87, 94, 96, 120,
    129–136, 178, 217, 231, 255,
    256, 258, 262–265, 269, 270
Horses
  age composition of, 131–132
  extinction of, 55, 225
Horsethief Draw, 30, 48, 227
Huckell, Lisa, xv
Hueyatlaco, Mexico, 135
Hunting camp. See Murray Springs
  Site, camp locality in
Hunting parties, estimated number of
  people in, 113, 129
Hunting techniques (strategies),
  128–129, 136, 200–201, 216–221
Hurley, CWO William S., 8
Hurley Mammoth Site, AZ, xiii, xiv,
  8

Ice-free corridor, xii
Intra-Allerød Cold Period (IACP), 54
Irwin, Henry, 6
Irwin-Williams, Cynthia, 6

Jacobs, G. Michael, xv
Jake Bluff, OK, bison kill at, xi, 221
Jasper
  debitage of, 108, 134, 135, 173,
    174, 176, 178, 179, 187, 196
  sources and artifact abundance of,
    188–191
Jones-Dabney Co., xiv
Juen, Jesse, xiv

Juniper (*Juniperus*), 40, 85

Kelso, Gerald, 15
Kendall Ranch Member (Stratum E_1),
  34–35
Kern County Land Co., xiii
Keven Davis Site, 215, 220
Kilby, J. David, xv
King, James E., xv
Kinkade, Gay, xiv
Knapping loci, 9, 106–108, 111,
  124–125, 132–135, 136, 157, 163,
  170–185, 211
Knapping of expedient tools, 123
Knapping techniques
  description of, 189–213
  hard hammer, 149, 162, 163, 166,
    167, 172, 176, 177, 180, 183,
    202, 204, 205, 209, 213
  percussion, 107, 113, 134, 197,
    199, 202, 209–210
  pressure flaking, 198, 200
  soft hammer, 107, 113, 134, 162,
    177, 180, 183, 197, 209, 213
  See also Edge angles; Hinge
    fractures
Knives, 13, 203, 211, 220
Koeppen, R. C., xv

Lagomorpha remains, 265
Laguna de Tagua Tagua, Chile, 135
Lance, John F., xiii, 1
Landscape learning, 217, 221, 223
Lange-Ferguson Site, SD, 215
Laury, Robert L., 28, 31
Lehner, Edward F., xii, xiv, 1, 5
Lehner Ranch Formation, 10, 18, 39,
  40, 44–45, 56, 85, 240, 269
Lehner Site, AZ, 40, 170
  age of Coro marl at, 33
  artifacts at, 1, 114, 159, 160–162,
    170, 187–189, 196, 198, 199,
    201–206, 208, 210, 220, 222
  bison at, 1, 218
  black bear at, 218
  black mat at, 1, 5, 243
  camel remains at, 218
  Clovis projectile points at, 1, 222
  dating at, xi, 237
  description of, xi
  dire wolf at, 103
  excavations at, 1, 5

hearth at, xi, 1, 218, 222
horse remains at, 218
knapping activities at, 184–185
mammoth remains at, 208, 217, 220, 222
molluscs at, 62–82
pollen record at, 40, 47, 49, 54, 55
post-Clovis evidence at, 5
rabbit remains at, 218
stratigraphy at, 85
tapir at, 218
Leikem, Slim, xii, 3
Leikem Site, AZ, 3, 195, 217, 222, 223
LeViness, Ed, xiv
Lewis Hills, 11, 16, 18, 21, 107, 155, 162, 188, 223
Lewis Springs, 35, 60, 82, 188
Liddicoat, Joseph, 33
Limestone
  cobbles of, 107
  sources of and artifact abundance of, 186, 188–189
Limestone, silicified
  Archaic tools of, 149, 155, 162, 165, 166, 172, 173, 183, 184, 190
  Clovis use of, 107, 162, 179, 185, 186, 188, 191, 210, 223
  source of, 188
Lindenmeier Site, CO, 158
Lindsay, Alexander J., Jr., 68
Lindsay, Everett H., xiii, xiv, 68
Lipscomb Site, TX, 139
Lithic artifacts. *See* Bifaces; Blades, Clovis projectile points; Cores; End scrapers; Gravers; Knives; Manos; Metates; Milling stones; Preforms; Scrapers; Unifaces; Utilized flakes
Lithic debitage, 107–108, 123, 124–125, 162–163, 166. *See also* Knapping loci
Lithic raw material
  conservation of, 194, 200–202, 211, 219–220
  Nexpa gravels poor source of, 31
  sources of, 40, 123, 149, 155, 156, 162, 163, 166, 167, 168, 183, 186–189, 213, 214, 222–223, 250–254. *See also* Cow Canyon; Government Mountain
  See also Basalt; Chert; Chalcedony;

Granite; Jasper; Limestone; Obsidian; St. David Chalcedony
Lithic technological organization, 186–213, 219–220
Little Boquillas Ranch, xiii
Llano complex, xi, 137
Lone Hill Site, AZ, 165
Long, Austin, xiv, 229, 230

Mammoth Kill Creek, 1
Mammoth (*Mammuthus columbi*) remains
  artifacts associated with, 106, 107, 108, 214, 203, 208
  at Big Bend of Curry Draw, 50
  at Donnet Site, 8
  at Escapule Site, 3, 8
  at Hurley Site, 8
  at Lehner Site, 1, 222
  at Leikem Site, 3
  at Murray Springs Site, 1, 6, 7–10, 13–14, 31, 32, 37, 40–42, 44, 46, 86–93, 149, 255–265
  at Naco Site, 1
  at Navarette Site, 3
  at Schaldack Site, 8
  stacking of, 8, 40, 219
Mammoth tracks, 8, 9, 18, 37, 38, 40, 41, 45, 46, 97, 102, 110, 112
Mammoths
  age composition of, 92, 93, 96, 102, 113, 136, 222
  extinction of, 55, 56, 84, 223–225
  gender of, 92, 93, 96, 97, 102, 113, 136
  processing of, 111, 113
Manos, 167–168. *See also* Milling stones
Manuports, 107, 123–124
Marrow extraction, evidence of, 126, 127
Martin, Paul S., xiii, xv, 5–6, 19, 83, 223–225, 229, 230
Martin-Schoenwetter-Mehringer (MSM) pollen profile, 50, 53, 55
Mastodons, extinction of, 55, 225
McCleary Canyon Site, AZ, 165
McCool, Grace, 21
McCool Ranch Member (Stratum G_{2b}, alluvium), 29, 50, 52, 53, 55, 56, 68, 70–76, 77–78, 80, 81, 232

McGrew, Paul, 138
Mead, Albert R., 82
Mehringer, Peter J., Jr., xiii, xiv, xv, 1, 5, 6, 8, 19, 29, 40, 50, 83, 229
Meighan, Clement W., xv, 109
Mesquite, 57–60, 64
Metasandstone cobbles, 209–210, 223
Metates, 50, 167–168. *See also* Milling stones
Metcalf, Artie L., 82
Mexican Highland Province of North America, 63
Miami Clovis Site, TX, xi
Microtus remains, 255, 258
Miller, Gifford H., 79
Miller, Walter B., 82
Milling stones, 5, 164. *See also* Metates
Millville Formation (Stratum Z, alluvium), 6, 7, 19, 29, 30, 31, 32, 37, 38, 40, 42, 46, 49, 50, 52, 54, 68, 70–76, 78, 84, 85, 87, 96, 124, 148, 150, 210
Mockingbird Gap Site, NM, 114
Mohave Desert, 60
Mollusc sampling locations, 32, 33, 238
Molluscan fauna, 32, 40, 62–82, 240
Morris, Col. Bud., xiv
Moson Ranch Member (Stratum D_1, sand), 31–32, 33, 37, 50
MUDR model, 217, 223
Murray, William (Pink), 21, 24
Murray Place
  Bakarich Ranch Member exposure at, 53
  history of, 19, 21–24
Murray Springs Formation, 30, 31–40, 54, 56, 84, 85, 238, 269
Murray Springs Site, AZ
  activity areas in, 16. *See also* Knapping loci
  artifacts at, 83–137, 170–215, 222–223
  camp locality in, 11–12, 15, 16, 44, 48, 146–169, 172, 182, 186, 207, 214–215, 222, 226. *See also* Murray Springs Area 6; Murray Springs Area 7
  dating of, 229–239
  erosion at, 11, 18, 24–27, 35, 37, 227, 266

Murray Springs Site, AZ (*continued*)
  geology of, 16–56
  hearths at, 12, 42
  history of Clovis discoveries at, 1–15
  mammoth tracks at, 8, 9, 18, 37, 38, 40–41
  modern environment at, 57–61, 62–68
  obsidian at, 40, 121, 123, 14, 155, 156, 163, 167, 175, 178, 183, 184, 187, 188, 195, 222, 250
  pre-Clovis evidence at, 226–227
  site integrity of, 8, 10–11, 96, 114 131, 168, 172, 240
Murray Springs Site Area 1
  artifacts in, 40, 86, 94, 95, 173–174, 269
  bison remains in, 95–96, 138
  bone preservation in, 86, 95
  dating of, 94, 95
  excavations in, 4, 6–11, 37, 86–96
  geology of, 30, 31, 40, 41, 45, 46, 49
  horse remains in, 94
  location of, 4
  mammoth remains in, 39–41, 86–93, 95–96, 113, 214, 230
  mollusc sample from, 79
Murray Springs Site Area 1 Extension
  artifacts in, 172–174, 226
  excavations in, 94–95, 173–174
  knapping loci in, 172–174
  location of, 4
Murray Springs Site Area 2
  bison remains in, 92, 93, 95–96, 138, 143
  bone preservation in, 86
  excavations in, 86–96
  faunal remains in, 4, 8, 35
  geology of, 40, 45
  horse remains in, 94
  location of, 4
  mammoth remains in, 87, 92, 93
Murray Springs Site Area 3
  artifacts in, 104–114, 159, 161, 174–176, 203–205, 210, 213, 222, 226
  bison remains in, 103, 138
  bone preservation in, 86, 97–103
  "buffalo wallow" in, 42, 97
  canid remains in, 103

  excavations in, 96–114
  knapping loci in, 172, 174–176, 222
  location of, 4
  mammoth remains in, 4, 8, 39, 40–41, 46, 97–103, 203, 214
  rodent remains in, 103–104
Murray Springs Site Area 3 Extension
  artifacts in, 170, 176–177
  excavations in, 94
  knapping loci in, 170, 176–177
  location of, 4
Murray Springs Site Area 4
  artifacts in, 121–125, 146, 177–178, 204, 205, 220, 241
  bison kill (bison remains) in, 4, 11, 41–42, 114–129, 136, 138–145, 176, 205, 214, 220, 222
  bone preservation in, 86, 115, 119, 120
  "buffalo wallow" in, 42, 120–121
  excavations in 114–129
  geology of, 45, 114
  hearths in, 120–121, 127, 239
  knapping loci in, 170, 177–178
  location of, 4
  refit flakes in, 146, 149, 155–156, 202
Murray Springs Site Area 5
  artifacts in, 129–130, 132–136, 161, 170, 178–179
  bison kill in, 41–42
  bison(?) tracks in, 4, 12–13
  bone preservation in, 86, 131
  excavations in, 129–136
  geology of, 45, 137
  horse kill in, 129–136, 180
  knapping loci in, 170, 178–179
  location of, 4, 129
Murray Springs Site Area 6
  Archaic period evidence in, 164–169, 190
  artifacts in, 44, 146–169, 180–182, 184, 202, 204, 207, 220
  excavations in, 4, 11, 13, 15, 146–169, 182, 183
  geology of, 48
  knapping locus in, 180–182, 184
  location of, 4
  patination on artifacts in, 156,159
  refit flake in, 146, 155–156, 202
Murray Springs Site Area 7
  Archaic period evidence in,

  167–169, 190
  artifacts in, 44, 146–169, 180–185, 203, 204, 206, 209, 212, 213, 220, 222, 223, 226
  bone preservation in, 86
  Cochise culture evidence in, 44
  excavations in, 4, 11, 13, 15, 146–169
  geology of, 48, 148
  knapping loci in, 180, 181, 182–184
  location of, 4
  mammoth remains in, 44
  patination on artifacts in, 162
  refit flake in, 149
Murray Springs Site Area 8
  anomalous features in, 42–43
  artifact in, 42, 43
  conduits in, 13, 14, 15, 226. See *also* Conduits
  excavations in, 32
  geology of, 33–34, 40
  location of, 4
Murray Springs Site Area 9
  bone exposed in, 27, 266, 267, 269, 270
  excavations in, 266–272
  geology of, 32, 37
  location of, 4, 267

Naco Site, AZ
  artifacts in, xi, 187, 195, 200, 202, 222
  Clovis evidence in, xi, 1, 170, 223
  excavations in, xi, 1
  mammoth remains in, xi, 1, 217, 219, 222
National Geographic Society, xii, xiii, 6, 14
National Historic Landmark proposal, xiv
National Park Service, xiv
National Science Foundation, xiii
Navarrete, Fred, xii, 1
Navarrete, Marc, xii, 1, 3
Navarrete Site, AZ, 3–4, 161, 195, 207, 215, 217, 222, 223
Neotoma remains, 258
Nexpa Formation (Stratum Y, gravels), 19, 22, 30, 31, 49, 124, 210

Oak woodland, 40, 64, 68, 78, 79, 80, 81, 82

Oak-grassland, 82
Oak-pine woodland, 68
Obsidian
   artifacts of, 121, 123, 148, 155, 156, 163, 167, 175, 178, 183, 184, 187, 188, 195, 222, 250
   hydration tests of, 109
   sources of, 40, 149, 183, 184, 188–191, 222, 223, 250–254. *See also* Cow Canyon; Government Mountain
Obsidian nodules (marekanite), 94, 95, 108–109, 123, 162, 176, 180, 188, 250, 251, 254
O'Donnell Cienega, 24
Older Dryas chronozone, 54
Oldest Dryas chronozone, 54
Olsen-Chubbuck Site, CO, 119, 138
Opuntia, 57

Paleoclimatic interpretations, 54–56
Paleoenvironmental reconstructions, 62–82
Paleosols, 17, 22, 29, 30, 49, 54, 84
Palli Aike Cave, Chile, 135
Palynological studies in the San Pedro Valley, 5
Patina, on artifacts, 85, 156, 159, 162, 164–167, 172, 182, 184, 188
Pavo Real Site, TX, 215
Peccary (*Platygonus*) remains, 120, 260
Peterson Ranch, 68
Petrified wood, Clovis projectile point of, 104, 188, 195, 223, 226, 254
Petrocalcic soil (horizons), 27, 31, 48, 49, 50, 57
Pine woodland, 79, 81
Pinto projectile point, 164–165
Pinyon, 40
Pinyon-juniper-oak woodland, 81
Plains-grassland, 80, 81, 82
Pleistocene (Rancholabrean) megafauna, extinction of, 5, 55, 56, 84, 223–225
Pleistocene-Holocene boundary, 40, 225
Pollen record, 5–6, 41, 47, 54, 55, 61, 81
Pollen sampling locations, 29, 32, 33, 39, 50, 53
Population densities. *See* Clovis people, population density of

Preboreal chronozone, 55
Precipitation, 16, 27, 46, 47, 55, 59–60, 82, 144, 225. *See also* Water table, fluctuations in
Pre-Clovis, xii, 226–227
Preforms (lithic), 106, 108, 113–114, 121, 124, 133, 134, 135, 137, 166 (Archaic?), 196
Prehistoric wells. *See* Wells
Procurement of bison. *See* Hunting techniques
Projectile points
   Archaic, 164–165, 172. *See also* Clovis projectile points
   post-Clovis, 220
Pyrolytic analyses, of black mat, 45, 245–247, 248–249

Quarries, in Lewis Hills, 18, 166. *See also* Lithic raw materials, sources of
Quarrying activities, evidence of, 188, 211, 212, 213
Quartz, Lehner Site artifacts of, 188
Quartzite
   artifacts and cobbles of, 107, 167, 175, 179, 184, 187, 210
   source and artifact abundance of, 188–191

Rabbit remains, at Lehner Site, 1, 218
Rabbitbrush, 58, 64
Radiocarbon ages
   at Lehner Site, 1
   at Murray Springs Site, 5, 8, 12, 28, 32, 33, 37, 39, 42, 46, 48–53, 79, 83, 94, 121, 136, 138, 229–239
   calibration of, xi, 1
   effect of nuclear fallout on, 79
   in Whitewater Draw, 5
   of hearth charcoal, 53
Rancho la Brea, CA, 145
Rancholabrean fauna, 5, 31, 32, 40, 55, 56, 84, 223–225. *See also* Extinction, of Rancholabrean fauna
Rancholabrean microfauna, 31
Refitted flakes, 11–12, 123, 132, 146, 149, 155–156, 165, 168, 174, 175, 176, 177–183, 189–191, 200, 202, 220
Roasting pit, at Lehner Site, 1. *See also* Hearths

Robinson, William J., xv
Rodent burrows, 3. *See also* Bioturbation
Rodentia remains, 103–104, 256, 257, 258, 262
Russell, Richard H., 64, 82
Ryan's Site, TX, 220

St. David Chalcedony
   artifacts of, 156, 159, 160, 162, 163, 173, 176, 177–184, 187–189, 191, 195, 201, 211, 213, 222–223
   source of, 187–188
St. David Formation (Stratum X), 6, 7, 16, 17, 19, 29, 30, 31, 50, 51, 53, 188, 222
Sample, Doris, xv
San Pedro projectile points, 164–165
San Pedro Riparian National Conservation Area, xiv, 16
San Pedro River Valley
   Clovis site concentration in, 1–5
   geology of, 16–56, 87
   occupational hiatus in, 223
   physiography and biomes of, 63
San Rafael del Valle grant, 24
Saunders, Jeffrey, xii, 15
Sayles, E. B., xiii 1, 5, 83, 229
Schaldack Site, AZ, xiii, 8
Schoenwetter, James, 5
Scottsbluff Site, NB, 139
scrapers, scraper/burin
   Archaic, 183
   at Murray Springs, 13, 44, 121, 124, 137, 146, 148, 158–159, 161, 168, 182, 185, 200, 202, 203–204. *See also* End scrapers
Sedges, 40, 46, 54, 64, 68
Shaft wrench, 9, 109–110, 114
Shawnee-Minisink Site, PA, 218
Sheehy Springs, environment at, 40, 64, 67, 77–78
Siltstone, silicified
   artifacts of, 160–163, 173, 183, 184, 187, 201, 205, 206, 207, 212
   sources and artifact abundance of, 188–191
Simon Site, ID, 191, 192, 211, 220
Simpson's coefficient, applied to mollusc studies, 76–78

Smiley, Terah L., xiii, 5
Smith, Jim, xiv
Snider, Ed, xiii
Sobaipuri Member (Stratum D, mud), 14, 32, 33, 34, 37, 38, 40, 42, 44, 49, 54, 68, 70-78, 93, 96, 114, 131, 148, 150, 155, 227, 235, 237-238, 241, 246
Sobaipuris, 31, 32, 61
Sonoran Desert, 60, 81
Southern Methodist University, xiv, 231, 240
Southwestern Molluscan Province, 63
Spanish arrival, 56
Spear thrower, xiv
Spude, Catherine H., xiv
Stahl Site, CA, 164-165
Stamp, Ellen, xv
Stratum F_2. See Black mat
Stromberg, Juliet, xiii
Stumpf, Gary, xiv
Sulphur Spring Stage, of Cochise culture, 5, 56
Sulphur Spring Valley, 5
Sumac, 58
Sycamore, 64
Sylvania Springs, 67-68, 76, 77

Tapirs
  at Lehner Site, 218
  extinction of, 55, 225
Tarbush, 27, 57, 59, 60
Tectonism, evidence of, 16, 51
Tellman, Barbara, xiii
Tenneco West Corporation, xiv

Teviston Member (Stratum H, alluvium), 29, 38, 50, 53-54, 56
Thomas, Albert, 24
Thompson, Raymond H., 64
Tombstone surface, 19, 48, 49, 60, 80
Tool kits, for butchering, 106, 123, 128, 135, 137
Tularosa Cave, NM, 164
Tule Springs Site, NV, 226
Turkey Creek, 24, 25, 48
Two Creeks interstade, xii

Unifacial tools
  Archaic, 164, 165, 166
  at Lehner Site, 3, 202, 203, 204, 222
  at Murray Springs Site, 106, 111, 121, 123, 124, 132-134, 149, 157-160, 172, 176, 178, 180, 186, 203-206
University of Arizona, xiv, 1, 5, 6, 241, 268, 270
University of New Mexico, 268
University of Texas, xiv, 231
U.P. Site, WY, xi, 143, 144
U.S. Army, xiv
U.S. Geological Survey, xiii

Vegetation, modern, 57-61
Velastro, Sam, xiv
Ventana Cave, AZ, 94, 135, 165

Walnut trees, 40, 54, 58
Wasley, William W., 1
Water hole, 9, 110, 136
  dug by mammoths, 9-10, 37, 38, 41, 55
  geology of, 41, 46
Water table, fluctuations in, 42, 44-46, 47, 49, 51, 54-56, 61, 80, 82, 85, 150, 227, 249
Weakly, Jannelle, xv
Weik, Alfred, xiv
Weik Ranch Member (Stratum G_1, alluvium), 29, 37, 49-51, 52, 53, 55, 56, 68, 70-76, 77, 80, 81, 232, 270
Wells
  of Archaic period age, 13, 38, 52, 131, 150, 164, 169
  of Clovis age(?), 42
Wendorf, Fred, xiv
Whetstone, Jack, xiv
Whitethorn acacia, 27, 57, 59, 60
Whitewater Draw, AZ, 5
Williamson Site, VA, 208, 212
Willow, 50, 58, 59
Wolf Creek, of Clovis age, 10, 36, 37, 39, 40, 41, 42, 44, 45, 48, 54, 86-96, 109, 115, 168
Wolf remains, 32, 96. See also Dire wolf
Woodcutter Draw, 58

X-ray fluorescence, 109, 123, 188, 250-254

Younger Dryas chronozone, 24, 47, 55, 56, 225, 237, 239, 266, 269, 272

Abstract

This opus reports on the interdisciplinary studies of one of the most significant Clovis sites yet discovered. The Murray Springs Site, in the upper San Pedro River Valley of southeast Arizona, is important because it contains a multiple bison kill, a mammoth kill, and possibly a horse kill in deeply stratified sedimentary context. In clear association with these animal remains is a camp site where the game was processed before the Clovis people, arguably the first Americans, moved on.

After a review of previous Clovis site finds in the upper San Pedro Valley, the geologic setting of the site in Curry Draw, an ephemeral tributary of the San Pedro, is presented in detail. Five geologic formations are defined that have widespread occurrence in the valley and provide a detailed stratigraphic framework for assessing the geochronology and site formational processes and associated paleohydrological changes over the past 40,000 years. The chronology of these events is well established on the basis of more than 120 radiocarbon age determinations.

A description of the modern vegetation provides a comparison with the paleoecology of the site. The detailed study of the molluscs found in the strata indicate that the site area was a riparian zone bordered by oak grassland during the Clovis occupation.

The excavations of the buried animal kills and processing localities revealed the killing of at least eleven bison (*Bison antiquus*) at one time and a young female mammoth (*Mammuthus columbi*) another time. Both were associated with a lowland area in and around a small spring fed stream system that had dried up as drought conditions worsened at the end of the Allerød postglacial climate episode. A water hole dug by mammoths appears to have been an important feature that attracted animals to the site. Detailed study of the dentitions of individual bison provided age estimates that indicated a kill in late fall or early winter.

Immediately after the Clovis abandonment, the occupation surface was buried by a unique algal black mat, fostering a preservation of the distributional integrity of the artifacts and debitage clusters that is exceptional for Paleoindian sites. Excavation of the

Resumen

Este es un reporte de los estudios interdisciplinarios en uno de los sitios Clovis más significativos que existen hoy. Murray Springs, localizado en el valle del alto Río San Pedro al sureste de Arizona, es importante porque contiene evidencia de múltiples matanzas de bisonte, una matanza de mamut y una posible matanza de caballo, todo lo cual se encuentra en un contexto sedimentario y estratificado. En clara asociación con estos restos de fauna se halla un campamento donde la caza fue procesada por la gente Clovis, quien pudo haber sido los primeros Americanos.

El reporte empieza con una revisión de sitios Clovis en el alto San Pedro Valley y continúa con una presentación del contexto geológico del sitio en la quebrada Curry, que es tributaria efímera del Río San Pedro. Se definen cinco formaciones geológicas de distribución amplia en el valle, y se provee un detallado marco estratigráfico para evaluar la geocronología y los procesos de formación del sitio en relación con cambios paleohidrológicos ocurridos en los últimos 40.000 años. La cronología de estos eventos es bien establecida en base a más de 120 fechas de radiocarbón.

Una descripción de la vegetación moderna sirve de comparación con la paleoecología del sitio. El detallado studio de moluscos encontrados en los estratos indica que el sitio fue una zona riparia rodeada de bosque de roble y de savana durante la ocupación Clovis. La excavación de los contextos de matanza y localidades de procesamiento revelaron que por lo menos 11 bisontes (*Bison antiquus*) fueron cazados en una ocasión y una mamut juvenil (*Mammuthus columbi*) en otra ocasión. Ambos eventos estuvieron asociados con la cuenca formada por una fuente de agua que se secó cuando las condiciones climáticas empeoraron al final del episodio climático posglacial Allerød. Un pozo de agua excavado por los mamuts parece haber sido un elemento importante que atrajo la atención de muchos animales. El studio detallado de la dentición de cada bisonte proveyó estimados de su edad e indicó que la matanza tuvo lugar en entre otoño e invierno.

Inmediatamente después de que la gente Clovis abandonó el sitio, la superficie de ocupación fue enterrada bajo una cubierta única compuesta de una capa

hunters' camp 50 to 150 meters south of the kills revealed artifactual evidence of typical hunting camp activity, including hide working and weapons repair. Impact flakes conjoining with Clovis points clearly tie the camp to the bison kill.

Detailed analyses of the lithic artifacts and debitage clusters showed discrete knapping loci and the use of at least 20 lithic materials. The location of five lithic source areas suggests a movement from northern to southeastern Arizona about 13,000 years ago. Before abandoning the area, the Clovis people had killed several mammoths at the Lehner Site about 10 miles farther south. The Naco mammoth with eight Clovis points and the Escapule mammoth with two points may be individuals that escaped from the Clovis ambushes only to die elsewhere.

Several deductions resulting from the Murray Springs research contribute to an understanding of Clovis paleoecology. Importantly, the faunal data and reconstruction of Clovis lithic technological organization at Murray Springs and other sites in the San Pedro Valley are consistent with a diet breadth and prey choice model prioritizing mammoth and bison as top-ranked prey species. Clovis activity within the valley appears intensive but is interpreted as being the result of either a single, extended foraging event by a single social unit or perhaps repeated occupations during a short interval of a few years. The Clovis people probably reached the valley by moving southward from the Little Colorado River Valley.

With regard to Pleistocene extinction, mammoth, *Bison antiquus*, horse, camel, dire wolf, tapir, as well as other animals disappeared immediately before the black mat buried the Clovis age landscape. As far as we can tell from the stratigraphic record, eight centuries passed before humans again reappeared in the San Pedro Valley some 12,200 years ago.

de alga negra, la que ayudó a la preservación e integridad de los razgos del sitio y sus artefactos, lo cual es excepcional en sitios paleoindios. La excavación del campamento localizado 50 a 150 metros al sur del lugar de matanza reveló evidencia artefactual de actividad típica en un campamento de cacería, incluyendo la producción de cuero y el reparo de proyectiles. El hallazgo de lascas que pertenecen a específicas puntas de proyectil Clovis indican claramente que el campamento está asociado con el sitio de matanza.

El análisis de concentraciones líticas y de artefactos reveló la presencia de áreas discretas de producción artefactual y el uso de por lo menos 20 materiales líticos. La localización de cinco áreas de proveniencia sugiere un movimiento del norte al sureste de Arizona hace 13.000 años atrás. Antes de abandonar el área, la gente Clovis cazó algunos mamuts en el sitio Lehner, a 10 millas hacia el sur. El mamut Naco con ocho puntas Clovis y el mamut Escápula con dos puntas, podrían ser individuos que escaparon de las trampas Clovis para morir en otro lugar.

Algunas deducciones resultantes de la investigación en Murray Springs contribuyen al entendimiento de la paleoecología Clovis. Es importante indicar que los datos de fauna y reconstrucción de la organización tecnológica lítica Clovis en Murray Springs y otros sitios del valle San Pedro son consistentes con una dieta que prefirió mamut y bisonte. La actividad Clovis en el valle parece haber sido intensiva pero se la interpreta como el resultado de un sólo evento de cacería por una sola unidad social, o tal vez ocupaciones repetidas durante un corto intervalo de pocos años. La gente Clovis probablemente alcanzó el valle durante su migración rumbo al sur desde el valle del Río Little Colorado.

En cuanto a la extinción pleistocénica, el mamut, *Bison antiquus,* caballo, camello, lobo, tapir y otros animales desaparecieron inmediatamente antes de que la capa de alga negra cubriera el paisaje de la era Clovis. Desde el punto de vista estratigráfico, ocho siglos transcurrieron antes de que grupos humanos reaparecieran en el valle San Pedro, aproximadamente 12.200 años atrás.

ANTHROPOLOGICAL PAPERS OF THE UNIVERSITY OF ARIZONA

1. Excavations at Nantack Village, Point of Pines, Arizona. David A. Breternitz. 1959. (O.P.)
2. Yaqui Myths and Legends. Ruth W. Giddings. 1959. *Now in book form.*
3. Marobavi: A Study of an Assimilated Group in Northern Sonora. Roger C. Owen. 1959. (O.P.)
4. A Survey of Indian Assimilation in Eastern Sonora. Thomas B. Hinton. 1959. (O.P.)
5. The Phonology of Arizona Yaqui with Texts. Lynn S. Crumrine. 1961. (O.P., D)
6. The Maricopas: An Identification from Documentary Sources. Paul H. Ezell. 1963. (O.P.)
7. The San Carlos Indian Cattle Industry. Harry T. Getty. 1964. (O.P.)
8. The House Cross of the Mayo Indians of Sonora, Mexico. N. Ross Crumrine. 1964. (O.P.)
9. Salvage Archaeology in Painted Rocks Reservoir, Western Arizona. William W. Wasley and Alfred E. Johnson. 1965. (O.P.)
10. An Appraisal of Tree-Ring Dated Pottery in the Southwest. David A. Breternitz. 1966. (O.P.)
11. The Albuquerque Navajos. William H. Hodge. 1969. (O.P.)
12. Papago Indians at Work. Jack O. Waddell. 1969.
13. Culture Change and Shifting Populations in Central Northern Mexico. William B. Griffen. 1969. (O.P.)
14. Ceremonial Exchange as a Mechanism in Tribal Integration Among the Mayos of Northwest Mexico. Lynn S. Crumrine. 1969. (O.P.)
15. Western Apache Witchcraft. Keith H. Basso. 1969.
16. Lithic Analysis and Cultural Inference: A Paleo-Indian Case. Edwin N. Wilmsen. 1970. (O.P.)
17. Archaeology as Anthropology: A Case Study. William A. Longacre. 1970.
18. Broken K Pueblo: Prehistoric Social Organization in the American Southwest. James N. Hill. 1970. (O.P., D)
19. White Mountain Redware: A Pottery Tradition of East-Central Arizona and Western New Mexico. Roy L. Carlson. 1970.
20. Mexican Macaws: Comparative Osteology. Lyndon L. Hargrave. 1970. (O.P.)
21. Apachean Culture History and Ethnology. Keith H. Basso and Morris E. Opler, eds. 1971.
22. Social Functions of Language in a Mexican-American Community. George C. Barker. 1972. (O.P.)
23. The Indians of Point of Pines, Arizona: A Comparative Study of Their Physical Characteristics. Kenneth A. Bennett. 1973. (O.P.)
24. Population, Contact, and Climate in the New Mexico Pueblos. Ezra B. W. Zubrow. 1974. (O.P.)
25. Irrigation's Impact on Society. Theodore E. Downing and McGuire Gibson, eds. 1974. (O.P.)
26. Excavations at Punta de Agua in the Santa Cruz River Basin, Southeastern Arizona. J. Cameron Greenleaf. 1975. (O.P.)
27. Seri Prehistory: The Archaeology of the Central Coast of Sonora, Mexico. Thomas Bowen. 1976. (O.P.)
28. Carib-Speaking Indians: Culture, Society, and Language. Ellen B. Basso, ed. 1977. (O.P.)
29. Cocopa Ethnography. William H. Kelly. 1977. (O.P., D)
30. The Hodges Ruin: A Hohokam Community in the Tucson Basin. Isabel Kelly, James E. Officer, and Emil W. Haury, collaborators; Gayle H. Hartmann, ed. 1978. (O.P.)
31. Fort Bowie Material Culture. Robert M. Herskovitz. 1978. (O.P.)
32. Artifacts from Chaco Canyon, New Mexico: The Chetro Ketl Collection. R. Gwinn Vivian, Dulce N. Dodgen, and Gayle H. Hartmann. 1978. (O.P.)
33. Indian Assimilation in the Franciscan Area of Nueva Vizcaya. William B. Griffen. 1979. (O.P.)
34. The Durango South Project: Archaeological Salvage of Two Late Basketmaker III Sites in the Durango District. John D. Gooding. 1980. (O.P.)
35. Basketmaker Caves in the Prayer Rock District, Northeastern Arizona. Elizabeth Ann Morris. 1980. (O.P.)
36. Archaeological Explorations in Caves of the Point of Pines Region, Arizona. James C. Gifford. 1980. (O.P.)
37. Ceramic Sequences in Colima: Capacha, an Early Phase. Isabel Kelly. 1980. (O.P.)
38. Themes of Indigenous Acculturation in Northwest Mexico. Thomas B. Hinton and Phil C. Weigand, eds. 1981. (O.P.)
39. Sixteenth Century Maiolica Pottery in the Valley of Mexico. Florence C. Lister and Robert H. Lister. 1982. (O.P.)
40. Multidisciplinary Research at Grasshopper Pueblo, Arizona. William A. Longacre, Sally J. Holbrook, and Michael W. Graves, eds. 1982. (O.P.)
41. The Asturian of Cantabria: Early Holocene Hunter-Gatherers in Northern Spain. Geoffrey A. Clark. 1983. (O.P.)
42. The Cochise Cultural Sequence in Southeastern Arizona. E. B. Sayles. 1983. (O.P.)
43. Cultural and Environmental History of Cienega Valley, Southeastern Arizona. Frank W. Eddy and Maurice E. Cooley. 1983. (O.P.)

44. Settlement, Subsistence, and Society in Late Zuni Prehistory. Keith W. Kintigh. 1985. (O.P., D)
45. The Geoarchaeology of Whitewater Draw, Arizona. Michael R. Waters. 1986. (O.P.)
46. Ejidos and Regions of Refuge in Northwestern Mexico. N. Ross Crumrine and Phil C. Weigand, eds. 1987. (O.P.)
47. Preclassic Maya Pottery at Cuello, Belize. Laura J. Kosakowsky. 1987. (O.P.)
48. Pre-Hispanic Occupance in the Valley of Sonora, Mexico. William E. Doolittle. 1988. (O.P.)
49. Mortuary Practices and Social Differentiation at Casas Grandes, Chihuahua, Mexico. John C. Ravesloot. 1988. (O.P.)
50. Point of Pines, Arizona: A History of the University of Arizona Archaeological Field School. Emil W. Haury. 1989.
51. Patarata Pottery: Classic Period Ceramics of the South-central Gulf Coast, Veracruz, Mexico. Barbara L. Stark. 1989.
52. The Chinese of Early Tucson: Historic Archaeology from the Tucson Urban Renewal Project. Florence C. Lister and Robert H. Lister. 1989. (O.P.)
53. Mimbres Archaeology of the Upper Gila, New Mexico. Stephen H. Lekson. 1990. (O.P.)
54. Prehistoric Households at Turkey Creek Pueblo, Arizona. Julie C. Lowell. 1991. (O.P.)
55. Homol'ovi II: Archaeology of an Ancestral Hopi Village, Arizona. E. Charles Adams and Kelley Ann Hays, eds. 1991. (O.P., D)
56. The Marana Community in the Hohokam World. Suzanne K. Fish, Paul R. Fish, and John H. Madsen, eds. 1992.
57. Between Desert and River: Hohokam Settlement and Land Use in the Los Robles Community. Christian E. Downum. 1993. (O.P., D)
58. Sourcing Prehistoric Ceramics at Chodistaas Pueblo, Arizona: The Circulation of People and Pots in the Grasshopper Region. María Nieves Zedeño. 1994.
59. Of Marshes and Maize: Preceramic Agricultural Settlements in the Cienega Valley, Southeastern Arizona. Bruce B. Huckell. 1995.
60. Historic Zuni Architecture and Society: An Archaeological Application of Space Syntax. T. J. Ferguson. 1996.
61. Ceramic Commodities and Common Containers: Production and Distribution of White Mountain Red Ware in the Grasshopper Region, Arizona. Daniela Triadan. 1997.
62. Prehistoric Sandals from Northeastern Arizona: The Earl H. Morris and Ann Axtell Morris Research. Kelley Ann Hays-Gilpin, Ann Cordy Deegan, and Elizabeth Ann Morris. 1998.
63. Expanding the View of Hohokam Platform Mounds: An Ethnographic Perspective. Mark D. Elson. 1998.
64. Great House Communities Across the Chacoan Landscape. John Kantner and Nancy M. Mahoney, eds. 2000.
65. Tracking Prehistoric Migrations: Pueblo Settlers among the Tonto Basin Hohokam. Jeffery J. Clark. 2001.
66. Beyond Chaco: Great Kiva Communities on the Mogollon Rim Frontier. Sarah A. Herr. 2001.
67. Salado Archaeology of the Upper Gila, New Mexico. Stephen H. Lekson. 2002.
68. Ancestral Hopi Migrations. Patrick D. Lyons. 2003.
69. Ancient Maya Life in the Far West Bajo: Social and Environmental Change in the Wetlands of Belize. Julie L. Kunen. 2004.
70. The Safford Valley Grids: Prehistoric Cultivation in the Southern Arizona Desert. William E. Doolittle and James A. Neely, eds. 2004.
71. Murray Springs: A Clovis Site with Multiple Activity Areas in the San Pedro Valley, Arizona C. Vance Haynes, Jr., and Bruce B. Huckell, eds. 2007.

Anthropological Papers listed as O.P., D are available as Docutech reproductions (high quality xerox) printed on demand. They are tape or spiral bound and nonreturnable.